Also by Martin A. Lee

Acid Dreams (with Bruce Shlain)
Unreliable Sources (with Norman Solomon)
The Beast Reawakens

SMOKE SIGNALS

A Social History
of Marijuana—Medical,
Recreational, and Scientific

Martin A. Lee

Scribner
New York London Toronto Sydney New Delhi

SCRIBNER
A Division of Simon & Schuster, Inc.
1230 Avenue of the Americas
New York, NY 10020

First Scribner hardcover edition August 2012

SCRIBNER and design are registered trademarks of The Gale Group, Inc., used under license by Simon & Schuster, Inc., the publisher of this work.

For information about special discounts for bulk purchases, please contact Simon & Schuster Special Sales at 1-866-506-1949 or business@simonandschuster.com.

The Simon & Schuster Speakers Bureau can bring authors to your live event. For more information or to book an event, contact the Simon & Schuster Speakers Bureau at 1-866-248-3049 or visit our website at www.simonspeakers.com.

Designed by Carla Jones

Manufactured in the United States of America

10 9 8 7 6 5 4 3 2 1

Library of Congress Control Number: 2012006737

ISBN 978-1-4391-0260-2
ISBN 978-1-4391-2793-3 (ebook)

CONTENTS

PROLOGUE

The tall, mustached Texan on horseback looks like the quintessential cowboy with his Stetson hat, red bandana, dusty boots, and jingly spurs. His sunburned arms and leathery face show the wear and tear of a rugged outdoorsman. But Howard Wooldridge isn't your typical cowboy. He's a retired police detective who's riding across the country to promote a provocative message—legalize marijuana and other drugs.

Wooldridge, then fifty-four, and his trusty, one-eyed mare, Misty, began their journey in Los Angeles in March 2005, and it would end seven months and 3,300 miles later in New York City. With a bedroll and a bag of carrots tied behind the saddle, they clippety-clopped from coast to coast, attracting attention and generating press coverage as they passed through cities and towns. Along the way, they had to contend with rattlesnakes in Arizona and New Mexico, and the blistering summer heat of the Great Plains. With the exception of a few death threats, the folks they encountered were usually friendly and many offered the veteran lawman a meal and a place to stay overnight. "The horse is a wonderful vehicle because people relate to the cowboy cop image," Wooldridge explained. "Then we start talking politics."

Another surefire attention-grabber was the T-shirt he often wore, with the slogan: COPS SAY LEGALIZE DRUGS. ASK ME WHY.

During his transcontinental trek, Wooldridge lectured on criminal-justice issues at several colleges and universities. He spoke in a disarmingly folksy "Yes, ma'am" manner as he challenged students and other citizens to rethink their ideas about marijuana prohibition and the war on drugs. Wooldridge discussed his eighteen years as a police officer in Michigan and how he never once received a call for help from a battered housewife or anyone else because of marijuana. Yet Lansing-area cops spent countless hours searching cars and frisking teenagers in order to find some weed when the police could have been addressing far more serious matters.

"Marijuana prohibition is a horrible waste of good police time," says

Wooldridge. "Every hour spent looking for pot reduces public safety." Based on his experience as a peace officer, he concluded that "marijuana is a much safer drug than alcohol for both the user and those around them . . . Alcohol releases reckless, aggressive or violent feelings by its use. Marijuana use generates the opposite effects in the vast majority of people." Officer Wooldridge decided to protect and serve the public by focusing on booze-impaired motorists. His efforts earned him the nickname "Highway Howie" and kudos from Mothers Against Drunk Driving.

Wooldridge did not condone or advocate drug use of any kind, but he had enough horse sense to recognize that by banning marijuana the U.S. government "essentially drives many people to drink." He felt that a substance should be judged by the actual harm it poses to the community. "From a law-enforcement standpoint," Wooldridge asserted, "the use of marijuana is not a societal problem . . . America needs to end pot prohibition."

Convinced that the laws against marijuana were a lot wackier than the weed, Wooldridge and several ex-cops formed a group called Law Enforcement Against Prohibition (LEAP) in 2002. Before long, LEAP would grow into a 40,000-member international organization composed of former prosecutors, undercover narcotics agents, judges, prison wardens, constables, and other disillusioned government functionaries who, after years of toiling in the trenches of a conflict with no conceivable end, had come to view the war on drugs as a colossal failure that fostered crime, police corruption, social discord, racial injustice, and, ironically, drug abuse itself, while squandering billions of tax dollars, clogging courtrooms and prisons, weakening constitutional safeguards, and impeding medical advances. LEAP condemned the war on drugs as America's longest-running bipartisan folly. Wooldridge called it "the most dysfunctional, immoral domestic policy since slavery and Jim Crow."

When law-enforcement veterans defect from prohibitionist orthodoxy, their arguments tend to be particularly potent. But Wooldridge understood that LEAP's views were very controversial. He knew that a long journey lay ahead, literally and figuratively, as he sought, one step at a time, to persuade Americans who had been exposed to years of government propaganda about the evils of marijuana. Many people reject the notion of legalizing drugs on moral and ideological grounds. They see marijuana first and foremost as a dangerous recreational drug, a harbinger of social decay. They believe the oft-repeated claim that smoking grass is a gateway to harder drugs.

The "devil's weed" has long been a favorite target of U.S. officials who misstate or exaggerate the physical and psychological effects of "cannabis," the preferred name for marijuana in medical and scientific circles. Although cannabis has a rich history as a medicine in many countries around the world, including the United States, federal drug warriors erected a labyrinth of legal and institutional obstacles to inhibit research and prevent the therapeutic use of the herb. They assembled a network of more than fifty government agencies and waged a relentless campaign against the marijuana "scourge," a crusade that entailed sophisticated aerial surveillance, paramilitary raids, border patrols, sensors, eradication sweeps, the spraying of herbicides, national TV ads, antidrug classes in schools, and mandatory-minimum prison terms for marijuana offenders, including an inordinate number of black and Latino youth.

In 2005, the year that Wooldridge and Misty hoofed across the states, more than 750,000 Americans were arrested on marijuana-related charges, the vast majority for simple possession. And the tally would continue to grow, irrespective of who was president or which political party was in power. Despite billions of dollars allocated annually to curb cannabis consumption, half of all American adults smoke the funny stuff at some point in their lives. An estimated fifteen million U.S. citizens use marijuana regularly.

Marijuana is by far the most popular illicit substance in the United States, with 10,000 tons consumed yearly by Americans in their college dorms, suburban homes, housing projects, and gated mansions. Pot smoking cuts across racial, class, and gender lines. It has become such a prevalent, mainstream practice that cannabis users are apt to forget they are committing a criminal act every time they spark a joint.

The history of marijuana in America has long been a history of competing narratives, dueling interpretations. As Harvard professor Lester Grinspoon, M.D., observed in his 1971 book *Marihuana Reconsidered,* some "felt that the road to Hades is lined with marihuana plants" while others "felt that the pathway to Utopia was shaded by freely growing *Cannabis sativa.*" And so it continues. At the center of this dispute is a hardy, adaptable botanical that feasts on sunlight and grows like a weed in almost any environment. Marijuana plants are annuals that vary in height from three to fifteen feet with delicate serrated leaves spread like the fingers of an open hand. Ridged down the middle and diagonally veined, cannabis leaves are covered, as is the entire plant, with tiny, sticky hairs. The gooey resin on the leaves and matted flower tops contains dozens of unique oily compounds, some of which, when ingested, trigger neurochemical changes in the brain. The hotter and sunnier the climate, the more psychoactive resin the plant produces during a three-to-five-month outdoor growing season. Known for its euphoria-inducing properties, "hashish" or "kif" is the concentrate made from the resin of female marijuana.

Ancient peoples during the Neolithic period found uses for virtually every part of the plant, which has been cultivated by humans since the dawn of agriculture more than 10,000 years ago. The stems and stalk provided fiber for cordage and cloth; the seeds, a key source of essential fatty acids and protein, were eaten as food; and the roots, leaves, and flowers were utilized in medicinal and ritual preparations. A plant native to Central Asia, cannabis figured prominently in the shamanistic traditions of many cultures. Handed down from prehistoric times, knowledge of the therapeutic qualities of the herb and the utility of its tough fiber slowly spread throughout the world, starting from the Kush, the herb's presumed ancestral homeland in the Himalayan foothills. The plant's dispersal across Eurasia into northern Europe followed the extensive migratory movements of the Scythians, aggressive charioteers in the second millennium BC. A famous passage in Herodotus' *Histories* (440 BC) refers to Scythians "howling with pleasure" in their hemp vapor baths.

Details gleaned from various academic disciplines—archaeology, history, anthropology, geography, botany, linguistics, and comparative mythology—indicate that marijuana's historical diffusion proceeded along two divergent paths, reflecting its dual role as a fiber crop and a psychoactive flower. One path moved westward from China into northern Europe, where cooler climes favored rope over dope, while the other path, the psychoactive route, hewed to trade lines that swung southward into India, Persia, the Arab Middle East, and Africa. As it traveled from region to region, the pungent plant never failed to ingratiate itself among the locals. Something about the herb resonated with humankind. Once it arrived in a new place, cannabis always stayed there—while also moving on, perpetually leaping from one culture to another.

Recent archaeological findings confirm that marijuana was used for euphoric as well as medicinal purposes long before the birth of Christ. In 2008, an international research team analyzed a cache of cannabis discovered at a remote gravesite in northwest China. The well-preserved flower tops had been buried alongside a light-haired, blue-eyed Caucasian man, most likely a shaman of the Gushi culture, about twenty-seven centuries ago. Biochemical analysis demonstrated that the herb contained tetrahydrocannabinol (THC), the main psychoactive ingredient of marijuana. "To our knowledge, these investigations provide the oldest documentation of cannabis as a pharmacologically active agent," concluded Dr. Ethan Russo, lead author of the scientific study. "It was clearly cultivated for psychoactive purposes" rather than for clothing or food.

The first reference to the medicinal use of cannabis also dates back to 2700 BC. It was subsequently recorded in the *Pen Ts'ao Ching*, the pharmacopeia of Emperor Shen Nung, the father of traditional Chinese medicine. Credited with having introduced the custom of drinking tea, Shen Nung recommended "ma" (marijuana) for more than a hundred ailments, including "female weakness, gout, rheumatism, malaria, constipation, beri-beri, and absent-mindedness." Shen Nung called "ma" one of the "Supreme Elixirs of Immortality." "If one takes it over a long period of time, one can communicate with spirits, and one's body becomes light," the *Pen Ts'ao Ching* advises. When consumed in excess, however, it "makes people see demons." Chinese physicians employed a mixture of cannabis and alcohol as a painkiller in surgical procedures.

In India, cannabis consumption had long been part of Hindu worship and Ayurvedic medical practice. According to ancient Vedic texts, the psychoactive herb was "a gift to the world from the god Shiva"—where the nectar of immortality landed on earth, ganja sprang forth. Longevity and good health were attributed to this plant, which figured prominently in Indian social life as a recreant, a religious sacrament, and a household remedy. Hindu holy men smoked hashish and drank bhang (a cannabis-infused cordial) as an aid to devotion and meditation. Folk healers relied on ganja, "the food of the gods," for relieving anxiety, lowering fevers, overcoming fatigue, enhancing appetite, improving sleep, clearing phlegm, and a plethora of other medical applications. Cannabis flower tops were said to sharpen the intellect and impel the flow of words. "So grand a result, so tiny a sin," the Vedic wise men concurred. There are no less than fifty Sanskrit and Hindu names for cannabis, all praising its attributes.

It's been said that language reflects the soul of a people. Eskimos have dozens of words for snowflakes, which underscores the centrality of snow in Inuit culture. So, too, with cannabis nomenclature: The versatile herb has generated an abundance of terms in many languages.

Cannabis comes from the Greek word *Kannabis,* which is related to the Sanskrit root *canna,* meaning "cane." In the Old Testament, *kanna-bosm* (Aramaic for "fragrant cane") is identified as an ingredient of the holy anointing oil, a topical applied by Hebrew mystics and early Christian healers. Galen, the influential Greek physician (second century AD), wrote of the medicinal properties of *kannabis,* but also noted that the herb was mixed with wine and served at banquets for pleasure. The first botanical illustration of the plant in Western literature appears in a Byzantine manuscript (AD 512) of Dioscorides, whose *Materia Medica* is the foundation for all modern pharmacopeias; he recommended covering inflamed body parts with soaked cannabis roots. Swedish botanist Carl Linnaeus, who laid the foundations for modern plant taxonomy, christened it *Cannabis sativa* in 1753.

Hemp, the common English name for cannabis through modern times, usually refers to northern varieties of the plant grown for rope, paper, fabric, oil, or other industrial uses. It derives from the Anglo-Saxon *henep* or *haenep.*

Differences in climate account for the paucity of hemp's resinous secretion compared with its psychoactive twin closer to the equator.

Of the multitude of terms associated with the cannabis plant, *marijuana* is the most universally recognized and widely used within the English-speaking world (even though it is not actually an English word). *Marijuana* is a Spanish-language colloquialism of uncertain origin; it was popularized in the United States during the 1930s by advocates of prohibition who sought to exploit prejudice against despised minority groups, especially Mexican immigrants. Intended as a derogatory slur, "marihuana"—spelled with a *j* or *h*—quickly morphed into an outsized American myth.

Slang words for marijuana in English are legion—*grass, reefer, tea, pot, dope, weed, bud, skunk, blunt, Mary Jane, spliff, chronic, doobie, muggles, cowboy tobacco, hippie lettuce* . . . And there are nearly as many terms for getting high, stoned, buzzed, blitzed, medicated. One could fill dictionaries with the shifting jargon related to cannabis. The profusion of idiomatic expression is in part an indication of the plant's unique allure as well as the perceived need for discretion and code words among users of the most sought-after illegal commodity on the planet. According to a 2009 United Nations survey, an estimated 166 million people worldwide—one in every twenty-five people between the ages of fifteen and sixty-five—have either tried marijuana or are active users of the herb.

Today, there is scarcely any place on earth that cannabis or its resinous derivatives are not found. A cannabis underground thrives from Greenland to Auckland to Tierra del Fuego. What accounts for marijuana's broad and enduring appeal? Why do so many people risk persecution and imprisonment to consume the forbidden fruit? Does cannabis cast an irresistible spell that bewitches its users? Is the herb addictive, as some allege? What happens when a society uses marijuana on a mass scale?

It is difficult to generalize about cannabis, given that its effects are highly variable, even in small doses. When large doses are imbibed, all bets are off. Marijuana can change one's mood, but not always in a predictable way. Immediate physiological effects include the lowering of body temperature and an aroused appetite. Flavors seem to jump right out of food. Realms of touch and taste and smell are magnified under the herb's influence. Quickened mental associations and a robust sense of humor are often accompanied by a tendency to become hyperfocused—"wrapped in wild observation of everything," as Jack Kerouac, the Beat scribe, put it. Similarly, Michael Pollan touted the "italicization of experience" that cannabis confers, "this seemingly virginal *noticing* of the sensate world."

There are detailed descriptions of the marijuana experience in literature that attest to the herb's capriciousness, its tricksterlike qualities. A cannabis-induced altered state can be calming or stimulating, soothing or nerve-racking, depending on any number of factors, including an individual's personality and expectations. Many people enjoy the relaxed intensity of the marijuana high; some find it decidedly unpleasant. It can make the strange seem familiar and the familiar very strange. Marijuana delinks habits of the mind, yet chronic use of the herb can also be habituating.

The marijuana saga is rife with paradox and polarity. It is all about doubles, twins, dualities: fiber and flower, medicine and menace, sacrament and recreant, gift and commodity. The plant itself grows outdoors and indoors. It thrives under a diurnal or a twenty-four-hour light cycle. It can be male or female, single-sex or hermaphroditic, psychoactive or nonpsychoactive. There are two principal types of cannabis—*sativas* and *indicas*. Recent scientific discoveries show that there are two sets of G-coupled protein receptors in the human brain and body that respond pharmacologically to cannabis. Marijuana's therapeutic mechanism is bimodal; it acts upon both the central nervous system and the peripheral nervous system, an unusual combination for a drug. Cannabis has biphasic properties, triggering opposite effects depending on dosage. As a healing herb, it is ancient as well as cutting-edge. It has been used as a curative and a preventive medicine. It is both prescribed and proscribed.

Cannabis has always lived a double life, and this also holds true for many marijuana smokers. An escape for some and a scapegoat for others, marijuana embodies the double-edged nature of the *pharmakon,* the ancient Greek word that signifies both remedy and sacrificial victim. Extolled and vilified, the weed is an inveterate boundary-crosser. Officially it is a controlled substance, but its use proliferates worldwide in an uncontrolled manner. It is simultaneously legal and illegal in more than a dozen U.S. states that have adopted medical-marijuana provisions.

California led the way in 1996, when voters in the Golden State broke ranks from America's drug-war juggernaut and approved Proposition 215, the landmark ballot measure that legalized cannabis for medicinal purposes. It's been an ugly, fractious battle ever since, as the federal government, working in tandem with state and local law-enforcement officials, responded to the medical-marijuana groundswell by deploying quasi-military units against U.S. citizens, trashing homes, ripping up gardens, shutting down cannabis clubs, seizing property, threatening doctors, and prosecuting suppliers. Much more was at stake than the provision of a herbal remedy to ailing Americans.

Smoke Signals is a cautionary tale about U.S. government corruption and constitutional rights under attack. It tells the story of several exemplary characters who struggled against heavy odds, a David-versus-Goliath chronicle in which resolute citizens challenged powerful vested interests and deeply entrenched policies. This book also draws attention to underreported scientific breakthroughs and addresses serious health issues that affect every family in America, where popular support for medical marijuana far exceeds the number of those who actually use the herb.

The wildly successful—and widely misunderstood—medical-marijuana movement didn't appear overnight. It was the culmination of decades of grassroots activism that began during the 1960s, when cannabis first emerged as a defining force in a culture war that has never ceased. In recent years this far-flung social movement has morphed into a dynamic, multibillion-dollar industry, becoming one of the phenomenal business stories of our generation. The marijuana story is actually many stories, all woven into one grand epic about a remarkable plant that befriended our ancestors, altered their consciousness, and forever changed the world in which we live.

1

HERBLORE

Black and Blue

Every Sunday in early nineteenth-century New Orleans, slaves gathered by the hundreds at Congo Square for an afternoon of song and dance. Uncoupled, limbs akimbo, some naked but for a sash around the torso, they gyrated to the beat of the *bamboulas,* the yowl of the *banzas,* shuffling, gliding, trance-stepping, crouching (a position that signifies vitality in Congolese culture), and mimicking the cries of animals. Some wore garments ornamented with ribbons, feathers, little bells, and shells. The dark-complexioned dancers were surrounded by men, women, and children "patting Juba," an African-derived technique for tapping rhythmically against parts of the body—striking their thighs, their chests, chanting, clapping their hands while others played drums, gourds, tambourines, makeshift marimbas, and banjo-like instruments.

The Sunday swoon in Congo Square, or Place des Nègres, as it was also called, provided a much-needed respite from the dehumanizing grind of plantation capitalism. This rite was reenacted on a regular basis until slave-owners began to suspect that the complex percussive beats were sending secret, subversive messages to restive blacks. Several years before the Civil War, African drumming was prohibited throughout the South. But music persisted as an indelible aspect of the dynamic cultural legacy transmitted across the ocean and passed along to generations of slaves and their descendents. From the African dances of the old days would come the driving energy of modern jazz.

Today Congo Square is an open area within Louis Armstrong Park, so named in honor of the jazz marvel, born and bred in New Orleans, who gained fame initially as a horn player and later as a vocalist, a musical ambassador, and a character of epic proportions. Although he lacked formal musical training, Armstrong rearranged the sonic terms of American popular culture and his innovations reverberated far and wide. More than anyone else, he taught the world to swing. Known affectionately as "Satchmo" and "Pops" to millions of adoring fans, he was a huge international celebrity. Before Bob Marley, before Muhammad Ali, Louis Armstrong was the original black superstar.

Armstrong grew up dirt poor, a shy, fatherless child who picked food out of garbage cans and ran errands for pimps and whores. Initially, he was raised by his grandmother, a former slave, in a country where black people were still considered less than fully human. American apartheid was imposed by vigilante terrorism and Jim Crow legislation that codified racial inequality. Armstrong not only had to ride at the back of the trolley like all African Americans in pigment-conscious New Orleans, he bore the brunt of additional prejudice because his skin was very dark.

For Armstrong, music was a siren call leading him out of misery. As a young man, he joined the great exodus of African Americans from the South who migrated to Chicago and other northern industrial cities in the 1920s, seeking jobs and a better life. Some bands in Chicago rejected Armstrong because his skin was so dark. But he was readily welcomed into the fraternity of marijuana-smoking musicians—*the vipers*—who gigged in the Windy City. During a break between sets at the Savoy Ballroom, the trumpet maestro inhaled his first stick of "gage," one of the preferred nicknames for cannabis in jazz circles. He liked the sweet smell and taste. It calmed his nerves and lifted his spirits. "I had myself a ball," he effused, adding: "It's a thousand times better than whisky."

Thus began Armstrong's enduring romance with "Mary Warner." From then on, he smoked reefer daily, and it didn't appear to compromise his musical dexterity or work ethic (three hundred concerts a year—no slacker was he). Pops swore by cannabis and often touted the benefits of the herb, telling jokes, jiving, proselytizing, and kidding endlessly with his cohorts. "We all used to smoke marijuana," a wistful Armstrong recounted years later. "Yeah, it's a thrill to think back to those beautiful times and wonderful cats who congregated to light up some of that *good shuzzit,* meaning, *good shit.*"

Stoned solidarity, the healing balm of community—smoking grass made Satch feel like he was one of the gang. "That's one reason we appreciated pot, as y'all calls it now, the warmth it always brought forth from the other person," said Armstrong, who confided: "It makes you feel wanted, and when you're with another tea smoker it makes you feel a special sense of kinship."

Armstrong made a point of blowing gage before he performed and recorded, and he encouraged his band members to get high with him. In December 1928, he recorded "Muggles," another slang for Satchmo's drug of choice and his best-known reefer tune. Showcasing solos by several musicians who passed the bluesy melody around like a burning marijuana cigarette—from piano to trombone to clarinet to soaring trumpet—this landmark instrumental signaled the transformation of jazz into an improvisatory art form with wide-open opportunities for individual expression. No one had ever made music like this before. The compilation known as the Hot Five and Hot Seven recordings, which included "Muggles," had tremendous popular appeal and established Armstrong's reputation as a jazz genius and one of the most important figures in twentieth-century music.

"If ya ain't got it in ya, ya can't blow it out," said Pops, who took Hollywood by storm, dazzling the likes of Charlie Chaplin, the Marx Brothers, and other cinema stars who flocked to see the jazz avatar, their ears avid for Armstrong. The Marx Brothers also shared a fondness for Satchmo's favorite herb. Groucho Marx got his nickname from a so-called grouch bag he wore around his neck. "In this bag, we would keep our pennies, our marbles, a piece of candy, a little marijuana," Chico quipped.

Armstrong himself appeared in some sixty films—singing, scatting, blowing his horn, and mugging for the camera. He was the first black American to be featured in A-list movies. His songs were broadcast every day on radio and listened to throughout the world. But Satchmo's fame did not always protect him from the cops.

In November 1930, Pops got popped by two Los Angeles narcs while smoking with Vic Berton, a white drummer, in the parking lot of the New Cotton Club. "Vic and I were blasting this joint, having lots of laughs and feeling good, enjoying each other's company," Armstrong recalled, when "two big healthy Dicks came from behind a car nonchalantly and said to us, 'We'll take the roach, boys.' "

Both musicians spent nine days in the Downtown Los Angeles jail awaiting trial for marijuana possession. They were each convicted and sentenced to six months in prison and a thousand-dollar fine. Strings were pulled and the judge was persuaded to suspend the sentences with the proviso that Armstrong leave California.

Although rattled by his close encounter with law enforcement, Armstrong continued to smoke pot for the rest of his life with little evidence of ill effect, according to Dr. Jerry Zucker, his personal physician. Armstrong couldn't understand why his beloved muggles was illegal. "It puzzles me to see Marijuana connected with Narcotics—Dope and all that kind of crap," he wrote. "It's actually a shame."

For Armstrong, cannabis wasn't just a recreational substance—it was a nostrum, a tonic, an essential element of his life. "We always looked at pot as a sort of medicine," he stated. Marijuana was part of Satchmo's overall health regimen. He never used hard drugs or popped pills, preferring to self-medicate with various herbs and home remedies, a custom he learned from his mother, who emphasized the importance of being "physics-minded." This practice, involving a mixture of African and Southern folk cures, was instilled in Louis during his impoverished childhood. His family was too destitute to see a professional doctor, so his mother would "go out by the railroad tracks, and pick a lot of peppers—grasses—dandelions, etc.," Armstrong remembered, and "she'd bring it home and boil that stuff and give us kids a big dose of it."

What exactly did Satchmo mean when he referred to marijuana as a medicine? What, in his case, was cannabis a remedy for? Armstrong said he used reefer to unwind, to relieve stress, to ease the chronic pain of racism. Smoking marijuana helped him deal with the daily humiliation meted out by Jim Crow—white society's relentless, sickening assault on his self-respect. As he told record producer John Hammond: "It makes you feel good, man. It relaxes you, makes you forget all the bad things that happen to a Negro."

Twenty years before Jackie Robinson swung a bat for the Dodgers, Armstrong slipped through whites-only portals, leaving doors slightly ajar behind him. A hero of his race, he became the first African American to host a national radio broadcast in 1937, the same year marijuana was outlawed by the U.S. government. Satchmo was one of few blacks to perform publicly with white musicians. Onstage, he was a megastar, but offstage Armstrong remained a second-class citizen of the United States. He and his band endured the indignities of touring in the South. They were harassed by police and barred from whites-only restaurants, hotels, and bathrooms. White supremacists bombed a theater in Knoxville, Tennessee, while Armstrong was playing for a racially mixed audience. Mob-controlled venues up north posed additional risks. "Danger was dancing all around you back then," he remarked.

Yet, despite all, Satchmo never abandoned his overriding belief that it's "a wonderful world." A few puffs of that *good shuzzit* helped him live and let live. As his fellow trumpeter Dizzy Gillespie put it, Armstrong "refused to let anything, even anger about racism, steal the joy from his life."

In the opening pages of Ralph Ellison's *Invisible Man,* the nameless narrator lights a reefer and listens to a recording of Louis Armstrong singing, "What did I do to be so black and blue," a soulful lament that epitomized the plight of African Americans. Armstrong's voice of musk and cinnamon imbues the lyrics with poignant emotion. Ellison's protagonist, absorbing the smoke and sound, is propelled into an eerie reverie, a surreal space, the American Dream

Louis Armstrong: "Mary Warner, you sure was good to me"
(Courtesy of Frank Driggs Collection/Getty Images)

in blacklight. To be invisible was not just to lack acknowledgment other than scorn from the pale man; it was the fundamental condition of black people in white America.

"Black and Blue" was the centerpiece of Armstrong's performance at an outdoor concert in Accra, Ghana, in 1956. More than 100,000 people thronged the city stadium on a sweltering afternoon to hear Satchmo sing this song with such intensity that it brought tears to the eyes of Kwame Nkrumah, Ghana's prime minister, a moment captured on film.

Louis Armstrong, the most visible of invisible men, traveled the world over, but this trip to the Gold Coast of West Africa was special. When he saw the women of Ghana, he recognized the face of his own mother. "I know it now. I came from here, way back. At least my people did," Armstrong asserted. "Now I know this is my country, too."

The prodigal son, the grandchild of a slave, had returned to his ancestral homeland, a land where the ceremonial use of roots and herbs had long been linked to animist spiritual beliefs. A staple of African shamanism, cannabis and other consciousness-altering flora were revered as "sacred plants" that provided access to hidden knowledge and curative powers.

Pollen samples indicate the presence of cannabis in sub-Saharan Africa for at least two millennia. Introduced by overland traders from the Arab Middle East and later by Portuguese seamen traveling from India, the herb quickly spread throughout the continent. Black Africans employed a variety of devices—clay pipes, gourds, bamboo stalks, coconut bowls—for inhaling "dagga," as marijuana was called by several tribes, who regarded it as a "plant of insight." According to the Tsongas of southern Africa, "Dagga deepens and makes men wiser."*

Earth-smoking, which entailed sucking cannabis fumes directly through a hole in a dirt mound, was an ancient tradition among Pygmies in the equatorial forest. The Zulus ingested psychoactive hemp via steam baths and enemas in addition to smoking it for pleasure; they also smoked it to boost their courage before going into battle. A Bantu tribe in the Congo dispensed cannabis as a means of punishment—miscreants were compelled to smoke a large quantity of marijuana until they either confessed to a crime or keeled over.

Cannabis had a medicinal reputation in Africa that varied from region to region. Cultivated as a source of fiber as well as for its remarkable resin, the versatile herb served as a remedy for a wide range of ailments, including dysentery, malaria, diarrhea, typhus, and rheumatism. The Hottentots, who applied it as a salve for snakebites, deemed dagga more valuable than gold. Sotho women used marijuana to facilitate childbirth, and Sotho children were fed ground-up hempseed paste while weaning. In West Africa, from whence Armstrong's ancestors hailed, cannabis was utilized as a treatment for asthma.

The roots of jazz and blues extend back through slavery to the collective rhythmic patterns of indigenous tribes in West Africa, where cannabis had thrived for centuries. Thrown upon bonfires, marijuana leaves and flowers augmented nocturnal healing rituals with drum circles, dancing, and singing that invoked the spirit of the ancestors and thanked them for imparting knowledge of this botanical wonder. It was only natch that Satch, the musical savant and dagga devotee, felt right at home as soon as he set foot on West African soil. "After all," he explained, "my ancestors came from here, and I still have African blood in me."

---

* The Bashilenge called themselves "Ben-Riamba" ("the sons of hemp") and they greeted one another with the expression "mojo," meaning both "hemp" and "life." They attributed magical powers to hemp, which was thought to protect against all kinds of evil.

New World Hemp

There is a general consensus among scholars that cannabis, a plant not native to "the New World," as the Europeans viewed it, was introduced to the western hemisphere in the sixteenth century through the slave trade. Black captives brought cannabis seeds (and seeds of other plants) with them aboard slave ships that made the perilous passage across the Atlantic. These ocean vessels were outfitted with sails, rope, and netting made of hemp, marijuana's durable, nonpsychoactive twin, which doesn't easily rot or wear when exposed to saltwater. In an era when sea power was paramount, saltwater-resistant hemp fiber was a crucial, strategic substance. For hundreds of years, all the major European maritime powers—the English, French, Dutch, Spanish, and Portuguese—depended on a quality hemp harvest to maintain their fleets. Christopher Columbus, Ferdinand Magellan, Sir Francis Drake, the Conquistadors, the Pilgrims who landed at Plymouth Rock—they all sailed ships equipped with hemp products. So did an estimated eleven million to twenty million African slaves, who were transported under conditions so horrible that up to a third died en route to North and South America.

The Portuguese were among the first Europeans to enslave Africans and bring them en masse to the Western hemisphere. This is how cannabis took root in Brazil, a Portuguese colony, in the early 1500s. Linguistic evidence in this case speaks volumes: nearly all the Brazilian names for cannabis—*macumba, diamba, liamba, pungo,* and so on—are African words from dialects spoken by the original slaves (many from Angola, where natives typically smoked cannabis in water pipes). Cannabis cultivation initially took hold on newly established sugar plantations in northeast Brazil. Black slaves seemed to handle the heat and fieldwork better when they smoked the fragrant herb, so Portuguese plantation owners allowed them to grow cannabis between rows of sugarcane. The word *marijuana* may have come from *mariguango,* Portuguese for "intoxicant."

After they came in contact with African slave laborers, some South American Indians began to puff marijuana. The aboriginal peoples of the New World were familiar with an array of psychoactive plants, which they used for religious rites, spirit journeys, divination, and therapeutic purposes. Thus, it was an easy transition for Native Americans to adopt cannabis and include it in their ceremonies.

It was only a matter of time before fishermen and dockworkers in the coastal cities of Brazil also were smoking pot, a practice that slowly spread through the northern half of South America, across the Panamanian isthmus, and into Mexico. As cannabis proliferated geographically, so did its medicinal applications in Latin America and the Caribbean. Tea made from boiled marijuana leaves was brewed to relieve rheumatism, colic, "female troubles," sleep disorders, and other common complaints. Marijuana purportedly had an analgesic effect on toothaches when packed on the gums near the painful area; leaves soaked in alcohol and wrapped around swollen joints were said to help arthritis.

The European colonial powers were less interested in the medicinal potential of cannabis than in the annual plant's tough fiber. In 1533, King Henry VIII commanded English farmers to grow hemp for its fibrous content or risk paying a stiff fine, an edict reiterated by Queen Elizabeth thirty years later. Similar measures were enacted in England's North American colonies. In 1619, eight years after colonists first planted hemp in Jamestown, the Virginia assembly passed a law requiring every household in the colony to cultivate the plant because it had so many beneficial uses—for making fabric, paper products, cord, and other items. Some of the earliest pioneers in North America were contracted to grow fiber hemp in exchange for safe transit to the New World. It was one of the first crops cultivated by Puritan settlers in the rich soil of New England, where hemp grew twice as high as in the British Isles.

Hemp farming and processing played an important role in American history. Its legacy is evident in the names of numerous towns and hamlets from the Atlantic coast to the Midwest—Hempstead, Hempfield, Hemp Hill, and variations thereof. Early American farmers and their entire families wore garments made from hemp, wiped their hands with hemp towels and hemp handkerchiefs, inscribed words on hemp paper, and sewed with hemp yarn. Hemp was considered so valuable that it served as a substitute for legal tender in seventeenth- and eighteenth-century America.

Several of the Founding Fathers, including George Washington, grew hemp—or tried to—and they urged other colonial farmers to do likewise. Among those heeding the call was Robert "King" Carter, an ancestor of President Jimmy Carter and a big-time hemp grower from Virginia who provided much of the fiber needed to make uniforms for Washington's soldiers.

Washington learned from firsthand experience that the sturdy stalk wasn't the easiest crop to process, and supplies of retted hemp never kept up with a voracious demand. One problem was the lack of a cultivation manual to assist colonial farmers. Such a manual had been printed in Italy (where hemp was referred to as *quello delle cento operazioni*, the "substance of a hundred operations"), but it was written in an Italian dialect and the prestigious hemp guilds of Venice preferred not to share inside information with foreign competitors. It was not until ten years before the American Revolution that an English-language guidebook for raising hemp became available in the colonies. The author of this how-to pamphlet, "A Treatise of Hemp-Husbandry," was Edmund Quincy, a cousin of John Adams, the first vice president and second president of the United States. George Washington was a close friend of the Quincy-Adams clan and he surely knew of the grow guide.

Quincy's treatise was published in 1765, the same year that Washington wrote in his diary about planting and harvesting hemp at Mount Vernon. The entry for May 12–13 states, "Sowed Hemp at Muddy hole by Swamp," and the notation on August 7 reads, "Began to separate the Male from the Female hemp . . . rather too late." Pot partisans have seized upon this statement as proof that Washington was trying to grow high-quality cannabis, the psychoactive kind, which entails separating the sexes to prevent pollination, thereby increasing the potency of unrequited, resin-oozing females. *Ipso facto,* Washington must have smoked pot. Otherwise why would he be so concerned with separating male and female plants?

"Sexing the plants" would become standard practice among growers of high-potency sinsemilla—seedless marijuana—in California two centuries after the American Revolution. But seedless hemp was likely the last thing George Washington wanted. He was obsessed with increasing the yield of hempseeds and saving them for next year's crop. Washington made several references to hemp in his diaries, including comments to his gardener, urging him to save the seeds. "Make the most of Indian hempseed. Sow it everywhere," Washington implored.

When Washington noted that he had separated male and female plants "rather too late," he was regretting his failure to follow directions that called for removing the male plants after pollination in a timely fashion so that the seed-bearing females had more room to bask and mature in the sun. "The remainder [of female plants] is to stand till the seed be ripened," Qunicy's manual instructed. In no uncertain terms, Quincy indicated that the males were to be separated from the females *after* seeds had been set on the latter. This is just the opposite of what sinsemilla cultivators strive for.

Washington was growing hemp for seed and fiber, not for smoke. There are no references in his diary to smoking any of that *good shuzzit*. Washington and other American revolutionaries were notorious boozers, not puffers. "Washington not only didn't smoke pot, he didn't know pot could be smoked," concluded Michael Aldrich, who, as a doctoral student at the State University of New York in Buffalo in the 1960s, researched Washington's hemp-growing efforts. "Why was Washington so keen on maximizing hempseed production? To develop a home supply," Aldrich explained, "so the colonies would not have to rely on another country, particularly England, for such a critical substance. This was a national-security issue."

The Founding Fathers didn't have to read tea leaves or hemp leaves to predict that war with Britain was approaching. Prior to the much-celebrated Boston Tea Party, hemp had already become a source of tension between the colonies and the mother country. One of the first ways the Americans asserted their independence was by refusing to send raw hemp fiber back to Britain. Instead, the Americans began to process hemp themselves in defiance of the Crown, which offered a lucrative price for every bale delivered from the colonies. Thanks, but no thanks, hemp entrepreneur Benjamin Franklin told the British ever so diplomatically—the Americans needed all the hemp they could get their hands on. Franklin owned a mill that converted hemp pulp into paper that American patriots used to propagate their seditious ideas of liberty.

Thomas Paine hyped hemp in *Common Sense*, his influential clarion call for independence that persuaded many Americans to support the revolution. Paine cited the fact that "hemp flourishes" in the colonies, providing a homegrown source of paper, clothing, rope, linen, oil, and other essentials, as an argument to convince the colonists that they could successfully secede from Britain. Without enough hemp, revolutionary forces would not have prevailed. Patriotic wives and mothers organized spinning bees with hempen thread to clothe the revolutionary army. The first American flags were made from hemp cloth.

Thomas Jefferson penned the original draft of the Declaration of Independence on Dutch hemp paper. Jefferson's second draft, also inscribed on hemp paper, was ratified on July 4, 1776, and then copied onto animal parchment. Jefferson not only raised and praised hemp (which he strongly favored over "pernicious" tobacco as a cash crop), he went to great lengths, unbeknownst to the British, to procure different varieties of hempseed from abroad. "The greatest service which can be rendered by any country is to add a useful plant to its culture," wrote Jefferson the hempseed smuggler.

In 1803, President Jefferson presided over the Louisiana Purchase, one of the largest land deals in history, whereby the United States paid France approximately $15 million (two and a half cents per acre) for more than 800,000 square miles of North American territory. At the time, Napoleon, the French emperor, desperately needed money to finance a military thrust to cripple the British navy by cutting off hemp supplies from Russia, then the world's leading exporter of this hardy fiber. British designs on securing access to hemp were also a factor in the War of 1812. Long before oil wars, nations fought over hemp, the plant that "fueled" international maritime trade and imperial expeditions by providing the best raw material for sails to harness wind power.

The domestic hemp industry prospered during the early days of the American republic in large part because black slaves were utilized to plant, harvest, and process the crop. It was arduous, backbreaking work—uprooting the hemp, pounding the tenacious husk, extracting the slippery raw fiber, and making it usable. So prized was hemp that some plantation owners even paid wages to slaves to encourage production. As the frontier moved westward, farmers established vast hemp-growing operations in Missouri, Mississippi, and especially Kentucky, where hemp was known as a "nigger crop" because of its association with slaves who worked the land.

After serving two terms as president, Jefferson retired to his Virginia estate in 1809 to raise fiber hemp, among other crops, with the help of his slaves. He eventually abandoned this project because it was too labor-intensive. "Hemp is abundantly productive and will grow forever in the same spot," he acknowledged after his 1815 harvest, but "breaking and beating it, which has always been done by hand, is so slow, so laborious, and so much complained of by our laborers, that I have given it up."

By mid-century, hemp was America's third-largest crop, exceeded only by cotton and tobacco. Seeking to boost his fiber-making capacity, John Augustus Sutter, a Swiss émigré, acquired a hemp-thrashing machine from Fort Ross, a Russian trading post in Northern California. Gold was subsequently discovered at Sutter's Mill by the American River in California on land where hemp grew. The news touched off an overnight stampede in 1849, as prospectors rushed in, manic for mineral wealth. Some made the journey overland to the Pacific in horse-drawn wagons covered with hemp canvas. In America's "Wild West," lynch mobs dispensed frontier justice using the "hemp collar"—otherwise known as the hangman's noose. More than one hundred years later, cannabis cultivation would precipitate another "gold rush" of sorts in Northern California as marijuana, the high-resin type, blossomed into the Golden State's most lucrative agricultural crop, boasting a multibillion-dollar annual yield despite its proscribed status.

Hemp was well established as a fiber crop in North America long before European settlers and their descendents discovered the psychoactive properties of cannabis. As new technologies, most notably the cotton gin and the steamship, eclipsed the urgency for hemp fiber, the resilient plant appeared in another guise—as a medicine for a wide range of infirmities. When the American Civil War began in 1861, fiber hemp had already begun to decline in commercial value, while the plant's reputation as a curative was surging.

Elixirs and Tinctures

The dual role of hemp as a healing herb and a source of fiber had deep roots in European culture. Hemp festivities were common throughout the continent long before Columbus set sail under the Spanish flag. Farmers, hoping for robust growth, sowed hempseed on days associated with tall saints. Peasants jumped for joy and danced in fields of hemp to usher in a bountiful harvest, and they plucked flowers from the venerable plant to protect themselves from the Evil Eye. The French had a saying, *"Avoir de la corde de pendu dans sa poche"*—"To have hemp in your pocket"—which meant to have luck on your side. Young women in the Ukraine and England carried hempseed as an amulet to attract a mate and hasten their wedding day. When a bride entered her new home after a Slavic marriage ceremony, well-wishers sprinkled her with hempseed for good fortune.

According to peasant folklore, the vapors from smoldering hemp possessed cleansing qualities that protected against disease. But given the low levels of psychoactive tetrahydrocannabinol (THC) typically present in northern strains of hemp, it's doubtful that many Europeans were getting stoned from inhaling the smoke. Unlike high-THC plants in India, Africa, and the Middle East, the variety of hemp that grew best in Europe's cooler climes didn't deliver much by way of euphoria. Nevertheless, European folk traditions still considered hemp a medicinal and magical plant, attesting to what twenty-first-century scientists would eventually confirm: THC is not the only therapeutic compound in cannabis, and certain nonpsychoactive compounds prominent in fiber hemp are powerful healing agents.

Cannabis sativa illustration

A familiar ingredient in European folk remedies, hemp served as a multipurpose medicine—for quelling fevers, soothing burns, relieving headaches, and dressing wounds with a disinfectant paste made of hemp flowers, wax, and olive oil. The curative powers of hempseeds, roots, leaves, and sap were well known in Germanic regions, where midwives placed sprigs of the mighty fiber over the stomach and ankles of pregnant women to prevent convulsions and difficult childbirth. It was customary to honor Freya, the German fertility goddess, with hemp as a pagan sacrament. In the twelfth century, Hildegard von Bingen, the legendary German folk healer, wrote about *hanaf* (hemp) in her *Physica*. The first written European reference to the medicinal use of hemp smoke appears in the *Kreuterbuch*, the massive sixteenth-century herbal compendium by Tabernaemontanus, a German doctor in Basel, Switzerland.

Linked to witches' unguents and potions, hemp was outlawed as heretical by papal fiat in 1484. Though forbidden by religious authorities for such purposes, the continued use of hemp as a medicament, lubricant, and anointing oil, and as a focal point for rural ritual was widely known. But few spoke of it openly so as not to arouse the wrath of the Holy Inquisitor. Pope Innocent VIII's demonization of cannabis was a continuation of the Church's war on pre-Christian traditions.

François Rabelais, the French Renaissance doctor, author, and humorist, referred cryptically to the "good herb pantagruelion," by which he meant hemp, in his satirical masterpiece *Gargantua and Pantagruel*, published in 1532. This early novel devoted three chapters to an allegorical plant that was used for making medicine as well as sails, cord, and hangman's nooses. Apparently his writing was not cryptic enough, for Rabelais's books were banned by the Roman Catholic Church.

William Shakespeare and several of his contemporaries often wrote in coded language to address topical social issues during a particularly volatile era in English history that was marked by intense religious and political strife. Professor Francis Thackeray, a South African paleontologist and a Shakespeare aficionado, suspected that the Bard may have been alluding to hemp when he mentioned "the noted weed" and "compounds strange" in one of his sonnets. It sounds like someone had the munchies in this couplet:

Like as, to make our appetites more keen,
With eager compounds we our palate urge.

Was Shakespeare obliquely extolling the virtues of the heretical herb? Did he actually smoke the noted weed? In 2001, Thackeray enlisted the aid of South African police forensic scientists, who used gas chromatography equipment to analyze two dozen clay pipe fragments that were excavated from the area of Shakespeare's Stratford-upon-Avon residence in early seventeenth-century England. Lo and behold, several of these fragments tested positive for hemp, a plant that had been cultivated in the British Isles at least since AD 400. Not surprisingly, tobacco residue was also found, along with traces of other curious substances.

Smoking tobacco was a new phenomenon in Shakespeare's time, having recently been introduced into English society. It was America's gift to Britain—part of a transatlantic swap: Hemp found a home in the New World while tobacco traveled in the other direction. The highly addictive nicotine habit spread like wildfire across Europe. Concerned that tobacco was undermining the social order, several European states imposed draconian punishments on smokers (such as the slitting of nostrils in Russia and the death penalty in Ottoman Turkey).

In seventeenth-century England, puffing tobacco was initially equated with plotting against the state. But the tobacco craze was unstoppable. After trying unsuccessfully to ban it, the British monarchy decided that smokers should pay with their money instead of with their lives. Tobacco commerce was heavily taxed, quickly filling the state treasury. To maintain their profit, merchants in turn raised the price of tobacco, which became worth its weight in silver to an addicted populace. And if the drug dealers of yore were anything like those of today, it's a safe bet that some cut their tobacco with less pricey leaf to boost their earnings. This could explain how traces of hemp, as well as coca leaf from Peru, ended up in the pipes found in Shakespeare's garden.

Shakespeare never explicitly mentioned pipes, smoking, or tobacco in any of his plays or poems. There's no proof that he smoked weed, "noted" or otherwise. But forensic science has shown that Shakespeare's neighbors—and perhaps the Bard himself—were inhaling some odd herbal mixtures that included hemp. And they may not have known exactly what was in those mixtures.

English-language accounts of hemp's utility as a medicine first appeared in 1621, five years after Shakespeare's death. The English clergyman Robert Burton cited hemp as a remedy for depression in his book *Anatomy of Melancholy.* Nicholas Culpeper's *Compleat Herbal*—the standard work on medicinal herbs for more than three hundred years after it was first published in mid-seventeenth-century England—recommended hemp for treating burns, gout, bowel problems, parasites, and skin inflammation, and as a general painkiller. (Culpeper remarked in his compendium that hemp was so well known among English housewives that he did not bother to indicate all its medicinal uses.) The *New London Dispensary* of 1682 added coughs and jaundice to the list of conditions for which hempseed decoctions were indicated, but warned that large doses had a side effect of filling the patient's head with "vapors."

The explorer Thomas Bowrey was the first Englishman to write about the recreational use of cannabis after he drank some bhang, a milk-based beverage infused with "gunjah" leaf and seed, while visiting India in the late seventeenth century. Referring to cannabis as the "admirable herbe," Captain Bowrey recorded in his journal: "In less than half an houre, its Operation will Shew it Selfe for the space of 4 or 5 hours." Bowrey indicated that his crewmen reacted to Indian hemp in different ways—the experience largely depended on the personality of the imbiber.

Carl Linnaeus, the father of modern botany, named the plant *Cannabis sativa* (*sativa* means "cultivated") in 1753. In his "Dissertation on the Sexes of Plants," the eminent Swedish scientist describes growing cannabis on his windowsill, an experience he greatly enjoyed.

> In the month of April, I sowed the seeds of hemp (*Cannabis*) in two different pots. The young plants came up plentifully . . . I placed each by the window, but in different and remote compartments. In one of them I permitted the male and female plants to remain together, to flower and bear fruit, which ripened in July . . . From the other, however, I removed all the male plants, as soon as they were old enough for me to distinguish them from the females. The remaining females grew very well, and presented their long pistilla in great abundance, these flowers continuing a very long time, as if in expectation of their mates . . . It was certainly a beautiful and truly admirable spectacle, to see the unimpregnated females preserve their pistilla so long green and flourishing, not permitting them to fade, till they had been for a very considerable time exploded, in vain, to access the male pollen . . .

Erasmus Darwin, the mid-eighteenth-century English physiologist, doctor, inventor, and poet, experimented with breeding methods to maximize the size of his cannabis specimens. A founding member of the Lunar Society, a discussion group of innovative industrialists and natural philosophers, he was also the grandfather of Charles Darwin. Charles was a contemporary of William B. O'Shaughnessy, the Irish scientist and physician who introduced cannabis to modern Western medicine.

Dr. O'Shaughnessy conducted an extensive study of Indian hemp while serving with the British East India Company in the 1830s. A man of many talents, he oversaw the construction of the first telegraph system in colonial

India, a 3,500-mile endeavor for which he was knighted by Queen Victoria. O'Shaughnessy also taught chemistry and practiced surgery at the Medical College of Calcutta. His interest was piqued by the Indians' widespread use of "gunjah," as he called it, for therapeutic, religious, and recreational purposes. "Almost invariably . . . the inebriation is of the most cheerful kind," he observed.

Seeking the advice of native doctors and scholars, O'Shaughnessy traveled to Nepal, Afghanistan, and Persia, where four or five people often shared cannabis smoke from a hookah.* "In the popular medicine of these nations, we find it extensively employed for a multitude of affections," O'Shaughnessy reported. He watched Ayurvedic healers mix ganja resin with ghee (clarified butter), creating a green, gooey remedy that was administered as a nerve tonic in India. After testing ganja tincture on animals and sampling it firsthand to better understand its effects, he decided it was safe to undertake scientific experiments with human subjects.

O'Shaughnessy investigated the drug's impact on various maladies and validated many of the folk uses of cannabis. He gave an oral extract to some of his Indian patients who suffered from rabies, cholera, tetanus, epilepsy, rheumatism, and other conditions that were very difficult to treat. The data he gathered from these clinical trials formed the basis of a groundbreaking forty-page monograph on the medicinal applications of Indian hemp. Published in 1842, it was the first modern medical article about cannabis to appear in a British scientific journal and it raised eyebrows on both sides of the Atlantic.

O'Shaughnessy noted the general effects of Indian hemp—"perpetual giggling," "ravenous appetite," "a sensation of ascending," "mental exultation"—and emphasized its efficacy as a painkiller, a muscle relaxant, and "an anti-convulsive remedy of the greatest value." In his paper, O'Shaughnessy also discussed ganja experimentation among his students that was not, strictly speaking, undertaken with a therapeutic intent. After swallowing "the spiritous tincture," a retiring young Scottish pupil behaved like "a rajah giving orders to his courtiers" and expounded upon "scientific, religious and political topics with astonishing eloquence." Likening his student's behavior to the trance channeling of the Delphic Oracles, O'Shaughnessy wrote that it "would be difficult to imagine a scene more interesting."

One of the curious characteristics of this "powerful and valuable substance," O'Shaughnessy observed, was the "contrary qualities" of medicinal hemp, "its

* In the Zend-Avesta, the ancient Persian religious text written around 700 BC, cannabis is mentioned as the most important of 10,000 medicinal pants.

stimulant and sedative effects." He found that hemp "possessed in small doses an extraordinary power of stimulating the digestive organs [and] exciting the cerebral system," while "larger doses induce insensibility or act as a powerful sedative." O'Shaughnessy expressed concern that "the incautious use of hemp preparations" could trigger "a peculiar form of delirium." Too strong a dose, he warned, might produce just the opposite of the desired medicinal outcome. The concluding sentence of his seminal study advised: "My experience would lead me to prefer *small* [emphasis in the original] doses of the remedy in order to excite rather than narcotise [*sic*] the patient."

O'Shaughnessy was describing what would become known in modern pharmacological parlance as the "biphasic" effect, whereby smaller amounts of a particular substance pack a potent therapeutic punch while larger doses have the opposite effect. (A large dosage might even make matters worse by exacerbating onerous symptoms.) The less-is-more dynamic intrinsic to the curative properties of cannabis dovetailed in significant ways with homeopathic medical practice, which, strange as it may seem, utilizes remedies that are diluted to enhance their impact. This notion conflicts with the assumptions of the allopathic school that would come to dominate Western medicine. Allopathic logic maintains that if low doses of a drug act as a stimulant, then a larger dosage should stimulate even more. But that's not how cannabis functions.

O'Shaughnessy respected the pioneering work of Samuel Hahnemann (1755–1843), the German founder of homeopathy, an alternative current within modern Western medicine. Hahnemann recommended microdoses of cannabis for certain people with nervous disorders. Drawing upon his analysis, the homeopathy journal *American Provers' Union* published the first U.S. report on the medicinal effects of cannabis in 1839, the same year O'Shaughnessy presented his initial scientific findings to the Medical and Physical Society of Bengal.

In 1842, O'Shaughnessy returned to England with a stash of Indian hemp. He gave some to Peter Squire, a London pharmacist, who developed and refined an alcohol-based tincture under O'Shaughnessy's supervision. Soon physicians in Europe and the United States were prescribing "Squire's Extract" and other cannabis concoctions for a variety of conditions, including nausea, delirium tremens, epilepsy, and painful spasms. Doctors often turned to cannabis preparations to treat ailments for which there were no known cures.

The U.S. Pharmacopeia first listed Indian hemp in 1854, along with a cautionary heads-up regarding the variable potency of cannabis products. By the end of the nineteenth century, more than a hundred articles had appeared in medical and scientific journals, documenting the benefits of this new wonder drug—or so it seemed at the time to many people.

The introduction of psychoactive hemp as a widely used therapeutic substance coincided with major changes in American medicine. Manufactured pills with precise dosages were replacing hand-me-down elixirs. And mom-and-pop apothecaries were becoming retail outlets for Eli Lilly, Parke-Davis, Squibb, and other fledgling U.S. pharmaceutical firms eager to sell their own cannabis cures along with a dizzying array of over-the-counter concoctions (including mixtures of cocaine, morphine, and Indian hemp). While the herb was usually ingested as a tincture, Grimault & Sons marketed ready-made cannabis cigarettes as an asthma remedy in the late 1800s. Indian hemp was a staple in most mustard plasters, poultices, and muscle ointments available in the United States. It was also a key ingredient in dozens of unlabeled patent medicines.

In 1860, the Ohio State Medical Society conducted the first official U.S. government study of cannabis, surveying the medical literature and cataloging an impressive array of conditions that doctors had successfully treated with psychoactive hemp, ranging from bronchitis and rheumatism to venereal disease and postpartum depression. The use of cannabis as an analgesic was so common that medical textbooks and journals identified several types of pain for which it should be administered. No less a figure than Sir William Osler, often called the founder of modern medicine, endorsed cannabis as the best treatment for migraine headaches. (In addition to easing headache pain, cannabis inhibited the nausea and vomiting associated with migraines.) And Sir John Russell Reynolds, Queen Victoria's personal physician, prescribed hemp tincture to Her Majesty to relieve painful menstrual cramps. He also recommended the herb for insomnia. "When pure and administered carefully, it is one of the most valuable medicines we possess," Reynolds asserted.

High on Hash

Dr. Jacques-Joseph Moreau de Tours, a trailblazing French psychiatrist, first learned about the mind-altering qualities of cannabis while traveling through the Middle East in the 1830s. In Egypt, a French colony since Napoleon invaded the country in 1798, Moreau was struck by the absence of alcohol and the prevalence of hashish (compressed cannabis resin), which Muslims from all walks of life consumed. The custom was particularly widespread among poor Arabs—the word *hashishin* became a pejorative for lower-class hashish users—yet few habitués seemed to suffer adverse consequences from the drug. Moreau concluded that hashish was a very safe substance: "[W]ine and liquors are a thousand times more dangerous." Noting that many of the diseases plaguing Europe were rare among Egyptians, he surmised that their indulgence in hashish and abstention from alcohol had a beneficial impact on their health.

But French colonial authorities in Cairo thought otherwise. They were so disturbed by the scale of hashish consumption among the native population that they tried to impose a ban on its use. Their alarm grew as French soldiers posted in Egypt partook of the habit in increasing numbers, despite regulations forbidding such behavior. After their tour of duty, some troops returned to France with hashish in their pockets. It was another example of how the use of cannabis in Western societies came from the colonized and the enslaved—the subject peoples of Europe and America.

Dr. Moreau also brought hashish back to Paris, where he sought to unravel the "mysteries of madness" by administering it to mental patients and studying how they reacted. Hashish seemed to calm them down, the doctor noted: Some hospitalized insomniacs were able to sleep well thanks to cannabis and the bleakest moods of a few depressed patients seemed to lift. But the results were inconsistent and, more often than not, fleeting. Still, Moreau felt that hashish could be a significant asset in treating mental illness and he urged doctors to avail themselves of the experience. Its greatest benefit, he maintained, was in enabling psychiatrists to gain insight into the mental worlds they were trying to comprehend and treat.

Walking the talk, as it were, Moreau found himself "rapt in a thousand fantastic ideas" after eating some hashish paste. Yet he never lost his lucidity or forgot that he had taken a drug. He was able to reflect upon his experience as everything unfolded, straddling a kind of double consciousness—stoned yet rational—while under the spell of cannabis. "To understand the ravings of a madman, one must have raved himself, but without having lost the awareness of one's madness," he wrote in *Hashish and Mental Illness*. Published in 1845, this landmark exposition postulated that insanity was caused by a chemical alteration of the nervous system rather than by physical damage to the brain. A large dose of hashish, according to Moreau, produced a model psychosis that temporarily mimicked symptoms of real mental illness.*

J.-J. Moreau's Parisian hashish experiments were instrumental in catalyzing the development of psychopharmacology as a field of study. But it was outside the scientific milieu where Moreau's project had a more immediate impact. He fed the cannabis-laced confectionary to poets, painters, sculptors, and

* Although the "model psychosis" concept was dubious, it had considerable influence on subsequent public-policy debates over cannabis and psychedelic drugs. Prohibitionists would go to town on the notion that marijuana makes you crazy.

architects, who were eager to explore the mental effects of hashish. Honoré de Balzac, Victor Hugo, Gustave Flaubert, Eugène Delacroix, Gérard de Nerval, and several other luminaries met each month at the elegant Hôtel Pimodan on Île Saint-Louis in Paris. They gathered beneath vaulted ceilings in an ornately decorated room with plush velvet curtains framing the door and tapestries on the walls. Dr. Moreau, the self-styled master of ceremonies, gave everyone a spoonful of greenish jelly paste made of pistachio, cinnamon, nutmeg, sugar, orange peel, butter, cloves, and, last but not least, hashish.

After everyone had eaten the green fudge—known as *dawamesc* in Arabic, which means "medicine of immortality"—they sat down for dinner. Some members of Le Club des Haschischins, as it was called, wore costumes with turbans and daggers, lending an exotic ambience to the conclave. Dr. Moreau, outfitted in Turkish dress, played the piano. By the end of the meal, they were feeling the effects of the hashish. Before long the dining hall was filled with laughter—a sure sign that the medicine was working.

The Hashish Eaters' Club was founded in 1844 by Moreau and his principal collaborator, Théophile Gautier, the French novelist best known for coining the bohemian battle cry: "Art for art's sake." Gautier wrote a famous essay, "Le Club des Haschischins," which described the proceedings in vivid detail. Gautier's baroque raptures generated wide attention among French intellectuals and artists. Before long, the Hashish Eaters' Club was the toast of Paris.

After the "convulsive gaiety of the beginning," Gautier wrote of his initiation into hashish, "an indefinable feeling of well-being, a boundless calm took over . . . I was like a sponge in the middle of the ocean. At every moment streams of happiness penetrated me, entering and leaving through my pores . . . I had never been so overwhelmed with bliss." Freed from his ego ("that odious and ever present witness"), he was seeing sounds and hearing colors.

"Soon the magic paste was completely digested and acted with more force in my brain," he reported. "I became completely mad for an hour. Every kind of gigantic dream-creature passed through my fantasies: goatsuckers, fiddle-faddle beasts, bridled goslings, unicorns, griffons, incubi, an entire menagerie of monstrous nightmares fluttered, hopped, skipped, and squeaked through the room."

The effects of cannabis, as Gautier discovered, could be quite capricious, especially when high doses are consumed. Whereas inhaling a few puffs of herb often produces a soft, dreamy, swimmy-headed high, eating hashish in sufficient quantities could precipitate a full-blown hallucinogenic experience more akin to magic mushrooms or LSD—with fast-moving kaleidoscopic imagery, physical rushes, flashes of insight, and, in some cases, intense anxiety and paranoia, although such feelings usually fade before the visions have run their course.*

Portrayed as a magic carpet ride to a boundless beyond within, hashish had a mystique that fascinated the French reading public. Alexandre Dumas, a notorious hashish eater and the most popular writer of his day, introduced the green jam to thicken the plot of his classic novel *The Count of Monte Cristo*. The enigmatic count, who calls himself "Sinbad the Sailor," offers a morsel of green paste to a wary visitor. "Taste this," Sinbad implores, "and the boundaries of possibility disappear, the fields of infinite space open to you, you advance free in heart, free in mind . . . Taste the hashish, guest of mine—taste the hashish . . . Open your wings and fly into superhuman regions."

Sinbad's obliging initiate is transformed by the drug: "His body seemed to acquire an airy lightness, his perception brightened in a remarkable manner, his senses seemed to redouble their power, the horizon continued to expand . . ." The hashish triggers a Dionysian gusher, an onrush of visual, musical, and erotic epiphanies, and when the dream passes, Sinbad's guest awakens to find himself stuck in a dark cave on a remote island, yearning to return to that tumultuous zone of enchantment.

The longing for the infinite and the use of drugs to satisfy this perennial urge were prominent themes in the poetry and prose of Charles Baudelaire. Although he lodged for a while at Hôtel Pimodan, Baudelaire did not regularly attend meetings of Le Club des Haschischins. Yet today Baudelaire is recalled as the writer most closely associated with the French hashish eaters. His books *On Wine and Hashish* and *The Artificial Paradises* are among the most admired of nineteenth-century drug writings.

Baudelaire praised the "superior sharpness" of his senses, "the glorious radiance," and the keen appreciation of music that he experienced under the potent sway of hashish. "It is as though one lives several lifetimes in the space of an hour," he mused. "It is like living some fantastic novel instead of reading

---

* Because of how it is processed in the body, orally administered cannabis releases psychoactive compounds more slowly than fast-acting cannabis smoke, which passes from the lungs, where the blood is oxygenated, directly into the bloodstream and the brain. When eaten, THC, the psychoactive component of cannabis, is transformed by the liver into a metabolite (11–hydroxy) that is four times more potent than THC itself, with delayed effects lasting for as long as eight hours. "A longer duration of effect makes oral cannabis preferable for those who are using it to treat sleep disorders," notes Dr. Mollie Fry, a California physician who was arrested in 2001 (and later imprisoned for violating the federal Controlled Substances Act) after she recommended that several of her patients use cannabis for this purpose.

it." But Baudelaire was ultimately critical of the moral and social implications of consuming the green paste. Although he says there are no dangerous physical consequences from hashish, he contends that the psychological risks are serious: "You have scattered your personality to the four winds of heaven, and how difficult it is now to recover and reconstruct it."

Referring to hashish as a "very tricky substance," Baudelaire said it acts like "a magnifying mirror" that "reveals nothing to the individual but himself." Hashish is psychodynamic, amplifying what already exists and drawing forth what is latent in the mind; thus it is important to be of sound mind and body, the poet advised, when embarking upon such an adventure. "Each man has the dream he deserves," according to Baudelaire, who concluded that hashish is "nothing miraculous, absolutely nothing but an exaggeration of the natural."

What did Baudelaire see when he gazed into the mirror of hashish? A pathetic syphilis-infected figure who botched a suicide attempt, an opium-addicted alcoholic whose overbearing mother, a devout Christian, was obsessed with Original Sin. Filled with self-hatred, Baudelaire projected his loathing onto "wretched hashish," that "chaotic devil," which he denounced after finding its effects too disturbing.

"I would have thought it better if you hadn't blamed hashish and opium, but only excess," Gustave Flaubert wrote in a letter to Baudelaire. Flaubert noted in the same letter that psychoactive hemp preparations, mostly in the form of alcohol-based tinctures, were on sale at French pharmacies, which meant that those enthralled by the literature of hashish could easily obtain the drug for experimental purposes. Such a prospect dismayed Baudelaire, who argued, "If by means of a teaspoonful of sweetmeat man can instantly procure all the blessings of heaven and earth, then he will not be prepared to earn one thousandth part of the same by hard work." In the end, he condemned the use of hashish as a doomed attempt to avoid requisite suffering.

While a growing number of French physicians utilized cannabis tinctures to treat patients stricken with various ailments, Dr. François Lallemand viewed the healing potential of hashish in broader social terms. A pioneer neuroscientist and Hashish Eaters' Club member, Lallemand was the first person to study the frontal lobes of the human brain and link them to language cognition and speech. He also wrote a utopian novel, *Hachych,* which was quite popular in mid-1800s France. The narrative begins at a dinner party where a doctor, just back from Egypt, feeds hashish to his guests, who experience "political ecstasies" and visions of a perfect society. Prefiguring the countercultural upheavals of the 1960s, Lallemand depicted hashish as a mental detonator, a catalyst for revolution, an anarchist weapon against the bourgeoisie.

Arthur Rimbaud, the *enfant terrible* of French arts and letters, didn't use cannabis until twenty years after Le Club des Haschischins dissolved and most of its members had passed away. A child prodigy with a gift for verse, Rimbaud was the rebel incarnate, the wild-eyed mystic, a desperate vagabond forever in search of "Christmas on earth." He ran away from home and joined the Paris Commune in 1871, but fled shortly before the bloody crackdown that put an end to the great working-class insurrection. "I had to travel, divert the spells assembled in my brain," the teenage renegade declared in *A Season in Hell*. Sleeping in the gutter, filthy, famished, and lice-infested, he took hashish and other drugs, including absinthe, the very strong, very bitter, and very addictive green liquor made from anise and wormwood.

For Rimbaud, hashish was at best a circuit-scrambling means to an end, not an end in itself. "The poet," he explained, "makes himself a visionary through a long, prodigious and systematic derangement of all his senses." The notion of some pie-in-the-sky paradise in a mythical afterlife elicited scorn from the young Rimbaud—he was all about the urgent here and now, the trials and tribulations of the flesh. "Hell hath no power over pagans," he proclaimed. Rimbaud got drunk and stoned with reckless abandon until he reached the point where he could say: "Finally I came to regard as sacred the disorder of my mind."

Rimbaud stopped composing poetry at the tender age of twenty, but his feverish verse, along with provocative accounts from first-generation French hashish eaters, would continue to entrance the literary world for many years to come. These evocative authors employed literary license to articulate some of the stranger aspects of the high-dose hashish experience. Through their writings, a large audience in modern Europe first learned about hemp's psychoactive properties. Around the same time, an awareness of cannabis as an inebriant was also starting to percolate in the United States, where homegrown hashish-swilling scribes were spinning a few yarns of their own.

Sex, Drugs, and the Occult

One morning in the spring of 1854, a precocious seventeen-year-old student named Fitz High Ludlow sauntered into his favorite hangout, Anderson's Apothecary in Poughkeepsie, New York. Reeking of "all things curative and preventive," the hometown pharmacy was "an aromatic invitation to scientific musing," said Ludlow, the son of an Abolitionist preacher. Anderson took a liking to the young man and allowed him to rummage through the store for hours on end. Ludlow had already sampled several psychoactive compounds, including ether, chloroform, and laudanum, an alcohol-based opium tincture, when Anderson informed him that a new product had arrived, something called Tilden's Extract. It was made from *Cannabis indica*, otherwise known as Indian hemp or "hasheesh." Ludlow picked up a vial of the odiferous, olive-brown elixir and sniffed its contents.

Tilden & Co., the U.S. subsidiary of the Edinburgh-based Smith Brothers (widely known for its cough medicines), was among the first to market solid as well as liquid hashish preparations. The company catalog touted *Cannabis indica* for "hysteria, chorea, gout, neuralgia, acute and sub-acute rheumatism, tetanus, hydrophobia and the like." But Fitz Hugh Ludlow, a quirky book-worm, was more interested in self-exploration than in using cannabis to cure a particular illness. He recognized that Tilden's Extract was, in essence, the same drug that he had recently read about in a story by Bayard Taylor, an American diplomat and travel writer, in the *Atlantic Monthly*. Taylor's account of eating a generous lump of hashish in Damascus was the first article in a popular U.S. magazine that discussed the psychoactive effects of cannabis. "I was encompassed by a sea of light . . . a vista of rainbows," Taylor rhapsodized. But after glimpsing paradise he got the willies and sank into an awful funk. Yet he did not regret trying hashish, for it revealed "deeps of rapture and suffering which my natural faculties never could have sounded."*

Ludlow took a cue from Taylor, whose experimentation with hashish was motivated not by hedonism but by a quest for knowledge, the desire to delve into unknown realms. For six cents, Ludlow purchased a box of Tilden's Extract from Anderson's; no doctor's note was necessary. Twice he swallowed the bitter potion to little effect. So Ludlow upped the dose substantially, and the third time worked like a charm—or at least it started out that way. He was "smitten by the hashish thrill as by a thunderbolt." Sparing no hyperbole, Ludlow waxed euphoric: "A vision of celestial glory burst upon me . . . I glowed like a new-born soul." But his mood quickly shifted. He suddenly noticed that the room was shrinking. People looked strange. Insane faces glared at him. The wallpaper came alive with satyrs. Panic set in. He oscillated wildly between deep beatitude and "uncontrollable terror."

Still awestruck the next day, Ludlow vowed to conduct additional experiments with the amazing extract. At the time, few people in the United States knew anything about cannabis, which was neither a narcotic nor an anesthetic but a substance of a whole different caliber. Ludlow had no one to guide him

---

* The first mention of hashish by an American author appears in a short poem by John Greenleaf Whittier in 1854: "Of all that Orient lands can vaunt of marvels with our own competing, the strangest is the Haschish plant and what will follow on its eating."

through the seductive labyrinth of hashish. Relying on his own devices, he took the drug frequently through the summer of 1854 and experienced a "prolonged state of hasheesh exaltation." Ludlow wasn't trying to mitigate pain or overcome illness; he was trying, perhaps impetuously, to gain insight into himself. Occasionally after ingesting a modest dose of *Cannabis indica*, Ludlow felt an overwhelming universal benevolence, which he referred to as a "catholic sympathy, a spiritual cosmopolitanism." He maintained that during high-dose hashish benders he underwent "metempsychosis," the movement of the soul out of the body, and seemingly traveled to far-off lands without physically going anywhere. After scouring the astral depths and suffering "the agonies of a martyr," he decided "to experiment with the drug of sorcery no more."

Ludlow embellished his stoned adventures in his book, *The Hasheesh Eater*, which was published anonymously in 1857 when he was twenty, although subsequent editions included the author's name. The book was well received among critics and inquisitive readers, from London literary salons to California gold camps. Some impressionable youth felt inspired to try the drug after reading Ludlow, including Brown University student John Hay, who later served as Abraham Lincoln's personal assistant, and secretary of state under Teddy Roosevelt. (Lincoln's widow was prescribed a cannabis tincture for her nerves after his assassination.) An instant curiosity, if not a classic, *The Hasheesh Eater* became the preeminent nineteenth-century American statement on the subject of mind-altering drugs. Ludlow was the first American scribe to stake his reputation on the claim that certain substances, especially cannabis, can enliven consciousness and arouse creativity—a belief that many young people would embrace with fervor in the 1960s. But Ludlow also warned of overindulgence with hashish and all drugs.

A rising star in the American literary firmament, Ludlow moved to Manhattan to pursue a career as a freelance journalist. He befriended a group of bohemian writers who hobnobbed at Pfaff's, a downtown restaurant, sharing tables with the likes of Walt Whitman and Mark Twain. Louisa May Alcott, the soon-to-be-famous author of *Little Women,* also caroused at Pfaff's.

In 1869, Alcott wrote a short story called "Perilous Play," which depicts the recreational use of cannabis. The story opens with a pronouncement by Belle Daventry, an attractive socialite: "If someone does not propose a new and interesting amusement, I shall die of ennui!" Dr. Meredith comes to the rescue, offering hashish pastries to Belle and her friends. "Eat six of these despised bonbons," he promises, "and you will be amused in a new, delicious and wonderful manner." When queried about the bonbons, the good doctor reassures her, "I use it for my patients. It is very efficacious in nervous disorders, and is getting to be quite a pet remedy with us."

Hashish was quite the pet remedy for Paschal Beverly Randolph, a mercurial mulatto intellectual, unstable occultist, bathtub chemist, and self-proclaimed master of "sex magic." A firebrand on the mid-nineteenth-century speaker's circuit, Randolph bequeathed hashish to the twilight world of American spiritualism. He touted the drug as a wondrous means of inducing clairvoyance and astral travel. "It will burst upon you like the crash of ten thousand thunders," he exclaimed, "and for hours you will be the sport of imaginations turned to realities of the queerest, strangest and weirdest, and perhaps terrific kind."

Randolph first tasted "the medicine of immortality" while traveling in France in 1855. He became a regular user and an enthusiastic proponent of hashish, claiming it was food for the soul, a replenisher of vital forces. But the true recipe for the green paste was known only "by adepts," according to Randolph, and it just so happened that he had access to an authentic source. At one point before the Civil War, Randolph "was probably the largest importer of hashish into the United States," his biographer, John Patrick Deveney, reports. Randolph was also the founder of the first Rosicrucian sect in North America. (Credited with being a repository of esoteric knowledge, the Brotherhood of the Rosy Cross debuted in Middle Europe in 1614 and has been the subject of conspiracy rumors ever since.) While ministering to his secret society, Randolph developed a formula for an Indian hemp concentrate and he created several patent medicines with cannabis as a key ingredient. During spirited lecture tours, he hawked his homemade hashish elixirs as "invigorants" and sex tonics for the erotically unfulfilled.

In large part due to Randolph's efforts, hashish experimentation became de rigueur within spiritualist circles in the United States and abroad. Russian-born mystic Helena Petrovna Blavatsky, the mesmerizing grande dame of occultism, was a dedicated hashish imbiber. "Hashish multiplies one's life a thousand-fold . . . It is a wonderful drug and it clears up profound mystery," she enthused. In 1875, the year Randolph committed suicide, Blavatsky founded the Theosophical Society, headquartered in New York City, which would attract a worldwide following of eclectic spiritual seekers who were interested in everything from Eastern mysticism and vegetarianism to Freemasonry and trance mediums. At times under the influence of hashish, Blavatsky wrote lengthy tomes filled with esoteric lore, introducing such concepts as karma, yoga, kundalini, and reincarnation to a Western audience. Replete with pagan legends, her books (*The Secret Doctrine* and *Isis Unveiled*) did not win over Bible Belt America. But Blavatsky, the most famous spiritualist of her age, was a big hit among U.S. and European devotees of the occult. She had a significant following in Paris, where a group of hashish-eating daredevils, under the leadership of Dr. Louis-Alphonse Cahagnet, had been experimenting with monster doses (ten times the amount typically ingested at the soirees of Le Club des Haschischins) to send the soul on an ecstatic out-of-the-body journey through intrepid spheres.

It was via Parisian theosophical contacts that the great Irish poet and future Nobel laureate William Butler Yeats first turned on to hashish. An avid occultist, Yeats much preferred hashish to peyote (the hallucinogenic cactus), which he also sampled. Yeats was a member of the Hermetic Order of the Golden Dawn and its literary affiliate, the London-based Rhymers Club, which met in the 1890s. Emulating Le Club des Haschischins, the Rhymers used hashish to seduce the muse and stimulate occult insight.*

Another member of the Hermetic Order of the Golden Dawn, Aleister Crowley, was a notorious dope fiend and practitioner of the occult arts. Crowley conducted magical experiments while bingeing on morphine, cocaine, peyote, ether, and ganja. He translated Baudelaire's writings on hashish into English and published excerpts in *The Equinox,* his occult periodical. Dubbed "the wickedest man in the world" by Britain's yellow press, Crowley came to the rather sober conclusion that a person's reactions to mind-altering drugs were specific to the individual and influenced by cultural variables. This was the gist of an essay he wrote, "The Psychology of Hashish," which quoted Fitz Hugh Ludlow's evocative comment about how hashish "loosens the girders of the soul." Crowley and H. P. Lovecraft, the American writer of supernatural fiction and another fin-de-siècle hashish eater, both greatly admired Ludlow's book.

The occult revival in the late 1800s was nourished by widespread insecurity over rapid changes in Western society and persistent anxiety about the future of humankind. The industrial revolution had reshuffled the deck economically and psychologically—the means of production and consumption were transformed, communication quickened, geographical distances shrank, populations shifted, and the working poor demanded a more equitable distribution of goods and resources. It was a period of profound uncertainty, as many people struggled to adapt to a new environment in which traditional human relationships—as well as one's place in the cosmos—were called into question.

---

* Rhymer mystery writer Algernon Blackwood published a story about a doctor-detective hired to investigate the case of a young comic who takes a hashish extract to make himself laugh. Instead, the comic is nearly driven mad by ghostly visitations. The detective's diagnosis: "[T]he hashish has partially opened another world to you by increasing your rate of psychical vibration, and thus rendering you abnormally sensitive" (Blackwood quoted in Boon, *The Road of Excess*, p. 146).

Doomsayers of every stripe had a field day. Occultists gleefully anticipated that "a terrible joy," in the words of Yeats, would soon "overturn governments, and all settled order." Believing that the end of civilization was imminent, Madame Blavatsky prophesied that a global catastrophe would usher in a Golden Dawn, after which the world would be governed by a beneficent psychic elite.

Whereas Blavatsky imagined a wondrous New Age emerging from the chaos, her contemporary Friedrich Nietzsche saw nothing but storm clouds of nihilism gathering on the horizon. Soon the ill winds of fascism would start to blow in Europe. Nietzsche, the German visionary, bemoaned the pervasive sense of alienation in modern society and the attempt by many to overcome it through intoxication, hedonism, disembodied mysticism, and "the voluptuous enjoyment of eternal emptiness." But Nietzsche, who called alcohol and Christianity "the two great European narcotics," was not averse to the therapeutic use of cannabis. "To escape from unbearable pressure you need hashish," Nietzsche wrote.

For all its sociopolitical and metaphysical contortions, the nineteenth century was an era of great personal freedom with respect to psychoactive substances. There were no laws against using hashish in Europe and North America, where any respectable person could walk into a pharmacy and choose from a range of cannabis tinctures and pastes. After the U.S. Civil War, Gunjah Wallah Hasheesh Candy ("a most pleasurable and harmless stimulant") was available via mail order from Sears-Roebuck. The average American pretty much was at liberty to use any drug that he or she desired.

Initially disseminated through medicinal channels, hashish was embraced by prominent writers on both sides of the Atlantic. Irish playwright Oscar Wilde wrote about cannabis, and a hookah-smoking caterpillar graced the pages of Lewis Carroll's *Alice's Adventures in Wonderland*. Robert Louis Stevenson (*Dr. Jekyll and Mr. Hyde*) also experimented with psychoactive hemp. And so did Jack London, who described a hashish-filled evening: "[L]ast night was like a thousand years. I was obsessed with indescribable sensations, alternative visions of excessive happiness and oppressive moods of extreme sorrow."

Inspired by first-person literary accounts and facilitated by local apothecaries, recreational use of cannabis among U.S. citizens slowly emerged during the patent-medicine era. In 1869, *Scientific American* reported, "The cannabis indica of the United States Pharmacopeia, the resinous product of hemp, grown in the East Indies and other parts of Asia, is used in those countries to a large extent for its intoxicating properties, and is doubtless used in this country for the same purpose to a limited extent."

Cannabis was on sale at the Turkish Hashish Pavilion, which generated a buzz during the American Centennial Exposition in Philadelphia in 1876.

Within a decade, there would be discreet hashish dens operating in every major American city. "All visitors, both male and female, are of the better classes . . . and the number of regular habitués is daily on the increase," H. H. Kane wrote of a New York City hashish parlor in *Harper's Magazine*. Published in 1883, the article depicted well-heeled patrons lounging in luxurious, dimly lit rooms, munching on cannabis edibles, smoking hashish, and drinking coca leaf tea.

For the most part, psychoactive hemp products were eaten in nineteenth-century America and Europe, not smoked. The growing number of hashish users in the West as the 1800s drew to a close was partly attributable to the belated realization that they could achieve a milder, quicker, and more manageable high by inhaling cannabis fumes instead of guzzling a tincture or chewing a pastry. Adopted by urban America's bohemian set, smoking hashish was not viewed as habit-forming or as an inducement to violence, addiction, or antisocial behavior; on the contrary, it was considered stylish and elegant. There was no stigma attached to cannabis and no cause for alarm until U.S. prohibitionists targeted "marihuana," the alien scourge, during an early twentieth-century upsurge of nativism, scapegoating, and political repression.

2

PROHIBITION

The Mexican Connection

High up in the rugged Sierra Madre mountains, fifty miles inland from the Pacific Ocean and a three-day journey on muleback to the nearest Mexican village, a terraced crop of marijuana is ready for harvest. Standing more than ten feet tall in blazing sunlight, hundreds of cannabis plants resemble thin bamboo shoots with clusters of long, serrated, fingerlike leaves swaying in the breeze. The gangly plants exude a distinctive, musky aroma. Concentrated on the upper leaves and on the thick tangle of matted flower tops known as the *cola* (Spanish for "tail"), minuscule mushroom-shaped trichome glands ooze resin containing psychoactive tetrahydrocannabinol (THC) and many other medicinal compounds. The resin—a kind of natural, frosty varnish—coats the leaves and acts both as a sunscreen and an insect repellant. Before harvesting, farmers test the resin content by squeezing the colas. If a sticky residue is left on their hands, they know the weed is good. Stripped and bundled, the cola-bearing branches are carried to a large shed and hung upside down on special drying racks for ten days. Then the marijuana is pressed into bricks and smuggled into the United States.

Long before it became an economic necessity for local farmers, the pungent herb was widely employed as a folk remedy by *curanderas* in Mexico, where marijuana patches were sufficiently plentiful in the countryside to be mistaken for an indigenous plant. The Tepehuan Indians in the Mexican highlands occasionally used cannabis—which they called Rosa Maria ("the Sacred Rose")—as a substitute for the peyote cactus in religious rituals. Indicative of its ability to stimulate collegiality and loquaciousness, Rosa Maria was known as the Herb That Makes One Speak.

By the early nineteenth century, when Mexican peasants first began smoking it as a means of relaxation and inebriation, cannabis seemed to grow wild everywhere. The abundance of *mota*, as Mexicans often referred to marijuana, may have derived in part from Spanish hemp fields left fallow during the colonial era. In 1545, the Spanish Crown ordered the cultivation of fiber hemp throughout its colonial territories—from the southern tip of Chile to Alta California. The extraordinary botanical flexibility of hemp enabled it to flourish in a wide range of soil types, altitudes, and weather. Epitomizing Darwin's survival of the fittest, hemp was so adaptable under stress that sex-starved plants could gender-bend and become hermaphroditic in order to pollinate and proliferate. Many hemp plants escaped from cultivation and, in the wild, underwent tricksterlike changes, according to Mexican historian Isaac Campos-Costero, who postulates that the fiber strains of Mexico's colonial era became the drug plants of the 1800s. He suggests that feral hemp, exposed to the scorching Mexican sun year after year for several centuries, adapted to the hot, dry climate by morphing into high-octane marijuana, a heliotropic (sun-loving) plant.

It was the hangover-free high that drew most people to the plant in Mexico, especially the multitudes of poor *campesinos* who utilized cannabis as a social lubricant and an antidote to drudgery and fatigue. There was a common saying among lower-class Mexicans, *"Esta ya le dio las tres"* ("You take it three times"), which referred to the exhilarating bounce from three puffs of marijuana. The fact that the use of cannabis, dubbed "the opium of the poor," was prevalent among underprivileged elements in Mexico (and in several other countries) may account for many of the persistent myths about the herb. Whereas the salt of the earth smoked pot as a palliative to help them cope with everyday tedium and despair, those of a more affluent standing tended to blame the problems of the less fortunate on the consumption of cannabis. Its initial association with the dregs of society—landless peasants, bandits, bootleggers, prisoners, and so on—made marijuana a convenient scapegoat for deep-rooted social inequities.

The military was one segment of the Mexican population that readily accepted marijuana. Conscripts enjoyed smoking the weed, which, in most cases, was cheaper than alcohol and easier to obtain. During the Mexican Revolution (1910–20), the first great social revolution of the twentieth century, Pancho Villa's guerrilla army, composed largely of peons and Indians, smoked marijuana during long marches and afterward to a celebrate a successful campaign. Known for their toughness, these pot-smoking peasants were valiant and tenacious fighters. Their stoned exploits in northern Mexico were immortalized in the well-known folk song "La Cucaracha" with the chorus about a hapless foot soldier ("the cockroach") who can't function unless he's high on marijuana:

La cucaracha, la cucaracha
Ya no puede caminar
Porque no tiene, porque no tiene
Marijuana que fumar

The cockroach, the cockroach
Is unable to walk
Because he doesn't have, because he doesn't have
Any marijuana to smoke

"Roach," modern-day slang for the butt of a marijuana cigarette, derives from this song, which inspired a dance and an Oscar-winning musical of the same name. Initially a battle hymn sung by Mexican rebels, "La Cucaracha" became a popular cultural phenomenon throughout North America. It is one of the first examples of how cannabis entered mainstream consciousness through mass media.

Although many of his troops were stoners, it's not known to what extent General Pancho Villa, the Sierra-bred ruffian, smoked marijuana. Known for his martial prowess and his skills as a horseman, he was lionized as the gentleman bandit who rescued orphans and wowed the ladies while chasing Yankee capitalists out of the country. In an age of stark disparities between the wealthy few and the impoverished many, Pancho Villa was Mexico's answer to Robin Hood. His military feats became legendary through popular ballads called *corridos*, which chronicled significant events of the day—from gun battles and government betrayals to love affairs and bountiful marijuana harvests. (*Narcocorridos*, a subgenre of folk songs devoted to marijuana smokers, smugglers, and drug-related bandidos, originated during this period.) More than just a form of entertainment, these ballads were a key source of news and political commentary that resonated with Mexico's illiterate masses. Some *corridos* glorified Pancho Villa's predawn cross-border raid in 1916 against a U.S. military garrison in New Mexico. Other songs lampooned General John Pershing, who sent an expeditionary force of 12,000 U.S. troops into Mexico in fruitless pursuit of the wily guerrilla leader.

Apparently some soldiers under Pershing's command could not resist the wiles of Mary Jane, the aromatic temptress. "After the guard went down to Mexico and came back, I saw the first white people who smoked the plant," a Texas-based U.S. Army physician told a federal fact-finding commission in the early 1920s. This practice found favor among U.S. troops stationed on the border, including black cavalry units, who smoked marijuana cigarettes either straight or mixed with tobacco.

The emergence of marijuana smoking in early twentieth-century America was catalyzed mainly by the tumultuous Mexican Revolution, which caused hundreds of thousands of brown-skinned migrants to flee to the U.S. Southwest in search of safety and work. Smoking grass became commonplace among dispossessed Mexicans in border towns such as El Paso, Texas, which passed the first city ordinance banning the sale and possession of cannabis in 1914. Public officials and newspaper reports depicted marijuana, the Mexican *loco weed,* as a dangerous vice, an alien intrusion into American life. Enacted in a climate of fear and hostility toward swarthy, Spanish-speaking foreigners, early marijuana legislation was a handy instrument to keep the newcomers in their place. Antidrug and vagrancy statutes, in addition to legally sanctioned segregation in housing, restaurants, and parks, comprised what one historian described as "a web of social controls" that were "mobilized to police Mexicans."

On a federal level, marijuana prohibition would be implemented in increments. In 1906, Congress passed the Pure Food and Drug Act, a landmark piece of reform designed to restrain abuses and rampant charlatanism in the patent-medicine industry. It was the first national legislation to mention cannabis, which was included—along with alcohol, opiates, cocaine, and chloral hydrate—on a list of intoxicating ingredients whose presence had to be identified on the product label. The prescription system had its origins in this law, which anointed the U.S. government as the watchdog over all drugs and medications that Americans took to make themselves feel better. While well intended, the law gave unprecedented power to federal bureaucrats to decide which drugs a person would be allowed to consume. Under the auspices of the Pure Food and Drug Act, U.S. officials would prohibit the importation of cannabis for anything other than strictly medical purposes.

Until 1906, there had been little concerted effort on the part of the federal government to regulate the manufacture, distribution, or consumption of psychoactive substances. Cocaine was still in Coca-Cola; heroin and hypodermic kits were available through Sears. No drug was illegal. The Harrison Act of 1914 extended federal control over narcotics so that a nonmedical consumer could not legitimately possess opiates or cocaine. For the first time, the U.S. government asserted a legal distinction between medical and recreational drug use. Physicians did not realize that they could be tricked into giving narcotics to a police informant, who pretended to need a painkiller. One study estimated that on the heels of the Harrison Act—which laid the foundation for contemporary drug prohibition—25,000 American doctors were arrested on narcotics charges, 3,000 served prison sentences, and thousands more had their licenses revoked in a bare-knuckle drive to prevent physicians from prescribing opiates to their patients.

Thanks to strong lobbying by the pharmaceutical industry, marijuana was not covered by the Harrison Act. From a federal perspective, cannabis didn't seem to pose much of a problem at the time. Most Americans were not yet aware of marijuana and few people, other than marginalized Mexicans and blacks, smoked it. While the feds dithered, several western and southern states proceeded to outlaw the herb, with California taking the lead in 1915, a move that served as a pretext for harassing Mexicans, just as opium legislation in San Francisco forty years earlier was directed at another despised minority, the Chinese.* In each case, the target of the prohibition was not the drug so much as those most associated with its use. Typically in the United States, drug statutes have been aimed—or selectively enforced—against a feared or disparaged group within society.

"All Mexicans are crazy, and this stuff [marijuana] makes them crazy," said one Lone Star state senator. Marijuana was outlawed in Texas in 1919 amid a wave of labor unrest. There were more than three thousand strikes throughout the country that year. Ignoring the rights of free speech, assembly, and due process, Attorney General A. Mitchell Palmer launched his infamous raids against aliens, "reds," and union members in dozens of American cities. The first "Palmer raids" in November 1919 were timed to coincide with the second anniversary of the Russian Revolution. The U.S. Supreme Court would soon outlaw picketing, abolish the minimum wage for women, and overturn child labor laws, while federal agents roamed the land, breaking up public meetings, seizing political literature, and patrolling freight cars for migrants. Side by side with "Bolshevik" labor leaders, state penitentiaries held significant numbers of Mexican American men serving time for drug crimes, according to sociologist Curtis Marez, who notes that "arrests and convictions of 'Mexican' workers for marijuana possession were most concentrated during the years of, and in the areas with, the highest levels of labor organization and action." The incarceration of Mexican workers, whether for smoking or striking, made the workforce as a whole easier to manage.

American society in the 1920s was a simmering cauldron of phobias—anti-Communist, antidrug, antiblack, antiforeigner. Law-enforcement operations against alleged "reds" and "dope fiends" (the two became conflated in the nativist mind) were bolstered by the Ku Klux Klan and other violent white vigilantes, who attacked left-wingers, Mexican immigrants, and other so-called un-American groups.

---

* Concurrent with the ban on opium, there were laws against wearing queues (ponytails), the traditional Chinese hairstyle, in San Francisco.

In 1925, the U.S. government convened a formal committee to investigate rumors that off-duty American soldiers based in the Panama Canal Zone were smoking "goof butts" for kicks. It was the first official U.S. inquiry into cannabis, and it concluded that marijuana was not addictive (in the sense in which the term is applied to alcohol, opium, or cocaine), nor did it have "any appreciable deleterious influence on the individual using it." On the basis of this assessment, previous orders prohibiting possession of the weed by military personnel were revoked in 1926.

Three years later, Congress passed the Narcotic Farms Act, which misclassified "Indian hemp" as a "habit-forming narcotic" and authorized the establishment of two hospitals in the federal prison system for treating drug addicts. The emerging consensus among lawmakers was that the nonmedical use of narcotics, like a cancer, had to be excised entirely from the body politic. The myth of the shiftless "marijuana addict," which surfaced during this period, was the figment of an early twentieth-century imagination desperate to define its own normality by highlighting the difference between "us" (the well-born and productive members of society) and "them" (the dirty, lazy, foreign-born pot smokers).* Since colonial times, Americans had been the arbiters of their own drug experiences; it wasn't considered the proper business of government to tell people what to smoke or swallow or what to avoid. Now the *federales* were keen to intervene, claiming a moral imperative to protect individuals from harming themselves—whether they liked it or not.

The Mighty Mezz

Once upon a time in the USA, alcohol was banned and cannabis was exempt from national crime legislation. The convivial consumption of alcohol became illegal when the Eighteenth Amendment to the Constitution went into effect on January 16, 1920, although wine was still allowed for religious services. Endorsed by the American Medical Association, the "noble experiment" of Pro-

---

* The medical concept of addiction was developed by German psychologists in the 1870s and was quickly adopted in France. But it was slow to catch on elsewhere. The first edition of Emil Kraepelin's classic textbook, *Compendium der Psychiatrie* (1883), lists neither drug intoxication nor drug addiction in its inventory of mental illness. The word *addiction* as a reference to drug use did not appear as an entry in the *Oxford English Dictionary* until 1906, and its first recorded use of *addict* as a noun was in 1909. The early 1920s witnessed the dramatic birth of a criminal class of addicts, a deviant social category that had not existed previously. Henceforth, the American drug addict, by definition, was a criminal.

hibition produced ignoble results during the thirteen years, ten months, and nineteen days that it lasted. A boon for organized crime, Prohibition inspired widespread corruption and contempt for the law. "The prestige of the government has undoubtedly been lowered considerably by Prohibition," Albert Einstein observed when he visited the United States in the early 1920s. "Nothing is more destructive of respect for the government and the law of the land than laws which cannot be enforced."

While the Twenties roared, Americans from all walks of life embarked upon an unbridled drinking spree, a festival of hedonistic lawbreaking. Babe Ruth, America's most celebrated sports star, regularly invited reporters to accompany him while he downed a dozen bottles of beer before playing baseball. Members of Congress, who spouted sanctimonious rhetoric about the evils of moonshine, had their own private club in the nation's capital, where they drank to their hearts' content. Speakeasies—known as "blind pigs"—catered to millions of adults who brazenly flouted the law against alcohol. The cocktail was invented around this time in an effort to disguise the awful taste of bootleg hooch. Liquor poisonings, not surprisingly, were commonplace.

Jazz flourished in the illicit social environment spawned by Prohibition, which was also conducive to the recreational use of marijuana, a much safer and less expensive intoxicant. The mood of America swung from manic to gloomy with the sudden onset of the Great Depression. With few employment options available, distilling and smuggling booze became a way of life for a new kind of American outlaw. The most notorious rumrunner of his day was Bill McCoy, whose exploits gave rise to the well-known expression "the real McCoy," which originally referred to the high quality of his liquor.

The "real McCoy" of marijuana was a Jewish kid from Chicago named Milton ("Mezz") Mezzrow. Born in 1899, Mezzrow got caught stealing a car with a couple of teenagers and ended up in reform school, where he befriended several black musicians. It was in the reformatory that Mezzrow rejected white society and vowed to "become" a Negro. He learned to play jazz clarinet, and soon after his release he was smoking tea with the boys in the band. Mezz claimed that he blew the horn better if he also blew some gage. In his autobiography *Really the Blues*, Mezzrow wrote that marijuana enabled him to "see things in a wonderful, soothing, easy-going new light. All of a sudden, the world is stripped of its dirty gray shrouds and becomes one big bellyful of giggles, a special laugh, bathed in brilliant, sparkling colors that hits you like a heat wave . . . You can't get enough of anything—you want to gobble up the whole goddamned universe just for an appetizer."

Mezzrow arrived in Harlem, the cultural capital of black America, shortly after the November 1929 stock market crash. Flat broke, he decided to sell marijuana cigarettes to make ends meet. Through his connections, Mezz had access to high-quality gold-leaf grass from Mexico. He began dealing to people he knew in the jazz scene, ten cents a reefer. Word quickly got around that the white dude had the best bud. Overnight, Mezz became "the most popular man in Harlem."

They called him "the Reefer King," "the Philosopher," "the Man with the Jive," "the Link Between the Races," "the Man that Hipped the World," and "Pops's Boy"—the last a reference to Mezzrow's close friendship with Louis Armstrong, who lived and worked in Harlem for several stretches during the late 1920s and early 1930s. Mezz made sure that Satch, the hottest act in town, always had plenty of that *good shuzzit*. As Armstrong's principal supplier of marijuana, Mezz had almost unlimited access to his hero at a time when Satchmo was at the height of his creative powers.

Once Satchmo started calling it "the Mezz," everyone in Harlem picked up on the new slang for gage. A "Mezzerola" was shorthand for a generous, well-rolled stick of tea. Before long "Mezz" became a byword in black hip-speak for anything that was "supremely good" or "genuine," especially good marijuana. When he was on the road, Armstrong would occasionally write personal letters to Mezzrow requesting more "Lo Zee Rose" and "Orchestrations," both euphemisms for primo weed.

Although Mezzrow's reputation as a dealer of wacky tobacky far surpassed his status as a jazz musician, he was in the studio in 1930 when Armstrong recorded "Hobo, You Can't Ride This Train." Mezz rang the locomotive bell that opens the song, which honored the legions of itinerant, downtrodden Americans who hit the road during the Great Depression. The economic collapse sent a chain reaction rippling through the United States. Flocking to soup kitchens, standing in long breadlines, hitching rides and hopping freight trains, these homeless "tramps" were the discards of capitalist America. They converged with other drifters in squalid "hobo jungles" that sprang up near rail terminals across the United States. It was not unusual, especially in the north, for poor whites to live side by side with Negroes and Mexicans in these camps, where there were no Jim Crow color lines and marijuana was used by all ethnicities as a cheap intoxicant that didn't ravage the mind and body like rotgut alcohol.

"Marijuana is popular because it is prepared without trouble and because it gives tremendous effect at very low cost," Box-Car Bertha Thompson wrote in her Depression-era autobiography, *Sister of the Road*, which chronicled the experiences of a young woman riding the trains and puffing reefers with a colorful assortment of transients. "Marijuana is called among the users, 'muggles,'" she explained. "It is really a form of hasheesh, slightly changed when grown on American soil. It came to this country first from Mexico. New Orleans and all the southern cities are full of it . . . It is available also in every northern city . . . One cigarette, if smoked by those who know the way, will give a thorough 'muggles jag' to at least three persons for an entire night."

Numerous jazz tunes from this period celebrated the joys of a thorough muggles jag. Bessie Smith sang "Gimme a Reefer," Ella Fitzgerald chimed "When I Get Low, I Get High," and Cab Calloway hi-de-ho'ed about "The Man from Harlem" who "got just what you need." Several musicians paid explicit tribute to Mezzrow for providing the herbal impetus for the looser, springier rhythms of a novel style of jazz, a unique subgenre known as "viper music." "If You're a Viper," written by Rosetta Howard and recorded by Stuff Smith, Fats Waller, and others, began with this frolicsome ditty:

Dreamed about a reefer five foot long
The mighty Mezz, but not too strong

For the early jazz artists, marijuana was a revelation. While high on gage, they experimented with melodic phrases, slurs, and offbeat syncopation that became the cutting-edge sound. They shared not only the experience of getting buzzed but also an empowered sense of cultural identity, a catchy slogan—*"Light up and be somebody!"*—and a jive way of talking that baffled outsiders. "Poppa, you never smacked your chops on anything sweeter in all your days of viping," said Mezzrow. The vipers, he asserted, "had a gang of things in common . . . We were on another plane in another sphere compared to the musicians who were bottle babies, always hitting the jug and then coming up brawling after they got loaded. We liked things to be easy and relaxed, mellow and mild, not loud or loutish . . ."

The smell of cannabis, the nutrient du jour among jazz artists at New York City nightclubs, lent an exotic ambience to already glamorous venues. Mezzrow described "acres of marijuana" being smoked openly by performers at the Lafayette Theatre, while some in the audience lit up as well. A growing number of white jazz fans mingled with African Americans at various nightspots, where the air was thick with marijuana smoke and all races were welcome. An ethnically diverse clientele also smoked muggles in hundreds of "tea pads" that flourished in New York City between the two world wars. Tea smokers, whether black or white, often prided themselves on being deliberate outsiders, scornful of the unhip world. Yet, at the same time, marijuana seemed to turn outsiders into insiders, as more would-be vipers in cities across the country were initiated into the fraternal order of the herb. The loose-knit clique of vipers included "anybody from all walks of life that smoked and respected gage," Armstrong explained.

On the path to racial integration, pot smokers and jazz musicians were years ahead of mainstream society. Marijuana served as a meeting ground between blacks and whites in nightclubs, as well as in hobo jungles. The precocious weed was disrupting highly sensitive social boundaries.

Mezzrow did three years on Riker's Island after the cops caught him entering a jazz club with sixty joints in 1940. When he got out of prison, Mezz moved to postwar France, where American jazz musicians were greeted with open arms. He lived in Paris for the rest of his days, feted as that "funny reefer man" who palled around with the legendary Louis Armstrong.

In the mid-1920s, when recordings of jazz became widely available, French surrealist writers, such as Jean Cocteau and Robert Desnos, were using hashish while they listened to Satchmo play "Cornet Chop Suey" and "Potato Head Blues" on the recently invented phonograph. During this period, Baroness Elsa von Freytag-Loringhoven graced the dance floors of Berlin, wearing a girdle of kitchen utensils at a ballroom extravaganza. This one-woman happening decorated her face with postage stamps and "smoked marijuana in a big china German pipe that must have held an ounce or more," Kenneth Rexroth recalled.

Walter Benjamin was one of several German intellectuals who experimented with hashish (as well as mescaline and opium) in the years between World War I and II. "Under the influence of hashish we are enraptured prose-beings raised to the highest power," he mused. Benjamin first ingested a cannabis tincture in 1927 as a volunteer for a research study at a Berlin clinic run by Drs. Ernst Joel and Fritz Frankel. These two left-wing physicians were pioneers in the field of "social psychiatry," which specialized in treating working-class drug addicts. (Morphine and cocaine addiction were rampant in Germany during the Weimar Republic.) In his 1929 essay on surrealism, Benjamin introduced the idea of a hashish-inspired "profane illumination," which could liberate the energies of the proletariat by shattering the hypnotic trance of modern life. The surrealists, he asserted, sought "to win the energies of intoxication for the revolution."

Benjamin projected high hopes onto hashish. He viewed it as a kind of social medicine that could provide temporary relief from the inebriating mind morass of capitalism, a hallucinatory world wherein citizens are estranged from themselves and the earth, indoctrinated by mass media and bewildered by the induced needs of consumer society. Benjamin suggested that a revelatory hashish dream might puncture and dispel the fever dream of capitalism, the phantasmagoria of advertising, shopping, and entertainment that was reshaping the modern psyche. There could be dire consequences if the impulse "to commingle with the cosmic powers" (via hashish or other means) was quashed, according to Benjamin, who maintained that humankind needs periodic rites of regeneration to avoid maniacal episodes of destruction.

Benjamin, a Jew, committed suicide in France while trying to elude the Nazi Gestapo. Dr. Fritz Frankel, the Jewish social psychiatrist who turned Benjamin on to hashish, fled to Mexico City, where he befriended Leon Trotsky, the exiled Russian Communist leader, and the muralist Diego Rivera. True to his Mexican heritage, Rivera was a marijuana smoker. Screen actor Errol Flynn recounted how he met Rivera during a visit to Mexico City. Rivera asked him if he had ever heard music coming from a painting. Then Rivera offered Flynn a reefer: "After smoking this you will see a painting and you will hear it as well." Flynn took a few puffs and, by his own account, he was swept up in a symphony that he could "see, feel and hear [but] never translate into words."

Voodoo Pharmacology

On August 11, 1930, Harry Jacob Anslinger became the director of the newly formed Federal Bureau of Narcotics (FBN) in Washington, D.C. He would run the FBN with an iron fist through six presidential administrations spanning more than three decades. An imposing, husky, bull-necked figure nearly six feet tall, he looked like a tough law-and-order drug buster. With a large square head, huge ears, a cleft chin, and glowering eyes, Anslinger took great pride in his role as the archnemesis of marijuana smokers. He was the Godfather of America's war on drugs, and his influence on public policy would be felt long after death stiffened his fingers in 1975.

Like most of his agents, Anslinger cut his teeth battling John Barleycorn. While serving as assistant prohibition commissioner, Anslinger called for draconian measures to arrest and punish liquor drinkers, including stiff jail terms and fines for anyone caught purchasing an alcoholic beverage. He believed that imposing harsh penalties was the only way to force compliance with the ban on liquor. In dissenting from a U.S. Supreme Court decision that permitted wiretapping to aid enforcement of alcohol prohibition, Justice Louis D. Brandeis referred to people like Anslinger: "The greatest dangers to liberty lurk in insidious encroachment by men of zeal, well-meaning but without understanding."

If Anslinger had his way, there would have been many more Americans locked up during Prohibition, which ended just in time to make Christmas that much merrier in 1933. Never before had a constitutional amendment been repealed—an occasion marked by dancing in the streets. It was an unequivocal rejection of an experiment in social engineering that had gone horribly wrong. Although alcohol prohibition was widely recognized as a public-policy disaster, Anslinger didn't see it that way.

When Anslinger grabbed the reins at the FBN, marijuana had already been banned in twenty-four U.S. states, but there still was no coordinated federal attempt to outlaw the plant. During its first few years, the FBN issued annual reports that minimized the marijuana problem, which Anslinger believed was best dealt with by state and local officials. The stuff grows "like dandelions," he complained. Trying to stamp out a plant that flourished everywhere in the world except Antarctica and the Arctic Circle seemed like a dubious proposition. Anslinger had only three hundred G-men on his roster, hardly enough to tackle heroin and cocaine let alone a common weed.

Anslinger didn't pay much attention to cannabis until 1934, when the FBN was floundering. Tax revenues plummeted during the Great Depression, the bureau's budget got slashed, and Harry's entire department was on the chopping block. Then he saw the light and realized that marijuana just might be the perfect hook to hang his hat on. A savvy operator and an extremely ambitious man, he set out to convince Congress and the American public that a terrible new drug menace was threatening the country, one that required immediate action by a well-funded Federal Bureau of Narcotics.

Determined to criminalize the herb and build his bureaucratic fiefdom, America's top narc promoted all the hoary myths about marijuana-induced mayhem and sexual depravity—stories of pot-crazed axe murderers, playground pushers, sordid drug dens, and buxom reefer babes whose lives were ruined by the drug. "If the hideous monster Frankenstein came face-to-face with the hideous monster Marihuana, he would drop dead of fright," declared the FBN chief. Anslinger pulled no punches as he orchestrated a nationwide campaign against marijuana, "the most violence-causing drug in the history of mankind." In the world according to Anslinger, cannabis was a deadly, addictive drug that enslaved its users and turned them into deranged criminal freaks. He fed titillating tidbits to reporters, who wrote articles that the FBN chief would then cite in making the case that society was in imminent danger of moral collapse because of marijuana.

Anslinger whipped up enthusiasm for the cause in speeches to temperance organizations, religious groups and civic clubs around the country. His anticannabis confabulations were given credence by hellfire-and-brimstone preachers who castigated hemp smokers as fallen sinners. A plant with an unimpeachable patriotic pedigree, a plant that provided the paper on which Guttenberg first printed the Bible, was denounced as "the Devil's weed."

Pulp fiction from the *Reefer Madness* era

Perhaps it was the constant pressure from waging war against a figment of his imagination or maybe his job was simply too demanding, but on April 1, 1935, an angst-ridden Anslinger checked into the U.S. Marine hospital in Norfolk, Virginia. The FBN chief complained of exhaustion and insomnia—he woke up too early and couldn't get back to sleep, a condition, ironically, which was treatable with cannabis. According to the medical director at the hospital, Anslinger was "suffering from a form of nervous strain incident to his professional duties."

While Anslinger convalesced, others picked up the slack. The FBN chief had a strong ally in the press baron William Randolph Hearst, a megalomaniac obsessed with marijuana, whose newspaper chain stretched across the nation. With an instinctual grasp of mass psychology, Hearst used his media empire to influence public policy (as when he pushed the U.S. government into war with Spain in 1898). His contempt for facts, his penchant for fabricated stories and doctored photos, and the hysterical tone of his newspapers gave rise to the pejorative expression "yellow journalism." Hearst launched a smear campaign against Mexican migrants and their herb of choice. "Murder Weed Found Up and Down Coast—Deadly Marihuana Dope Plant Ready for

Harvest That Means Enslavement of California Children," the *Los Angeles Examiner* screeched in 1933.*

By stigmatizing marijuana and the "foreigners" who smoked it, Hearst succeeded in exacerbating anti-Mexican sentiment during the Great Depression, when many Anglos felt they were competing with brown-skinned migrants for scarce jobs. More than two million Mexicans, who had been welcomed while the U.S. economy boomed in the 1920s, were deported when it faltered in the 1930s—a policy of ethnic cleansing vociferously championed by the Hearst conglomerate.

Hearst also cheered the rise of fascist forces in Europe. "Mussolini Leads Way in Crushing Dope Evil" was the headline of a Hearst press screed that combined two of the owner's pet passions—his support for fascism and the war on narcotics. Hearst Sunday papers published columns by German Nazi leaders, who conveyed Hitler's point of view to thirty million readers without space for rebuttal. During the Third Reich, the verminization of religious and ethnic minorities went hand in hand with *Rauschgiftbekämpfung*, the "combating of drugs" to promote racial hygiene. Nazi racialist policies and the demonization of marijuana by Anslinger and Hearst were parallel historical phenomena—both exploited fear and hatred of the Other.

The FBN commissioner understood that the likelihood of prohibitory legislation increased if the substance in question was associated with ethnic minorities. Thus, Anslinger disclosed in 1936 that 50 percent of violent crimes committed in districts occupied by "Mexicans, Greeks, Turks, Filipinos, Spaniards, Latin Americans, and Negroes may be traced to the use of marihuana." The headlines and the plotlines were antidrug and anticrime, but the subtext was always about race. Anslinger brandished the non-English term like a truncheon to emphasize the weed's connection to alien elements that crept over the Mexican border into the United States. Popularized during the Depression, the new name *marihuana* was, in effect, the evil twin of *cannabis*, a word familiar to Americans as a medicinal ingredient. Anslinger eschewed references to benign-sounding *cannabis* and *hemp*, while calling for a federal ban on *marihuana*. Very few Americans knew that marijuana, the weed that some blacks and Chicanos were smoking, was merely a weaker version

* For Hearst, vilifying cannabis users was more than just a scheme to boost circulation; it was a personal vendetta. He harbored an animus toward Mexicans ever since Pancho Villa occupied the media mogul's 800,000-acre ranch in Chihuahua in 1916 and seized some cattle-grazing land.

of the concentrated cannabis medicines that everyone had been taking since childhood.

To gain public support for his crusade, Anslinger depicted marijuana as a sinister substance that made Mexican and African American men lust after white women. One of the worst things about marijuana, according to the FBN chief, was that it promoted sexual contact across color lines. "Marijuana causes white women to seek sexual relations with Negroes," Anslinger frothed. He rang alarm bells in segregated America, warning that blacks and whites were dancing cheek-to-cheek in tea houses and nightclubs, where pot-maddened jazz bands performed what the Hearst papers called "voodoo-satanic music."

In addition to hexing blacks and Mexicans, Anslinger's antimarijuana diatribes served as a not-so-subtle reminder to white women, who had only recently won the right to vote, that they still needed strong men to protect them from the "degenerate races." He never tired of telling new versions of the same morality tale, which featured a vulnerable young white woman whose tragic downfall is triggered by smoking marijuana with dark-skinned rogues.

During the run-up to federal legislation that banned cannabis, Anslinger pounded home the message: White women are in mortal peril because of marijuana—and so are American children. That was the upshot of a July 1937 magazine article by Anslinger, entitled "Assassin of Youth," which led with the usual purple prose:

> The sprawled body of a young girl lay crushed on the sidewalk the other day after a plunge from the fifth story of a Chicago apartment house. Everyone calls it suicide but actually it was murder. The killer was a narcotic known to America as marihuana, and history as hashish. It is a narcotic used in the form of cigarettes, comparatively new to the United States and as dangerous as a coiled rattlesnake.

"How many murders, suicides, robberies, criminal assaults, holdups, burglaries, and deeds of maniacal insanity it causes each year, especially among the young, can only be conjectured," the FBN chief warned.

With Anslinger pitching script ideas, cannabis was demonized in several low-budget exploitation flicks, some of which were financed by major distilling companies that stood to lose sizable sums if marijuana were a legal competitor. The film *Marijuana!* (1935) featured the lurid tagline "Weird orgies! Wild parties! Unleashed passions!" But when it came to ridiculous antimarijuana propaganda, nothing could top Hot Fingers Pirelli, the bug-eyed piano player who pounds out jazz tunes in *Tell Your Children* (1936), better known by its later title *Reefer Madness*. A perverted pot addict, Pirelli sneaks into a closet and fires up the Devil's doob, prompting frightful facial twitches as he morphs into an insane killer. Drug-policy critic Jacob Sullum calls it "voodoo pharmacology"—the idea that certain substances are molecularly programmed to compel weird, immoral behavior.

Although it bombed at the box office, *Reefer Madness* was destined to become a cult humor classic among American college students in later years. A vivid example of the national frenzy that set the stage for federal pot prohibition, this film epitomized the synchronicity among Washington, Hollywood, and mainstream media in the war against cannabis.

In April 1937, Representative Robert L. Doughton of North Carolina introduced House Bill 6385, which sought to prohibit the use of marijuana by imposing an exorbitant tax on the drug. When he testified before the House Ways and Means Committee, Harry Anslinger trotted out examples from the "Gore File," his infamous scrapbook full of Hearst press editorials, racial slurs, and anecdotal accounts of horrific murders falsely attributed to marijuana smokers. Bereft of actual scientific data to back up his reefer madness claims, the FBN director presented no evidence of a statistical correlation between marijuana use and criminal behavior.

Members of Congress held only two one-hour hearings to consider the Marihuana Tax Act. The final witness and lone voice of dissent was Dr. Wil-

Harry Anslinger, commissioner of the Federal Bureau of Narcotics, testifies before Congress
(Courtesy of Historical Collections and Labor Archives, Special Collections Library, Penn State University)

liam Woodward, the legislative counsel for the American Medical Association (AMA), who challenged Anslinger's claim that cannabis was a dangerous drug with no therapeutic value. AMA doctors, Woodward asserted, were wholly unaware that the "killer weed from Mexico" was actually cannabis. He accurately predicted that federal legislation banning marijuana would strangle any medical use of the plant.

By this time, the use of cannabis as a remedy had been supplanted by newer medicines such as aspirin, barbiturates, and morphine. All the newer drugs were water-soluble and therefore could be injected with a hypodermic needle—unlike fat-soluble cannabinoid compounds, which couldn't be administered intravenously. The practical problems posed by marijuana's insolubility and its variable impact contributed to an early twentieth-century decline in the medicinal use of cannabis tinctures. Despite that, dozens of pharmaceutical preparations containing cannabis extracts—pills, syrups, topical ointments—were still widely available in August 1937 when a clueless U.S. Congress, hoodwinked by Anslinger, approved legislation that effectively banned all forms of hemp through prohibitive taxation.*

Just four years after relegalizing the consumption of liquor, Congress overwhelmingly passed the Marihuana Tax Act by a voice vote without a recorded tally. Signed by President Franklin D. Roosevelt without fanfare, the law went into effect on October 1, 1937. It was a day of infamy for pot smokers everywhere. Yellow journalism, racial bias, and political opportunism had triumphed over medical science and common sense.

A Truth Drug

The purpose of the Marihuana Tax Act was to control behavior, not to raise revenue. Even if someone sought to pay the exorbitant levy formally required for any commercial transaction involving cannabis, the U.S. government would not sanction the sale by issuing a tax stamp. The new law was little more than a thinly veiled ruse to bust pot smokers. Local police, aided occasionally by Anslinger's agents, were primarily responsible for apprehending reefer suspects.

---

* Few members of Congress knew anything about cannabis when they voted to outlaw the herb. "What is this bill about?" a congressman asked House Majority Leader Sam Rayburn from Texas, who replied, "It has something to do with a thing called marijuana. I think it is a narcotic of some kind." USC law professor Charles Whitebread described the hearings and the vote as "near comic examples of dereliction of legislative responsibility."

The first person arrested for violating the Tax Act was fifty-eight-year-old Samuel R. Caldwell, an unemployed Colorado farmhand. On October 2, 1937, the day after the Tax Act became law, Caldwell got caught selling a couple of marijuana cigarettes to a man named Moses Baca. For this crime, Caldwell was sentenced to four years of hard labor at the federal penitentiary in Leavenworth, Kansas, and fined a thousand dollars; Baca got eighteen months in the same prison. Harry Anslinger was seated in the Denver courtroom when U.S. District Judge J. Foster Symes threw the book at the two convicted felons. "Marijuana destroys life," the judge declared. "I have no sympathy with those who sell this weed." Elated by the verdict, the FBN chief weighed in: "Marijuana has become our greatest problem . . . It is on the increase. But we will enforce the law to the very letter."

Enforcing the letter of the law meant incarcerating small-fries like Caldwell and Baca. Their cases were typical—a peddler pawning a few joints to a consenting adult. During the last three months of 1937, the FBN seized about 500 pounds of bulk marijuana and 2,852 reefer cigarettes—a rather paltry law-enforcement harvest given all the hoopla about the deadly weed. In a confidential memo to all his district supervisors on December 14, 1937, Anslinger noted that "a great many marihuana cases of a comparatively minor type are being reported." He urged his agents to engage in "more strenuous efforts . . . to ascertain sources of supply" and to develop larger cases "which could command more respect in the courts."

But there was no big-time marijuana racket for the FBN to tackle. The black-market cannabis trade was grassroots, low-key, and decentralized. "It can be grown easily almost anywhere, hence it tends to be inexpensive as drugs go," *Time* magazine reported in 1943. "Its recent prices [ten to fifty cents a cigarette] have placed it beneath the dignity of big-time racketeers. But its furtive preparation and sale provide a modest living to thousands." Among those who earned their modest living from selling reefers at New York City jazz venues during this period was a young hustler known as Crazy Red, who landed in prison and transformed himself into Malcolm X.

When the U.S. government outlawed marijuana in 1937, an estimated 50,000 Americans, mainly blacks and Chicanos, were smoking the herb. Within a decade, according to *Newsweek*, that number had doubled. Rooted in the "racy" parts of town, the illicit cannabis scene spread at a steady pace thanks in part to the indefatigable efforts of Commissioner Anslinger. Few U.S. citizens had ever heard the word *marihuana* until the FBN chief embarked upon his reefer-madness crusade. Anslinger gave the weed a lot of bad publicity. He also aroused the curiosity of a small but growing cadre of skeptics who saw through his puerile propaganda. They wanted to know what all the fuss was about, so they tried a few puffs and couldn't help but notice that the official rant didn't match their experience.

Anslinger habitually exaggerated the incidence of marijuana use in the United States and the national dimensions of "the problem." He insisted that marijuana was inherently criminogenic, that it made people aggressive and violent. But his bluster appeared to backfire when several attorneys took advantage of the prevailing hype against the weed by successfully arguing that their clients were not guilty as charged due to diminished responsibility from reefer-induced insanity.*

The FBN moved methodically to choke off access to medicinal cannabis. Brushing off scientific data that conflicted with his hard-core ideology, Anslinger adamantly maintained that marijuana was not a therapeutic substance. Doctors were no longer able to prescribe cannabis-derived medications. Due to onerous licensing rules, wholesale pharmaceutical dealers stopped distributing cannabis tinctures. By 1941, thanks to arm-twisting by the commissioner, cannabis was officially removed from the *United States Pharmacopeia and National Formulary,* wherein Indian hemp had previously been listed as a remedy for more than one hundred ailments.

More than anything else, Anslinger needed to show some visible results from his law-and-order crusade. The capture of a major dealer or a sizable haul of marijuana would have helped, but since neither had materialized, he would have to find some other target. After running roughshod over the medical community, Anslinger set his sights on the jazz scene. He envisioned a coordinated, nationwide roundup of jazz musicians, culminating in a series of high-profile marijuana busts on the same day. In a memo dated September 7, 1943, he ordered his field agents to gather information on "musicians of the swing band type," but not to make any arrests until the commissioner gave the word. "If possible," Anslinger emphasized, "I should like you to develop a number of cases in which arrest would be withheld so as to synchronize with arrests to be made in other districts."

Being a jazz musician automatically made one suspect in the eyes of Anslinger. He kept a special FBN file, "Marijuana and Musicians," which read

---

* Called to testify by defense lawyers, federal narcotics agents stated that marijuana could indeed make people crazy enough to commit awful crimes against their will. Dr. James C. Munch, a court-certified expert on marijuana and an Anslinger ally, supported the testimony of a murder defendant who claimed temporary insanity simply because he had been in the same room with a bag of marijuana. The defendant was subsequently acquitted.

like a who's who of the jazz world. Anslinger ordered his agents to gather incriminating information on dozens of well-known artists and their band members, including Duke Ellington, Charlie Parker, Count Basie, Billie Holiday, Dizzy Gillespie, Lionel Hampton, Jimmy Dorsey, and Thelonious Monk. The FBN's dossier on Louis Armstrong noted his 1930 marijuana arrest and conviction in Los Angeles.*

FBN agents arrested Gene Krupa, the famous white drummer and swing band leader, for marijuana possession in San Francisco in 1943. Krupa, a wild, shaggy-haired percussionist, spent eighty-four days in jail. Prosecutors eventually dropped the case, but not before it caused the breakup of his jazz orchestra. The world-renowned diva Anita O'Day, who had been "Krupa's canary" (the singer in his band), was busted for pot a few years later. "I smoked some grass," O'Day admitted, "but I wasn't an every-dayer." She fondly recalled how it was before marijuana prohibition when "you could buy a joint at the corner store, if not nearer." Then the law changed. It didn't make any sense to O'Day: "One day weed had been harmless, booze outlawed; the next, alcohol was in and weed led to 'living death.' They didn't fool me. I kept on using it, but I was just a little more cautious." Hollywood idol Robert Mitchum could only wish that he had been more cautious on the day of his high-profile marijuana arrest in 1948.

Not content to nail a few big-name tokers here and there, Anslinger continued to fantasize about a single-day dragnet that would apprehend jazz musicians throughout the country. But his hopes for a major publicity coup faded as it became increasingly apparent that FBN agents weren't able to infiltrate the jazz milieu. Anslinger fumed when he learned that Fats Waller, the popular pianist and composer, had been asked to record a song of his own choosing for American GIs during World War II. Produced as an Armed Forces radio "V-Disc," Waller's recording was an inspired version of the classic marijuana missive "If You're a Viper," in which he "dreamed about a reefer five foot long."

---

* Anslinger's dislike of jazz was so intense that he even took a dim view of certain animated cartoon characters. Jazz musicians supplied the soundtrack for popular early cartoons such as Betty Boop and Popeye the Sailor. "Spinach," Popeye's signature edible, was yet another jazz-transmitted code word for cannabis. (Julia Lee's "Spinach Song" celebrated the pleasures of cannabis without referring by name to the plant: "I used to run away from the stuff / But now somehow I can't get enough.") Popeye gained superhuman strength by sucking a wad of green leaf through his corncob pipe.

As if this wasn't enough of an affront, Anslinger was obliged to defer to the U.S. armed forces and the Department of Agriculture, which jointly released a 1942 motivational film, *Hemp for Victory*, urging American farmers to grow lots of hemp to support the war effort. The patriotic plant was back in demand just five years after the Marihuana Tax Act wiped out America's domestic hemp industry (despite Anslinger's solemn promise that industrial hemp production would not be affected by marijuana prohibition). During World War II, Japan invaded the Philippines, a principal supplier of plant fiber to the United States. That's when military necessity trumped political concerns in Washington about any link between hemp and marijuana. Hemp for Victory meant hemp rope for U.S. Navy battleships, hempseed oil as an aviation lubricant, and hemp cloth for parachutes, like the kind that saved the life of the future president George Herbert Walker Bush, who jumped to safety in the Pacific Theater. Hemp for Victory also meant generous government subsidies for farmers, who cultivated more than 300,000 acres of the fiber crop to help Uncle Sam. Ironically, in the years ahead American law enforcement and National Guard units would spend countless hours and waste lots of taxpayers' money trying to eradicate barely psychoactive "ditch weed" that descended from the Hemp for Victory fields.

While the armed forces were promoting hemp production, the Office of Strategic Services (OSS), the Central Intelligence Agency's wartime predecessor, embarked upon a clandestine mission to develop a "truth drug" capable of eliciting vital information from enemy spies and other tight-lipped suspects. Sodium pentothal, a barbiturate, was hailed by law enforcement as a "truth serum" when it debuted in 1936, but it made people drowsy and didn't deliver surefire results. So in 1942, the OSS established a secret Truth Drug committee, which considered a range of chemical mood-changers, including alcohol, caffeine, and peyote, before selecting a highly concentrated liquid acetate of *Cannabis indica* as the best speech-inducing substance for espionage interrogations. (As noted earlier, the Tepehuan Indians in Mexico described cannabis as the Herb That Makes One Speak.)*

Referred to as "T.D." (Truth Drug) in once-classified OSS documents, this potent marijuana derivative was odorless, colorless, tasteless, and therefore difficult to detect when inserted into a tobacco cigarette or added to food. The effects of T.D. were described as follows:

---

* Among the Sanskrit names for cannabis, *vakpradatava* meant "speech giving." A Tibetan pharmacopoeia notes that hemp, among its many attributes, "produces feelings of elation and . . . makes a person talkative" (Rätsch, *Marijuana Medicine*, p. 44).

> It accentuates the senses and makes manifest any strong characteristics of the individual. Sexual inhibitions are lowered, and the sense of humor is accentuated to the point where any statement or situation can become extremely funny to the subject . . . It may be stated that generally speaking, the reaction will be one of great loquacity and hilarity.

This behind-the-scenes intelligence assessment, which likened marijuana to Giggle Weed, was rather tame compared with the Killer Weed hysteria fomented by Harry Anslinger, who secretly collaborated with the OSS team. The spooks were not about to blow their own cover and expose Anslinger's public falsehoods, especially when one of the FBN's top men, George Hunter White, was assisting sensitive OSS interrogations. White covertly administered T.D. cigarettes to high-value targets, including German POWs and U.S. Army personnel suspected of Communist leanings. On September 23, 1943, he visited Manhattan Project security officer John Lansdale in San Francisco to give the Truth Drug treatment to scientists who were developing America's atomic bomb.*

White found that in some cases T.D. loosened the reserve of unwitting subjects and stimulated a "rush of talk," while other people grew wary and clammed up after they unknowingly absorbed a dose of the supercharged cannabis compound. The lack of a consistent reaction was a major drawback that undermined the utility of T.D. as an espionage tool. The OSS had no way to predict how different individuals would respond to the drug. This was especially problematic, OSS officials surmised, because an overdose of T.D., although it "will not have serious physical results," could make a person "aware some foreign substance has been administered to him."

In the end, America's World War II spymasters were stumped by T.D. "The drug defies all but the most expert and searching analysis," a lengthy OSS report concluded, "and for all practical purposes can be considered beyond analysis."

---

* During the 1950s and early 1960s, George Hunter White freelanced for the CIA while serving as a high-ranking Federal Bureau of Narcotics officer. Operating out of CIA safehouses decorated as bordellos in New York City and later in San Francisco, White used prostitutes to give LSD and other psychoactive drugs to unwitting American citizens. Marijuana is referred to as "sugar" in once-classified documents pertaining to the CIA's Cold War mind-control research (Lee and Shlain, *Acid Dreams*, pp. 32–35).

Cold War Cannabis

Harry Anslinger never bought into the notion that marijuana or any derivative thereof was a truth drug. For the FBN chief, "truth" was a function of power rather than factual accuracy. Truth was not something that one searched for or discovered; it was created and imposed by a governing elite. During his tenure as FBN director, Anslinger constructed what French philosopher Michel Foucault would later refer to as a "regime of truth." This hegemonic process entailed a protracted campaign to suppress the facts about cannabis by deriding and marginalizing the commissioner's critics. Anslinger used his authority to stymie independent scientific inquiry and banish competing ideas. When necessary, he wasn't above destroying the careers of those who disagreed with the party line. Simply put, he would solidify his regime of truth by silencing the opposition.

Anslinger's efforts to dictate how marijuana would be perceived by the American public faced its first serious challenge in 1944 with the publication of the La Guardia Report. Five years earlier, Mayor Fiorello La Guardia of New York City had appointed a blue-ribbon committee of doctors and scientists from the New York Academy of Medicine to assess just how harmful marijuana was and what threat, if any, it posed in the Big Apple. The ensuing investigation, which entailed pharmacological, clinical, and sociological research, was the most thorough and extensive study of cannabis since the massive 1894 Indian Hemp Commission report.* The La Guardia committee examined and debunked virtually every claim that Anslinger made about marijuana. All the catastrophic reasons he gave for outlawing cannabis were refuted by this com-

---

* Troubled by the widespread use of ganja in India, a British colony, British officials formed a committee of experts to study the matter in the late 1800s. The seven-volume, three-thousand-page report by the Indian Hemp Commission found no evidence of a link between the use of hemp drugs and crime—and nothing to support claims that ganja drove men mad. Excessive ganja consumption was the exception, not the rule, the report emphasized, whereas the "moderate use of hemp . . . appears to cause no appreciable physical injury of any kind . . . no injurious effects on the mind . . . and no moral injury whatever." Overall, the commission was impressed by "how little injury society has hitherto sustained from hemp drugs." This authoritative report, published in 1894, concluded that the "suppression of the use of hemp would be totally unjustifiable" and any attempts to control or ban it would likely lead to far more serious problems with alcohol. Better to collect taxes and tariffs from ganja merchants, the study counseled, than to impose an unpopular and unnecessary prohibitionist policy.

mittee, which concluded that Americans had been needlessly frightened about marijuana's supposed dangers.

For starters, La Guardia's experts asserted that it was incorrect to call marijuana a *narcotic,* a term for a potentially lethal drug or poison that reduces sensibility by depressing brain function. "In point of fact," the report noted, "cannabis is a mild euphoriant." Influenced by various cultural, social, and psychological factors, an individual's complex personality is not going to vanish in a puff of marijuana smoke, the La Guardia scientists asserted: "Prolonged use of the drug does not lead to physical, mental or moral degeneration, nor have we observed any permanent deleterious effects from its continued use." The report stated categorically that marijuana is not addictive and it does not cause insanity, sexual deviance, violence, or criminal misconduct.

The La Guardia Report also recommended further investigation into the curative properties of cannabis and its derivatives. In his summary, the committee chairman, George B. Wallace, emphasized the medicinal potential of the herb: "The lessening of inhibitions and repressions, the euphoric state, the feeling of adequacy, the freer expression of thoughts and ideas, and the increase in appetite for food, brought about by marijuana suggests therapeutic possibilities."

Anslinger was livid. He publicly berated Mayor La Guardia and threatened doctors with prison terms should they dare carry out independent research on cannabis. The FBN chief called the La Guardia Report a "government-printed invitation to youth and adults—above all teenagers—to go ahead and smoke all the reefers they feel like." He charged that the findings of the copious study were seriously flawed because the committee neglected to scrutinize the use of marijuana in real-life settings (something the FBN never bothered to do). This was another blatant falsehood. In addition to conducting controlled experiments on human subjects, the mayor's team dispatched undercover police to observe the use of marijuana in New York City tea pads (houses that hosted pot parties), playgrounds, schoolyards, and anywhere else that Gotham residents might congregate to smoke marijuana.

The mayor's committee disclosed that marijuana smoking was largely confined to the poorer neighborhoods of New York, particularly Harlem. Contrary to Anslinger's scare stories, there was no marijuana trafficking in schoolyards and youthful hangouts. After they examined the records of the Children's Court of New York City and interviewed experts on this subject, La Guardia investigators determined there was no link between juvenile delinquency and marijuana smoking. On the whole, they found that illicit tea pads were mellow, congenial places with no violence or explicit sexual activity. "A constant observation was the extreme willingness to share and puff on each other's cigarettes," the report stated.

In order to discredit the La Guardia committee and minimize the impact of its findings, the FBN chief strong-armed the American Medical Association. As late as 1942, the AMA continued to raise the possibility that cannabis had therapeutic uses. Following the release of the La Guardia Report, however, the AMA did an extraordinary about-face and joined Anslinger's crusade against marijuana. The *Journal of the American Medical Association* excoriated the mayor's committee in an April 1945 editorial that read as though Anslinger had written it (he probably did). The La Guardia Report, according to the AMA's influential mouthpiece, "has already done great damage to the cause of law enforcement. Public officials will do well to disregard this unscientific, uncritical study, and continue to regard marijuana as a menace wherever it is purveyed."

Since then, the AMA steadfastly maintained a position on cannabis that hewed closely to drug-war orthodoxy. And because the FBN controlled the licenses for the importation of opiates, Anslinger also received the support of drug companies and their trade organization, the American Pharmaceutical Association, which had previously criticized sensationalistic press coverage of marijuana. The capitulation of these two giants of the medical establishment enabled Anslinger to consolidate his regime of truth. With Anslinger running interference, the mayor's committee received scant press attention, even in the hometown *New York Times,* which buried a summary of the La Guardia Report on the last page.

Even though credible studies disproved Anslinger's outrageous allegations, his campaign would skew public policy for many years to come. Future "drug czars" carried on his legacy by casting marijuana as the lynchpin of the drug war. Holding the line on marijuana, medical as well as recreational, would persist as an essential element of prohibitionist strategy. Drug-war catechism maintained that moderate use of the herb was impossible—all use was abuse, no questions asked.

Scarcely a decade after telling Congress that cannabis was "the most violence-causing drug in the history of mankind," Anslinger did a 180-degree switcheroo and declared marijuana a threat because smoking the herb turned people into docile zombies—to the point where stoned U.S. citizens would be neither willing nor able to fight the Red Menace within and without. According to the FBN chief, cannabis was now part of a Commie plot to sap America's strength. "Marijuana leads to pacifism and Communist brainwashing," Anslinger asserted in a 1948 congressional testimony.

Anslinger was all over the map, yet Congress and mass media swallowed the new antireefer rationale hook, line, and sinker. Major rhetorical zigzags were a hallmark of Anslinger's regime of truth, as he reversed positions in response to the changing political climate of the Cold War. Once again, facts mattered less than the power to define them. During the 1937 Tax Act hearings, the FBN commissioner had unequivocally nixed the notion of any link between marijuana and heroin.* Yet a dozen years later, Anslinger was pushing the domino theory of drug abuse. He contended that marijuana, by arousing a desire for greater kicks, was the first of a series of falling dominos that inevitably led the user to hard drugs, and hard drugs led to doom and self-destruction. Most young addicts "started on marihuana smoking . . . and graduated to heroin," Anslinger told Congress. "They took to the needle when the thrill of marihuana was gone." The FBN's latest take on cannabis meshed well with the politically fashionable domino imagery of International Communism toppling one country after another. Marijuana was the gateway, the stepping-stone to heroin addiction, Anslinger insisted, and heroin addiction was the result of a Communist conspiracy to weaken the United States and the Free World.

Once again, U.S. officials were attributing America's drug problem to the devious work of foreign devils intent on turning the United States into a nation of addicts. During the Second World War, Anslinger accused the Japanese of pushing narcotics to undermine America's resolve to fight. The Germans had been fingered as drug-dealing culprits during the previous Great War. Now it was China's turn to star as the nefarious narco-bogeyman flooding the West with drugs. In a May 1951 speech to the American Legion, Commissioner Anslinger denounced the Yellow Peril for "producing and shipping large quantities of heroin which is finding its way into this country." When testifying at Senate hearings on "Communist China and illicit narcotics traffic," Anslinger claimed that Red China was "the greatest purveyor in history of habit-forming drugs." The FBN chief ominously warned of "a great concentration of Communist heroin in California."†

---

* "I am just wondering whether the marijuana addict graduates into a heroin, an opium, or a cocaine user?" asked Rep. John Dingell. Anslinger's response: "No, sir. I have not heard of a case of that kind. I think it is an entirely different class. The marijuana addict does not go in that direction" (Hearings before the Committee on Ways and Means, U.S. House of Representatives, 75th Congress, 1st Session, April and May 1937: House Marijuana Hearings, p. 24).

† Typical was this headline from the *Los Angeles Times* (May 25, 1951): "Dope's Flow Said to Have Red Backing." In 1968, John Ingersoll, who headed one of the successor agencies to the FBN, was asked whether there was any evidence to support charges that the People's Republic of China was engaged in drug trafficking. Ingersoll rolled his eyes and admitted, "That was the sort of thing that went on in politics in those days. It was all just McCarthyism and making Communist China the bogeyman."

During the early years of the Cold War, drug addiction was depicted as a threat to national security. Those who took illegal substances were said to be aiding and abetting communism. To contain the drug—and the Communist—threat, Anslinger pressed for tougher federal laws against cannabis, opiates, and cocaine. In 1951, Congress passed the Boggs Amendment, which upped the penalties for all narcotics offenses and specified the same mandatory-minimum punishment for marijuana and heroin violations: two to five years in prison for first-time possession. Repeat drug offenders were denied parole consideration—a truly draconian twist considering that rapists and murderers were granted parole.

Congress enacted the Boggs Amendment, which made no distinction between drug users and traffickers, at the peak of the McCarthy witch-hunt craze. Writing of this era, Anslinger disclosed in his memoir, *The Murderers,* that he arranged a regular supply of morphine for "one of the most influential members of Congress," who had become an opiate addict. Anslinger's biographer, John C. Williams, asserts that the well-connected addict was none other than Senator Joseph McCarthy. Apparently, Anslinger felt it was necessary to dispense morphine to the bourbon-swilling Tail Gunner from Wisconsin so that the Communists would not be able to manipulate McCarthy in a moment of drug-dependent despair.

A fervent cold warrior, Anslinger embraced the new order that gave top priority to the shadow war against the Soviet Union and its Communist allies. The FBN chief faithfully subordinated the mission of his drug-control apparatus to suit the needs of the fledgling Central Intelligence Agency (CIA) and the national security state. For many years, Anslinger concealed evidence that U.S. espionage agencies were sponsoring and supporting zealously anti-Communist forces abroad that profited from trafficking in illegal drugs. Camped in the poppy-rich Golden Triangle region of Southeast Asia, the CIA-backed Chinese Nationalist Kuomintang Army was heavily involved in the opium trade—to cite but one example. While spreading propaganda about Commie drug plots, the FBN turned a blind eye to dope smuggling by CIA collaborators. As it was back then, so it would continue throughout the Cold War and after: So-called national security interests trumped those of U.S. drug enforcement agencies.

To underscore that illicit drugs were a matter of grave concern to his administration, President Dwight Eisenhower called for "a new war on narcotics addiction at the local, national and international level" in 1954. Two years later, Congress increased penalties for marijuana yet again with the passage of the Narcotics Control Act. It wasn't an easy time to be a viper, as Louis Armstrong recalled in his inimitable way: "Mary Warner, honey, you sure was good to me . . . But the price got a little too high to pay (law wise). At first you was a 'misdemeanor.' But as the years rolled on you lost your *misdo* and got *meaner* and *meaner*."*

Writing the Reality Script

A key aspect of cannabis as a social phenomenon has been its boundary-crossing quality, how it leapt like a flame from one culture to another. So did jazz. The music and the weed were fellow travelers, so to speak, joined at the juncture of hip. Even after the onset of federal prohibition, when viper lyrics were distinctly out of favor, contraband cannabis could be procured at jazz clubs such as Minton's Playhouse on 118th Street in New York City. That was where the great saxophonist Lester ("Prez") Young gave Jack Kerouac, the fledgling writer, his first taste of marijuana in 1941. It would prove to be a seminal, flame-leaping moment.

Kerouac and a small circle of friends, soon to be dubbed the "Beat Generation," started to smoke pot and hang out at jazz joints in the mid-1940s just as the swing era was evolving into music known simply as "bop" or "bebop." Bop was jazz for the modern age—fast, emotional, turbulent, yet lyrical and subtle in its rhythms. The new music exalted the cult of the soloist improvising off the top of his head from deep in his gut. When Charlie Parker blew, it was the

* Ironically, Armstrong and several other jazz greats, who had been in Anslinger's crosshairs for years, would become strategic assets in a U.S. government public-relations offensive that showcased top musicians during the Cold War to demonstrate America's commitment to cultural freedom—despite institutional racism back in the States. Jazz stoners played to enthusiastic crowds in Europe, Africa, and Asia on tours discreetly underwritten by the CIA and State Department in the 1950s and early 1960s. Anslinger wanted to cancel the passports of all jazz musicians with a marijuana conviction, but the FBN chief was overruled by his superiors in the Treasury Department. "Jazz musicians, the old ones and the young ones, almost all of them I knew smoked pot, but I wouldn't call that drug abuse," said Dizzy Gillespie, who was one of the jazz luminaries enlisted by the federal government to serve as an unofficial goodwill emissary. U.S. diplomatic strategists recognized the importance of jazz as a dynamic American art form that personified freedom, a powerful, uplifting music appreciated by millions around the world. To rebut charges that America's racism and imperial policies made a mockery of Uncle Sam's claim to lead the free world, even the Grey Lady, the staid *New York Times*, touted the geopolitical significance of jazz: "America's secret weapon is a blue note in a minor key [and] its most effective ambassador is Louis Armstrong." The Soviets could boast about *Sputnik*, the recently launched space probe, but the United States had "the hot jazz trumpet" of Ambassador Satch.

sound of freedom calling, the naked cry of an individual defying the weight of the world. To Kerouac and his literary comrades, jazz represented the uninhibited expression of the soul's impulses. They wanted to write like Charlie Parker and Dizzy Gillespie played music. Kerouac, who often composed while high on reefer and Benzedrine, called his writing "bop prosody" and compared his technique to "a tenor man drawing a breath and blowing a phrase on a saxophone till he runs out of breath, and when he does, his sentence, his statement's been made."

Like Mezz Mezzrow, the quintessential "White Negro" and legendary pot dealer, the Beats shared a deep affinity for black culture at a time when racial segregation was the norm. The publication of Mezzrow's life story, *Really the Blues,* in 1946 coincided with the advent of the Beat circle in New York. These brash young writers believed that only the most daring commitment to personal creativity would overcome the stifling conformity of the early Cold War years. The use of illegal drugs was an integral part of their search for transcendence. They smoked marijuana and experimented with whatever else they could get their hands on—heroin, speed, hallucinogens—often to the point of excess in the spirit of Rimbaud, a poet the Beats greatly admired. They sought to discover and articulate a "New Vision," a phrase they borrowed from Rimbaud. The Beats were intent on writing this New Vision into existence.

Kerouac and his cohorts got high together in small groups, much like the bohemian writers who congregated at the Hashish Eaters' Club in mid-nineteenth-century Paris. The Beats were conscious of their link to this great stoned lineage of European artists, which included the Dadaists, Surrealists, Symbolists, and others who defied convention and labels. Kerouac's cabal loved the associational fluidity engendered by cannabis, how it loosened the powers of analogy and unleashed the spoken word. They stayed up all night smoking fat marijuana bombers, listening to jazz, reciting poetry, and confiding their deepest secrets, their hopes and fears, in protracted, stoned rap sessions. Marijuana was a truth drug, of sorts, for the Beats. As the Beat poet Allen Ginsberg recalled: "All that we knew was that we were making sense to each other, you know talking from heart to heart, and that everybody else around us was talking like some kind of strange, lunar robots in business suits."

Ginsberg and Kerouac, along with William S. Burroughs, comprised the core group of Beat writers who refused to live according to the rules set by "straight" society. During the deep freeze of the Cold War, when reflexive obedience to authority was rewarded, they offered a biting critique of America the Beautiful. At a time when few middle-class Americans doubted the fundamental goodness of their society, the Beats railed against the spiritual bankruptcy of consumer culture and the deadening routine of nine-to-five. At a time of expanding nuclear arsenals and ghoulish strategies of "Mutually Assured Destruction," Ginsberg told America: "Go fuck yourself with your atom bomb." As pot prohibition became increasingly punitive, he declared in the same poem: "I smoke marijuana every chance I get." In an era when homes across the land were sprouting TV antennae that transmitted a relentlessly cheerful and confident message, Ginsberg and his companions felt utterly *beat*, as in burned out, beaten down, emotionally and psychologically exhausted.

The term came from an offhand remark by Kerouac, who despondently told a friend in 1949, "I guess you might say that we're a beat generation." The word had a dual connotation in keeping with the culture of doubles associated with cannabis: *beat* implied beaten down and it also meant "beatific, to be in a state of beatitude like St. Francis, trying to love all life," Kerouac insisted. It could refer to someone who was beaten up or upbeat or both. Part citified and part nomadic, the Beats were "subterraneans," self-selecting outcasts who became internal exiles. To smoke pot in those days was to take sides, to affiliate with an underground community, "a community of the excluded," as Ted Morgan described the Beats, a fraternity of "the unlike-minded" who were out of sync with the national mood.

In 1947, a charismatic, streetwise hipster named Neal Cassady, age twenty-one, arrived on the scene, radiating a boundless energy that captivated the Beats. When he got going after a few puffs of reefer, this blue-eyed, curly-haired rebel without a cause could rap for hours nonstop, weaving a yarn that kept his listeners spellbound. Raised by his hobo dad on Denver's skid row during the Depression, Cassady, a teenage jailbird, experienced satori behind the wheel of a stolen car and never looked back. He became, quite literally, the driving force behind the Beats.

With Cassady burning rubber at ninety miles an hour, he and his new-found friends traversed North America several times on madcap pilgrimages with no final destination. Their marathon travels became the stuff of legend in the writings of Jack Kerouac. *On the Road,* Kerouac's most famous novel, mythologized the story of his interstate automobile adventures with Cassady, aka Dean Moriarty, the impulsive protagonist who was "out of his mind with real belief." The book chronicled their search for Dean's itinerant father, who was nowhere to be found. Instead they found the raw beauty of terra firma and the revivifying power of the open road. ("Gone on the road" was Cassady's phrase for being high on grass.) Told from the point of view of two desperados who opted out of the American Dream, *On the Road* is a rhapsodic tour de force of male-bonding, girl-chasing, drug-induced visions and nonstop chatter, ending up in a Mexican whorehouse where they smoked huge spliffs of reefer rolled from newspaper.

While Kerouac and Cassady sought to outrun the boredom and stasis of late '40s America with sheer speed and cunning, William Burroughs (thinly disguised as "Old Bull" in *On the Road*) was holed up at a remote, broken-down ninety-nine-acre farm in rural East Texas, where he tried his hand at growing marijuana. After Cassady helped harvest the pot crop, which grew between persimmon and oak trees several miles from the nearest dirt road, he drove Burroughs and a trunk full of weed back to New York.

Busted on narcotics charges, Burroughs fled the United States, a nation he had come to loathe. In 1953, he journeyed to the Amazon jungle on a quest to systematically derange his senses by imbibing *ayahuasca,* a foul-tasting, industrial-strength hallucinogen brewed by rainforest shamans. Since his youth, Burroughs had been "searching for some secret, some key" with which he could "gain access to basic knowledge, answer some of the fundamental questions." The trail of clues led to Tangiers, Morocco, where he spent much of the 1950s and early 1960s as an expatriate, smoking *kif* (powdered hashish) in cafés, eating *majoun* (hashish candy), and writing *Naked Lunch,* his wildly surreal and morbidly satiric breakthrough novel.*

In *Naked Lunch,* heroin addiction serves as an all-encompassing metaphor for social relations in a world ruled by maniacal power addicts who employ various "clinical" procedures to rehabilitate deviants and befuddle the masses into accepting their own servitude, their masochistic addiction to authority. Written, as Burroughs put it, "to make people aware of the true criminality of our times," *Naked Lunch* portrays addiction not as a personal vice but as the basic condition of everyone in consumer capitalist society. It describes a loveless, predatory environment in which giant industries rely on cynical marketing tactics to sell an enormous quantity of useless stuff—junk—that could only satisfy artificial needs induced by commercial media. From a mercantile perspective, junk is the perfect product; the consumer addict will crawl through the sewer again and again, if necessary, to score. Addicts of all persuasions inhabit a Bosch-like landscape in *Naked Lunch*—junkie doctors wielding scalpels for sport, sadistic cops hooked on brutalizing people, and bizarre characters such as A.J., the sex fiend, who spikes the punch with hashish and ayahuasca at a U.S. embassy Fourth of July confab, precipitating an orgy. In

* "Unquestionably [marijuana] is very useful to the artist, activating trains of association that would otherwise be inaccessible," Burroughs explained. "I owe many of the scenes in *Naked Lunch* directly to the use of cannabis" (William S. Burroughs, "Points of Distinction Between Sedative and Consciousness-Expanding Drugs," in Solomon, ed., *The Marijuana Papers*, pp. 445–46).

Naked Lunch, the emperors not only have no clothes, they prance through the pages as simians and purple-assed baboons.

Copies of *Naked Lunch* were seized by U.S. officials, who unsuccessfully prosecuted Burroughs and his publisher, Grove Press, in a landmark obscenity case that smashed barriers against free expression. U.S. government stiffs also tried to block the publication of *Howl and Other Poems* by Allen Ginsberg, but he, too, was exonerated of obscenity charges. Both books were deemed by the court to have socially redeeming value.

Arguably the most important American poem of the twentieth century, "Howl" captured the sense of doom and desperation that haunted many people in the wake of Hiroshima and the Holocaust. An epic, raging incantation, it scandalized Americans with graphic references to illicit drugs and men who "screamed with joy" as they were anally penetrated by "saintly motorcyclists." Ginsberg bemoaned the "narcotic tobacco haze of capitalism" and everything in our mechanistic civilization that smothers the spirit. He reminded Americans of hopes and possibilities that were suppressed in the 1950s, a decade dominated by redbaiting, loyalty oaths, blacklists, and the cancerous growth of the military-industrial complex. "Holy the groaning saxophone!" the poet wailed. "Holy the bop Apocalypse! Holy the jazzbands marijuana hipsters peace peyote pipes & drums!"

With melancholy, soulful eyes looking out from horn-rim glasses, Ginsberg was a textbook outsider—gay, Jewish, left-wing, pacifist. It took considerable courage for him to come out of the closet as an unrepentant queer and a pot smoker when homophobia and repressive drug laws were core elements of the Cold War consensus. Ginsberg didn't expect that "Howl" would make him world famous when he read parts of it aloud for the first time at the Six Gallery in San Francisco on October 13, 1955. Kerouac and Cassady were in the audience that evening, goading and cheering as Ginsberg, age twenty-nine, swayed like a prophet and intoned his electrifying screed: *"I saw the best minds of my generation destroyed by madness . . ."*

Reciting "Howl" in public was an act of cultural sedition. It was also a galvanizing event for the bohemian community that had nestled in North Beach, an Italian American neighborhood in San Francisco, where Ginsberg lived while composing "Howl." North Beach was a haven for eccentric artists and other offbeat characters. The hub of the dissident subculture in North Beach was City Lights bookstore, run by the poet Lawrence Ferlinghetti, who published *Howl* and various edgy texts in inexpensive paperback editions. The area even had its own latter-day Mezz Mezzrow, a self-proclaimed "Johnny Potseed." He was none other than Neal Cassady (also "N.C., secret hero of these poems" in *Howl*), who supplied North Beach residents with marijuana that he smuggled over the Mexican border while working as a brakeman on the Southern Pacific Railroad. Cassady was a cannabis evangelist; he gave away much of his herb, turning on hundreds of Bay Area locals. Before long, according to *San Francisco Chronicle* columnist Herb Caen, the smell of pot was stronger than the smell of garlic in North Beach. Caen mockingly referred to the scruffy, pot-smoking crowd as *beatniks* because, like *Sputnik*, the Soviet space probe, they were way out there.

During the so-called beatnik summer of 1958, frequent police raids targeted San Francisco's homosexual subculture, as well as the cannabis underground. Cassady's generosity got him in trouble when he was busted for offering a few joints free of charge to a couple of plainclothes cops. Convicted and sentenced to two terms of five years to life, he ended up serving a couple of years in San Quentin. Ginsberg visited him in prison and they talked about how unfair it was that Cassady had been punished so severely for what was meant as a Good Samaritan gesture. The 1958 arrest and imprisonment of Cassady, an early martyr to America's harsh antimarijuana statutes, catalyzed Ginsberg's subsequent efforts as a trailblazer for drug-law reform. "It was becoming clear to me," Ginsberg explained, "that the only way people like Neal and myself who smoked marijuana as part of a way of life would ever be safe was when the laws were changed."

Ginsberg believed that the U.S. government prohibited cannabis, a consciousness-altering botanical, as a means of enforcing conformity among its citizens. Conformity of consciousness, the most insidious kind of conformity, had become a hallmark of Cold War America. The crusade against cannabis resembled and reinforced the 1950s anti-Communist crusade. During this period, there was little public debate about marijuana. Scholars and social scientists were reluctant to address the subject. Marijuana was never mentioned in Hollywood films without Commissioner Anslinger's approval. To question the probity of pot prohibition—or the self-righteousness of anticommunism—was to invite public ridicule and scorn.

The publication of *Howl* (1956) and *On the Road* (1957) ignited a firestorm of criticism. *Time* magazine, in a typical attack, called Kerouac "the latrine laureate of Hobohemia" and denigrated *Howl* as "an interminable sewer of a poem." But nothing could gainsay the fact that the Beats had touched a raw nerve in American society. They gave voice to an undercurrent of alienation and discontent bubbling beneath the surface calm of the Eisenhower era. By proclaiming their enthusiasm for marijuana in poetry and prose, the Beats shattered taboos of conformity and silence. They connected pot smoking to a potent ethos of freedom and rebellion. The Beats encouraged everyone to be adventurous and open-minded, to plumb their own experience, to question conventional wisdom about marijuana and much else.

On the last night of 1959, while Cassady stewed behind bars and Burroughs lingered in Tangiers, Kerouac uncorked a bottle of wine and poured a glass for Ginsberg and a friend. They sat on the roof of Ginsberg's East Village apartment building in New York City, conversing through the wee hours. As they watched the first sunrise of the New Year, Ginsberg and Kerouac bid adieu to the dwindling darkness of the old decade and wondered what the Sixties would bring.

3

REEFER REBELLION

Seeds of Change

J. Edgar Hoover, the pugnacious director of the Federal Bureau of Investigation (FBI), put it country-simple for a lay audience when he declared in a widely quoted 1961 speech: "The three biggest threats to America are the Communists, the Beatniks, and the Eggheads."

America's secret police chief with the bulldog visage was exaggerating when he fingered the reds, for he knew that the Communist Party USA by this time was largely a front for government spies masquerading as authentic members. As for the eggheads—Hoover never bothered to explain who they were or why they were dangerous. But he was right about the Beats, even though the full scope of their disruptive impact had yet to be felt.

The Beats actually did pose a threat to the status quo, though not in a conventional political sense. Convinced that any serious attempt to transform mainstream society was futile in the forlorn Fifties, the Beats did not advocate organized political engagement. Theirs was more a call to consciousness than a call to arms. The task of remodeling themselves by pursuing experiences outside the cultural norm took precedence over changing political institutions. Other than a commitment to radical individualism and personal freedom, the Beats did not share a unified political outlook: Ginsberg was a red diaper baby and a left-wing libertarian; Burroughs was a conservative anarchist and a bit of a gun nut; and Kerouac retained some of the reactionary political views of his French Canadian Catholic working-class parents. Yet, by helping to jump-start a cultural revolution, this trio of writers was arguably as influential in shaping American lives as the three branches of the U.S. government.

"Woe unto those who spit on the beat generation," Kerouac warned, "the wind'll blow it back." As cultural expatriates, the Beats linked cannabis to a nascent groundswell of nonconformity that would develop into a mass rebellion in the years ahead. They were the key transmission belt for the spread of marijuana into mainstream America. A trickle of white, middle class pot smokers, once confined to jazz clubs, would become a nationwide torrent during the social tumult loosely known as "the Sixties." By the end of the decade, FBI undercover agents would be smoking marijuana and hashish in an effort to burnish their counterculture credentials and infiltrate radical groups.

A devout enemy of the herb, J. Edgar Hoover maintained that a marijuana user "becomes a fiend with savage 'cave man' tendencies. His sex desires are aroused and some of the most horrible crimes result." The FBI had it in for Ginsberg, in particular, because of the pot-smoking poet's unabashed homosexuality. This was a touchy issue for Hoover, a closet queer obsessed with hoarding information about other peoples' sex lives for blackmail purposes. Hoover pegged Ginsberg "potentially dangerous" and the FBI opened a case file on him.

Imbued with the zeal of a crusader, Irwin Allen Ginsberg was the original culture warrior for cannabis, a one-man, anti-reefer-madness wrecking crew determined to shake the foundations of pot prohibition. On February 12, 1961, he sang the praises of marijuana during a live appearance on a televised talk show anchored and moderated by John Crosby. Ginsberg was joined by anthropologist Ashley Montagu and novelist Norman Mailer. The poet quickly steered the discussion toward cannabis. All the guests agreed that ganja was a relatively benign substance that should not be illegal. Even the host acknowledged that the laws against marijuana were far too severe. Ginsberg later described the show as a "lucid advertisement for pot." The controversial segment on "Hips and Beats" generated extensive press coverage. This was the first time that the virtues of marijuana had been extolled on national television.

The Federal Bureau of Narcotics responded with a seven-minute videotaped rebuttal, which aired the following month over the objections of Crosby, who wrote a syndicated newspaper column complaining about the U.S. government's heavy-handed interference. Crosby called the FBN's retort "a lot of alarmist nonsense concerning pot, about which our Narcotics Bureau knows very little."

In the early 1960s, few Americans were aware of the history of marijuana and how it came to be criminalized. Anslinger's rabid fictions still held sway among mass media. Young people were taught that pot was a deadly menace. Ginsberg stood the mainstream view of marijuana on its head, recasting Anslinger's killer weed as something positive, a source of enrichment, a valuable tool for introspection, something healthy, refreshing, and enjoyable. In an effort to generate a serious discussion about drug policy, Ginsberg circulated copies of the La Guardia Report, the seminal study that roundly debunked the notion that marijuana was a dangerous substance. Ginsberg tried to persuade commercial publishers to reissue the neglected La Guardia Report, but there were no immediate takers.

Ginsberg believed that marijuana could play a major role in opening hearts and minds and sensitizing people to social injustice. This is what he intuited while high on grass: "It was the first time I ever had solid evidence in my own body that there was a difference between reality as I saw it myself and reality as it was described officially by the state, the government, the police and the media. And from then on I realized that marijuana was going to be an enormous political catalyst because anybody who got high would immediately see through the official hallucination that had been laid down and would begin questioning, 'What is this war? What is this military budget?' "

Ginsberg maintained that smoking marijuana could be an educational experience, especially for someone who is intellectually curious. "Grass should be used with mindful attentiveness, rather than just for kicks," he advised. He credited the herb with provoking a more deeply sensual awareness, an aesthetic kind of concentration. Ginsberg said that under the influence of cannabis he grasped the complex, inner structure of jazz and classical music compositions. Occasionally, he would smoke some "tea" and visit an art museum, where he gazed upon the works of Cézanne and other great painters. He became acutely aware of "awe and detail" while stoned, as he explained with poetic precision: "Marijuana consciousness is one that, ever so gently, shifts the center of attention *from* habitual shallow, purely verbal guidelines and repetitive secondhand ideological interpretations of experience to more direct, slower, more absorbing, occasionally microscopically minute engagement with sensing phenomena."

But Ginsberg—who grew up tormented by his mother's mental illness and her death in a psychiatric institution—found that cannabis could also amplify unpleasant experiences, ingrained insecurities, free-floating anxiety. (Latin Americans had a name for panic reactions under the influence of marijuana—*muerta blanca,* or "white death.") At various times in his life, Ginsberg abstained from smoking pot entirely because it seemed to exaggerate his paranoia, a difficulty he attributed in part to the climate of illegality and the very real fear of arrest that hexed pot smokers in the USA.

Ginsberg saw some of the best minds of his generation crippled by habitual drug use, and he was careful never to get hooked on anything. He felt that overindulgence could have negative consequences even with a substance as benign as grass. Unlike Kerouac, Ginsberg never got into a fifteen-reefers-a-day routine. (Even Cassady, whose middle name was not Moderation, criticized Kerouac's obsessive pot smoking in Mexico.) Ginsberg's interest in cannabis and other drugs was largely experimental, whereas several of his close, excess-prone friends became addicted to alcohol and opiates. Unable to cope with his own notoriety and the media-skewed trajectory of the Beat scene, Kerouac would slowly drink himself to death.

A few weeks after Kennedy was elected president of the United States by a narrow margin, Ginsberg and his partner, Peter Orlovsky, visited Harvard University, JFK's alma mater, to participate in a psilocybin experiment conducted by psychology professor Timothy Leary. Psilocybin, a hallucinogenic drug derived from magic mushrooms, triggered fantastic visions similar to lysergic acid diethylamide-25 (LSD), an even more potent, mind-altering fungoid compound that Leary would also administer to volunteer subjects. Like cannabis, LSD was well regarded among scientists for its medicinal potential long before it gained a reputation for recreational abuse. Grass and acid would both be instrumental in catalyzing the countercultural rebellion that erupted later in the decade. Initially, however, cannabis was frowned upon by Leary's circle in Cambridge, Massachusetts. "Instinctively, Leary stayed away from marijuana because it was illegal. He didn't want to get involved with it at all," recalls Ralph Metzner, Leary's Harvard collaborator. LSD, on the other hand, was still legal and would remain so for a few more years.

Discovered in 1943 by Dr. Albert Hofmann, a Swiss chemist with Sandoz Pharmaceuticals, LSD was odorless, colorless, tasteless, and extremely powerful—properties that stoked the interest of American spies and military strategists during the early years of the Cold War. While U.S. Army brass were smitten by the notion of using LSD to wage psychochemical warfare, the CIA wielded the hallucinogen as a cloak-and-dagger weapon to disorient people and elicit information from uncooperative targets. Ironically, around the same time, many reputable psychiatrists were touting LSD as an adjunct for psychotherapy, a promising healing modality that could help neurotic patients confront and overcome their problems. A tiny dose of LSD seemed to have an uncanny ability to make the subconscious conscious, to illuminate long-hidden sources of stress by bringing to the surface whatever might be lurking in the depths of the mind; hence the word *psychedelic,* which literally means "mind manifesting."

When Leary launched his research project at Harvard in 1960, psychedelic drugs were one of the hottest topics of study in psychiatry. Although he was hardly a pacesetter in this regard, Leary became an instant convert. He was convinced that LSD held the key to unlocking the prison of personality. Leary and Ginsberg agreed that psychedelics could dissolve the old conditioned self and stretch the mind to hitherto unknown limits, allowing a radical new being to emerge. In their messianic enthusiasm, they projected the therapeutic potential of LSD onto the social landscape. Leary began to trumpet acid as a cure-all for a sick society, a species-catalyst capable of catapulting humanity to the next evolutionary level. This was a tad too much for Harvard authorities, who fired Leary and his research associate, Richard Alpert, in May 1963 amid rumors of LSD-laced sugar cubes circulating among impressionable undergraduates. Undaunted, Leary embraced the role of Pied Piper with relish, brandishing his trademark grin and a knack for memorable one-liners. "Turn on, tune in, and drop out" was his well-publicized clarion call. Exiled from academia, he threw caution to the winds and promoted LSD as a miracle drug for seekers of everything from personal fulfillment and spiritual truth to better orgasms.

Ginsberg was traveling in Asia when Leary got his walking papers from Harvard. The poet's metaphoric and geographical journey to the East included a fifteen-month stay in India, where Ginsberg smoked hashish with naked *sadhus* (ascetics) near burning funeral pyres on the banks of the Ganges. *"Bom Bom Mahadev!"* the yogis shouted while raising the ganja pipe to their brows before inhaling. Dubbed "the leaf of heroes" and "the joy-giver," the resinous plant was central to everyday religious and social life in India and had been for many centuries. The Sanskrit root word for ganja meant "knowledge."

Ginsberg came to India hoping to learn from a culture with a living spiritual tradition. In addition to smoking a lot of ganja and drinking bhang, the ubiquitous cannabinated beverage, he studied meditation, mantra chanting, and other nondrug techniques of altering consciousness. He toured ashrams (religious communities) and various pilgrimage sites, joining two million devotees at the mind-boggling Kumbh Mela festival in Haridwar, held once every twelve years. The lessons Ginsberg brought back to the United States—and his subsequent Buddhist practice—would influence legions of Western youth who came of age in the 1960s hungry for alternatives to Judeo-Christian canon.

The zeitgeist was beginning to shift in the United States. JFK declared that a torch had been "passed to a new generation." A charismatic commander-in-chief and an elegant first lady—it seemed like a fresh start for America after the insipid Eisenhower era. What passed for change in Camelot, however, was often more style than substance and did not include the jettisoning of fundamental Cold War assumptions. But there were signs that the Kennedy administration was serious about revamping federal drug-control policy.

In a long-overdue move, JFK sacked Harry Anslinger in 1962. Kennedy wasn't enamored of Anslinger's roughneck cop mentality and his organization's chronic disregard for constitutional rights. With Anslinger forcibly retired, top FBN officials engaged in rancorous infighting. Corruption was rampant among FBN agents in New York, Miami, and other cities; several narcotics officers were later shown to be actively colluding with heroin traffickers and street pushers. The Federal Narcotics Bureau, the most notoriously compromised department of the federal government, was a scandal waiting to blow wide open.*

It was time to set a new course. Kennedy authorized a committee to study America's narcotics problem. In 1963, the White House Conference on Narcotics and Drug Abuse concluded that the hazards of smoking marijuana were "exaggerated" and that harsh criminal penalties (which in Georgia, for example, included the death penalty for selling pot to a minor) were "in poor social perspective." For a country punch-drunk on antimarijuana hysteria, it was a momentary jolt of sobriety.

Kennedy was in no rush to affix his Hancock to the United Nations Single Convention on Narcotic Drugs, which Anslinger had vociferously championed. The 1961 Single Convention Treaty required all signatory countries to adopt and maintain domestic legislation and penal measures against cannabis and other drugs. Drafting and lobbying for the Single Convention's section on marijuana was Anslinger's last hurrah as FBN chief, the coup de grâce that would make it impossible for the U.S. government to relax its marijuana policies, or so he believed. "We've got it locked up so tightly now they'll never change the law," Anslinger exulted. But caveats in the text exempted hemp's medicinal and industrial applications from the new international treaty, which was formally ratified by the United States in 1968.†

After JFK was assassinated, there were whispers alleging that Kennedy had smoked pot in the White House with various female friends. Some claimed

---

* In 1968, it became known that a number of federal narcotics agents in the New York office were in the business of selling narcotics or protecting dope dealers. FBN agents stole money, seized drugs (and did not turn them in), and looted apartments they raided. According to the Wurms Report, the FBN itself had been the major source of supply and protection of heroin in the United States. Several FBN agents were indicted, and eventually nearly every agent in the New York office was fired, forced to resign, or transferred. The Knapp Commission subsequently investigated and documented mass corruption in the NYPD (Epstein, *Agency of Fear*, pp. 105, 246; Ball, *Allen Verbatim*, pp. 63–65).

† Article 46 of the 1961 U.N. Single Convention Treaty stipulated that any signatory country can withdraw from the Treaty, and if enough countries choose to do so it shall cease to exist. The Treaty also asserts: "The medical use of narcotic drugs continues to be indispensable for relief of pain and suffering and . . . adequate provisions must be made to ensure the availability of narcotic drugs for such purposes . . ."

the president used the herb to soothe his back pain. Such rumors, though not implausible, remain unsubstantiated. But this much can be confirmed: During the Kennedy presidency, marijuana smoking increased exponentially among white middle-class youth, including some of America's best and brightest college students. And now that the genie was out of the bottle there was no way to put it back in.

In 1963, Caucasians for the first time comprised more than half of those arrested for marijuana violations in California, a bellwether state. Contrary to the usual scare stories, most people weren't tricked into puffing by a devious pusher. In ever-increasing numbers, American youth were introduced to cannabis by their friends. That fateful first joint or pipeful did not lead to ruin. It didn't turn them into miserable addicts or psychos or couch potatoes. More often than not, it relaxed them and gave them the munchies and the giggles. And it also set their skeptical minds in motion: If government authorities habitually lie about marijuana, what else do they lie about? If pot prohibition is based on blatant falsehoods, are other laws just as arbitrary, capricious, and groundless?

Once they tried marijuana, many Americans wondered if they could trust the government to tell the truth about anything. Not surprisingly, pot smokers in the early 1960s tended to harbor antiestablishment attitudes. It wasn't the chemical composition of cannabis that engendered a general skepticism toward authority—it was the chasm between lived experience and official antimarijuana mythology enshrined in federal legislation that mandated five years in prison for possessing a single stick of grass.

As more Americans discovered the gentle euphoria and the angst-assuaging effects of cannabis, grassroots user networks reached a critical mass and became visible as distinct countercommunities in major cities and college towns. The seeds of change planted by Ginsberg and Kerouac were sprouting across the country in dozens of small-scale bohemian enclaves, where students, artists, marijuana smokers, bongo bangers, folk singers, jazz buffs, leftist intellectuals, and other coffeehouse patrons discussed the burning issues of the day—civil rights, the death penalty, the recent Cuban revolution, and the threat of nuclear war.

Born and raised in Duluth, Minnesota, Robert Zimmerman took up the guitar as a teenager and started hanging out in Dinkytown, the Twin Cities' bohemian district. Situated near the University of Minnesota, it offered a congenial environment for young malcontents who were seeking their own generational identity and looking to cop some weed. This is where Zimmerman first came into contact with marijuana in 1959. Beat literature also made a big impression on him during this period. "It was Ginsberg and Kerouac who inspired me at first," he acknowledged. Soon he changed his name to Bob Dylan and moved to New York City to pursue his dream of becoming a folk singer.

Dylan was nineteen when he arrived in Greenwich Village, the cradle of the folk music revival. Unpolished and ambitious, he sang in a nasal twang that challenged conventional tastes while tapping into a rich vein of youthful alienation. Folk music was antiestablishment music that supported desegregation, labor unions, nuclear disarmament, and social justice. En route to becoming the foremost singer-songwriter of his era, Dylan initially rode the coattails of Joan Baez, the reigning queen of folk, whose talented sister, Mimi, was married to Dylan's close friend Richard Farina.* They were quite a foursome, according to David Hajdu, who reports that Richard and Bob shared a "fondness for marijuana," though Dylan seemed "far more interested in the literal effects of the drug than in its social cache."

A society that seemed so humdrum and predictable just a few years earlier was undergoing a series of convulsions. As the timidity of the 1950s mind-set began to abate, it dawned on an entire generation of Americans that they had the power, in the words of Thomas Paine, "to begin the world over again." Driven by moral outrage and the conviction that their country was more democratic in name than fact, scores of Americans from all walks of life took part in a civil rights movement that included dangerous voter-registration campaigns in the Deep South, where police savaged nonviolent protestors with billy clubs, attack dogs, and water cannon. Dylan went to Mississippi to support the "Freedom Summer" voting rights drive and his song "Blowin' in the Wind" became both a Top Ten hit (sung by Peter, Paul, and Mary) and an anthem for the civil rights movement. Dylan performed this song with Joan Baez for 200,000 people at the legendary rally in Washington, D.C., where Rev. Martin Luther King, Jr., delivered his stirring "I have a dream" speech on August 28, 1963.

Exactly one year later to the day, Bob Dylan ascended the elevator of the Delmonico Hotel on Park Avenue in Manhattan for a momentous first meeting with the Beatles, who were touring the United States. Beatlemania was then at its peak, and twenty police stood guard in the corridor as Dylan entered the Beatles' sixth-floor hotel suite.

---

* Farina, a folk musician and an author, died in a motorcycle accident in 1966, shortly after his first novel was published. A cult classic among counterculture buffs, *Been Down So Long It Looks Like Up to Me*, describes the travails of Gnossos Pappadopoulos, the archetypical student outcast who rejects approved avenues of advancement as too narrow, too compromised, or simply too dull to abide, while indulging in a complete collegiate pharmacopeia—grass, hash, peyote, paregoric-soaked cigarettes, and whatever else he could find.

After an exchange of courtesies, Dylan suggested that they all smoke some grass. He was surprised to learn that the Beatles were marijuana virgins. Dylan had a bag of weed with him and he rolled a sloppy joint. Blinds were drawn and towels carefully placed before locked doors to hide the smell. Dylan sparked a reefer and a few minutes later everyone was laughing uproariously.

"We were kind of proud to have been introduced to pot by Dylan," Paul McCartney later remarked. "That was rather a coup."

Cannabis was quite different from the purple hearts and other uppers that the Beatles had taken to keep pace with the rigors of the late-night club circuit. Marijuana eased them into a soft yet lively space, a cushioned reprieve from the bizarre fishbowl sensation—the hysterical fans, the constant media attention—that accompanied their vertiginous rise to rock stardom. From that day forward, the Beatles would consume cannabis on a regular basis. And whenever John Lennon felt like getting stoned, he would say, *"Let's 'ave a larf!"*

The Riddle of THC

On August 28, 1964, the day Dylan lit up and handed the Beatles their first joint in a New York City hotel room, Dr. Raphael Mechoulam was working intently in his laboratory at the Hebrew University in Jerusalem. The young Israeli chemist and his research partner, Yechiel Gaoni, would soon become the first scientists to fully isolate and synthesize delta-9-tetrahydrocannabinol, or THC, marijuana's principal psychoactive component.

Mechoulam's groundbreaking research was subsidized by the U.S. National Institutes of Health (NIH), which had suddenly become desirous of more objective information about the herb. As the use of marijuana soared among middle-class youth, officialdom started to get anxious, especially when the sons and daughters of prominent politicians were caught smoking it. Queried by members of Congress as to whether pot caused brain damage, the NIH scurried to gather basic scientific data. But hard science was hard to come by in large part due to the stubborn refusal of the Federal Bureau of Narcotics to sanction laboratory research. For a long time, the illegality of cannabis acted as a deterrent to research in the United States.

From a scientific perspective, the riddle of THC was not easy to unravel. The small number of researchers who studied cannabis over the years found the herb difficult to work with because many of its 421 distinct compounds are "lipophilic" (soluble in fat but not in water), which means they can't be separated and scrutinized without sophisticated equipment. Scientists would

Israeli scientist Raphael Mechoulam first synthesized THC, marijuana's principal psychoactive ingredient, in 1964. In the early 1990s, Mechoulam's team discovered endogenous cannabinoid compounds in the mammalian brain and body that protect neurons, stimulate adult stem-cell growth, and regulate the immune system, glucose metabolism, and other crucial physiological processes.
(Courtesy of The Hebrew University in Jerusalem)

eventually ascertain that at least a hundred of these lipophilic compounds—known as "cannabinoids"—are unique to the marijuana plant.* In addition to the cannabinoids, a term coined by Mechoulam, marijuana contains various alkaloids, flavonoids, and terpenoids (essential aromatic oils).

The isolation and synthesis of THC would prove to be a highly significant event in the history of psychopharmacology. Mechoulam, then thirty-four, an-

* Plant cannabinoids have twenty-one carbon atoms in ring structures, with hydrogen and oxygen molecules attached at different points.

nounced his discovery in a letter to the editor of the *Journal of the American Chemical Society* on July 20, 1965. Although he didn't realize it at the time, Mechoulam had lit a slow-burning fuse that would detonate a revolution in medical science.

Scientists noted that THC had two asymmetrical centers and existed in both left- and right-handed forms. (The molecular structure of THC has a "double" quality in keeping with the twin spirit of cannabis.) Mechoulam and his Hebrew University colleagues proceeded to isolate and elucidate the chemical structure of dozens of other cannabinoids, which composed a new class of compounds different from any other drugs. Mechoulam understood that marijuana had a therapeutic history dating back thousands of years, and he believed that the cannabinoids were "a medicinal treasure trove" waiting to be tapped. Much of his early research was devoted to exploring the healing potential of THC, which caused the psychoactive buzz sought by pot smokers. When smoked, THC is absorbed into the bloodstream via the lungs and nasal passages and quickly crosses the blood-brain barrier.

The variability of THC became evident to Mechoulam when he administered the compound to a group of people in a social setting. Everyone "had a different reaction," Mechoulam recalled after his first and only THC experience. "I think I enjoyed it. I was just sitting there and feeling above everything else. One person became a little anxious; another became a little aggressive." A member of the Knesset (the Israeli parliament) who ingested THC talked a blue streak for several hours.*

Mechoulam and his associates conducted clinical studies with THC at a hospital in Jerusalem, and found that it showed promise for treating a wide range of conditions, including neuropathic pain, Tourette's syndrome, hypertension, and chronic hiccups (which can wreak havoc on a person's health). Israeli physicians also gave THC to children undergoing cancer chemotherapy in order to alleviate nausea and prevent them from vomiting; it worked in every case.

During this period, the U.S. Army was also very interested in THC—but not for therapeutic purposes. "We weren't looking for medical benefits," re-

* In a 1970 article in *Science* magazine, Mechoulam speculated (incorrectly, it turned out) that the body metabolized THC into another chemical, which acted on a molecular level to cause the marijuana high. Later Mechoulam found a THC metabolite—a compound generated by the breakdown of THC—in mammalian urine. But this metabolite was not psychoactive. Nevertheless, Mechoulam's discovery laid the basis for today's urinalysis industry because the presence of this THC metabolite in urine meant that marijuana had been consumed. To his everlasting regret, Mechoulam neglected to patent his discovery.

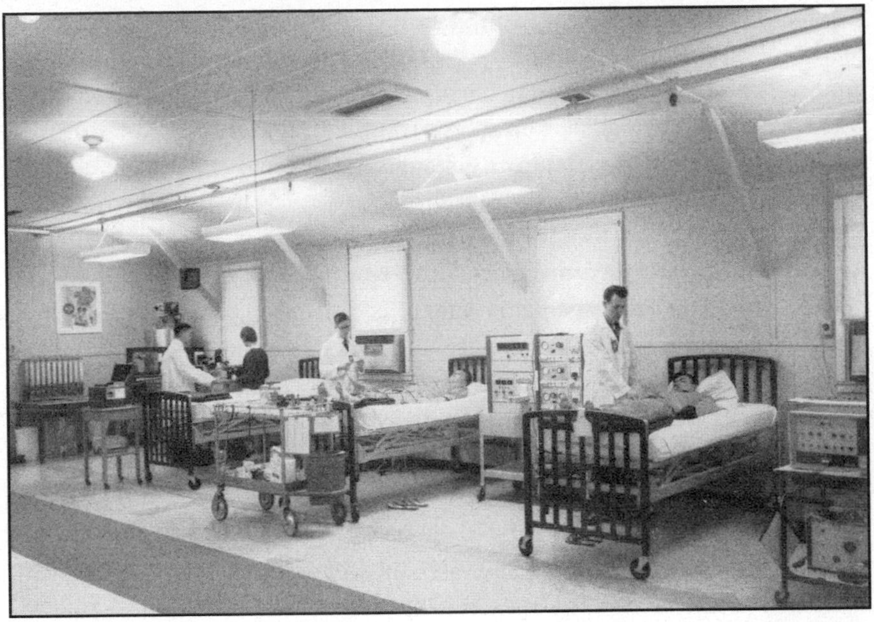

Edgewood Arsenal, Maryland, where the U.S. Army Chemical Corps tested potent THC-like molecules on GI volunteers
(Courtesy of James Ketchum)

called Dr. James S. Ketchum, a retired colonel. "We were trying to subdue people." Ketchum was referring to his work at Edgewood Arsenal, headquarters of the Army Chemical Corps, in the 1960s, when American national security strategists were high on the possibility of developing a so-called humane weapon that could knock people out without necessarily killing them. Top military officers hyped the notion of "war without death," conjuring visions of aircraft swooping over enemy territory releasing clouds of "madness gas" that would disorient the bad guys and dissolve their will to resist, while specially equipped U.S. soldiers moved in and took over.

"Paradoxical as it may seem, one can use chemical weapons to spare lives, rather than extinguish them," contends Ketchum, who oversaw a secret research program at Edgewood (located twenty-five miles northeast of Baltimore), where an array of mind-bending drugs were tested on American soldiers, including an exceptionally potent synthetic marijuana derivative. Obtained from major pharmaceutical corporations and other sources, most of these drugs had no medical names, just "experimental agent" (EA) numbers designated by army officers.

The Chemical Corps's marijuana research began several years before

Raphael Mechoulam succeeded in isolating and synthesizing pure THC. In the late 1950s, the army tested "EA-1476"—a potent cannabis concentrate hitherto known as "Red Oil" in scientific circles—on U.S. soldiers at Edgewood Arsenal. When asked to perform routine numbers and spatial reasoning tests, the stoned GIs couldn't stop laughing. But Red Oil was not an ideal chemical-warfare candidate. For starters, it was a "crude" plant extract that contained many hard-to-separate components besides psychoactive THC. Army scientists surmised that pure THC would weigh much less than Red Oil and would therefore be better suited as a chemical weapon. They were intrigued by the possibility of amplifying the active ingredient of marijuana, tweaking the mother molecule, as it were, to enhance her psychogenic effects. So the Chemical Corps set its sights on developing a synthetic variant of THC that could clobber people without killing them.

Enter Harry Pars, a scientist working with Arthur D. Little, Inc., based in Cambridge, Massachusetts, one of several pharmaceutical companies that conducted chemical-warfare research for the U.S. Army. A frequent visitor to Edgewood Arsenal, Pars synthesized a new cannabinoid compound, dubbed "EA 2233," which was significantly stronger than Red Oil.

The U.S. Army Chemical Corps began clinical testing of EA 2233 on GI volunteers in 1961, the year Ketchum began his military career as a staff psychiatrist at Edgewood. "There was no doubt in my mind that working in this strange atmosphere was just the sort of thing that would satisfy my appetite for novelty," he later recounted. Ketchum rose swiftly in rank and became chief of clinical research at the army's hub for chemical-warfare studies. Although the Geneva Convention had banned the use of chemical weapons, the U.S. government never agreed to this provision, and Washington poured money into the search for a nonlethal incapacitant.

Colonel Ketchum found that EA 2233, when ingested at sufficient dosage levels, lasted up to thirty hours, far longer than the typical marijuana buzz. In a videotaped interview seven hours after he had been given EA 2233, a GI volunteer described feeling numb in his arms and unable to raise them, precluding any possibility that he could defend himself if attacked. "Everything seems comical . . . I just feel like laughing," he told his interlocutor, Dr. Ketchum.

Q: Does the time seem to pass slower or faster or any different than usual?

A: *No different than usual. Just—just that I mostly lose track of it. I don't know if it's early or late . . .*

Q: Suppose you have to get up and go to work now. How would you do?

A: *I don't think I'd even care.*

Q: Well, suppose the place were on fire?
A: *It would seem funny.*
Q: It would seem funny? Do you think you'd have the sense to get up and run out or do you think you'd just enjoy it?
A: *I don't know. Fire doesn't seem to present any danger to me right now . . . Everything just seems funny in the army. Seems like everything somebody says, it sounds a little bit funny . . .*
Q: Is it like when you're in a good mood and you can laugh at anything?
A: *Right . . . It's like being out with a bunch of people and everybody's laughing. They're just—*
Q: Having a ball?
A: *Yeah. And everything just seems funny.*
Q: Would you do this again? Take this test again?
A: *Yeah. Yeah. It wouldn't bother me at all.*

EA 2233 was actually a mixture of eight stereoisomers of THC. (An isomer is a rearrangement of the same atoms within a given molecule; a stereoisomer entails different spatial configurations of these atoms.) Eventually, Edgewood scientists would separate the eight stereoisomers and investigate the relative potency of each of them individually in an effort to separate the psychoactive wheat from the chaff and reduce the amount of material needed to get the desired effect for chemical warfare.

Only two of the stereoisomers proved to be of interest; the others didn't have much of a knockdown effect. When administered intravenously, low doses of these two synthetic cousins of tetrahydrocannabinol triggered a dramatic drop in blood pressure to the point where test subjects could barely move. Standing up without assistance was impossible. Cautious army doctors construed this as a warning sign—a sudden plunge in blood pressure could be dangerous—and human experiments with single THC stereoisomers were suspended.

Looking back on these studies, Colonel Ketchum wonders whether his colleagues made the right decision. "This hypotensive [blood pressure reducing] property, in an otherwise nonlethal compound, might be an ideal way to produce a temporary inability to fight, or do much else, without toxicological danger to life," Ketchum stated in a 2007 interview. Given the high safety margin of THC—no one has ever died from an overdose—and the likelihood that the stereoisomers would display a similar safety profile, Ketchum believes the army may have spurned a couple of worthy prospects that were capable of filling the knock-'em-out-but-don't-kill-'em niche in America's chemical-warfare armory.

As for the two exemplary stereoisomers weaned from EA 2233, Ketchum speculates: "They probably would have been safe in terms of life-sparing activity . . . But a person who received them would have to lie down. If he tried to stand up and get his weapon, he would feel faint and lightheaded and he'd keel over. Essentially he would be immobilized for any military purpose until the effects wore off."

The colonel's assessment: "A safe drug that knocks people down—what more could you ask for?"

With THC isomers on the back burner, the U.S. Army Chemical Corps focused on several other compounds that were thought to have significant potential as nonlethal incapacitants: LSD, PCP, Ritalin (now widely prescribed in the USA for hyperactive children), and a delirium-inducing ass-kicker known as "BZ." By the time the clinical testing program had run its course, 6,700 volunteers experienced some bizarre states of consciousness at Edgewood. Sequestered in padded rooms, soldiers under the influence of powerful mind-altering drugs rode imaginary horses and ate invisible chickens. Other GIs took showers in full uniform while smoking phantom cigars. Some of their antics were so over the top that Ketchum had to admonish the nurses and other medical personnel not to laugh at the volunteers even though it was unlikely that they would remember such incidents once the drugs wore off.

One morning, Ketchum arrived at his office in Edgewood and found "a large black steel barrel, resembling an oil drum, parked in the corner of the room," as he recounted. Overcome by curiosity, he opened the barrel and examined its contents. There were a dozen tightly sealed glass canisters that looked like cookie jars; the labels on the canisters indicated that each contained about three pounds of EA 1729, the army's code number for LSD. By the end of the week, the forty pounds of government acid—enough to blow several hundred million minds—vanished as mysteriously as it had appeared. Ketchum never found out who put the LSD in his office or what became of it.

But this much he knew: Several officers at Edgewood were dipping into the army's stash for their own personal use. "Some of my colleagues took LSD more often than was necessary to appreciate its clinical effects," Ketchum admitted. "They must have liked it."

During the mid-1960s, when young Americans in large numbers were first turning on to reefer, the colonel occasionally got together with a few friends and smoked pot while on leave from Edgewood. "I enjoyed it," Ketchum conceded. "It was very sensuous. But I didn't use it very often. I didn't have any of my own."

After sixteen years in the service, the colonel retired and moved to California. When residents of the Golden State passed the 1996 ballot measure that legalized medical marijuana, Ketchum got a recommendation from his family physician to use the herb for insomnia. "I have personally found it helpful, especially for sleep," he divulged. "I've had problems with sleep for a long time. When I started smoking pot more often, my sleep improved. As a result, I no longer needed to take Valium regularly."

Colonel Ketchum, the man who tried to harness THC as a weapon of war, found solace in the healing qualities of cannabis. As a private citizen, he supported the efforts of drug-policy critics working inside and outside the system to end pot prohibition. "It's the refusal to look at the evidence that keeps cannabis illegal," the colonel asserted. "It's a much safer drug than many legal substances. They misrepresented marijuana as an evil weed."

Grass and Acid

Ken Kesey knew how to throw a party.

It all started when this burly, blue-eyed, ex–high school wrestling champ with a gift for gab heard about an experiment being conducted at the Veterans Hospital in Menlo Park, California. Volunteers were paid $75 to serve as guinea pigs in a U.S. government-sponsored study of hallucinogenic drugs. Kesey, then a graduate student in Stanford University's creative writing program, had smoked marijuana, but he had never tried LSD, a drug that was not yet generally available for public consumption. In the spring of 1960, Kesey took "acid" for the first time courtesy of Uncle Sam. It changed his life. And he changed America.

A few weeks after his initial shell-shattering trip to "Edge City"—Kesey's name for the outer limits of consciousness he experienced on LSD—he finagled a job at the Veterans Hospital. The young writer proceeded to help himself to a generous array of psychedelic compounds, which he shared with his adventurous friends in Perry Lane, the collegiate bohemia of Palo Alto. While working as a night attendant on the hospital's psychiatric ward, Kesey got the idea for his first novel, *One Flew over the Cuckoo's Nest,* about a group of mental patients who battled the repressive authority of the Big Nurse. The asylum inmates were depicted as less crazy than their keepers, an apt metaphor for America circa '62, when *Cuckoo's Nest* was published to great critical acclaim. That was the year of the Cuban missile crisis: The United States and the Soviet Union went eyeball to eyeball and the world held its breath. The turn of a key could have triggered nuclear war and the mass extinction of the human species. The whole thing seemed suicidal, completely insane, yet it was precisely this irrationality that gave the superpowers their credibility in the modern world.

That year also saw the publication of *Silent Spring,* Rachel Carson's deeply disturbing exposé of environmental pollution and the peril it posed to animal genetics and the entire biosphere. Hers was literally a prophetic voice crying out from the wilderness, a portent of impending ecological doom. Poisons everywhere, weapons of mass destruction, glaring social inequality, idiotic drug laws—it all seemed like Cuckoosville. The early Sixties were pervaded by a sense of daily apocalypse. Those who came of age during these anxious times made their stand not only as a "lost generation" but also as potentially the last generation.

Kesey's antiauthoritarian fable was a harbinger of the youth rebellion that would soon sweep the land—student protest, peace demonstrations, grass and acid, the hippie counterculture, black power, women's liberation, gay rights, and more. Flush with earnings from his book, Kesey bought an old school bus, painted the exterior in bright, swirly, psychedelic colors, and filled it with a passel of like-minded friends, the Merry Pranksters, who dressed in Day-Glo apparel and American flag outfits. They put a hole in the roof so folks could sit atop the bus, which became a funhouse on wheels. In the summer of 1964, the Pranksters set off on a mythic journey across America, smoking lots of marijuana and guzzling LSD-laced orange juice while spreading the gospel of psychic freedom in a country not yet thoroughly homogenized by monotonous chain stores and inane television. They were on a quest to "stop the coming end of the world," said Kesey, the charismatic chief of this rolling medicine show.

The driver of the psychedelic bus was the Beat legend Neal Cassady. After serving two years in jail for a minor marijuana infraction, Cassady hooked up with Kesey and resumed his wandering, weed-smoking ways. "With Cassady at the throttle, the bus perfected an uncanny reverse homage to *On the Road,* traveling *east* over Eisenhower's interstates," former Prankster Robert Stone observed. Well-muscled and shirtless behind the wheel, Cassady wore a straw cowboy hat while driving like an utter maniac all the way to New York and back. "He never ate, never slept, and never shut up. He also thought it a merry prank to slip several hundred micrograms of LSD into anything anyone happened to be ingesting. No one dared eat or drink without secure refuge from Neal," Stone recalled in his memoir, *Prime Green.*

Nineteen Sixty-four was an election year—conservative GOP spear-carrier Barry Goldwater versus Democrat Lyndon Johnson, the sitting president. To baffle the clueless as they careened through the heartland, Kesey and Cassady painted a sign on the side of the bus—"A Vote for Goldwater is a Vote for Fun." An ardent anti-Communist and staunch militarist, Goldwater famously declared: "Extremism in defense of liberty is no vice." Ironically, that could have been the Merry Pranksters' motto, as well. The Pranksters were an example of the kinds of characters that a society invents every so often to correct its own imbalance. These holy fools sought to subvert "an entire nation's burning material madness," as Kesey put it. They were like a dose of LSD coursing through the veins of the American body politic.

When they got to the Big Apple, Cassady fetched Kerouac and brought him to meet Kesey and crew. But Kerouac was withdrawn and taciturn during an anticlimactic encounter with Neal's new pals. Unlike Cassady and Ginsberg, Kerouac sat out the Sixties and watched from the sidelines while his prophetic vision of a "great rucksack revolution" unfolded—"thousands or even millions of young Americans wandering around," as he wrote in *The Dharma Bums,* a horde of "Zen Lunatics" hitchhiking cross-country, "refusing to subscribe to the general demand that [they] work, produce, consume, work, produce, consume . . ."

Next, the Pranksters swung by Millbrook, the sprawling, 2,400-acre psychedelic commune two hours north of New York City where Timothy Leary, the ex-Harvard professor, had taken up residence. But that impromptu meeting didn't go well either. Hankering for the big revelation—that elusive, penultimate zap of White Light—never topped the to-do list of the Pranksters, who were on a different trip than the spiritual strivers at Millbrook. Kesey's posse split after a brief visit and headed back to California.

With outdoor speakers in the redwoods blaring songs by Dylan and the Beatles, Kesey's rural home in La Honda, fifty miles south of San Francisco, became a magnet for an ever-changing cast of beatniks, bikers, college kids, marijuana smokers, and acid eaters, witting and unwitting. They all partied like there was no tomorrow. Gonzo scribe Hunter S. Thompson, a buddy of Kesey's, called the scene at La Honda "the world capital of madness. There were no rules, fear was unknown and sleep was out of the question."

Kesey got busted for pot in April 1965, but instead of lying low he and the Pranksters staged a series of public psychedelic initiations up and down the West Coast. The notorious Electric Kool-Aid Acid Tests (as chronicled in Tom Wolfe's famous book) turned on hundreds of people at a time. Kesey's idea was to host a big Dionysian bash where everyone took LSD and experienced a collective cosmic breakthrough not by meditating on mandalas but by courting the unexpected via all-out sensory overload. The acid tests were weird carnivals with flashing strobes, light shows, free-form dancing, and live, improvised rock 'n' roll by the Grateful Dead, the Prankster house band. If the cops crashed an acid test, they wouldn't know where to begin.

LSD was still legal in 1965 when Augustus Owsley Stanley III, a fixture at the acid rituals and the Dead's patron, began manufacturing millions of tabs for intrepid trippers. The Beatles sampled some of Owsley's finest and were thrust into a world of "tangerine trees and marmalade skies." As the Beatles quickly discovered, LSD was way stronger than smoked cannabis, which doesn't threaten to overwhelm the cognitive mechanism as psychedelic drugs sometimes do. Grass and acid both slow down the passage of time and intensify the present moment. But LSD triggers a departure from normal waking consciousness so preternaturally vivid that a few puffs of pot seem tame by comparison. Dropping acid could engender a bizarre, discomfiting sense of depersonalization to the point where some astronauts of inner space had a hard time reentering the earth's atmosphere.

While Owsley was mixing up the medicine in the mid-1960s, Dr. Harris Isbell, a perennial CIA contract employee, conducted a scientific study to compare the effects of LSD and synthetic THC. After giving both drugs to inmates at the federal narcotics hospital in Lexington, Kentucky, Dr. Isbell concluded that a very high dose of THC could trigger hallucinations similar to lysergic acid. Both drugs were said to produce a state of mind similar to schizophrenia. LSD madness (*Life* magazine called acid "a one-way ticket to an asylum") would occupy the same place in the American imagination in the late 1960s that reefer madness held three decades earlier. Just as marijuana had been demonized, LSD, a once-promising therapeutic adjunct, became the target of scare stories about acidheads cooking their babies in ovens and going blind by staring at the sun. Public officials promoted baseless allegations that LSD causes genetic damage and birth defects. Identical bogus charges would be leveled at marijuana.

Although LSD never achieved the social popularity of marijuana, the two substances were closely linked during the rebel Sixties. Grass and acid were like a one-two punch that wobbled the American psyche. Ever the contrarian, Ken Kesey had his own, unique perspective on pot. He maintained that cannabis was essentially a Christian herb by virtue of its propensity to engender feelings of well-being and benevolence. Marijuana, according to Kesey, makes a person more thoughtful and more tolerant toward others in keeping with Christ's compassionate teachings. "[T]o be peaceful without being stupid, to be interested without being compulsive, to be happy without being hysterical . . . smoke grass," Kesey counseled.

Marijuana was always around Kesey's scene. "We smoked a lot of pot," said Prankster mainstay Carolyn ("Mountain Girl") Garcia. But she and her comrades usually refrained from reefers during an acid test. "LSD and marijuana don't mix," Mountain Girl explained. "If you're high on 250 mics, you can smoke pot all night and you won't notice any effects from it. It's a waste.

Plus you'd be making yourself stick out at a time when grass was illegal and acid was not." But a few puffs of primo weed sure could come in handy "if you are rushing too hard from acid," according to MG. "It's good for that. It can bring you back a little bit. Some people used it that way. Coming down from acid is a good time for pot."

Kesey and the Pranksters were trendsetters. Their outrageous antics sparked California's counterculture. They provided the template for much of what transpired during the heyday of the psychedelic era when legions of long-haired youth lay prostrate before the gates of awe. The party that started in La Honda followed the Pranksters "out the door and into the street and filled the world with funny colors," said Stone. The mind-altering ripple effects from grass and acid were felt in music, cinema, fashion, literature, and the visual arts, as well as in the fledgling home-computer industry pioneered by turned-on whiz kids in Palo Alto, not coincidentally the birthplace of Pranksterdom. These taboo substances decisively influenced how popular dissent was expressed during a very turbulent decade. A large-scale, multifarious, grassroots movement for social change was, in Kesey's words, "salted with revelation."

Life seemed to be one grand eruption of youthful enthusiasm in the mid-1960s. It was a period of high-flying optimism, a moment saturated with possibility when cultural and political radicals, each in their own way, endeavored to "break on through to the other side." Nearly everything was being challenged and most things tried in an orgy of experiment that shook the nation at its core.

The notion that all types of personal and social experimentation were somehow wisdom-instilling and therefore positive became both the creed and the pitfall of the cultural insurgency that was cranking up in the Haight-Ashbury district of San Francisco. Unbeknownst to the rest of America, a frothy broth, seasoned with cannabis and LSD, was brewing in the Haight, a diverse community of working-class whites, poorer blacks, San Francisco State University students, and beatnik refugees from North Beach.

Each weekend Bay Area youth got high on grass and acid and danced with reckless abandon at concert halls such as the Fillmore and the Avalon Ballroom while liquid blobs of light pulsated across the walls and local bands played inventive, mind-melting music known as "acid rock." Jefferson Airplane sang "Feed your head," Quicksilver Messenger Service implored "Take another hit," Country Joe and the Fish crooned "Don't bogart that joint, my friend," and a boozy chick singer named Janis Joplin left it all onstage with Big Brother and the Holding Company. And, of course, there was the Grateful Dead, the premier psychedelic band. These first-rate Bay Area acts attracted international attention.

As news media began to notice what was happening in Haight-Ashbury, the City by the Bay became a magnet for lost souls and utopia seekers who didn't fit in anywhere else. They gravitated to San Francisco, where they could be "out of step together," as the Jefferson Airplane's drummer, Spencer Dryden, put it. Or perhaps they were a step ahead together as they groped for a way of life that didn't damage the planet. "Why San Francisco?" asked Herb Caen. "Because this is where the winds of freedom blow. And because there has been an atmosphere of abandon here since the Gold Rush days. And because this city has always taken the oddball and the alien to its heart . . ." Caen called the latest wave of oddballs "hippies," and before long the Haight was clotted with barefoot, bedraggled youngsters begging for spare change.

But the love generation hit a few speed bumps on the highway to Nirvana. California outlawed LSD in 1966 and the rest of the country soon fell in line. And marijuana remained unequivocally illegal—which was useful for peevish authorities. The cops couldn't bust people because they had long hair and dressed funny. It supposedly wasn't a crime to think differently in the United States, but possessing an illicit substance was grounds for immediate arrest. Official disapproval of marijuana had less to do with what the weed actually did than with what it seemed to represent: disrespect, bad manners, licentious sex, a lack of patriotism, laziness, permissiveness in general.

As the use of marijuana increased so did the number of individuals who were hassled and arrested for smoking the herb. To dramatize this growing problem, the San Francisco Mime Troupe performed *Search and Seizure*, a skit written and directed by Peter Berg, a Haight-Ashbury community activist. Berg cast his friend Emmett Grogan in the lead role as a belligerent law-enforcement officer. His acting was so fierce and persuasive that when Grogan and another "cop" burst into the Matrix, a popular San Francisco nightclub, and started roughing people up, the audience thought they were real policemen busting folks for drugs. *"Calm down everybody, this will only take a little while,"* Grogan bellowed as he grabbed someone in the audience, dragged him onstage, and started asking: *"Where did you get the drugs?" "Who did you take them with?" "Do you know what kind of danger you are to children?"*

The line between spectator and spectacle was deliberately blurred during this riveting episode of "guerrilla theater," a phrase coined by Berg, who explained: "I was after an emotion that would build a culture of resistance." He and Grogan split from the Mime Troupe in 1965 to form the Diggers, a group of artists, anarchists, and street toughs who staged food giveaways and imaginative street theater that catered to the needs of a community increasingly under siege.

Drug busts were occurring all the time. Ken Kesey and Mountain Girl were nailed one night while sharing a joint on a San Francisco rooftop. It was Kesey's second marijuana arrest (the first case was still pending) and the legal implications were grim. Kesey ran off to Mexico, a traditional place of refuge for gringo stoners and cultural expatriates. He hid there for several months with some Prankster friends, including Mountain Girl, who gave birth to Kesey's daughter while they were on the run. They drifted apart after Kesey snuck back into California, where the FBI caught up with him; he did six months on a work farm.

By this time, Mountain Girl had left the Pranksters and moved in with her future husband, Jerry Garcia, and the other members of the Grateful Dead. They all lived together in a thirteen-room communal house on Ashbury Street until the cops stormed the premises and busted eleven people for marijuana. A spokesperson for the Dead pulled no punches after the raid: "The arrests were made under a law that classifies marijuana along with murder, rape and armed robbery as a felony. Yet almost everyone who has ever studied marijuana seriously and objectively has agreed that marijuana is the least harmful chemical used for pleasure and life-enhancement. The law encourages an even greater evil. It encourages the most outrageously discriminatory type of law enforcement."

A Tipping Point

Pot and political protest went hand in hand in the cacophonous Sixties. Much of the turmoil took place on college campuses. The Free Speech Movement (FSM) at the University of California in Berkeley staged the first student takeover of an administration building in the fall of 1964, after police arrested a young civil rights activist for distributing political literature on school grounds. FSM leaders gave impassioned speeches critical of impersonal university policies geared toward turning students into fodder for corporate America. Roused by calls for social justice and for greater student say in higher education, several hundred demonstrators occupied four floors of Sproul Hall and demanded that their First Amendment rights be respected.

The Free Speech Movement energized students throughout the country by emphasizing that personal alienation and private problems were relevant political issues. They believed that, as young citizens, they could collectively transform their lives. Student activism became the core of an insurgent New Left, which was unusual in many respects. For the first time in U.S. history, the force at the cutting edge of radical change was distinguished principally by age rather than by race or class.

The so-called Baby Boom generation was a unique demographic phenomenon—by 1965 half of America was under thirty. It was a decade of unparalleled economic prosperity and middle-class affluence; the U.S. Gross National Product doubled during the 1960s. But student dissidents rejected the notion that an expanding GNP was necessarily the best measure of human happiness. Some felt encumbered by "the chains of privilege." The scarcity they rebelled against was not a material scarcity but a lack of meaning, an inner emptiness, the prospect of a comfortable life that was dull and unfulfilling. In keeping with the popular slogan of the day, "Don't trust anyone over thirty," these young radicals were wary of any set, hand-me-down ideologies that genuflected to either the industrial proletariat or the "free market." At the portals of the New Left, one had to curb one's dogma.

The phenomenal growth of the New Left in the mid-1960s coincided with marijuana's emergence as the collegiate drug of choice. Cannabis was no longer just a weed smoked by Mexicans and African Americans. An illicit substance previously confined to the lower socioeconomic strata in the United States, marijuana made a quantum leap and suddenly found favor among white middle-class youth. This curious development was noted in articles with headlines such as "Dope Invades the Suburbs" and "The College Drug Scene." What the magazines called "drug abuse" was almost entirely a matter of young people smoking grass.

As the times changed, so did the arguments against marijuana—the "killer weed" of yore morphed into the '60s "drop-out drug," which allegedly blunted ambition and stifled motivation, thereby causing users to detach from society. No single factor could account for why marijuana proved so attractive to large numbers of people on a continuing basis around this time. In some unexplained way, cannabis met the needs of young Americans as they grappled with "growing up absurd" in a catch-22 world.

A tipping point for cannabis in the United States occurred in 1964. That was when white America discovered pot and *marijuana* became a household word. It was also the year when the U.S. surgeon general released a widely publicized report on the health hazards of cigarette smoking. For the first time, it became common knowledge that cigarettes caused cancer and other serious diseases, killing hundreds of thousands of Americans annually.* Yet the U.S. govern-

* Doctors had first linked cigarettes to lung cancer in 1946, but the American Medical Association downplayed the danger for many years while railing against what the AMA referred to as "socialized medicine." According to ancient Native American lore, the gods craved tobacco. To please the gods, one offered them tobacco during shamanic rites. In effect, the

ment continued to subsidize tobacco growers. The hypocrisy of singling out marijuana for criminalization, while sanctioning tobacco, a deadly, addictive poison, was glaringly obvious to anyone with a half-open mind.

Miltown, Librium, Valium, and other highly addictive hypnotics and tranquilizers—known as "dolls" in mid-Sixties happy-speak—were also readily accessible along with a cavalcade of uppers and diet pills. Physicians routinely prescribed millions of uppers and downers to help Mom and Dad get through the day and fall asleep at night, and these drugs were often misused. Overconsumption of alcoholic beverages was even more commonplace. President Lyndon Johnson's Advisory Commission on Narcotics and Drug Abuse noted that "the rarest or most abnormal form of behavior is not to take any mind-altering drugs at all. Most adult Americans are users of drugs, many are frequent users of a wide variety of them." This being the case, it seemed arbitrary and capricious for the government to sanction drugs that were demonstrably harmful while banning marijuana.

Marijuana's status as a forbidden substance added to its allure. Smoking herb entailed an elaborate ritual—copping the weed, removing the seeds and stems (an antiquated folk art in the sinsemilla era), rolling a joint or packing a pipe, and sharing it with others behind drawn shades while incense burned to mask the smell. "When a young person took his first puff of psychoactive smoke, he also drew in the psychoactive culture as a whole, the entire matrix of law and association surrounding the drug, its induction and transaction. One inhaled a certain way of dressing, talking, acting, certain attitudes. One became a youth criminal against the State," said Michael Rossman, a leader of the Berkeley Free Speech Movement.

There's an old joke among stoners that if pot were legal, it would stop working. Imbued with the intrigue of sneaking behind enemy lines, marijuana's popularity was inextricable from the outlaw ethos surrounding its use. While antimarijuana legislation did not act as a deterrent, it did cause young people to be more cynical about the establishment. The U.S. government lost credibility among teenagers and twentysomethings who tried cannabis and found that, contrary to shrill warnings, it didn't wreck their lives. Although the ef-

---

gods were dependent on the generosity and goodwill of human beings, who could withhold tobacco if the gods became peevish with harvests, food supplies, and other essentials. Tobacco leveled the playing field by empowering native people to bargain directly with the divine spirits. But the rules of the game were broken when white folk took tobacco from the Indians and consumed it without offering any to the gods, who retaliated with a vengeance. Thus came to pass the scourge of addiction, lung cancer, emphysema, and a plethora of nicotine-related diseases.

fects of marijuana wore off in a couple of hours, the attitudes changed by the herb would persist. Skepticism regarding marijuana policy encouraged doubts about officialdom in general. By eroding confidence in the powers-that-be, cannabis functioned as an antiestablishment catalyst, just as Ginsberg had anticipated that it would. Cannabis was like compost starter for cognitive dissidence that spread across the social landscape.

In 1965, President Johnson dramatically escalated American military involvement in Vietnam, increasing U.S. troop strength from 23,000 to 184,000. Opposition to the war became the preeminent New Left issue. Students burned draft cards, picketed ROTC classes, and rallied against university ties to military contractors. As it gained momentum on and off campus, antiwar protest became more imaginative and more combative. Cannabis was intimately associated with the grassroots movement that led Americans to question, reevaluate, and oppose their nation's bully-boy foreign policy. "You couldn't separate laws against drugs from the war," said Paul Krassner, editor of *The Realist,* who declared at a peace demonstration that he "wouldn't *stop* smoking pot until it was legal."

For many young people, getting high on grass was an affirmation of generational solidarity, a badge of identity. It was also an act of defiance, a way of saying "No!" to authority. Not everyone who smoked grass became politically engaged, but there was considerable overlap among cultural and political rebels—the "heads" and the "fists," as author and journalist Laurence Leamer called them. A broad (and at times uneasy) alliance formed between the two camps. This convergence was reflected in the *L.A. Free Press, Berkeley Barb,* and other underground newspapers that sprang up everywhere in the mid and late '60s. The underground press covered a wide range of subjects—everything from magic mushrooms to Mao Tse-tung—and blended a spectrum of radical viewpoints. Replete with stoned humor, "comix," such as R. Crumb's *Mr. Natural* and Gilbert Shelton's *Fabulous Furry Freak Brothers,* were featured in several hundred underground media outlets. Even high school kids published underground newspapers that called for the legalization of marijuana.

But cannabis and LSD also comprised an axis of division among rebellious youth who debated the political implications of recreational drugs. Some felt the key to social change lay, first and foremost, in personal transformation. Free your mind—with pot, LSD, whatever—and the rest will somehow follow. Others were less sanguine about the notion of "better living through chemistry," as the famous '60s poster (and DuPont ad) proclaimed. They worried that marijuana and psychedelics would divert energy from the political struggle against rapacious capitalism and U.S. imperialism. And the capitalist system, in their view, had extremely toxic side effects—or main effects—that no drug alone could cure.

Allen Ginsberg felt that both arguments had merit. He was not averse to holding contradictory ideas at the same time, embracing each of them emotionally without reconciling them logically. Ginsberg's willingness to abide ambiguity was an asset during the Sixties as he sought to bring various strands of cultural and political rebellion into the most intimate possible interplay. He considered the cross-hatch of New Left activism and bohemian outrage to be both workable and exciting. Ginsberg straddled both worlds. A key link between Beats and hippies, he was, in the words of Ted Morgan, "the bridge . . . the culture carrier and transmitter, the electrician who connected the wires."

Even though he was over thirty, Ginsberg became a trusted spokesman for the younger generation. He had a major impact not only on the fledgling counterculture, but also on student radicals and New Left activists during the 1960s. In a direct carryover from the Beats, Sixties rebels broadened the very definition of politics to include problems of everyday existence, loneliness, interpersonal relationships, and various lifestyle choices, such as smoking pot. They pursued a dual-pronged radical project that involved individual as well as social transformation. They were intent on changing their own lives while also trying to change the world. The legalization of marijuana was one of the causes embraced by Sixties activists, and Ginsberg would be their mentor.

Legalize It!

On August 16, 1964, a young Haight-Ashbury resident named Lowell Eggemeier strutted into a San Francisco police station, calmly lit a reefer, took a big toke, and exhaled slowly. "Arrest me," he challenged the cops, who promptly did just that.

Eggemeier's in-your-face gesture marked the beginning of the marijuana legalization movement in the United States. By boldly puffing where no man had puffed before, he made explicit what was already implicit to millions of Americans: Smoking marijuana was unavoidably a political act, an act of nonviolent civil disobedience. ("If a law is unjust, it's your responsibility to break it," said Gandhi.) The decision to smoke cannabis was not just a departure from cultural convention; it was a decision to violate the law.

In a marriage of political opposites that prefigured an ongoing trend within the pro-pot movement, Eggemeier retained as his attorney James R. White III, an ultraconservative civil libertarian who described himself as "to the right of

Goldwater." For White as well as for Eggemeier, smoking pot was above all a personal-freedom issue. They strongly believed that what a person chose to imbibe for recreational or medical purposes was nobody else's business but their own—not the government's, and certainly not the cops'.

White's legal briefs for Eggemeier, who insisted on going to trial, included reprints of excerpts from the Indian Hemp Commission study and the La Guardia Report. As part of his defense strategy, White formed a group called LEMAR (*Le*galize *Mar*ijuana). It was the first U.S. organization devoted to overturning legislation that banned cannabis. LEMAR sponsored several public demonstrations on behalf of marijuana law reform. Eggemeier was eventually convicted of possession, served a short sentence, and then vanished, leaving others to build a nationwide grassroots movement that his lone act of civil disobedience foretold and inspired.

Allen Ginsberg happened to be in the Bay Area in December 1964 when LEMAR held its initial protest against marijuana prohibition. The peripatetic poet was sufficiently impressed to think that this just might be the right moment to walk the talk and raise the cannabis issue to another level. When Ginsberg returned to New York City, he huddled with Ed Sanders, a shaggy-haired, Zapata-mustached classics scholar, age twenty-five, with a flair for humor and energetic agit-prop. They proceeded to set up a LEMAR chapter in the Big Apple "to get people who use marijuana to stand up and agitate for its legalization," as Sanders explained.

A former Boy Scout from Missouri, Sanders had read *Howl* when he was a teenager, and, as he put it, "My life changed overnight." He migrated to New York's East Village in the early 1960s and fell in with a loose-knit cadre of literary bohemians who sought to translate the Beat critique into political activism. After Sanders served a sixty-day prison term for challenging nuclear proliferation, he befriended Ginsberg and the two poets became lifelong collaborators.

On a cold day in January 1965, Ginsberg and Sanders led a pro-marijuana march outside the New York Women's House of Detention on Sixth Avenue, where several left-wing war resisters were imprisoned for civil disobedience. LEMAR supporters chanted slogans and waved placards, resulting in one of the quintessential images of the Sixties: a photograph of Ginsberg, snowflakes on his beard and head, holding a sign that said, POT IS FUN. Published around the world, it made quite a splash. Another picket sign read: POT IS A REALITY KICK.

Afterward, the Lemarians shambled across lower Manhattan and gathered at the Peace Eye Bookstore, which Sanders had recently opened on Tenth Street in the East Village, a block away from Ginsberg's apartment. The Peace Eye had converted a butcher's shop into an incubator for alternative ideas and a

Allen Ginsberg protesting in front of the New York Women's House of Detention, January 10, 1965 (Courtesy of Benedict J. Fernandez)

"scrounge lounge," as Sanders described his storefront, which still had "Strictly Kosher" on its window. Peace Eye offered an eclectic variety of books and journals, including *Fuck You / A Magazine of the Arts*, edited and produced by Sanders, which featured poetry and prose by Ginsberg, Burroughs, and other writers. Every mimeographed issue of *Fuck You* was a no-holds-barred attack on the state of the planet. In keeping with Sanders's avowed mission to wage a "total assault" on mainstream American culture, a mimeograph machine in the back room of Peace Eye churned out pro-cannabis leaflets and assorted missives—including two issues of the *Marijuana Newsletter*—in an effort to "liberate pot from the grouches of the überculture," as Sanders put it.

Before long, the NYPD raided Peace Eye, seizing books and pro-pot literature, and sending Sanders back to jail—this time on obscenity charges. Ginsberg did a benefit poetry reading to help pay legal fees, and Sanders eventually beat the rap in court. It was all grist for the mirth-mill of the Fugs, an underground folk-rock band founded by Sanders and Tuli Kupferberg. In addition to composing poems, cartoon illustrations, and a how-to booklet, *1001 Ways to Live Without Working*, Kupferberg published *Birth*, a small-press periodical that devoted an entire issue to marijuana and other psychoactive drugs. Notorious for their irreverent and bawdy lyrics, the Fugs (the name was a euphemism for the sex act) cut several record albums and performed songs such as "Kill for Peace," "Group Grope," and "CIA Man" during cross-country concert tours that rankled Hoover's smut-obsessed FBI, which vicariously monitored the Fugs' activities.

Despite frequent run-ins with police, the Fugs earned enough money to finance *The Marijuana Review*, LEMAR's hip-zine for heads, which included detailed reports on the price of pot, what was available on the street, legal and scientific developments, activist campaigns, and other examples of reefer rabble-rousing. *The Marijuana Review* was largely the bailiwick of Michael Aldrich, a soft-spoken, studious young man, who had discovered cannabis as an undergraduate at Princeton after seeing the word *marijuana* in print for the first time in Ginsberg's *Howl*. A South Dakota native, Aldrich smoked hashish in India while on a Fulbright scholarship, and then completed his graduate studies at the State University of New York in Buffalo, where he organized a LEMAR chapter and wrote his doctoral thesis on "Cannabis Myths and Folklore." Aldrich briefly worked as Ginsberg's secretary. Nicknamed "Dr. Dope," the genial hemp historian with the PhD would continue to play a notable role in the legalization movement for many years.

Small LEMAR affinity groups sprang up in several cities in the mid-1960s, including Boston, Chicago, Los Angeles, Berkeley, and Toronto. The poet-activists d. a. levy in Cleveland and John Sinclair in Detroit both ran afoul of the law after forming LEMAR chapters in their respective locales. The Cleveland Narcotics Squad raided levy's Asphodel Book Store and carted off nine crates of printed matter, including levy's self-published *Marrahwanna Quarterly*. "I am part of a movement trying to make this planet more civilized," he told local reporters after his arrest. Out of disdain for the municipal authorities, levy wrote a gonzo novel called *youcanhaveyourfuckingcityback*. Indicted on obscenity charges and continually harassed by the police, he committed suicide in 1968.

When he wasn't traveling, Ginsberg spent lots of time with Sanders at Peace Eye, crafting LEMAR position papers and strategizing about how to respond to the latest wave of heavy-handed government censorship. The authorities' ace-in-the-hole was the cabaret license system, whereby musicians and spoken-word artists needed a city-certified card to perform in public. Talented artists lost their ability to earn a livelihood when their cabaret cards were canceled because they got busted for weed or for any other transgression that resulted in a police record. New York City censors revoked the cabaret cards of

Charlie Parker and Thelonious Monk for several years in the 1950s, although neither was ever convicted of a narcotics charge. Even poets were required to register with the police in order to read—for free, no less—at coffeehouses and art galleries.

Led by poets and musicians, a grassroots citizens' movement to rescind the cabaret card requirement would succeed after several years of struggle. This, however, was small consolation to Lenny Bruce, the social critic/comic who ruffled prudes and rankled squares with razor-sharp riffs on topics ranging from the narcotics heat to America's congenital racism and the bishops of Religion Incorporated. His use of profanity undermined long-standing barriers against free expression and challenged people to ask themselves what was truly obscene—four-letter words or the depravities of modern warfare? But Bruce paid the price. The king of existential absurdity was arrested numerous times on drug and obscenity charges. In 1964, he was sentenced to four months in prison. His routines from this period were peppered with frequent references to oral sex, sodomy, suppositories, syringes, Zig-zag rolling papers, and *schtupping*, Yiddish for "fucking," a word he wasn't supposed to utter in English onstage. He did anyway. Occasionally during his performances, Bruce circulated a satiric pamphlet about pot smoking entitled "Stamp Out Help." In 1966, Bruce, age forty, overdosed on a lethal combination of cops and heroin. Before he shed his mortal coil, dozens of artists, including Allen Ginsberg and Bob Dylan, came to his defense.

For Ginsberg, the struggle against censorship and the fight against pot prohibition were inseparable. After visiting Professor Alfred Lindesmith, an early drug-policy critic, in Bloomington, Indiana, and studying his extensive files on the history of U.S. narcotics legislation, Ginsberg penned a prose essay on the merits of marijuana. Called "First Manifesto to End the Bringdown," it appeared in the *Atlantic Monthly* in November 1966. The Federal Narcotics Bureau, according to Ginsberg, had perpetrated an "insane hoax on public consciousness." He drew attention to the racist origins of America's drug laws and explicitly linked the "suppression of Negro rights" to marijuana prohibition. Ginsberg proposed the formation of an impartial national commission to study the marijuana issue and make recommendations regarding the herb's legal status.

Ginsberg also wrote about his own hassles with the narcotics police. Thanks to J. Edgar Hoover, Allen's name appeared on the government's list of suspicious persons. A spurious reference in Ginsberg's FBI file to his "reported engagement in drug smuggling" was a convenient pretext for keeping tabs on him. On several occasions he was strip-searched by vice squad or customs officers looking for dope. They never found anything. Ginsberg was always squeaky clean when he traveled, and he warned visitors not to bring illicit drugs into his apartment. He had good reason to be cautious.

In 1965, Ginsberg learned of a scheme by the Federal Bureau of Narcotics to set him up on a pot bust. A jazz musician named Jack Martin was arrested for marijuana possession, and four narcotics agents met with him privately and threatened to raise his bail from five grand to one hundred grand unless he helped them get Ginsberg. Martin refused to cooperate and blew the whistle on the feds. Sanders banged out a news release and LEMAR denounced the plot to entrap Ginsberg at a press conference that named names. The Fugs played at a hastily organized rally protesting "the rudeness, brusqueness, crudeness & violence" of the FBN, which maintained a dossier on Ginsberg that included a photograph of the famous poet "in an indecent pose." The picture was marked "for future use" and kept in a vault at FBN headquarters. "I feel like the noose of the police state is closing in on me," Ginsberg told *The New York Times* after he got wind of several other attempts to frame him for drugs.

There was plenty of marijuana circulating in the Village and other New York City neighborhoods in the mid-Sixties. But smoking it was very hush-hush. "It wasn't being done openly. It was done with a lot of fear—*great gobs of fear*, in fact, always looking over your shoulder," Sanders told journalist Martin Torgoff.

The pervasive paranoia surrounding the use of illegal substances was evoked by Bob Dylan in "Subterranean Homesick Blues," the opening song on his 1965 album *Bringing It All Back Home*. Composed while he chain-smoked reefers, this high-energy rant portrayed the pitfalls of pot puffing in Anytown, USA, where the narc in "the trench coat" has a "bad cough" and wants to be "paid off." It was Dylan's most pointed statement about the outlaw aspect of the mid-Sixties drug scene. In a video that accompanied the release of "Subterranean Homesick Blues," Allen Ginsberg was seen loitering in an alley while Dylan sang like someone who couldn't fall asleep at night.

By this time, Dylan had angered folk music purists by strapping on an electric guitar and belting out incredible tunes that reinvented rock 'n' roll as a medium of social criticism and much more. His next album, *Highway 61 Revisited*, featured the international chart-buster "Like a Rolling Stone." Freighted with spiritual turmoil, it was a paean to a generation in motion yearning for freedom and adventure, a transcendent hymn for restless youth who'd been twisted out of shape by society's pliers. Dylan's chemically fueled burst of creativity in the mid-1960s marked a shift from straightforward topical protest songs to strange, elusive compositions that implied soul searching, rejuvenation, and open-ended change. During this period, he smoked lots of grass, dropped acid, and tried just about everything else to "open his head," according to his biographer Tony Scaduto.

Dylan the trickster got his band high on grass and booze—and all the musicians supposedly switched instruments at his request—before they recorded "Rainy Day Women #12 and 35," his boisterous, rollicking song about pot and public opprobrium. "I would not feel so all a-*lone*," Dylan moaned, as if prescribing a subversive, do-it-yourself remedy for adolescent alienation: "Everybody must *git* stoned!" Released in 1966, it was a shot across the bow in America's escalating culture war, a bull's-eye blast that defined an era. It became the biggest hit of Dylan's recording career, even though many radio stations in the USA and Britain refused to play the song because of its reefer-rowdy refrain. The message spread far and wide on the wings of Dylan's double entendre—getting stoned could mean the psychoactive buzz or the biblical punishment. Tens of millions of fans took his injunction to heart. And many would be punished for their transgression.

Flower Power

The music was key. Urgent, rebellious, and emphatically pro-pot, rock 'n' roll dominated the airwaves, providing an audacious soundtrack for a decade of cultural tumult and generational self-assertion. "The political and societal juggernaut of the 1960s rolled on wheels of music," said novelist Tom Robbins. Revered by impressionable youth, rock musicians were cultural arbiters as well as ardent marijuana smokers. They played a crucial role in the proliferation of recreational reefer during this period. Just as the jazz vipers of an earlier era had portrayed reefer as a kick not to miss, rock stars promoted a similar message to a huge audience. Numerous rock songs contained subtle and not-so-subtle allusions to cannabis.

"Got to Get You into My Life," one of several druggy tunes on the Beatles' *Revolver* album, was "entirely about pot," according to Paul McCartney, who acknowledged that marijuana had a huge impact on the Fab Four in the mid-Sixties. After the Beatles got into grass, they began to think of themselves as artists, not just performers. The herb triggered a creative surge that altered their approach to writing and recording songs. ("We were smoking marijuana for breakfast," Lennon jibed.) Cannabis opened the door to new dimensions of popular music, and the Beatles carried the youth of the world with them across the psychoactive threshold.

During the mid-1960s, London's burgeoning "spontaneous underground" embraced marijuana and LSD along with a bevy of British rock 'n' roll bands (the Animals, Moody Blues, Pink Floyd . . .) that were into both drugs. If this countercultural movement had an unofficial headquarters, it was the Indica Bookshop and Gallery, named after the kind bud, *Cannabis indica*. Paul McCartney was involved in planning the bookshop-gallery venture, and when the right venue was found he helped remodel the interior, drilling, sawing, hammering away, plastering the walls and installing bookshelves. McCartney was Indica's first customer the day it opened; he purchased several paperbacks, including *Peace Eye* poems by Ed Sanders (Peace Eye and Indica were sister stores) and Robert DeRopp's *Drugs and the Mind*, a subject of keen interest to the Beatles. Every so often, McCartney and Lennon would drop by to browse books and attend Indica gallery openings. This was where Lennon met Yoko Ono, an edgy Japanese artist whose work was featured at Indica.

International Times (IT), an underground newspaper that operated out of Indica's basement, swapped stories with a worldwide network of comrade publications that advocated for ending the war in Vietnam and legalizing marijuana—two overarching concerns of Sixties rebels. Once again, McCartney pitched in, laying out ads for the paper and providing emergency funds to keep the operation viable. "Changing the lifestyle and appearance of youth throughout the world didn't just happen—we set out to do it," Lennon asserted a few years later. "We knew what we were doing."

The British authorities also knew what they were doing when a dozen plainclothes police officers raided Indica in the winter of '67, allegedly looking for dirty books while ignoring the hard-core porn shops just a stone's throw away in Soho. The cops seized copies of *IT*, deemed it obscene, and temporarily shut down the newspaper in a brazen attempt to criminalize and throttle dissent. Like their American counterparts, the Brits were using legal excuses to wage a moral battle. *IT* fought back with wit and verve, at times straining to accommodate disparate factions within "the Movement," which was never really a single, unified phenomenon.

When he visited London, Ginsberg stayed with Indica and *IT*'s cofounder Barry Miles, who introduced him to the Beatles. They all became fast friends. The world's most famous poet was seemingly everywhere in the 1960s—Moscow, Tokyo, Havana, Rome, Tel Aviv, Bombay, Vancouver, Prague. Like a molecule at full boil, Ginsberg zipped around the globe, reading poetry and touting the benefits of marijuana and LSD at every opportunity, even though his own drug intake was relatively modest during this period.

Ginsberg chanted "Om" onstage at the first Human Be-in in San Francisco's Golden Gate Park in January 1967. Twenty thousand day-trippers, beaming stoned-out optimism, attended this fabled assemblage, which featured an all-star lineup of poets, rock bands, and counterculture celebrities. It was Ginsberg, now with long, thinning locks and a full rabbinical beard, who coined the expression "flower power" to describe the drug-fueled cultural effervescence bubbling in the Haight.

What transpired on that unseasonably warm winter afternoon passed instantly into the hagiography of the marijuana subculture. Although the name smacked of "sit-in" and "teach-in" (two successful modes of New Left activism), the Be-in was not convened to protest anything in particular. It was more like a huge pot party than a political demonstration. Countless joints were smoked openly. The police wisely chose not to intervene as Be-in revelers engaged in an impromptu public nose-thumbing at cannabis prohibition.

Billed as "A Gathering of the Tribes," the Be-in generated extensive news coverage, nationally as well as internationally, and set in motion a chain of overhyped events that led inexorably to the much-ballyhooed "Summer of Love." Prior to the Be-in, Haight-Ashbury had been an improvised work in progress, an evolving community of the creatively alienated. Then, all of a sudden, the psychedelic city-state was floodlit by mass media and transformed into a prurient freak show with gawkers outnumbering potheads. The once vibrant neighborhood would soon be overrun by junkies, speed freaks, pimps, runaways, and cops. By summer's end, Haight Street looked a lot like Desolation Row.

Meanwhile, ripples from the Haight had spread across America and beyond, inspiring a spate of mini be-ins and love-ins all over the world. New York City cannabis activists organized four successive weekend smoke-ins in the leafy refuge of Tompkins Square Park, a favorite hangout of East Village hippies. At the initial smoke-in in June 1967, Dana Beal tossed handfuls of joints into a thankful crowd, which sent everyone scrambling. The same ritual was enacted a few weeks later when the Grateful Dead performed a free concert at another Tompkins Square smoke-in. (It was the Dead's first visit to the Big Apple.) By throwing down the gauntlet in such a fashion, Beal and his gang of pot provocateurs sought to force the police to choose between busting hundreds of people or letting them smoke in public. The cops caved.

The Tompkins Square puff-ins coincided with a series of pot protests in London, where several high-profile rock musicians had recently been arrested on drug charges. Detective Sergeant Norman Pilcher, from London's Metropolitan Police Drug Squad, made it his mission to bust as many pop stars as possible. First he nailed Donovan (who was fined £250 for marijuana possession), then Keith Richards and Mick Jagger of the Rolling Stones. The Stones had made drug motifs a central part of their music—only to face the music themselves when narcs crashed a party at Richards's house. "I don't have a drug problem," Richards famously sniffed. "I have a police problem." (His conviction for allowing the use of marijuana on his premises was reversed on appeal, and Jagger's three-month prison sentence for possessing four amphetamine tablets that he had bought legally in Italy was reduced to a conditional discharge.) Two members of the Beatles, John Lennon and George Harrison, were also arrested by Pilcher, who later got a taste of his own medicine when he was sentenced to four years imprisonment for perjury and evidence tampering.

"If I smoke, will I get caught?" asked the underground journalist Richard Neville, who answered his own question: "Only if you're stupid, unlucky or a pop star." John ("Hoppy") Hopkins, cofounder of the *International Times*, was one of the unlucky ones. A photographer by trade, he got busted for a small quantity of pot stashed at his London flat. But instead of showing remorse in court, he chose to make a forthright political statement. Hoppy told the jury that marijuana was less harmful than alcohol and the law was unjust. The judge didn't buy it. "You are a pest to society," he declared before consigning Hoppy to Wormwood Scrubs for nine months.

Hoppy's friends held an emergency summit in the back room of Indica. Steve Abrams, an Oxford-educated American expatriate who ran a drug-policy reform group called SOMA (an affiliate of LEMAR), urged that they undertake a multifaceted activist campaign to highlight the iniquities of marijuana prohibition. Cannabis had been banned in Great Britain since 1928, and recreational reefer remained on the margins, confined mainly to Caribbean migrants, until flower power blossomed in Merry Olde England. On July 16, 1967, Abrams emceed Britain's first "Legalize Pot" rally in London's Hyde Park. Allen Ginsberg addressed the gathering, which quickly morphed into a smoke-in of sorts as a few protestors lit up and passed joints.

A week later, SOMA placed a full-page advertisement in *The Times* of London, criticizing Britain's marijuana laws as "immoral in principle and unworkable in practice." The ad was signed by sixty-five British luminaries, including two members of Parliament, a dozen prominent physicians and clergymen, and numerous artists and writers. It called upon the government to:

- allow scientific research into cannabis;
- remove cannabis from the list of dangerous drugs and make possession punishable by a fine;
- permit the use of cannabis in private premises;
- and release everyone imprisoned for marijuana possession.

Among the signatories were notables such as novelist Graham Greene; Nobel laureate Francis Crick, the codiscoverer of the double-helix shape of DNA; and the four Beatles, who paid for the ad.

The advertisement caused a furor, but its impact paled in comparison with the latest Beatles album. The release of *Sgt. Pepper's Lonely Hearts Club Band* was an epochal event in the history of popular music. Synchronous with the millennial spirit of '67, it tapped into a collective generational mood that had been altered by psychotropic drugs. The Beatles were speaking to—and for—millions of reefer rebels around the world who embraced the counterculture's inchoate flower-power ideal.

"Do you know what caused *Pepper*?" McCartney told a reporter. "In one word, drugs. Pot."

"But you weren't on it all the time."

"Yes, we were. *Sgt. Pepper* was a drug album," McCartney insisted.

The drug imagery on the album cover (which included a marijuana plant amid a montage of famous people) and throughout the lyrics was hard to miss. Ringo Starr rhapsodized about "getting high with a little help" from his friends. McCartney "had a smoke" and "went into a dream." And Lennon cooed: "I'd love to turn you on." The BBC proceeded to ban several of the songs from its playlist, including "Lucy in the Sky with Diamonds," on the grounds that they promoted the use of illegal drugs. This ungainly attempt to censor the Beatles, who were at the zenith of their influence, underscored Britain's befuddled—some might say schizoid—attitude toward marijuana and its most influential proponents. The Beatles, after all, had recently been honored by the Queen. Lennon would later claim they smoked bud in the bathroom at Buckingham Palace.

The release of the 1968 Wootton Report, a comprehensive study by the British Parliament's advisory committee on Drug Dependence, sparked a heated public debate when it gave cannabis something very close to a clean bill of health. Headed by Baroness Wootton of Abinger, a social scientist of great repute, the advisory committee indicated that an increasing number of people in all classes of British society were using marijuana regularly for social pleasure. The Wootton Report drew a clear distinction between hard and soft drugs, a distinction hitherto unrecognized by the British legal system. Cannabis, according to the report, was "very much less dangerous than opiates, amphetamines, and barbiturates, and also less dangerous than alcohol [and] it is the personality of the user, rather than the properties of the drug, that is likely to cause progression to other drugs."

At one time or another, the report noted, tea and coffee as well as alcohol and tobacco had been condemned in much the same terms as cannabis was dissed in the Sixties. The committee poked holes in various popular fallacies about marijuana, noting that it did not lead to violence, psychosis, or dependence in otherwise normal people; nor did it create a vast constituency of junkies. "Having reviewed all the material available to us," the Wootton Report asserted, "we find ourselves in agreement with the conclusion reached by the Indian Hemp Drugs Commission appointed by the Government of India (1893–94), that the long-term consumption of cannabis in moderate doses has no harmful effects." It went on to state that "the long-asserted dangers of cannabis are exaggerated and that the law is socially damaging, if not unworkable." Specifically, the report criticized official pot policy for needlessly interfering with civil liberties. The committee recommended that cannabis law be changed so that no one would "go to prison for an offense involving only possession for personal use or for supply on a very limited scale."

Those who had become habituated to viewing marijuana as a beastly menace were mortified by the report. As soon as Baroness Wootton presented her study, stodgy British officials denounced its findings. For the Beatles and millions of their pot-smoking fans, it was just another day in the life.

High Spies

"Out, demons, out!" boomed the voice of Ed Sanders, who stood on a flatbed truck with the Fugs, chanting to a raucous throng of antiwar protestors in front of the Pentagon in Washington, D.C.

"Out! Out! Out!" the crowd roared in unison, as they sought to levitate the imperious, multimillion-ton structure three hundred feet into the air.

A phalanx of military police stood guard, forming a ring around the high church of the military-industrial complex. Stiff and expressionless, the soldiers faced down a motley assemblage of hippies, peaceniks, and direct-action stalwarts who had come to believe after several years of polite protest that the only way to stop the carnage in Southeast Asia was to disturb the peace at home. Hundreds of marijuana cigarettes were dispersed among the colorfully costumed agitators, who "looked like the legions of Sgt. Pepper's band," as Norman Mailer wrote in *Armies of the Night*, his celebrated account of the anti–Vietnam War rally on October 21, 1967. This demonstration, which drew an estimated 75,000 people, marked a turning point for America's peace movement when a sizable contingent broke off from the main rally at the Lincoln Memorial, marched across the Potomac, and surrounded the five-sided command center of America's armed forces. For the first time at an antiwar rally, a group of radicals tried to break through police lines and resist the efforts of federal marshals to arrest them. Amid all the commotion, Sanders and the Fugs intoned the "Pentagon Exorcism."

"Out, demons, out!"

Despite their incantations, the Pentagon did not budge. But the levitation ritual nonetheless had an upside, gifting to the world the indelible photographic image of daisies sprouting from the barrels of M16s held by dutiful young soldiers. The Pentagon was humbled, brought to its metaphoric knees by an authentic expression of flower power, which had gotten a lot feistier of late. In one fell swoop, that photo demystified the heavy-metal omnipotence of the U.S. military.

The Exorcism of the Pentagon epitomized the cross-fertilization between cultural and political radicals in the mid-1960s—a fusion championed by Allen Ginsberg and other pot-smoking activists. "A new man was born while besieging the Pentagon . . . A stoned politico. A hybrid mixture of New Left and hippie coming out something different," exulted Jerry Rubin, the Berkeley Free Speech Movement veteran who was instrumental in organizing the Pentagon protest.

Rubin attended a strategy session in New York City with a dozen other comrades who had been involved in planning the Pentagon action. Ed Sanders was there along with another East Village rabble-rouser, Abbie Hoffman. They smoked some Colombian and brainstormed about how to build on the momentum, which, they felt, was moving swiftly in their favor. Paul Krassner came up with the perfect expression to describe the stoned politico, the head who was also a fist. He was a *Yippie!*—an activist hippie. By the time the meeting was over, they were the "Youth International Party"—the full name for Yippie, an essentially mythical organization that combined New Left politics with marijuana and LSD in an effort to bring diffuse young rebels into the activist fold.

"Yippie!" was also a shout of joy in keeping with the zany antics of these political pranksters, who played upon the media's insatiable appetite for shock and sensation. Hoffman and Rubin, the two Yippie ringleaders, were adept at staging bombastic, made-for-TV events that conveyed a radical critique, such as when they burned dollar bills on Wall Street. Convinced that political protest should never be boring, they favored smoking cannabis over long-winded, leftist analysis. "Every time I smoke pot it is a revolutionary act," declared Hoffman. One clandestine Yippie caper entailed mailing thousands of rolled joints, along with a Yippie flyer, to a random list of New Yorkers.

The Yippies understood that smoking marijuana was a relatively easy way for incipient rebels to express their outrage against the establishment and flout its laws. To get access to youth culture, one had to get high. Otherwise one would be an outsider looking in. The illegal status of cannabis proved to be a useful recruiting opportunity for left-wing organizers, some of whom went so far as to *oppose* the legalization of marijuana because they felt severe penalties for possession aided their efforts by making pot smokers angry at the society that overreacted to a nonexistent danger. Selling black-market cannabis also provided a source of income for cash-strapped causes, according to Rubin, who admitted years later that "a lot of marijuana money was re-channeled among activists and cultural aspects. All those crazy right-wingers were always saying we are getting our money from Russia, but we were getting it from marijuana smoking. How else could the movement have been financed?"

The drug issue figured prominently in Yippie tactics. After forty-three students at the State University of New York in Stony Brook were arrested for pot possession in January 1968, a hundred or so "Keystone Kop" Yippies staged a mock predawn raid on campus to protest the coordinated police roundup. It was the first big Yippie media event, and it kicked off a turbulent year at colleges and universities throughout the United States. Antiwar actions became more militant and confrontational as U.S. troop levels in Indochina peaked at 542,000 in 1968 and aerial bombardment of North Vietnam exceeded the total tonnage dropped during World War II.

The turmoil on college campuses was not confined to the United States. In 1968, the barricades went up in student redoubts throughout Europe, Latin America, Africa, and parts of Asia. The Sorbonne insurrection in Paris during May and June triggered strikes and rioting in several French cities, which nearly toppled the national government. "Be realistic, demand the impossible," the wall graffiti proclaimed. At one point, young rebels occupied the Bourse (the French stock exchange) and a large victory flag—emblazoned with the image of hand-rolled reefer—was flown from the roof.

On the other side of the Iron Curtain, Soviet teenagers were turning to marijuana as an antidote to East Bloc boredom. "With pupils dilated from the drug," the Moscow weekly *Krokodil* reported, "the youngsters rolled cigarette tobacco in their sweaty palms, mixed in with a few specks of hashish or grass, lit up and inhaled deeply." A Warsaw-based student magazine, *ITD*, noted the emergence of a pot-smoking hippie scene in Poland. Ditto for youngsters in Belgrade and also in Prague, where protestors adopted the song "San Francisco," the hippie anthem, during Czechoslovakia's nonviolent uprising in the spring of 1968 that was crushed by the Soviet Union.

In their stoned reverie, the New York Yippies mistook the demographic proliferation of pot-puffing youth for raw political power during a very violent period in American history. If 1967 was the summer of love, then '68 was the summer of civil strife. The assassination of Dr. Martin Luther King in April ignited a spasm of arson and rioting in U.S. cities from coast to coast. Presidential candidate Senator Robert Kennedy, the next likely occupant of the Oval Office, was murdered in June. The steady drumbeat of violence continued to build while the Yippies announced plans for a massive protest at the Democratic National Convention in Chicago in August. "We will burn Chicago to the ground!" a Yippie press release sneered. "We demand the Politics of Ecstasy!" Other demands included the legalization of marijuana, an end to censorship, and the abolition of money and pay toilets.

The local press had a field day when the Yippies threatened to put LSD in Chicago's water supply. They also promised that Yippie gamines posing as hookers would give acid to delegates, while Yippie studs would seduce delegates' daughters and wives. And thousands of protestors would run naked through the streets. "We are dirty, smelly, grimy, foul . . . we will piss and shit and fuck in public . . . we will be constantly stoned or tripping on every drug known to man," the Yippies hyperbolized. These foul-mouthed subversives were determined to provoke a reaction from law enforcement, thereby exposing the true nature of the system for all to see. Force the Man to show his fascist face and the people will finally see the light. Such was their flawed logic.

Allen Ginsberg, among others, expressed concern for the safety of those who intended to demonstrate in the Windy City, where badge-heavy police and National Guardsmen were armed to the teeth. Ginsberg wondered whether the Yippies were leading lambs to slaughter by luring young people into a direct confrontation with forces they were ill equipped to defend themselves against. His fears were born out when city authorities refused to grant a permit for protestors to congregate at a public park during the convention. About ten thousand people showed up anyway, far fewer than the Yippies had hyped. While Ginsberg *ommmmed* to keep the peace, a lot of folks got very stoned on honey spiked with superpotent amber hash oil that mysteriously appeared on the streets of Chicago, adding to the general sense of anarchy and confusion. Several activists were knocked out of commission by the honey, prompting conspiracy theories in the underground press that the cannabinoid concoction was a CIA or FBI plot to immobilize the movement.

Getting loaded on hash-oil concentrate doubtless had an incapacitating effect, but these stoners may have helped themselves—albeit inadvertently—when they ingested the honey mixture: scientific studies would later establish that cannabinoid compounds have significant neuroprotective properties that mitigate the impact of traumatic brain injuries. This particular aspect of cannabis certainly was a plus given how many heads got smashed by billy-club-swinging cops, who went on a televised rampage in Chicago, cracking the skulls of protestors, reporters, and innocent bystanders. Many were hospitalized. A government commission, the Walker Study Team, would later call it a "police riot." But a majority of Americans, fed up with snotty Yippie shenanigans and eager for a paternal whip, sided with the boys in blue who went berserk. Richard M. Nixon, pledging to restore law and order, rode the backlash all the way to the White House.

CBS News, citing U.S. Army intelligence reports, later revealed that nearly one out of six protestors in Chicago was an undercover agent. Jerry Rubin's pot-smoking bodyguard was always stirring up trouble, throwing stones at cops, leading crowds in militant chants, desecrating the American flag, and exhorting protestors to tie up traffic and set fire to buildings. The Yippies never suspected that Rubin's bodyguard was a mole; after all, smoking marijuana was inherently a "revolutionary act" and no cop could keep his identity secret under the herb's truthful influence. Or so the Yippies thought.

The government's use of informants and provocateurs who spouted inflammatory rhetoric in order to incite others to violence was part of a no-holds-barred covert campaign to disrupt, fragment, and neutralize the forces of dissent in the late 1960s. Law-enforcement personnel enjoyed vast discretionary powers to monitor, infiltrate, and sabotage liberal and leftist organizations. A quarter of a million Americans were under "active surveillance" by various U.S. intelligence agencies, and dossiers were maintained on the personal lives and lawful political activities of millions more.

"Hoover University," located at Quantico Marine Base in Virginia, specialized in teaching spooks how to penetrate left-wing networks. Students who attended this elite FBI academy were instructed not to wash for several days in order to project the appropriate counterculture image when they approached radical groups. The more astute spies recognized that if they insinuated themselves into the radical wing of the antiwar movement, they might be expected to share a joint now and then with their newfound comrades.

Smoking marijuana during an undercover assignment "required a much higher degree of training than merely smoking a cigarette," acknowledged former FBI agent Cril Payne, who wrote about his time as an undercover leftie. During breaks between lectures on the New Left, drug abuse, and FBI procedure, Payne and several G-men would sneak away to get stoned. "We were definitely a happy group as we floated over to the dining hall," Payne recalled. "Just as we had suspected, the food did taste better, especially the second helpings." Payne could hardly keep from laughing as he watched his classmates "systematically appropriate ever-increasing portions of the official Bureau stash."

Payne fooled his surveillance targets by posing as a pot dealer. This way he could easily explain how he was able to support himself without a regular job and why he split the scene for brief interludes. "And since there was a certain aura of mystery and intrigue surrounding marijuana dealers, many of whom were viewed as modern day folk heroes, I wouldn't be expected to divulge extensive information about myself," Payne later explained. The fact that he supplied, rolled, and smoked reefer further enhanced his credibility as a dealer and a counterculture radical. "My undercover experiences brought me to the point where I considered marijuana use a normal social occurrence," said Payne, who confided that he found the altered state of awareness brought on by cannabis to be "both pleasurable and relaxing." He eventually left the FBI, disillusioned with the suits who ran the Bureau and somewhat sympathetic to the earnest young radicals he consorted with during his days and nights undercover.

Pot-smoking politicos were prime targets of FBI dirty tricks conducted under the auspices of COINTELPRO, the Bureau's political counterintelligence program, which entailed a multipronged assault on the New Left, antiwar activists, black power proponents, and the underground press. In a once-classified directive to FBI field offices, J. Edgar Hoover delineated a far-reaching twelve-point plan to neutralize left-wing leaders and journalists. "Since the use of marijuana and other narcotics is widespread among members of the New Left, you should be on the alert to have them arrested on drug charges," Hoover ordered. "Any information concerning the fact that individuals have marijuana or are engaging in a narcotics party should be immediately furnished to local authorities and they should be encouraged to take action."

Nearly every major police department in the United States initiated under cover operations against the hippie subculture, underground weeklies, and political protest groups. Marijuana laws provided police with all the leverage they needed to harass young people, racial minorities, and anyone else with nonregulation haircuts. Some pot arrests were clearly politically motivated. Lee Otis Johnson, a black militant and antiwar organizer at Texas Southern University, was sentenced to a thirty-year jail term for sharing a joint with a narc. (In Texas, the average jail term handed down in murder cases was ten years.) A federal court later annulled the verdict on the grounds that Johnson had been targeted because of his political opinions.

John Sinclair, a cultural worker and community organizer in Detroit, was sentenced to ten years in state prison for giving a couple of joints to an undercover cop who had repeatedly nagged him for some weed. In addition to forming a LEMAR chapter for Wolverine weed-lovers, he launched the White Panther Party, which was renamed the Rainbow People's Party after it relocated to Ann Arbor in 1967. He urged his youthful followers to join in a "total assault on the culture," a phrase popularized by Sinclair's friend Ed Sanders.

Built like a giant panda with exploding curly hair and wire-rimmed glasses, Sinclair was an outspoken supporter of the Black Panther Party, which the FBI pegged as public enemy number one in the late 1960s. The Panthers emphasized self-determination for the black community and proclaimed the necessity of bearing arms for self-defense. While Panther leaders occasionally smoked reefer, they told their members not to use drugs while engaged in party activities. Marijuana was never central to Black Panther politics like it was for Sinclair. While in jail, Sinclair wrote "The Marijuana Revolution," a panegyric to pot. He believed that cannabis heightened his awareness of the world, boosted his creativity, and promoted solidarity among different peoples—a credo from which he has never deviated.

As word of Sinclair's cruel but not entirely unusual punishment circulated via the underground press, he became a cause célèbre among marijuana smokers. "Free John Now" posters and bumper stickers appeared in counterculture enclaves across the country. Abbie Hoffman ran onstage during the Woodstock rock festival in August 1969 and tried to deliver a message about the plight of John Sinclair to half a million people who had made the pilgrimage to Max Yasgur's 600-acre farm in upstate New York. Just as he started to talk, the microphone went dead and Peter Townshend of the Who bonked the Yippie leader over the head with an electric guitar. This brief snafu hardly dimmed the luster of the three-day "Aquarian Exposition," which featured thirty-two musical acts, with Jimi Hendrix performing a stirring acid rock rendition of "The Star Spangled Banner" for the grand finale.

It was the counterculture's greatest moment in the sun, even though torrential downpours turned the festival site into a huge, muddy mess. Beset by a critical shortage of food, toilets, and medical supplies, Woodstock could have easily been a disaster. But the stoners somehow kept it together and America did a double take. Journalists noted that marijuana smoke was ubiquitous at Woodstock and according to police there was not a single fight. "It was a chance to show the world how it could be if we were running the show," said veteran Merry Prankster Wavy Gravy, a Woodstock emcee. Never before in the USA had a joyful declaration of dissent come from so many people collectively breaking the law. Woodstock was the biggest smoke-in of all, and there weren't enough jail cells in the entire state to hold all the people who were openly puffing grass and hash.

Woodstock was where the youth rebellion crested and the Sixties counterculture swelled to mainstream proportions. By the end of the decade, estimates of the number of pot smokers in America ran as high as 25 million. With the possible exception of jaywalking and speeding on highways, pot smoking had become the most widely committed crime in the United States. Meanwhile, the truly criminal war in Southeast Asia continued to grind on. President Nixon, ignoring public opinion, which had turned against the war, tried unsuccessfully to pound Vietnam into submission.

Faced with the realization that five years of street demonstrations and other forms of protest had had little tangible impact on U.S. foreign policy, antiwar activists grew increasingly frustrated and desperate. Shortly before Woodstock, Students for a Democratic Society, the nation's largest New Left organization (with 100,000 members and 350-plus chapters), imploded and gave birth to the Weather Underground, a violent splinter group with Armageddon fantasies. Firepower eclipsed flower power as the Weather fanatics vowed to "bring the war back home." They embarked upon a bombing spree that targeted property rather than people. After an explosion leveled the Whitehall Induction Center, where military draftees enlisted in New York City, a Weather dispatch claimed responsibility for the attack, asserting that it was meant to show support for the Vietcong, "love," and "legalized marijuana." Such acts unintentionally gave credibility to Nixonian hard-liners, who seized upon incidents of violence (often provoked by government agents) in an effort to quash political dissent in America. The antiwar movement as a whole was tainted by the unfavorable impression generated by its ultramilitant wing.

In the late 1960s, the social fabric of the United States appeared to be unraveling. Bombarded by daily television images of street fighting, campus upheavals, black power radicals, and pot-smoking longhairs, an increasing number of Americans feared their country was on the verge of collapse. To many onlookers, the widespread consumption of marijuana was a symptom, if not the cause, of public disorder and moral decay. Henry Giordano, who succeeded Anslinger as chief of the Federal Bureau of Narcotics, told Congress that calls to legalize pot were "just another effort to break down our whole American system."

The serrated marijuana leaf had become a totem of rebellion, a multivalent symbol of societal conflict. Condemning cannabis was a way to denounce the social and political movements that were in open revolt against "the American way of life." And continued support for criminal penalties against marijuana served as a symbolic means of asserting the legitimacy of the dominant culture. Denigrated by politicians and deified by dissidents, the little flower that millions liked to smoke would end up being the focus of "an immeasurably costly game of cops and robbers," as Robert Stone put it, "that made our difficulties with drugs, a marginal problem in most civilized countries, into an endless pep rally for repression."

4

THE BIG CHILL

This Means War

September 21, 1969. The line of cars and trucks stretched backward as far as the eye could see, while U.S. officials, looking for psychoactive contraband, stopped and searched every cargo that eked across the border from Tijuana. There were similar logjams at checkpoints all along the two-thousand-mile border with Mexico. Whereas usually U.S. customs inspectors would wave nineteen out of twenty vehicles through without close scrutiny, today was different. It was Day One of Operation Intercept, the Nixon administration's indelicate attempt to reduce the smuggling of marijuana into the United States. This unilateral interdiction effort continued for three weeks, wreaking economic havoc on both sides of the border and making life miserable for millions of commuters and legitimate commercial traders.

Intercept, the opening salvo of Richard M. Nixon's as yet undeclared war on drugs, failed to stem the influx of Mexican marijuana. (The running joke was that interdiction efforts failed more often than Hollywood marriages.) The amount of reefer seized during the controversial operation did not exceed the average twenty-day border haul. Apparently, most smugglers took a brief vacation, figuring that the full-court press wouldn't last. They knew it was not possible to police the entire border region traversed by cannabis couriers.

But that was not the main purpose of Operation Intercept. Its principal goal was to force a reluctant Mexican government to crack down on domestic cannabis cultivation at a time when the herb accounted for nearly 10 percent of the country's total exports. (A Mexican marijuana farmer could earn up to forty times the income that any legal crop might provide.) In effect, Washington was using economic blackmail and political coercion to make Mexico toe

Uncle Sam's rigid antipot line. As G. Gordon Liddy, one of Nixon's gung-ho henchmen, noted in his autobiography: "For diplomatic reasons the true purpose of the exercise was never revealed. Operation Intercept, with its massive economic and social disruption, could be sustained far longer by the United States than by Mexico. It was an exercise in international extortion, pure, simple, and effective, designed to bend Mexico to our will."

The Mexican Congress knuckled under and passed legislation that prohibited marijuana cultivation. Equipped with U.S. weaponry, Mexican police went through the motions and burned a few marijuana fields in the mountains. "We hope to drive the price [of marijuana] so high it will be unavailable to students in colleges and high schools . . . who are using it so commonly today," explained U.S. Deputy Attorney General Richard Kleindienst. Would marijuana users turn to street crime, as heroin addicts often did, to score more expensive herb? "Since marijuana is not addictive, we don't think that our students and young people will resort to crime in order to get it," Kleindienst remarked. His bland assertion that "marijuana is not addictive" contradicted one of the perennial myths promoted by the Federal Bureau of Narcotics, which had recently been renamed the Bureau of Narcotics and Dangerous Drugs (BNDD).

Nixon's law-and-order cabal may have been riding top-saddle for the moment, but what really counted in this instance was the law of unintended consequences. The higher the price that cannabis commanded, the more enticing it became for adventurers and high-rolling entrepreneurs, who diversified, so to speak, and availed themselves of other smuggling routes by land and sea. While Mexican marijuana still dominated the American market, excellent bud from Jamaica, Colombia, Thailand, and Hawaii reached a growing constituency of cannabis connoisseurs. Tons of high-grade hashish also turned up in Europe and North America during the late 1960s and early 1970s. As the Western appetite for *charas* increased, young travelers foraged "the hippie trail" through the Near East, Afghanistan, India, and Nepal, and returned with bricks of hash in body packs and false-bottom luggage.

The Brotherhood of Eternal Love, an elusive underground network of surfers and bikers-turned-LSD-evangelists, smuggled large slabs of Afghani hashish and distributed them throughout North America. Bought for $20 a kilo in Kandahar, the same quantity sold for more than $2,000 back in the States. Stuffed in car panels and shipped to Vancouver and other West Coast ports, a single consignment of dark brown Afghani Primo netted nearly a half million dollars for the Brotherhood, which also manufactured gallons of gooey, superpotent hash oil at a lab near Kabul. Known for its couch-lock THC levels, hash oil took up less space than regular hashish, was easier to conceal, and proved to be even more lucrative for the Brothers, who used the cash to subsidize their principal passion—the dissemination of millions of hits of free LSD. Orange Sunshine was the crème de la crème, the gold standard of black-market acid, and this brotherhood of true believers felt it was their spiritual duty to spread the psychedelic sacrament in accordance with the philosophy of their friend and mentor, Timothy Leary.

Several members of the Brotherhood were indicted by a California court in 1972, and a few would do jail time. But other Brothers picked up the slack and continued to smuggle vast quantities of LSD and hashish with Interpol and American narcotics agents in hot pursuit. Leary, meanwhile, was saddled with his own legal problems stemming from a 1966 pot bust in Laredo, Texas, when he was caught trying to cross the border with less than an ounce of marijuana. Sentenced to thirty years in federal prison for this infraction, the notorious LSD advocate fought the case all the way to the U.S. Supreme Court. His lawyers argued that the punitive Marihuana Tax Act of 1937 entailed a form of double jeopardy—if a person sought to acquire a marijuana tax stamp, as the law required, then he or she would be admitting an intention to commit a crime. In other words, Leary's attorneys reasoned, the Marihuana Tax Act was unconstitutional because it violated the Fifth Amendment right not to incriminate oneself. The Supreme Court agreed, ruling unanimously in Leary's favor on May 19, 1969, in a landmark decision that struck down the legal basis for marijuana prohibition.

It proved to be a Pyrrhic victory. Before the smoke cleared, the feds filed new charges against Leary and retried him on a technicality. The High Priest, who freely admitted to using marijuana, was convicted and sentenced to a decade in prison. Another pot bust—Orange County cops had found two roaches in Leary's car in December 1968—resulted in another ten-year sentence to run consecutively with the first. Dubbed by President Nixon as "the most dangerous man in America," Leary was denied bail. With little chance of early release, the forty-nine-year-old counterculture icon faced a virtual life sentence in jail. It was obvious to Allen Ginsberg that Leary was incarcerated not for a picayune stash of pot but for expressing politically incorrect views about psychoactive drugs. After seven months in captivity, Leary flew the coup with the help of the Weather Underground. The Brotherhood of Eternal Love had provided money to finance the prison escape, and Leary lived on the lam for more than two years until BNDD agents caught up with him in Afghanistan.

The fact that Leary, of all people, had instigated the legal challenge that threw federal pot prohibition into limbo was particularly irksome to Nixon. The president pulled out all the stops to make sure that a new antimarijuana law was passed before the midterm elections. On October 27, 1970, Congress ratified the Controlled Substances Act, which was part of a larger piece of legislation (the Comprehensive Drug Abuse Prevention and Control Act) that gave a green light to "no-knock" raids by narcotics agents and placed all drugs into five different categories or "schedules," ranking each according to their safety, their medical uses, and their potential for abuse.* Attorney General John Mitchell labeled marijuana a Schedule I narcotic, a category reserved for drugs of maximum danger that had no therapeutic value. The designation was supposed to be temporary, pending further review by a presidential commission.

Heroin and LSD were also deemed Schedule I; cocaine and methamphetamine were labeled Schedule II, a lower category of abuse, because they had medical applications. This made little sense to Dr. Leo Hollister, a Veterans Administration expert on psychoactive drugs, who raised pointed questions about the hasty manner in which cannabis had been classified. "The unfortunate scheduling which groups together such diverse drugs as heroin, LSD and marijuana perpetuates a fallacy long apparent to our youth. These drugs are not equivalent in pharmacological effects or in the degree of danger they represent to individuals and to society," Hollister told the House Ways and Means Committee. He predicted that the new law would "become a laughingstock."

But it was no laughing matter to Nixon, who viewed marijuana as a useful wedge issue that he could play for political advantage. Nixon linked cannabis to loudmouthed radical protestors. "They're all on drugs," he brusquely told an aide. Susceptible to bouts of paranoia, the commander-in-chief blamed "the Jews" for spearheading efforts to legalize cannabis. "You know it's a funny thing, every one of those bastards that are out for legalizing marijuana is Jewish. What the Christ is the matter with the Jews, Bob?" Nixon asked his closest adviser, H. R. Haldeman. In private conversations with his inner circle, Tricky Dick also savaged African Americans. "[Nixon] emphasized that you have to face the fact that the whole problem is really the blacks. The key is to devise a system that recognizes this while not appearing to," Haldeman wrote in his diary.†

The "system" that Tricky Dick devised in response to this "problem" was the war on drugs, which would disproportionately target people of color. At

---

* 1,899 Americans died from illegal drugs in 1970, the year the Controlled Substances Act was passed; far more Americans died that year from food poisoning and falling down stairs (Baum, *Smoke and Mirrors*, p. 47).

† "We understood that drugs were not the health problem we were making them out to be, but it was such a perfect issue for the Nixon White House that we couldn't resist it," Nixon White House counsel John Erlichman later acknowledged.

a press conference on June 17, 1971, Nixon opened the floodgates by lumping marijuana together with hard narcotics and declaring, "America's public enemy number one is drug abuse. In order to fight and defeat this enemy, it is necessary to wage a new, all-out offensive." Nixon doubled down on the Anslinger lie, and soon marijuana-related arrests would exceed the number of arrests for all violent crimes combined in the United States.

For Nixon, the antidrug crusade was more than just a formula for padding arrest statistics and cracking down on crime. It was also a symbolic means of stigmatizing youth protest, antiwar sentiment, rock 'n' roll music, and other expressions of cultural ferment—underscoring once again that pot prohibition had little to do with the actual effects of the herb and everything to do with who was using it. By disparaging marijuana smokers, the president cast aspersions on all the troublesome currents flowing out of the Sixties youth rebellion. Nixon's declaration of all-out war against illicit drugs, in general, and marijuana, in particular, marked the opening act of a protracted national drama, a decades-long vendetta against what the Beats and their putative heirs had unleashed. The reactionaries were sharpening their knives. The pendulum had started to swing back.

The White House hoped to recruit a few youth-oriented celebrities to serve as antidrug shills. Elvis Presley volunteered for the cause at a hastily arranged meeting with Nixon shortly before Christmas 1970. A memo by Egil "Bud" Krogh, deputy counsel to the president, summarized what transpired. Nixon told Presley that "those who use drugs are also in the vanguard of anti-American protest. Violence, drug usage, dissident protest all seemed to merge in generally the same group of young people." Elvis agreed that illegal drugs and the hippie counterculture were destroying American society, and he offered his services to the president as an antidrug spokesman who knew how to communicate with a young audience. An appreciative Nixon indicated that they should keep their relationship secret to preserve Presley's credibility, and he gave the erstwhile king of rock 'n' roll a BNDD badge, which Elvis carried around like a talisman. Presley liked to show off his federal narcotics badge while voicing disapproval of the Beatles and other rock groups that were known to use marijuana.

Presley's antidrug shtick was ironic, and sad, given that he was high as a kite when he visited Nixon. Addicted to a combination of barbiturates, painkillers, and amphetamines for most of his adult life, Elvis died of a polydrug overdose in 1977. Yet even while he was slowly committing suicide by abusing pharmaceuticals, Presley didn't think of himself as a drug addict. Elvis took a hard line against cannabis, but rationalized his habitual excess because his meds were obtained legally, duly prescribed by several government-licensed doctors. The gallons of pills he consumed day-in and day-out were not the Schedule I street drugs that Nixon had vowed to wage war against.

As part of the Controlled Substances Act, a National Commission on Marihuana and Drug Abuse was established to assess the dangers of cannabis and make long-term policy recommendations. Nixon handpicked most of the commission members, including Michael Sonnenreich, ex–deputy chief counsel of the BNDD. Stacked with drug-war hawks and chaired by former Pennsylvania Governor Raymond Shafer, a law-and-order Republican, the blue ribbon commission nevertheless took its work very seriously. It conducted fifty research projects and solicited input from scientists, doctors, law enforcement, and concerned citizens. A clean-shaven Allen Ginsberg, wearing a necktie and a porkpie hat, made a surprise appearance before the commissioners at a public fact-finding forum in San Francisco. Ginsberg testified that cannabis was a creative tool for artists and no one should be put in jail for using it.

The Shafer Commission, as it was known, also conferred with foreign government officials, who parroted the standard line—marijuana use was very problematic and they were deeply concerned and wanted to work with Washington to stamp it out. "Then, at night," a commission member disclosed, "we'd go out drinking with them, and they'd tell us the truth: they thought marijuana was harmless, but the Nixon administration wanted a hard line and they feared economic reprisals if they didn't go along."

When Nixon got wind that the commission might be more sympathetic to cannabis than he had expected, the president made his displeasure known during a private meeting with Shafer. The president indicated in no uncertain terms that he "had very strong feelings" about marijuana. He warned Shafer to get control of his commission and avoid looking like a bunch of soft-on-pot "do-gooders." They also discussed Shafer's potential appointment to a federal judgeship. "I want a goddamn strong statement about marijuana . . . one that just tears the ass out of them," Nixon growled shortly before the Shafer Commission released its final report—1,184 pages long—in March 1972.

Called "Marihuana: A Signal of Misunderstanding," this report was the most comprehensive review of cannabis ever conducted by the federal government. The Shafer Commission estimated that 24 million Americans had smoked pot at least once. Experimentation with the herb "is motivated primarily by curiosity and a desire to share a social experience," the report asserted. "The most notable statement that can be made about the vast majority of marijuana users—experimenters and intermittent users—is that they are essentially indistinguishable from their non-marijuana using peers by any fundamental criterion other than marijuana use."

"Why has the use of marijuana reached problem status in the public mind?" The answer, according to the commission, did not lie in the plant's pharmacological properties: "Many see the drug as fostering a counterculture which conflicts with basic moral precepts as well as with the operating functions of our society." Cannabis had become "more than a drug." It had become "a symbol of the rejection of cherished values." Skeptical of claims that cannabis caused biological or psychological harm, large numbers of young people openly defied the law by smoking pot in public, the commission noted. "Seldom in the nation's history has there been a phenomenon more divisive, more misunderstood, more fraught with impact on family, personal, and community relationships than the marijuana phenomenon," said Governor Shafer, who recognized "the extensive degree of misinformation about marijuana" and the need for "a more rational discussion of marijuana policy." "The time for politicizing the marijuana issue is at an end," Shafer asserted.

The Shafer Commission found no evidence that marijuana causes physical or psychological harm or any tortuous withdrawal symptoms following the sudden cessation of chronic, heavy use—no brain damage or birth defects, no compulsion to use hard drugs, and no evidence that a single human fatality has resulted solely from marijuana intoxication. "Neither the marijuana user nor the drug itself can be said to constitute a danger to public safety," the report concluded. In essence, the Shafer Commission reaffirmed the findings of the Indian Hemp Drugs Commission, the Panama Canal Study, the La Guardia Commission, and the Wootton Report.

Given how widespread marijuana smoking had become in the United States, law-enforcement officials were simply powerless to stop it. The Shafer Commission report recognized this and cited several adverse effects of marijuana prohibition, including selective enforcement, selective prosecution, misallocation of resources, and disrespect for the law among youth. The Shafer Report also took note of "the nation's philosophical preference for individual privacy" and emphasized that legislation against marijuana possession represented a departure from America's constitutional roots: "We believe that government must show a compelling reason to justify invasion of the home in order to prevent personal use of marijuana. We find little in marijuana's effects or in its social impact to support such a determination."

According to the Shafer Commission, the existing marijuana-prohibition system did not serve the national interest of the United States of America. For marijuana users, the potential harm of getting arrested was much greater than any harm from using the herb. In effect, Nixon was told that the real marijuana problem derived not from the drug but from the war on drugs. The Shafer Report recommended that state and federal laws be changed to remove criminal penalties for "possession of marijuana for personal use" and for "casual distribution of small amounts of marijuana" involving little or no remuneration. But growing or selling pot for profit should remain felony offenses, advised the commission, which favored decriminalization rather than outright legalization of cannabis. The Shafer Commission also recommended that cannabis be investigated for possible medical benefits.

Nixon never even read the report before he rejected its policy recommendations. Cannabis would remain a Schedule I drug, meaning that it was deemed unsafe for use even under a doctor's supervision—a determination made not by medical experts but by the U.S. Justice Department. And Governor Shafer, needless to say, never got appointed to the federal bench.

Dr. Mikuriya's Medicine

Tod Hiro Mikuriya was a man on a mission. At a time when the therapeutic use of marijuana had been abandoned in the United States, Mikuriya rediscovered the forgotten medical literature and brought it to the attention of physicians and scientists. The tall, handsome psychiatrist sought to remedy a historical injustice by fighting to restore cannabis to its proper place in the Western pharmacopeia. Almost single-handedly, he kept the issue alive while very few Americans—even pot smokers—were aware of marijuana's medicinal history.

Born in 1933 and raised on a small farm in eastern Pennsylvania by his German mother and his Japanese father, Mikuriya experienced double-whammy bigotry as a child during World War II. Although his father, a convert to Christianity, worked at a defense plant, the Mikuriyas were visited by the FBI and threatened with confinement in an internment camp. "My sister and I were shot at, beaten up, spat upon, called names. The local kids chased us like a pack of dogs," Mikuriya recalled. "I realized that people could be brainwashed and trained to hate. The same thing has been done with marijuana and marijuana users. I learned to fight back."

Mikuriya earned his medical degree from Temple University in Philadelphia. His interest in marijuana was piqued when he perused an unassigned chapter in a pharmacology textbook, which included a brief reference to the curative qualities of cannabis. A voracious reader, he scoured the library at Temple for more information about the herb. During a break between semesters in the summer of 1959, he traveled to Mexico and purchased a small quantity of *mota* from a street dealer. He smoked his first reefer after watching his guide take a few puffs "just to see that it wasn't poison," as Mikuriya later explained.

In August 1966, Mikuriya traveled to North Africa to investigate what proved to be spurious claims of *kif*-induced madness. (*Kif*—pronounced "keef"—is a potent form of hashish powder.) Dr. Mikuriya wrote articles for several academic journals on traditional *kif*-smoking communities in the rugged Rif Mountains of Morocco. "They had never seen any Westerners there before," Mikuriya reported. He shared pipefuls of *kif* with Berber tribesmen, who had resisted previous attempts by the French colonial government to stamp out cannabis smoking. Mikuriya dined with the local chief of police who stated, "My policy is, if it's under two kilograms, it's for their own personal use."

After visiting Morocco, Dr. Mikuriya returned to his job as director of the New Jersey Neuropsychiatric Institute Drug Addiction Treatment Center, a detox facility for heroin and barbiturate addicts, in Princeton. A casual cannabis smoker, Mikuriya had never ingested an oral preparation of Indian hemp, so when opportunity knocked he volunteered for an experiment conducted by the Princeton-based researcher Carl C. Pfeiffer. Hooked up to various instruments in Pfeiffer's laboratory, Mikuriya was given low-, medium-, and high-dose hashish extracts. His brain waves, blood pressure, and pulse were monitored through each session. Mikuriya later learned that Pfeiffer had been secretly contracted by the CIA to undertake mind-control experiments involving LSD and other psychoactive drugs.

Mikuriya's respectful relations with Pfeiffer and other well-connected drug scientists at Princeton helped smooth the way for his next job. In July 1967, Mikuriya was recruited by the National Institute of Mental Health (NIMH) to direct its marijuana research program. He was rather idealistic at the time, thinking that all he needed to do to reform government policy was to make a fair and rational case for marijuana as a safe and effective medicine.

While employed by the NIMH, Dr. Mikuriya undertook a thorough survey of all the scientific and medical reports on cannabis that were archived at the National Library of Medicine. He discovered a long-ignored copy of the seminal 1838 study of Indian hemp by Sir William O'Shaughnessy, the Irish physician who introduced "gunjah" to Western medicine. Mikuriya found various papers that confirmed O'Shaughnessy's findings and reported several additional uses for cannabis. He combed through 3,281 pages—all nine volumes—of the 1893–94 Indian Hemp Drugs Commission Report, which indicated that cannabis had been used as a therapeutic substance on the Indian subcontinent for millennia. Mikuriya learned that cannabis tinctures were commonly prescribed for a wide range of maladies in the United States, Britain, and France during the nineteenth century. But since the U.S. government effectively outlawed marijuana in 1937, the American medical establishment had forgotten what was once known about the herb's valuable therapeutic attributes.

Mikuriya soon became mired in bureaucratic quicksand at the NIMH, which authorized research that sought only to justify the total prohibition of cannabis. "The government wanted bad things found out about marijuana," Mikuriya stated, "and I didn't find them." Away from the office, he smoked pot with several NIMH staffers, who were sympathetic to Mikuriya's views. But few had the temerity to risk their careers by offending the Federal Bureau of Narcotics. "One also had to worry about antediluvian congressional types that had it in their power to smite us mightily where it hurt—right in our appropriation," explained Mikuriya, who saw that the game was rigged. Every marijuana-related grant proposal was screened by a series of squeamish, politically correct committees that hewed to an "ethic of inoffensiveness." Therapeutic-oriented research was not on the agenda.

Mikuriya crafted a detailed position paper on marijuana calling for major policy changes. He emphasized that cannabis was not a dangerous drug and he urged the U.S. government to fully research its versatile medicinal properties. But Mikuriya's superiors at the NIMH were less interested in marijuana's therapeutic applications than in its impact on wayward Sixties youth. He was dispatched to Northern California on an undercover operation. "I was assigned by the NIMH to spy on hippie communes to find out what influence marijuana was having on this subculture. My colleagues regarded these communes as the potential end of civilization," said Mikuriya, who added: "If you think a hippie commune is strange, you ought to work for the federal government. The hippies ask, 'What's your [astrological] sign?' Within the government, they ask, 'What's your GS [government service] level?' "

Mikuriya realized that as far as cannabis was concerned he had more in common with the reefer rebels he visited in Northern California than with the "repressed bureaucrats" who debriefed him when he returned from the West Coast. The NIMH shirts "seemed obsessed with the image of hippie chicks without bras," Mikuriya recalled. After less than four months in the belly of the beast, Mikuriya went native, so to speak, and resigned from the NIMH.*

---

* Not long after he defected from the NIMH, Mikuriya was contacted by Dr. Van Sim, medical director of the U.S. Army's secret chemical-warfare research program at Edgewood Arsenal during the late 1950s and 1960s. Sim said he wanted to get the army's THC research declassified because of the medically useful properties the Chemical Corps had inadvertently discovered. While searching for an antidote to nerve gas, the Edgewood crew had stumbled upon marijuana's powerful anticonvulsive properties. Sim concluded that cannabis "is probably the most potent anti-epileptic known to medicine." But the army studies were never declassified due to bureaucratic inertia and the hostile official climate toward

Mikuriya moved to Berkeley, California, and went into private practice as a psychiatrist. In March 1968, he participated in a panel discussion, "Current Problems of Drug Abuse," hosted by the California Medical Association. He provided an overview of the medicinal history of cannabis, citing examples from ancient China, India, Greece, and the Muslim world, along with recent scientific studies conducted outside the United States, which found that THC controlled epileptic seizures in children more effectively than approved pharmaceuticals (that had serious side effects). "Because cannabis does not lead to physical dependence, it was found to be superior to opiates for a number of therapeutic purposes," he stated. Mikuriya also noted favorable results in treating opiate addiction withdrawal and alcoholism with cannabis.

An early proponent of what would become known as "harm reduction," Mikuriya advocated the use of nonlethal, nonaddictive marijuana as a substitute for heroin or booze. In 1970, he published a report in *Medical Times* about a patient who weaned herself from alcohol by smoking cannabis. After medical marijuana was relegalized in California, Mikuriya treated hundreds of alcoholic patients who got their lives back after switching to pot. In general, he found that an increase in the consumption of marijuana correlated with a reduction in the consumption of alcohol. As far as Mikuriya was concerned, marijuana was not a gateway drug to addiction—it was an exit drug.

Mikuriya, meanwhile, had compiled a definitive bibliography of scholarly writings on every aspect of cannabis. The most important articles were included in *Marijuana: Medical Papers*, a groundbreaking anthology edited by Mikuriya, who wrote in the introduction: "In light of such assets as minimal toxicity, no buildup of tolerance, no physical dependence, and minimal autonomic disturbance, immediate major clinical investigation of cannabis preparations is indicated in the management of pain, chronic neurologic diseases, convulsive disorders, migraine headache, anorexia, mental illness, and bacterial infections." It was intended as an "everything-you-never-learned-in-med-school" type of textbook for fellow physicians.

The publication of Mikuriya's compendium in 1973 marked the beginning of the modern renaissance of medicinal cannabis. For several years, he would carry on his shoulders a nascent social movement that subsequently grew into a widespread populist revolt against conventional medicine and extraconstitutional authority. Unable to change the system from within, he surmised that the solution to pot prohibition lay in grassroots citizen activism. In February

marijuana (Sim quoted in Alfred D. Berger, "Marijuana," *World Medical News*, July 16, 1971).

Dr. Tod Mikuriya in his smock with the cannabis caduceus after California legalized medical marijuana in 1996. Mikuriya unearthed the lost history of medicinal hemp and his efforts sparked a revival of interest in cannabis therapeutics.

(Courtesy of Marcio Jose Sanchez/Associated Press)

1969, he networked with cannabis agitators at the "New Worlds" Drug Symposium in Buffalo, New York, organized by Michael Aldrich of LEMAR. It was at this conference that Mikuriya first met Allen Ginsberg and a young researcher from Harvard named Andrew Weil, who went on to become a prominent practitioner of holistic healing and the author of several best-selling books on integrative medicine.

In 1970, Aldrich moved to the Bay Area, where he reconnected with Mikuriya and teamed up with a pot activist named Blair Newman. They launched a new group, Amorphia (the successor to LEMAR), which funded itself by selling Acapulco Gold rolling papers made entirely of hemp. (The hemp rolling papers were produced in Spain.) All the proceeds from this co-operative business venture were devoted to supporting political action for the legalization of cannabis. When the Shafer Commission held a public forum in San Francisco, Aldrich, the pony-tailed pot scholar, punctuated his testimony with a raised fist as he shouted Amorphia's slogan: "*What we want is free, legal, backyard marijuana!*"

The release of the Shafer Report was a big boost for the fledgling marijuana reform movement, which drew support from across the political spectrum. William F. Buckley, the most influential conservative intellectual in America, endorsed the recommendations of the Shafer Commission, noting that "the existing anti-marijuana laws are excruciatingly anachronistic." Concerned that anticannabis conservatives were alienating young voters, Buckley and his tribune, *National Review*, came out in favor of legalization. In 1972, *National Review* published a controversial cover story by Richard Cowan, the Yale-educated cofounder of the right-wing student group Young Americans for Freedom. Cowan urged conservatives to reconsider their knee-jerk views on cannabis. He argued that penalizing marijuana consumption made a mockery of conservative principles: "The hysterical myths about marijuana . . . have led conservatives to condone massive programs of social engineering, interference in the affairs of individuals, monstrous bureaucratic waste."

A scion of Texas oil money, Cowan enjoyed smoking pot with the upper crust in the Lone Star State, despite the fact that marijuana possession was a felony punishable by up to life imprisonment in Texas. Cowan became an early supporter—and later the executive director—of the National Organization for the Reform of Marijuana Laws (NORML), based in Washington, D.C. Launched in 1970 by a young attorney named Keith Stroup, NORML lobbied federal officials and state legislatures and mounted a legal challenge to get marijuana removed from the list of Schedule I controlled substances so that it could be prescribed by a doctor. NORML's star-studded advisory board included pacifist pediatrician Benjamin Spock; human rights activist Aryeh Neier; former deputy director of the Bureau of Narcotics and Dangerous Drugs John Finlater; and Harvard Medical School professor Lester Grinspoon, who was frequently called upon to refute the ridiculous claims about cannabis that prohibitionists continued to promulgate.

In 1972, NORML hosted the first People's Pot Conference at the St. Mark's Episcopal Church on Capitol Hill, attended by three hundred delegates from thirty-six states. They were an unusual mix of long-haired leftists, suit-and-tie liberals, and conservative libertarians, underscoring that marijuana law reform was a "big tent" issue whose time had arrived. Michael Aldrich, representing Amorphia, met his wife-to-be, Michelle Cauble, at this conclave. Shortly thereafter, Cauble left her job with the National Coordinating Council on Drug Education, moved to San Francisco, and devoted herself full-time to the 1972 California Marijuana Initiative (CMI), a decriminalization ballot measure spearheaded by Amorphia and Bay Area attorneys Leo Paoli and John Kaplan.

It was the first time that Americans would have a chance to vote on marijuana law reform. Officially known as Proposition 19, this initiative stipulated that no one over the age of eighteen could be punished for growing, transporting, possessing, or using cannabis in the Golden State—in other words, "free, legal, backyard grass." (It did not entail legalizing the sale of marijuana or its cultivation for profit.) Aldrich asked NORML to help with the CMI campaign, but initially he got a tepid response from Stroup, NORML's chief, who didn't think mass-based voter propositions were a smart strategy. NORML was more into inside-the-Beltway sparring than Amorphia-style, grassroots rabble-rousing.

Amorphia recruited Gordon Brownell, a twenty-eight-year-old Republican lawyer with experience running statewide campaigns, to coordinate CMI's political operations. Brownell cut his teeth with the 1964 Goldwater presidential bid and later worked as an administrative aide in the Nixon White House. Privy to the inner workings of the Nixon administration, Brownell could see that marijuana was a lightning rod for much of the anger that Tricky Dick and "his people" felt toward the antiwar counterculture. At a CMI press conference, Brownell explained: "The lack of government credibility on marijuana has helped foster a growing drug abuse problem in America. The facts regarding marijuana's relative harmlessness have been known but disregarded for many years." Brownell had high hopes that the California Marijuana Initiative would "serve as an example to the entire nation that government 'by the people' will not wither away in the face of an intransigent bureaucracy."

Brownell was the kind of conservative who believed in minimal government interference with individual freedoms. Consciousness is private, not a domain for armed agents of the state, and, as citizens of a free society, we should have the right to put into our bodies whatever we wish, according to Brownell, who felt that choosing to smoke a nightly bowl of weed or experimenting once in a while with a psychedelic drug was perfectly compatible with life, liberty, and the pursuit of happiness. His decision to abandon the Nixon White House and join the pro-pot cause was triggered in part by an epiphany he had while tripping on mescaline (an LSD-like substance) with his girlfriend in the Grand Canyon.

Brownell barnstormed throughout the state with Dr. Tod Mikuriya, who also played a major role in the CMI campaign. "In Tod, I found another libertarian Republican—a not yet extinct species—who talked about individual freedom and keeping government out of our homes and private lives," said

Brownell. Like Brownell, Mikuriya was a registered Republican who later bolted and joined the Libertarian Party. Young CMI volunteers listened with rapt attention as Mikuriya regaled them with stories about cannabis and the British army in India in the 1800s, the Indian Hemp Drugs Commission Report, and Dr. William Woodward of the AMA, one of his heroes, who resisted Harry Anslinger's efforts to outlaw marijuana.

Mikuriya was the first physician to unearth and publicize the lost history of medicinal cannabis. But Dr. Tod, as his patients liked to call him, believed that marijuana's full potential as a therapeutic substance could not be realized unless recreational use was legalized. A member of the CMI board of directors and the CMI steering committee, Mikuriya composed medical fact sheets, information brochures, and an educational pamphlet, "Thinking About Using Pot" (coauthored with Dr. Andrew Weil), which were distributed during the campaign. He did a benefit tour for the initiative, showing the *Reefer Madness* film from the 1930s, which elicited howls and belly laughs at every venue. Mikuriya and Yippie veteran Keith Lampe (Amorphia's "entertainment director") formed Jocks for Joynts, enlisting pro-pot athletes such as former star NFL linebacker Dave Meggyesy. Film idols, musicians, the cast of *Hair*, and other celebrities pitched in.

When the final results were tallied, Proposition 19 was defeated by a wide margin. But Aldrich was heartened that a third of California voters (2.7 million people) had pulled the lever for de facto marijuana legalization; moreover, the pot proposition got a 52 percent majority in San Francisco, while across the bay in Berkeley support topped 70 percent. The election revealed the existence of a sizable but hitherto unrecognized political constituency. Politicians took note and in 1976 the California legislature approved the Moscone Act, which reduced the penalty for possessing less than an ounce of pot from a felony to a misdemeanor punishable by a maximum $100 fine—a prudent fiscal move that would save Californians more than $100 million a year over the next decade in enforcement costs alone.

By this time, Amorphia had merged with NORML. Brownell took over as NORML's West Coast coordinator, and Aldrich became curator of the Fitz Hugh Ludlow Memorial Library (named after America's nineteenth-century hashish trailblazer), a unique archive of drug literature and counterculture rarities. He continued to collaborate with Dr. Mikuriya, whose passion for cannabis would never waver during the years of cultural rollback that lay ahead.

The Euphoria of Secrecy

They called it a "Bed-in for Peace." In May 1969, John Lennon and Yoko Ono, wearing pajamas and reclining throughout, staged a Yippiesque media event in their room at the Queen Elizabeth Hotel in Montreal. This is where they recorded their popular antiwar anthem, "Give Peace a Chance." During the weeklong vigil, they were visited by a succession of friends and counterculture notables, including Allen Ginsberg and Timothy Leary.

While in Montreal again later that year, Lennon and his wife were interviewed by the Le Dain Commission of Inquiry into the Non-Medical Use of Drugs. For ninety minutes they shared their views on marijuana, the youth scene, and the generation gap with Canadian government investigators. "The one thing that can be said about marijuana is it's non-violent," Lennon commented. "If any government wanted to use it to calm people, they have got the ultimate weapon."

After completing its work in 1972, the Le Dain Commission issued a final report, widely praised for its thoroughness, which urged the Canadian government to legalize marijuana for personal use and called upon provincial authorities to implement controls similar to those regulating the consumption of alcohol. The use of marijuana for pleasure, the Le Dain report noted, must not be interpreted to mean that the motivation is trivial. Once again, an official government inquiry gave cannabis a passing grade—and once again its recommendations would be ignored by public officials.

John and Yoko, meanwhile, had moved to New York City and applied for U.S. citizenship. They befriended several prominent radical activists and immersed themselves in left-wing causes, often speaking out against the Vietnam War and for marijuana legalization. In addition to writing and recording his own songs, Lennon produced a few albums by other musicians, including *The Pope Smokes Dope* by David Peel and the Lower East Side, a scruffy East Village stoner band.

In December 1971, Lennon appeared at a mass rally in Ann Arbor, Michigan, to protest the imprisonment of John Sinclair, the left-wing cultural activist who had thus far served twenty-nine months of a ten-year sentence for giving two joints to a narc. It was Lennon's first live performance in the United States since the breakup of the Beatles. "So flower power didn't work," Lennon told the crowd, "so let's try something new." Allen Ginsberg and Ed Sanders spoke at the eight-hour rally for their erstwhile LEMAR collaborator, and several other big-name musicians rocked the packed arena. Michigan native Stevie Wonder introduced one of his songs by saying, "This is to any undercover agents in the crowd" and proceeded to play "Somebody's Watching You." Sure enough, FBI agents and undercover cops were in the audience.

Three days after the benefit concert, the Michigan Supreme Court released Sinclair from prison and his conviction was subsequently overturned in a historic decision that struck down Michigan's marijuana laws as unconstitutional. Sinclair's saga sparked a local tradition, the Ann Arbor Hash Bash, an annual rite-of-spring smoke-in held on the first Saturday of April. In 1972, the year of the initial Hash Bash, the Ann Arbor city council overrode state laws by making marijuana possession a $5 fine. It was the prelude to a national trend of marijuana decriminalization by eleven state legislatures during the 1970s, a policy shift precipitated by the incarceration of John Sinclair and the publicity his case received, thanks most of all to John Lennon.

John and Yoko considered the Ann Arbor gig a trial run for a national antiwar tour in a dozen U.S. cities. At each stop, local organizers would urge young people to register to vote and to vote against the war, which meant voting against Richard Nixon. Lennon had talked about concluding the tour with a giant rock concert/protest rally near the Republican National Convention in Miami, where President Nixon was slated to be renominated in August 1972. Although Lennon dropped the idea of a rock 'n' roll peace campaign, his presence in the United States inflamed the paranoia of Nixon's inner circle, which viewed the ex-Beatle as a threat to the president's reelection chances. The last election had been a squeaker and Nixon would stop at nothing to win a second term.

"If Lennon's visa was terminated, it would be a strategic counter-measure," a FBI report suggested. J. Edgar Hoover, on his last legs, classified the Lennon problem as a "security matter." Shortly thereafter, the U.S. Immigration and Naturalization Service (INS) initiated deportation proceedings against the British superstar. The Nixon Justice Department instructed Hoover to nail Lennon on a drug charge, which would have been grounds for immediate expulsion. A July 1972 FBI memo described "John Winston Lennon" as a "heavy user of narcotics" and emphasized that local law-enforcement agencies should keep him under surveillance and arrest him "if at all possible on possession of narcotics charges." When a pot bust didn't pan out, Nixon administration officials tried to use Lennon's 1968 marijuana arrest in London (instigated by a corrupt British cop) as an excuse to deport him. But Lennon's lawyers duked it out in the courts and eventually he got the okay to remain in the United States.

The Nixon administration's effort to neutralize Lennon was a small part of a tangled skein of illegal activities designed to silence dissent and ensure the president's reelection. Driven by political rather than legitimate law-enforcement considerations, the persecution of the former Beatle typified the massive abuses of power that culminated in the Watergate scandal, which was inextricably linked to both the war in Vietnam and the war on drugs.

On June 17, 1971, exactly one year before the Watergate break-in, Nixon officially declared "war" on marijuana and other illicit substances. Right from the get-go, the war on drugs was primarily a war on marijuana smokers. By depicting pot smokers as combatants in a war, Nixon succeeded in militarizing a health issue. But Nixon's antidrug histrionics were soon overshadowed by the release of the *Pentagon Papers*, the documents that exposed the fraudulent basis for U.S. military intervention in Southeast Asia.

Obsessed with plugging the leak that led to the publication of the *Pentagon Papers* and protecting other incriminating secrets, Nixon authorized the formation of a clandestine White House intelligence unit that operated almost entirely outside the Constitution. Known euphemistically as "the plumbers," this privately financed police-state squadron specialized in dirty tricks against Nixon's opponents. The original plan to bypass the existing espionage bureaucracy called for using the drug war as a pretext to create an all-powerful covert action capability. Narcotics control provided an ideal cover for Nixon's cronies, who surmised that if push came to shove few politicians would dare challenge the president lest they risk being branded "soft on drugs."

Nixon's goons engaged in break-ins, wiretaps without court orders, character assassination, and other forms of "rat-fucking," as they called it. Apparently no scheme was too far fetched for the rat-fuckers, who plotted to kidnap radical protestors and incapacitate selected individuals by surreptitiously dosing them with LSD. Deputy Attorney General Kleindienst envisioned a time when "concentration camps" might be required for "ideological criminals."

The plumbers honed their skills by sabotaging the peace movement and then set their sights on the Democratic Party and its nominee for president, George McGovern. During the 1972 Democratic Convention in Miami, a Nixon operative arranged for a plane to fly overhead with a large banner that read: "Peace Pot Promiscuity—Vote McGovern." A master at dissembling who first gained political office by shamelessly redbaiting the opposition, Nixon sought to win votes by falsely portraying McGovern as the candidate who favored marijuana legalization. Pot-baiting may have only served to reinforce the bias of those who would have voted to reelect Nixon anyway, but this kind of chicanery underscored the extent to which marijuana remained a volatile symbol in American politics.

Nixon, a heavy drinker, drew a rather fuzzy distinction between marijuana and alcohol. "A person doesn't drink to get drunk . . . A person drinks to have fun, while a person smokes pot to get high," the president told a friend. But the president wasn't having much fun while hitting the bottle during his truncated second term. Addicted to sleeping pills and amphetamines and often soused on liquor, Nixon staggered through the White House in a daze, talking to portraits of past presidents that hung on the walls. As the Watergate scandal escalated, he became increasingly unstable, "a walking box of short-circuits" (in the words of a *Newsweek* reporter), raising serious doubts as to whether Nixon was the right man to have his finger on the nuclear trigger. "If the president had his way, there would have been nuclear war each week," Secretary of State Henry Kissinger grumbled.

Richard Nixon resigned in disgrace in August 1974, but the drug war he set in motion would become a mainstay of American politics. One of Nixon's parting gifts to the American people was the Drug Enforcement Administration (DEA), the most powerful and costly narcotics control apparatus ever assembled. Created by presidential fiat in 1973, the DEA recruited personnel from various government agencies, including several dozen former CIA spooks and numerous narcs from the corruption-ridden (and now defunct) BNDD. By the mid-1970s, the DEA had some 10,000 agents stationed throughout the world.

Busting drug rings was the ostensible purpose of the DEA, but right from the start the superagency performed various functions that exceeded its mandate. When Lieutenant Colonel Oliver North needed bagmen to transfer cash during the Iran-contra weapons scam of the 1980s, DEA agents were readily available. And when the CIA needed protection for anti-Communist "freedom fighters" neck-deep in the narcotics trade, the DEA dutifully looked the other way.

During the Vietnam War, the CIA allied itself with various tribal warlords in the mountainous Golden Triangle region (which included parts of Burma, Laos, and Thailand), where opium was the most lucrative cash crop. Instead of pressuring the warlords to forsake the drug business, the CIA provided them with airplanes, helicopters, and other military equipment, which enabled these longtime producers of local opium to greatly increase their poppy acreage; soon they were synthesizing high-grade heroin. In the late 1960s and early 1970s, more than 80 percent of the heroin sold on America's streets came from Southeast Asia. And in a macabre, metaphoric twist, packets of heroin were smuggled to the United States in body bags with dead soldiers returning from Vietnam.

When Allen Ginsberg got wind of the CIA's collaboration with big-time heroin traffickers in Southeast Asia, he started to investigate the issue. He spoke with several former CIA operatives, who confirmed that top U.S.-backed South Vietnamese officials were profiting from the heroin business. Ginsberg shared his findings with Al McCoy, author of the soon-to-be-published book *The Politics of Heroin in Southeast Asia*, which meticulously documented (through numerous on-the-record interviews with participants in the heroin trade) the sordid history of U.S. government involvement in illegal opium trafficking. When Ginsberg tried to interest *The New York Times* in the story, foreign affairs columnist C. L. Sulzberger told him that he was "full of beans."*

By the spring of 1971, U.S. media were reporting a significant heroin problem among GIs fighting overseas. Some accounts indicated that 25 percent of American troops stationed in Vietnam were doing smack. The Nixon administration announced that the use of heroin by U.S. servicemen in Vietnam had reached "crisis proportions" and vowed to intensify the war on drugs.

Marijuana was also easy to come by in Vietnam.† American GIs smoked weed en masse to deal with the mind-bending pressures of being in a combat zone, where atrocities and accidental deaths were commonplace and, as Michael Herr wrote, "It was a privilege just to be afraid." Among soldiers, joints were traded for tobacco cigarettes at a one-for-one rate. Others used rifle butts as bongs—a real smoking gun!—to inhale potent strains of *Cannabis sativa* that grew in the Vietnamese highlands. Reefers laced with opium, known as "o-jays," were also cheap, plentiful, and widely used by GIs.

As many as three out of four American servicemen tried cannabis during their tour of duty, and three out of ten were regular marijuana smokers. "Even in combat situations and on week-long patrols in the jungle, we smoked pot several times a day," a machine-gunner recalled. His experience was not unusual. A Congressional Medal of Honor winner said he was stoned on marijuana the night he fought off two waves of Vietcong soldiers and earned America's highest military honor.

Ubiquitous marijuana use among American troops in Vietnam was ironic given that the U.S. Army Chemical Corps had tried to develop THC into a battlefield weapon. With so many grunts smoking grass and tripping on psychedelics, an authentic subculture took root in the trenches, reinforced by the male bonding ritual of passing a joint, water pipe, or rifle butt. For some soldiers, smoking marijuana was a political statement as well as a coping mechanism.

---

* Sulzberger (a member of the family that published and owned controlling interest in the New York Times Co.) later apologized to Ginsberg. "Indeed you were right," Sulzberger acknowledged in a letter to Ginsberg dated April 11, 1978. Ginsberg provided a copy of this letter to the author.

† Cannabis seeds, leaves, stalks, and flower tops had long been used for medicinal purposes in Vietnam and other Southeast Asian countries to treat pain, nausea, skin disorders, burns, constipation, premature aging, blood poisoning, and to stimulate the production of mother's milk.

"Vietnamese pot became our path to sanity, our lifeline," a veteran helicopter pilot confided. "It was a simple yet very effective way of maintaining peace of mind amidst the chaos of the conflict—an escape from the horrendous reality of our daily lives." Many U.S. soldiers found marijuana, which inhibits dream and nightmare recollection, to be the safest and most effective treatment for what would later be diagnosed as posttraumatic stress disorder, or PTSD.

Seeing Is Believing

With the United States on the verge of defeat in Indochina, a Senate subcommittee headed by James Eastland held hearings on the "Marijuana-Hashish Epidemic and Its Impact on U.S. Security." The Yankee pussyfooters may have been willing to write off Vietnam as a failure, but Senator Eastland and the hard-line political forces he represented were not about to raise the white flag of surrender in the war on drugs. An unabashed racist and reactionary, Eastland had previously accused the civil rights movement of promoting the destruction of "the American system of government" and the "mongrelization of the white race." The Mississippi Democrat decried the use of marijuana as immoral and warned that "subversive groups played a significant role in the spread of this epidemic," which began, according to Eastland, at the University of California in Berkeley during the Free Speech Movement uprising. Nothing less than the fate of Western civilization was hanging in the balance. "If the epidemic is not rolled back," the senator drawled, "our society may be taken over by 'marijuana culture'—a culture motivated by the consuming lust for self-gratification, and lacking any higher moral guidance. Such a society could not long endure."

Convened in the spring of 1974, the Eastland hearings were explicitly designed to discredit the work of the Shafer Commission. Two dozen witnesses weighed in against marijuana, which was said to cause brain damage, lung disease, broken chromosomes, birth defects, impotence, sterility, obesity, impaired immune function, social backwardness, and an insatiable hunger for hard drugs. Only those who supported the strict prohibition of cannabis were invited to testify. "We make no apology for the one-sided nature of our hearings—they were deliberately planned that way," Eastland asserted.

The star of the show was Gabriel Nahas, professor of anesthesiology at Columbia University and a consultant to the United Nations Commission on Narcotics. Nahas claimed to have uncovered "the first direct evidence of cellular damage" in humans from marijuana, a dangerous herb, in his view, which "weakens the body's immune defenses." Habitual pot smokers are therefore more prone to cancer and infectious diseases, according to Nahas, who purported to show causal links between THC and various clinical symptoms, including "cerebral atrophy." Nahas wrote two alarmist books, *Keep off the Grass* and *Deceptive Weed,* which advocated for tight controls over marijuana and its users "before it's too late for America." But it was Nahas's own research methodology that proved to be deceptive and his work was the target of scathing criticism in periodicals such as the *New England Journal of Medicine.* His work was so shoddy that even the U.S. National Institute on Drug Abuse (NIDA), always hankering for dirt on cannabis, declined to continue his research grants.

Nahas maintained that the subjective effects of marijuana—unlike the effects of caffeine, alcohol, and tobacco—are inimical to successful societies. "Hashish addiction," as he saw it, played a major role in the long period of decline in the Arab world, an era marked by intellectual and cultural stagnation. The abuse of cannabis was to blame for this historical impasse—not poverty, illiteracy, colonialism, religious fundamentalism, and/or government repression. During his testimony before Eastland's subcommittee, Nahas raised the specter of a lethargic, zombified populace perpetually stoned on pot, a "stupefying drug" that posed a dire threat to the American way of life. Several other Eastland witnesses extrapolated on the dangers of marijuana-induced "amotivational syndrome," a sluggish, apathetic, and unproductive condition that allegedly afflicted chronic pot smokers.

Antimarijuana zealots invoked the amotivational syndrome to explain adolescent indolence and indifference toward conventional goals and values. Eastland's experts had a field day denigrating marijuana as a drop-out drug, and, by inference, the entire counterculture of drop-outs who lost the desire to work and compete in a go-gettum, dog-eat-dog world. Therein lay the basis for the stereotype of the lazy, pot-smoking stoner, the slacker couch potato bumbling through the day. Dr. Andrew Weil took issue with the prevailing dogma when he suggested that "amotivation [is] a cause of heavy marijuana smoking rather than the reverse."

Founded in 1973, the National Institute on Drug Abuse poured money into researching the amotivational syndrome and every other negative claim about cannabis made at the Eastland hearings. And time after time, the new evidence against marijuana fell apart upon close scrutiny.* The confabulations,

* Case in point: A 1974 rhesus monkey study by Dr. Robert Heath at Tulane University—trumpeted during the Eastland inquisition and touted for years as evidence that cannabis

distortions, and utter mendacities promoted by the drug-war bureaucracy comprised "a kind of latter-day *Malleus Maleficarum,*" as Dr. Lester Grinspoon put it, against heathen hemp. According to well-publicized tall tales, smoking marijuana made men grow large breasts and rendered one unable to resist homosexual advances. The compilation of charges was so over-the-top that pro-pot activists for a laugh began circulating the published transcript of the Eastland proceedings, which included an appendix with recipes for marijuana edibles (brownies, chili, banana bread, etc.).

Harry Anslinger, the retired narcotics chief, and a lot of other straight-laced folks didn't get the joke. Blind, hard of hearing, and dependent on morphine to ease the pain of his last days, Anslinger died of heart failure on November 14, 1975, at age eighty-three. Once a powerful figure in Washington, he and his life's work had become the target of public ridicule. Since he demonized the weed and led the campaign to make it illegal, marijuana went from being an obscure plant that few Americans had ever heard of to the most widely used illicit substance in the United States.

As the social consensus around cannabis crumbled in the 1960s, the regime of truth Anslinger had assiduously constructed gave way to a regime of confusion. Anslinger's outrageous lies about homicidal hopheads may have run their course, but misinformation and omission would remain major weapons in the federal government's ongoing crusade against cannabis.

"No one is more controllable than a confused person; no society is more controllable than a confused society," wrote psychologist Anne Wilson Schaef. Beholden to pseudo-objective standards, mainstream journalists typically played the "on the one hand, on the other" game while covering the marijuana story, giving weight to both sides while neglecting to evaluate the veracity of

---

damages the brain—was exposed as a textbook case of scientific fraud. (Like UCLA's Louis "Jolly" West, who coined the phrase "amotivational syndrome," Heath had been a contract employee of the CIA's MK-ULTRA drug research program.) Shackled in airtight gas masks, Heath's monkeys were forced to inhale the equivalent of 63 high-potency marijuana cigarettes in five minutes. Lo and behold, the primates suffered brain damage from suffocation and carbon monoxide poisoning, but Heath attributed the results to marijuana toxicity. His findings were never replicated. Several studies, including an experiment involving rhesus monkeys at the National Center for Toxicological Research (a division of NIH), repudiated Heath's work. No claim of brain damage caused by cannabis was ever proven. On the contrary, numerous peer-reviewed scientific reports would demonstrate that cannabinoid compounds are neuroprotective and stimulate neurogenesis (brain cell growth) in mammals (Novak, *High Culture*, p. 205; Mike Gray, *Drug Crazy*, p. 177; Iversen, *The Science of Marijuana*, p. 183; and Conrad, *Hemp: Lifeline*, p. 156).

either until nothing seemed clear. Even if one didn't believe all the negative charges that were leveled against cannabis, the steady drumbeat of deceptions conveyed the overall impression that there must be something bad about the weed.

Whereas Anslinger systematically blocked all scientific research into cannabis, NIDA's regime of confusion pursued a more selective strategy. NIDA splurged on studies that sought to highlight harmful aspects of cannabis but impeded studies of the herb's potential benefits. The U.S. government would spend billions of dollars in an effort to establish the dangers of marijuana so that the DEA and local narcotics police could justify the arrest of millions of pot smokers.

Despite NIDA's institutional bias, scientists in the United States and elsewhere made some amazing discoveries while assessing the safety profile of cannabis. In 1974, U.S. government-funded researchers at the Medical College of Virginia found that injections of cannabinoid compounds "slowed the growth of lung cancers, breast cancers and a virus-induced leukemia in laboratory mice, and prolonged their lives by as much as 36 percent." In the only news story that mentioned this study, *The Washington Post* reported that the "active chemical agent in marijuana . . . may also suppress the immunity reaction that causes rejection of organ transplants."

Rather than eliciting hosannas of joy and serious support for follow-up studies, the discovery of the antitumoral properties of cannabis was suppressed by federal bureaucrats. The war on drugs took precedence over—and undermined—the war on cancer. A quarter century would pass before Dr. Manual Guzmán of Complutense University in Madrid, Spain, and scientists at the Hebrew University in Jerusalem rediscovered the cancer-fighting qualities of THC and other cannabinoids.

The prestigious *New England Journal of Medicine* reported in 1975 that THC successfully minimized chemotherapy-induced nausea and vomiting in twenty cancer patients after standard antiemetics were found to be ineffective. Additional therapeutic possibilities were postulated by Dr. Raj K. Razdan, a senior scientist at Arthur D. Little, which had been contracted by the U.S. Army Chemical Corps to develop THC into a battlefield weapon. Razdan, the first chemist to create a water-soluble version of THC, found that certain THC analogs showed promise for treating depression and as an anesthetic adjunct. Dr. Tod Mikuriya was convinced that if therapeutic-oriented marijuana studies had not been discouraged by federal authorities, numerous medical uses would already have been validated.

In 1975, Mikuriya participated in a NIDA-sponsored conference that brought together leading marijuana scientists, including Raphael Mechoulam, the Israeli chemist who isolated and synthesized THC a decade earlier. Mechoulam predicted a bright future for cannabis-based medicines. He suggested that within ten years marijuana-derived meds might replace 10 to 20 percent of all prescription pharmaceuticals—and that in time perhaps 40 percent of marketed medicines would contain a cannabis extract or a synthetic cannabinoid compound. The scientists unanimously agreed that more resources should be devoted to exploring the medical potential of cannabis. But NIDA catechism maintained that marijuana is a drug of abuse, not a drug of healing, and promising leads fell by the wayside.

The following year, Robert C. Randall, a young college professor living in Washington, D.C., made medical and legal history by successfully suing the federal government for access to cannabis, the only remedy that controlled his glaucoma. Randall was twenty-four when a doctor told him the awful news that he would be completely blind in both eyes before his thirtieth birthday because of irreversible damage caused by this incurable inflammatory disorder. Glaucoma, the leading cause of blindness in the United States (afflicting two million Americans and more than sixty million people worldwide), occurs when fluid builds up within the eyeball, triggering abnormally high intraocular pressure that injures the optic nerve. Randall tried surgery; it didn't help. Nor did any prescribed pharmaceuticals, which all had adverse side effects. His eyesight continued to deteriorate. His prospects were—literally—quite dim.

Then, one evening in 1973, Randall smoked a joint that a friend had given him. After a few puffs, Randall noticed while staring out the window that the tricolor halos he usually saw around a nearby streetlight had disappeared. Optical halos were one of the telltale symptoms of his disease and—voilà!—they were gone. Immediately he made the connection: "You smoke pot, your eye strain goes away. Ganja is good for you." He began a program of self-medication, using marijuana on a regular basis—with positive results. Regular checkups with his eye doctor confirmed that cannabis significantly reduced his intraocular pressure. Randall had serendipitously discovered that marijuana, a plant millions of people smoked for fun, was "more than a recreational drug." The "goofy relaxant" turned out to be "a critical medication" for his illness.

But Randall was not always able to obtain a sufficient supply of his herbal medicine from the black market. To tide him over through the dry spells, he grew a few pot plants in his yard. Upon returning from a summer vacation in 1975, he found his plants missing, his home ransacked, a search warrant on his kitchen table, and a note from the D.C. police demanding that he turn himself in. He was busted.

Randall could have pled guilty to misdemeanor possession, paid a fine, and gotten on with his life. Instead he became the Rosa Parks of the medi-

Robert Randall, the Rosa Parks of the medical-marijuana movement, made legal and medical history when he successfully sued the U.S government for access to cannabis, the only remedy that controlled his glaucoma
(Courtesy of Alice O'Leary)

cal marijuana movement. Rather than copping a plea, he chose to fight the criminal charges on the basis of "medical necessity," a legal principle that in theory justifies breaking the law when obeying it would cause greater harm. The only problem with this defense strategy was that it had never worked in a U.S. courtroom.

Randall's search for allies soon led to the Washington, D.C., office of NORML, the marijuana reform group led by attorney Keith Stroup. The head of NORML pledged his support and pointed Randall toward several contacts within the U.S. government. One of them gave Randall a copy of a recent NIDA report that referred to a 1971 study by UCLA ophthalmologist Robert Hepler, who had conducted government-sponsored research to ascertain marijuana's effect on the eye so that police could identify illicit drug users. Dr. Hepler failed to detect pupil dilation, but he observed a significant decrease in eye pressure in his test subjects. He proceeded to treat several glaucoma patients with cannabis and he reported his findings in the *American Journal of Ophthalmology*. Randall was stunned when he realized that U.S. officials had solid evidence of marijuana's efficacy as a treatment for glaucoma.

To prepare for his case, Randall underwent ten days of rigorous testing at UCLA under the supervision of Dr. Hepler, who concluded that large doses of smoked marijuana effectively lowered Randall's intraocular pressure into a safe range. In a sworn affidavit Hepler asserted that without marijuana Randall would go blind. During a two-day nonjury trial in D.C. Superior Court, the defendant argued that any sane person would break the law to save his or her eyesight. Judge James A. Washington agreed and Randall was acquitted. The widely publicized verdict established an important legal precedent. "Medical evidence suggests that the prohibition [of marijuana] is not well-founded," Judge Washington wrote in a carefully crafted decision, adding: "Reports from the [Shafer] Commission and the Department of Health, Education and Welfare have concluded that there is no scientific evidence of any harm attendant upon the use of marijuana. According to the most recent HEW study, research has failed to establish any substantial physical or mental impairment caused by marijuana. Reports of chromosome damage, reduced immunity to disease, and psychosis are unconfirmed; actual evidence is to the contrary."

But Randall's groundbreaking acquittal in and of itself did not solve the problem of obtaining a steady, legal supply of cannabis. Randall learned from one of his doctors that the U.S. government grew marijuana on an experimental farm at the University of Mississippi. His dander up, Randall filed a petition demanding that Uncle Sam provide him with enough marijuana to meet his medical needs. The federal government reluctantly agreed to his request, then dragged its feet when pressed to follow through. At every step of the way, Randall encountered bureaucratic resistance. First he was told he could use marijuana only in a hospital under a doctor's supervision. He said no way. Then he was told that he had to keep his pot at home in a 750-pound safe. Yeah right. When Randall tried to get a letter from the DEA indicating that he was legally allowed to smoke marijuana—in case he was ever stopped by police—the DEA refused.

What irked the feds most of all was Randall's penchant for singing the praises of marijuana during frequent TV and press interviews. National and international news coverage unhinged the bureaucrats, who threatened to cut off his allotment of cannabis. Every month, Randall was supposed to receive three hundred prerolled joints in a tin canister courtesy of Uncle Sam's pot farm at the University of Mississippi. Unwilling to be silenced, he vowed to go to court again, if necessary, to defend his First Amendment rights. "Having won, why go mum? There are sick people to save," Randall explained. "Better to trust my fellow citizens and shout into the darkness than rely on a devious government dedicated to a fraudulent prohibition."

A living refutation of the amotivational syndrome, Randall felt it was important to speak out and do all that he could to help others who might benefit from medical marijuana. His indefatigable efforts compelled the Food and

Drug Administration to establish a special "Compassionate" IND [Investigational New Drug] Program, whereby desperately ill patients, if they were very persistent and lucky, could gain access to government-grown cannabis. For twenty-five years until his untimely death in 2001, Randall smoked ten legal marijuana cigarettes a day. And he never went blind.

Rasta Vibration

In mountain caves overlooking Kingston, the capital of Jamaica, skinny old men with long dreadlocks brew their "culture drink," a ganja-infused blend of medicinal roots and herbs. A majority of Jamaicans consume cannabis in one form or another—smoking it, applying it as a topical ointment or salve, ingesting it as tea, cooking it in soup and other dishes. Used both curatively and prophylactically by Jamaicans of all ages, marijuana is a common household remedy for arthritis, stomach ailments, insomnia, and many other troubles. Some island residents claim that ganja "brainifies" them, that it's good for concentration and problem solving. They medicate to meditate.

Cannabis was introduced to Jamaica by indentured servants from India who had been brought over by the British during the mid-nineteenth century (hence the use of the Hindi word *ganja*). Legislation banning the cultivation, distribution, and consumption of marijuana in Jamaica was imposed by colonial decree in 1913. Fifty years later, Jamaica became independent of British rule, but ganja remained illegal and the police continually harassed the poor, mostly for their flagrant consumption of marijuana.

Over the years, the greatest police brutality was reserved for the Rastafari, an Old Testament–oriented Christian mystical sect that uses ganja for religious purposes. The Rastas claimed that the "wisdom weed," as they referred to marijuana, grew on the grave of King Solomon. They cited biblical passages to justify their belief that cannabis is the Tree of Life, a divine herb that cleanses the spirit and brings people closer to the earth, to God, to each other. According to Rasta lore, the holy smoke helps the righteous attain a state of "iration," the highest level of existence where no falsehood intrudes. Rastafarianism emphasizes universal brotherhood, moral rectitude, and a natural "ital" lifestyle, which entails strict dietary rules and abstention from alcohol.

The Rastas dreamed of returning to Africa, their ancestral homeland, where dagga was traditionally revered as a "plant of insight." Vehemently opposed to all forms of injustice, they viewed Western society as the modern kingdom of Babylon. They wanted no part of a corrupt political and economic "shitstem" that was built upon the backs of the oppressed. One day Babylon will fall, they prophesied—until then the quirky Rastas refused to cut their hair, which they twisted into long, matted dreadlocks.

Word of the Rasta creed would travel far beyond that small Caribbean island thanks primarily to Robert Nesta Marley, the legendary reggae performer. A high school dropout, Marley and a few friends formed a band called the Wailers—so named because they wailed for the suffering masses. Bob Marley spoke for the voiceless, he sang for the earth's dispossessed. Just when the momentum of the Sixties seemed to be petering out, he emerged from wretched circumstance to become the Third World's first international superstar. Marley was huge, and his influence did not diminish after he died of cancer at age thirty-six in 1981.

A handsome, Christ-like figure, his hair twined in natty tresses, Marley introduced reggae to a worldwide audience. He was the Rasta apostle, a pot-puffing "buffalo soldier," who urged everyone to "get up, stand up" for their rights. His songs paid homage to black freedom fighters and other revolutionaries. Soothingly mesmeric yet seething with ethno-political attitude, reggae was protest music for the global underclass. It was also marijuana music. Reggae's slow-moving cadence resonated with the laid-back attentiveness of ganja. The herb helped people down-regulate from Babylon speed.

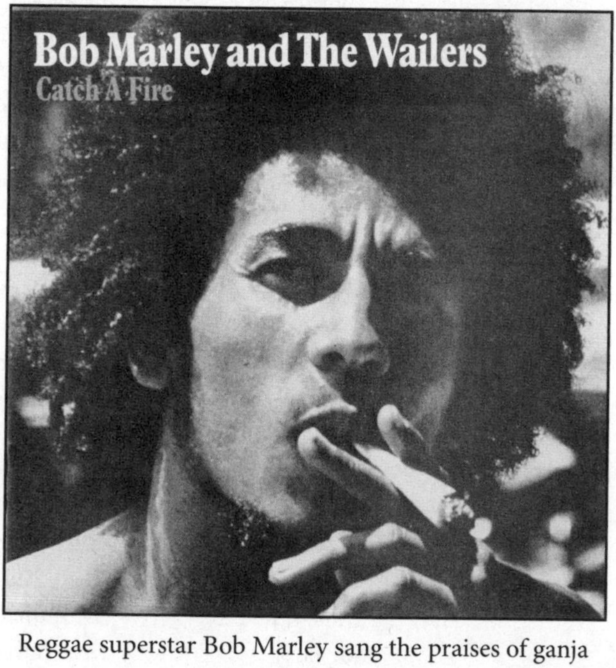

Reggae superstar Bob Marley sang the praises of ganja

Marley recorded several songs in praise of cannabis and was often photographed smoking a spliff, a large, conical cannabis cigar. He preached a kind of stoned liberation theology, rejecting the hedonistic use of marijuana while affirming its importance as a daily spiritual sacrament in keeping with his Rastafarian faith. "Herb is the healin' of the nation," said Marley, who once remarked to a Canadian journalist: "You mean they can tell God that it's not legal?"

In the early 1970s, a U.S. research team went to Jamaica to assess the long-term impact of marijuana use on the native population. Sponsored by NIDA, this three-year multidisciplinary project focused on chronic ganja consumption by Jamaican workers and their families. The NIDA study, involving a comprehensive battery of psychological and physiological tests, found no evidence of harmful changes in brain function or personality in Jamaicans who smoked pot as part of their everyday routine. There were no significant differences between ganja smokers and nonsmokers in terms of perceptual-motor functioning, conceptual capability, social skills, or any other area analyzed by the American researchers. Written by anthropologists Vera Rubin and Lambros Comitas, the lengthy NIDA report concluded that the chronic use of potent cannabis is not toxic to the human mind or body. The authors were unable to ascertain any causal link between marijuana and psychosis (ganja smokers were underrepresented in Jamaican mental hospitals) or pot smoking and criminal behavior, except insofar as possessing ganja itself was a crime. Nor did the authors find any evidence that daily marijuana smoking caused physical addiction or severe withdrawal symptoms when cannabis use was abruptly terminated. Instead, the NIDA investigators discerned that ganja smokers drank much less alcohol than nonsmokers, lending credence to the notion that widespread marijuana use was the main reason for significantly lower levels of alcoholism in Jamaica than anywhere else in the Caribbean.

NIDA's Jamaica study also called into question claims that marijuana caused amotivational syndrome. Jamaican fisherman smoked marijuana to ward off fatigue while at sea and they noticed that their night vision improved when they got stoned, enabling them to steer boats better in the dark. Scientists who investigated these claims found that the fishermen could see better at night for the same reason that Robert Randall was able to control his glaucoma with cannabis—the anti-inflammatory herb greatly reduces pressure on the eyeball, thereby improving nocturnal sight.

Three out of four Jamaican laborers consumed ganja on a regular basis. Almost without exception cannabis smokers asserted that ganja energized them and eased the burden of tedious, repetitive work. Given the demographics of ganja smoking on the island, Jamaica's antimarijuana laws served as a vehicle for establishing and maintaining social control over an exploited labor force—step out of line and you go to jail for sparking a spliff. Pot prohibition in Jamaica was in essence a form of class warfare.

NIDA sponsored two other major long-term-use studies during the 1970s—an analysis of chronic cannabis consumption in Costa Rica and hashish smoking in Greece. Again researchers found no palpable harm inflicted by the resinous herb. Neuropsychological and personality tests failed to reveal significant differences between cannabis smokers and nonsmokers.

Flummoxed by these reassuring reports, NIDA officials dug in their heels and downplayed the significance of the three U.S. government-funded studies that were supposed to provide definitive answers to crucial questions about the long-term use of marijuana. Instead of breathing a sigh of relief that hundreds of millions of cannabis users around the world were not putting themselves at serious risk, NIDA continued to fixate on presumed adverse effects. Although proof of harm to adults remained elusive, NIDA bureaucrats assumed that rigorous scientific inquiry would show marijuana consumption by pregnant women threatened the well-being of their children. So NIDA financed yet another investigation in Jamaica.

During the 1980s, Melanie Dreher and her colleagues at the University of Massachusetts Nursing Education Department undertook a long-term "longitudinal" study to evaluate the health of Jamaican infants and children whose mothers ingested ganja during pregnancy and continued to use cannabis while breast-feeding. Many Jamaican women smoked ganja to quell morning sickness, lessen labor pains, and speed up the birth process by facilitating uterine contractions. "All the mothers considered the effects of marijuana on nausea and fatigue to be good for both themselves and their infants," Dreher reported. Jamaican women claimed that "smoking and drinking ganja was good for the mother and the baby because it relieved the nausea of pregnancy, increased appetite, gave them strength to work [and] helped them relax and sleep at night." Older women recommended that newborns be washed with ganja leaves. Cannabis was sometimes added to baby's milk or juice to ease infant distress and to help babies sleep. Jamaican mothers prepared ganja teas and tonics for their children to "make them smarter and stronger," U.S. researchers were told. Some Jamaican mothers drank marijuana tea to alleviate postpartum depression.

In her NIDA study, Dreher matched thirty cannabis-using pregnant women by age and socioeconomic status with thirty pregnant nonusers. Dreher's team, using several standard tests and measurements, compared the course of these pregnancies and their neonatal outcomes. The ganja moms and their kids did not appear to be harmed by marijuana exposure in the womb; there were no physical abnormalities, no cognitive deficits, and no neonatal complications; nor were there any discernible disparities between the three-day-old babies of mothers who used marijuana and the three-day-old nonexposed babies.

Dreher was surprised to discover that after one month the babies of mothers who had used ganja throughout their pregnancy (whether nauseous or not) were actually healthier, more alert, and less fussy than one-month-old infants whose mothers did not take cannabis. Test results for one-month-old infants whose mothers also ingested ganja while breast-feeding were "even more striking," according to Dreher. Heavily exposed babies were more socially responsive and more autonomically stable than babies not exposed to cannabis through their mother's milk: "alertness was higher, motor and autonomic systems more robust, they were less irritable, less likely to demonstrate imbalance of tone, needed less examiner facilitation . . . than the neonates of non-using mothers." When all the children were retested at ages four and five, Dreher's team "found absolutely no differences" between the children of ganja moms and the children of nonusers.*

The idea that marijuana was safe, even in pregnancy, to mother and child—and might actually confer benefits—was blasphemous to keepers of the NIDA flame. Dreher's findings cut against the grain of widely held assumptions in the United States, where government officials, opinion leaders, and many a Jane and John Doe viewed smoking the illicit weed during pregnancy as way beyond the pale—harmful, deviant, appalling, something to shun at all cost. Although the upshot of Dreher's study, indicating no negative impact from prenatal marijuana use, was borne out by subsequent epidemiological investi-

* In 1993, the year before Dreher's controversial report was published in the journal *Pediatrics*, archaeologists discovered evidence of a young woman using hashish to alleviate labor pains in ancient Israel. Additional archaeological and written records attest to the use of cannabis as a widespread, cross-culture remedy for various obstetric and gynecological issues. As early as the sixteenth century BC, an Egyptian papyrus indicated that cannabis was used to aid the birthing process. An old Chinese herbal text prescribed hempseed to hasten delivery and to promote lactation for suckling infants. The Sotho women of Africa used marijuana for similar reasons. Ditto for women in India, according to the Indian Hemp Drugs Commission, which noted that "gunjah" was a traditional remedy for menstrual problems. Midwives in medieval Europe were also well acquainted with medicinal hemp. "Those women who have cramps in the womb, for them hemp should be burned and held to the nose," Tabernaemontaus recommended in 1564. The use of cannabis to treat menstrual cramps and to reduce labor pains without anesthesia was cited in several European and North American medical texts, including the 1854 *Dispensatory of the United States*.

gation, NIDA gave her the cold shoulder when she sought support for follow-up research.

Even before the U.S. government was forced to acknowledge marijuana's utility for controlling glaucoma, American midwives had begun to resurrect the age-old practice of hemp-assisted childbirth. Haight-Ashbury veteran Ina May Gaskin is the woman most responsible for catalyzing the modern home-birth movement and the renaissance of midwifery in the United States. Gaskin recognized that cannabis worked wonders for hyperemesis gravidarum, a severe form of morning sickness characterized by intense nausea and frequent vomiting, malnutrition, and weight loss during pregnancy—a condition suffered by 1 to 2 percent of pregnant women globally. During the early 1970s, Gaskin and several other "roots women" (as Jamaicans refer to conscientious, down-to-earth, ganja-smoking mothers) established an on-site midwifery clinic and training center on the Farm, a large counterculture commune located in the backwoods of Tennessee. To the midwives on the Farm, cannabis seemed like an eminently sensible option as a birthing asset, and the herb was used safely and discreetly for this purpose.

The possibility that a woman could have painless labor became an idée fixe of H. L. ("Doc") Humes, a literary wunderkind and MIT science prodigy who developed some intriguing theories about cannabis. When his wife was giving birth at their home on July 4, 1977, they tried an experiment involving marijuana, breathing exercises, and massage. Humes gave her some pot to inhale just before each contraction and this helped her immensely.

Marijuana is "among the most forgiving medicines we know," said Humes, who described cannabis as a "neurological laxative" that "acts to surface anxiety which the user holds within himself." Doc touted the weed as the best remedy for stress, "the necessary medicine for the nation's anxiety-tension problem." "America is so sick," he declared, "and cannabis is the specific medicine for the disease that afflicts us." *

Ganja's biphasic qualities allowed smokers to "equilibriate" the nervous

* Chronic "anxiety-tension," Humes explained, "is a state of general blockage that shows up most obviously at an individual's 'weakest link,' so it can have a wide variety of physical and emotional symptoms, as well as being generally debilitating . . . Most of the common elements from which people suffer are really symptoms of anxiety-tension, including headache, backache, insomnia, fatigue, irritability, GI disturbances such as constipation and ulcers, overweight, arthritis, and so on. Anxiety-tension has also been very clearly implicated in more deadly disorders such as high blood pressure, heart disease, cancer proneness, and premature aging . . . Depression is frequently a symptom of anxiety-tension" (H. L. Humes, "Notes on Painless Detoxification from Narcotics Addiction," unpublished manuscript).

system. Consumed in appropriate quantities, the herb could calm the hyper or invigorate the sluggish. "The medical use of cannabis depends precisely on managing its psychoactive properties," Doc counseled. "In heavy dosage, it functions like a hypnotic. In a light dosage it functions like an illuminant." Humes saw early on that the widespread "recreational use of cannabis is also a form of self-medication," even if most marijuana smokers did not acknowledge this to themselves. He lamented the fact that hundreds of thousands of young people are arrested each year for using the most efficacious and least harmful medication available to cope with the stress of living in the modern world.

In Your Face

The mid-1970s were boom years for the marijuana trade, especially in Florida. The southern part of the state was a frequent landing zone for air and maritime consignments of Colombian and Jamaican grass. Despite scores of pot seizures, the DEA barely made a dent in the steady flow of cannabis ferried via "mother ships" (as they were called in smuggler's parlance) to prearranged locations off the Florida coast. Filled with bales of grass, these big sea vessels transferred their cargo onto a fleet of speedy hydroplanes that could outrace Coast Guard cutters. The mother ships then returned to their source country for more marijuana and another U.S.-bound delivery.

Interdiction strategies were destined to fail because the political legislation that the DEA sought to enforce was less powerful than the economic law of supply and demand that made the smuggling and distribution of cannabis such a highly lucrative venture. A pound of primo weed that wholesaled for $25 in Latin America changed hands for $175 in Arizona or $250 in Massachusetts—a 1,000 percent markup from the producer's price and a 100 percent rise above the top price in the late 1960s. Every time narcs busted a marijuana smuggling ring, they unintentionally subsidized all the other traffickers they didn't catch. With prohibition propping up prices, the profits in pot were so vast that the DEA could not possibly keep the herb out of circulation.

The early pot entrepreneurs were for the most part independent adventurers and hippie types who liked to smoke grass and maneuver below the radar. Few of them had criminal records. They supplied intermittent kilos of cannabis to a counterculture constituency. Back then smuggling was primarily a "little guy" business, though some astute operators amassed huge fortunes. While they built their networks separately, the more successful traffickers evolved similar techniques for moving weed, setting up stash houses and elaborate communication systems, concealing their activities behind dummy companies, and washing tainted cash.

Given the incredible sums at stake, the cannabusiness underground not surprisingly began to attract professional gangsters, spies-for-hire, ex-cons, and other shady players who viewed the weed strictly as a way to make a buck. Tempted by quick profits, a Miami-based cadre of anti-Castro Cubans with CIA and Mob connections commandeered planes and boats with illicit payloads of grass and coke, rationalizing that the money would help the anti-Communist cause. If a Bay of Pigs veteran got caught during a drug run to Florida, his ties to U.S. intelligence, erstwhile or current, usually served as a get-out-of-jail-free card.

The Mafia definitely had its hooks in the marijuana trade, but nobody could dominate the market sufficiently to manipulate prices. Decentralized, expanding, and forever in flux, marijuana commerce was wide open to anyone with a talent for logistics and a yen for serious risk-taking. Thomas King Forçade, the consummate pot smuggler who fancied himself a hippie Robin Hood, became notorious in underground circles for his daring exploits. Discharged from the U.S. Air Force after convincing his superiors that he was mentally unbalanced, he proceeded to fly copious quantities of grass into the United States from Mexico and Colombia. On one occasion, he was spotted transferring nine tons of weed into a camper, but Forçade, a veteran hot-rodder, eluded the cops who chased him into an Everglades swamp.

Born Kenneth Gary Goodson in Phoenix, this pale, slightly built man with a dark beard and wispy mustache earned a college degree in business administration from the University of Utah. Then he changed his name to Forçade (an intentional play on "façade") and reinvented himself as a slow-talking, long-haired hipster who drove a black Cadillac with wing tips and a plexiglass bubble. Brilliant, mercurial, and self-consciously mysterious, Forçade used the wealth he accrued from smuggling to unleash a frontal attack on marijuana prohibition.

In 1969, Forçade moved to New York City and took over the Underground Press Syndicate (UPS), which served as a clearinghouse for hundreds of radical journals and college newspapers that shared articles about cannabis, psychedelic drugs, youth culture, the antiwar movement, identity politics, government corruption, and other pertinent topics. UPS affiliates in several cities were busted by police who said they found marijuana on the premises (often true, sometimes planted). After cops roughed up peaceful pot smokers in the Los Angeles area, the *Free Press* responded with a front-page editorial that listed the names of local narcotics agents.

Forçade launched his most ambitious media project in 1974—a slick, glossy publication wholly devoted to recreational drugs. By this time, the surge of marijuana-enhanced optimism among American youth that characterized the previous decade had given way to widespread disillusionment. Many activists felt burned out. Cynicism and distrust of political authority were rampant in America—an enduring contribution of the Sixties—but elite power structures remained entrenched. "The movement was over and I needed something to keep from killing myself out of boredom," Forçade remarked. So he started *High Times* magazine.

Right from the get-go, *High Times* was a runaway success, even though its publisher was a fugitive marijuana smuggler who dodged the limelight. Forçade's name did not appear on the masthead. Subscribers were assured that the magazine's mailing list would be kept under lock and key and would not be shared with anyone else "under any circumstances, period." Within three years, the circulation of this uppity monthly grew to 400,000 with a pass-along readership of 4 million. The phenomenal growth of *High Times* was a testament to Forçade's intuitive understanding that among America's 25 million pot smokers there were many who identified with "a vast underground society [which] had its own myths and folklore, social etiquette and pecking order, songs and language, heroes and humor," as Albert Goldman, a frequent *High Times* contributor, put it.

High Times emerged from this underground milieu and parted the curtain on a labyrinthine world of pot pilots, dope lawyers, gourmet ganja growers, stoned mountain trekkers, and big-time adventurers who journeyed to exotic places—from the Himalayas to the Amazon—in search of the best mind-altering drugs on the planet. In addition to tantalizing stories that romanticized smuggling, *High Times* ran interviews with pot-smoking celebrities such as Bob Marley, William S. Burroughs, and Hunter S. Thompson, along with a list of fluctuating black-market prices for different kinds of cannabis in each issue. "Highwitness News," another regular feature, kept readers abreast of late-breaking developments about the DEA, pot busts, drug-dealing cops, scientific research, and efforts to relegalize the herb. Forçade's magazine also included a full-color centerfold of an exotic psychoactive specimen—usually a prodigious marijuana bud or gummy morsel of hash. In the years ahead, close-up pictures of various cannabis strains with outrageous *colas* would comprise a unique, visually compelling photobotanical genre.

But *High Times* was not just a reefer rag. Herein lay the basis for the magazine's financial stability. Despite its revolutionary pretensions, *High Times* embraced what sociologist Christopher Lasch described as "the propaganda of commodities"—hawking products and an ethic of conspicuous consumption as a substitute for inner satisfaction. Advertisements for T-shirts, comic books, concert tours, getaway vacations, debugging equipment, rolling papers, and all manner of drug-related paraphernalia (the magazine's bread and butter) brought in several million dollars annually and filled the pages with gaudy images of scantily clad women inviting the reader to enjoy the good life. (How about a penis-shaped water pipe with a babe climbing the stem?) Using sex to make a sale was hardly a departure from mainstream mercantile methodology. Nor did it jive exactly with Seventies New Age spirituality, which also had roots in a precommoditized cannabis subculture. "In this way," wrote alternative press historian David Armstrong, "drugs paradoxically sparked a spiritual renaissance in American life and contributed to its debasement. *High Times* played a leading role in this cultural passion play."

Even though his publication was raking in dough, Forçade continued to smuggle muggles while juggling several projects at once. Many hippie partisans cast a wary eye when the punk scene emerged, but Forçade gave it a thumbs-up, backing *Punk* magazine and bankrolling a documentary of the Sex Pistols' 1978 U.S. rock tour, *DOA* ("Dead on Arrival"). *High Times* ran a photo of Johnny Rotten smoking a joint.

Forçade also collaborated with a radical East Village clique that denounced veteran Yippie impresarios Abbie Hoffman and Jerry Rubin as has-beens, old fogy sellouts. This Yippie breakaway faction engaged in fisticuffs with their opponents and launched unremitting personal attacks against other activists. After Hoffman went underground to avoid facing cocaine charges and Rubin immersed himself in a smorgasbord of New Age therapies, Forçade's acolytes coalesced into a self-styled cannabis liberation squad centered around red-haired Yippie renegade Dana Beal.

Thanks to Forçade, there was always plenty of grass around, and dealing it (via a telephone pot-delivery service or other means) became the primary income source for these hard-core neo-Yippies, who staged occasional rock against racism concerts and pro-pot rallies for the faithful. Based at a brick tenement on 9 Bleecker Street, this unkempt gaggle of marijuana misfits, militants, and street brawlers included the likes of A. J. Weberman, the infamous "garbologist" who popularized the practice of searching through people's trash for journalistic clues, and phone phreak "Captain Crunch," a socially challenged proto-hacker who devised ingenious ways to make free long-distance calls. There was also Aron Kay, a rotund guerrilla prankster with idiot savant tendencies who threw cream pies at right-wing Christian fundamentalists, conservative pundits, lapsed left-wingers, and various public officials. Ex-CIA chief William Colby and *Rolling Stone* publisher Jann Wenner were among those symbolically assassinated by the Yippie pie man.

The New York neo-Yippies had an ultraradical affiliate in Washington, D.C., where Ben Masel, then in his early twenties (and the youngest person to make Nixon's enemies list), mentored a group of teenage activists who called themselves the Outlaws Collective. They lived together at the D.C. Yippie house, an urban commune and crash pad for runaways and street kids. Led by a hyper-capable high school dropout named Steve DeAngelo, the Outlaws became the organizing hub for the annual Fourth of July smoke-in in the nation's capital.

The Outlaws spent much of the year preparing for the D.C. smoke-in, which drew ten thousand pot-puffing protestors to Lafayette Park, just across the street from the White House, during the late 1970s. Rock bands played, oodles of joints were given away freely, and a large contingent of stoners marched to DEA headquarters, chanting slogans, smoking weed, and protesting with a zeal that bordered on the obnoxious.

The Fourth of July smoke-in was somewhat of an embarrassment to Keith Stroup, director of NORML, the national drug-policy reform organization run out of Washington. Although the Yippies and NORML both favored marijuana legalization, they parted company when it came to activist strategy. The Yippies were anything but "normal," and they had little interest in working within the "shitstem" to bring about piecemeal change. Come hell or high water, these unrepentant tie-dyed rebels would wave the freak flag high. They went out of their way to show how different they were from mainstream America. The folks at NORML, by contrast, were trying to convince the heartland that they were just like everyone else—decent, reasonable, hardworking, normal folks who happened to like bud more than Budweiser.

In a way, the Yippies were a useful prop for Stroup, who could always plead to reporters that NORML was a respectable outfit—unlike them crazy Yippies! A nine-to-five guy, Stroup dressed in a jacket and tie like any straight attorney while shmoozing state and federal officials. His persistent efforts bore fruit. In 1973, Oregon became the first state to end criminal penalties for less than an ounce of marijuana by making possession a $100 fine. Two years later, Alaska legalized pot for personal use. Before long, marijuana possession would be decriminalized (reduced to a misdemeanor) in ten other states: California, Maine, Colorado, Ohio, New York, Nebraska, Minnesota, Mississippi, North Carolina, and Nevada. And the federal government seemed poised to follow suit.

President Jimmy Carter ushered in a brief period of ganja *glasnost* (the Russian term for "openness") when he told Congress in 1978, "Penalties against drug use should not be more damaging to the individual than the use of the drug itself. Nowhere is this more clear than in the laws against possession of marijuana in private for personal use." Carter cited the Shafer Commission's conclusions that marijuana should be decriminalized: "I believe it is time to implement those basic recommendations." The U.S. Justice Department disclosed that it would no longer make marijuana prosecution a priority, nor did it "have the resources to do so."

If the laws are more harmful than the crime, then the laws must be changed. Who could argue with that? A groundswell was building for marijuana decriminalization. Conservative congressman Dan Quayle, the Indiana Republican who would later become vice president, announced that he favored a reduction in penalties for pot. "We should concentrate on prosecuting the rapists and burglars who are a menace to society," Quayle argued. The American Bar Association, the Consumers Union (which published *Consumer Reports*), the National Council of Churches, National Education Association, American Public Health Association, and several other influential organizations cued up for marijuana law reform.

At the outset of the Carter administration, it seemed that marijuana legalization was no longer a pipe dream but an inevitable outcome. The new regime definitely had a more tolerant attitude toward pot-puffing than its predecessors. *Ladies' Home Journal* described a summer jazz festival on the White House lawn where "a haze of marijuana smoke hung heavy under the low-bending branches of a magnolia tree." The question on everyone's lips was *when*—rather than *would*—pot be decriminalized by the federal government.

Although relatively few marijuana users were prosecuted under federal law, "decrim" at the federal level would send a powerful message across the country, where local and state arrests for marijuana possession continued to rise despite Carter's call for a change of policy. In 1977, 458,000 people were arrested on marijuana charges in the United States—the biggest single-year tally thus far. Most were popped for simple possession. A nationwide household survey that year indicated that 31 percent of U.S. youth aged twelve to seventeen smoked grass; 53 percent of Americans from eighteen to twenty-five puffed; and 55 percent of all college students had tried pot.

The whiff of impending triumph was in the air when NORML held its sixth annual conference at the Hyatt Regency in downtown D.C. in December 1977. But not everyone was stoked by the prospect of decriminalization. Averse to bundling more lenient pot policy with a problematic crime-bill package, the Yippies viewed decrim as a meek compromise that retained the vestiges of prohibition and social disapproval while recognizing the obvious fact that large numbers of people would continue to break the law. Factionalism within the pro pot movement surfaced during the NORML colloquium when Joe Nellis, chief counsel for the House Select Committee on Narcotics Abuse and Control, spoke on a panel about drug policy. Without warning, Aron Kay waddled toward the lectern and—splat!—a cream pie landed on Nellis's face.

It was a bittersweet moment for Stroup and the folks at NORML who had tirelessly cultivated contacts on Capitol Hill only to learn that the Carter administration decided to continue spraying Paraquat, the herbicide used in Mexico to destroy marijuana plants. NORML strongly objected to the poisoning of marijuana fields south of the border, claiming that it threatened the health of Mexican farmers as well as American cannabis consumers. Stroup filed a lawsuit against the federal government to stop it from backing the herbicide program. He felt personally double-crossed by Peter Bourne, Carter's otherwise liberal-minded drug-policy point man, who wouldn't budge on the Paraquat issue. Angry at the latest turn of events and egged on by the Yippies, Stroup exacted revenge by leaking scandalous information to the press about Bourne's presence at a Capitol Hill cocaine-sniffing party. Bourne was forced to resign, a move that derailed Carter's reform agenda. Hard-liners would quickly reassert themselves. In effect, Stroup had snatched defeat from the jaws of victory. "It was probably the stupidest thing I ever did," he later acknowledged.

On November 17, 1978, a few months after the Bourne debacle, NORML suffered another setback when one of its key patrons gave up the ghost. Prone to manic-depressive mood swings, Tom Forçade had been acting erratically. He fired the entire staff at *High Times,* cut the phone lines with a switchblade, and trashed the office, yelling and screaming at everyone, only to rehire the same personnel a few days later. Haunted by who knows what demons, Forçade gobbled a fistful of Quaaludes, grabbed his pearl-handled .32-caliber revolver, and blew his brains out. He was thirty-three years old. Before his death, Forçade had been donating $50,000 a year to NORML, which was also given free ad space in *High Times.*

Forçade's will designated NORML as the sole beneficiary of a lucrative charitable trust held by Trans-High Corporation, the parent company of *High Times*. But NORML never benefited from the trust because of posthumous legal maneuverings that involved Forçade's relatives, several attorneys, and possibly Stroup himself, who was fired by the NORML board. Badly wounded, NORML would sputter on as a rump organization in the Eighties, a bleak stretch for pot advocates.* *High Times,* the magazine Forçade founded to finance and advance the agenda of the Yippie marijuana activist movement, would continue to publish on a monthly basis during an inhospi-

* In subsequent years, there would be dozens of organizations working for drug-policy reform, including the Criminal Justice Policy Foundation, Drug Policy Alliance, Marijuana Policy Project, Students for Sensible Drug Policy, Law Enforcement Against Prohibition, and Americans for Safe Access.

table era, its fortunes largely tied to ad revenue from the drug paraphernalia industry.

By this time, so many people were smoking pot in America that its radical edge had become diluted and diffused throughout mainstream society—the counterculture was seemingly everywhere and nowhere at the same time. Affluent professionals and business executives were as likely to use marijuana as factory workers, truck drivers, and the girl next door. The remnant Yippies, for their part, soldiered on. Quixotic culture warriors to the bitter end, they would keep the flame burning while laws against marijuana in America continued to carry penalties and consequences far more damaging than the actual use of the herb.

5

JUST SAY NEVER

Reefer Sadness

On the evening Ronald Wilson Reagan was elected president of the United States, his daughter, Patti Davis, pulled off Sunset Boulevard, parked her car on a Los Angeles side street, got a joint out of her purse, lit it, and took a deep drag. She was on her way to the Reagan victory party on November 4, 1980, but she wasn't in a celebratory mood. Ms. Davis, then twenty-eight, feared for the future. She worried about the fate of her family, the fate of her country, the fate of the planet, with her father in the White House. So she smoked some grass to calm her nerves and steady herself.

It wasn't simply a matter of not subscribing to the same political opinions as her dad. Ronald Reagan, a B-movie-actor-cum-politician, lived in a simplistic, make-believe, *Father Knows Best* world where good-guy cowboys always vanquished bad-guy injuns. His personal charm notwithstanding, Reagan was ideologically rigid, detached, and largely impervious to the consequences of his own decisions. His frequent mental slippage between real life and the silver screen was emblematic of a country in denial, a political culture unable to distinguish fact from fiction. President Reagan acted like a rootin' tootin' cinema cowboy who spoke in all seriousness when he blamed trees for pollution and asserted that marijuana was "the most dangerous drug in America."

What wasn't he smoking?

Reagan divided the world into the forces of good and the forces of evil and attributed all troubles at home and abroad to a single conspiratorial source: international communism. That's how he saw it when, as president of the Screen Actors Guild, he led the fight to drive alleged subversives out of Hollywood during the early years of the Cold War. That's how he saw it when he became governor of California in 1966 by fulminating against hippies, pinkos, student radicals, and black militants. And that's how he still saw it when, as president of the United States, he excoriated the "Evil Empire," his description of the Soviet Union, for seeking to overthrow foreign governments around the world. The impulse to demonize—a deep-rooted American trait—was such that the ends always justified the means for Reagan, even if the ends and means mirrored those of the archenemy. His administration sought to bring about violent regime change in several Latin American, Asian, and African countries during the 1980s—exactly what he accused the Soviets of doing.

The Reagan narrative equated the evils of communism with the threat of drugs and crime; the common thread was demonology. Empowered by the lofty language of virtue and the might of the state, the president used his bully pulpit to frame the discussion of illicit drugs as a clear-cut, black-and-white issue with no shades of gray, an absolutist approach well suited for martial tub-thumping and an overall push-back against perceived liberal permissiveness. Reagan's Manichean mind-set meshed well with the politics and psychology of the ascendant religious right, which, along with free-market fundamentalists and die-hard militarists, comprised the nuts and bolts of the conservative coalition that backed the Gipper.

The culture warriors of the religious right turned a blind eye to deadly ethical violations by pharmaceutical, tobacco, and alcohol companies, and corporate America in general, while demonizing cannabis. Marijuana epitomized everything right-wing revivalists hated about the 1960s, a decade that continued to stick in their craw. They were hell-bent on waging a religious war against a symbol of that era. The fight over marijuana was in many ways a fight over the memory of the Sixties.

While the religious right played up marijuana as a moral issue, the president's decision to relaunch the war on drugs was inspired not so much by God's word as by the fierce conviction that it was still possible to enforce discipline and impose order in a world that seemed increasingly chaotic. Reagan's much-trumpeted drug war started primarily as an antimarijuana campaign. But the issue wasn't really about smoking pot—it was about disobedience, rocking the boat, a willingness to question authority and stray outside the law.

Reagan picked up where Nixon left off and called for a "full scale anti-drug mobilization," a "nationwide crusade . . . to rid America of this scourge." In a radio address on October 2, 1982, Reagan conflated all drugs, including cannabis, into one ultimate bogeyman: "We're making no excuses for drugs—hard and soft, or otherwise. Drugs are bad, and we're going after them . . . We've taken down the surrender flag and run up the battle flag. And we're going to win the war on drugs."

Thus began yet another zero-tolerance jihad that refused to distinguish between casual use and serious abuse of proscribed substances. It was "déjà vu all over again," as Yogi Berra once said. Just as Nixon had dismissed the Shafer Report without even looking at it, Reagan ignored a hefty 1982 study, comprising six years of research, from the prestigious National Academy of Sciences (NAS), which found "no convincing evidence" that marijuana damages the brain or nervous system or decreases fertility. The NAS report concluded that marijuana should be decriminalized and that states should regulate its sale and distribution. Such a policy, according to the eighteen-member NAS panel, would bring "substantial savings" to law enforcement and society at large, by keeping small-scale users out of the penal system.

Instead, Reagan would resurrect Nixon's failed policies that emphasized targeting the drug source, disrupting contraband routes, and cracking down hard on consumers. Reagan placed Vice President George H. W. Bush in charge of the National Narcotics Border Interdiction System, which was supposed to stop marijuana, cocaine, and heroin from entering the United States. Spending on interdiction efforts tripled during the Reagan administration; the operative premise was that the demand for cannabis and other drugs could be curbed by eliminating supplies. This hopeless strategy married intellectual myopia—supply leads to demand—with the pragmatic impossibility of eliminating the urge to alter human consciousness via exogenous means.

For political purposes, however, Reagan's strategy worked like a charm. Although candidate Reagan had campaigned on a promise to cut big government down to size, President Reagan did just the opposite when he granted the DEA and other federal agencies extraordinary powers to wage a no-holds-barred battle against marijuana and other drugs. The revamped, well-funded drug war would transform the criminal-justice system into one of the top growth industries in the United States. Law-enforcement jobs at every government level grew by 36 percent and prison-related jobs by 86 percent under Reagan, who championed tougher penalties for drug crimes. Reagan wanted—and got—more authority to wiretap drug suspects. For the first time, selling pot paraphernalia, everything from roach clips to bongs, became grounds for imprisonment. Reagan's attempt to enforce compliance with cannabis prohibition would entail activities on the part of cops and narcs that were similar to those prevalent in police states.

Pitting law enforcement against a cultural and economic force was a dumb idea to begin with. But Reagan went even further than Nixon by deploying active-duty military personnel in a holy crusade against the forbidden herb. Reagan broke with long-standing legal tradition, which forbade the U.S. military from engaging in domestic law enforcement. The president insisted that the armed forces play an active role in the fight against illegal drugs. By casting drug importation as a threat to national security and elevating narcotics policy to warfare status, Reagan convinced Congress to amend the 1878 Posse Comitatus Act so that U.S. soldiers could enforce civilian law on American soil. With Reagan leading the charge, the war on drugs became a real war and the once sacrosanct distinction between military ops and civilian policing evaporated. Because of the drug war, law enforcement throughout the United States would become militarized. In the name of domestic security, Reagan rationalized cutting social programs and channeling funds into military hardware (helicopters, tanks, high-tech surveillance equipment) and paramilitary training for SWAT teams and other police units, whose main task entailed serving drug-related search warrants in cities and towns across the country.

Military modus operandi and law-enforcement procedure were not a smooth fit. "Where the military sees 'enemies' of the United States, a police agency, properly oriented, sees 'citizens' suspected of crimes but innocent until proven guilty in a court of law. These are two different views of the world," noted Colonel Charles J. Dunlop, who was uncomfortable with the military's growing involvement in domestic policing.

The federal escalation of the drug war in the 1980s had a major impact on local and state police, according to Joseph McNamara, former police chief in Kansas City, Missouri, and San Jose, California. McNamara contends that cops were "indoctrinated to hate drug users and to see them as the enemy." Throughout the United States, police departments received much of their funding and training from federal officials who stressed the need to focus on drug arrests. "The drug war is a holy war," said McNamara, "and in a holy war you don't have to win, you just keep fighting."

In 1984, Congress passed the Comprehensive Crime Control Act, which raised federal penalties for marijuana possession, cultivation, and sales. It also made drug busting easier for cops, who were given wide latitude to seize the property of suspected pot dealers. A house, real estate, cars, jewelry, or any other assets that theoretically could have been purchased with illicit drug proceeds were fair game for law enforcement, which usually got to keep or sell the booty. Goods could be seized without a court order before charges were filed against a cannabis suspect, and even those who were exonerated in court had to jump through near-impossible hoops to reclaim their property. Most people who lost property under drug forfeiture statutes didn't bother fighting back, because the odds were so stacked against them. Accused rapists, murderers, and kidnappers—unlike marijuana suspects—did not have their assets confiscated without a trial.

During the Reagan years, asset seizures and convictionless forfeiture became a cash cow for law enforcement and a pretext for routine official looting. Gross receipts of seizures nationwide grew from about $100 million in 1981 to over $1 billion in 1987; 80 percent of all forfeited property belonged to people who were never charged with a crime. Police departments went on a buying spree, stocking up on semiautomatic weapons, computer equipment, body armor, and perhaps even a chopper or two to monitor outdoor grow-ops from the air. Nearly half the police forces in the United States relied on drug seizures and forfeitures to supplement their budgets. By fostering an insidious police dependency on seized assets, the 1984 crime bill ensured that the drug war would achieve a self-perpetuating life of its own. As Christian Parenti observed, "Forfeiture, contrary to its purported goals, does not take the profit out of drug dealing. Instead, the laws merely deal law enforcement into the game."

Although the Fourth Amendment guarantees against "unreasonable searches and seizures," a Supreme Court ruling in 1984, redolent with Orwellian implications, gave law enforcement a near-blanket authorization to search for marijuana on private property without a warrant. Henceforth, police in paramilitary gear could break into people's homes with impunity and ransack the premises looking for cannabis. Legal scholar Steven Wisotsky called it "the drug exception to the Bill of Rights."

Under the guise of drug-war urgency, the Supreme Court continued to chip away at the Constitution, ruling in 1985 that schoolchildren basically have no right to privacy. School officials could detain students at will, frisk and strip-search them, and rifle through their possessions without obtaining a search warrant. Courts upheld searches of high school lockers and college dorm rooms on the flimsiest of justifications. Hidden cameras recorded students in school bathrooms. Such incursions were a necessary response to "the veritable national crises in law enforcement caused by smuggling of illegal narcotics," stated Chief Justice William Rehnquist, whose publicly visible struggle with prescription pharmaceutical medication had long been a source of Washington gossip.

Rehnquist was often pixilated on Placidyl, a "sedative-hypnotic" developed to help insomniacs sleep, which he started taking in 1971. Soon he was seriously addicted to the heavy downer. But his longtime chemical dependence did not disqualify him from serving on the High Court, no pun intended. An FBI probe noted that in 1981 Rehnquist became so disoriented while hospitalized because of his tranquilizer habit that he ran into the lobby in his pajamas and tried to escape, fearing that the CIA was out to get him. That year, Rehnquist cast the deciding vote in a shocking decision, which ruled, in response to an appeal by the state of Virginia, that a forty-year prison term for selling a small amount of marijuana was not cruel and unusual punishment in the case of

Roger Davis. A black man married to a white woman in rural Virginia (where hemp growing was once mandatory by law), Davis and the ACLU maintained that his "crime" was more about miscegenation than marijuana. But according to Rehnquist the real issue was that federal courts shouldn't interfere with sentences handed out under state law.

American citizens, meanwhile, were treated to sanctimonious finger-wagging by First Lady Nancy Reagan, who admonished everyone to "just say no" to drugs. "There is no moral middle ground," she declared, calling for a "new intolerance" toward marijuana smokers and other illicit imbibers. "If you're a casual user, you're an accomplice to murder," she proclaimed.

Nancy Reagan was not a casual user. She was a chronic user, a prescription tranquilizer addict, according to Patti Davis, who suspected that her mother's high-profile antidrug advocacy may have been a form of denial and "a subconscious cry for help." "To my knowledge she never addressed the vast numbers of people who become addicted to prescription drugs that they got, perfectly legally, from doctors," said Davis, who grew a few cannabis plants in the backyard of her Topanga Canyon home before Reagan became president.

"Just say no," the Reagan drug-war mantra, meant that the prohibition of every use of cannabis, medical as well as recreational, had to be maintained without exception to safeguard the American people from the evils of substance abuse. "Just say no" was allegedly all about protecting the kids—a theme that animated a network of federally funded antipot parents' groups that rose to prominence during the Reagan administration. "We're in danger of losing our whole next generation," the First Lady told leaders of the National Federation of Parents for a Drug-Free Youth. The rhetoric of child protection was the calculated cornerstone of drug-war public relations. To protect the children, parents' groups (that were about as grassroots as AstroTurf) began to monitor federal publications with the goal of weeding out comments favorable to marijuana use. NIDA director William Polin ordered his staff to purge any NIDA-published booklets, papers, and monographs on marijuana that contained the word *social.* Sixty-four publications, some predating NIDA's inception in 1974, were blacklisted, and every public library in the United States received a letter from NIDA, suggesting that the offending documents were outdated and ought to be pulled.

To protect the children, the just-say-no zealots said *shush!* to serious public discussion at a time when Americans could have benefited from honest discourse about drugs. To protect the children, parents groups and other government-financed fronts churned out antipot propaganda so ridiculously one-sided that it read in sum like a rabid religious tract, a litany of unending horrors—marijuana causes cancer, brain damage, schizophrenia, homosexuality, uncontrollable weight gain, birth defects, and, yet again, the amazing allegation that pot makes men grow large breasts!

The parents' groups were given an influential forum by *Reader's Digest,* which ran an alarming three-part series called "Marijuana Alerts." The last installment, "The Devastation of Personality," contrasted the chronic pot smoker unfavorably with the heavy drinker, who sobers up and "becomes himself again," whereas the pothead, according to the article, remains in a perpetual "state of sub-acute intoxication." The article quoted a despondent teenage boy who says, "I'm like an empty shell. There is nothing left that I like about myself. And pot did it." The final comments were reserved for Carlton Turner, Reagan's drug-policy adviser, who claimed that marijuana smoking threatened the "future of our families and our nation."

It's been said that truth is the first casualty of war, and the war on drugs was no exception. The Reagan administration conducted a psychological warfare campaign, a "psy-op" in espionage parlance, targeting the American population. Schoolchildren were bombarded with fallacious antimarijuana propaganda. To underwrite this effort, Reagan operatives turned to the Sultan of Brunei and the Saudi Arabian monarchy—the same oily benefactors that covertly financed U.S.-instigated "contra" wars in the Third World that claimed tens of thousands of civilian lives. Known for staging public decapitations of accused drug smugglers, the Saudi royal family contributed generously to Nancy Reagan's favorite antimarijuana organizations. Tobacco, liquor, and pharmaceutical corporations also filled the tax-deductible coffers of the Partnership for a Drug-Free America, which ran hyperbolic ads on radio and television telling young people to eschew illegal drugs. "A mind is a terrible thing to waste," warned one antimarijuana advertisement. Another ad showed an egg simmering in a frying pan: "This is your brain on drugs."

The Drug Abuse Resistance Education program (D.A.R.E.)—also a recipient of tax-exempt largesse from Big Pharma, Big Tobacco, and Booze Inc.—dispatched uniformed police to schools throughout the United States to enlighten students about the absolute evil of marijuana and other illicit drugs. School kids were instructed to rat on their parents and neighbors if they smoked pot. Founded in 1983, D.A.R.E. was the brainchild of Los Angeles police chief Daryl Gates, who maintained that casual drug users were guilty of "treason" and should be "taken out and shot." Although tobacco and alcohol were by far the most widely used and abused substances by teenagers, they were not the focus of D.A.R.E.'s educational efforts. Nor did Nancy Reagan ever refer to cigarette manufacturers or liquor companies as "accomplices to murder."

Subsequent studies called into question the efficacy of D.A.R.E., which taught schoolchildren that smoking grass would lead to perdition. But Uncle Sam cried wolf too often: First marijuana was said to create maniacal killers, then to produce inert masses of lazy indulgers. When teens caught on that they weren't getting the straight dope about marijuana, they were more likely to ignore warnings about genuinely dangerous drugs. "The kids try marijuana and say, 'Hey, this isn't bad. They must be lying to me about coke, speed, and smack.' That's how a steppingstone works," Dr. Mikuriya noted.

Mayor Ross Anderson of Salt Lake City criticized the federally approved D.A.R.E. program, calling it "a complete fraud" that actually did "a lot of harm." Other marijuana-policy critics exposed the depravities of drug war "boot camps" for children, such as Straight, Inc., which "harmed scores of American kids in the name of saving them from drugs," as Arnold Trebach reported. Straight, Inc., shut down its operations in several states after journalists exposed the torture and confinement of children and young adults at the tough-love rehab facility. "Because we so irrationally fear drugs as a nation, we say that you can practically destroy children to prevent them from using drugs," Trebach warned.

During the 1980s, federal marijuana policy was shaped by fanatics and ideologues who behaved as though they were trying to stamp out a heresy rather than a vice. The drug warriors carried on as though there were something embedded in the chemical structure of cannabis that made it an inherently wicked substance. They projected their fear and loathing onto the herb, thereby committing what Alfred North Whitehead, the twentieth-century British philosopher, referred to as "the fallacy of misplaced concreteness"—mistaking an abstract belief for a concrete or physical reality. Some pro-pot enthusiasts made a similar mistake when they claimed that smoking marijuana automatically causes one to question authority and became a revolutionary. Combatants on both sides of the drug war erred in thinking that marijuana's magic—or malevolence—was all in the herb.

Dr. Andrew Weil said it best: "There are no good or bad drugs; there are only good and bad relationships with drugs." By deeming every pot smoker a drug abuser, the U.S. government created "an insoluble marijuana problem of enormous proportions," Weil warned.

Dr. Weil emphatically rejected the view that altering one's consciousness is implicitly a dereliction of human nature. Scientists have noted that intoxication persists as a fundamental drive throughout the animal kingdom, which suggests that the desire to go beyond normal waking consciousness is deeply instinctual. "The ubiquity of drug use is so striking that it must represent a basic human appetite," said Weil, who underscored the importance of recognizing the value of other states of consciousness in order to teach people, particularly young people, to satisfy their needs without engaging in self-destructive behavior.

The Laughing Cure

The 1980s were grim years for American marijuana advocates. The pro-cannabis tide that had been building during the Sixties and Seventies came to a standstill with Reagan at the helm. His administration resurrected the notion that drug abuse was a moral not a medical issue and that marijuana offenders, therefore, deserved to be punished. Once again, pot smokers were pegged as the enemy—even medical users. Law enforcement at every level refused to differentiate between recreational tokers and people who smoked or ingested cannabis explicitly with a therapeutic intent.

On July 7, 1987, Kentucky state police raided the 90-acre farm of James Burton, a thirty-nine-year-old glaucoma patient. Burton, a Vietnam veteran, told the cops that he was growing thirty pot plants to keep from going blind. A jury believed his medical-necessity argument and found him guilty of simple possession, not the more serious charge of manufacture with intent to distribute. As Dan Baum recounted in his classic study *Smoke and Mirrors*, Burton "was sentenced to a year in federal prison without parole. In addition, U.S. District Judge Ronald Meredith ordered Burton's entire farm confiscated and gave the Burtons ten days to clear out of their home of eighteen years. Burton wasn't allowed to testify on his own behalf and no witnesses were called during the confiscation hearings. 'There is no defense against forfeiture,' the Judge explained."

Burton was busted a decade after Robert Randall, another glaucoma sufferer, became the first American to gain legal access to marijuana for medicinal purposes. Since that landmark 1976 court decision, Randall and his partner, Alice O'Leary, had dedicated themselves to expanding this unique privilege so that others in serious need could consume cannabis to prevent blindness, ease muscle spasms, and quell the nausea of chemotherapy. Randall heard testimonials from pot-smoking cancer patients who not only endured chemotherapy without vomiting, they even got the munchies.

A half million Americans each year underwent chemotherapy and 70 percent experienced nausea and vomiting; as many as 40 percent of cancer patients who underwent chemotherapy didn't respond well to standard anti-emetics. Thanks to marijuana, patients found they could just say no to starvation, chronic pain, convulsions, and the living hell of cancer pharmaceutical side effects. Randall was an articulate and powerful proponent for the growing number of ailing Americans who confronted a major dilemma regarding the use of medicinal cannabis. As drug-policy analyst Kevin Zeese explained, "They could obey the law, suffer the consequences of their disease and possibly die or they could break the law by acquiring and possessing marijuana and perhaps face criminal prosecution."

In 1981, Randall and O'Leary formed the Alliance for Cannabis Therapeutics (ACT), a nonprofit organization dedicated entirely to legalizing medical marijuana. Recreational use was not on ACT's agenda. Randall traveled extensively, often speaking about the therapeutic benefits of cannabis. On various occasions he shared a podium with Dr. Tod Mikuriya. Both men pressed the flesh in state capitals as part of a concerted effort to push through laws that recognized marijuana's healing properties and afforded safe access for patients. By 1983, thirty-four states plus Washington, D.C., passed bills in support of medical marijuana. A half dozen states, starting with New Mexico in 1978, also authorized therapeutic research programs that involved giving marijuana to patients with cancer, glaucoma, and other serious ailments and studying the effects of the herb. But these efforts foundered when the federal government refused to supply experimental cannabis, thereby rendering the state laws symbolic rather than real. Marijuana was readily available on the street, but scientists were hogtied by bureaucrats who blocked access to the herb for research purposes.

With state measures mired in red tape, grassroots activists took matters into their own hands. After her son suffered through gut-wrenching chemo, Mae Nutt, known affectionately as "Grandma Marijuana," launched the Green Cross delivery service, which provided cannabis edibles and herb to cancer patients and other ailing citizens in Michigan during the late 1970s and 1980s. Underground green aid networks operated discreetly in other areas of the country, as well.

In addition to honing in on state governments, Randall lobbied federal officials to advance the cause of medicinal cannabis. He was instrumental in drafting legislation that would have established a full-scale federal marijuana program for U.S. citizens with life- or sense-threatening diseases. Cosponsored and introduced by Representative Newt Gingrich, a rising GOP star who later became Speaker of the House, this bill initially attracted considerable interest on both sides of the aisle. In a March 1982 letter published in the *Journal of the American Medical Association,* Gingrich stated that "the outdated federal prohibition" of medical marijuana was "corrupting the intent of state laws and depriving thousands of glaucoma and cancer patients of the medical care promised them by their state legislatures." Gingrich went on to denounce "the hysteria over marijuana's social abuse" and "bureaucratic interference" by the federal government, which was preventing "a factual [and] balanced assessment of marijuana's use as a medicament."

But congressional support for medical marijuana waned when President Reagan relaunched the war on drugs. Gingrich, who had smoked pot while in graduate school, tersely withdrew his endorsement of the bill. "The medical case for the use of marijuana is sustainable, but the cultural case isn't," he wrote to Randall.

The vast social consumption of marijuana spawned many criminal medical users who, like Randall, had inadvertently discovered that cannabis was good for their illness. ACT helped scores of patients fill out the tedious forms necessary to qualify for the Compassionate Investigational New Drug program, which the U.S. government was forced to create as a result of Randall's legal victory. Since its inception, however, federal officials did everything possible to limit the scope of the program that was supposed to supply marijuana free of charge to qualifying patients. The onerous qualification process was designed to deter applicants and their physicians, who had to wade through mountains of paperwork and endure various indignities, including a background check and a visit from DEA agents. Only a handful of people managed to jump through all the requisite hoops.

On November 20, 1982, after four and a half years of Kafkaesque bureaucratic contortions, Irvin Rosenfeld became the second person in the United States to obtain a federal license to smoke marijuana. As a child and adolescent, Irv underwent seven operations to remove more than thirty bone tumors associated with a rare and excruciatingly painful disease called multiple congenital cartilaginous exotosis. His skeleton was riddled with more than two hundred tumors; he wasn't expected to live much past his teenage years.

The first time he smoked marijuana in a social setting, Rosenfeld didn't get high, but his muscles relaxed to the point where he hardly noticed that he had been sitting for a half hour while playing chess. Ordinarily, because of his infirmity, he couldn't sit for more than ten minutes without succumbing to painful spasms. Before long, Irv discovered that if he smoked pot every couple of hours, he didn't have to rely on doctor-prescribed muscle relaxants, opiates, and grog-inducing tranquilizers to get by. Although he felt no euphoric effects from cannabis, the herb somehow kept his disease in check, inhibiting tumor growth and enabling him to fully participate as a productive member of society.

As vice president of a Fort Lauderdale–based brokerage firm, Rosenfeld handled millions of dollars in investments for thousands of clients while smoking ten government-issued joints every day—morning, noon, and night. It was the same skanky weed from the federal pot farm at Ole Miss that Randall had been receiving in monthly allotments. On a five-acre plot encircled by barbed wire, guard towers, and motion-activated alarms, taxpayer-funded scientists grew confederate cannabis with uniformly meager THC content. The weed was harvested, dried, chopped to bits—seeds, stems, and leaves included—and passed through a sieve. Much of this deracinated reefer was shipped to the Research Triangle Institute in Raleigh, North Carolina, where it was rolled into standardized cigarettes and stored in a freezer, pending delivery to Randall, Rosenfeld, and a few other patients who managed to enlist in the Compassionate IND program. As a group they comprised a unique fraternity of disabled freedom fighters and all-American hell-raisers who refused to back down when it came to asserting their human right to avail themselves of medical marijuana.

U.S. government-grown ganja from Ole Miss was also used to train drug-sniffing police dogs so they could identify marijuana smokers, including medical users who weren't authorized by the feds. "It's a lethal irony, that's for sure. The same government project that saved my life is also used to destroy the lives of other patients," said George McMahon, a federally authorized pot patient from Texas who was stricken with nail-patella syndrome, a disease characterized by abnormalities of the arms and legs, bones that break easily, kidney dysfunction, and glaucoma.

McMahon wasn't impressed by the quality of Uncle Sam's weed. Male and female plants were mixed together. The smoke was harsh. It lacked that zesty, perfumed aroma. It was not the *good shuzzit*. But he and the other federal patients didn't complain about the cannabis. Their criticism was directed at cruel and incoherent federal policies that punished people for using a nonlethal herb to ease their suffering. "Compared to all the patients who live in fear of arrest and pay hundreds of dollars each month to get black market medicine of questionable quality, I have it easy," McMahon acknowledged. "I just cut open the joints, clean out the seeds and stems, moisturize the herb [in a baggy with lettuce] and reroll the joints with my own papers."

Under the terms of the Compassionate Use Protocol, the U.S. government was supposed to treat each medical-marijuana patient as a research subject. In theory, American officials were supposed to collect data on the therapeutic effectiveness of marijuana. But, as Rosenfeld pointed out, the Compassionate IND program "existed in name only." "I'm living proof that cannabis works as a medicine," Rosenfeld asserted, adding: "I'm also living proof that the government doesn't want to know how well it works." The Food and Drug Administration (FDA) never investigated whether those who got cannabis from the feds were actually benefiting (or harming themselves) by smoking the herb.

NIDA, which sponsored the program, neglected to conduct the mandated follow-up investigations.

In an effort to ascertain the safety and efficacy of chronic cannabis use sanctioned by Uncle Sam, a nongovernmental team of scientists led by Dr. Ethan Russo, a neurologist in Missoula, Montana, examined four of the federal patients who were still alive in 2001, including a chipper Rosenfeld, then in his late forties. Each medical user was put through an extensive battery of MRI brain scans and other tests to assess the impact of marijuana on immunological, pulmonary, endocrine, and neuropsychological functions. Russo found no physical or mental impairment attributable to cannabis. The Missoula study concluded:

> Results demonstrate clinical effectiveness in these patients in treating glaucoma, chronic musculoskeletal pain, spasm and nausea, and spasticity of multiple sclerosis. All 4 patients are stable with respect to their chronic conditions, and are taking many fewer standard pharmaceuticals than previously . . . These results would support the provision of clinical cannabis to a greater number of patients in need. We believe that cannabis can be a safe and effective medicine."

But NIDA wasn't keen on providing "clinical cannabis to a greater number of patients in need"—and NIDA controlled access to muggles from Ole Miss, the only legal source of reefer for research purposes. The same agency that was politically hostile to medical marijuana served as the gatekeeper of its supply. Dr. Charles Schuster, who headed NIDA during Reagan's second term, recalled that he was under considerable pressure to "find something wrong with marijuana." Consequently, NIDA spent a major portion of its budget looking for marijuana's elusive negative effects. In the 1980s, federal money for research into risks associated with cannabis increased almost tenfold. "For many years, we tried to determine whether marijuana produced brain damage. We didn't," said Schuster.

While consistently blocking therapeutic-oriented research into smoked cannabis, the federal government favored drug companies that sought to pharmaceuticalize the plant by synthesizing its key active ingredient and creating a "pot pill" with a standardized dosage. The result was dronabinol—synthetic THC mixed with sesame oil, patented and produced by Solvay Pharmaceuticals, a Belgian firm, and sold under the brand name Marinol. The U.S. government provided most of the R&D funds for Marinol, which was fast-tracked and approved by the FDA in 1985 as an antinausea drug for cancer patients.

The Reagan administration wanted Marinol—pure THC—rushed to market as a substitute remedy to placate those clamoring for medical marijuana. The drug warriors figured there would be no need to smoke the herb if prescription pills were available. Somehow logic got lost in the bureaucratic shuffle: The U.S. government maintained that marijuana, a Schedule I substance, had no medical value, while certifying its principal psychoactive component, THC, as a medicine.

According to the feds, pot was dangerous, but THC was not. In 1999, the DEA downgraded Marinol from Schedule II to Schedule III, a category designated for medically useful drugs with minimal abuse potential. There is a simple explanation why Marinol, unlike some prescription medications, would never become a drug of abuse. Many people, even those who benefited from Marinol, found the experience to be highly disagreeable. An hour or so after ingesting the pill, it comes on like gangbusters. People often got way too stoned from pure, orally administered THC and panic attacks were not uncommon.*

The synthetic concoction just didn't work as well as good, old-fashioned cannabis. "The government's preference for synthetic or single compound drugs, as opposed to natural marijuana is more based on prejudice than any other rationale," Dr. Mikuriya asserted in a 1987 legal affidavit petitioning the DEA to reschedule cannabis. Inhaling natural marijuana is often preferable to swallowing a standardized THC capsule "as the patient is better able to control the dose through self-adjustment . . . A pill is a fixed dose while a cigarette can be varied to suit the needs of the patient," explained Mikuriya, who questioned the wisdom of administering an antinausea medication in pill form to someone who couldn't keep anything down. Smoking a joint made more sense and provided instant relief. Yet marijuana continued to face official vilification and Marinol (approved initially only for cancer patients) enjoyed legitimacy and government backing. Sick people were punished, some severely, for self-medicating with botanical THC, while patients taking synthetic THC got insurance coverage. If you were among the tens of millions of Americans who lacked health insurance, then forget about the pot pill—Marinol was prohibitively expensive.

But the main drawback of Marinol was that it lacked marijuana's full range

---

* Orally consumed THC produces a much more powerful and longer-lasting effect than inhaled THC. When marijuana is eaten, the liver hydroxylates THC into other chemicals, including the highly potent metabolite 11-hydroxy-THC, which is four times as strong as THC itself.

of therapeutic attributes. Synthesized in a lab, Marinol was a single-molecule medicine—only THC. Cannabis, by contrast, has more than four hundred natural compounds, including dozens of cannabinoids, terpenoids, and flavonoids, each with a unique medicinal impact, which interact synergistically in a way that buffers THC's tricky psychoactivity. This synergistic interaction—described by Raphael Mechoulam as an "entourage effect"—yields a pharmacological result that is greater than the sum of the plant's parts.

"We have no reason to believe that a synthetically manufactured product will be as safe or as effective as the natural product," said Dr. Andrew Weil, whose studies indicated that "the synthesis of natural plant products into pharmaceutical preparations invariably increases the potential for adverse effects, but may not enhance therapeutic action." The federal regulatory system, however, was primed to handle synthetic molecules not botanicals. The FDA approval process privileged single-compound products invented, owned, and patented by large pharmaceutical firms. Big Pharma had little financial incentive to shepherd cannabis, an unpatentable plant, through expensive new drug trials. Of course, marijuana was not a new drug, having been used therapeutically two thousand years before Christ. But that didn't matter to the sticklers at the FDA, which refused to recognize cannabis as a traditional natural medicine and grandfather it as such.

Left to their own devices, a growing number of pot smokers in the United States and elsewhere found that cannabis not only helped ease their ailments, it also seemed to mitigate some of the toxic side effects from corporate pharmaceuticals. Marijuana users typically reported that they needed less prescription medication when they smoked cannabis. Some people used marijuana to get off alcohol, opiates, cocaine, and barbiturates, as well as prescription antidepressants such as Prozac, Eli Lilly's blockbuster, which flooded the market by the end of Reagan's second term.

Introduced in 1988, Prozac quickly became the standard treatment for the blues. Prozac wasn't just a pharmaceutical. It was a cultural icon—the Coca-Cola of mental health medications. Drug companies and corporate media promoted the idea that depression is caused by a chemical imbalance in the brain. The pharmaceutical response to this seemingly widespread condition entailed mood elevation by manipulating neurotransmitter levels. When it came to depression, serotonin was something like a magic bullet for the masses. Doctors pushed Prozac, which works by increasing the presence of serotonin in the brain, as a remedy for millions of unhappy people, including shy children and out-of-sorts pregnant women, who were presumed to be lacking in sufficient amounts of this important neurochemical. Soon one in ten Americans was taking Prozac or another overprescribed "serotonin selective reuptake inhibitor" (Paxil, Zoloft, Lexapro, etc.), which began to turn up in the water supply, an alarming sign of the pervasive use of pharmaceutical antidepressants.*

For the Prozac generation, it was mourning in America. Although some clinically depressed patients achieved positive results with prescription antidepressants, many did not. The FDA approved these drugs—for adults and children—despite numerous studies showing that they worked no better than a placebo. What's more, Prozac and other serotonin-boosting compounds had nasty side effects—headaches, nausea, loss of appetite and libido, liver failure, bone-density depletion, and increased risk of stroke, heart disease, and suicidal behavior. A study of American mothers and their babies found that fetal exposure to Prozac disrupted neurological development and increased the risk of autism and newborn heart defects. Nearly one in three infants born to women taking antidepressant drugs showed signs of withdrawal. Exposed neonates had seizures, bluish skin from lack of oxygen, feeding difficulties, low blood sugar, rapid breathing, and other symptoms.

People in chronic pain are often depressed. But taking Big Pharma antidepressants along with certain kinds of painkillers increased the likelihood of bleeding from the stomach. Cannabis, a healing herb long used as an analgesic and a mood enhancer, posed no such risks. (Nor has marijuana ever been shown to harm the fetus or increase the risk of miscarriage.) Medical writings from ancient India, Persia, and Greece mentioned the antidepressant properties of cannabis. Robert Burton, the English clergyman, touted the herb as a remedy for melancholy in 1621. During the mid-1800s, Dr. J.-J. Moreau de Tours spoke of the "mental joy" of hashish intoxication and recommended it as a treatment for depression. Early twentieth-century medical texts cited cannabis in a similar context. It was not for nothing that some latter-day pot smokers referred to marijuana as "green Prozac." Many people with serious chronic illnesses said that marijuana boosted their spirits.†

---

* An ABC News poll found that one in eight Americans took an antidepressant at some point in the 1990s (Greider, *The Big Fix*, p. 115). Antidepressant use more than doubled in the United States between 1996 and 2005, according to a study published in the *Archives of General Psychiatry*. In 1994, Princess Diana criticized British doctors for prescribing "too many pills" to women; she didn't say which pills but hinted at antidepressants, which polluted the British water supply ("Report: Prozac Found in Britain's Drinking Water," Reuters, August 8, 2004). Prozac and other medications also poisoned America's watersheds (Kelli Whitlock, "Casting Prozac Upon the Waters," *University of Georgia Research Magazine*, Summer 2005).

† In 2005 the *Journal of Psychopharmacology* examined cannabis smoking among people with bipolar affective disorder who used the psychoactive herb as a mood stabilizer. For

A peer-reviewed study published in the journal *Addictive Behaviors* in 2005 concluded that marijuana smokers, in general, were less depressed and less encumbered by somatic discomfort and psychiatric problems than their non-smoking counterparts. By this time, Brazilian and American scientists probing the neurobiology of depression had discovered that cannabidiol (CBD), a unique natural substance present only in cannabis and hemp, activates brain receptors that modulate the ebb and flow of serotonin. This is one of many ways, according to recent findings in medical science, that marijuana produces an antidepressant effect.

Self-medication for mild to moderate depression underlies a great deal of recreational marijuana use. Recreational as in "Pot is Fun"—à la Ginsberg. Therapeutic as in Proverbs 17:22—"A cheerful heart does good like a medicine: but a broken spirit makes one sick." In ancient Greece, the word *euphoria* meant "having health," a state of well-being. The euphoric qualities of cannabis, far from being an unwholesome side effect, were deeply implicated in the medicinal value of the plant. "We should be thinking of cannabis as a medicine first," said Dr. Mikuriya, "that happens to have some psychoactive properties, as many medicines do, rather than as an intoxicant that happens to have a few therapeutic properties on the side."

Marijuana makes people laugh, and laughter is therapeutic. Laughter is excellent medicine for reducing stress, boosting the immune system, and increasing oxygenation and blood flow by dilating the endothelium tissue that forms the inner lining of the blood vessels. A good belly laugh can exercise the heart more efficiently than a physical workout. Laughter can even help type-2 diabetics process sugar better.

There's a reason why marijuana is called the funny stuff. Cannabis and comedians forged deep bonds in the twentieth century—Groucho Marx, Lord Buckley, Lenny Bruce, Rodney Dangerfield, George Carlin, and many other satirists were pot smokers. Richard "Cheech" Marin and Tommy Chong, the stoner duo, rose to fame in the '70s and '80s, giggling across the silver screen with their giant spliffs, their ridiculous drug paraphernalia, and their taboo, minority-centric humor. *Up in Smoke*, their first film together, became a cult

---

some self-medicating patients, cannabis was an effective substitute for lithium carbonate, the conventional bipolar remedy; they said that marijuana took the edge off manic episodes and kept the lows under control (C. H. Ashton et al., "Cannabinoids in Bipolar Affective Disorder: A Review and Discussion of Their Therapeutic Potential," *Journal of Psychopharmacology* [May 2005]). A 2009 study by Norwegian scientists published in the journal *Psychological Medicine* linked cannabis with improved neurocognition in bipolar patients.

hit and inaugurated the stoner movie genre. Cheech and Chong satirized the slacker pothead stereotype in the same spirit that smoking a joint during the Reagan era might be prefaced with the exhortation "Let's get stupid!" Marijuana smokers jestfully incorporated official antipot rhetoric into their self-appraisals. Weed culture was full of self-deprecating humor. If you were a pot smoker back then, you had to laugh to keep from crying.

Home Grown

In 1982, U.S. law-enforcement agencies made record seizures of domestic marijuana. The tally included a spectacular $2 million bust less than ten miles from President Reagan's ranch in Santa Barbara, California. The amount of homegrown cannabis seized that year was 38 percent *higher* than official estimates of the entire American crop. And the narcs got only a small fraction of what was actually out there. What's more, homegrown weed, by some estimates, accounted for up to 15 percent of the total amount of marijuana consumed in the United States.

U.S. government efforts to crack down on smuggling from Mexico and Colombia, the principal suppliers of cannabis smoked by Americans, spurred a big leap in domestic cultivation. With spy satellites monitoring the border and crop dusters spraying toxic herbicide on foreign fields, homegrown cannabis seemed like a safer and more attractive option than imported weed. It turns out that American farmers excelled at growing marijuana—and they were growing a lot more of it than anyone realized. An indigenous cannabis industry initially took root in the lush rural landscape of Northern California and Oregon and from there it spread across the country en route to becoming America's number one cash crop—a remarkable accomplishment for a proscribed plant.

The Reagan administration launched an aggressive nationwide program, involving federal, state, and local law enforcement, which sought to crush domestic marijuana production. The DEA identified several pot hot spots in the continental United States. Topping the list was the so-called Emerald Triangle, a 10,000-square-mile swath of California redwoods, grapes, and ganja, encompassing Mendocino, Humboldt, and Trinity counties. A hundred miles or so north of San Francisco, the Emerald Triangle was the cannabis breadbasket of the Pacific Northwest, the heartland of domestic cultivation. Drug enforcement agents described California as a "source nation" because of the vast amounts of reefer grown in this region.

Marijuana horticulture in the Emerald Triangle evolved into a risky, high-stakes game that pitted tough, resourceful, and fiercely independent guerrilla growers against heavily armed government agents. Bereft of professional training and forced to maneuver in the shadow of a repressive drug war, American pot farmers nevertheless managed to transform "homegrown"—an erstwhile putdown for lousy ditch-weed—into the best, stoniest, and most expensive herb in the world.

When Carolyn ("Mountain Girl") Garcia, the matriarch of the Grateful Dead, started cultivating marijuana in her backyard in the early 1970s, making money wasn't part of the homegrown equation. For Mountain Girl and her husband, Jerry Garcia, cannabis was always more sacrament than commodity. Their home in Marin County, just north of San Francisco, attracted a steady stream of visitors and world travelers, including some who brought marijuana seeds from exotic places. Mountain Girl, the daughter of a botanist, had a way with plants in general and cannabis in particular. She planted a few pot seeds from Vietnam in a secluded spot in her outdoor garden and by summer's end the Dead and their extended family were getting blitzed on MG's "Marble Buddha" weed. It was stronger than any pot they had smoked. "Two hits of this stuff and you were gone, you'd turn into a marble Buddha," said Mountain Girl.

Mountain Girl shared her growing techniques with other eager gardeners. "I had a whole circle of friends who were doing it . . . this whole group of women growers who started in Mendocino," she recalled. As more would-be pot growers turned to her for advice, Mountain Girl put her thoughts down on paper. *Primo Plant,* the first cannabis cultivation handbook written by a woman, included homespun tips on composting, ground preparation, greenhouses, soil mixes, pruning, and cultivating a deeper relationship with one's plants. She felt that a grower's personal vibe became part of the plant's vibe. "Thai farmers pray and meditate in their gardens," MG noted.

One of Mountain Girl's infamous associates from the psychedelic Sixties had his own ideas about how to augment a marijuana crop. Augustus Owsley Stanley III, the legendary underground chemist who produced some 12 million doses of LSD before running afoul of the law, also got into growing reefer. He studied Rudolph Steiner's writings on biodynamic gardening and applied them in a rather idiosyncratic way to marijuana horticulture. Owsley maintained the herb grew better if you made love in your pot patch.

Cannabis cultivators had something else in mind when they spoke of "sexing the plants," a practice that entailed identifying and uprooting all the males to prevent the female marijuana plants from being pollinated. The sexually frustrated females produce bigger flower clusters with more sticky, aromatic resin in an attempt to catch pollen that never arrives. Known as *sinsemilla* (Spanish for "without seeds"), the unfertilized females buds, oozing psychoactive THC and other phytocannabinoids, are the most prized part of the marijuana crop.

This ancient method of cultivating potent, seedless reefer was rediscovered and resurrected by American horticulturists in the 1970s. Sexing the plants was simple—all you needed to know was what the male and female flowers looked like in their earliest stages. Mountain Girl wrote about it. So did Mel Frank and Ed Rosenthal in *The Marijuana Grower's Guide*. Cannabis, a hearty, adaptable plant that almost anyone could grow, also lent itself to sophisticated breeding and cultivation techniques, such as cloning and crossing strains, which were explained scientifically in Robert Connell Clarke's *Marijuana Botany*. These books would influence an up-and-coming generation of ganja gardeners who quickly picked up on the rule—if you want great stuff, snuff the males.

Homegrown sinsemilla was an instant hit among American pot smokers, who were willing to pay more for premium herb. Big Sur Holy Weed, one of the first commercially available sinsemilla strains from Santa Cruz, California, set a high standard. It rivaled Maui Wowie, the best smoke from Hawaii, another pot hot spot, according to the DEA. (In 1978, Hawaiian police estimated that *pakalolo*—"crazy weed"—had surpassed sugar to become the biggest cash crop in the fiftieth state.) Before long, tens of thousands of mom-and-pop pot growers on the mainland were harvesting small plots of tangy, seedless bud.

Thus began the golden age of marijuana cultivation in America. The advent of sinsemilla coincided with another crucial development—what Clarke referred to as "the great revolution" in cannabis genetics. Up until the early 1970s, nearly all the grass that Americans smoked were varieties of *Cannabis sativa,* which thrived in tropical or semitropical regions below the 30th latitude on either side of the equator. These were the great, landrace "heritage strains" (Acapulco Gold, Panama Red, Thai stick, etc.) that evolved in specific locales over countless generations. *Cannabis indica,* a different kind of marijuana, flourished between 30 and 50 degrees north and south of the equator. Indica was native to the Hindu Kush Mountains of Afghanistan and Pakistan. Traditionally, it has been used to make hashish in northern India, Nepal, and in Arab countries.

Whereas sativas typically are tall, slender plants with thin, light green leaves, indicas are usually compact and bushy with wider, darker leaves. Sativas are said to produce a soaring, cerebral high; indicas are known for a more sedative, dreamy, body-oriented buzz. Rebel smugglers associated with the Brotherhood of Eternal Love were among the first to bring indica seeds from Afghanistan, one of the world's oldest hashish cultures. Unlike *Cannabis sativa,* this type of marijuana grew well in cooler, harsher North American climates. Some indicas flowered as far north as Alaska. The introduction of indica seeds during the 1970s had a major impact on the trajectory of the homegrown ganja scene, enabling citizens in all fifty states to cultivate cannabis.

American horticulturists soon discovered that they could create unique hybrids by cross-pollinating indica and sativa plants. Pioneer pot agronomists used selective breeding techniques to coax desired traits into prominence: fast growth, early maturation, smaller (and more easily hidden) plants with bigger buds and higher THC potency. In the early 1980s, the Sacred Seed Company, an elusive underground network, began distributing some of the remarkable new crosses, such as Haze, Northern Lights, and Skunk #1. Derived directly from the pure landrace varieties, these vigorous hybrids served as building blocks for a surfeit of subsequent strains—each with its own particular look, smell, taste, and psychoactive subtleties. The complexity of gourmet ganja would reach a level of artistry comparable to the wine industry.

"The range of flavors expressed by the genus cannabis is extraordinary. No other plant on the planet can equal the cacophony of smells and tastes available from cannabis," says DJ Short, the breeder-artisan who conjured True Blueberry from several original heritage strains. Drenched in chromatic resin that shimmered like tiny silver ball bearings, True Blueberry became a popular mother plant utilized by talented outlaw gardeners who transformed marijuana into one of the most phenomenal success stories in the annals of modern horticulture. By varying the ratios of indica and sativa, self-taught botanical wizards were able to fine-tune the quality of the cannabis high. Together they comprised a secretive guild of world-class pot breeders who swapped seeds and insights with guerrilla growers at annual, below-the-radar harvest festivals on the Left Coast.

Cultivating high-quality cannabis wasn't rocket science, but it involved strenuous, time-consuming work and considerable attention to detail. Lots of things could go wrong. A single undetected male plant could pollinate all the females and ruin an entire crop. Mold was another disaster. From preparing the soil and adding the right nutrients to drying and meticulously curing and manicuring the harvested buds, the whole process was fraught with potential problems. "There is always a hint of danger in the air. The very nature of the game breeds anxiety," said one Emerald Triangle resident, who described pot growing as "farming with attitude."

For some outlaw horticulturists, growing sinsemilla wasn't merely a job—it was a calling, a passion, a personal statement of rebellion and independence. And it also happened to pay well. The price of pot quadrupled from the mid-'70s to the mid-'80s. Sweet sinsemilla, retailing for as much as $400 an ounce, was nearly worth its weight in gold. But cannabis horticulture offered rewards that went beyond simple cash. There was something deeply satisfying about tending a garden and watching marijuana plants mature into full-size botanical beauties with sticky, perfumed colas arching skyward and glistening like jewels.

Weed was the new wampum. In the Emerald Triangle, marijuana money seeded business start-ups and nurtured innovative firms that specialized in solar energy and green technologies. Others found that a modest cannabis crop afforded the ways and means to fight for wilderness and implement bioregional restoration projects. In Petrolia, a small coastal town in Humboldt County, a handful of green guerrillas who grew pot on the side took it upon themselves to reintroduce wild salmon into streams in the Mattole East River watershed. Vietnam vets, scattered in remote nooks and crannies throughout the Emerald Triangle, also grew cannabis to get by moneywise and to ease posttraumatic stress.

Marijuana made possible a quiet rural renaissance in Northern California, where some 30,000 pot growers took part in the largest illicit agricultural movement in American history. Cannabis was good medicine for the local economy. Farmers in the early 1980s could sell their sinsemilla for between $1,400 and $2,200 per pound—a phenomenal amount of cash compared with any other field crop. Thanks to donations from anonymous pot growers, volunteer fire departments had new equipment and community theater productions were amply funded. "As far as I'm concerned," said one redneck convert, "marijuana is the best thing that ever happened to Humboldt County."

Cannabis farming, historian Ray Raphael noted, "fit in with the tradition of rural anarchy [in] the coastal hills of California," which had long been a stronghold of rugged, don't-tread-on-me individualism. Growing pot was the "perfect embodiment of a people's capitalism," according to Raphael, who described the grassroots cannabis scene as "the first truly populist form of agriculture since homesteading the original frontier." The Jeffersonian ideal of a patchwork of self-reliant independent farmers was alive and well in the Emerald Triangle and adjacent counties. Sustained by frontier adventurism and good old Yankee ingenuity, cannabis farming was as American as apple pie.

The Reagan administration set its gun sights on the cannabis industry in the Emerald Triangle and turned the once-tranquil territory into a combat zone, a key battleground of the newly militarized war on drugs. Throughout the 1980s, narcs in camouflage fatigues ran roughshod over local residents, wielding machetes and hacking through pot gardens, large and small, under the auspices of CAMP, the federally funded Campaign Against Marijuana Planting. The foot soldiers for this annual summer offensive were drawn from several different agencies, including the State Highway Patrol, the FBI, National Guard, U.S. Forest Service, and, of course, the DEA. CAMP officers ran the gamut from ex–Green Berets with buzz cuts to military reservists, local cops, and sheriff's deputies, all convinced of the righteousness of their cause. They stood guard at twenty-four-hour checkpoints on roads during harvest season, while Huey helicopters buzzed homes and marijuana eradication squads invaded private property without search warrants. It was a time when Northern California "rejoined, operationally speaking, the Third World," as Thomas Pynchon wrote in *Vineland,* his novel set in America's prime pot-growing region during the Reagan years.

The fact that the Emerald Triangle was the chosen home of many Sixties radicals who remained active in green causes may have been one of the reasons this place was singled out for selective, paramilitary overkill. "There [was] a visceral hostility towards those people that could now be vented," explained Eric Sterling, a former congressional staffer who helped write Reagan-era drug war legislation and later became an outspoken drug-policy critic. DEA agents in uniform marched through one Northern California town, chanting "*War on drugs! War on drugs!*"

Local residents banded together to defend their civil liberties. They monitored and videotaped CAMP abuses and filed suit in court to thwart the de facto military occupation of their communities. In 1985, a federal judge, citing the high probability of harm to Mendocino County residents, formally enjoined all CAMP personnel "from entering by foot, motor vehicle, or helicopter any private property other than open fields without a warrant." The judge also ordered federal and local police to refrain "from using helicopters for general surveillance purposes, except over open fields" and not within "five hundred feet of any structure, person, or vehicle."

As soon as Reagan sent in the troops, the risks for commercial cultivators increased and, consequently, they charged—and got—more for their product. Mandatory-minimum sentencing automatically meant five years in prison for growing one hundred plants. Thanks to prohibition's distortion of the laws of supply and demand, pot profits were so vast that some folks simply couldn't afford not to grow marijuana. "That's my price support system," said one ganja farmer, pointing to a CAMP helicopter crisscrossing the sky.

What started as an outdoor hobby pursued by hippies and organic gardeners in Northern California became an economic lifeline for an estimated 100,000 to 150,000 commercial pot growers scattered throughout the country in the mid-1980s. Growing sinsemilla made dollars as well as sense for American farmers struggling to keep afloat at a time when one-third of family farms in the United States was being driven into insolvency by political decisions made in Washington, which rigged the game in favor of a few agribusiness giants. Out of desperation, some Midwest farmers started planting marijuana to save their farms from foreclosure. This practice also caught on among farmers in Kentucky, the Ozarks, eastern Oklahoma, and parts of the Deep South.

On August 5, 1985, the federal government launched the largest coordinated antimarijuana crackdown in American history. "Operation Delta-9" deployed 2,200 federal, state, and local law-enforcement agents in all fifty states to destroy a quarter million cannabis plants in three days. In response to these intensified efforts to wipe out domestic marijuana, resilient growers survived by adapting to the harsh political environment much like the plant itself endured in the wild. When federal legislation made it easier for law enforcement to seize the property of drug suspects, shadowy marijuana moguls started planting on public lands so as not to incur forfeiture penalties. Many growers moved their operations indoors to avoid detection via helicopter and U-2 aerial surveillance.

No matter what the U.S. government did, marijuana wouldn't go away. By targeting overseas supplies, the Reagan administration provided a substantial boost for domestic pot farmers. Uncle Sam's assault on outdoor ganja gardens triggered a rapid increase in the number of indoor grow-ops. Nearly every major technological development that improved marijuana cultivation was driven by law-enforcement intervention.

Outlaw horticulturists, based primarily in California and the Pacific Northwest, created new hybrids that thrived in a controlled indoor setting. Indica-dominant strains did especially well indoors. Updated cultivation manuals offered advice on sophisticated ways to speed photosynthesis and increase yield by gorging plants on just the right amount of special nutrients, water, carbon dioxide, and twenty-four-hour light exposure. By abruptly altering the light cycle, the indoor grower could force the plants to flower before they were two months old. Hydroponics stores, specializing in the latest equipment for indoor gardeners, supplied high-pressure sodium lamps, halide lights, and various irrigation, heat, and moisture-control gizmos. Spicy, genetically enhanced bud could now be nurtured in garages, attics, and walk-in closets in every city and town in America.

"The plant adapted more brilliantly to its strange new environment than anyone could have expected," Michael Pollan wrote in *The Botany of Desire*. "For cannabis, the drug war is what global warming will be for much of the rest of the plant world, a cataclysm some species will turn into a great opportunity to expand their range." It's ironic, he noted, "that the creation of a powerful new taboo against marijuana led directly to the creation of a powerful new plant."

Going Dutch

As the U.S. government intensified its campaign against homegrown marijuana, American pot agronomists and seed breeders, feeling the heat, sought and found refuge in the Netherlands, a nation long known as an oasis of social, political, and religious tolerance. During the 1980s, a wave of expert cannabis cultivators from the West Coast migrated to Amsterdam, where state-licensed coffee shops were permitted to sell small quantities of hash and grass to patrons eighteen years or older. These American expatriates brought with them marijuana seeds and sinsemilla know-how. They helped set up seed banks and breeding programs that enabled many Dutch ganja growers to get started. To the dismay of hapless U.S. officials, Holland bombarded the world with pot seeds, which were mailed in nondescript envelopes to growers in North America and across the globe.

Transported across the ocean by American botanical specialists, carefully crafted cannabis genetics landed on fertile turf in the Netherlands, a country with a passionate horticultural tradition dating back to the seventeenth-century tulip craze. Cannabis buds had initially been brought to Holland by black migrants from Surinam, the former Dutch colony in South America. But marijuana didn't catch on among the Dutch until the mid-1960s when the pot-puffing "Provos," the vanguard of Europe's lyrical left, launched a campaign of political surrealism and anarchy that shattered the spell of linear protest on the continent.

The Provos—the name was short for *provocateur*—combined avant-garde art and communard politics not unlike their contemporaries in the San Francisco Bay Area, the Merry Pranksters and the Diggers. The Dutch radicals unrolled reams of newsprint through the streets of Amsterdam to protest the "daily newspapers which brainwash our people." When denied a permit for a demonstration, the Provos showed up anyway with blank banners and handed out blank leaflets to passersby. Marijuana smoking figured prominently at Provo happenings on the Spui, a busy Amsterdam plaza, where weekly confrontations between the police and the "provotariat" attracted lots of media attention. Amsterdam cops, overreacting to pinprick provocations, roughed up nonviolent pot smokers and arrested hundreds of people. As a result, cannabis became associated with civil unrest and Dutch authorities deemed marijuana advocates a public nuisance.

After the group disbanded in 1967, two erstwhile Provo ringleaders, Kees Hoekert and Robert Jasper Grootveld, immersed themselves full-time in cannabis activism. In 1969, they founded the Lowlands Weed Company, the "first ever pure hemp outlet," which sold inexpensive marijuana plants that were openly displayed on a multicolored houseboat floating in a quaint Amsterdam canal. They claimed to have discovered a loophole in Dutch law that prohibited the possession or sale of the dried tops of marijuana plants but said nothing about the seeds or whole plants.*

Dutch officials cast a benign but wary eye on music and dance venues such as the Melkweg and the Paradiso, where young people in Amsterdam could purchase hashish, LSD, cocaine, and heroin from dozens of street dealers who hovered inside and outside these government-supported youth clubs. Then one day in the spring of 1972, a Dutch student named Wernard Bruining and a klatch of hippie friends took over an abandoned bakery and opened a marijuana "tea house" on Weesperzijde, an inconspicuous side street in Amsterdam. They called it Mellow Yellow, after the song by Donovan, and began serving food, weed, hashish, and nonalcoholic beverages to customers who flocked to Holland's first low-key over-the-counter cannabis retail store. "A few tokes of good cannabis can dissolve the spider webs that are woven around us by authorities," Bruining opined.

By the time it shut its doors after six years and several police raids, Mellow Yellow had inspired a handful of imitators. In 1975, Maarten Brusselers opened a more upscale cannabis café called Rusland ("Russia") and Henk de Vries launched the eye-catching (and soon-to-be world famous) Bulldog coffee shop in Amsterdam's Red Light district; hard drugs were strictly forbidden at both commercial outlets. Arrested on numerous occasions, these Dutch marijuana pioneers practiced civil disobedience as if it were a martial art. They were committed to remaking the law by breaking the law.

During this period, the Dutch government was reevaluating its drug policies. In response to the upsurge of cannabis smoking in the rebel Sixties, Dutch officials appointed psychiatrist Pieter Baan to head an inquiry into the root causes of drug use among youth and make appropriate recommendations. The Baan Commission presented its findings to the Dutch Minister of Health in 1972, the same year the Shafer Commission delivered its report to President Nixon and the Le Dain Commission weighed in in Canada. The three commissions reached the same conclusions concurrently: decriminalize, destigmatize,

* Grootveld, a performance artist, liked to play games with the authorities. At times he dressed up as an American Indian and ambled into a police station to engage in friendly chats about cannabis. To confuse the cops, he called at all hours, passing along tips about nonexistent pot parties and triggering raids for nothing. He even called the police on himself to underscore the idiocy of marijuana prohibition.

above all recognize that in the case of cannabis, "it's more sensible for a society to live with it than to fight its use," as Dr. Lester Grinspoon reasoned.

Whereas U.S. authorities rejected the Shafer Commission's policy prescriptions and Canadian politicians ignored the Le Dain report, the Dutch government decided to implement Baan's proposals. Dutch officials understood that the goal of a drug-free society was unrealistic. Rather than tilting at just-say-no windmills, the Netherlands opted out of Washington's global anticannabis crusade and embraced a harm-reduction approach that sought to minimize excessive and inappropriate drug consumption while encouraging less dangerous alternatives. The Dutch recognized that cannabis was a much safer substance than heroin, cocaine, alcohol, and nicotine.

In 1976, the Dutch parliament essentially legalized marijuana possession for personal use and retail sale, while increasing police efforts against (and penalties for) hard drugs. Technically cannabis remained illegal in keeping with Holland's commitment to the United Nations Single Convention on Narcotic Drugs, but the Dutch Ministry of Justice simply chose not to enforce the law against marijuana. In a rebuke to American gateway theorists who argued that marijuana stimulates an appetite for addictive narcotics, Dutch experts determined that social factors rather than the pharmacological properties of cannabis were germane to hard-drug use. While marijuana smoking in and of itself did not function as a stepping-stone, marijuana prohibition put cannabis consumers in contact with pushers selling an array of illicit substances. In order to minimize the temptation to experiment with heroin and cocaine, it was crucial to disentangle cannabis from the hard-drug market and create a tightly controlled distribution network for the herb, as the Baan Commission had counseled. The nascent coffeehouse system in Amsterdam fit in well with this plan.

Thanks in large part to the Netherlands' open-minded health minister Irene Vorrink, the Dutch government created a set of guidelines under which coffee shops could sell marijuana and hashish without fear of criminal prosecution. The basic rules included a ban on advertising, no underage sales, a five-gram limit on individual transactions, and absolutely no white powder or needles on the premises.

Soon there were hundreds of licensed cannabis coffee shops in Amsterdam and hundreds more scattered throughout the Netherlands. Most featured a particular theme or ambience with various amenities and different styles of music—from bebop to reggae to punk or rock 'n' roll. Pictures of Bob Marley adorned many a coffee shop window. With names like Bluebird and Grasshopper, cannabis cafés were more than just distribution points for depenalized weed and hashish; they were multicultural institutions, a place to socialize and meet people of various ethnicities and nationalities, share a smoke and conversation, read a magazine, shoot pool, play chess. Dutch cannabis cafés became a favorite hangout of American soldiers on leave from military bases in Europe—which perturbed U.S. officials to no end.

Millions of "flower tourists" from all over the world descended upon Amsterdam to partake and indulge. "The expression 'going Dutch' took on a whole new meaning. Now it meant going to the Netherlands to get high in a coffee shop!" remarked Nol van Schaik, a prominent cannabis activist who owned several coffee shops in picturesque Haarlem.

But even as the coffee shop system became institutionalized in Holland, there was no law that permitted domestic marijuana cultivation or the importation of cannabis from abroad. Consequently, coffee shop owners, who formed their own association and political lobby, would continue to operate in a legal limbo, openly selling cannabis to retail customers while maneuvering in the shadows to obtain a wholesale supply. It wasn't an ideal arrangement, but it worked. The Dutch government profited, as well, by collecting taxes on gray-market sales.

Initially, the typical coffee shop menu included cannabis-infused pastries called "space cakes" and a dozen or so varieties of hashish and marijuana smuggled from different regions around the world. It wasn't until the early 1980s that the Dutch started to cultivate their own *Nederwiet* (Netherweed), a development precipitated by the arrival of a legendary American pot grower named Ed Holloway, who relocated to Holland in 1979 after his organic marijuana crop in the States got raided. Known affectionately as "Old Ed" to his Dutch acolytes, Holloway, then in his early sixties, looked like a slim version of Santa Claus, with long white hair and a generous beard. This gentle soul came bearing gifts—most notably his forbidden knowledge of cannabis genetics and sinsemilla cultivation, which Old Ed shared with Wernard Bruining, the original Mellow Yellow coffee shop crusader. Old Ed's seeds were the first to be sold commercially in Amsterdam, by the Lowlands Weed Company, which Bruining and Kees Hoekert, the ex-Provo, launched in 1980.

Old Ed had a colorful history. A former aeronautical engineer with General Dynamics, he went AWOL from the military-industrial complex and started smoking pot and letting his hair down in the 1960s. This highflier with an astronomical IQ got turned on to grass by his son, who came back from an early tour of duty in Vietnam with some scintillating sativa. Old Ed liked it so much that he embarked upon a personal quest to cultivate exceptional cannabis. He said he learned the tricks of the trade by listening to his plants. That was Old Ed's message—listen carefully to the plants, grow organic, share information, spread the seeds, and never give up. When asked what cannabis meant to him, Old Ed smiled: "Marijuana is our medicine. It makes us feel good. What else do we need to know?"

Old Ed inspired Bruining and a handful of other "sinsemilla guerrillas" who made it their mission to transform Holland into the Jamaica of Europe. The "Dream Team," as they called themselves, developed a way to mass-produce clones (cuttings that are genetic duplicates) from exemplary mother plants so that ganja greenhouse growers were assured of a uniform, high-quality female crop. By the early 1980s, Old Ed's green army was supplying homegrown sinsemilla—*Nederwiet*—to the Bulldog and other coffee shops.

Bruining also established Positronics, the first cannabis superstore in the Netherlands, which sold seeds, clones, hydroponics equipment, indoor grow lights, and anything else a cannabis cultivator might need. ("If you don't smoke it, don't grow it" was the Dream Team's motto.) Within a few years, the production of sinsemilla was widespread in small-scale greenhouses throughout the country. *Nederwiet* became the new tulip mania.

Catalyzed by the Dream Team, the sinsemilla revolution in Holland spread like wildfire to other parts of the continent. Amsterdam remained the epicenter of the burgeoning Eurocannabis industry, a multibillion-dollar juggernaut personified by feisty Dutch entrepreneurs such as Ben Dronkers. With an ever-present spliff in hand, Dronkers built a formidable commercial empire that serviced pot-growing customers around the world. A multitasking seed magnate, marijuana breeder, coffee shop owner, and resolute hemp activist, he rode the crest of the green tsunami, the Dutch cannabusiness boom. His love for cannabis and his innate Dutch business instincts made him very wealthy, even though he was arrested more than eighty times by Dutch police.

While sparring with fickle authorities, Dronkers founded Sensi Seeds, the cornerstone of his family-run business operation. It became the biggest player in the lucrative ganja seed market, the Baskin-Robbins of seed banks, with many varieties to choose from. Built upon the pioneering efforts of American expatriates, Sensi Seeds and a dozen or so friendly Dutch competitors collected, preserved, and interbred hundreds of different cannabis strains. These seed companies kept scrupulously detailed records of genetic ancestry, which helped Dutch breeders develop additional hybrids. Each new designer strain produced and sold by Dutch companies began with a hybrid seed that encoded the plant's unique genetic blueprint. Cannabis was no longer identified by the region where it grew, but by its genetically jumbled parentage. Certain seed banks trademarked the names of their strains, but some veteran breeders from the States weren't keen on the idea and enforcing these trademarks was problematic due to the illegal status of the plant.

In 1985, Dronkers opened the Hash, Marijuana, and Hemp Museum in

Amsterdam, which offered information to visitors about the many historical and modern uses of cannabis for medicinal, industrial, religious, and recreational purposes. It included a real marijuana garden, pipe and roach clip collections, and an 1836 Dutch Bible made of hemp paper, along with samples of hemp fabrics, hemp rope, and other cannabusiness items. Dronkers recruited an American comrade, Ed Rosenthal, to serve as the museum's first curator. Rosenthal—not to be confused with Old Ed—was involved in the Dutch sinsemilla scene from the very beginning.

A California-based cannabis advocate with a crusty sense of humor, Rosenthal was described by *The New York Times* as "the pothead's answer to Ann Landers, Judge Judy, Martha Stewart and the Burpee Garden Wizard all in one." Well known for his "Ask Ed" advice column in *High Times*, the unrepentant Yippie was instrumental in steering indoor growers toward high-intensity sodium lamps and other technological gadgetry that he flagged as a journalist. "I just give advice on how to cultivate a better garden. It's not my fault that marijuana, the plant that is my specialty, is illegal," he explained.

Rosenthal kept his readers abreast of new developments in the cannabis underground, such as the Dutch "sea of green" gardens, wherein dozens of genetically identical plants grown from clones are crammed together in greenhouses under a perpetual blaze of light, hot-wired to the same nutrient regimen and forced to flower in lockstep. These pampered plants had identical hairy calyxes with the same cannabinoid-terpenoid-flavonoid mix, the same resinous medicament.

Rosenthal and Dronkers were among the stoned cognoscenti who gathered at the inaugural Cannabis Cup, hosted by *High Times* in Amsterdam in 1987, underscoring once again that Holland was the place to be if you were into marijuana. What began as a one-day contest evolved into a weeklong celebration of all things hemp, an annual psychoactive soirée that attracted thousands of ganja fans from around the world. There were speeches, strategy sessions, new product demonstrations, and lots of pot parties, leading up to the climactic moment when the judges reached their decision and crowned the year's best cannabis strain, a verdict based on superb look, flavor, aroma, and quality of the high. The winner of the first Cannabis Cup, the Oscars of pot, was Skunk #1, an Afghan-sativa cross created by David Watson, from Santa Cruz, California. A mercurial genius, Watson had been at the forefront of the great migration of American talent to the Netherlands.

Watson's award-winning weed was a potent, adaptable hybrid and its genetics would be woven into countless modern strains. (In the years ahead, pot prohibitionists misappropriated the term *skunk* and used it as a generic way of referring to any strong reefer.) Watson "the Skunkman" and his perspicacious business partner, Robert Connell Clarke, obtained a license from the Dutch government to pursue advanced scientific research into cannabinoid botany. Their company, HortaPharm, was not a commercial seed bank or grow operation. Formed in 1989, HortaPharm broke new ground in horticultural pharmacology.

Watson and Clarke isolated various phytocannabinoids and terpenes in order to explore their medicinal potential. This dynamic duo took cannabis science to a whole other level. They were the first to breed "chemovar" plants—marijuana plants that express just one cannabinoid. HortaPharm developed a THC chemovar and a CBD chemovar—and that was just the beginning. They also created a seed library with hemp germ plasm they had gathered from all over the world, a priceless collection that included old landrace cannabis strains threatened with extinction because of ecocidal U.S. drug-war policies.

Drug-War Doublespeak

Barry Seal was sitting behind the wheel of his white Cadillac in a Salvation Army parking lot in Baton Rouge, Louisiana, on February 19, 1986, when two men carrying machine guns approached him and opened fire gangland-style. Seal died instantly, his head, neck, and chest riddled with bullets. Federal officials called it a professional assassination. One of the biggest drug traffickers ever brought before a U.S. court of law had been slain in broad daylight.

By his own admission, Seal had made more than $50 million hauling marijuana and other drugs since the mid-1970s. A gung-ho pilot and inveterate hustler, "he could fly anything with wings," said one of Seal's smuggling associates. Seal moved marijuana in ever-increasing quantities and then graduated to cocaine, which was even more profitable and easier to handle. He also smuggled Quaaludes, explosives, guns, and other contraband. Indicted on drug and money-laundering charges, Seal flipped and cut a deal with the feds to avoid a prison sentence. In 1984, he became a key DEA witness in the U.S. government's case against the leaders of the Medellín cocaine cartel. Later that year he was caught flying a big load of marijuana into Louisiana, but charges were mysteriously dropped.

Nineteen eighty-four was also the year that Congress passed the Boland Amendment, which expressly forbid U.S. military aid to the "contra" rebels who were fighting to overthrow Nicaragua's left-wing Sandinista government. Hell-bent on defeating the Sandinistas, Reagan operatives broke U.S. and international law by establishing a secret arms pipeline to sustain the contras. Seal's aviation talents were appreciated by Lieutenant Colonel Oliver

North, who supervised the illicit contra supply effort in cahoots with CIA director, William Casey, and Vice President George H. W. Bush's office. Seal and several other highfliers worked both sides of the street under U.S. government protection—transporting weapons to the contras and returning with weed or white powder. The quid pro quo was simple and time-tested: If you helped the CIA's proxy army, then U.S. authorities would look away while you smuggled drugs into the United States.

Pegged by the DEA as one of the largest marijuana smugglers in the United States during the 1980s, Michael Palmer flew contra missions for Vortex, a CIA proprietary front. When Palmer was indicted in Detroit in 1986 for marijuana smuggling and again in 1989 in Louisiana on charges of bringing 150 tons of cannabis into the country, he invoked his CIA ties and got off scot-free. "The whole thing is too sleazy for words," remarked a State Department official regarding Palmer's untouchable status.

In 1983, U.S. Attorney General William French Smith had secretly granted the CIA an exemption sparing it from a legal requirement to report on drug smuggling by agency assets. This loophole applied to the Cuban exile Frank Castro, a longtime CIA asset based in Miami. In the mid-1970s, Castro was involved with a right-wing Cuban umbrella organization known as CORU, which united several extremist factions under its banner. CORU was linked to a wave of kidnappings, murders, and terrorist attacks throughout the Americas, including the 1976 midair bombing of a Cubana Airlines passenger jet that killed all seventy-three people on board. Frank Castro became the target of a U.S. Justice Department investigation for his role in a plot to smuggle 425,000 pounds of marijuana through Beaumont, Texas, in 1983. By this time, Castro was neck-deep in the contra-supply imbroglio, ferrying weapons and providing drug profits to contra leaders camped in Costa Rica, and the Texas drug charges were quietly dropped. He was identified in a CIA cable dated March 7, 1986, as the principal liaison between the Colombian cocaine barons and anti-Communist Cuban militants in Miami.

"Drugs and covert operations go together like fleas on a dog," said former CIA analyst David MacMichael. Scratch the surface of the narcotics trade and once again it seems that certain drug dealers were okay by the CIA as long as they snorted the anti-Communist line. In 1989, Lt. Col. North and three other U.S. officials were banned for life from Costa Rica after that country's parliament found hard evidence of CIA complicity in cocaine trafficking. A report by Inspector General Frederick Hitz of the CIA subsequently identified more than fifty contras and contra-related entities that were implicated in the drug trade—all while the Reagan administration was purporting to wage a no-holds-barred war on illicit substances! For sheer hypocrisy, this was hard to top. Official rhetoric emphasized the importance of ending drug abuse, but federal policies had the opposite effect, particularly with respect to cocaine.

Coke, blow, rock, snow, nose candy, Peruvian marching powder—by whatever name, cocaine is an addictive stimulant that can be snorted, smoked, or injected. Movie director Oliver Stone called it "a bad breath drug." His 1987 film *Wall Street* captured the frenetic, go-go capitalism of the Reagan era, with its aggressive individualism, cocaine bingeing, and ruthless, profit-über-alles obsession. If the Seventies were the Me Decade, then the Eighties were the Fuck You Decade. In an age of unfettered corporate greed, cocaine evoked dreams of the eternal high, the economic boom that never ends. Coca powder, popular among fashionistas and young professionals, revved up Wall Street during the Reagan presidency, while crack, "the 'fast food' of the cocaine world," decimated America's impoverished inner cities.

During the 1980s, according to data gathered by the Institute for Social Research at the University of Michigan, the use of marijuana declined among high school seniors while the use of cocaine increased—the exact opposite of what the gateway theory would have predicted. An article of faith among American drug warriors, the gateway theory maintained that smoking pot was a stepping-stone to addictive narcotics: the more people who smoked weed, the more junkies and coke fiends. Numerous studies, however, have debunked this idea. In 1982, the National Academy of Sciences (NAS) reiterated the findings of the Shafer Commission: Cannabis is not a gateway drug. Contrary to prohibitionist liturgy, statistical evidence indicated that *less* marijuana was associated with the wider use of more dangerous substances.

The Reagan administration remained indifferent to the spread of crack cocaine until the summer of 1986, when college basketball star Len Bias died of heart failure from cocaine poisoning. A few days later, Cleveland Browns defensive back Don Rogers followed him to the grave, another drug casualty. Mass media had a field day as antidrug pandemonium engulfed the nation's capital. *The Washington Post* called it "the legislative equivalent of a cattle stampede" with Congress "rushing pell mell to approve a sweeping anti-drug bill." Eager to appear tough on crime, leaders of both parties outdid each other ratcheting up the drug-war rhetoric. South Carolina Republican congressman Thomas Arnett went so far as to proclaim that "drugs are a threat worse than nuclear warfare or any chemical warfare waged on any battlefield."

A 1986 *New York Times*/CBS poll listed illicit drug abuse as the "nation's leading overall concern." The full-blown moral panic culminated in the near-unanimous passage of the Anti–Drug Abuse Act, breathtaking in its scope, which Reagan signed into law in October. Twenty-nine new mandatory minimums with dizzyingly steep sentences went into effect immediately, including the newly defined crime of selling marijuana within a thousand feet of a school. In addition to nixing the possibility of probation or parole even in minor possession cases, these harsh mandatory-minimum guidelines left federal judges with no discretion when it came to punishing drug offenses.

Within a year, most states had enacted similar mandatory-minimum sentencing provisions. Instead of targeting major dealers, police and narcotics agents focused on low-level, nonviolent offenders. To save their own hide, many drug defendants copped a plea and/or cut deals with law enforcement and became snitches, thereby creating a "cottage industry of cooperators," as one defense attorney put it.

The result was predictable: Incarceration rates exploded. In 1980, roughly 500,000 people were locked up in state and federal prisons; by the time Reagan left office in 1989, the number of prisoners had doubled. The rate of incarceration in the United States per capita dwarfed that of other industrialized nations. Drug sentences represented the largest growth segment of America's penal population. And cannabis, which was like low-hanging fruit for cops, accounted for the lion's share of drug arrests and convictions. Marijuana offenses had become "so ubiquitous that they might be said to be driving the entire criminal-justice system," Rutgers University professor Douglas Husak observed.

Even though whites and blacks used illegal drugs at about the same rate, blacks were arrested, prosecuted, and jailed at much higher rates than whites. Getting caught with a joint meant being photographed, fingerprinted, and permanently entered in a vast criminal database. Perhaps marijuana functioned as a gateway after all—feeding hundreds of thousands of minority youth each year into the maw of the criminal-justice system. People of color, particularly young African Americans, were the main targets of Reagan's drug war, even though most illegal drug users were white. The incarceration of minorities skyrocketed during the Reagan years to the point where black prisoners outnumbered white inmates for the first time since slavery.

The war on drugs was integral to the post-'60s conservative ascendancy, which depended heavily on racial backlash. Although unadulterated bigotry (à la Harry Anslinger) was no longer part of prohibitionist discourse, illicit substances still offered the Reaganites a way to express racist themes in code. The Anti–Drug Abuse Act of 1986 mandated much longer sentences for possessing crack than for powder cocaine, a measure aimed at black ghetto dwellers. Crack dealers were punished far more severely than powder cocaine suppliers. "These racially targeted patterns affect more than imprisonment: They have effectively eroded much of the voting rights victories won by the civil rights movement during the 1960s," explained Ira Glasser, director of the American Civil Liberties Union.

Glasser noted that nearly five million Americans are "barred from voting because of felony disenfranchisement laws. . . . In the states of the Deep South, thirty percent of black men are barred from voting because of felony convictions." The drug war provided a means of perpetuating Jim Crow under a less obvious guise. "Just as Jim Crow laws were a successor system to slavery in the attempt to keep blacks subjugated, so drug prohibition has become a successor system to Jim Crow laws in targeting black citizens, removing them from civil society and then barring them from the right to vote," said Glasser, who called the drug war "a major, though largely unrecognized, civil rights issue."

During the 1980s, the official response to illicit-drug use increasingly assumed the form of attacks on the civil and political rights of minorities. The have-nots and have-littles bore the brunt of Reaganomics, which widened the gap between rich and poor, resulting in greater inequality, social dislocation, and an estimated two million homeless Americans. Reagan-era economic restructuring was accompanied by an intense criminal-justice crackdown. The war on drugs served as a pretext to keep plenty of police armed and ready should popular unrest ever reach a boiling point. The police used drugs as a surrogate—it allowed them to arrest and harass a large segment of society.

For everyone else, there were piss tests. During the coke-crazed summer of '86, Reagan asked that government workers in crucial occupations be required to take random urine tests to ensure that the workplace was "drug free." To get the ball rolling, the president, the vice president, and seventy-eight other White House officials took time out from their jobs to urinate for a drug-free America.

After this golden-shower publicity stunt, peeing into a bottle became an all-American ritual in schools and industry. Soon a majority of Fortune 500 companies required their employees and job applicants to submit urine samples. In some fields, such as transportation, sports, and civil service, nearly every worker would undergo urine tests, which were geared toward identifying pot smokers rather than users of hard drugs or alcohol. An occasional toker who had puffed at a party three weeks earlier might test positive, while another worker who had snorted coke or binged on booze a couple of days before the test would pass with flying colors. That's because nonpsychoactive cannabinoid metabolites remain in the body much longer than traces of cocaine or booze.

Urine tests don't measure on-the-job impairment. But they could disclose if you're the kind of person who enjoys smoking weed now and then. At a time when anticommunism was on the wane as a mobilizing ideology, drug tests functioned much like the loyalty oaths of the McCarthy era. Disloyal subjects could find themselves out of a job. Urine testing gave rise to a cottage industry of start-ups hawking products and techniques designed to fool the exam.

Marijuana use in the distant past was also held against people. The career of federal judge Douglas H. Ginsburg, a Reagan Supreme Court nominee, hit a roadblock in 1987 when National Public Radio revealed that he had smoked pot as a young law professor in the early 1970s. This disclosure, which torpedoed his Supreme Court nomination, came amid a much bigger Reagan administration drug scandal. The Iran-contra affair blew wide open when Nicaraguan soldiers shot down an American C-120 cargo plane (once owned by the drug smuggler Barry Seal) that was illegally delivering weapons to anti-Sandinista rebels. In a move that deflected attention from the CIA's drug-related misdeeds in Latin America, the White House acknowledged that U.S. operatives had sold missile parts to America's archenemy, Islamic fundamentalist Iran, and diverted the profits to finance the contra war.

While Congress fumbled the Iran-contra investigation, a Senate Foreign Relations subcommittee chaired by Massachusetts Democrat John Kerry launched an extensive probe into the role of the contras in marijuana and cocaine trafficking. Over a two-year period, the subcommittee held twenty-three days of hearings, took testimony from forty-seven witnesses, and produced a 1,166-page report that was largely ignored by the American press. "There was substantial evidence of drug smuggling . . . on the part of individual Contras, Contra suppliers, Contra pilots, mercenaries who worked with the Contras, and Contra supporters throughout the region," the Kerry report concluded. "U.S. officials involved in Central America failed to address the drug issue for fear of jeopardizing the war against Nicaragua . . . Senior U.S. policy makers were not immune to the idea that drug money was a perfect solution to the Contras' funding problems."

Yet another narco-quagmire was brewing in the Golden Crescent of Southwest Asia, where the highlands of Afghanistan, Pakistan, and Iran converge. This region became the largest source of heroin in the world during the 1980s while the CIA trained and supplied the mujahideen rebels who were fighting against a Soviet-backed regime in Kabul. The price tag for the operation was \$3.2 billion—the most expensive undertaking in CIA history. The CIA essentially told the DEA to get lost for the duration of the war while Afghan mujahideen factions and their U.S.-backed Pakistani benefactors profited mightily from the opium trade. The Reagan administration was mum regarding massive amounts of unaccounted-for U.S. aid to the mujahideen, which helped grease a major arms-for-heroin pipeline in the war zone. And U.S. newsmedia, forever marveling at the Teflon president, lacked the gumption to report the obvious: Reagan's war on drugs was a sham so long as American intelligence supported groups that peddled narcotics.

Photographed behind huge piles of cash and a cache of heroin or cocaine seized by law enforcement, Reagan blithely proclaimed that America was winning the war on drugs. In 1988, his last year in office, Congress passed yet another round of harsh antidrug legislation, which authorized the eviction of public housing residents if any member or guest of the household was involved in a drug offense. If a black teenager smoked a joint on the corner, his grandmother could lose her apartment. Forfeiture laws were expanded and a billion dollars in grant money was designated for state and local fuzz under the Edward Byrne Memorial State and Local Law Enforcement Assistance Program. An additional $5.5 billion was earmarked to equip and train police. The 1988 Anti–Drug Abuse Act also established a cabinet-level "drug czar" to oversee the newly formed Office of National Drug Control Policy. In the same bill Congress declared it the "policy of the United States Government to create a Drug-Free America by 1995."

The notion that the war on drugs was winnable may have been little more than a pipe dream, but the collateral damage was real.

The Hemperor

"*What do we want legalized?*" a voice blared through a bullhorn at an April 1989 rally in Chicago's Grant Park.

"*Marijuana!*" screamed several hundred protestors who never succumbed to just-say-no.

"*What's going to save the family farmer?*" the bullhorn bellowed.

"*Marijuana!*" the crowd effused.

"*What's going to save the country?*"

"*Marijuana!*"

The featured speaker at this Midwestern smoke-in was Jack Herer, a charismatic, six-foot-three-inch, 230-pound former Goldwater Republican with a scraggly gray beard and a deep, resonant voice. Imbued with righteous rage, this barrel-chested firebrand proclaimed the wonders of hemp, spouting statistics gleaned from government documents and waving a copy of his self-published treatise, *The Emperor Wears No Clothes*, which revealed the lost history of hemp. First published in 1985, this book was instrumental in cata-

Jack Herer, patron saint of cannabis for medicine, fiber, food, and recreation
(Courtesy of Dan Skye)

lyzing a renewed interest in the many forgotten industrial uses of a plant once prized by America's Founding Fathers. Translated into several languages, it became a worldwide underground bestseller, the bible of the modern-day hemp movement.

While most pot smokers preferred to keep a low profile during the Reagan years, Herer (rhymes with *terror*) refused to kowtow to a prohibitionist regime that he saw as utterly corrupt and depraved. "The Hemperor" had a knack for turning the tables on his opponents, asserting that the laws against cannabis were criminal, not the plant itself. Herer believed that hemp should be legal because it is an eco-friendly source of fiber, fuel, medicine, and food. He depicted the much-maligned weed as a virtual panacea for humankind.

Before he turned on to cannabis in 1969, Herer hated hippies, environmentalists, and antiwar youth. "I was a normal American nerd," he confessed. "I had never gotten high. Nobody ever told me about marijuana." That changed when the Los Angeles–based corporate salesman fell in love with a pot-smoking woman who convinced him to give it a go. "She tried three times to get me high. Finally it worked, and I had the most incredible sex I'd ever had,"

Herer recounted. After they finished making love, his first words were: "Why is this against the law?"

The mind-blown businessman soon traded in his polyester suits for tie-dyed T-shirts and got involved in the fledgling cannabis reform movement. One day, while volunteering for the 1972 California Marijuana Initiative, Herer met veteran pot proponent Michael Aldrich, who showed him some rolling papers that were made from hemp. "You mean there's something else you can do with cannabis besides smoke it?" a wide-eyed Herer asked. Back then few pot smokers in the USA knew much about hemp. Aldrich explained that it was a versatile fiber crop suitable for making clothes, paper, building material, insulation, biofuel, and much else.

For Herer, this was a game-changer. He embarked upon a quest to learn all that he could about the hidden history of hemp. He scoured libraries and newspaper archives, searching for information. Soon he could rattle off dozens of little-known facts about hemp's role in American history, such as the 60 tons of hemp rigging used on the USS *Constitution* (the legendary "Old Ironsides" battleship) and the price of the hemp canvas used on covered wagons driven west across the Great Plains. Rudolph Diesel designed his engine to run on hemp oil, and Henry Ford, vowing to "grow automobiles from the soil," built a car with body panels and other components made from supertough hemp fiber instead of metal and plastic.

Herer got hold of a 1916 U.S. Department of Agriculture study that forecast the invention of a harvesting and decorticating machine that would transform hemp into America's number one cash crop, replacing wood pulp as the main raw ingredient for paper and other products. The USDA extolled hemp as a high-yield, low-maintenance crop, noting that an acre of fiber hemp grown during a 120-to-180-day season produced the same amount of paper as four acres of twenty-year-old trees. What's more, hemp doesn't require pesticides and harsh fertilizers. It actually enriches and replenishes the soil and "provides an excellent rotation crop," according to the USDA report.

In the fall of 1974, while high on LSD, Herer had a Eureka moment: Anything made from trees or petroleum could instead be made from hemp! This multipurpose plant possessed a near limitless potential for phasing out environmentally destructive industries. Rather than cutting down forests for wood and paper, Americans could grow hemp, a hearty annual that thrives in all fifty states. By fully utilizing hemp, America and the rest of the world could overcome its pernicious addiction to oil and petrochemicals and avert environmental catastrophe. Jack's vision pointed the way toward a new society, a hemp-based ecotopia that has no need of fossil fuels or plastic or synthetic fibers, a society where children are fed protein-rich hempseed oil rather than obesity-inducing corn syrup and neurotoxic diet drinks, a world where self-reliant citizens of all nations use natural, hemp-derived medicines to maximize their health.

Every industrial product made from hemp is legal but the plant itself is illegal in the United States, the only industrialized nation that prohibits industrial hemp cultivation. How could the U.S. government outlaw such an amazing, beneficial plant? Herer asked. A fast-growing annual that produces biomass (usable plant material) like nothing else? A plant with a superior ability to capture carbon emissions that contribute to global warming and climate change? A plant that has no earthly equal among nontoxic, renewable resources?

Arrested after speaking at a pro-pot rally in Los Angeles in 1980, Herer scrawled the first draft of his influential hemp manifesto while serving time in Terminal Island federal prison. He cited a 1938 article in *Popular Mechanics*, which had trumpeted the recent invention of a superefficient decorticating machine that stripped hemp fiber from stalk and changed the economics of hemp production. Published under the headline "New Billion-Dollar Crop," the article predicted a bonanza for Depression-era American farmers. *Mechanical Engineering* magazine likewise hailed hemp as "the most profitable and desirable crop that can be grown."

At the time, the case for industrial hemp had a lot of momentum. But its resurgence was cut short by the demonization and prohibition of marijuana, hemp's psychoactive twin. The Marihuana Tax Act of 1937, which banned the roots, stems, and smokable flower tops of cannabis, effectively dealt a death blow to industrial hemp in America, despite assurances from top narc Harry Anslinger that the legislation would not interfere with the legitimate production of fiber hemp.

Why did such a promising agricultural crop bite the dust? Herer's pursuit led him into a murky thicket of corporate-government collusion. Influential petrochemical and timber companies, fearing a major competitor, pulled strings to put the kibosh on hemp, he concluded. Herer pegged DuPont, which had patented a synthetic nylon fiber, as the chief villain in the antihemp conspiracy. Industrial hemp could have advanced the growth of a sustainable, carbohydrate-based economy instead of a noxious, hydrocarbon-based economy, but that dream was shoved aside by DuPont and other synthetic chemical firms, according to Herer, who alleged: "If hemp had not been made illegal, eighty percent of DuPont's business would never have materialized, and the great majority of the pollution which has poisoned [our] rivers would not have occurred."

When cannabis was outlawed, DuPont's chief financial backer, Andrew Mellon of the Mellon Bank in Pittsburgh, was also treasury secretary of the

United States. Secretary Mellon was Anslinger's boss. (The Federal Narcotics Bureau was a branch of the Treasury Department.) And Anslinger, it just so happened, was married to Mellon's favorite niece. Herer presumes—but never proves—that Mellon leaned on Anslinger to block a natural alternative to DuPont's synthetic schemes.

Herer also drew a bead on the press lord William Randolph Hearst, whose newspaper empire had waged a protracted smear campaign against "marihuana," a term that Hearst was largely responsible for introducing to the American public. According to Herer's conspiracy theory, Hearst feared that hemp would undermine the value of his vast timber holdings. But the Hearst chain, the nation's largest purchaser of newsprint, always needed more paper, and it seemingly would have been in Hearst's interest to promote hemp as an inexpensive, renewable paper source.

Even if one did not accept the notion of an antihemp cabal, Herer's spiel was substantive and compelling enough to be taken seriously. His unified field theory of cannabis as medicine, recreant, and multifaceted sustainable resource rang true to many people who were inspired by the Hemperor's save-the-world vision and his passionate denunciations of pot prohibition. "We have found a way that you could live longer, have less stress, have a good time, and it's illegal, and it's got to be made lawful!" Herer thundered. "It's the safest, smartest, best medicine on the planet. You'd be stupid not to use it!"

Wherever he went, Herer was surrounded by a coterie of young acolytes who helped distribute ever-evolving versions of his manuscript, a *J'Accuse*-like screed that included news clips, old photographs, photocopied primary source material, and various miscellanea such as postage stamps from countries around the world marking their hemp harvests. Herer found a receptive audience at Grateful Dead concerts, where he set up a mobile information booth and spun hemp yarns for anyone willing to listen.*

* While many rock bands and political cadres had come and gone since the heady days of flower power, the Dead kept on truckin'. The roving Deadhead scene, an unmistakable carryover from the psychedelic Sixties, was a never-ending party, a grassroots celebration of community and continuity, past, present, and future. By the 1980s, Haight-Ashbury had become a station of the cross and the Dead emerged as the rock 'n' roll equivalent of a Christian cult, albeit with a different set of sacraments. Every Dead conclave was "a no-holds-barred orgy of pot, LSD, nitrous oxide, and other substances that seemed to worry only curmudgeonly columnists and the occasional small-town-minded police department," the Dead spokesperson Dennis McNally observed. The Grateful Dead were the number one concert draw in the United States throughout the Eighties. They rarely played to an empty seat, despite zero advertising and hardly any press.

It was at a Dead concert in 1987 that Jack Herer initially crossed paths with Rick Pfrommer, an eighteen-year-old Washington, D.C.–based pot enthusiast who hosted the Hemperor when he arrived in the nation's capital the following year. Herer was hot on the trail of the U.S. government's World War II propaganda flick *Hemp for Victory*, which was referenced in the National Archive. Herer got ahold of the fourteen-minute black-and-white motivational film and made a duplicate copy for himself. With snatches of "Anchors Aweigh" and other upbeat songs playing in the background, *Hemp for Victory* showed images of Old Glory wafting in the breeze while U.S. troops prepared for battle. American farmers were instructed how and where to plant hemp, how best to harvest it, and the many good reasons for doing so: "Hemp for light-duty fire hoses," for "parachute webbing," for "countless uses on ship and shore"—"Hemp for Victory!"

Herer made a continuous video loop of the film and projected it twenty-four hours a day at a licensed stall a stone's throw from the Washington Monument, where he set up a mini hemp museum to protest the Smithsonian's omission of hemp from its historical exhibits. For days on end, this irascible, boisterous fanatic held court near the big obelisk, his beard and hair askew, a latter-day Jeremiah raving about cannabis the savior—while *Hemp for Victory* played over and over again in the background. Fortified on grass and psychedelics, Herer was firing on all synaptic cylinders. He was in the clime of rhyme, a man possessed. "Jack had an almost messianic ability to influence people," Pfrommer recalled. "He would get high as a kite on acid at the Washington Monument and preach like a messiah."

When he wasn't perched by a national landmark, Herer and his traveling menagerie stayed with Pfrommer and a dozen other D.C. marijuanistas, who lived together in a ten-bedroom communal Victorian on Butternut Street, close to Walter Reed Hospital. In the late 1980s and early 1990s, the Butternut House, or the "Nut House," as it was known to residents, emerged as action central for the East Coast reefer resistance. "Boycott white powder, bring back herb" was the motto of this motley crew, which welcomed Herer with open arms as the patron saint of hemp. He was a father figure to a nascent social movement.

"We had this little fire going, and then Jack came along and blew gasoline all over it," said Steve DeAngelo, the thirty-year-old leader of the Nut House collective. "Just the energy of this one guy fired up a whole new generation of activists. We were there. We were waiting for him. We were keeping our powder dry. Our heads were down a little in the '80s, but we were ready. And then Jack brought his New Testament and showed us this plant, which we already loved, in a whole new light, a holistic light. He told us to stand up for our rights, to stand up for this plant, in a completely uncompromising way."

DeAngelo, or "Stevie D," as his friends called him, kept the Nut House afloat in more ways than one. He was perhaps the biggest marijuana dealer in D.C. during this period. "*We sell cannabis*" was printed on his business card. DeAngelo supported Herer financially while the Hemperor was in Washington updating his book. And when Jack was ready to hit the road with the new edition and spread the word, Stevie D kicked in fifty grand to underwrite a fourteen-city "Hemp Tour" in the heartland. "The plant financed her own liberation," DeAngelo later remarked.*

DeAngelo's keen business instincts were aroused as he observed how instinctively people responded to Jack's rolling hemp museum. They loved to touch and feel samples of hemp yarn and fabric, which blocked the sun's ultraviolet rays more effectively than any other textile. In the early '90s, Stevie D split from the roadshow to focus on building his new company, Ecolution, which specialized in hemp clothing and accessories. The recent collapse of Soviet Bloc communism opened up unprecedented commercial opportunities and DeAngelo was quick to pounce. For the next ten years, he imported hemp textiles and paper from Eastern Europe. A handful of other start-ups, including Don Wirtshafter's Ohio Hempery, brought a variety of new hemp products to market. During this period, the first hemp stores popped up in North America, but these small retail ventures didn't pan out financially in the long term.

While hemp start-ups and independent retailers struggled, several well-established companies, such as Calvin Klein and Adidas, successfully incorporated hemp into their product lines. The Body Shop, an international cosmetics chain, sold hemp lip balm, hemp soap, hemp-oil shampoo and hair conditioner, and hemp-enhanced skin moisturizer. Hemp had considerable cultural cachet in no small part because of its association with marijuana. Hemp backpacks, hemp sneakers, hemp surfboards, packing foam made from hemp—there were no fewer than 25,000 known industrial uses for the plant.

By misclassifying hemp as a drug, the U.S. government essentially ceded a lucrative agricultural field to China, Russia, and the European Union (which offered subsidies to hemp growers). In 1988, Chris Conrad launched the Business Alliance for Commerce in Hemp and three years later he founded the

* Launched in the spring of '89, Hemp Tour was the brainchild of Ben Masel, DeAngelo's oft-jailed Yippie comrade from the previous decade. The ponytailed Masel had migrated to Madison, Wisconsin, where he organized the annual Midwest Harvest Festival, a pro-cannabis jamboree. Herer's unconventional tome made a big impression on Masel, who reconnected with DeAngelo and enlisted his participation in what would be the first of several national hemp tours.

American Hemp Council to advance the interests of the fledgling domestic hemp industry. A can-do California journalist, Conrad was already deep into hemp politics when he met Jack Herer and offered to revise and update *The Emperor Wears No Clothes* for its 1990 printing. Conrad added some of his own research and turned Jack's uneven manuscript into a well-written and well-designed coffee-table-size book.*

But some industrial-hemp advocates were not enamored of Herer's eccentric, over-the-top manner and his tendency to overstate his case. They sought to distance themselves from Jack's minions who believed that cannabis could solve most if not all the world's problems. The more staid pro-hemp forces would have been quite content if the U.S. government decided to legalize industrial hemp without lifting the ban on pot. Hemp industry lobbyists tried to persuade public officials that it was wrong to equate hemp with marijuana, even though taxonomically they were the same species. The difference lay in their respective cannabinoid profiles: industrial hemp was relatively high in nonpsychoactive CBD and had only trace amounts of THC, "the high causer," whereas just the opposite was true for most of the new marijuana strains.

Herer adamantly maintained that it was a mistake to parse hemp into separate legal categories. Legalize the plant for everything—medicine, recreation, industrial uses. That was his approach and it had a certain philosophical consistency that appealed to ganjafied Gen X'ers as well as veteran weed smokers. The Hemperor broadened the scope of the marijuana reform movement and injected some much-needed oomph into an activist scene that was largely moribund. While pot proponents debated the pros and cons of growing hemp for biofuel and other specifics, Jack's unbridled exuberance set the stage for the reefer resurgence of the 1990s.

* In the early 1990s, Conrad and his wife, the activist Mikki Norris, worked as consultants for Sensi Seeds, the cannabis research and breeding facility in the Netherlands owned by Ben Dronkers. Conrad and Norris upgraded the Hash, Marijuana, and Hemp Museum in Amsterdam that Dronkers founded. The Dutch seed magnate and hemp promoter eagerly embraced Herer's ideas and named an award-winning cannabis strain in his honor. A skunky, sativa-dominant hybrid that earned top honors at the seventh *High Times* Cannabis Cup, "Jack Herer" was described as "the champagne of strains" in the Sensi Seeds catalog.

6

FROM BLUNTS TO BALLOTS

Bush v. Weed

"Marijuana in its natural form is one of the safest therapeutically active substances known to man."

This was the unequivocal conclusion of Francis L. Young, the DEA's chief administrative law judge, who asserted in a stunning sixty-nine-page opinion on September 6, 1988: "By any measure of rational analysis marijuana can be safely used within supervised routine medical care." To deny cannabis to patients who need it would be, in Young's words, "unreasonable, arbitrary and capricious."

Young's finding was the latest twist in a lengthy legal battle that began in 1972 when NORML and the American Public Health Association petitioned the Bureau of Narcotics and Dangerous Drugs, the DEA's forerunner, to recognize marijuana's medical value and remove it from Schedule I classification so that doctors could prescribe it. Several other parties joined the rescheduling petition in the intervening years, but the narcs refused to budge. Initially, the DEA rejected the petition without "a reflective consideration and analysis," according to a U.S. appeals court in Washington, D.C., which reprimanded America's top antidrug agency and demanded that it justify marijuana's status as a Schedule I drug.

Finally, in the summer of December 1986, the DEA reluctantly commenced fifteen days of court-ordered public hearings on the matter of rescheduling cannabis. No one believed that Judge Young would rule in favor of the pro-pot petitioners. After all, he was the Drug Enforcement Administration's leading law judge. A confident trio of drug-war heavy-hitters—the U.S. Justice Department, the National Federation of Parents for Drug-Free Youth, and the

International Association of Chiefs of Police—filed affidavits opposing the reclassification request on the grounds that it would send the wrong signal that marijuana is okay for recreational use. Weak on factual evidence, they made a circular argument—marijuana has no medical value because the law says it has no medical value.

Young also heard from doctors, nurses, patients, and researchers extolling the benefits of cannabis. Irv Rosenfeld from Florida, one of a handful of people who received marijuana cigarettes each month from the U.S. government, testified about his rare medical condition and how cannabis had spared him of a life of misery and an early death. Robert Stephan, the conservative attorney general of Kansas and a cancer patient, told of his travails and the need for prescription marijuana to mitigate the horrible side effects of chemotherapy. Mae Nutt from Michigan described how she had to buy pot from a street dealer to help her twenty-two-year-old son suffering from testicular cancer.

Young, who spoke with a gentle Louisiana lilt, was swayed by these and other testimonials, which he discussed in a written decision that affirmed marijuana's safety and efficacy as medicine. The judge was particularly struck by the case of a three-year-old boy with cancer who underwent surgery at a hospital in Spokane, Washington. The child vomited for days after each chemotherapy treatment. He could barely eat. He lost weight and strength. His immune system was compromised. The boy's mother heard that marijuana might provide relief. She got some pot from a friend and baked marijuana cookies for her child. She brewed marijuana tea. "When the child ate these cookies or drank this tea in connection with his chemotherapy, he did not vomit. His strength returned. He regained lost weight. His spirits revived. The parents told the doctors and nurses at the hospital of their giving marijuana to their child. None objected. They all accepted smoking marijuana as effective in controlling chemotherapy-induced nausea and vomiting," Young noted.

Soon, the three-year-old who medicated with cannabis was riding a tricycle in the hallways of the hospital following chemo treatments. The other children with cancer were racked with nausea. "When your kid is riding a tricycle while his hospital buddies are hooked up to IV needles, their heads hung over vomiting buckets, you don't need a federal agency to tell you marijuana is effective," the pot-savvy mom told Young. "The evidence is in front of you, so stark it cannot be ignored."*

Young learned that large numbers of paraplegic and quadriplegic pa-

* In October 1988, a month after Judge Young issued his historic ruling, the *New York State Journal of Medicine* published a peer-reviewed report on "Inhalation Marijuana as an Anti-

tients, particularly in Veterans Administration hospitals, routinely smoked marijuana to reduce spasticity. "While this mode of treatment is illegal, it is generally tolerated, if not openly encouraged, by physicians in charge of such wards who accept this practice as being of benefit to their patients," the judge observed. Cannabis was also a godsend for many multiple sclerosis patients who used the herb illicitly with their doctors' consent. "In strict medical terms marijuana is far safer than many foods we commonly consume," Young stated, adding: "There has never been a death attributed to an overdose of marijuana."

The DEA's top judicial expert determined that the law didn't just permit moving marijuana to Schedule II, the law required it. According to Young, the Controlled Substances Act of 1970 did not give the DEA the power to tell doctors if they could or should not include cannabis in their medical practice. The matter of scheduling marijuana was supposed to have been resolved by the medical community, not by law enforcement.

But the ruling of an administrative law judge is a recommendation, not a binding order, and Young's ruling would be ignored by the DEA director, John Lawn. As it had under Nixon and Reagan, the federal government under George H. W. Bush again chose to disregard the results of its own investigation. The Bush administration would continue the long tradition of federal stonewalling with respect to marijuana law. Cannabis would remain a Schedule I substance. As the *Merck Manual of Diagnosis and Therapy* stated in no uncertain terms: "The chief opposition to the drug rests on a moral and political, and not toxicological, foundation."

On September 5, 1989, in a televised speech from the Oval Office, President Bush announced a major escalation of the war on drugs. Like all the previous drug-war declarations, this one was presented as the decisive assault, the battle royal. Boosted by a $7.8 billion federal antinarcotics budget, law enforcement would pursue marijuana offenders with renewed vigor. The drug war would get even uglier, the penalties stiffer, the rhetoric more absurd.

Leading the charge was William Bennett, America's first "drug czar," a boorish, overweight nicotine addict and self-proclaimed moral arbiter who had served as education secretary under Reagan. Bennett was also a compulsive gambler who lost millions in Las Vegas. This holier-than-thou hypocrite wrote several books advising young people on how to be virtuous. Never use illegal drugs, he counseled. The notion that someone could smoke marijuana and escape a horrible fate was anathema to Bennett and the other faux moral-

---

emetic for Cancer Chemotherapy" by V. Vinciguerra and his colleagues, which underscored the usefulness of smoked marijuana for cancer patients.

ists who directed the war on drugs. As far as Bennett was concerned, casual drug users were the most dangerous of all because they "impart the message that you can use drugs and still do well in school or maintain a career and family."

In other words, the casual use of marijuana is especially bad because it doesn't appear to be especially bad. That was the muddled message emanating from the Office of National Drug Control Policy (ONDCP), headed by Bennett, which was supposed to develop a long-term strategy to win the war against the evil weed and bring about a "drug-free society." Attacking casual drug use would comprise the core of Bennett's hyperbolic, moralistic crusade. America's drug problem was not a public-health crisis but a moral one, traceable back to the "do your own thing" counterculture and its disrespectful attitude toward authority, according to Bennett: "Somewhere along the way, in the late 1960s and 1970s, part of America lost its moral bearings regarding drugs."

The drug czar, nursing a two-pack-a-day cigarette habit, dismissed as left-wing pabulum the rather obvious notion that a person's choices are influenced by social circumstances. Marijuana smokers and other drug users, in his view, were immoral, irresponsible individuals lacking in self-control. Bennett called for "a massive wave of arrests" and a rapid expansion of the nation's prison system. He urged prosecutors to go after weekend pot smokers—not just big-time pushers.

Given that marijuana's proscribed status turned a large proportion of the citizenry into criminals, police were under constant temptation to use the marijuana laws to bring certain people to heel—not because they smoked pot but because they fit the demographic profile of a potential troublemaker. Urban African Americans and Latinos bore the brunt of Bennett's zero-tolerance campaign, which clogged the courts and jails with young, low-level offenders. By 1990, there were 610,000 black males (one in four) between the ages of twenty and twenty-nine locked up, on probation, or on parole in the United States, but only 436,000 blacks of the same age were enrolled in college.

Bennett complained that drug suspects were entitled to due process of law and a fair trial ("that kind of slows things down") and he publicly endorsed the beheading of drug dealers ("morally I don't have any problem with that at all"). His overblown rhetoric was having an impact. A February 1990 survey by the Drug Policy Foundation disclosed that 65 percent of the U.S. population shared Bennett's puritanical belief that the use of any illicit drug solely for the purpose of intoxication was morally and ethically wrong. Sixty-two percent of Americans said they would "give up some freedoms" to fight drug abuse. And a majority favored drug tests for all citizens.

Bennett lobbied for a rollback of marijuana decriminalization in states with less punitive pot laws. Drug czar *numero uno* also called for a "vigorous program" to wipe out domestically grown pot. The Bush administration announced it would double the funds for eradicating homegrown marijuana. But the narcs apparently had a hard time telling dope from rope. More than 90 percent of the cannabis plants destroyed by the DEA during this period were actually ditch weed, the feral offspring of the World War II–era "Hemp for Victory" campaign.

As military-style attacks on outdoor pot gardens escalated, more growers retreated indoors. Team Bush responded by launching a national assault on indoor horticulturists. On October 26, 1989, known as "Black Thursday" in cannabis lore, the DEA and local law enforcement raided garden-supply vendors and warehouses in forty-six states in a coordinated attempt to cripple the hydroponics industry and shut down the indoor production of marijuana. Code-named Green Merchant, this multiyear covert operation targeted the entire hydroponics industry, even though only a small percentage of hydroponics farmers grew cannabis. Undercover agents posing as hippies, bikers, military vets, and, most cynical of all, medically needy folks visited hydroponics stores, wearing secret recording devices while trying to trick the proprietors into engaging in incriminating discussions about marijuana. "They offered us women, guns, and money if we'd show them how to grow pot and sell them gear," a hydroponics retailer recounted.

Under the auspices of Green Merchant, the DEA seized irrigation equipment, lights, plant nutrients, books, and customer records from hundreds of stores and mail-order houses that specialized in indoor-gardening supplies. DEA sleuths could always count on public utility companies for access to private data pertaining to suspiciously high home energy use. Within a year, Green Merchant generated more than 50,000 investigative leads, an indication of just how extensive indoor pot cultivation had become in the United States. It was also a clue as to how the DEA frittered away much of its time—snooping on gardener hobbyists in an effort to catch small-time marijuana growers. By the end of 1991, Green Merchant had snagged $17.5 million in assets, arrested 1,262 people, dismantled hundreds of indoor grows, and destroyed 57,000 pot plants.

Tom Alexander, publisher of *Sinsemilla Tips*, the unofficial trade journal of cannabis horticulture, lost his hydroponics business when a DEA squad invaded the Full Moon garden-supply store in Corvallis, Oregon, and seized his entire inventory at gunpoint during the early stages of Green Merchant. Although Alexander was never charged with a crime, the civil forfeiture laws were such that to contest the DEA's theft of his property would have cost him more than what his inventory was worth. "They used the law as a tool of extortion. It wasn't worth my remaining assets to fight these assholes," said Alexander, who stopped publishing his grow-zine after ten years to avoid further harassment by the feds.

By 1991, seven years after Congress revised civil forfeiture laws to permit the seizure of drug money, the Justice Department had collected more than $1.5 billion in alleged drug-related assets. And during the next five years that figure would double. Police had an incentive to seize property because they profited directly from forfeiture. A growing number of law-enforcement units depended on seized drug assets to make their annual budget. As former New York City police commissioner Patrick Murphy explained in congressional testimony, forfeiture laws "created a great temptation for state and local police departments to target assets rather than criminal activity."*

In 1992, seventeen major European cities signed the Frankfurt Charter, agreeing to tolerate the social use of cannabis, but the United States was moving in the opposite direction. Some 340,000 people in the United States were busted for pot that year, including Jim Montgomery, a paraplegic who used marijuana to relieve muscle spasms. Montgomery was arrested at his home in Oklahoma and charged with felonious possession of two ounces of pot (found in his wheelchair pouch). Montgomery was sentenced to life in prison plus sixteen years. A judge later reduced his sentence to a mere ten years. James Geddes, another victim of Oklahoma's draconian pot laws, got ninety years for cultivating five marijuana plants. And Okie justice saddled William Foster, a rheumatoid arthritis patient, with a ninety-three-year sentence for growing a medicinal pot garden.

Official efforts to make an example of individual pot smokers by meting out excessive penalties had little deterrent effect. More than twenty million Americans continued to smoke marijuana on a regular basis and a third of the population fourteen and older tried the herb. Eradication programs hardly put a dent in America's annual multibillion-dollar marijuana crop.

When laws are flouted on such a huge scale, the laws themselves start to look ridiculous. As the futility of marijuana prohibition sank in, a small but

---

* Asset-hungry cops were on the prowl on October 2, 1992, when an antidrug task force with thirty-one officers from various law-enforcement agencies stormed Donald Scott's 200-acre ranch in Malibu, California, ostensibly looking for marijuana plants. Scott's wife screamed when she saw the armed intruders, and Scott, a sixty-one-year-old multimillionaire, grabbed a gun, thinking that robbers had broken into his home. He was shot dead by the police, who never found any marijuana on the premises. One day Scott was a rich man, the next day he was drug-war roadkill, one more example of collateral damage in the antimarijuana crusade (Joel Miller, *Bad Trip*, pp. 40, 133).

growing number of public officials and policy wonks, some with impeccable conservative credentials, began to criticize the federal government's misguided war on drugs. "We need at least to consider and examine forms of controlled legalization of drugs," said George Shultz, Reagan's secretary of state, who supported medical marijuana. Lyn Nofziger, an aide to Reagan and Nixon, also spoke out in favor of allowing patients to use cannabis after his daughter underwent chemotherapy: "If doctors can prescribe morphine and other addictive medicines, it makes no sense to deny marijuana to sick and dying patients when it can be provided on a carefully controlled, prescription basis."

In an open letter to William Bennett published in *The Wall Street Journal* in September 1989, the Nobel Prize economist Milton Friedman declared: "Your mistake is failing to recognize that the very measures you favor are a major source of the evils you deplore." Friedman, the darling of the Reaganite "free market" crowd, was a strong advocate for legalizing pot. He denounced prohibition as "an attempted cure that makes matters worse." The drug war was doomed to fail and would shred the Constitution and grind up freedom in the process, Friedman warned: "The path you propose of more police, more jails, use of the military in foreign countries, harsh penalties for drug users, and a whole panoply of repressive measures can only make a bad situation worse."

Drug-policy critics in the late 1980s ran the gamut of the entire political spectrum. Gary Johnson, the Republican governor of New Mexico, declared the drug war "an expensive bust" and came out in favor of legalizing marijuana. Baltimore Mayor Kurt Schmoke, a Democrat, called for a drug-war strategy "led by the Surgeon General not the Attorney General." A circle of liberal academicians, led by Ethan Nadelmann of Princeton, made a strong case for harm reduction and legalization rather than punitive approaches to illicit-drug use. Nadelmann would soon be hired by the billionaire hedge-fund manager George Soros to run a drug-policy think tank.

But fighting illegal drugs had become nearly as big a business as selling them in the fin de siècle Nineties, and powerful vested interests felt well served by the status quo. The drug war was simply too serviceable for Team Bush to abandon during a key transition period as the bipolar certainties of the Cold War gave way to the instabilities of a new geopolitical era. It's no coincidence that official antidrug and anticrime rhetoric intensified just "when the largest military-industrial complex in the world [was] losing its forty-year-long justification for its existence and growth," law-enforcement historian Peter Kraska observed.

The end of the Cold War demagnetized everybody's compass and precipitated a shift in U.S. foreign-policy discourse. Drug-war rhetoric supplanted anti-Communist rhetoric as the justification for U.S. intervention in Latin

America. Uncle Sam was behaving like a drug-war addict; he desperately needed "an intervention." In December 1989, 24,000 U.S. soldiers invaded Panama, ostensibly to overthrow and capture General Manuel Noriega, the country's leader, who was involved in drug running and money laundering on a massive scale. The CIA, which kept Noriega on its payroll for several years, had winked at the general's cocaine-pushing proclivities as long as he stayed in lockstep with U.S. foreign policy. When Noriega defied the United States, President George W. H. Bush, a former CIA director, sent in the troops.*

The Brain and Marijuana

Up until the late 1980s, marijuana research remained a rather esoteric field involving a small number of scientists in the United States and abroad. Their efforts were circumscribed by the politicized agenda of the National Institute on Drug Abuse, which subsidized studies designed to prove the deleterious effects of cannabis, while blocking inquiry into marijuana's potential benefits. But rather than discrediting cannabis, NIDA inadvertently helped to facilitate a series of major discoveries about the inner workings of the human brain. These breakthroughs spawned a revolution in medical science and a profound understanding of health and healing. "By using a plant that has been around for thousands of years, we discovered a new physiological system of immense importance," says Raphael Mechoulam, the dean of the transnational cannabinoid research community. "We wouldn't have been able to get there if we had not looked at the plant."

Since the identification and synthesis of THC by Mechoulam's team in Israel in 1965, scientists had learned a great deal about the pharmacology, biochemistry, and clinical effects of cannabis. Everybody seemed to have an opinion about marijuana, but no one really knew how it worked. Smoking pot got you stoned, but what it actually did inside the brain on a molecular level to alter consciousness was still unknown. No one could yet explain how cannabis worked as an appetite stimulant, how it dampened nausea, quelled seizures,

---

* According to a 1991 GAO report, Panama continued to function as a haven for drug money after Noriega was captured by U.S. troops. Associates of Noriega's U.S.-backed successors, President Guillermo Endara and Vice President Guillermo Ford, were major drug money launderers. Carlos Eleta, the Panamanian CIA agent who dispersed millions of U.S. dollars to Endara's political party, was arrested in April 1989 in Macon, Georgia, for conspiring to bring more than half a ton of cocaine each month into the United States (Lee and Solomon, *Unreliable Sources*, p. 317).

and relieved pain. No one understood how smoked marijuana could stop an asthma attack in seconds, not minutes. No one knew why it lifted one's mood. Although there was considerable evidence that cannabis could ameliorate a wide range of disease symptoms, it took scientists a long time to figure out how marijuana produced its myriad effects.

When American researchers at Johns Hopkins University identified receptor sites in the brain capable of binding with opiates in 1973, some scientists expected that the discovery of receptor sites for marijuana would soon follow. But these were difficult to pin down. Fifteen years would elapse before a government-funded study at the St. Louis University School of Medicine determined that the mammalian brain has receptor sites—specialized protein molecules embedded in cell membranes—that respond pharmacologically to compounds in marijuana resin. Every cell membrane has lots of receptors for many types of messenger molecules, which influence the activity of the cell.

Initially identified by Professor Allyn Howlett and her graduate student William Devane, cannabinoid receptors turned out to be far more abundant in the brain than any other G-protein-coupled receptors.* Tagged radioactively, a potent THC analog synthesized by Pfizer ("CP55,940") enabled researchers to begin mapping the locations of cannabinoid receptors in the brain. These receptors were found to be concentrated in regions responsible for mental and physiological processes that are affected by marijuana—the hippocampus (memory), cerebral cortex (higher cognition), cerebellum (motor coordination), basal ganglia (movement), hypothalamus (appetite), the amygdala (emotions), and elsewhere. There are few cannabinoid receptors in the brain stem, the region that controls breathing and heartbeat—which is why no one has ever suffered a fatal overdose of marijuana.

On July 18, 1990, at a meeting of the National Academy of Science's Institute of Medicine, Lisa Matsuda announced that she and her colleagues at the National Institute of Mental Health (NIMH) had achieved a major breakthrough—they pinpointed the exact DNA sequence that encodes a THC-sensitive receptor in the rat's brain. People have the same receptor, which consists of 472 amino acids strung together in a crumpled chain that squiggles back and forth across the cell membrane seven times. Cannabinoid

* Cannabinoid receptors belong to the superfamily of G-protein-coupled receptors, which includes opioid receptors. When these receptors sense certain molecules outside the cell, a biochemical response is triggered via specific "signal transduction pathways." G-protein-coupled receptors are involved in many disease processes and are reportedly the target of approximately 40 percent of all modern pharmaceuticals.

receptors function as subtle sensing devices, tiny vibrating scanners perpetually primed to pick up biochemical cues that flow through fluids surrounding each cell. Matsuda also disclosed that she had successfully cloned the marijuana receptor.

The cloning of the cannabis receptor was crucial. It opened the door for scientists to sculpt molecules—new drugs—that "fit" these receptors somewhat like keys in a slot. Some keys ("agonists") turned the receptor on; others ("antagonists") turned it off.* In addition to synthesizing cannabinoid receptor agonists and antagonists, scientists experimented with genetically engineered "knockout" mice that lacked this receptor. When administered to knockout mice, the THC had nowhere to bind and hence could not trigger any activity. This was further proof that THC works by activating cannabinoid receptors in the brain and central nervous system. Finally, after fifty centuries of medicinal usage, the scientific basis of cannabis therapeutics was coming into focus.

Researchers soon identified a second type of cannabinoid receptor, dubbed "CB-2," which is prevalent throughout the peripheral nervous system and the immune system. CB-2 receptors are also present in the gut, spleen, liver, heart, kidneys, bones, blood vessels, lymph cells, endocrine glands, and reproductive organs. THC stimulates the CB-2 receptor, but this does not result in the psychoactive high that pot is famous for (because CB-2 receptors are not concentrated in the brain); THC binding to CB-1, the central nervous system receptor, causes the high. The CB-1 receptor mediates psychoactivity. CB-2 regulates immune response. Marijuana is such a versatile substance because it acts everywhere, not just in the brain.

Just as the study of opium resulted in the discovery of endorphins, the brain's own morphinelike substance, so, too, marijuana research would lead to the discovery of a natural, internal THC-like compound, our "inner cannabis," so to speak. In 1992, Raphael Mechoulam, in collaboration with NIMH research fellow William Devane and Dr. Lumír Hanuš, found a novel neurotransmitter, a naturally occurring endogenous (meaning "made internally") cannabinoid. This "endocannabinoid" attaches to the same mammalian brain cell receptors as THC. Mechoulam decided to call it "anandamide," deriving from the Sanskrit word for "bliss." In 1995, his group discovered a second major endocannabinoid

---

* Cannabinoid receptors recognize and respond to three kinds of agonists (turn-on keys): endogenous fatty acid cannabinoids found in all mammals; phytocannabinoids concentrated in the oily resin on the buds and leaves of the marijuana plant; and potent, synthetic cannabinoids concocted in university and drug company laboratories.

molecule—"2-AG" [2-arachidonoylglycerol]—which binds to both CB-1 and CB-2 receptors.*

By tracing the metabolic pathways of THC, scientists had stumbled upon a hitherto unknown molecular signaling system that plays a crucial role in regulating a broad range of biological processes. This molecular signaling system modulates how we experience pain, stress, hunger, sleep, our circadian rhythms, our blood pressure, body temperature, bone density, fertility, intestinal fortitude, mood, metabolism, memory retention, and more.

Scientists call it "the endocannabinoid system"—so named after the plant that led to its discovery. The name suggests that the plant came first, but in fact, as Dr. John McPartland explained, this ancient internal signal system started evolving more than 500 million years ago (long before cannabis appeared), when the most complex life-form was sponges. Endocannabinoids and their receptors are present in fish, reptiles, earthworms, leeches, amphibians, birds, and mammals—every animal except insects. Its long evolutionary history indicates that the endocannabinoid system must serve a very important and basic purpose in animal physiology.

Drug-company investigators paid close attention to cutting-edge developments in cannabinoid research, which few people outside the scientific community were privy to.† Endocannabinoids and their receptors emerged as a hot topic among scientists who shared their findings in highly technical peer-reviewed journals and at annual conclaves hosted by the International Cannabinoid Research Society (ICRS). Advances in the burgeoning field of cannabinoid studies would pave the way for new treatment strategies for vari-

* Anandamide and 2-AG impact the organism in ways that are "predominantly local and specific," says Mechoulam. "Their actions are ubiquitous. They are involved in most physiological systems that have been investigated" ("Conversation with Raphael Mechoulam," *Addiction* 102[2007]: 887–93; see also "The New Science of Cannabinoid-Based Medicine: An Interview with Dr. Raphael Mechoulam," in David Jay Brown, ed., *Mavericks of Medicine*.

† In a lengthy 2006 review, "The Endocannabinoid System as an Emerging Target of Pharmacology," scientists with the National Institutes of Health reported that cannabinoid compounds held "therapeutic promise" for disparate pathological conditions "ranging from mood and anxiety disorders, movement disorders such as Parkinson's and Huntington's disease, neuropathic pain, multiple sclerosis and spinal cord injury, to cancer, atherosclerosis, myocardial infarction, stroke, hypertension, glaucoma, obesity/metabolic syndrome, and osteoporosis," as well as other diseases that are seemingly beyond the reach of orthodox medicine (Pal Pacher, Sándor Bátkai, and George Kunos, "The Endocannabinoid System as an Emerging Target of Pharmacotherapy," *Pharmacology Review* 58[3][2006]: 389–462).

ous pathological conditions—cancer, diabetes, neuropathic pain, arthritis, osteoporosis, obesity, Alzheimer's, multiple sclerosis, and several odd diseases of unknown etiology that seemed to have as their common denominator an inflammatory or autoimmune dysfunction.

The discovery of the endocannabinoid system has breathtaking implications for nearly every area of medicine, including reproductive biology. Dr. Mauro Maccarrone at the University of Teramo, Italy, describes the endocannabinoid system as the "guardian angel" or "gatekeeper" of mammalian reproduction. Endocannabinoid signaling figures decisively throughout the reproductive process—from spermatogenesis to fertilization, ovuductal transport of the zygote, embryo implantation, and fetal development. Cannabinoid receptors proliferate in the placenta and facilitate neurochemical "cross-talk" between the embryo and the mother. A misfiring of the endocannabinoid system could result in serious problems, including ectopic pregnancy and miscarriage. Appropriate levels of endocannabinoids in maternal milk are critically important for the initiation of suckling in newborns. Infant colic has been attributed to a dearth of endocannabinoids.

Israeli scientist Ester Fride observed that knockout mice missing CB receptors resemble babies who suffer from "failure to thrive" syndrome. (Mice lacking CB receptors don't suckle and they die prematurely.) This is one of many enigmatic conditions that may arise because of a dysfunctional endocannabinoid system. Individuals have different congenital endocannabinoid levels and sensitivities. University of Washington neurologist Ethan Russo postulates that "clinical endocannabinoid deficiency" underlies migraines, fibromyalgia, irritable bowel disease, and a cluster of other degenerative conditions, which may respond favorably to cannabinoid therapies.*

For Big Pharma, cannabinoid research became a tale of knockout mice and men. Using genetically engineered rodents that lacked CB receptors, researchers were able to prove that cannabinoid compounds can alter disease progression and attenuate experimentally induced symptoms. An "animal model" of osteoporosis, for example, was created in normal mice and in knockout mice without cannabinoid receptors. When a synthetic cannabinoid drug was given to both groups of osteoporotic mice, bone damage was mitigated in the nor-

* Recent research has established that clinical depression is an endocannabinoid-deficiency disease. Matthew Hill, a scientist at the University of British Columbia, analyzed the "serum endocannabinoid content" in depressed women and found that it was "significantly reduced" compared with controls. Hill observed that this reduction "negatively correlated to episode duration," meaning "the longer the depressive episode the lower the 2-AG content."

mal mice but had no effect on rodents sans CB receptors—which means that cannabinoid receptors are instrumental in regulating bone density.*

Other experiments would establish that CB receptor signaling modulates pain and analgesia, inflammation, appetite, gastrointestinal motility, neuroprotection and neurodegeneration, along with the ebb and flow of immune cells, hormones, and other mood-altering neurotransmitters such as serotonin, dopamine, and glutamate. When tickled by THC or its endogenous cousins, cannabinoid receptors trigger a cascade of biochemical changes on a cellular level that put the brakes on excessive physiological activity.

The human immune system, an amazing physiological wonder, kicks on like a furnace when a fever is required to fry a virus or bacterial invader. And when the job is done, endocannabinoid signaling turns down the flame, cools the fever, and restores homeostasis. (Cannabinoids—endo, herbal, and synthetic—are anti-inflammatory; they literally cool the body.) But if the feedback loop misfires, if the pilot light burns too high, if the immune system overreacts to chronic stress or mistakes one's body for a foreign object, then the stage is set for an autoimmune disease or an inflammatory disorder to develop.

Endocannabinoids are the only neurotransmitters known to engage in "retrograde signaling," a unique form of intracellular communication that inhibits immune response, reduces inflammation, relaxes musculature, lowers blood pressure, dilates bronchial passages, increases cerebral blood flow (a rush of thoughts!), and normalizes overstimulated nerves.† Retrograde signaling serves as an inhibitory feedback mechanism that tells other neurotransmitters to cool it when they are firing too fast.‡

---

* A German research team would later demonstrate that CB-2 receptor activation restrains the formation of bone reabsorbing cells, known as osteoclasts, by down-regulating osteoclast precursors, thus tipping the balance in favor of osteoblasts, cells that facilitate bone formation.

† The human brain has about 100 billion neurons that communicate through neurotransmitters (endogenous messenger molecules) that operate in the space between cells, the "synaptic cleft." The synaptic cleft is where two nerve tendrils converge without actually touching; it's in the space between nerve endings that messages are chemically communicated (transmitted) from one cell to the next. Whereas every other neurotransmitter (serotonin, dopamine, GABA, etc.) enables nerve impulses to jump across the synaptic cleft, endocannabinoid compounds travel backward and interact with CB receptors strategically situated on "presynaptic" nerve axons. CB receptor retrograde signaling facilitates a process known as "presynaptic inhibition," which interrupts and slows down the release of other neurotransmitters.

‡ This is the basis of marijuana's biphasic effect: The body synthesizes endocannabinoids that act as a "slow down" mechanism when nerve cells are stimulated by excitory neurotransmitters such as norepinephrine and glutamate; and cannabinoid receptors also trans-

Prior to the discovery of the endocannabinoid system, retrograde signaling was known to occur only during the embryonic development of the brain and nervous system. Endocannabinoids choreograph "a broad array of developmental processes in the embryonic brain," explains Dr. John McPartland, including neural stem cell proliferation and differentiation, a process guided by extracellular cues conveyed via CB receptors. Scientists would learn that cannabinoid receptor signaling also regulates adult neurogenesis (brain cell growth) and stem cell migration.

High endocannabinoid levels in the brain are triggered by strokes and other pathological events—attesting to the neuroprotective function of the endocannabinoid signaling. A major function of the endocannabinoid system—and therefore a significant effect of the cannabinoids in marijuana—is neuroprotective in nature: protecting brain cells from too much excitation. The endocannabinoid system, according to Mechoulam, is part of the body's "general protective network, working in conjunction with the immune system and various other physiological systems." His discoveries posed a direct challenge to scientific orthodoxy by revealing that the brain has a natural repair kit, an in-built mechanism of protection and regeneration, which can mend damaged nerves and brain cells.

Ironically, the U.S. government's unending search for marijuana's harmful properties yielded astonishing scientific insights that validated the herb's therapeutic utility. By stimulating CB-1 and CB-2 receptor signaling, marijuana functions as a substitute "retrograde messenger" that mimics the way our bodies try to maintain balance. Cannabis is a unique herbal medicine that taps into how our bodies work naturally. Thanks to this plant, scientists have been able to decipher the primordial language that nerve and brain cells use to communicate. From womb to tomb, across countless generations, the endocannabinoid system guides and protects.

But a big disconnect existed between the world of science and the general public. Aside from certain segments of the scientific community, few people knew about the endocannabinoid system. Doctors, journalists, public officials—hardly anyone was clued in to the latest scientific research that went a long way toward explaining why marijuana is such a versatile remedy and why it is, by far, the most-sought-after illicit substance on the planet.

---

mit chemical signals that "slow down" the release of sedative neurotransmitters such as GABA (which binds to the same receptor as Valium and alcohol). By slowing down or inhibiting GABA activity, the endocannabinoid system speeds things up.

Hip-Hop Hemp

It was "Hash Wednesday" at the University of Illinois in Champaign-Urbana in 1988. Several hundred students had gathered for the annual outdoor pot-smoking celebration, held during the third week of April. Debby Goldsberry, a nineteen-year-old sophomore, looked forward to a pleasant afternoon, a stoned frolic on the campus commons, as she and a few friends shambled toward the festivities.

But the police were in no mood for fun and games. A melee ensued as cops in riot gear bloodied peaceful participants with billy clubs and arrested nine people. This unprovoked assault was a galvanizing event for Goldsberry. It catapulted her into a lifelong career as a cannabis activist. The tall, statuesque beauty from the Illinois cornfields would play a pivotal role in jump-starting a nationwide grassroots movement for marijuana law reform.

"We were motivated. We realized we had to get organized," said Goldsberry, as she recounted the senseless beating that took place at her college. Marijuana was mainly a personal-freedom issue, a pro-choice issue, for this young woman, who vowed to carry on the Hash Wednesday tradition. She contacted people at other schools and reached out to *High Times* and NORML, inviting them to send speakers for the next Illini smoke-in, in April 1989, which happened to coincide with the Midwest Hemp Tour launched by Jack Herer's neo-Yippie comrades Ben Masel and Steve DeAngelo. So the Hemp Tour, with its museum-on-wheels, rolled through Champaign-Urbana.

Goldsberry hopped on board and never looked back. She dropped out of college and soon was getting paid a bare-bones salary to plan and coordinate the next Hemp Tour, a seventeen-state excursion that featured a rotating cast of speakers—Jack Herer, Ed Rosenthal, Dr. Tod Mikuriya, and several other prominent marijuana advocates. "Everywhere we went, people had been abused by the war on drugs," said Goldsberry. She attended the 1989 Fourth of July Washington, D.C., smoke-in when park police started clubbing pot smokers at the end of a concert headlined by the Butthole Surfers. Ten thousand young folks turned out for this protest rally, which was staged to promote "hemp consciousness" in the nation's capital.

Goldsberry wowed the guys at the Butternut House, who had organized the Washington smoke-in. They gave her unlimited use of their office and a place to crash whenever she needed it. During strategy sessions at the Nut House, she and her comrades brainstormed about how to unlock the political potential of marijuana's enduring cultural popularity. In the momentous fall of '89, while the Berlin Wall teetered, they came up with the name for a

Debby Goldsberry, founder of the Cannabis Action Network, at the *High Times* Cannabis Cup in Amsterdam
(Courtesy of *High Times*)

new organization that would spread the gospel of hemp throughout America. Henceforth, they called themselves the Cannabis Action Network (CAN).

Cofounded by Goldsberry and Rick Pfrommer, CAN grabbed the reins of Hemp Tour and ran with it. For the next five years, they were on the move nonstop, stumping for cannabis, shouting "Hemp, hemp, hurray!" on the steps of state capitols, asserting their right to free speech while bringing Jack Herer's evangelical message directly to the masses. They were the Hemperor's disciples. They crisscrossed America, setting up information booths on town squares and college campuses, selling thousands of (otherwise hard to find) books and magazines about pot, handing out free literature, and imparting what one reporter described as "a sexy urgency" to the cannabis cause.

Soon there were two CAN caravans and sometimes three on the road at the same time in different parts of the country. During the fall of '91, they did 125 events in thirty-three states—debates, teach-ins, rallies, hempfests, smoke-ins—and each year the tour kept growing. They always attracted a lot of attention by displaying a large banner with the controversial leaf.

Like retrograde messengers, CAN cadres traversed the back roads and byways of America, fanning out across the country from coast to coast on a mission to restore hemp's good name. They were doing pro-cannabis PR. "We never wanted to be a group that people formally joined," explained Goldsberry. "We never saw ourselves as building CAN chapters all over the place. We wanted to be a fomenting agent, a catalyst . . . We were planting seeds, networking, delivering resources to people and getting them excited, making them feel that change was possible."

CAN framed marijuana legalization as an ecological issue, arguing that the plant should immediately be granted amnesty in the war on drugs because it's a sustainable source of fiber, fuel, medicine, and paper. Liberating the weed wasn't just about smoking pot to get high—it was also about improving the environment and healing the sick. CAN's green credo emphasized a whole-plant approach to public outreach. They developed multiple pitches that affirmed all the different reasons why people might use cannabis. CAN activists touted the industrial, therapeutic, ecological, and civil libertarian aspects of hemp. Their efforts resonated in many rural redoubts where fiber hemp had once been part of the local culture.

Of all the arrows in CAN's quiver, perhaps none was as potent as the argument for medical marijuana. They got a big boost when forty-six-year-old Elvy Musikka, one of the few Americans given cannabis by the federal government for therapeutic reasons, joined the CAN road crew. Cheerful, feisty, and legally blind, Musikka was the third person approved for the Compassionate Investigational New Drug program, the second glaucoma patient to qualify, and the first woman to get prescription pot from Uncle Sam. Born with congenital cataracts, she credited cannabis with partially restoring and preserving her sight in one eye after several botched surgeries. "If you smoke or eat marijuana, your whole system gets so much better," said Musikka, who became a federal patient in 1988 shortly after a Florida judge declared her innocent of marijuana charges on the grounds of medical necessity. (She had been busted for growing a few plants in her backyard.)

Musikka felt compelled to speak out for people in need of medicinal cannabis. She had the time of her life touring the country with the CAN cavalcade. "Those kids were wonderful. They worked their little fannies off—that's for sure," Musikka reminisced. "They were determined to put everything aside and go out and educate people. They had the same idea as I did. We've got to tell people! If people knew the truth, they would not keep this prohibition."

Musikka gave CAN instant credibility. She was a walking, talking repudiation of the official fiction that cannabis had no therapeutic benefit. Her very existence exposed the knotted lie at the heart of marijuana prohibition. "The medicinal aspect was crucial—that's what the press wanted," said Goldsberry. "And we had Elvy. It seemed like everywhere we went Elvy appeared on the front page of the newspaper the next day. She toured with us constantly for several years. She lived in the van with us. It was like having your grandmother along."

There was no generation gap on this caravan. They were all united by their devotion to cannabis. "It's a holy weed. I thank God for it every day of my life," said Musikka. Whereas some medical-marijuana advocates were squeamish about conflating recreational and therapeutic consumption, Elvy didn't mince words: "It's a very positive, mind-altering experience. It enhances creativity . . . I enjoy the high."

Every month or so, Musikka visited a pharmacy in Miami, Florida, to pick up a tin canister of three hundred government-issue reefers. ("Use 10 cigarettes every day, smoked or eaten," read the instructions.) She always brought her medicine when she toured with the Cannabis Action Network. She also traveled with a letter from her lawyer explaining that the federal government permitted her to possess and use marijuana, which she smoked openly at public gatherings. That didn't smell right to local law enforcement. Elvy was arrested several times while campaigning against the drug war. "If looks could kill, I wouldn't be here right now," said Musikka after an incredulous cop in Amarillo, Texas, reluctantly returned her stash on orders from the feds. She was turned away at the border by Canadian customs officials, who prevented her from speaking at a CAN event in Vancouver.

CAN had frequent run-ins with cops. But the hempsters knew their constitutional rights (they memorized the ACLU guidebook), and they always stood their ground politely but firmly when dealing with the police. Occasionally CAN convoys protested at state courthouses where judges were dispensing severe mandatory-minimum prison sentences to marijuana offenders. CAN mainstay Monica Pratt would help launch Families Against Mandatory Minimums, a grassroots civil rights organization with the motto "let the punishment fit the crime."

In the early 1990s, the Cannabis Action Network set up its national headquarters in Kentucky, a centrally situated and economically depressed state once known for its abundant hemp fields. The locals were receptive to CAN's message and welcomed their presence. Hard times had fallen upon farmers throughout the region, and many desperate families, lacking other sources of income, were cultivating marijuana to survive.

To combat cannabis farming, the DEA sprayed forests in the Bluegrass State with Paraquat, the herbicide that killed foliage indiscriminately and poisoned the watershed. Anger at the government was palpable in rural pot-producing counties, where state police were refused food and gasoline during harvest season. It got very personal. "Why does your husband want to take Christmas away from our children?" the wife of a state trooper was asked.

Gary Earl Shepherd, a crippled forty-five-year-old Vietnam vet who used marijuana to relieve pain and posttraumatic stress, was sitting on the front porch of his home in Broadhead, Kentucky, on the afternoon of August 8,

1993, when a black helicopter landed on his property and a team of narcs in battle fatigues appeared. "Are these your plants? We're going to cut them down," they announced. To which Shepherd responded, "You'll have to kill me first." For the next six hours, he sat by his medicine patch with rifle in hand, guarding a half dozen cannabis plants. Suddenly, without warning, Shepherd was shot dead by police snipers hiding in the woods. Lethal government violence (often drug-related) and frequent aerial pot patrols by black helicopters stoked the frenzy of right-wing militias and untethered "Christian Patriots"—the homegrown Timothy McVeighs who were sprouting like flowers of evil in the American heartland.

Hemp was a lightning rod for discontent in Kentucky. In 1996, hometown hero Woody Harrelson, the famous actor, was arrested after he brazenly planted four hemp seeds in full view of the county sheriff's office in Lexington. "Industrial hemp can help meet our fiber needs while also revitalizing our struggling rural economies," Harrelson told the press at the time of his arrest. He had long been outspoken against government policies that allowed the clear-cutting of old-growth forests while at the same time prohibiting the cultivation of hemp, which would lessen the need for timber. Thanks to Harrelson's celebrity status, his symbolic act of civil disobedience made national headlines. Later that year, the American Farm Bureau, the largest U.S. farming organization, urged federal and state authorities to reconsider the ban on growing hemp. The American Farm Bureau called hemp "one of the most promising crops in half a century . . . [It] could be the alternative crop farmers are looking for."

Kentucky farmers were among the most boisterous in supporting the return of hemp. They had a champion in Gatewood Galbraith, a big, raw-boned, Bunyanesque character, who ran unsuccessfully for governor several times as a maverick Democrat and an independent on a pro-hemp, pro-pot platform. Galbraith advocated legalizing the plant for all uses. He was joined on the campaign trail by Willie Nelson, the legendary pigtailed country-western singer from Texas, who shared Galbraith's enthusiasm for cannabis. They drove across Kentucky together in a Mercedes powered by hempseed oil and other biofuel to underscore the economic potential of industrial hemp.

A prodigious pot smoker, Nelson promoted hemp at his concerts for Farm Aid, which raised money to help America's struggling family farmers who were losing ground, literally, to corporate agribusiness monopolies. "Hemp is petroleum. Hemp is food. Hemp is clothing. Hemp is paper. It's a shame that our farmers aren't allowed to grow this again," Nelson lamented. "They used to do all right with it . . ."

Nelson often sang the praises of marijuana. "I would have been dead if it hadn't been for pot, because when I started smoking pot I quit smoking cigarettes and drinking," he told Country Music Television's *Inside Fame* program. America's greatest country music star endorsed the herb's curative properties: "The highest killer on the planet is stress, and so many people medicate themselves in one way or another. But the best medicine for stress, if you have to take something, is pot."

Musicians were some of the biggest supporters of the Cannabis Action Network. In 1992, the Black Crowes played for 50,000 at an Atlanta festival to legalize the weed. CAN was at the concert, handing everyone fliers about hemp. "There's value in actually looking people in the eye, having a verbal exchange, shaking hands, giving them some literature—it motivates people in a different way," said Goldsberry. "Everyone was fed up with the war on drugs. They were hungry for information. They knew something was wrong, and they wanted to know why . . . And the best way to get information out is to put it down on a piece of paper and start passing it around all over the place."

In the waning days of the pre-Internet era, Goldsberry and her cohorts conducted one of the great pamphleteering operations of all time. CAN crews piggybacked on several major rock 'n' roll tours simultaneously—Fishbone, Primus, Green Day, Lollapalooza, H.O.R.D.E., and others. At every venue, CAN teams worked the crowds and spread the word about hemp to a receptive audience.

While following the Grateful Dead, CAN activists befriended a couple of guys from Marin County who called themselves "the Waldos." Twenty years prior, the teenage Waldos and their buddies met every day after high school at exactly 4:20 in the afternoon to smoke marijuana—or so goes the story. "420" became the numerical code for getting high among those in the know, a way for youthful members of an illegal subculture to communicate without exposing themselves. CAN adopted the 420 lingo and projected it well beyond Northern California. Before long, a 420 toke became a daily ritual in the United States, and marijuana lovers everywhere would celebrate April 20 as an international pot-smoking holiday, a worldwide rite of unity and civil disobedience.

In the early 1990s, CAN volunteers handed pro-pot literature to roughly five million concertgoers. CAN's grassroots push to legalize hemp in all its forms penetrated mainstream consciousness. Its efforts coincided with an increase in marijuana use among Americans aged twelve to twenty and a spike in reefer-related arrests. After more than a decade in the drug-war doldrums, pot was becoming cool again. Industrial hemp and medicinal cannabis played well throughout the country—from Peoria to South Central Los Angeles. Marijuana's resurgent popularity during this period paralleled the remarkable scientific advances that led to the discovery of the endocannabinoid system. The CAN team sensed a cultural shift, a change in public opinion. As the momentum continued to build, they felt "the spirit of the plant" moving through them.

In 1992, Cypress Hill, the hugely popular Cuban American/Latino hip-hop band from LA, did their first solo performance in New York City at a benefit for the Cannabis Action Network. It was a watershed moment for CAN, a cross-cultural melding of hemp and hip-hop activism. Cypress Hill albums featured many an ode to getting stoned, with titles such as "Hits from the Bong," "Something for the Blunted," and "Stoned Is the Way of the Walk." During media interviews, Cypress Hill's B-Real lauded cannabis not only for its pleasurable smoke but also as a valuable fiber. "Legalizing marijuana could bring a lot of jobs back," B-Real asserted.

The hemp movement found favor in the inner city, where smoking blunts (hollowed-out cigars stuffed with ganja) had become a daily ritual, especially among young African American males. This practice soon jumped its ghetto borders thanks to marijuana-positive music videos and hip-hop songs with not-so-cryptic instructions on how to convert Phillies, White Owls, Dutch Masters, and other cheap cigars into phallic-shaped doobies. Big-name hip-hop artists celebrated potent pot strains in their lyrics. Dr. Dre's album *The Chronic* went platinum in 1992—with a bright green marijuana leaf emblazoned on the CD. Snoop Dogg, Dr. Dre's protégé, personified the high-profile, pot-smoking gangsta who rapped about the grim realities of the street. For gang members, rolling a big phatty and chilling with some chronic was a much healthier way to deal with the stress of ghetto life than smoking crack or shooting junk.

Cannabis was indisputably part of hip-hop culture. The small serrated leaf replaced the X (for Malcolm X) on baseball caps worn by many who came of age in the early 1990s. Hip-hop "was the kind of tidal wave that rolls through once in a generation and takes everyone with it," wrote Jeff Chang. Born of social and economic breakdown in the South Bronx, hip-hop was a shout against invisibility and hopelessness, a furious lyrical assault on the politics of abandonment at a time when one third of black America and 45 percent of black children lived below the poverty line. Hip-hop unleashed an enormous surge of creative energy from the bottom of American society. It quickly spread beyond the ghetto en route to becoming the most popular musical genre on the planet. Ultimately, hip-hop evolved into something more than music. It was the lingua franca of a worldwide, multiracial youth movement. The hip-hop explosion and the reefer renaissance coalesced in the early Nineties. Both were at the center of global capitalist currents that generated billions in revenue.

Russell Simmons, Def Jam Recordings cofounder and Phat Farm clothing entrepreneur, was instrumental in launching the Hip Hop Summit Action Network, which made opposition to the drug war one of its main issues. Hip-hop activists in New York forged a coalition of rappers, academics, music industry execs, civil rights leaders, and politicians to push for social change. Hip-hop's multicultural army waged successful pre-Obama voter registration drives while fighting to overturn the onerous Rockefeller drug laws, which required harsh mandatory-minimum sentences for possession of even small amounts of drugs, regardless of the person's role in the crime. (Enacted in 1973, the notorious Rockefeller antidrug laws, then the most punitive in the nation, penalized some first-time drug violators more severely than murderers.) Ninety-four percent of those sentenced under the Rockefeller drug laws were black or Latino. The hip-hop community's high-profile involvement in this issue would help sway New York State officials to implement drug-law reform.

In the world according to hip-hop, marijuana is an everyday therapeutic, a preventive medicine for the masses, a nice buzz, and, in some cases, a user-friendly escape route from the clutches of cocaine, alcohol, heroin, and other addictive substances. Chronic is street med with street cred. A 2001 study of twenty-three U.S. cities found that as the use of cannabis increased, the use of crack and heroin declined, casting serious doubt (once again) on the theory that marijuana leads to harder drugs and bolstering the notion that smoking herb is a form of harm reduction and self-medication for many inner-city residents.

The marriage of hemp and hip-hop marked an important milestone in the drug war. Hip-hop's global triumph, a resounding cultural landslide, was a decisive rebuke to ten years of just-say-no. The Cannabis Action Network and allied hempsters turned the soil while hip-hop widened the social space for the medical-marijuana insurgency that was brewing across the country, especially in the Golden State.

To Live and Die in San Francisco

Ever since gold was discovered near a hemp patch at Sutter's Mill in 1848, California had occupied a special place in the American imagination, a place where the harried and the hopeful came in search of a better ending for their story. The "coast of dreams" beckoned to the beleaguered and the brokenhearted, the poor and displaced, the outlaw and the misfit.

Likened by Kevin Starr to "a prism through which the larger American identity, for better or worse, could be glimpsed," California often incited hyperbole. If it were an independent country, the Golden State would have ranked as the world's seventh-biggest economy in the final years of the twentieth century. Topographically fabulous and demographically diverse, it became a great social and political laboratory, a pacesetter for the rest of the nation. Thanks to the progressive reforms of the pre–World War I era, California voters could directly enact legislation and recall elected officials by placing proposed measures on the ballot through petition.

Residents of the Golden State had long displayed a penchant for exploring new directions. California led the way in the computer and film industries, aircraft manufacture, viticulture, sexual and drug experimentation, and much else. For decades, the San Francisco Bay Area had been a spawning ground for radicals—dockworkers, Wobblies, Beats, Pranksters, Diggers, Panthers, hippies, gays. The City by the Bay, with its twin legacies of bohemian self-renewal and left-leaning dissent, was America's cannabis capital. The Bay Area was "the spiritual Bethlehem of the pro-pot movement . . . it's Alpha and Omega," as Gordon Brownell put it. San Francisco would lead the nation in many areas of drug-policy reform.

Dennis Peron fell in love with San Francisco when he passed through California on a three-week furlough en route to Vietnam in 1967. The nineteen-year-old Long Island native was stationed in Saigon during his tour of duty. "Saigon was filled with the sweet smell of marijuana," Peron recounted. "The day I arrived, I saw lots of American soldiers turning on, smoking pot all over the place."

Peron had smoked grass in high school to relieve "parental stress syndrome," as he'd put it, but Indochinese reefer was better than any weed he'd tried back home. Like many other GIs, Peron endured the daily horrors of the Vietnam War by smoking cannabis. (One of his assignments was to stack bodies in the morgue.) He got high during the Tet Offensive and made love in a bunker to a fellow soldier while rockets exploded nearby and Vietcong fighters overran much of the city. It was his first sexual experience as a gay man.

Discharged in December 1969, Sergeant Peron gave a snappy salute as he slipped past customs with two pounds of Thai weed in his Air Force duffel bag. Peron started dealing ounces as soon as he settled in San Francisco, the city with the largest percentage of gays and counterculture denizens in the United States.

Impish, quixotic, and quick on his feet, the five-foot-six-inch Peron tilted against the confining rules of American society, especially its drug laws. He grew his hair long and rented a two-bedroom flat, which became home base for more than a dozen like-minded communards. Together they set up the Big Top, a pot-selling salon, and before long Peron's pad in the Castro district was crammed with new acquaintances. Thus began the legendary career of the man who would become California's most vocal, effective, and controversial marijuana activist. Busted so many times he lost count ("I'm a professional defendant," he quipped), Peron always went back into business. An unlikely working-class hero, he more than anyone else was responsible for catalyzing the dynamic grassroots social movement that culminated in the passage of Proposition 215, the Golden State's landmark medical-marijuana law.

One of five children in an Italian American family of modest means, Peron never fancied himself a highbrow intellectual or political sophisticate. But he had lots of energy and determination. Pushing the envelope was second nature for Peron. He refused to accept the idea that someone could tell him that he didn't have a right to partake of this amazing plant. "And the right to smoke it means the right to get it," he insisted, "which means the right to grow it and sell it."

In 1974, two years after the first cannabis café sprouted in Amsterdam, Peron and a few pals renovated an old storefront and opened the Island, a one-of-a-kind, reefer-friendly health food restaurant in the heart of the Castro. The décor was secondhand California hippie: an eclectic array of tables, chairs, plates, silverware, found art, wall hangings. Nothing matched. But the mostly vegetarian fare was tasty and the place was usually packed. Everyone who patronized this festive community dining hall was given a free joint, courtesy of Peron, the gregarious proprietor. "It was the only restaurant in the world where marijuana smoking was nearly mandatory," he explained.

Downstairs there was food and entertainment; upstairs the Big Top collective ran a bustling marijuana supermarket with pounds of weed, some acid, a few peyote buttons, and the occasional magic mushroom or two. No hard drugs changed hands at this after-dinner speakeasy. "It was kind of one-stop shopping," said Peron. "Hostesses. Baskets of pot. No waiting. You could tell them what you wanted and they would give it to you: Colombian, Cambodian, whatever. About 200 to 300 people a day came. I treated them with respect and gave them their money's worth. It was like a dream. People loved it."

A mecca for sexual exiles and political intrigue, Peron's bistro required that anyone who purchased pot on the premises must also register to vote. For two and a half years, the Island (named after Aldous Huxley's last novel, about a short-lived psychedelic utopia) hosted fund-raisers, book signings, and other gatherings for every hip cause imaginable. "It became a home for political change in San Francisco," said Peron. Gays and lesbians, greens, civil libertarians, and various progressive groups held press conferences and planned protests at his pot parlor. Paul Krassner, the Sixties veteran who had coined the word *Yippie,* called it "a little oasis."

Peron himself was a Yippie of sorts—a counterculture pothead committed to community service and social activism outside the two-party system. East Coast radicals had inaugurated a tradition of smoke-ins to protest marijuana prohibition, and Peron advanced this legacy of direct action and civil disobedience at his eatery. For a while, he supplied California sinsemilla to Yippie pot dealers in New York and Washington, D.C. In the years ahead, Peron participated in the Hemp Tour as an occasional speaker. Had it not been for the ganja that funded such efforts, Hemp Tour and several of Peron's initiatives would not have been possible.

While Peron viewed marijuana legalization as an essential part of the struggle for social justice in America, much of his activist energy was devoted to the gay rights movement in the Bay Area. He befriended Harvey Milk, the charismatic civil rights leader and populist coalition-builder who would, with Peron's help, become the first openly gay person to be elected to California public office. Milk got his start in electoral politics in 1972 when he circulated petitions for the California Marijuana Initiative in the Castro, going door to door in the same precincts that would, five years later, elect him to the San Francisco Board of Supervisors. For a while, Milk used the Island restaurant as his campaign headquarters.

Milk's electoral breakthrough reflected the growing sense of freedom and empowerment that gays and lesbians were discovering in San Francisco. Their swelling ranks translated into political clout. Henceforth, no major local official could get elected without gay support or without paying heed to gay concerns. And the gay community was strongly in favor of marijuana law reform. Advocates for gay rights and marijuana legalization believed in the same basic principle—that people should not be punished for personal lifestyle matters that are nobody's business but their own. The two issues were analogous in many ways. Like homosexuals who remained in the closet, pot smokers often hid the fact that they used marijuana for fear of being ostracized by their neighbors, coworkers, or disapproving family members.

For many years, San Francisco police had targeted gay bars and other places where homosexuals gathered. The cops conducted a virtual shakedown operation; those who were arrested often preferred to pay bribes rather than face exposure in the local press. The medical establishment compounded the stigma by viewing homosexuality as a disease. (Up until 1974, the American Psychiatric Association listed homosexuality as a pathology in its diagnostic manual.) Guilt and self-hatred drove many homosexuals to alcoholism and suicide.

When Peron first arrived in San Francisco, city police were still arresting several thousand gay people yearly for holding hands in public. Considerable animosity toward homosexuals persisted among Bay Area cops as Milk's supporters began to flex their political muscle. Widespread homophobia was demoralizing and debilitating for gays and lesbians, who, not surprisingly, were more likely than others to use cannabis and other mood-altering agents to relieve stress.

In July 1977, the San Francisco narcotics squad raided the Big Top. Officer Paul Mackavekias shot an unarmed Peron in the leg, shattering his femur. The cops seized 200 pounds of marijuana and $8,000 in cash. Peron and thirteen others were arrested. A wounded Peron continued to sell cannabis from his bedside while recovering at St. Joseph's Hospital. Milk publicly defended Peron after the latest bust. "He's the opposite of a profiteer," said Milk. "My experience has been one where I've seen his money and his energy going back to the community."

Given that California had recently decriminalized marijuana so that possession of an ounce or less would entail no more than a fine, Peron and his flamboyant trial lawyer, the ponytailed Tony Serra, argued for acquittal by emphasizing contradictions inherent in the new law. They based their defense strategy on what Peron referred to as the "miracle ounce"—if it's illegal to buy, sell, or grow marijuana, then how could a person acquire depenalized weed if not by some miracle?

During a courtroom break, Peron teased Mackavekias, "Hey, sweetheart, I like your shoes." The macho narc exploded, calling Peron "a motherfucking faggot" and saying within earshot of several bystanders that he wished he had killed Peron "so there would be one less faggot in San Francisco." As a result of this outburst, the officer's testimony was thrown out of court and Peron got off with a relatively light sentence. During a six-month stint in San Bruno County jail, he wrote a letter to *High Times* in which he declared: "Watch the light from San Francisco; it will light up the world."

Peron saw the future before anyone else. While in prison, he drafted and launched a campaign for a local ballot measure that directed the police and the district attorney to stop arresting and prosecuting people who "cultivate, transfer or possess marijuana." Proposition W won easily. Although the citywide referendum was nonbinding, it sent a clear signal that a large majority of San Franciscans felt that cannabis should be legal. Mayor George Moscone notified the police that they should respect the will of the people and ignore minor marijuana infractions. But the new policy was derailed when the mayor and Supervisor Harvey Milk were assassinated by Dan White, a homophobic ex-cop, on November 27, 1978.

Milk's life was cut short at a time when the alternative communities he represented and the progressive coalition he was building had started to seriously challenge the Bay Area status quo. A gifted public speaker, Milk was a strong advocate of rent control and measures to restrict real estate speculation; he befriended local labor leaders and challenged downtown corporate interests by opposing redevelopment plans; and he introduced an antiapartheid resolution in an effort to close the South African consulate in San Francisco. "Harvey was not just for gay rights. He was for the repeal of marijuana prohibition, justice for working people, human rights for all people . . . Harvey wanted to give dignity to people who had no dignity," explained Peron, who grieved the loss of a close friend.

Dan White, the assassin, was exonerated of murder charges after his lawyer persuaded a jury (from which all gays and nonwhites were excluded) that he suffered from diminished capacity due to a high-sugar, junk-food diet—the so-called Twinkie defense. White was found guilty of manslaughter and sentenced to four and a half years in jail, less than the mandatory minimum for some marijuana violations. The verdict triggered an outpouring of rage. Tens of thousands of people took to the streets and rioted, torching police cars, smashing windows at the Civic Center, and demanding justice. Many were tear-gassed during the all-night fracas.

And then—the epidemic.

On June 5, 1981, a brief note appeared in the *Morbidity and Mortality Weekly Report* from the U.S. Centers for Disease Control and Prevention, which mentioned a peculiar cluster of pneumonia and other symptoms in five otherwise healthy gay men. It was the first official mention of a terrible, infectious disease that as yet had no name, no treatment, and no cure. Within five years, 25,000 men in San Francisco would die from Acquired Immune Deficiency Syndrome, or AIDS, as it came to be known. Transmitted through sexual contact, blood transfusions, and intravenous drug use, the HIV virus ravaged America's gay communities and quickly spread throughout the heterosexual world. The AIDS epidemic—described by the United Nations as the "most destructive in human history"—would claim 25 million lives by 2006.

More than any other single factor, it was the AIDS epidemic that made medical marijuana an urgent, cutting-edge issue. No city in America was more devastated by this voracious illness than San Francisco. And no one played a more significant role in providing cannabis to AIDS patients than Dennis Peron, the Bay Area's most notorious pot dealer. As the AIDS crisis deepened, Peron increasingly catered to rail-thin men with gaunt, blemished faces. The wasting syndrome was one of the telltale signs of HIV infection—and the leading cause of death. Sickened gays found that marijuana, an appetite stimulant, was the most effective and least toxic treatment for HIV-associated anorexia and weight loss. Without cannabis many AIDS patients would not have been able to tolerate the severe nausea and other harsh side effects of potent, lifesaving protease-inhibitor drugs when they finally became available in the late 1980s. For people with AIDS, marijuana was a matter of life or death.

While President Reagan failed to respond to an escalating public-health crisis, ACT UP and other pro-pot community activists took matters in their own hands. They built extensive support networks and staged boycotts, demonstrations, "die-ins," cannabis giveaways, and other forms of nonviolent civil disobedience to publicize the disaster that was unfolding.

Mary Jane Rathbun did her part by baking as many as 15,000 marijuana brownies a month and distributing them free of charge to HIV-infected patients in the AIDS ward at San Francisco General Hospital. Nicknamed "Brownie Mary," this plump, grandmotherly figure with curly gray hair and a sweet disposition began volunteering as a nurse's assistant at the outset of the crisis when few were willing to work with HIV-infected people. Like every other public hospital in California, S.F. General was financially strapped and the overextended staff in the AIDS wing needed all the help they could get. For thirteen years, Mary comforted AIDS patients ("my kids," she called them), sharing her "magically delicious" brownies, and doing whatever else needed to be done.

After waiting tables in diners for most her adult life, Brownie Mary had found her calling. A self-described "anarchist," she believed in the rejuvenating power of direct action and the medicinal efficacy of marijuana. A "Thank you for pot smoking" sticker adorned her senior housing apartment door. She was a longtime cannabis consumer who often sampled her own wares, typically eating half a brownie in the morning and another half in the afternoon. Without the kind bud, Mary claimed, she couldn't walk much on her artificial knees.

The notion that Rathbun was some sort of self-medicating Mother Teresa didn't carry much weight with antimarijuana law-enforcement officers who arrested her on several occasions. Her repeated, tragicomic run-ins with the law made Brownie Mary a visible and much beloved public figure, a cause célèbre who focused national attention on San Francisco's burgeoning medical marijuana underground. Refusing to plea-bargain after her third bust in the early 1990s, Brownie Mary asserted in a manner that would have made Mae West proud: "I'm going to be vindicated in the state of California . . . I'll be damned if I give in to their bullshit." She appeared on ABC's *Good Morning America* and said the federal government ought to be paying her to bake brownies. "Walk a mile in my shoes, Middle America, and tell me what I'm doing is wrong," she stated shortly before her case was thrown out of court.

San Francisco Supervisor and later District Attorney Terence Hallinan (*on right*) called Brownie Mary (*left*) the "Florence Nightingale of the medical-marijuana movement"
(Courtesy of Fred Gardner)

This refreshingly irreverent woman was honored by the San Francisco Board of Supervisors, which declared August 25, 1992, "Brownie Mary Day." San Francisco Supervisor Terence Hallinan called her the "Florence Nightingale of the medical-marijuana movement." A heroine to the gay community as well as a steadfast advocate for legalizing the herb, Brownie Mary maintained that cannabis was a legitimate treatment for stress and scores of ailments. With marijuana donated by Dennis Peron, her comrade-in-arms, she continued to bake brownies for those in dire need until old age prevented her from doing so. At the peak of her baking operation, there were so many sick people asking for brownies that she had to pull names from a cookie jar.

Inspired by Brownie Mary's charitable work and her culinary contributions, Dr. Donald Abrams sought to conduct a rigorous scientific inquiry into how marijuana affected HIV-infected patients at San Francisco General Hospital. A professor of medicine at the University of California in San Francisco and a renowned Stanford-educated AIDS expert, Abrams was one of the first physicians in the United States to recognize and treat the disease. In 1985, he became chairman of a community consortium of Bay Area HIV health providers that pooled public and private clinics to test various treatment options and share vital information. As chief of hematology and oncology at San Francisco General, Abrams designed a pilot study to assess whether smoked marijuana or synthetic THC pills helped people with AIDS overcome the deadly wasting syndrome.

For several years, Abrams fought an uphill battle to get legal approval for his research project. "Every place I turn there is an obstacle in my way," he complained. "It's not medical—it's political." Abrams needed authorization from eight academic and government agencies, including NIDA, the FDA, and the DEA, to proceed. After navigating through a daunting thicket of regulations, he was denied access to cannabis from Uncle Sam's pot farm in Mississippi. Nearly anyone could get marijuana in San Francisco—except a doctor who wanted to study the herb's medicinal properties. But NIDA had final say in the matter. "Donald, we are the National Institute *on* Drug Abuse, not *for* Drug Abuse," NIDA's Alan Leshner explained.

Abrams kept getting the runaround from federal bureaucrats while scores of AIDS patients were dying in his hospital. He wouldn't let the matter rest. NIDA eventually relented and agreed to supply him with marijuana after he redesigned his research protocol. Instead of focusing on possible beneficial outcomes, Abrams proposed to investigate whether marijuana harmed immune-compromised HIV-infected patients by interfering with the body's ability to break down protease inhibitors. His conclusion: Cannabis helped AIDS patients gain weight without weakening the immune system. A subsequent study conducted by Abrams found that marijuana eases the extremely painful and otherwise untreatable AIDS-related condition known as peripheral neuropathy, which also afflicts advanced cancer patients and diabetics.*

"I think marijuana is a very good medicine," said Abrams. "I see cancer patients every day who suffer from loss of appetite, weight loss, pain, anxi-

* In 2008, scientists at Harvard Medical School and Northeastern University found that cannabinoid receptor activation strengthens the blood-brain barrier. Breakdown of the blood-brain barrier is frequently observed in patients with HIV-associated dementia (T. S. Lu et al., "Cannabinoids Inhibit HIV-1 GP120-Mediated Insults in Brain Microvascular Endothelial Cells," *Journal of Immunology* 181[9][2008]: 6406–16). Researchers at the University of Catania, Italy, showed that a synthetic cannabinoid (WIN 55,212–2), which binds to both CB-1 and CB-2 receptors, decreases the viability of Kaposi's sarcoma cells, as reported in the *European Journal of Pharmacology* in June 2009. Kaposi's sarcoma is a cancer that is often observed in AIDS patients. And in 2012, researchers at Mount Sinai School of Medicine in New York City reported that cannabinoids that bind to CB-2 receptors activate other receptors on certain human immune cells that can directly inhibit the HIV-virus in Late-Stage AIDS (C. M. Costantino et al., "Cannabinoid Receptor 2-Mediated Attenuation of CXCR4-Tropic HIV Infection in Primary CD4+ T Cells," *PLoS One,* March 20, 2012 [in press]).

ety, depression, insomnia, and nausea. With cannabis, I can recommend one medicine instead of writing prescriptions for six or seven."

The Pot Club

Shortly before midnight on January 27, 1990, ten narcotics officers, armed with sledgehammers and a search warrant, burst into Dennis Peron's walk-up apartment in the Castro. They ordered Peron and his twenty-nine-year-old lover, Jonathan West, to lie on the kitchen floor while the cops ransacked their home looking for marijuana. West was gravely ill with AIDS. He had Kaposi's sarcoma lesions on his face and the police made a big to-do of putting on rubber gloves while cracking sick jokes about his condition. "Do you know what AIDS means?" said one of the narcs as he put his boot on West's neck. "Asshole in deep shit." When they saw a photograph of Peron with Harvey Milk, the cops went into a harangue about how they hated "that fag."

The police found only four ounces of sinsemilla—no scales or packing equipment anywhere. Despite the modest haul, they arrested and booked Peron on the usual charges of possession with intent to sell and carted him off to jail, leaving West by himself. Peron thought of poor Jonathan home all alone, helpless, without any marijuana to quell his nausea and his pain. Later that night it came to him in a dream—he saw sick people, people in wheelchairs, men and women, young and old, black and white, all sitting in a large room, laughing, hugging, and sharing cannabis. That's how Peron got the idea for a public medical-marijuana dispensary, a place where people like Jonathan could gather and smoke pot with friends, unashamed of their skin abrasions and their obvious infirmities.

Six months later when the case came to trial, an emaciated West, weighing ninety pounds and barely able to walk, testified on Peron's behalf. One could hear a pin drop in the courtroom as West slowly approached the witness stand. He was so weak and wobbly that several minutes elapsed before he sat down and took the oath. Peron's attorney Tony Serra asked him about the cannabis. West said it was his. He said Peron kept it for him and rolled joints for him. The judge threw out the charges and scolded the arresting officers, telling them that he never wanted to see another case like this in court. West died two weeks later. "He lived to testify at my trial and then he let go of life," said Peron.

The Castro district was the epicenter of the AIDS epidemic in the United States. For a while it seemed that everybody Peron knew and loved was dying. He vowed to dedicate the rest of his life to helping "other Jonathans," as Peron put it. Henceforth, he would concentrate on making cannabis available for those in medical need. He rallied the troops and launched another citywide ballot initiative, Proposition P, which urged the state of California and the California Medical Association to legalize "hemp preparations" for medical purposes. It passed with a whopping 80 percent of the vote in November 1991. Most city officials and opinion leaders had endorsed the measure, including the former police commissioner Jo Daly, who acknowledged that she had smoked marijuana while undergoing chemotherapy for colon cancer. "I can't explain to anyone how violently ill you become after chemotherapy. You lose control. It's like a nuclear implosion inside your body. The word *nausea* doesn't even come close," she stated. "But with marijuana, just a tiny bit, it went away almost instantly."

Buoyed by Proposition P's lopsided victory at the polls, Peron founded the San Francisco Cannabis Buyers' Club in a small apartment on Sanchez Street in late 1991. It signaled the coming-out of California's medical-marijuana movement after many years in hiding. Peron knew that he had the backing of the local electorate and he was willing to risk incarceration in pursuit of his vision. He felt he had a moral obligation to force the issue by breaking the law—proudly, publicly, and defiantly. "It's not just about marijuana," Peron often insisted. "It's about America. It's about how we treat each other as people."

Peron and several colleagues who launched the fledgling dispensary assumed they'd all end up in prison for selling cannabis. But local officials turned a blind eye and the cops stayed away on orders from Mayor Frank Jordan, a Republican. "I am sensitive and compassionate to people who have legitimate medical needs," said Jordan. "We should bend the law to do what's right." By not enforcing antimarijuana statutes, the San Francisco Police Department was spared the bad publicity of busting terminally ill people.

With the tacit approval of City Hall, the Cannabis Buyers' Club quickly grew into a unique San Francisco institution, thereby setting the stage for a major confrontation with the federal government. Peron, the pot dealer-turned-healer, soon moved his operation to a bigger location on Church Street, where several hundred patrons purchased marijuana over the counter at below-market prices. Supply was never a problem. Peron tapped into a well-developed network of organic growers who kept the cupboards filled with different varieties of reefer.

As word of marijuana's therapeutic benefits spread among people with AIDS, small underground cannabis clubs took root in thirty other cities, including New York, Baltimore, Pittsburgh, Cincinnati, Little Rock, Key West, Seattle, and Washington, D.C. But none of these "green cross" facilities operated openly with the support of the local government like in San Francisco. Across the country, tens of thousands of desperately ill patients broke the law every day by consuming the forbidden herb. Demand for legal medical access was building.

In 1991, Kenneth Jenks and his wife, Barbara, became the first AIDS patients to receive marijuana from the U.S. government under the auspices of the Compassionate IND program established during the Carter presidency. A hemophiliac living in Florida who had contracted AIDS through a tainted blood transfusion, Jenks unknowingly infected his spouse. (Ninety percent of hemophiliacs in the United States were HIV-positive in the early '90s.) Stricken with chronic nausea and hardly able to eat, Kenny and Barbara tried dozens of different drugs but nothing helped. The mere smell of food made them puke. They were slowly starving to death. When the Jenkses heard about medical marijuana from an AIDS support group, they were initially skeptical. But they had little to lose, so they tried it. Both found that smoking cannabis provided immediate relief and restored their appetite. From then on they self-medicated on a daily basis—until they got busted.

To save money and avoid buying weed of unknown quality from street dealers, Kenny and Barbara grew a couple of pot plants behind their live-in trailer. The police, acting on a tip from an informant, arrested the couple. In Florida, marijuana cultivation was a felony, and both faced up to five years in prison. Their case generated national publicity when a state appeals court ruled that their use of cannabis was an act of medical necessity and therefore not a crime. Never before had a medical-necessity defense been successfully invoked by an AIDS patient. But the Jenkses still had no way of obtaining marijuana legally. After a bruising battle with the federal bureaucracy, they began receiving monthly shipments of government-grown reefer. Barbara Jenks died shortly thereafter and her husband soon followed her to the grave.

At a national AIDS conference in San Francisco in 1991, Robert Randall and a group of medical-marijuana activists distributed information packets to help ailing Americans apply to become legal federal patients. Soon the FDA was flooded with hundreds of applications from desperately ill AIDS sufferers seeking cannabis. The Bush administration responded by abruptly shutting down the entire Compassionate IND program in March 1992. No new candidates would be accepted. The eight patients who were already getting ganja from Uncle Sam would continue to receive their medication thanks to a grandfather clause. Everyone else, in effect, was told to drop dead.

U.S. Public Health Service director James O. Mason defended the policy change by blaming the victim. AIDS patients who use cannabis "might be less likely to practice safe behavior whether it's sharing needles or sexual behavior," he suggested. Moreover, there were better and safer treatments than smoked marijuana for treating chemotherapy-induced nausea and appetite suppression, according to Mason, who hyped Marinol (the THC pill) as an alternative to cannabis, even though most patients found that the pricey pharmaceutical provided limited relief compared with the less expensive, natural herb. Marinol had been available since the mid-1980s, but it was never cited as a reason to close the Compassionate IND program until Bush Senior's final year in office. The real reason was painfully obvious: If the federal government provided marijuana to hundreds of AIDS patients, then the medicinal value of cannabis would be indisputable. And that might send "the wrong signal" to impressionable Americans, especially young Americans. "If it is perceived that the Public Health Service is going around giving marijuana to folks, there would be a perception that this stuff can't be so bad," said Mason.

Medical-marijuana advocates were hopeful that things would change for the better when William Jefferson Clinton from Hope, Arkansas, was elected president in November 1992. Born and raised in Hempstead County (once a prime hemp-growing area in the Razorback State), Clinton had spoken out against mandatory-minimum sentences for nonviolent drug offenders while campaigning for the White House. He also expressed sympathy for seriously ill Americans who medicated with cannabis. "When I'm president, you'll get your medicine," candidate Clinton told Jacki Rickert, a Wisconsin resident who suffered from Ehlers-Danlos syndrome, a rare and painful connective-tissue disorder. Rickert's application to participate in the Compassionate IND program had been approved shortly before it was terminated by the Bush administration; consequently, she never got any marijuana from the feds.

Clinton's promise to Jacki Rickert was overshadowed during the campaign by his laughable assertion that he once smoked a joint but didn't inhale—a comment that spoke volumes about the U.S. political establishment's inability or unwillingness to be truthful about cannabis. One of marijuana prohibition's pernicious side effects was a baseline level of cultural hypocrisy that America's chattering class and much of its misled public could not get beyond.

Faux moralists and knee-jerk politicians jumped all over Joycelyn Elders, President Clinton's initial choice for surgeon general, when she expressed her opinion that physicians should have the right to prescribe marijuana as a medicine. Many doctors agreed with her. A 1991 Harvard University survey of more than a thousand cancer specialists found that 44 percent had recommended marijuana to their patients and more would do so if the herb were legal; 80 percent of the oncologists said that cannabis should be legally available by prescription. Elders also had the temerity to suggest that marijuana legalization might be worth studying—a remark that drew immediate fire from drug warriors who screamed for her head. Clinton, the first Baby Boomer president, solemnly swore through his press secretary that he firmly opposed legalizing cannabis. Not long thereafter Surgeon General Elders, never one to mince words about drugs, sex education, and other controversial subjects, tendered her resignation.

Once in office, Clinton failed to pursue any meaningful drug-policy reform. On the contrary, he escalated the war on drugs. The president who didn't inhale broke his campaign promise and declined to reinstate the Compassionate IND program for seriously ill Americans, thereby forcing tens of thousands of people into the unenviable position of having to obtain their medicine through illicit means. Like his Republican predecessors, Clinton adamantly resisted efforts to allow any therapeutic use of the herb despite pleas from sick and dying citizens and mounting evidence of marijuana's efficacy for a wide range of ailments. *Marihuana: The Forbidden Medicine*, a groundbreaking 1993 compendium coauthored by Harvard Medical School professor Lester Grinspoon and Yale scholar James Bakalar, featured compelling first-person accounts of the benefits of pot smoking for physically and emotionally distressed individuals. Banning the use of marijuana is "scientifically, legally and morally wrong," Dr. Grinspoon subsequently wrote in the *Journal of the American Medical Association*.

If, as Albert Einstein once said, "The definition of insanity is doing the same thing over and over again and expecting a different result," then Clinton and his same-old, same-old "New Democrat" entourage were prime examples when it came to marijuana policy. Clinton's first drug-war budget continued Bush's heavy emphasis on law enforcement with ever more money allocated for prisons, the DEA, and stepped-up helicopter raids against pot growers in the Emerald Triangle. With Slick Willie in the Oval Office, the drug-war budget doubled and record numbers of Americans would be arrested on marijuana charges.

House Speaker Newt Gingrich called Bill and Hillary Clinton "counterculture McGoverniks," even though nearly four million Americans were arrested on marijuana charges during the Clinton presidency, the vast majority, as usual, for simple possession. The number of jail sentences nationwide for marijuana offenders during Clinton's two terms was 800 percent higher than during the twelve years under Reagan and Bush Senior. Eager to outdo GOP law-and-order zealots, Clinton signed legislation that cut off federal aid to student marijuana offenders and other drug violators. Armed bank robbers, meanwhile, remained eligible for federal aid.

Clinton's abject refusal to restore the Compassionate IND program had the unintended effect of fueling the rise of the medical-marijuana movement. With the last legal option foreclosed by the feds and nowhere else to go, ailing patients in the San Francisco Bay Area flocked to the Cannabis Buyers' Club.

Dennis Peron in the doorway of the San Francisco Cannabis Buyers' Club on Market Street, 1996 (Courtesy of Fred Gardner)

To accommodate a deluge of new members, Dennis Peron moved his mission of mercy in 1995 to a converted five-story warehouse at 1444 Market Street, a busy locale near the San Francisco Civic Center.

Entering this expansive, well-lit concrete-and-glass structure, marked only by a red cross in the front window, was a mind-altering experience in and of itself. To join the San Francisco Cannabis Buyers' Club, one had to produce a photo ID and a doctor's note certifying that one had a condition that could be helped by marijuana. Senior citizens were granted automatic admission. ("People in the autumn or sunset of their lives have a right to any medicine that helps them feel better," Peron insisted.) The walls and ceilings of the top three floors, where patients congregated, were cluttered with masks, fans, found art, marionettes, rainbow flags, and origami paper birds. Bulletin boards posted notices about AIDS treatments, wheelchair maintenance classes, and memorials to those who recently passed away. Half of the club's 11,000 members and most of the staff were people with AIDS.

The San Francisco Cannabis Buyers' Club employed close to one hundred people—food servers, "bud tenders," janitors, clerical workers, carpenters, security guards. The club featured a Jerry Garcia elevator with piped-in rock music and several large rooms where members lounged on mismatched secondhand couches and easy chairs, casually passing joints and pipes while engaging in animated conversation. After they inhaled a few puffs of a doobie, the disabled and the dying seemed to forget their most onerous symptoms. Raucous laughter often filled the air, which reeked of thick, aromatic fumes. "People are smoking pot openly here!" blurted a breathless CBS *48 Hours* correspondent.

Patrons lined up at counters to choose from a daily menu of pot specials—smokables, edibles, tinctures, and topicals. Several strains of bud were displayed beneath a sign that read "The Island," a memento from Peron's first cannabis café in the Castro. Wholesome food went for a dollar a plate; the cooler stored juice and liquid supplements. For dessert or snacks, the "Brownie Mary Bar" offered baked goods with a range of potencies. The club also sold hemp clothing and smoking paraphernalia, along with copies of *Brownie Mary's Marijuana Cookbook & Dennis Peron's Recipe for Social Change,* which included some homegrown advice: "Mix, in a big country, a magic herb, a blend of people (do not separate), and lots of chutzpah. Pour off prohibition, strain out and discard unjust laws. Use no DEA. Whip media into frenzy. Smoke remainder for several days. Serve."

The bustling pot dispensary was always crowded on Tuesdays and Thursdays when Peron gave away free bags of marijuana to poor patients—not just people with AIDS, but also those suffering from cancer, multiple sclerosis, spinal cord injuries, glaucoma, arthritis, and other degenerative conditions. Nor did Dennis dismiss those suffering from "common afflictions" just because their pain or disability didn't entail chemo or a wheelchair.

The San Francisco Cannabis Buyers' Club wasn't only about smoking grass. "Marijuana is part of it, but the biggest part of healing is not being alone," said Peron, who intuitively grasped a profound truth that experts often overlooked in the age of high-technology medicine: social isolation is bad for one's health. The pot club was therapeutic by design—a setting where wheelchair-bound patients and other chronically ill individuals could hang out, smoke reefer, make new friends, and interact with those who shared their plight. It was a place where people came to laugh for the last time before they died.

"Sick people tend to withdraw, and that's the worst thing they can do," Peron explained. "We don't have a delivery service, because we want them to get out of the house." His club pioneered what sociologists would later refer to as the "San Francisco model"—the marijuana dispensary that allows on-site medication and encourages patients to socialize, form support networks, and avail themselves of counseling and recreational facilities. The social aspect of the Cannabis Buyers' Club played a crucial, salutary role, improving the quality of life and perhaps even prolonging the life of many of its members.

Dr. Tod Mikuriya, the Berkeley-based psychiatrist who briefly directed marijuana studies at the NIMH in late 1960s, viewed the pot club across the bay as a real-world laboratory, a "unique research opportunity." The physician who reintroduced cannabis to Western medicine wasn't going to wait for U.S. government approval to get a research grant. When Peron launched the San Francisco Cannabis Buyers' Club, Dr. Tod immediately volunteered as medical coordinator. He began interviewing members who were willing to take part in a study. Mikuriya listened to hundreds of patients describe their conditions, their cannabis intake, and changes in their health. "Medicinal applications reported by self-medicating buyers would appear to reconfirm descriptions in clinical literature before the drug was removed from prescriptive availability," Mikuriya concluded. "Further clinical study is warranted. Restoration of cannabis to prescriptive availability is indicated."

As more and more people joined the pot club, Dr. Tod continued to interview patients and expand his master list of ailments helped by cannabis—colitis, lupus, postpolio pain, alcoholism, Crohn's disease, involuntary movement disorders . . . the list kept expanding. During this period, Mikuriya, a biofeedback pioneer, maintained a private practice while serving as a psychiatric consultant at several Bay Area hospitals.

In the early 1990s, Mikuriya became part owner of a hemp store in San Francisco. The Hemporium on Haight Street employed several veteran activists from the Cannabis Action Network, which had moved its headquarters from Kentucky to Berkeley shortly after Peron opened his pot club. "Tod Mikuriya convinced us to come out to California," recounted Debby Goldsberry, who wanted to be closer to the action and to lend a hand, if possible, as the medical-marijuana movement gained traction in the Bay Area. She and her CAN comrades tipped their hats to Peron, "that merry little elf," as Goldsberry called him: "Nobody was thinking as big as Dennis was thinking. Nobody was thinking we're going to find the magic formula that would blow the lid off this whole thing like Dennis did with medicinal cannabis."

Crossing the Rubicon

For several years, Dennis Peron had been nursing the idea of a statewide ballot initiative that would legalize medical marijuana in California. A lot was at stake. If such a ballot measure passed, it would be a major defeat for the federal drug-control regime. A successful ballot measure might mean the effective end of cannabis prohibition in America's most populous state. It could spark a national upheaval strong enough to shake the foundations of the law-and-order establishment.

Peron and his allies realized that to succeed in their quest to legalize medical marijuana they had to decouple state law from federal law. In the mid-1990s, several pot club members in wheelchairs along with widowers of medical-marijuana patients visited Sacramento. They successfully lobbied the state legislature, which passed two bills that allowed the use of medical marijuana for a limited number of conditions. But the Republican governor, Pete Wilson, vetoed both bills. The only way to get around the logjam in the state capital was through the grassroots initiative process, which enabled voters to directly formulate and enact public-policy options when state officials failed to represent the popular will. Such a ballot measure, if approved, would not be subject to a veto by the governor.

In early 1995, Peron began hosting weekly meetings at the San Francisco Cannabis Buyers' Club, where he and a rotating cast of organizers hashed out plans for a full-scale grassroots ballot campaign. Dale Gieringer, director of California NORML, who held a PhD in economics from Stanford, played a key role in launching the initiative. Other participants in these early strategy sessions included Vic Hernandez, who would open a second med-pot social club in San Francisco; harm-reduction activist Michelle Aldrich; hospice organizer Valerie Corral from the Wo/Men's Alliance for Medical Marijuana in Santa Cruz, another pro-cannabis stronghold; Scott Imler, who opened a dispensary in Los Angeles; the East Bay lawyers Bill Panzer and Robert Raich; Lynette Shaw and Pebbles Trippet, from Marin and Mendocino counties, respectively; Michael Petrelis of ACT UP; Bob Basker, a labor organizer and longtime ally of Peron; and, last but not least, John Entwistle, Peron's go-to guy and closest political confidant. They were all seasoned activists in a grassroots reform movement.

Gieringer from NORML raised seed money to conduct a poll, a feasibility study, and a direct-mail test. The numbers looked good. Depending on the phrasing, between 59 and 66 percent of Californians expressed support for a medical-marijuana initiative. (One third of those surveyed in another poll said they knew someone who used marijuana for medical reasons.) Several months passed as Peron, Gieringer, and several other activists painstakingly debated and tweaked the wording of the ballot measure. It went through many versions before the editing process was concluded.

Dr. Tod Mikuriya played a crucial role in drafting the language of the initiative. He contributed the most critical phrase in the first sentence, which stipulated that a patient has a right to use cannabis not only for a short list of specified diseases but also for *"any other illness for which marijuana provides relief."* Some drug-policy reformers worried that the language was too broad, that it might turn off uncertain voters. But Peron steadfastly backed Mikuriya and they would not waver on this key point. Dr. Mikuriya had documented a myriad of conditions helped by marijuana, and Peron adamantly maintained that the new law should reflect this significant medical truth. And Peron had final say in the matter. After all, he was the recognized leader of the medical-marijuana movement. Day in and day out, he was doing the risky work of providing illicit medicine to people in need. Peron had the moral authority and a battalion of willing and disabled volunteers. "We have a lot of sick and dying people willing to stand up for their rights," he explained.

Peron signed off on the text of the Compassionate Use Act, which was filed in Sacramento on September 29, 1995. The wording of the initiative did not set age limits for medical-marijuana use. It did not address the tricky issue of how patients would obtain their medicine. It did not limit the number of medicinal plants someone could grow. It did not spell out rules for entrepreneurs who wanted to sell the herb. The carefully crafted ballot measure did not directly conflict with federal law because, technically speaking, it did not legalize cannabis. It simply created a doctor-recommended exception to state enforcement.

Peron's resistance to watering down the language of the proposition proved prescient. But his headstrong attitude was counterproductive during the early stages of the petition drive, which began as a volunteer crusade and succeeded despite its dysfunctional tendencies. More than once the medical-marijuana initiative appeared dead in the water. Under California law, the organizers had 150 days to gather 433,269 valid signatures (5 percent of the total votes cast in the last presidential election) for the proposition to qualify as a ballot measure. Gieringer and others pleaded with Peron to hire professionals who had experience running statewide initiatives. They estimated that it would cost a million dollars to conduct a successful petition drive and a lot more to run a viable campaign if the measure qualified.

Dennis demurred. He didn't have that kind of money. Nor, in his opinion, did he need a professional signature-gathering company. Peron stubbornly maintained that his network of dedicated patient-activists could do the job. He assumed the same tactics that had previously delivered the vote in San Francisco would also work for a statewide campaign.

Launched on December 1, 1995, the signature drive was organized out of an office on the mezzanine level of the San Francisco Cannabis Buyers' Club, which functioned as a nerve center for activism as well as a sanctuary for the sick. By mid-January, it became apparent that the all-volunteer effort was coming up way short. Some activists wondered if the freewheeling Peron had bitten off more than he could chew. They were concerned about his erratic, seat-of-the-pants management style. For more than two decades in the drug-war trenches, Peron operated as an outlaw. Improvising was his M.O. That's how he got by at the pot club. Apparently he kept no business records. No one tracked inventory or cash flow on a consistent basis. If Peron felt like donating to a worthy cause, he simply grabbed a bunch of cash and gave it away. Dennis conducted the statewide petition drive the way he ran his pot business—on faith, hunch, and impulse.

Insiders knew the campaign was floundering. It was too casual. It needed more discipline and a lot more money. Public sentiment was there, but chances of getting on the ballot were becoming increasingly remote. Short on cash and strained by personality conflicts, the grassroots coalition behind the initiative desperately needed help.

As fate would have it, a *New York Times* reporter picked up on an offhand comment by Peron, who exaggerated the number of signatures they had gathered for the medical-marijuana proposition. (Gieringer called it "luck of the Dennis kind.") This inflated figure caught the eye of drug-policy critic Ethan Nadelmann, who convinced a quartet of reform-minded billionaires, led by George Soros, to contribute big bucks at a crucial moment. Their nick-of-time intervention rescued the medical-marijuana ballot initiative from the brink of failure, lending credence to Hunter S. Thompson's memorable adage: "When the going gets weird, the weird turn pro."

The Hungarian-born Soros disagreed with the long-entrenched view that the best way to fight drug abuse is through the criminal-justice system. Averse to all forms of totalitarian politics, he knew from firsthand experience what it was like to grow up under both fascism and communism. His opposition to the drug war was entirely consistent with his vision of an antiauthoritarian "open society," which he promoted through various philanthropic endeavors. "A drug-free America is simply not possible," wrote Soros, who maintained that the war on drugs "is doing more harm to our society than drug abuse itself."

Soros became interested in drug policy after he met Allen Ginsberg. The intellectually engaging poet told Soros about how he had spent an entire summer researching the files of Indiana University sociologist Alfred Lindesmith, the first prominent U.S. academic to challenge America's heavy-handed war on drugs. In 1994, Soros founded the Lindesmith Center, an independent drug-policy institute, which favored harm-reduction, medical marijuana, and an end to discriminatory drug laws. He tapped Nadelmann, a Princeton political scientist, to head the new think tank, which soon merged with another organization to form the New York–based Drug Policy Alliance (DPA).

Backed by Soros, Nadelmann negotiated with several Deep Pockets, including Cleveland insurance magnate Peter Lewis and University of Phoenix founder John Sperling, who each committed more than a quarter of a million dollars to the California medical-marijuana campaign. George ("I guarantee it!") Zimmer, CEO of Men's Warehouse, and Lawrence Rockefeller pitched in, as well. But the infusion of money that Nadelmann promised to the California activists came with strings attached. He insisted on replacing Dennis Peron with a professional campaign manager. Nadelmann bore no personal animus toward Peron, who just a few months earlier had received a citizen action achievement award from the DPA. Thanks largely to Peron, majority support for medical marijuana already existed in California by the time the billionaires entered the fray. It was clear, however, that the preoccupied pot club proprietor was not up to the task of conducting a successful statewide voter initiative.

Nadelmann recruited Bill Zimmerman, a Los Angeles–based PR strategist, to take over. An organization called Californians for Medical Rights was formed to oversee the petition drive and the subsequent campaign. Zimmerman intended to concentrate on winning votes across the state. He did not anticipate expending a lot of effort in the Bay Area, where support was assured. Henceforth, the initiative would be headquartered in Santa Monica, near Zimmerman's office, rather than in Peron's pot club. The new leadership emphasized that it was important for the campaign to speak with one voice and stay "on message." Several old-guard activists felt brusquely pushed aside during the transition. The personal and strategic quarrels that surfaced during the heat of battle would linger long past Election Day.

Zimmerman's first move was to hire Angelo Paparella's Progressive Campaigns, a top-notch signature-gathering organization that could mount a full-scale petition drive at a moment's notice. When Paparella examined the names that had already been collected, he was dismayed to discover far fewer valid signatures than had been reported by *The New York Times*. His audit precipitated a crisis that threatened to derail the entire campaign. With the deadline less than eight weeks away, they had to gather more than a half million signatures—a Herculean task.

Paparella suggested the most sensible plan would be to suspend the petition drive and try again in two years. But Nadelmann signaled his willingness to pay Paparella's crew one dollar per signature—an incentive that inspired renewed effort. Peron's unpaid volunteers also rose to the occasion as did the Berkeley-based Cannabis Action Network and signature-gatherers organized by Chris Conrad and Mikki Norris. Jack Herer—who initially refused to endorse the initiative because it sought to legalize hemp only for medical purposes without addressing industrial and recreational uses—dispatched his followers to supermarkets, shopping malls, and health food stores with petitions in hand. Together, they somehow managed to amass more than three quarter of a million signatures for the medical-marijuana measure. Paparella was amazed. On June 6 state officials announced that they had certified the ballot initiative. It would be called Proposition 215.

But the shotgun marriage between the East Coast pros and the West Coast activists quickly soured. A behind-the-scenes tussle erupted over the text of a 500-word argument for the California ballot pamphlet that would be mailed to fourteen million registered voters. "Police officers can still arrest everyone for marijuana offenses," the pros asserted in their ballot argument rebuttal. "Proposition 215 simply gives those arrested a defense in court, if they can prove they use marijuana with a doctor's approval." Peron objected to the notion that the medical-marijuana initiative merely provided an affirmative defense for arrested patients. The purpose of the initiative, as he conceived it, was to stop cops from arresting people in the first place. He submitted a different ballot argument to Sacramento without telling the pros, who subsequently cut off all communication with Peron. Confronted with having to choose between competing pro-215 ballot arguments, bemused state officials went with the pros' weaker version, which included the affirmative defense clause. Intent on making the initiative as appealing as possible to the general public, Zimmerman had unwittingly given antimarijuana law enforcement officers a significant weapon they could exploit after the November vote.

While focus groups and opinion polls showed strong support for medical marijuana, fewer than 25 percent of Californians wanted to legalize recreational reefer. Accordingly, Zimmerman's pro-215 TV ads framed the issue in terms of patients' rights, treatment options and compassion, while steering clear of anything that smacked of hippies in tie-dyed T-shirts. One TV advertisement featured an oncologist who stated: "Morphine works. Marijuana works. Let us physicians treat you with every medicine that can help." In another ad, Anna Boyce, a registered nurse (and official cosponsor of Proposition 215), was shown in a cemetery placing flowers on her husband's grave while speaking of how medical marijuana had helped him before he died. "Vote yes on 215," she implored. "God forbid, someone you love may need it."

Adversaries of Prop. 215 could not muster an effective response to heart-stirring testimonials from patients and loved ones. The opposition, led by Attorney General Dan Lungren and the California Narcotics Officers' Association (CNOA), was caught flat-foot by the medical-marijuana initiative.

The drug warriors had grown complacent over the years, believing their own stereotypes of stoners as slackers incapable of doing much of anything. Mired in ideological quicksand, state law-enforcement officials drew from the same dog-eared antipot playbook as the feds. There wasn't a whiff of clinical proof establishing that smoked marijuana was a medicine, they claimed. In 1996, the CNOA blithely asserted that "more than 10,000 studies" had documented the harmful effects of marijuana, but, when challenged, the narcs were unable to substantiate this claim.

More than a hundred California law-enforcement officials publicly opposed the medical-marijuana initiative, including dozens of sheriffs, police chiefs, and fifty-seven of the state's fifty-eight district attorneys (San Francisco's Terence Hallinan being the sole supporter). Prop. 215 naysayers framed their arguments around several concerns—the inappropriateness of practicing medicine by popular vote, the permissive wording of the proposition, 215's conflict with federal law, and that old standard, the danger of sending the wrong message to children. According to the narcs, the whole concept of medical marijuana was a "cruel hoax," a cleverly designed ploy to legalize recreational reefer. They made hay over a comment by Richard Cowan, erstwhile executive director of NORML, who had stated a few years earlier: "The key is medical access, because once you have hundreds of thousands of people using marijuana under medical supervision, the whole scam is going to be brought up . . . Then we will get medical, then we will get full legalization."

Warnings from law-enforcement groups, however, did not have the same emotional tug as poignant stories from patients and health-care providers. Unable to win the medical argument, opponents of 215 tried to turn the vote into a referendum on Dennis Peron and his loosely run Cannabis Buyers' Club. "This bill was written by a dope dealer from San Francisco," declared Brad Gates, the Orange County sheriff who cochaired the "No on 215" campaign.

For several months, California narcotics officers had staked out 1444 Market Street. Undercover agents with forged doctors' notes infiltrated the San Francisco club and purchased weed to prove that Peron, the silver-haired bad boy of pot politics, was not just dealing to needy patients. The narcs went to elaborate lengths to gain membership at his club. They forged letters on fabricated doctors' letterheads and set up a dedicated phone line that would reach an agent pretending to be a physician's receptionist, who "confirmed" the phony medical diagnosis.

On Sunday, August 4, 1996, early in the morning, some one hundred heavily armed, black-clad police used a battering ram to bust open the front door of the Buyers' Club. Dispatched by the California Bureau of Narcotics Enforcement on orders from Attorney General Dan Lungren, the uniformed raiders confiscated 150 pounds of sinsemilla, $60,000 in cash, 400 indoor plants, lots of marijuana edibles, all the medical records of club members, and files of the "Yes on 215" campaign. They even ripped the marijuana menu off the wall. Black curtains were draped over the windows so people on the street couldn't watch the narcs tear up the place. "This is nothing more than an obscene effort to win with guns what they can't win at the ballot box," said Peron, who was out of town when the raid occurred.

Once again, the mercurial Peron was a lightning rod for controversy—much to the chagrin of the pros down south, who were trying to run a disciplined "on message" campaign. At the official Prop. 215 headquarters in Santa Monica, they considered the scene in San Francisco an unpredictable sideshow with the potential to blow up in their faces. Californians for Medical Rights publicly distanced itself from Peron and called for him to withdraw from the pro-215 campaign following the police raid. But the irrepressible pot club pioneer wasn't about to go away. Newsmedia continued to focus on Peron, the high-profile, telegenic champion of medical marijuana, and he continued to speak freely with the press.

The fallout from the raid was unkind to Attorney General Lungren, who claimed that he was compelled to act, given how ostentatiously Peron had been flouting the law. To many Bay Area observers, it seemed like a bare-knuckled attempt by state law enforcement to cripple an unwanted political campaign. District Attorney Terence Hallinan, a strong proponent of medical marijuana, called the raid "a cheap political trick" and said that his office had not been informed beforehand, a departure from usual procedure. The San Francisco Medical Society unequivocally condemned the confiscation of private medical records.

Lungren was lampooned in the popular *Doonesbury* cartoon in which Zonker's friend says, "I can't get hold of any pot for our AIDS patients. Our regular sources have been spooked ever since the Cannabis Buyers' Club in San Francisco got raided." Lungren tried to convince newspaper editors to drop the widely syndicated comic strip, and the press had a field day reporting on California's top lawman duking it out with a fictitious cartoon character.

The attorney general scored a Pyrrhic victory when his office convinced a California Superior Court judge to issue a temporary restraining order prohibiting Peron's club from providing medical marijuana to its clientele. With medicinal access abruptly cut off, thousands of hapless patients looked elsewhere for herb. Several San Francisco churches began distributing cannabis as a humanitarian effort. Some folks went across the bay to the Oakland Cannabis Buyers' Cooperative, a new, well-run facility sanctioned by the Oakland city government.

During the run of the medical-marijuana campaign, General Barry McCaffrey, President Clinton's recently appointed drug czar, weighed in heavily on behalf of the "No on 215" forces. Although the Hatch Act explicitly prohibited federal funds from underwriting intervention in a state election, the retired four-star general made four high-profile visits to California to rally the troops against the grassroots voter initiative. Two weeks after law enforcement shut down the San Francisco Cannabis Buyers' Club, General McCaffrey announced with great fanfare while touring the Bay Area on the taxpayers' dime: "There is not a shred of scientific evidence that shows that smoked marijuana is useful or needed. This is not science. This is not medicine. This is a cruel hoax that is more like something out of a Cheech and Chong show." He would repeat the Cheech and Chong line on several occasions. But the stoner duo never said anything as stupid as the drug czar when he insisted that cannabis had no medical value.

Former presidents Carter and Ford also made statements opposing Proposition 215. So did California's senators, Dianne Feinstein and Barbara Boxer, former surgeon general C. Everett Koop, and several Clinton administration officials. Proposition 215 was the target of doomsday predictions by McCaffrey, who warned in Chicken Little fashion that legalized medical marijuana in California would lead to "increased drug abuse in every category." The word-slurring drug czar asserted that if the measure passed, he would order federal agents to arrest any physician in California who recommended cannabis to a patient.

Peron's retort: "What in the world is a retired army general doing telling doctors what to do?"

As Election Day drew closer, Soros and a few other Deep Pockets kicked in a million more for a down-to-the-wire advertising blitz that helped transform the image of the pot smoker from a scruffy, long-haired ne'er-do-well into a decent, ailing American who took a few puffs a day to keep the pain away. A number of prominent health-care organizations, including the California Nurses Association, the California Academy of Family Physicians, and the San Francisco Medical Society, endorsed Proposition 215. The medical-marijuana campaign was on a roll.

There was one mother of a party among cannabis activists in San Francisco on the night of November 5, 1996, when the Compassionate Use Act triumphed by a healthy margin at the polls. 4,870,822 Californians voted for Proposition 215, nearly a quarter million more than those who cast their ballot to reelect President Bill Clinton (who easily carried the state over the GOP nominee, Bob Dole). Medical marijuana had revealed its transideological appeal: liberals, conservatives, independents, and progressives all believed that doctors had the right to recommend and patients to use therapeutic cannabis. Fifty-six percent of those who voted had come to the conclusion that criminalizing sick people who smoked pot was bad public policy.

The victory set off a celebration at the shuttered buyers' club on Market Street. A smiling Peron stood before the TV cameras holding Pinky, his miniature Pomeranian. He lit a big phatty, inhaled, and slowly blew smoke in America's face. "This is a great moral victory. This is about who we are as a people and where we're going as a nation," he beamed. Throughout the Golden State, revelers freely passed joints and rejoiced.

In yet another unscripted departure from the on-message campaign, Peron was quoted in *The New York Times* saying: "All marijuana use is medical." What he actually said was more nuanced: "In a society where kids are prescribed Prozac for shyness, all marijuana use is medical."

But there was nothing nuanced about the political earthquake that had just shaken California. The passage of 215 put the most populous state in the country on a collision course with the federal government and the entire, multibillion-dollar U.S. drug-war behemoth. At exactly one minute past midnight on November 6, 1996, Proposition 215 became section 11362.5 of the California Health and Safety Code, meaning that with a doctor's recommendation, it was legal to possess and cultivate marijuana for personal use under state law.

7

FIRE IN THE BELLY

Counterattack

All eyes were on California attorney general, Dan Lungren. The drug-war zealot and ardent foe of medicinal cannabis was in an awkward position. His sworn duty as California's chief law-enforcement official was to uphold state law—even if it clashed with federal law. This was true for all California law-enforcement personnel, not just Lungren, a Republican ex-congressman whose father had been Richard M. Nixon's longtime physician and close friend.

Under the supremacy clause of the U.S. Constitution, federal law supersedes state law when they conflict. But America's Founding Fathers had the foresight to create a system of governance that encouraged states to be "laboratories of democracy" by giving them significant latitude to pursue different approaches to issues. While Proposition 215 did not prevent the DEA or other federal agencies from enforcing the Controlled Substances Act, it was not the job of local or state police to enforce legislation enacted in Washington, D.C. And without the cooperation of California law-enforcement agencies, which employed ten times more narcs on the ground in the Golden State than the DEA, it would be impossible for the feds to impose their will. In short, medical marijuana represented the most significant challenge to federal drug prohibition since the passage of the 1937 Marihuana Tax Act.

"This thing is a disaster," Lungren told the *Los Angeles Times* the day after the election. "We're going to have an unprecedented mess." Lungren said the new law would lead to "anarchy and confusion." He promised to use every legal means to fight it.

Lungren had fire in the belly. As he saw it, the medical-marijuana initiative was riddled with ambiguities and loopholes and it was up to him to dictate how to interpret and implement the voter initiative. As soon as the vote was tallied, he faxed a three-page memo to California district attorneys, police officers, and sheriffs regarding "the challenge that the new law presents to law enforcement and prosecutors." Lungren promised that he would confer with federal officials "to determine how they will enforce federal law."

The people of California had spoken. But the feds said nope to medicinal dope and continued to treat all marijuana as equally illicit, making no exceptions even for the gravely ill. Unwilling to allow a crack in the prohibitionist façade that might threaten the entire drug-war edifice, public officials—both Republicans and Democrats—sought to thwart the implementation of California's medical-marijuana provision. Instead of enforcing state law, Attorney General Lungren and other California law-enforcement personnel secretly conspired with federal authorities to crush what they saw as an incipient grassroots rebellion, a challenge to the existing order. State and local officers who had sworn to uphold the ballot measure would prove to be willing, often eager, accomplices in a concerted federal attack on state law—an attack that began midway through Bill Clinton's "I didn't inhale" presidency and escalated after the contentious handoff to George W. Bush.

The assault on California's Compassionate Use Act would turn courtrooms into stages for show trials, send the innocent to prison, deny medication to the seriously ill, and terrorize America's weakest citizens with fascistic paramilitary raids that ransacked their homes and property. Doctors, caregivers, dispensary operators, ganja growers, patient-activists, and other qualified therapeutic users would be targeted by a law-enforcement juggernaut intent on rolling back the gains that medical-marijuana supporters thought they had achieved through democratic means.

In a November 9 press release, the drug czar's office stated: "The passage of [Proposition 215] creates a significant threat to the drug-control system that protects our children." General McCaffrey was quick to emphasize that California's medical-marijuana provision did not change federal law. He was not trying to be subtle: "The decision to bring appropriate criminal or administrative enforcement action will be, as always, decided on a case-by-case basis." The voters "must have been asleep at the switch," McCaffrey condescendingly suggested. He blamed George Soros and his billionaire allies for duping a well-intentioned but gullible electorate. As usual, McCaffrey described medical marijuana as "a cruel hoax," a Trojan horse for drug legalizers who exploited sympathy for the sick to advance a hidden agenda.

On November 14, a scant nine days after the watershed election, California law-enforcement heavies huddled privately with America's drug-war high command in Washington, D.C., where they plotted to sabotage a voter initiative they were unable to defeat at the ballot box. McCaffrey hosted the summit. Attendees included DEA chief, Thomas Constantine, "No on 215" cochair Sheriff Brad Gates (from Orange County), and some forty other federal and state officials, along with representatives from a few ostensibly private antidrug groups, such as Partnership for a Drug-Free America.

Those who participated in this closed-door meeting—the first of four such gatherings of "the interagency working group" from mid-November to late December 1996—were not seeking, as Proposition 215 mandated, "to implement a plan to provide for the safe and affordable distribution of marijuana to patients." Instead, police and prosecutors from California requested federal help in overturning the new law and snuffing out the medical-marijuana movement. Thomas F. Gede, Lungren's special assistant, asked the DEA to deputize California cops and prosecutors so they could enforce federal legislation. The conferees knew they were treading on thin ice as they pondered ways for Uncle Sam to impose his will and limit the impact of state law. As Paul Jellinek, vice president of the Robert Wood Johnson Foundation, noted, "The other side would be salivating if they could hear [the] prospect of the feds going against the will of the people." Endowed by Johnson and Johnson, the world's biggest pharmaceutical firm, the Robert Wood Johnson Foundation channeled many millions of dollars to groups that campaigned against marijuana law reform.

A major concern discussed at the federal-state powwow was how to prevent the medical-marijuana contagion from spreading beyond California. The drug warriors were unnerved by Bill Zimmerman's publicly stated intention to put medical-marijuana initiatives on the ballot in a half dozen more states. "We hope to establish the right to medical marijuana for patients nationwide," Zimmerman announced shortly after the ballot measure became California law. His organization, Californians for Medical Rights (the official sponsor of 215), renamed itself Americans for Medical Rights (AMR) and set its sights on the '98 midterm elections, leaving grassroots California patient-activists largely to fend for themselves.

Arizona was already infected by the med-pot plague—citizens of the Grand Canyon State voted by a 65–35 margin in favor of Proposition 200, which went even further than Cal's 215 by allowing doctors to prescribe marijuana, heroin, cocaine, or any drug they saw fit. An Arizona law-enforcement delegation joined the Interagency Working Group, which explored potential legal challenges to both state initiatives. They found an easy way to scuttle the Arizona law. Although Proposition 200 carried by more than a three-to-two margin, the yes votes did not comprise a majority of the state's registered voters, a technicality that enabled the Arizona state legislature to gut the bill.

Proposition 215 posed a much bigger challenge to the drug warriors. The authors of California's medical-marijuana measure had cleverly crafted the language so that it did not directly conflict with federal law—it merely allowed physicians to recommend the herb and legitimate patients to use it without breaking state law. Prop. 215's use of the word *recommend* rather than *prescribe* was, in effect, an end run around the Controlled Substances Act, which outlawed the manufacture, possession, and distribution of marijuana, but said nothing about recommending cannabis for therapeutic use. This flustered Justice Department and DEA lawyers, who worried that a direct legal assault on 215 might backfire. They were cool to pleas from California officials that the U.S. government should quickly assert its authority through the courts and sue to have 215 overturned on the grounds of federal supremacy. While the feds mulled their legal options, General McCaffrey promised to come up with big bucks for a nationwide antidrug ad campaign to counter the medical-marijuana surge.

Attorney General Dan Lungren did not personally attend the November 14 strategy session, but he consulted with federal drug-control honchos during subsequent visits to Washington. They were on the same page about how California law enforcement should proceed with respect to medical marijuana. On December 3, 1996, Lungren presided over an "Emergency All-Zones Meeting" in Sacramento, where three hundred California district attorneys, police chiefs, sheriffs, and narcotics officers were advised, basically, to continue arresting and prosecuting as if 215 had never passed. Lungren and his deputies maintained that the new law did not shield marijuana suspects from arrest or prosecution but merely provided them with an "affirmative defense" to invoke at a trial. In a subsequent bulletin to California law-enforcement agencies, Lungren asserted that it is "not incumbent on a police officer to inquire whether the individual cultivating, possessing, or using marijuana is doing so for medicinal purposes. It is the responsibility of an individual to claim that he/she has an affirmative defense."

Ironically, it was Zimmerman, Prop. 215's campaign chief, who gave Lungren and McCaffrey the weapon to eviscerate the medical-marijuana provision. Zimmerman's ballot argument characterized 215 essentially as an "affirmative defense" option in a courtroom—although this was not the intention of the original activists who launched the initiative. Two weeks after the election, Zimmerman reiterated during a CNN *Crossfire* debate with Lungren: "What Proposition 215 does is create a medical necessity defense for people arrested for marijuana. Anybody in California can still be arrested for marijuana."

The drug czar's office made this policy explicit in a seven-page action plan, "The Administration's Response to the Passage of California Proposition 215 and Arizona Proposition 2000," released at a Washington, D.C., press conference on December 30, 1996: "State and local law enforcement officials will be encouraged to continue to execute state law to the fullest by having officers continue to make arrests and seizures under state law, leaving defendants to raise the medical-use provisions of the proposition only as a defense to state prosecution." Marijuana still wasn't medicine in Uncle Sam's mind. Flanked by Health and Human Services Secretary Donna Shalala, NIDA's director, Alan Leshner, and U.S. Attorney General Janet Reno, General McCaffrey told reporters: "Federal law-enforcement provisions remain in effect. Nothing has changed."

The drug czar pegged physicians as the weakest link in the med-pot chain; cut them out of the picture and there would be no way for folks to secure the requisite recommendation. So McCaffrey took aim at the doctors first, threatening to arrest them and revoke their prescribing licenses if they so much as mentioned to a patient that cannabis might help in some way. McCaffrey indicated that doctors who recommended cannabis would be subject to IRS audits. He also said that marijuana medics should be barred from treating Medicare and Medicaid patients.

During the year-end news conference, McCaffery unveiled a made-for-TV visual—a large poster listing dozens of conditions that marijuana was said to be good for. (One of the conditions was misspelled as "Migranes.") The data was lifted from the list that Dr. Tod Mikuriya had been compiling since the late 1960s, when he directed marijuana research for the National Institute of Mental Health. The drug czar publicly denounced Mikuriya, the physician most closely identified with Proposition 215, as if the Berkeley psychiatrist was a snake-oil salesman peddling a cure-all.

On the morning after Election Day, Mikuriya had called the California Bureau of Narcotics Enforcement and volunteered to help state officials chart a new course with respect to medical marijuana. Dr. Tod suggested that all interested parties—law enforcement, county health departments, and the medical-marijuana community—should cooperate and figure out a workable system. Such was the road not taken. Instead, America's drug-war general singled out Mikuriya for ridicule. McCaffrey mocked Mikuriya's most important insight—that marijuana has a multitude of medicinal applications by virtue of its scientifically proven ability to modulate immune cell migration and slow down the rate at which neurotransmitters are released in the human body.

A group of physicians and patients, with help from the ACLU and the Drug Policy Alliance, promptly sued the U.S. government to prevent federal agencies from punishing doctors for recommending marijuana. "The government has no place in the examination room," asserted Dr. Marcus Conant, the lead plaintiff and well-respected AIDS specialist, who regretted that physicians' hands were tied because they couldn't use a herb that "is effective and has a reasonable place in the medical armamentarium." The suit, called *Conant v. McCaffrey*, would work its way through the federal court system, resulting in a federal injunction issued on First Amendment grounds that upheld a doctor's right to discuss the pros and cons of cannabis as a treatment option.

In a January 1997 editorial entitled "Federal Foolishness and Marijuana," the prestigious *New England Journal of Medicine* criticized the U.S. government's attempt to gag physicians and quash the California ballot initiative. Dr. Jerome Kassirer, the journal's editor-in-chief, derided the federal response to Proposition 215 as "hypocritical" and "out of step with the public." "I believe that a federal policy that prohibits physicians from alleviating suffering by prescribing marijuana for seriously ill patients is misguided, heavy-handed and inhumane," he wrote. Kassirer called for the rescheduling of cannabis in recognition of its medical utility.

The American Medical Association didn't go that far, but the largest doctors' organization in the United States managed to pass a resolution backing a physician's right to discuss marijuana therapy with a patient. The AMA also came out in favor of more federally funded research into marijuana's healing potential. McCaffrey, changing his tune, agreed: More research was necessary to ascertain if cannabis had any merit as a curative. He commissioned another study from the National Academy of Sciences to assess marijuana's medical value. To critics of the drug war, this seemed like yet another stalling tactic. "When politicians say 'More research is needed,' they really are saying 'More prohibition is needed,'" opined Irv Rosenfeld, the federally supplied marijuana patient from Florida.

On April 11, 1997, U.S. District Court Judge Fern Smith, a Reagan appointee, issued a temporary restraining order blocking any federal government action to punish California doctors who recommended cannabis until the *Conant v. McCaffery* lawsuit was settled. "[The] plaintiffs have raised serious questions as to the constitutionality of the defendants' 'policy' regarding Proposition 215," Judge Smith noted in her decision. The plaintiffs also presented evidence that "physicians have been censoring their discussions with patients about medical marijuana out of fear that the government will either prosecute them or take away their prescription licenses for conducting such discussion." The restraining order was made permanent in 1999; it was upheld by the U.S. Ninth Circuit Court of Appeals on October 29, 2002.

Despite this pivotal federal court ruling, doctors continued to fear the wrath of officialdom. Unschooled in cannabis therapeutics, many physicians shied away from recommending marijuana to their patients. Their fears were justified. Unable to muzzle the medics, the feds passed the baton to the California attorney general's office, via its agents in the Medical Board's enforcement division, which targeted physicians specializing in cannabis consultations. Topping the hit list was Dr. Tod Mikuriya.

On October 28, 1997, John Gordnier, Attorney General Dan Lungren's senior assistant, sent a memo to all California law-enforcement personnel and county district attorneys, requesting that they forward any information in their jurisdictions pertaining to medical-marijuana recommendations signed by Dr. Tod Mikuriya and another pro-cannabis physician, Eugene Schoenfeld. Although specific language in Proposition 215 exempted doctors from retaliation by state officials, the Medical Board would initiate legal proceedings against Mikuriya and several other physicians based on evidence gathered by undercover narcs who feigned symptoms to obtain a medical recommendation.

Unchartered Waters

Outside the doors of 1444 Market Street, a crowd gathered on a chilly, wet morning. Hundreds of people, some hobbling on crutches, others in wheelchairs, many suffering from AIDS and cancer, slowly made their way past a crush of TV cameramen. They had come to witness the official ribbon-cutting ceremony that marked the reopening of the San Francisco Cannabis Buyers' Club on January 15, 1997, under a new name (the Cannabis Cultivators' Club) and old management.

A week earlier, Superior Court Judge David Garcia had ruled that the passage of Proposition 215 entitled the club—closed since it was raided in August—to resume operations. Garcia ordered Dennis Peron and his colleagues to operate as a nonprofit entity for medical purposes only and to maintain records "showing that they have been designated as primary caregiver by the members [with] recommendations from physicians." Attorney General Lungren immediately indicated he would appeal Garcia's decision. California's top lawman rejected the notion that a pot club could legitimately function as a caregiver.

Peron felt personally vindicated by the passage of Proposition 215. He called Lungren "a bully" and "a crybaby" and lampooned him at every opportunity. Meanwhile, Peron still faced felony charges that he sold marijuana to minors and to undercover agents bearing notes from imaginary doctors. The Cannabis Buyers' Club was pilloried by state prosecutors as a lax, freewheeling, for-profit operation. Dennis could have avoided the possibility of a multiyear mandatory-minimum prison term by pleading guilty to a lesser charge of conspiracy to commit a public nuisance. Instead of plea-bargaining, he used the opportunity to make a political statement about every California patient's right to grow, possess, and, if necessary, purchase herb from their friendly neighborhood marijuana store.

Just a stone's throw from City Hall, Peron's cannabis collective retained the support of the local political establishment. A former state senator cut the ribbon to reopen the dispensary. "America is never going to be the same," Dennis crowed as he handed a ceremonial bag of herb to Milahhr Kemnah, an AIDS patient, to great applause. Soon club members were lighting joints, passing pipes, and eating THC-laced brownies inside the five-floor reefer sanctuary.

Peron, aged fifty-one, his hair shorter and whiter, felt that he was building a social movement that followed in the footsteps of the movement for civil rights, women's rights, gay rights, and environmental justice. "There's no sense in having a law if you're not going to implement it," he asserted. Tampering with Proposition 215 would be tantamount to "rescinding civil rights legislation," according to Peron. "People who are sick are not going to go back to sitting in the back of the bus. They're not going to go out into the street to get their medicine." What would Martin Luther King, Jr., have said about medical marijuana? Would King have believed it a crime to follow the advice of one's doctor? Peron didn't think so. For Dennis the drug warrior's menace, it was never just about changing the marijuana laws. It was about changing the country. It was about pursuing King's dream of a "society at peace with itself."

As winter segued into the spring of '97, some fifteen cannabis dispensaries were up and running in various parts of California, along with several delivery services that catered to homebound patients' needs. Some clubs that had been operating underground became a public presence in their communities. The founders of these fledgling "gray market" marijuana retail outlets were mainly people with compelling personal stories of illness and recovery who dared to stick their necks out and venture into unchartered territory after the passage of Proposition 215.

The new law provided no real road map for citizens and local officials on how to proceed. Many patients who were smoking pot or thinking about using marijuana for therapeutic purposes still had lots of questions about their legal status. The Compassionate Use Act definitely gave them the right to possess, use, and grow their own marijuana (no plant limits specified) if they had a note from a doctor. But would California physicians, threatened by the feds, be willing to write recommendations? And where would people get their medicine if they were too ill to cultivate it or if they didn't have the right facilities to grow cannabis? While Proposition 215 encouraged government officials to set up a safe and affordable distribution system for cannabis, it did not mention anything about dispensaries or pot clubs. Nor did it explicitly exempt patients and caregivers from existing laws against marijuana grow-ops, sales, and transportation. No one knew how things would play out in the brave new world of medical marijuana.

It was virgin territory for law enforcement, as well. Attorney General Lungren moved quickly to chart a course that all but nullified the voter initiative. He relied on bureaucratic and administrative procedures to discourage or prevent the implementation of a viable medical-marijuana distribution system. The attorney general's office peppered law-enforcement departments throughout California with advisories and bulletins emphasizing that 215 did not protect patients or caregivers from arrest and did not legalize the sale of marijuana in any way, shape, or form. Lungren maintained that providing marijuana to anyone, even giving it away for free, qualified as illicit drug trafficking and was therefore punishable by law.

Lungren gave local fuzz carte blanche to exercise unilateral power in deciding if cannabis growers had more plants than they, the officers, believed was justified by their medical condition. (Peron's retort: "You would not ask the doctor to arrest a mugger. Don't ask a peace officer to treat an illness.") The county-by-county response to 215 varied widely with prosecutors in each region improvising as they went along. In certain pot-friendly places, a cop might turn the other cheek; elsewhere, he'd slap the cuffs on a weed smoker. Some municipalities banned cannabis dispensaries, while other jurisdictions would make marijuana, medical and recreational, the lowest law-enforcement priority.

Occasionally, run-ins with the cops had a happy ending—charges were dropped against a few obviously ill patients with letters of recommendation, and seized marijuana was returned to its rightful owners. For the most part, however, local police remained stuck in a punitive mode. "Marijuana is not medicine"—that was the official line of the California Narcotics Officers' Association. A deep-rooted culture of resistance to medical marijuana permeated much of the law-enforcement community, particularly in rural areas where officials pursued an "arrest first and let the courts sort it out" policy, per Lungren's instructions, which put the onus on the defendant to prove that he or she was a bona fide patient. Local law enforcement had ample incentive to cooperate with the federal government, which lavished funds in the form of Byrne grants, CAMP overtime, and other pork for interagency marijuana eradication squads that ran amok throughout the Golden State. Lots of drug busts meant lots of cash from seizures and forfeitures to pad the budget. It was a cushy arrangement for small-town cops as well as big-city narcs, who served on joint task forces, led by the DEA, which persisted in waging a no-win crusade against cannabis through its local, cross-deputized proxies.

Proponents of Proposition 215 had hoped that it would remove the sick and wounded from the battleground of America's war on drugs. Instead, qualified medical users found themselves thrust onto the front lines of what seemed like an endless conflict. Numerous patients and caregivers were apprehended for possession or cultivation of marijuana. California NORML, in its October 1997 newsletter, reported frequent complaints of "police harassment, raids on gardens, and improper treatment by authorities."

One of the first patients to test the new law in the courts was Alan Martinez, a thirty-nine-year-old epileptic arrested for growing fewer than ten plants in Santa Rosa. Martinez said that smoking cannabis made his convulsions less severe and less frequent. His lawyer Bill Panzer, who helped draft Prop. 215, argued at a pretrial hearing that the initiative was meant to protect medical-marijuana users like Martinez from being dragged through the criminal-justice system. But the judge bought the prosecution's contention that 215 merely provided a defense that people could use in court after they had been arrested. On July 3, 1997, while waiting trial, Martinez died in a solo car crash when his car veered off the road and hit a tree. A few days earlier, Martinez had suffered a seizure and a brief blackout. Because of his precarious legal predicament, he had ceased using cannabis to control his epilepsy. "He was pretty stressed out," his partner and caregiver, Jason Miller, explained. And being stressed out made him more seizure-prone. At a memorial gathering in Sonoma County, medical-marijuana activists extolled Martinez as a martyr. It was "the first death directly caused by government resistance to implementing Prop. 215," said Northern California activist Pebbles Trippet.

Lungren kept a running tab on dozens of marijuana prosecutions in which a medical recommendation was cited by the defense. He was particularly irked by the emergence of more than a dozen cannabis clubs scattered around California after the election. "The state's position is that a buyers' club is not allowed under law," a spokesperson for the attorney general asserted. Public pot dispensaries were like clay pigeons for cops. Undercover narcs pretending to be weed-needy patients purchased reefer from storefront dispensaries, and the state pressed charges. If local law enforcement wasn't up to the task, Lungren could always play tag-team with the feds. Together they waged a coordinated campaign to close all the cannabis clubs in the state. Protracted court battles would ultimately determine the outcome of their attempt to dismantle California's grassroots dispensary network.

In April 1997, federal narcotics agents swooped down on Flower Therapy, a medical-marijuana retail operation in San Francisco's Mission District, seizing more than three hundred pot plants, lots of herbage, patient records, and growing equipment. The early-morning, kick-down-the-door raid sparked an uproar of protest. San Francisco district attorney Terence Hallinan leaped to Flower Therapy's defense. (The club reopened the next day.) In no uncertain terms, Hallinan told the feds to butt out and stop meddling in Frisco's affairs. He said if charges were pressed he would testify on behalf of the defendants that they were trying to abide by state law.

Whereas the DEA typically informed local officials before it mounted an operation in their area, Hallinan was purposely kept out of the loop. A strong supporter of medical marijuana, San Francisco's DA was the son of Vincent Hallinan, a flamboyant lawyer famous for defending Bay Area radicals and their causes. Terence Hallinan was the only prosecutor in the state who endorsed Proposition 215 and after the vote he immediately assembled a task force of patients, caregivers, and city health officials to develop a program to regulate cannabis dispensaries and issue patient and caregiver ID cards.*

With the pillars of the local political establishment standing four square in favor of cannabis therapeutics, the San Francisco Bay Area became an oasis of experiment, a safe haven for alternative healing. In June 1997, Oakland City Council passed a resolution protecting medical-marijuana users. Lynette Shaw, for several years a mainstay at Peron's pot club, set up a dispensary in marijuana-friendly Marin County. Farther north in the Humboldt County city of Arcata and in the Southern California city of West Hollywood, patient-centered distribution facilities enjoyed strong local backing. In Santa Cruz, Valerie and Mike Corral's cannabis hospice collective, Wo/Men's Alliance for Medical Marijuana, received nonprofit status from the state.

---

* "Terence Hallinan's finest hour," according to Fred Gardner, a journalist who would serve as Hallinan's public information officer, "came a few weeks after Prop. 215 passed, when Lungren summoned every DA, police chief and sheriff in California to an 'Emergency All-Zones Meeting' in Sacramento. It took not just political courage but almost physical courage to stand up in front of 250 very hostile, self-righteous men with guns on their hips and tell them they ought to follow the law." Hallinan later recounted what he said at the meeting: "I reminded them that the voters had spoken and that they ought to respect that. I told them that it wasn't a hoax, that marijuana really did have medicinal effects and to think of it and treat it as a medical matter, not a law-enforcement matter. I told them we had a plan in San Francisco that had been working, involving the Department of Public Health. I told them they had a chance to get marijuana off the street and have a safe a controlled distribution system instead of a public nuisance . . . I think I got through to at least some of them."

But beyond a few autonomous zones, medical-marijuana patients and growers encountered stiff resistance from law enforcement. The DEA raided the home of Bryan Epis, who was instrumental in starting a medical cannabis dispensary in Chico. An electrical engineer with no prior convictions, Epis had been using marijuana to treat chronic neck and upper back pain after he fractured two vertebrae in a near-fatal car accident. Arrested for growing more than four hundred pot plants with four other physician-approved patients, he became the first California medical user to be convicted in federal court post-215. Under federal rules of evidence, testimony about the medical use of marijuana and Proposition 215 was excluded by the judge. Shortly after Epis began serving a mandatory minimum of ten years in federal prison, billboards appeared around the state with a photo of his eight-year-old daughter holding a sign that said: "My Dad Is Not a Criminal."

Meanwhile, in hardscrabble Calaveras County, med-pot patient Robert Galambos was tried and convicted for growing a 380-plant garden that supplied Northern California cannabis clubs. Commenting on the verdict, his attorney Tony Serra wryly observed, "They've legalized the milk, but outlawed the cow."*

A market demand existed for medical marijuana and dispensaries were trying to fill it. Pot clubs offered many advantages to patients who preferred not to buy from strangers on the street. But every dispensary in California operated at the whim and mercy of the DEA and local law enforcement. Cannabis club proprietors knew they could be busted at a moment's notice.

It was smooth sailing for Peter Baez (cousin of folksinger Joan Baez), who ran a dispensary in Santa Clara County, until Chief Lou Cobarruviaz of the San Jose Police retired and Interim Chief Walt Adkins, a staunch opponent of 215, took over. The next day, the San Jose club was raided and closed. Baez, who had AIDS and cancer, was taken into police custody and booked for selling marijuana to an undercover cop without a valid physician's recommendation.

Shortly after 215 passed, representatives from more than a dozen California pot clubs met in Santa Cruz at the invitation of activist Scott Imler to draw up a code of conduct for the "legal and ethical distribution" of medical marijuana. They agreed to verify the diagnosis of all applicants, distribute only

---

* In August 1997, the attorney Tony Serra (the model for James Woods's character in the film *True Believers*) sent out a press release disclosing that he was a member of the San Francisco Cannabis Buyers' Club and that he used marijuana as an antistress medication. He said he was going public to encourage other lawyers and stressed-out professionals to "come off booze and get on the cannabis."

to qualified patients, and keep prices low. Dispensary owners pledged not to blur the line between medical and nonmedical uses of marijuana. Some clubs prohibited on-site pot smoking in deference to local authorities. Dennis Peron felt that the guidelines were too restrictive and he refused to endorse the protocols. "It sounded like you had to be dead to get marijuana," he complained. Peron's pot collective continued to service senior citizens without asking for a doctor's note. When critics called his club "a circus," Peron took it as a compliment.

The San Francisco Cannabis Buyers' Club was the first big crack in the bureaucratic wall, which opened the way for other dispensaries to follow. Without Peron, they never would have gotten this far. But his tendency to shoot from the lip and antagonize law enforcement complicated matters for those who sought to ingratiate themselves with officialdom in the post-215 era. Some low-key dispensary operators hoped that exemplary citizenship and operational transparency would carry the day and win over skeptics. Dennis, the inveterate prankster, wasn't helping.

"We're sick and tired of spending ninety percent of our time explaining away the excesses of Dennis Peron and 1444 Market Street," said Imler, a former ally. Imler was not alone in insisting on the importance of drawing a clear line between therapeutic and recreational cannabis consumption. Most marijuana smokers in America were not lighting up to ease an acute or incurable ailment. And those in dire need weren't smoking pot simply to cop a buzz—they were people in pain trying to make it through the day. A lot of folks used the herb to get high, many others took it medicinally to get by—and never the twain shall meet, according to Imler, who held that the arguments for legalizing therapeutic use were substantially different from arguments for legalizing the recreational use of marijuana.

The Peronistas, by contrast, were not fixated on distinguishing between medical and recreational reefer. Life is stressful, pot is good for stress, and relieving stress is beneficial to one's health. Therefore, Peron reasoned, anyone who smokes pot is self-medicating, whether consciously or not. If people take Big Pharma meds for anxiety, social awkwardness, and various stress-related conditions, then why shouldn't cannabis be used to ease stress and lighten one's mood? Why is that not therapeutic? Pot and med-pot, after all, are two sides of the same serrated leaf. The very idea of what constitutes "medical" use as opposed to "recreational" use is largely a social construct, a matter of convention. Such distinctions are apt to go up in smoke as soon as one sparks a doobie and phytocannabinoids start tickling the brain receptors. Pot can be fun, as well as healthy—it's healthy in part because it's fun. That's how Peron saw it.

But the "fun" part of the funny stuff rubbed some people the wrong way—and still does. Embedded in America's cultural DNA, a lingering Puritan distrust of pleasure gave rise to "the haunting fear that someone somewhere may be happy," as H. L. Mencken famously said. Latter-day zealots for zero tolerance were a direct extension of old-fashioned Puritanism, which values hard work, discipline, and order, while shunning intoxication and merriment for their own sake as inherently immoral. To ardent drug warriors, all marijuana use is recreational. They maintain that medical marijuana is merely a decoy, a pretense for getting high, a ruse perpetrated by reprobates and apostates who want to legalize all narcotics.

Dennis Peron wasn't trying to be cute or controversial when he said, "All marijuana use is medical." He spoke a broad truth that called into question sharply defined categories of cannabis intake—medical versus nonmedical. Ironically, the Peronistas and the drug warriors concurred on this point: The boundary between recreational and medical use is often tenuous at best.

For many marijuana smokers, the medical-versus-recreational argument was moot. It was all "personal use" and it should be legal, pure and simple, according to the Cannabis Action Network, which pushed the envelope even further during the stormy aftermath of Prop. 215. In 1997, CAN launched the Cannabis Consumers' Union, which openly sold marijuana at a steep discount to anyone eighteen or over—no medical recommendations necessary—from a Berkeley, California, storefront one day a week. Smoking pot was permitted on-site. "It was a direct action campaign," explained Debby Goldsberry. "We knew it was risky, but we were trying to make a point. No one else was focusing on personal use." After nine months of shaking and baking, Goldsberry and several of her cohorts were arrested by Berkeley cops. CAN proceeded to sue the city, claiming that it was illegal to bust people for pot in Berkeley because voters two decades earlier had overwhelmingly passed an initiative in support of legalized adult access to cannabis. They eventually settled out of court and the city paid CAN's legal fees.

The dawning of the post-215 era coincided with the dot-com boom and the emergence of e-mail and the World Wide Web as household phenomena. Marijuana-related websites flourished as soon as the Internet caught on in the mid-1990s. Medical-marijuana activists were early Netactivists. The Web made it much easier to share long-suppressed information and respond quickly to police raids and other emergencies. Now anyone could log on and find tips on growing sinsemilla and baking pot brownies. Hitherto hard-to-get cannabis cultivation books were easily available via online booksellers. Pot seeds could be purchased through Dutch and Canadian e-commerce outlets.

The Internet catalyzed a surge in homegrown cannabis on the heels of Proposition 215.*

Net-savvy CAN veterans no longer needed to embark upon cross-country expeditions to get their message out to the masses. Instead, CAN functioned as a training school for organizers, a ruckus academy for pot activists. Etienne Fontan, an injured Gulf War I vet, learned the ropes on the Hemp Tour and would serve as codirector, with Goldsberry, of the Berkeley Patients Group, a medical-marijuana dispensary launched in 1999. CAN graduates Don Duncan and Steph Sherer would go on to form Americans for Safe Access, a spunky nationwide grassroots support network for medical-marijuana patients. Jeff Jones, another articulate CAN recruit, established the Oakland Cannabis Buyers' Co-op (OCBC), a model facility that would spark the transformation of a hitherto run-down urban neighborhood into the bustling, pot-friendly enclave known as "Oaksterdam."

Jones arrived in the Bay Area in 1994, a gangly twenty-three-year-old hemp advocate from South Dakota. He cut his hair short, donned a jacket and tie, and began cultivating cordial relations with Oakland's political establishment. His impeccable, by-the-book manner won over the city council and the local police department, which certified ID cards that an earnest, fresh-faced Jones issued to OCBC members. What started as a semiunderground East Bay delivery service morphed into a well-run public pot dispensary. Situated on the third floor of a nondescript downtown building on Broadway, the OCBC sold herb, tinctures, edibles, cannabinoid creams, and vaporizers to a steady flow of customers. The co-op posted a sign by the front door indicating that it accepted cash and debit or credit cards. "We don't want to be flagrant. We know we are changing society," said Jones, the confident cannabis crusader.

The OCBC was one of six Northern California cannabis clubs named in a civil suit brought by the Clinton administration in an effort to enforce federal laws against marijuana distribution. Filed in January 1998, it was the opening salvo of a precedent-setting legal battle, which seesawed back and forth for the duration of Clinton's second term. By initially pursuing civil litigation rather

---

* Marijuana and psychedelic drugs were popular from the outset among Silicon Valley "techies" and cybersavants who sparked the '90s dot-com boom, which thrust the world willy-nilly into the vortex of the information economy. A high percentage of people who worked in the tech industry smoked pot. John Markoff reports that Stanford students used ARPAnet, a precursor to the Internet, in the early 1970s, to facilitate cannabis transactions. "Before Amazon, before eBay, the seminal act of e-commerce was a drug deal. The students used the network to quietly arrange the sale of an undetermined amount of marijuana" (Markoff, *What the Dormouse Said*, p. 109).

than criminal prosecution in an effort to close the clubs, the U.S. Justice Department avoided the risk and potential embarrassment of a jury trial.

Cited as a codefendant in the federal suit, Jones faced civil conspiracy charges and a potential criminal indictment if he persisted in breaking federal law by dispensing cannabis. He joined with other club proprietors and challenged the feds in a case that came to be identified most prominently with the Oakland Cannabis Buyers' Cooperative. The city of Oakland had deputized the OCBC as a city agency in an unsuccessful effort to shield the club from federal attempts to shut it down. In so doing, Oakland became the first U.S. metropolis to officially distribute cannabis for medical use.

From a purely legal standpoint, it looked like curtains for California's medical-marijuana experiment when U.S. District Judge Charles Breyer ordered the six clubs to shut down ASAP or risk being held in criminal contempt. With U.S. marshals poised to move against the OCBC, it ceased to operate as a medical-marijuana dispensary in October 1998. But other potpreneurs in Oakland picked up where the OCBC left off and did a brisk business while Jones fought the good fight all the way to the U.S. Supreme Court. It would be the first time the high court heard a case involving medicinal cannabis. The OCBC maintained that the marijuana it provided was a medical necessity for seriously ill co-op members (who were named in legal briefs). U.S. Justice Department attorneys did not contest the clinical and scientific evidence. Instead the feds argued that Congress put cannabis in Schedule I and no court had the legal authority to nix or amend this decision; only Congress could do that.

In April 2001, the Supreme Court ruled unanimously against the OCBC in an opinion that cast a long shadow over the medical-marijuana movement. No medical-necessity defense in a case involving marijuana would be allowed in federal court as long as cannabis was a Schedule I drug that officially had no medical use. Although the narrow ruling by the court did not overturn Proposition 215 or address other constitutional issues, the OCBC decision delighted drug-war hawks and gave President George W. Bush his first chance to ramp up the federal assault on California's fragile medical-marijuana infrastructure.

By this time, legal maneuvering by the California attorney general's office had succeeded in putting the San Francisco Cannabis Buyers' Club out of business. "This whole thing is about the Sixties. It has nothing to do with marijuana as a medicine," an unrepentant Peron declared shortly before the doors of the Market Street dispensary were permanently padlocked on May 25, 1998, on orders from a state appellate court. For several years Peron had flaunted his club's borderline legality, refusing to file for a business license or pay taxes on the grounds that his operation was based on a doctrine of nonviolent civil disobedience. Now the jig was up. Lungren had finally cornered his archnemesis.

But Peron, as usual, had the last word. "Yes, I did sell marijuana to kids," he admitted. "They were sixteen- and seventeen-year-olds, they had cancer, and to the shame of America, they had AIDS."

Southern Exposure

Less than two years after the passage of Proposition 215, medical-marijuana dispensaries in California were fast becoming an endangered species. Attorney General Dan Lungren trumpeted the state appeals court decision against Dennis Peron to justify his effort to close every cannabis club in the Golden State. One by one they fell. Undercover narcs entrapped and arrested the proprietors of a San Diego cannabis club and an antidrug task force raided the Monterey County Medical Marijuana Care Center, seizing patient records and a small amount of herb. Sacramento authorities warned would-be dispensary operators that they would be promptly prosecuted if they tried to open a pot club in the state capital. Nathan Sands, communications director of the Sacramento-based Compassionate Coalition, compared the situation to "the Jim Crow laws, where they gave people the right to vote but not to practice it." Writing in mid-1998, *Orange County Register* editor Alan Bock concurred: "Except in a few areas, it would be stretching to say that [Proposition 215] is now the law of the land in practice."

Marijuana arrests soared in California, despite the passage of Proposition 215. Police apprehended cannabis smokers, many with valid medical recommendations, at a record pace: 57,677 pot arrests in the Golden State in 1997. (That year, there were 695,201 pot arrests nationwide—then the highest tally in U.S. history.) Unprepared for the backlash, patient-activists were hamstrung by prosecutors and judges who rejected the notion that 215 legalized the buying and selling of marijuana for therapeutic purposes.

The ongoing harassment and punishment of patients and caregivers in the aftermath of 215 went largely unreported by influential, big-city news media. One exception was the sensational raid of an ornate turreted mansion, built to resemble a castle, in the ritzy Bel Air neighborhood of Los Angeles. On July 27, 1997, fifty heavily armed, flak-jacketed LA County sheriff's deputies paraded over a drawbridge, crossed a moat, and descended upon the fairytale-like ziggurat. Inside they found secret rooms, a dungeon, a king's quarter, and more than four thousand marijuana plants in various stages of development that filled virtually every nook and cranny of the five-story fortress—the bathrooms, the dining hall, the patio, the yard. A spokesperson for the LA County sheriff's office said it was the largest marijuana seizure his department had ever made.

The prodigious pot garden was the work of twenty-six-year-old Todd McCormick, an amateur horticulturist and medical-marijuana patient who insisted he was breeding various cannabis strains to treat different diseases. A childhood cancer survivor, McCormick had undergone nine surgeries before his teenage years, resulting in five fused neck vertebrae and a stiff gait. His hippie mom encouraged him to smoke pot for health reasons and he subsequently joined the front lines of the battle for medical marijuana. McCormick founded an underground compassion club in San Diego in 1995. Then he fled to Amsterdam for a yearlong instructional sabbatical with Old Ed, the legendary American expatriate with the green thumb for ganja. While under Old Ed's tutelage, McCormick discovered that strains rich in cannabidiol (CBD), a nonpsychoactive compound, worked best for pain relief in his own case.

McCormick had been exploring the possibility of crafting cannabis hybrids to exert pinpoint therapeutic effects when he was lured back to California by the best-selling author and publisher Peter McWilliams. A gay, pot-smoking Libertarian, McWilliams had written *Ain't Nobody's Business If You Do* (on the absurdity of consensual crimes in a free country) and several how-to books on subjects ranging from personal computing to surviving the loss of a loved one. Diagnosed with AIDS and non-Hodgkin's lymphoma, McWilliams used marijuana to quell the horrible nausea from multiple medications.

McWilliams offered McCormick a hefty book advance to write about breeding cannabis for curative purposes. A few months after the passage of 215, McCormick rented the unconventional Bel Air castle—not far from the homes of actress Elizabeth Taylor and former president Ronald Reagan—and resumed his reefer research. Before long, the so-called marijuana mansion became a place where celebrity pot puffers from Tinseltown partied with the cannabis cognoscenti.

"I thought I could share what I knew about growing medical marijuana with other patients in California. I thought the people of California had voted to let sick people have their medicine and I thought the government would listen to the people and go chase murderers instead of medical-marijuana users. I guess I thought wrong," said McCormick after the cops raided the castle and arrested him. His bail, set at $100,000, was posted by actor Woody Harrelson, the hemp activist.

Given the large number of plants seized, Los Angeles law enforcement deferred to the feds, who pursued the case with a vengeance. The Clinton Justice Department indicted nine Southern California residents for their involvement with McCormick's setup, including a young artist named Renee Danielle Boje, who had been hired to sketch cannabis specimens. Boje fled to Canada, where she sought political asylum, while McCormick and McWilliams, stripped of their right to mount a medical defense in federal court, pled guilty. Pegged as "a drug kingpin," McWilliams collapsed and died in 2000, a few months after a federal judge denied him access to medical marijuana. McCormick would ultimately serve a five-year sentence.

Under the gun in the same city, South Central LA's Sister Somayah Kambui, a former Black Panther, survived numerous police invasions. The cops tore up her backyard cannabis crop around harvest time several years in a row (before and after the enactment of Proposition 215). "We are the vanguard," said Sister Somayah, the dreadlocked founder of the Crescent Alliance, a self-help group for people with sickle-cell disease. Describing herself as "the most-raided medical-marijuana user" in the state, she chided the authorities: "If local police are left to interpret the law, we're in trouble. Their interpretation is a noose around our necks."

Sickle-cell anemia is a painful, hereditary red blood cell disorder that afflicts 1 in 650 African Americans (and rarely anyone without African ancestry). Somayah learned she had the disease while serving in the U.S. Air Force during the Vietnam War. An air force doc prescribed large doses of morphine and sent her on her way, feeling like a zombie. It wasn't until her father disclosed that he, too, suffered from sickle-cell anemia and shared his home remedy that she found a folk treatment that worked best for her—marijuana tea. "Not only is cannabis a vasodilator—which opens up your blood vessels and allows those cells to become unblocked—but it is a fantastic analgesic as well, reducing pain to a bearable level," Somayah explained.*

Sister Somayah's Crescent Alliance sought to educate the public about sickle-cell anemia and how cannabis—smoking it and eating it—helped control the symptoms of this painful illness. Somayah also emphasized the importance of treating sickle cell (and other diseases) nutritionally with whole foods and lots of nonpsychoactive hempseed oil, which is very rich in essential fatty acids.† She pressed her own hempseed oil and shared it with many sickle-cell sufferers. "Sister Somayah has been a pioneer in nutritional therapy for

---

* More than one third of sickle-cell patients in Great Britain report using cannabis to obtain therapeutic relief, according to the *British Journal of Haematology* (October 2005). A subsequent survey of patients with sickle-cell disease in Jamaica also showed a high prevalence of cannabis use (J. Knight-Madden et al., "The Prevalence of Marijuana Smoking in Young Adults with Sickle-Cell Disease: A Longitudinal Study," *West Indian Medical Journal* 55[4] [2006]: 224–27).

† Essential fatty acids form the biochemical building blocks of endogenous cannabinoid compounds that lubricate the CB-1 and CB-2 receptors.

sickle-cell disease," said Dr. William S. Eidelman, who confirmed that cannabis was beneficial for her illness. "As it happens, oil from the hempseed has the perfect blend of omega fatty acids for humans, and this oil is beneficial in most (or all) of the same ways as fish oil, without the risk of mercury. It is anti-inflammatory and pro-health."

Somayah, the community health activist, was continually harassed by the LAPD. She spent sixty-two days in jail, at great cost to her health, until she finally got a court order for the cops to lay off. But the police returned anyway year after year to uproot her modest medicine patch without bothering to arrest her. Frequent "rip 'n' runs" by California cops in the post-215 era deprived ailing patients of a viable herbal remedy. "You've got kids so sick they're having to remove major organs because of sickle cell and the oxygen depletion that results," Somayah lamented, "and we could get it all taken care of if only the government would accept cannabis and hemp oil and publicize the issue and the cure."

To the south in notoriously conservative Orange County, medical-marijuana patient-activist Marvin Chavez faced multiple charges stemming from several busts. A high school dropout from East LA, Chavez suffered from a rare genetic disorder, ankylosing spondylitis, which causes crippling bone abnormalities, chronic pain, and ultimately paralysis. After a doctor recommended cannabis, he found that the herb worked much better than Big Pharma painkillers. Soon Chavez was able to wean himself from prescription pharmaceuticals. He proceeded to launch the Orange Country Patient, Doctor, Nurse Support Group, which provided medicinal cannabis, often free of charge, to needy Californians.

Chavez was taken down by a police sting operation. An undercover dick who had posed as a patient with fake ID testified in court that he obtained marijuana from Chavez in exchange for a donation to his cannabis club. Questioned by Chavez's attorney, the narc admitted that he had only vaguely heard of Proposition 215, wasn't familiar with its provisions, and had never had any training about how the new law might impact his work. Chavez's lawyer also asked the cop if he had ever heard of a drug dealer who handed out membership cards, donation slips, and free pot to people who couldn't afford it. Although the case wasn't being tried in federal court, Judge Thomas Borris instructed the jury not to consider Proposition 215 in its deliberations.

"I received kangaroo justice," Chavez asserted after he was found guilty. He would serve three years of a six-year sentence handed down by the judge, who deemed a lengthy stint in jail appropriate punishment given that Chavez had a prior conviction for cocaine possession and he refused to cease his medical-marijuana advocacy. Judge Borris later wrecked his car while driving under the influence of twice the legal alcohol limit.

Local law enforcement also came down hard on David Herrick, a Vietnam veteran and former San Bernadino County sheriff's deputy, who assisted Chavez at the short-lived Orange County dispensary. Herrick used marijuana to treat disabling neck and back injuries that had forced him to retire from the police force. In March 1997, Herrick was arrested with several small bags of cannabis marked "Not for Sale: For Medical Purposes Only." Convinced that he had done nothing wrong, Herrick refused to plea-bargain. When the case went to trial, Judge William Froeberg barred the defense from mentioning Proposition 215 or any relevant medical information, even though federal rules do not apply in state court. The ex-cop was convicted and sentenced to four years in prison. Herrick served twenty-nine months before the verdict was reversed due to prosecutorial misconduct.

For several years after the passage of Proposition 215, medical marijuana in California remained largely a tug-of-war shadow world with ambiguous law, erratic enforcement policies, gray-area business schemes, and uncertain consequences. In terms of patients' rights, it was a classic example of two steps forward and one and a half steps back, as dozens of judicial rulings and precedent-setting cases began to sort out what was legal and what was not under the statewide voter-enacted amendment to the California Constitution. Home-growers and medical-marijuana activists insisted that state and local law-enforcement agencies must return improperly seized herbal medication. The cops resisted. It would be a while before the dust settled and clarity emerged on various issues, including plant limits for qualified patients, driving under the influence of cannabis, and workplace law.

Some California employers were caught between the Scylla of Prop. 215 and the Charybdis of having to enforce company drug-use policies based on federal legislation. In general, the state high court would deem that the ballot initiative had changed criminal law but not employment law. If you had a valid medical-marijuana recommendation, you still could get fired. But if the cops took your weed, they would probably have to give it back or compensate you in some way. Transporting the medicine was another tricky legal issue. Growers obviously needed a way to get the herb to patients and dispensaries. Patients had to go places. And that meant people had to drive (or be driven) with marijuana in their car.

Traveling with cannabis within or beyond California was problematic for patients and caregivers. On March 20, 1998, U.S. customs officials arrested basketball Hall of Famer Kareem Abdul-Jabbar at a Canadian airport. The big man was carrying a small stash, which a doctor had recommended to treat his intense, nausea-inducing migraines. The former Los Angeles Lakers center and all-time leading NBA scorer was busted again for marijuana possession in 2001.

Abdul-Jabbar was one of many NBA stars who used cannabis therapeutically. It was an open secret that a majority of pro basketball players smoked pot to relax and take the edge off the inevitable pounding they sustained on the court. With upward of 70 percent of the NBA rank-and-file smoking weed, pot busts involving high-profile hoopsters became a so-what news story. (Ditto for dozens of other pot-smoking professional athletes.) The inside joke was that if the league ever got serious about cracking down on cannabis, the National Basketball Association would not be able to field an all-star team.

The National Football League also had its share of pot-smoking all-pros. Mark Stepnoski, five-time consecutive pro-bowl center and two-time Super Bowl champ with the Dallas Cowboys, earned all-decade honors for the 1990s while smoking the funny stuff. It didn't seem to hinder his athletic performance or his desire to excel. "I have used marijuana, and it's never prevented me from accomplishing what I wanted to accomplish," said Stepnoski. He smoked marijuana to ease the pain from his banged-up right knee and the six surgeries he underwent as an athlete. "From my own personal experience, it seemed inherently less harmful than alcohol," Stepnoski explained. "When you're playing football in 105 degrees, and then you drink a couple of six-packs, you can't go out the next day and perform. That's just not the case with marijuana." After he retired, Stepnoski became the president of the Texas chapter of NORML, the drug-policy reform group.*

Cannabis-smoking was not uncommon among world-class athletes—soccer stars, swimmers, skiers, boxers, baseball players, the gamut—who found marijuana, a pain-management and stress-reducing medicine, to be well suited for the injurious lifestyle of an athlete. Canadian Ross Rebagliati, the first snowboarder to win Olympic gold, was almost stripped of his medal after he tested positive for marijuana in 1998. He said he had inhaled second-hand pot smoke at a party. Within extreme winter sports circles "marijuana

* The NFL star running back Ricky Williams was once a poster boy for Paxil, a prescription antidepressant that's supposed to alleviate a condition known as "social anxiety disorder." But the Heisman Trophy winner decided to stop using Paxil because of adverse side effects. "Marijuana is ten times better for me than Paxil," he declared. Williams touted the herb's medicinal and spiritual value. He told the *San Francisco Chronicle* that he smoked pot and practiced yoga "to find that place of clarity" (Fred Gardner, "Ricky Williams Protests Drug Testing by Quitting Football," *O'Shaughnessy's*, Autumn 2004).

culture is widely accepted and is not something looked down upon," according to Rebagliati.

In bygone days, a marijuana bust might have torpedoed a promising athletic career. But this was '98—year of "the Dude," the pot-smoking slacker played by Jeff Bridges in *The Big Lebowski*. Throughout the wide world of sports and celebrity entertainment, it was indisputable—the Weed, like the Dude, abides.

Falling Dominos

General Barry McCaffrey was all business and no smiles as he unveiled the U.S. government's national drug-control strategy for 1998 at a Washington, D.C., press conference. The latest battle plan was short on novelty and long on promises to cut youth drug use in half in ten years. National surveys indicated that marijuana smoking was widespread among teenagers and twentysomethings. Fifty-four percent of the U.S. population admitted that they had tried cannabis by age twenty-five. A majority of American teens said they could find someone at their school to sell them weed in less than an hour.

During Clinton's second term, marijuana would be the main focus of a two-billion-dollar television ad campaign aimed at discouraging young people from using illicit psychoactive substances. The Clinton administration's spending spree put it in elite company with major brand-name advertisers such as Nike and American Express. As the drug czar explained: "If Corporate America uses mass media to sell everything from sneakers to soda, we've got to use the full power of mass media to unsell drugs to children."

The crusade against cannabis, medicinal as well as recreational, remained the casus belli of federal drug policy. It was the main reason for drug testing in the workplace and antidrug classes in schools: get kids early before they pass through the dangerous gateway. The drug czar confronted a three-headed menace in marijuana—medical advocates, hemp advocates, and those fighting for the right to party. Behind it all "there is a carefully camouflaged, exorbitantly funded, well-heeled elitist group whose ultimate goal is to legalize drug use in the United States," McCaffrey warned the Senate Foreign Relations Committee in June 1998.

The medical-marijuana issue, in particular, had become a pounding headache for the general, a veteran of four combat tours, at a time when he was preoccupied with Plan Colombia, the Clinton administration's controversial multibillion-dollar "counter-narcotics" program ostensibly aimed at curbing coca cultivation and drug trafficking in South America. The general's military experience made him an ideal choice to oversee a full-scale counterinsurgency campaign that armed, trained, and advised Colombian soldiers in their fight against left-wing guerrillas, trade unionists, and community organizers. McCaffrey said it was "silly" to try to differentiate between antidrug efforts and the war against insurgent groups.

Plan Colombia included a far-ranging effort to spray herbicide on coca crops grown by poor farmers in rural regions. These aerial fumigation forays came under verbal fire because they damaged legal crops and had adverse health impacts upon villagers and campesinos who worked the fields. Meanwhile, U.S.-backed Colombian security forces were supporting or tolerating human rights abuses and cocaine commerce by right-wing paramilitary forces. Given these unsavory relationships, it's not surprising that Plan Colombia would barely put a dent in that country's drug trade.*

With a four-star general riding top saddle in the drug czar's office, the militarization of U.S. narcotics policy escalated at home and abroad. In May 1997, eighteen-year-old Enrique Hernandez of Redford, Texas, a U.S. citizen, was shot to death on his own property by camouflaged marines on border patrol duty as part of a drug-interdiction operation. No drugs or weapons were found on Hernandez, who had never been arrested for any criminal activity. Nonplussed, McCaffrey posted additional active-duty military personnel on the U.S.-Mexican border.

Stopping the influx of marijuana and cocaine from Mexico was, in many ways, the crux of McCaffrey's antidrug strategy. During a law-enforcement conclave in Mexico City, the U.S. drug czar bonded with his Mexican counterpart, General Jesús Gutiérrez Rebollo, praising him as "a guy of absolute, unquestioned integrity." Shortly thereafter, Gutiérrez was arrested for working with Amado Fuentes, one of Mexico's most ruthless drug barons.

Such a faux pas might have given pause to a less determined man, but McCaffrey plunged ahead. He rejected recommendations by the U.S. Sentencing Commission for equalizing racially imbalanced penalties for crack and powder cocaine. He refused to support needle-exchange programs and other proven harm-reduction initiatives. And he opposed American farmers who

---

* By threatening to "decertify" foreign governments as uncooperative players in the global drug war, the State Department wielded considerable leverage over Third World countries. Drug-war decertification would mean the loss of U.S. aid and the loss of American support for assistance from multilateral lending institutions, such as the World Bank and the International Monetary Fund. The expatriate African American author James Baldwin cut to the chase: "The drug laws can be used selectively and sporadically against the poor or the otherwise undesirable, which is by no means incidental. Their enforcement is a tremendous political and economic weapon against what we call the Third World."

wanted to grow nonpsychoactive industrial hemp. On McCaffery's watch, the U.S. government commenced a hush-hush R&D project at Montana State University, where scientists sought to breed a superfungus to attack cannabis and coca plants.

In the summer of 1998, McCaffrey undertook a "fact-finding" tour of several European countries, including the Netherlands, a nation known for its liberal marijuana policies. Before he set foot in Holland to gather the facts, he denounced the Dutch approach to drugs as "an unmitigated disaster." McCaffrey was not above hyperbolizing to drive home his message. "The murder rate in Holland is double that in the United States. The overall crime rate in Holland is probably 40 percent higher than the United States. That's drugs," the general said, scowling.

Point of fact: The murder rate in the United States during this period was four and a half times higher than in the Netherlands. The Dutch Foreign Office not only sent a formal diplomatic protest to Washington, it briefly considered barring McCaffrey from the country.

While in Amsterdam, McCaffrey refused an offer to visit a marijuana coffee shop. Nor did he pay a visit to the Cannabis College, near the red-light district, which had recently opened its doors. Along with educational material on the medicinal, recreational, and historical uses of marijuana, the college featured a "Human Rights and the Drug War" exhibit that highlighted the long jail sentences U.S. courts imposed on drug offenders, the absurd incarceration rates in American prisons, and the terrible toll the war against marijuana and other illicit substances has inflicted on families and communities in the United States and abroad.

Instead, McCaffrey toured a Dutch Health Ministry center, where addicts had access to free heroin. Afterward, he attended a dinner with Health Minister Els Borst. When Borst told McCaffrey she would prefer that young people experiment only with marijuana, the drug czar fell silent and looked the other way.

In the world according to McCaffrey, the notion that smoking marijuana leads to hard-drug use was an a priori truth. The Dutch experience proved otherwise. "As for a possible switch from cannabis to hard drugs, it is clear that the pharmacological properties of cannabis are irrelevant in this respect. There is no physically determined tendency toward switching from marijuana to harder substances. Social factors, however, appear to play a role," the Netherlands Institute of Mental Health and Addiction reaffirmed in 1997.

Dutch harm-reduction policies yielded impressive results by erecting a barrier between the retail market for cannabis (coffeehouse sales) and the retail market for hard narcotics (illicit underground sales). Annual surveys revealed that a significantly lower percentage of Dutch youth and adults used illegal drugs, hard and soft, compared with user levels in the United States, Canada, Great Britain, France, and many other countries. And the percentage of young people in the Netherlands who tried cannabis and then started using the harder stuff was also much less than in the United States. This pattern would continue throughout the next decade and beyond.

The permissive Dutch approach laid the foundation for a taxable, multibillion-dollar economic sector, attracting millions of visitors each year and generating substantial revenue for the government. Resources previously devoted to busting marijuana smokers were instead used to combat the production and smuggling of hard drugs. While the coffee-shop system underwent minor modifications over the years, the core principles remained the same. Problems attributable to the abuse of marijuana in the Netherlands were either rare or difficult to document. "The coffee shops are living proof that prohibition of cannabis is not necessary, that it's a useless and harmful policy," said Frederick Polak, a psychiatrist with the Amsterdam Municipal Health Service.

When McCaffrey visited Europe, support for punitive, American-style pot prohibition was unraveling on the continent. Influenced by the Dutch model, the European Parliament voted to decriminalize the possession of marijuana and other drugs for personal adult use in 1995. Soon Belgium, Luxembourg, Switzerland, Spain, Portugal, Denmark, Italy, Greece, and the Czech Republic would emulate the Netherlands and remove (or ignore) criminal penalties for cannabis as part of a continent-wide shift toward harm reduction.

"Most of Europe prefers to deal with marijuana as a health issue rather than a criminal one," observed Rick Steves, the American travel writer, tour guide, and TV personality. "Europe has learned you can't legislate personal morality. It's futile. It is counterproductive . . . You can tolerate alternative lifestyles or you can build more prisons. In Europe they'd rather tolerate alternative lifestyles."

The British legal system was beginning to bend on the issue of medical marijuana. In November 1998, the House of Lords Select Committee on Science and Technology published a report, *Cannabis: The Scientific and Medical Evidence,* which recommended that clinical trials of marijuana medicaments be conducted "as a matter of urgency." The report noted that cannabis tinctures had a long history of human use and were part of the British pharmacopeia until 1948.

"What's extraordinary is to have so many reputed applications for something that doesn't even legally exist as a medicine," Geoffrey Guy told the

House of Lords. "I've gotten beyond the point of being surprised by anything this plant can do." An astute businessman with a background in botany and pharmaceuticals, Guy had his sights set on developing a cannabis extract that could be marketed legally as an under-the-tongue spray. When Guy floated the idea by British officials, they needed little convincing. "They were almost relieved I had turned up. I was pushing on a door that sprang right open," he recounted.

Spooked by the prospect of multiple sclerosis patients in wheelchairs leading street protests for marijuana legalization, the British government granted a license to Guy's startup company, GW Pharmaceuticals, to grow and possess cannabis for the purpose of conducting medical trials. GW purchased the seed stock and breeder's rights to a variety of high-grade strains from HortaPharm, the Dutch firm established a decade earlier by the American expatriates David Watson and Robert Clarke. Soon GW scientists were overseeing a large cannabis grow-op inside a hangar-sized greenhouse at a secret location in southeastern England.

GW's flagship product, Sativex, is not a conventional, single-molecule medicine like Marinol, the THC pill. Sativex is a whole-plant extract containing equal amounts of THC and nonpsychoactive CBD, along with trace elements of the full range of cannabinoid compounds that are unique to marijuana. Sativex also contains aromatic terpenes and other components that may contribute to its therapeutic value. GW scientists believed that all the components of the cannabis plant act together to provide a better effect. As a mouth spray, Sativex delivered fast-acting medicinal doses in quantities smaller than those required to get high, so that MS patients could navigate the borderland between crippling pain and intoxication. Clinical trials in several European countries confirmed the safety and efficacy of Sativex for different patient groups. The cannabinoid spray was approved initially in Canada (2005) and later in Great Britain, Spain, Denmark, Germany, Sweden, the Czech Republic, New Zealand, Austria, and several other countries as a remedy for multiple sclerosis pain and spasticity.

The formal launch of Sativex constituted a milestone in the treatment of MS, a degenerative neurological illness that afflicts 25 million people around the world. But Sativex was not yet a treatment option for Americans such as former TV talk show host and Emmy award-winner Montel Williams, who suffered from multiple sclerosis. The U.S. government lagged behind the international community in this area of medicine, despite several peer-reviewed studies by American scientists that demonstrated the beneficial effects of cannabinoids on symptoms of MS. Williams, a military veteran, said that smoked marijuana was more effective than Big Pharma meds in treating the pain, depression, and sleep disorders caused by his degenerative illness. "I'm breaking the law every day and I will continue to break the law," Williams told journalists and state legislators grappling with proposed medical-marijuana legislation.

On November 4, 1998, five more U.S. states became conscientious objectors to the federal government's war on drugs, as citizens in Alaska, Nevada, Oregon, Washington, and Arizona voted to legalize medical marijuana. (Arizonans showed their displeasure at the state legislature's gutting of the 1996 medical-marijuana measure by passing another initiative.) The clean sweep by medical-marijuana supporters provided a big morale boost to California's besieged pot clubs and sent a clear signal to the entire nation that what had happened at the ballot box two years earlier in the Golden State wasn't a fluke.

Unlike California's Proposition 215, which enabled doctors to recommend cannabis for any condition they saw fit, the new state laws allowed the use of marijuana only for a handful of specific diseases and limited patients to small quantities of the herb. California remained the only state with a significant aboveground marijuana business.

In 1998, a lame-duck U.S. Congress registered its displeasure with the state ballot initiatives by passing House Resolution 117, which opposed medical marijuana and denounced cannabis as dangerous and addictive. But the feds didn't have the resources, the backbone, or the political support to contain the nationwide medical-marijuana groundswell. Advice columnist Abigail ("Dear Abby") van Buren spoke for a majority of Americans when she wrote: "I agree that marijuana laws are overdue for an overhaul. I also favor the medical use of marijuana—if it's prescribed by a physician. I cannot understand why the federal government should interfere with the doctor-patient relationship, nor why it would ignore the will of the majority of voters who have legally approved such legislation."

Federal officials ignored the will of the majority in the District of Columbia, where Initiative 59, a California-style medical-marijuana measure, was on the ballot in 1998. Exit polls indicated a landslide vote to legalize medical marijuana in the nation's capital. But a couple of weeks before Election Day, Representative Bob Barr, a Republican from Georgia (who opposed lawsuits against tobacco companies), had slipped into D.C.'s 1999 budget a proviso that no funds could be allocated to count the results of the medical-marijuana proposition. So the final tally was not officially disclosed. The bill also barred the district's use of its own funds to support needle-exchange programs for drug addicts. "This is democracy held hostage," said Wayne Turner, a local activist who spearheaded the D.C. medical-marijuana campaign while his partner was battling AIDS.*

Barr's maneuver triggered protests by medical-marijuana advocates. Jim Miller was arrested after he lifted his wife, Cheryl, a crippled multiple sclerosis sufferer, out of her wheelchair and placed her in a sleeping bag to block the doorway of Barr's congressional office. (A few years earlier, Jim had pushed Cheryl's wheelchair fifty-eight miles across the state of New Jersey, where they lived, to draw media attention to the need for medical marijuana.) The Clinton Justice Department announced that it would defend Congress's right to nix the D.C. medical-marijuana initiative by prohibiting the vote count. The Clinton administration called the Barr amendment "sensible."

The political gamesmanship on Capitol Hill would have lethal consequences for Jonathan Magbie, a twenty-seven-year-old African American quadriplegic paralyzed from being hit by a drunken driver. As a child, Magbie became a poster boy for Mothers Against Drunk Driving. He even had his picture taken with President Ronald Reagan. Busted in 2004 for possessing a small amount of marijuana, Magbie was sentenced to ten days in jail by D.C. Superior Court Judge Judith Retchin, even though he was a wheelchair-bound first-time offender who needed round-the-clock nursing assistance. Retchin was angered by Magbie's refusal to swear off pot. She could have given him probation; instead she chose to punish Magbie because he answered honestly when asked if he intended to smoke marijuana again. Yes, he said—it was the only thing that made him feel better. So off he went to jail. He died four days later, unable to breathe without a ventilator. Only a country caught in the grip of a deep psychosis, a full-blown outbreak of reefer madness, would imprison a quadriplegic for using cannabis as a medicine.

The Stake-Out

Medical-marijuana advocates in the Golden State were heartened by the 1998 election of Democrat Bill Lockyer to succeed Dan Lungren as California's attorney general. A veteran lawmaker from the East Bay, Lockyer had voted for Proposition 215 and he criticized Lungren for blocking its implementation.

* In 2002, the federal law that nixed the D.C. medical-marijuana ballot initiative was overturned as an unconstitutional restriction on political speech. Another medical-marijuana proposition passed by a wide margin in the nation's capital in 2010—and this time the votes were counted.

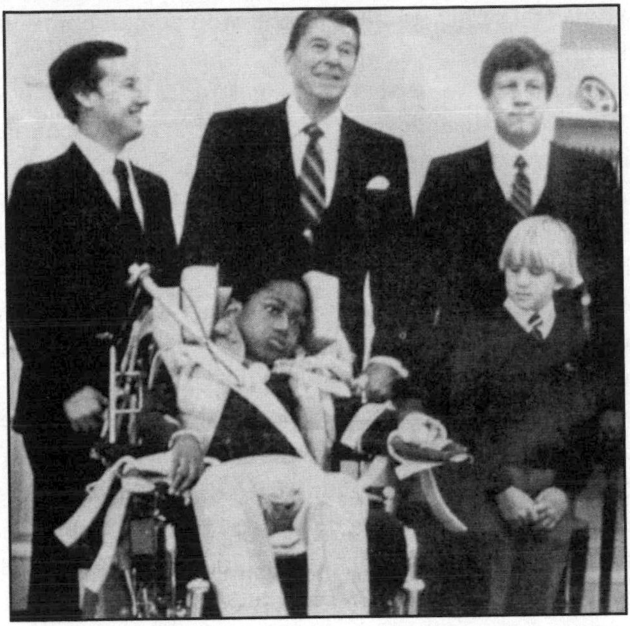

President Ronald Reagan posing with Jonathan Magbie, a wheelchair-bound quadriplegic poster child for victims of drunk drivers. Unable to breathe without a ventilator, Magbie died in a Washington, D.C., jail while serving time for a minor marijuana violation.

(Courtesy of American Association for Respiratory Care)

Lockyer said all the right things about wanting to make Proposition 215 work. He called his predecessor "overly zealous in opposing [Prop. 215] even after the voters had adopted it." He joked that sometimes he thought Lungren "had a copy of *Reefer Madness* at home."

Shortly after he took charge of California's Department of Justice, with its three hundred Bureau of Narcotics enforcement agents and nine hundred attorneys, Lockyer convened a medical-marijuana task force to "clarify" and implement the Compassionate Use Act. But the task force, which was chaired by State Senator John Vasconcellos and included law-enforcement lobbyists and patient-activists, struggled to reach a consensus. Medical marijuana remained a political hot potato. Aware that Prop. 215 was still very unpopular within the ranks of California law enforcement, Lockyer promised to cooperate with local authorities even if they pursued different approaches to the issue. He rebuffed pleas from medical-marijuana supporters and some public officials to set statewide standards for police to follow. Consequently, enforcement of the Compassionate Use Act would continue to vary significantly across California's fifty-eight counties.

Where support for Proposition 215 was strongest, especially in the San Francisco Bay Area, patients could obtain locally issued medical-marijuana ID cards and purchase their herb from retail storefronts. Lockyer conferred with District Attorney Terence Hallinan and gave a thumbs-up to Frisco's city-regulated medical-marijuana dispensaries. "If local law enforcement is supportive of implementation of Proposition 215 and their policies don't provoke [federal] prosecution, I have no intention of intervening," Lockyer asserted. At the same time, however, he was reluctant to rein in the cowboy cops who were terrorizing patients and caregivers in the Other California—Red-State California, as it were.

A brutal story (largely unnoticed by the state's metropolitan press corps) was unfolding in small, remote communities in the Eastern District of the California federal court system, a sprawling jurisdiction that covers Sacramento, Bakersfield, Lake Tahoe, the Sierra Nevada mountains, and the San Joaquin Valley. Cross-deputized by the DEA, county law-enforcement officers manhandled and arrested disabled cannabis patients in several Eastern District redoubts. "You know, if you take away the badge and the gun, there's no difference between us and the Hell's Angels," a disgruntled California narc confided to freelance journalist Patrick McCartney, who investigated police corruption in the Eastern District.

In Tuolumne County, sheriff's deputies arrested thirty-five-year-old Myron Mower, blind and seriously ill from childhood diabetes, while he lay on a hospital bed tethered to a morphine drip. His alleged crime: growing marijuana. Mower, who was upfront about his use of cannabis, had repeatedly run afoul of the sheriff's department for cultivating a pot garden after a doctor recommended reefer to help him cope with nausea, vomiting, near constant pain, and other complications from his life-threatening disease. Mower's residence had already been subjected to two no-warrant searches. During the first raid, the deputies discovered he was growing seven plants, but they left without pressing charges. The Tuolumne County Sheriff's Department subsequently adopted a three-plant limit for patients without disclosing this policy to the public. Mower's home was searched again, and this time the cops found thirty-one plants. They removed twenty-eight, leaving Mower with only three plants, which were later stolen. "My health was all in that garden," cried Mower. "You guys don't know what you've done to me."

At Mower's trial in 1998, the prosecution introduced Special Agent Mick Mollica, the Forrest Gump of marijuana eradication, who always seemed to turn up at the scene of important antipot operations in California. Employed by the state attorney general's office, this veteran narcotics operative had worked closely with federal drug warriors over the years. When he testified against Mower and other medical-marijuana patients, Mollica performed his usual role of narco-numerologist, inflating plant-yield estimates so that the defendant would invariably be portrayed as a greedy commercial grower hiding behind the state med-pot law.

Mollica claimed that Mower's harvest would have produced up to 62 pounds of marijuana (more than he needed for his personal medical use). But this calculation was way too high, according to expert witness Chris Conrad, who cited criteria set forth in a 1991 DEA analysis, which identified fresh weight and canopy diameter as the best predictors of plant yield. Smitten by the men in badges, the jury needed just ninety minutes to find Mower guilty of felony cultivation—the accused had grown more plants than county authorities deemed necessary, and nothing else mattered. Mower was sentenced to five years probation and a thousand-dollar fine.

Mower appealed, and his conviction was subsequently overturned by the California Supreme Court in a landmark decision that gave patients the right to seek early dismissal of charges by claiming medical use at a pretrial hearing. The ruling shifted the burden of proof to the prosecution, where it belonged. The state high court affirmed that California is responsible for enforcement of its own marijuana laws and not those of the federal government. But the Mower ruling did little to protect patients from being arrested in the first place. And the court declined to set a statewide standard for plant numbers or possession amounts.*

Steve Kubby, an outspoken medical-marijuana patient, was busted for growing his own in Placer County, another Eastern District redoubt. Diagnosed with a rare and highly aggressive form of adrenal cancer, Kubby was once a ski racer, a mountain climber, a deep-sea diver, and a pilot with top-secret security clearance who broke the sound barrier flying an F-5 fighter jet. But Kubby's world caved in when he learned that his body was riddled with malignant tumors. Doctors found the cancer had spread to his bladder, stom-

* In *People v. Mower* (2002), the California Supreme Court observed that "the possession of marijuana . . . is no more criminal . . . than the possession and acquisition of any prescription drug with a physician's prescription." The court held that the law grants a defendant a limited immunity from prosecution, a defense that can be raised in a pretrial motion or at trial to set aside an indictment or information.

ach, liver, and spleen. Kubby underwent four major surgeries, chemotherapy, and several debilitating rounds of radiation. Medical experts pronounced his condition terminal.

Kubby was in his late twenties when he learned he was dying of pheno-chromocytoma, a cancerous condition that causes sudden spikes in adrena-line and other hormones. At any moment, his tumors could secrete a lethal or near-lethal amount of adrenaline, triggering a heart attack, a stroke, or an aneurysm. Kubby's energy was draining away when his former college room-mate, Richard "Cheech" Marin (of the stoner comedy duo Cheech and Chong), dropped by one day to cheer him up. Cheech lit a joint for old times' sake and told his compañero, "Hey, if you're going to die, then why not die happy?" Kubby took a few hits, and, wow, he hadn't felt that good in a long time. With little left to lose, he began to self-medicate with marijuana on a regular basis.

A miracle of premodern medicine, Kubby survived by smoking up to an ounce of high-THC cannabis every day. Adhering to a strict dietary regimen, he supplemented his steady intake of THC with generous swabs of cholesterol-lowering hempseed oil—highly rich in protein and essential fatty acids—which he spread on toast. "I don't have a medicine cabinet. I don't take any pharmaceutical drugs, except for a rare dose of antibiotics. I don't drink coffee, tea, or soda," he explained.

Outraged by the federal government's heavy-handed efforts to stymie the implementation of Proposition 215, Kubby ran for governor on the Libertar-ian Party ticket in 1998 to highlight the issue of medical marijuana. Kubby, then fifty-one, stood on the steps of the state capitol in Sacramento, held up a bottle of aspirin and a big bud of homegrown cannabis, and asked which was more dangerous—the aspirin that kills more than two thousand Americans a year or marijuana, which has never been known to kill anyone?

Law enforcement did not take kindly to his theatrics. On January 19, 1999, twenty heavily armed SWAT team members battered down the door of Kubby's rented home near Squaw Valley, confiscated his 265-plant marijuana garden, and hauled him and his wife, Michele, off to the Placer County jail. Three days in jail without reefer nearly did him in. His captors mocked his requests for medicinal cannabis and went out of their way to punish him. "I was forced to attend breakfast where my repeated bouts of vomiting could be witnessed by the rest of the inmates who were trying to eat their meal," Kubby recounted.

The police, meanwhile, had seized nearly everything the Kubbys owned, including all their office equipment, which they used to operate an online magazine devoted to extreme winter sports. As a result, Kubby lost his busi-ness and was forced into bankruptcy. He also had to deal with the hassle and expense of obtaining enough cannabis on the black market for his medical needs. A costly wrangle in court loomed as both Kubbys were charged with conspiring to cultivate and sell marijuana.

When Dr. Vincent DeQuattro, one of the world's leading specialists on adrenal cancer, heard that Kubby had been busted, he couldn't believe that his former patient was still alive. Every other patient whom he treated for this terminal illness "had died long ago," DeQuattro wrote in a letter to the judge. "Only Kubby had survived." DeQuattro examined Kubby and concluded that cannabis stabilized his adrenal function: "In some amazing fashion, this medication has not only controlled the symptoms of phenochromocytoma, but in my view, has arrested growth." If Kubby is deprived of cannabis, according to DeQuattro, adrenaline will overwhelm his system and his blood pressure will spike to dangerous levels, which could result in a fatal seizure. In short, marijuana was keeping Kubby alive.

The Mayo Clinic, one of the most prestigious medical centers in the world, also studied Kubby's medical condition. "[W]e can't explain it, but whatever you're doing, keep doing it," the Mayo Clinic urged. But Kubby couldn't keep "doing it"—smoking high-THC reefer all day long—while residing in prison, which is where he feared he'd end up if a Placer County jury found him guilty as charged. Dr. DeQuattro testified on Kubby's behalf; so did Dr. Tod Mikuriya, whose letter of recommendation entitled Kubby to use cannabis as a medicine in California. After a lengthy trial and four days of deliberation, Kubby and his wife were exonerated of marijuana charges. But the jury found him guilty of felony possession of a peyote button and a magic mushroom. Judge John Cosgrove sentenced Kubby to 120 days of home detention and three years probation.

A defiant Kubby refused to accept a guilty verdict of any sort. "Make no mistake," he asserted in memos and press releases to his supporters, "this trial is no more about marijuana than the Boston Tea Party was about tea." Unwilling to countenance another life-threatening stint in jail, the Kubbys fled the country with their two small children. In the spring of 2001, they slipped across the border into Canada and applied for political asylum on the grounds that they had a "well-founded fear of persecution" by drug warriors in the United States.

Michael Baldwin, a Placer County dentist who used marijuana for chronic lower back pain and sciatica, was closely watching developments in the Kubby case. Baldwin's home had been raided on September 23, 1998, even though he and his wife, Georgia Chacko, both had recommendations to medicate with cannabis from Dr. Alex Stalcup, a leading authority on illegal drugs. (Stalcup taught classes on the subject to narcotics agents at the behest of the California Narcotics Officers' Association.) According to Baldwin, the uniformed invaders held guns to their heads, pinned them to the ground, and kneed them in the back. "Proposition 215 doesn't apply in Placer County," a deputy told Baldwin during the bust. The next day, the Placer County Sheriff's Department issued a press release announcing that the Baldwins had been arrested for cultivation and sales of a controlled substance based on the seizure of 146 plants (mostly seedlings) that were growing on their property. The negative publicity from the bust ruined Baldwin's dental practice.

Financially strapped and embittered toward the government, Baldwin began looking into the activities of the federally funded Placer County marijuana eradication squad. Led by a gung-ho sheriff's deputy named Tracy Grant, the Placer antidrug squad conducted numerous raids against marijuana suspects in the late 1990s. In Placer and adjacent counties where Grant's team operated, zero-tolerance dogma empowered a certain kind of fanatical, belligerent cop who viewed pot smoking as a grave social pathology. Several people claimed they were roughed up and abused by Grant, whose predatory behavior epitomized a criminal-justice system gone haywire. The targets of Grant's antimarijuana witch hunt included patients with valid medical recommendations and others who had grown nothing more scandalous than lettuce.

As he prepared to mount a defense in court, Baldwin reached out to other medical-marijuana patients who had been busted by Grant's unit. Baldwin befriended Amy Breeze, a Sacramento resident who was severely disabled by a horrific workplace accident a few years earlier. Breeze smoked pot to ease her pain and to wean herself from an excessive regimen of doctor-prescribed painkillers. Early one morning in December 1998, Grant and a team of uniformed narcs barged into her home and ransacked the premises looking for weed. She had a medical recommendation and was growing a few plants indoors. "I asked him not to handcuff me behind my back," Breeze later recounted. "He said, 'Don't give me that disabled bullshit. We've seen you walk. If you keep claiming disability, things will get really bad for you.'"

Chris Miller had a similar story. Seriously injured in a motorcycle accident, he used marijuana as a painkiller and a mood enhancer. His home near Sacramento, where he tended a small ganja garden, was assaulted at dawn by pistol-waving Placer County deputies. Soon other folks started to come out of the woodwork, claiming that they, too, had been victimized by Grant and his passel of power-crazed narcs. It was only a matter of time before Grant's overzealous antics would get the best of him.

On July 1, 1999, at seven a.m., the Placer County antidrug unit raided the home of eighty-year-old retiree Sandy Sanborn and his wife, Grace. The narcs searched high and low for marijuana but didn't find any. They had no idea that Sanborn, a lifelong Republican and member of the Rotary Club, was a friend and political associate of Ronald Reagan. The next day Placer County Sheriff Edward Bonner apologized to Sanborn. But Bonner was at a loss to explain why one of his deputies had stated in a search warrant affidavit that they had found "fresh, green" marijuana in Sanborn's trash bin a week earlier.

Baldwin, Breeze, and Miller joined forces with several other Placer County marijuana defendants. They began combing through every search warrant executed by Grant's law-enforcement unit during a two-year period. They examined court files, sworn affidavits, and other pertinent records. Comparing notes, they found that every search warrant used the exact same wording to justify raiding their homes. In each case, a sheriff's deputy claimed to have found "marijuana . . . fresh, green and still moist" in their trash. This was peculiar, to say the least, given that most cannabis cultivators took pains to avoid incriminating themselves. It looked like a cut-and-paste job—the same falsehood repeated over and over again. Probing further, the defendants discovered that they had something else in common. They all shopped at a Sacramento nursery called Greenfire, which sold gardening supplies and hydroponics equipment for indoor cultivation. The Sanborns shopped there, as well.

Intoxicated by the prospect of dragooning more drug users and seizing more property, Grant's henchmen had staked out the nursery. But Greenfire was never mentioned in any of Grant's search-warrant affidavits, which contained suspicious information that suggested a pattern of police misconduct. "Just the fact that people shop in a hydroponics store doesn't mean what they're buying is something for an illegal purpose," said Kate Wells, an attorney who filed litigation on behalf of some of the Greenfire defendants. "It's like saying because some people shoplift, that you're automatically presumed guilty when you walk into a store."

Baldwin and the other Greenfire patrons believed the cops targeted them because they happened to shop at this particular nursery, which was under surveillance by Grant's goons, who mounted four dozen Greenfire-related raids. Some Greenfire customers were able to convince judges and jurors that their pot cultivation was legal under California law. In other cases, defendants had little choice but to accept the best deal the prosecutors offered. Unable to afford legal counsel, they were coerced into pleading guilty. The drug warriors held a trump card that dangled like the sword of Damocles over any courtroom contest—the feds could step in at any time and press additional charges against a defendant who would not be permitted to invoke medical necessity at a trial.

Greenfire patron Robert Whiteaker refused to plea-bargain with Sacramento prosecutors after a SWAT team had ransacked his home in Rio Linda on May 10, 1999, and destroyed a small medicinal-pot garden that he was growing under his doctor's supervision. Whiteaker and his wife were arrested and their traumatized children were taken into custody by Sacramento County Child Protective Services for several days. Unwilling to capitulate, Whiteaker turned the tables on the cops and won the right to a legal hearing on the validity of the search warrant issued in his case. During the hearing, a reluctant Tracy Grant disclosed that U.S. Attorney Samuel Wong had given him a stack of blank subpoenas, which Grant's team used to wage a vendetta against dozens of marijuana suspects. While not technically illegal, it is highly improper for a federal prosecutor to give blank subpoenas to a county narc for application in a state case. Shortly after the search-warrant hearing, the U.S. Attorney's office in Sacramento informed Whiteaker that he would be indicted on federal drug charges if he pursued the matter any further. Faced with the possibility of life in federal prison, he had no recourse other than to accept an eighteen-month jail sentence for a crime he didn't commit.

The saga of the Greenfire defendants would play out in the courts for several years. In multiple claims and civil lawsuits against Placer County, Greenfire resisters accused Grant's government-sponsored gang of committing perjury and violating their civil rights. They believed that dishonest police work led to their arrest. They accused the Placer County narcs of lying and falsifying evidence in order to secure a search warrant.* Convinced that they had uncovered a can of worms, several Greenfire defendants filed a federal racketeering suit accusing local and federal law enforcement of conspiring to undermine California's medical-marijuana provision.

After criminal charges against Michael Baldwin and his wife were dismissed, they pressed their case against Placer County law enforcement in civil court. They submitted declarations from a dozen individuals who had been targeted by the Placer County marijuana-eradication team. When Grant and his cohorts sought qualified immunity, the Ninth Circuit U.S. Court of Appeals filed an opinion that strongly favored Baldwin and his wife. The opinion cited excessive force by Placer County deputies, judicial deception, and conspiracy on the part of the law-enforcement team: "On the basis of the facts conceded as undisputed by the county, for purposes of this appeal, we hold that Placer County violated established constitutional rights of the plaintiffs . . . The Fourth Amendment is the guarantee of every citizen that his home will be his

* Allegations of perjury on sworn affidavits have become almost commonplace within the criminal-justice system. "It's the real deep dark secret of the war on drugs," said the Seattle attorney Jeff Steinberg. "Perjury has become commonplace on search warrants. It's the currency of search warrants, and the courts tolerate it."

castle, safe from the arbitrary intrusion of official authority. It is no barrier at all if it can be invaded by a policeman concocting a story that he feeds a magistrate." Despite this finding, all charges against Grant and Placer County were dismissed "with prejudice" by U.S. district court judge Garland E. Burrell, a decision that ensured that police corruption in the Eastern District would go unpunished.

While Grant and his henchmen were wreaking havoc and turning people's lives upside down, the National Academy of Sciences' Institute of Medicine (IOM) was putting the final touches on a report that had been commissioned by the drug czar's office shortly after the passage of Proposition 215. The IOM, an independent, nonprofit think tank considered by many to be the "gold standard" of American medicine, conducted an eighteen-month study of the therapeutic potential of cannabis. It held a series of public workshops and solicited input from various sources, including several cannabis clinicians and medical-marijuana patients.

During a site visit to the Oakland Cannabis Buyers' Cooperative (prior to its closure), IOM researchers met with Dr. Tod Mikuriya, the OCBC's medical consultant. "The passage of Proposition 215 has made clinical research possible again," said Mikuriya, who explained the intake forms that patients filled out in an effort to gather data about individual use patterns and how cannabis impacted their conditions. OCBC's director, Jeff Jones, demonstrated how to use a "vaporizer," a new delivery system that heated plant matter to a temperature just below combustion. A vaporizer enabled patients to inhale cannabis fumes rather than smoke, thereby minimizing exposure to carcinogens and harmful particulates.

The IOM delegation also paid a house call to Dennis Peron at the San Francisco Cannabis Buyers' Club and to CHAMP (Californians Helping Alleviate Medical Problems), another SF dispensary that had adopted the "social club" model. CHAMP cofounder Michael Aldrich (Ginsberg's LEMAR colleague from the '60s) believed that the key to CHAMP's success lay in the ability and willingness of its affluent members to subsidize the pot purchases of less fortunate patients.

Published by the National Academy of Sciences in March 1999, *Marijuana as Medicine: Assessing the Science Base* contained a diplomatic mix of carefully phrased findings. First and foremost, the 250-page IOM report confirmed that cannabis has legitimate medical uses. The IOM study included a lengthy technical exegesis on cannabinoids and animal physiology. For the first time, a major U.S. government study discussed the CB-1 and CB-2 receptors; the endocannabinoids that bind to these crucial receptors; how endocannabinoid signaling affects human immune response; and findings from recent knockout mice experiments demonstrating the role of endocannabinoid signaling in neuroprotection, pain perception, and various biological systems.

The IOM report indicated that marijuana has been shown to provide relief for a wide range of ailments. Patients suffering nausea, pain, and appetite loss might get "broad spectrum relief not found in any other single medication" by using cannabis, according to IOM investigators, who found that the risk of developing dependence on marijuana is slight: "[F]ew users develop dependence" and for those that do, withdrawal is "mild and short-lived." The report debunked the notion of cannabis as a gateway drug that leads to cocaine and heroin use: "In fact, most drug users do not begin their drug use with marijuana—they begin with alcohol and nicotine, usually when they are too young to do so legally." Furthermore, the IOM noted that marijuana use among the general population "is not associated with increased morbidity" and, unlike tobacco, cannabis has never been shown to cause cancer. The IOM concluded there was no evidence that allowing sick people to use medical marijuana would cause an increase in recreational drug use.

The IOM acknowledged that marijuana's side effects are well within the range that is tolerated for other medications. But the authors of the study expressed concern about potential harm from smoking: "Smoked marijuana is a crude THC delivery system that also delivers harmful substances." What the IOM report intended as a cautionary lament—"cannabinoid effects cannot be separated from the effects of inhaling [marijuana] smoke"—had a double-edged significance: It also meant that the smoke contained the significant beneficial elements—the oily cannabinoids, terpenes, and flavonoids, which can be inhaled via combustion or vaporization.

Ignoring the advent of vaporizers, the IOM strongly endorsed additional research geared toward developing cannabinoid-like compounds that could exert multifarious therapeutic effects via "rapid-onset, reliable, and safe delivery systems." The authors acknowledged the inherent difficulty in marketing a nonpatentable herb. Without a patent, where's the profit for Big Pharma? Accordingly, the IOM predicted "there is little future in smoked cannabis as [an] approved medication."

Drug czar McCaffrey and the political establishment reacted to the IOM study in predictable fashion—by publicizing the knock on smoking and ignoring the positive findings. A broad scientific consensus had emerged in support of therapeutic claims for cannabis, but the sorry record of official stonewalling would drone on. The DEA and the California Narcotics Officers' Association continued to insist that marijuana is not a medicine, proving once again, in the words of Barbara Ehrenreich, that "Prohibition is right up there with heroin and nicotine among habits that are hell to kick."

Veterans for Drug-War Peace

Sometimes all it took was a loud noise or the smell of diesel or barbecued meat. Instantly it all came back: the unspeakable horror of war, suffering so intense that it changes the way a person's brain functions. Ambushes, booby traps, "improvised explosive devices," fallen comrades, napalmed flesh, limbless children—the mind-altering pressure of being on high alert 24/7 made active-duty soldiers susceptible to violent mood swings, emotional meltdowns, and homicidal fantasies. These were telling signs of posttraumatic stress disorder, otherwise known as PTSD, a crippling mental illness that afflicts a high percentage of U.S. military veterans.

Legions of American vets have returned from their tour of duty psychologically shattered, strung out on drugs, and fearful of government retribution if they reported their mental problems. Studies on the problems of military vets demonstrated strong links between combat-related posttraumatic stress and high rates of unemployment, homelessness, substance abuse (particularly alcoholism), suicide, domestic violence, criminality, and imprisonment. Fifty-eight thousand American soldiers died in Vietnam; nearly twice that number would kill themselves after the war.

"PTSD is not a disorder. It's a rational response to what you've seen," contends Al Byrne, a retired career navy officer. "I was terrified in Vietnam, I was scared to death and anybody who tells you they weren't wasn't there."

A tall, strapping New Englander, Byrne was a starting fullback on Notre Dame's rugby team before he joined the navy and served in Southeast Asia in the early 1970s. Exposed to Agent Orange (a highly toxic U.S. chemical weapon) and struggling with combat-related anxiety, Byrne joined a support group for veterans after the war and became a peer counselor for those disabled by PTSD. He spent much of the late 1980s in the Appalachian Mountains, seeking out troubled, disillusioned military vets who had gone into hiding. Many Vietnam veterans found that nothing could calm the storm that raged in their heads like a few puffs of weed.

"Eighty to ninety percent of the vets I counseled used cannabis—with good results," said Byrne. "In some cases, they gave up harder drugs. They drank less alcohol. They could sleep through the night. If you can't sleep, your world goes to hell in a hand basket real fast. The ability to sleep was instrumental in getting everything else straightened out. For many veterans, cannabis was literally a lifesaver."

When Byrne visited Veterans Administration hospitals, wounded soldiers would confide that they much preferred marijuana to Valium and other pharmaceutical mood enhancers prescribed by VA docs. "Guys would come up to me and say, 'Al, you see these pills the doctor gave me? You know what we do with them? We either sell them on the street or swap them for pot.'" According to Byrne: "It was an open secret at any number of VA hospitals in the United States that if you needed to smoke cannabis just go on the roof. Somebody up there always had a match."

Byrne's wife, Mary Lynn Mathre, ran a substance abuse program for veterans. Trained as a Vietnam-era navy nurse, she was both an addictions specialist and an outspoken advocate for medicinal cannabis. In 1995, Mathre and Byrne formed Patients Out of Time (POT) to educate health-care professionals and the general public about medical marijuana. The group's name was chosen to emphasize the urgent situation faced by many ailing Americans: People were dying; patients were literally running out of time. They could not afford to wait for long-delayed research studies to yield results. They needed cannabis immediately. That was the message Mathre conveyed to the American Nurses Association, which declared in 2003 that every registered nurse in America should be educated "regarding current, evidence-based therapeutic use of marijuana/cannabis." Uncle Sam, meanwhile, continued to supply three hundred marijuana cigarettes each month to Randall and a few other Compassionate IND patients—Irv Rosenfeld, Elvy Mussika, George McMahon, and MS sufferer Barbara Douglass—who served on POT's board.

In addition to lobbying professional organizations to endorse patient access to cannabis, Mathre and Byrne arranged for doctors, nurses, drug counselors, and social workers to earn continuing-education credit for attending seminars on medical marijuana. Held every other year, POT's national conference featured scientists explaining the latest discoveries about the endocannabinoid system; doctors attesting to marijuana's safety and efficacy; and patients telling personal stories of grief and redemption.

Dr. Tod Mikuriya treated several Desert Storm veterans who wrestled with atrocities that had been seared into their consciousness during the 1991 Persian Gulf War. Like many Vietnam vets, they smoked marijuana to mitigate the nightmare flashbacks and the sudden fits of anxiety, fury, and deep depression that are associated with PTSD. "Cannabis use enhances the quality of sleep," Mikuriya reported in a paper on marijuana as an "easement" for posttraumatic stress. "The importance of restoring circadian rhythm of sleep cannot be overstated in the management of PTSD. Avoidance of alcohol is important in large part because of the adverse effects on sleep . . . Restorative exercise and diet are requisite components of treatment of PTSD and depression. Cannabis does not leave the patient too immobile to exercise, as do some analgesics, sedatives, benzodiazapenes, etc." Marijuana's side effects seem "especially benign when contrasted with those of the prevailing mainstream treatments,"

Mikuriya noted. He concluded that "cannabis should be considered first in the treatment of post-traumatic stress disorder."*

Some military veterans in post-215 California emerged as fervent crusaders for medicinal cannabis. One of Mikuriya's patients, Charles "Eddy" Lepp, was a manic, pot-growing Vietnam vet who suffered from PTSD, chronic pain, and several other medical challenges. He, too, had fire in the belly. The sign in front of the pathway leading up to his rural Lake County home read: "Eddy Lepp's Medicinal Garden and Chapel." In July 1997, local narcs busted Lepp for cultivating fifty-one plants in his backyard, which straddled the southern tip of the Emerald Triangle. A Lake County jury acquitted Lepp after he testified on his own behalf. "I told them, 'I've done nothing wrong.' I'm a white, middle-class, goddamn war hero—military intelligence . . . Ninety percent of what's wrong with me can be traced to my service years. I need marijuana . . . I get bad when I drink alcohol. On weed, I've never met anyone who doesn't like me.' "†

Lepp was the Energizer Bunny of outdoor herbage—he kept on growing and growing and growing. In August 2004, a DEA strike force, accompanied by several California highway patrolmen, arrested Lepp for cultivating more than 32,000 marijuana plants, some in excess of ten feet tall, which were clearly visible on both sides of Route 20, a county road that cut through his land. Lepp's agricultural operation—with precise rows of ganja fed by an extensive drip irrigation system—looked more like a corporate wine country vineyard than an outlaw cannabis crop. The DEA called it "the largest, most sophisticated marijuana garden in the world." Lepp was busted yet again a few months

---

* Preclinical research has shown that endocannabinoid signaling in the amygdala, a brain area where CB-1 receptors are concentrated, plays a key role in encoding and extinguishing aversive memories. Scientists found that aversive memory extinction did not occur in genetically altered mice lacking CB-1 receptors or mice given a CB-1 antagonist that blocked the receptor (Jean Marx, "Drugs Inspired by a Drug," *Science* [January 20, 2006]; see also G. Marsicano et al., "The Endogenous Cannabinoid System Controls Extinction of Aversive Memories," *Nature* 418[2002]: 530–34).

† B. E. Smith, another Vietnam vet, was busted in the summer of 1997 for growing eighty-seven plants on land rented from a friend in Trinity County. Tried in federal court in Sacramento, Smith testified that he began using marijuana in Vietnam, that he subsequently used it as a substitute for alcohol, and that he was growing it for himself and other patients. Woody Harrelson testified as a character witness on his behalf. (They had met while protesting to save the Headlands old-growth forest in Humboldt County.) Judge Garland Burrell refused to allow medical evidence to be introduced in court. Convicted on charges of possession and "manufacturing" marijuana, Smith was sentenced to twenty-seven months in federal prison.

later when law-enforcement officers found several hundred clones in a greenhouse on his Lake County spread.

Farmer Lepp was also minister of a self-styled Rasta church that embraced ganja both as a medicine and a daily sacrament.* But Lepp's "freedom of religion" defense failed to sway U.S. District Judge Marilyn Patel, who deemed he could not credibly claim that his faith compelled him to distribute thousands of pounds of marijuana to parishioners he had never met. Au contraire, Lepp insisted: With the requisite physician's recommendation and a modest payment to cover costs of cultivation, a qualified medical patient who belonged to his church would be assigned a small plot on Lepp's land. And after a bountiful harvest, Lepp's assistants would distribute the yield of each plant to a designated medical sharecropper. A kamikaze pilot for cannabis who flew headlong into the prohibitionist fortress, Lepp, aged fifty-three, was sentenced to a ten-year mandatory-minimum prison term. Patel called the sentence "excessive," but said she had no choice under federal law.

Under federal law, cannabis is not a medicine—even though irrefutable proof of marijuana's therapeutic utility is merely a mouse click away for anyone with access to the Internet. The analgesic effects of THC were documented in the *Journal of Clinical Pharmacology and Therapeutics* in 1975. Subsequent scientific studies would show that THC combined with nonpsychoactive cannabidiol works better than THC alone for chronic pain. People seek medical help for pain more often than for any other symptom.†

At the annual meeting of the U.S. Society for Neuroscience in October 1997, a team of researchers from Brown, Michigan, and UC San Francisco unveiled the discovery of a biochemical pathway that pain signals follow as

---

* Lepp's multidenominational Chapel of Cannabis and Rastafari was one of several ersatz ganja churches that cropped up in the post-215 era. They went by various names—Tree of Life, Church of Cognizance, Temple of Advanced Enlightenment, Universal Life Church, Church of Reality, 420 Temple, etc. The law generally took a dim view of these reefer religions. When Lepp stood trial in federal court on charges of criminal cultivation and distribution of marijuana, his lawyers tried unsuccessfully to get the case dismissed on religious grounds. A 2006 U.S. Supreme Court ruling upheld the right of an American religious group to use ayahuasca, the Amazon brew, which contains a powerful Schedule I hallucinogen.

† Long before the days of Hippocrates, Ayurvedic healers in India utilized ganja to soothe pain, while Chinese physicians employed medicinal hemp as an anesthetic for surgery. Pliny the Elder, the Roman naturalist born in AD 23, cited the painkilling properties of cannabis in his encyclopedia. In nineteenth-century America, patent medicines containing cannabis tinctures were widely used to treat migraines and other kinds of pain.

they travel from the site of an injury through the spinal cord to the brain. It turns out that there's an abundance of cannabinoid receptors in brain areas that control analgesia. When you feel pain, your body responds by releasing endocannabinoids, which activate receptors in the brain and nervous system to ameliorate discomfort. The latest research showed that THC and other plant cannabinoids, by mimicking the effect of the body's endocannabinoids, had a direct impact on pain perception. These studies also indicated that, unlike the current crop of opiate-based painkillers, cannabinoids are not addictive and they do not require increasing doses to achieve relief. The Society for Neuroscience concluded that "substances similar to or drawn from marijuana . . . could benefit more than 97 million Americans who experience some form of pain each year."

California cannabis clinicians and their patients found that pain was often best managed with marijuana as the primary medication. Smoked cannabis provided quick relief. People could titrate the amount they took into their bodies, adjusting as needed to achieve a desired effect. By self-medicating with marijuana, some patients were able to alleviate intense pain that even huge doses of morphine could not conquer. That's because cannabis and opiates act in different ways on the brain and nervous system. Many patients found that marijuana eased chronic pain without all the problems caused by opiates, which can make people nauseated, constipated, and too run-down to function. Some opiate addicts used cannabis to blunt withdrawal symptoms and maintain an opiate-free regimen thereafter—a testament to marijuana's potential as a harm-reduction medication.

Within the medical-marijuana community, it was well known that cannabis helped patients cut down or eliminate heavy doses of narcotic painkillers.* Any doubts about marijuana's painkilling capabilities should have been allayed

* Sandra Welch at the Medical College of Virginia demonstrated that morphine was fifteen times more active in animals with the addition of a small dose of THC, and the pain-relief effectiveness of codeine was enhanced nine hundredfold. Methadone's therapeutic utility was also magnified by cannabis. Additional studies found that cannabinoids act synergistically in combination with nonsteroidal anti-inflammatory drugs (NSAIDs) to reduce chronic pain. These findings confirmed anecdotal accounts from pain patients who—thanks to pot—were able to cut back on their consumption of aspirin, ibuprofen, and other potentially lethal NSAIDs, which are a leading cause of gastrointestinal bleeding and kidney failure. Acetaminophen, a NSAID widely used as an over-the-counter pain reliever for children, has been linked to asthma and other ailments. NSAIDs reportedly contribute to more than 100,000 hospitalizations and 16,500 deaths annually in the United States.

by the 1999 Institute of Medicine report, which noted that cannabinoids can have a substantial analgesic effect. The IOM noted that cannabinoids showed great promise in treating peripheral neuropathy, an excruciatingly painful condition caused by nerve injury that affects an estimated 1 percent of the world's population. FDA-approved analgesics were at best only marginally effective in reducing this type of pain. But marijuana, Sativex (GW Pharmaceuticals' whole-plant cannabis extract), and some single-molecule synthetic cannabinoids were able to attenuate neuropathic symptoms associated with AIDS, cancer, diabetes, multiple sclerosis, and rheumatoid arthritis. The IOM cited cases in which cannabis is said to have relieved postoperative pain, pain associated with spinal cord injuries, and phantom-limb pain suffered by amputees—agonies all too familiar to disabled war veterans.

In 1998, scientists at the National Institute of Mental Health disclosed that naturally occurring compounds present only in marijuana may protect brain cells from the effects of stroke and acute head injuries. Traumatic brain injuries cause the excessive release of glutamate, a neurochemical messenger that interacts with the endocannabinoid system; glutamate overload destroys gray matter and blows out the brain's circuitry. The research of Aidan Hampson and his NIMH colleagues demonstrated that THC and CBD are powerful antioxidants that protect brain cells against glutamate toxicity. Hampson was particularly impressed with cannabidiol, which showed greater antioxidant potency than standard antioxidants such as vitamin C and vitamin E.

On the basis of Hampson's research, the U.S. Department of Health and Human Services secured a patent titled "Cannabinoids as Antioxidants and Neuroprotectants." Awarded in October 2003, US Patent 6,630,507 asserts that "Cannabinoids have been found to have antioxidant properties [and] are found to have particular application as neuroprotectants, for example in limiting neurological damage following ischemic insults, such as stroke and trauma, or in the treatment of neurodegenerative diseases, such as Alzheimer's disease, Parkinson's disease and HIV dementia." But there was little institutional support to pursue clinical studies while drug-war boosters in Washington prattled on about pot causing brain damage.

Thousands of U.S. soldiers who fought in Iraq and Afghanistan will spend the rest of their lives coping with severe head wounds, neurological pain, and PTSD. These are the signature injuries of the wars launched by George W. Bush. When distressed troops sought help, military doctors prescribed the usual regime of synthetic opiates, antidepressants, and antipsychotic meds to blur the pain. Medicating with cannabis, however, was forbidden by Veterans Administration higher-ups, even though ample evidence showed that medicinally active compounds in marijuana were beneficial for treating posttraumatic stress, nerve damage, and traumatic brain injuries.*

Throughout the Bush years, the U.S. military and an overburdened VA system continued to deal with mental health problems in an ad hoc way while record numbers of active-duty soldiers and veterans committed suicide.† VA docs were barred from even discussing with patients that marijuana might help them. Vets who acknowledged using cannabis risked losing their VA benefits.

Michael Krawitz, a disabled Virginia-based air force veteran, was told by VA physicians that he had to sign a "pain contract" to get opiate medications. The contract stipulated that he could not use marijuana or other Schedule I drugs. When Krawitz refused to sign and submit to drug tests, his VA care was cut off. "Frankly, I felt like I deserved to smoke a joint after all I had been through," Krawitz later remarked. Krawitz formed Veterans for Medical Marijuana and doggedly lobbied the VA to reconsider its antiquated rules and recognize the therapeutic value of cannabis. For several years, he worked closely with Martin Chilcutt, a Michigan-based Korean War vet. Their efforts were instrumental in getting the Veterans Administration to change its policy. In 2010, the Obama administration announced that the VA would no longer penalize veterans for using the kind bud if they had a valid recommendation from a doctor in a state where medical marijuana was legal. It was a huge victory for military veterans, for chronic-pain patients, for medical-marijuana advocates, and for common sense.

---

* These afflictions were common among American soldiers returning from Iraq, where *azalla* (ancient Mesopotamian for hemp) was once a commonly used medicinal herb. In the old days, Mesopotamians referred to *azalla* as the "plant of forgetting worries," a fitting—and ironic—description given the epidemic levels of PTSD that ravaged American veterans who fought in Iraq ("Suicides, Mental Health Woes Soar Since Start of Iraq War, Study Finds," ABC News reported on March 8, 2012).

† During this period, the U.S. Army's suicide-prevention manual advised military chaplains to promote religiosity—specifically, Christianity—to dissuade distraught soldiers from killing themselves. The Department of Veterans Affairs undersecretary for benefits Daniel Cooper responded to criticism over a backlog of injured vets' disability claims by saying that Bible study was more important than his work; he resigned shortly thereafter (Aaron Glantz, "Embattled Veterans Official Resigns Post," IPS, February 29, 2008; and Jason Leopold, "Army Manual Promotes Christianity to Combat Epidemic of Suicides," January 3, 2009, http://www.militaryreligiousfreedom.org/press-releases/tpr_armymanual.html).

8

GROUND ZERO

Narcs Gone Wild!

When George W. Bush placed his hand on the Good Book and took the oath of office on January 20, 2001, American news media genuflected. "A new drama of invention starring Mr. Bush is beginning to unfold," gushed a *New York Times* editorial. That's how the Grey Lady referred to the inauguration of the forty-third president of the United States. GOP speechwriter Doug Gamble offered a less starry-eyed, insider's assessment: "Bush's shallow intellect perfectly reflects an increasingly dumbed-down America . . . To many Americans, Bush is 'just like us,' a Fox-TV president for a Fox-TV society."*

Before he embarked upon a career in politics, George W. Bush had a drug problem. Arrested twice for driving under the influence during his self-described "young and irresponsible" days, Bush was an alcoholic who got re-

* George W. Bush's Oval Office aspirations directly benefited from the racially skewed war on drugs. Bush would never have become president if not for the astonishing number of black Floridians who were denied the right to vote or whose ballots were disqualified. According to Human Rights Watch, no less than 31 percent of all African American men residing in the Sunshine State were barred from polling stations in November 2000 because of a felony conviction. The disenfranchised included many drug violators who had paid their debt to society and were no longer under criminal-justice supervision. Factor in the hundreds of thousands of Florida residents whose names had been incorrectly purged from voter rolls, the transportation tie-ups, police blockades, short voting hours, dimpled chads, and faulty equipment in predominantly African American districts—all of which contributed to undercounting the black vote—and the stage was set for a stolen election.

ligion and sobered up. In secretly taped conversations with his friend Doug Wead, Bush implicitly acknowledged that he had smoked pot, but he wouldn't elaborate: "You know why? Because I don't want some little kid doing what I tried."

Youthful irresponsibility apparently runs in the Bush family. Jenna and Barbara Bush, the president's twin daughters, were both cited for underage drinking. The actor Ashton Kutcher told *Rolling Stone* that the Bush twins smoked pot at a party at Kutcher's house in 2002. Their cousin Noelle Bush (daughter of Governor Jeb of Florida) was arrested that year for trying to use a fraudulent prescription to buy Xanax, the antianxiety drug, at a Tallahassee pharmacy. She was later sentenced to ten days in jail and led away in handcuffs for hiding crack cocaine in her shoes while in drug rehab. If America's drug laws were applied evenly and consistently, Jeb Bush and his family would have been evicted from their publicly funded mansion, just as poor people living in public housing were thrown out of their homes when a household member was busted for using illicit drugs. But Noelle Bush and other drug offenders from wealthy families were typically given every break in the book. Only poor students were punished for drug violations by having their financial aid revoked; wealthy students, who didn't need financial aid for education or rehab, were not affected by this penalty.

When George W. Bush was governor of Texas (1995–2000) he opined that medical marijuana was an issue for each state to decide. But Dubya flip-flopped while residing in the White House and made med-pot a top federal law-enforcement priority. The Bush administration played rougher than Clinton, filing criminal charges instead of civil lawsuits. It became open season on cannabis clubs in California. Assisted by local narcotics units, the U.S. Justice Department, led by Attorney General John Ashcroft, went after dispensaries, grow-ops, and high-profile activists throughout the state. "I want to escalate the war on drugs. I want to refresh it, relaunch it," declared Ashcroft. During his four-year tenure as America's chief lawman, Ashcroft ordered all federal prosecutors to notify the Justice Department whenever federal judges imposed lighter penalties for drug convictions than called for in federal sentencing guidelines.

Dubya's choice for drug czar, John P. Walters, was an Anslinger throwback who had previously served as deputy director of the Office of National Drug Control Policy during Papa Bush's administration. As the right-hand man of America's first drug czar, faux moralist William Bennett, Walters was instrumental in crafting drug policies that wasted billions of dollars, shattered millions of lives, eroded civil liberties, and exacerbated social discord. "Walters' record reveals the consummate doubletalk skills necessary to fulfill the office's task of redefining disaster as success, while simultaneously warning that worse disaster looms," wrote sociologist Mike Males.

At a time when 460,000 nonviolent drug offenders languished behind bars (more than the total number of prisoners for all crimes combined in Western Europe), Walters dismissed those who claimed that America's jails were too full. He ridiculed the notion that black men and other minorities were disproportionately punished for using illegal drugs as one of "the great urban myths of our time." Walters called for escalating the military's role in the drug war at home and abroad, particularly in South America. His rabid enthusiasm for armed interventions was a trait he may have picked up from his father, Vernon Walters, the multilingual CIA deputy director and presidential aide whose diplomatic postings always seemed to coincide with U.S.-backed military coups in the Third World during the 1960s and 1970s.

Described by the *Austin Chronicle* as "the Doctor Strangelove of our country's absurd drug war," Walters was obsessed with marijuana. He sent a letter to every prosecutor in the United States, urging them to make cannabis crimes a high priority and to fight efforts to weaken drug laws. "For Walters, it's all marijuana all the time," said Graham Boyd, director of the ACLU's drug-law reform project. Dubya's drug czar frequently referred to cannabis as "poison." He favored longer jail sentences for marijuana users. Instead of expanding drug treatment, the Bush administration expanded drug testing, which, in effect, meant marijuana testing because cannabinoid metabolites stay in the system for several weeks. Walters launched a nationwide initiative to persuade schools to force students to pee in a cup. Nothing sent him into a tizzy quicker than the thought of a socially well-adjusted teenager who smoked pot and got good grades in school. "Marijuana use, especially during the teen years, can lead to depression, suicide and schizophrenia," Walters insisted.

Walters flatly denied that marijuana had any therapeutic uses. He churlishly maintained that feeling better was not a valid measure of a drug's effectiveness. Although federal officials aren't supposed to poke their noses in state elections, Walters made dubious visits to several states in an attempt to influence voters and legislators who were considering a medical-marijuana bill or broader legalization initiatives. By the end of Bush's second term, several more states would jump on the medical-marijuana bandwagon—Maine, Colorado, Hawaii, Montana, Vermont, Rhode Island, New Mexico, and Michigan.

The drug czar, a Catholic, sought to enlist church-based youth projects and other religious programs in the Bush administration's antidrug efforts. Walters directed John DiIulio, head of the White House's faith-based initiative office, to allow religious groups engaged in antidrug activity to receive federal funds. With the blessings of the president, the drug czar launched "Faith—The Anti-

Drug," a multimillion-dollar propaganda campaign designed to encourage the religious community to incorporate marijuana abstinence into their spiritual teachings. "Faith plays a powerful role in preventing youth marijuana use," Walters asserted. "We are urging youth ministers, volunteers and faith leaders to integrate drug prevention messages and activities into their sermons and youth programming, and are providing them with key tools and resources to make a difference."

Walters's faith-based approach appealed to George W. Bush, a practicing Methodist who "accepted Jesus Christ into [his] life" fifteen years before he became president. Only by submitting to God's will could a person be safe from the temptations of illegal drugs, according to Bush, who maintained that recreational pot smokers must undergo a religious conversion to achieve abstinence. Dubya believed that someone with a changed heart would be less likely to relapse into addiction. But the president's views clashed with the teachings of the United Methodist Church (the third-largest denomination in the United States, with eight million members), which recognized the medicinal value of marijuana.

John Walters explicitly referred to the war on drugs as "a conservative cultural revolution." In his view, the antimarijuana insurgency waged by the Office of National Drug Control Policy was part of a larger, high-stakes culture war that had been raging in the United States since the 1960s. That unsettled conflict entered a new phase during Bush's first year in the White House when two commercial jets commandeered by Islamist terrorists crashed into the World Trade Center towers, killing 3,056 people.

The toxic dust had hardly settled upon lower Manhattan when Congress passed the Patriot Act, which gave the U.S. government wide-reaching power to designate anyone a terrorist and to spy on its own citizens with little judicial oversight. Championed by Attorney General Ashcroft, the Patriot Act created the Department of Homeland Security, a cumbersome bureaucracy that included a counternarcotics office. The September 11 attacks would be used to justify the indefinite detention and torture of terrorist suspects, secret military tribunals, covert operations against U.S. peace groups and green activists, and other disreputable government actions. When critics complained about the erosion of the Bill of Rights, President Bush defended the Patriot Act by pointing out that the government was already employing many of the same tactics to combat drug trafficking. By September 11, 2001, America's Constitution had already been shredded by the war on drugs, a process that set the stage for an extended assault on civil liberties under the guise of the war on terror.

Prior to September 11, the Bush administration was so fixated on illicit drugs in general and marijuana in particular that tracking terrorists got short shrift. Four months before the attack on the Twin Towers, Ashcroft misled Congress when he said that the Justice Department had no higher priority than preventing terrorism. Thanks to America's crippling addiction to the war on narcotics, the FBI, the Department of Defense, the DEA, and other federal agencies squandered precious time and resources on ineffective drug enforcement while Osama bin Laden dispatched suicide squads to the United States. A few months after 9/11, the FBI discreetly transferred four hundred agents from antidrug to antiterrorism duties.

John Walters, meanwhile, was eager to hitch an increasingly unpopular drug war on to a very popular war on terror. "If you use drugs, you are standing against the rule of law," Walters warned. "You are standing against freedom. You are standing against those who fight against terrorism." A government-funded antimarijuana advertising campaign, which equated using drugs with aiding terrorists, debuted on Super Bowl Sunday 2002. Puffing pot put cash directly into Al Qaeda's pocket—that was the upshot of the TV commercials that bombarded America in the aftermath of 9/11. The drug war was all the more necessary because of terrorism, according to Walters, who would never acknowledge that the drug trade was highly profitable—and therefore a potential source of revenue for terrorists—because of the illegality of controlled substances, not because of the drugs themselves.

Conventional wisdom among pundits held that September 11 "changed everything," but some things hardly changed at all. The U.S. military continued to invade other countries based on trumped-up allegations just like it did before 9/11. The CIA continued to ally itself with unsavory elements involved in opiate trafficking. And federal officials continued to ignore or manipulate scientific data in order to "make marijuana seem more dangerous than it is," according to Matthew Robinson, a criminal-justice professor at Appalachian State University, who analyzed the history of claims made by the Office of National Drug Control Policy. "What they say simply doesn't match reality," Robinson concluded. "They claim it's a gateway drug . . . but the vast majority of marijuana users don't go on to use harder drugs."

Suppressing science to suit prohibitionist drug policies was nothing new for U.S. authorities. But the Bush administration escalated the war on science to unprecedented levels. Federal officials mounted systematic attacks on global-warming evidence, stem-cell experiments, reproductive research, and anything that smacked of evolution, a theory pooh-poohed by the president of the United States. A survey by the Union of Concerned Scientists (UCS) found that the Bush administration routinely censored and falsified important environmental and health research. During the Bush years, twelve hundred federally employed scientists reported that they feared retaliation from their superiors because the results of their research threatened corporate or political interests. "When science is falsified, fabricated or censored, Americans' health and safety suffer," said UCS director Francesca Grifo, a former government scientist.

A mass of scientific data validating medical marijuana meant little in terms of federal policy. The Bush administration took advantage of the perfect authoritarian storm brewing in the wake of 9/11 to wage asymmetrical combat against pot clubs, patients, and caregivers in California, despite national polls that showed overwhelming public support for medical marijuana. The DEA hammer came raining down on the Golden State, the principal battleground in the cannabis culture war. The timing of the anti-medical-marijuana offensive—which began less than a month after the 9/11 terrorist attacks—raised eyebrows as well as questions about skewed government priorities.

On September 28, 2001, a convoy of a dozen unmarked SUVs driven by federal agents arrived at the home of Dr. Marian ("Mollie") Fry and her husband, attorney Dale Shafer, in rural El Dorado County in California's Eastern District. The narcs emerged from the vehicles with guns drawn. "They threw me down on the ground, on my face," Fry recounted. "They handcuffed me and left me lying in the dirt for twenty minutes while they secured the house." They found thirty pot plants and some loose cannabis, which federal marshals seized as evidence. They took the children's computers. They took (and never returned) Fry's wedding ring and the crucifix that she wore around her neck. And they also seized the confidential medical records of more than six thousand patients that Fry, a practicing physician, had stored at home for safekeeping.

At the time of the raid, Fry was one of a handful of California doctors who specialized in cannabis therapeutics. She learned firsthand of marijuana's medicinal attributes after she was diagnosed with breast cancer in 1997. Fry underwent a double mastectomy and used marijuana to cope with the wrenching side effects of chemotherapy. She refused to wear prosthetics. Marijuana helped her adjust psychologically to her new life. When Mollie heard that many doctors were reluctant to recommend cannabis, she felt it was her duty to assist people who could benefit from the herb.

In 1999, Fry and Shafer created the California Medical Research Center in the Sierra foothill town of Cool. They advertised themselves as an attorney-physician team that provided professional guidance to those who were eligible for medical marijuana under Proposition 215. They offered clones and starter kits so that qualified patients could save money by growing their own cannabis. "The whole idea was to get our patients away from the black market, and away from the police," Shafer explained. Fees were discounted or waived for poor people living on social security or welfare.

On two occasions, Shafer invited local law-enforcement personnel to visit their home and examine their modest marijuana garden. Shafer maintains that he and Fry were misled by El Dorado County officials, who assured the couple that their business was in compliance with state law—while the same officials were secretly conspiring with U.S. authorities to enforce federal law. Unable to discuss the Compassionate Use Act in a federal courtroom, Fry and Shafer were found guilty of manufacturing and distributing marijuana. After losing their appeal, both were sentenced to sixty months in federal prison. Ironically, an inscription carved near the entrance of the federal courthouse in Sacramento, where they turned themselves in, read: "There are not enough jails, not enough policemen, not enough courts to enforce a law not supported by the people."

On the same day the feds busted Mollie Fry and her husband, another DEA strike force confiscated more than two hundred plants from a medicinal pot farm in Ventura County. Veteran hemp activists Judy and Lynn Osburn had been cultivating marijuana for the Los Angeles Cannabis Research Center, a squeaky-clean dispensary founded by Scott Imler shortly after Proposition 215 became state law. Based in West Hollywood, Imler's club established excellent relations with city officials. But his aboveboard, by-the-book approach failed to placate Uncle Sam. DEA agents raided Imler's dispensary four weeks after the feds uprooted the Osburns' pot crop. The narcs seized more than $300,000 that the city of West Hollywood had loaned to the center to purchase a building.

These DEA operations signaled a major escalation in the federal war on medical marijuana. Nearly three dozen public dispensaries were operating in California when Bush took office. Any of them could be next on the hit list. The narcs were "running wild in the laboratories of democracy," as Jacob Sullum put it, "smashing experiments in reform and injuring innocent bystanders." But the DEA may have overreached when it raided the Wo/Men's Alliance for Medical Marijuana (WAMM), a Santa Cruz cannabis hospice service run by Valerie and Mike Corral.

WAMM was born out of Valerie's efforts to alleviate her frequent grand mal epileptic seizures and excruciating migraines, which began when she suffered head trauma and other serious injuries in a car accident in 1973. Valerie, then twenty, was one of the 25 percent of epileptics whose condition did not improve when treated with Big Pharma medications. Anticonvulsant drugs with dangerous side effects left her in a perpetual stupor. "It was like living underwater," Valerie explained. She turned to marijuana after her husband read an article in a medical journal in which researchers reported that cannabis successfully controlled seizures in laboratory animals. Valerie found that if she smoked pot as soon as she felt a seizure coming on, she could avoid convulsions or mitigate their intensity. By maintaining a steady level of marijuana in her system, she got a new lease on life. A few puffs a day kept the seizures away. She stopped taking noxious pharmaceuticals and her health improved dramatically.*

Valerie and Mike grew a half dozen pot plants in their rustic garden every summer to ensure that they had sufficient herb for their needs. When cops busted the couple in 1992, Valerie Leveroni Corral, hailing from an Italian family of radical pacifists, became the first person in California to successfully challenge the marijuana laws in state court by pleading medical necessity. Charges against the Corrals were dropped by the Santa Cruz County district attorney's office, which concluded that it would be impossible to win a conviction before a sympathetic local jury. The DA told the Santa Cruz police to leave them alone. Their case generated a lot of publicity. Inundated with inquires, Valerie and Mike Corral began to provide organic cannabis free of charge to seriously ill individuals.

The Corrals helped draft Proposition 215, and shortly after it passed they

---

* In 1997, the U.S. National Institutes of Health held a workshop on medical marijuana and concluded that cannabinoid compounds held promise in the treatment of epilepsy, a nervous disorder that affects about 1 percent of the population. A subsequent study in the *Journal of Pharmacology and Experimental Therapeutics* (2003) noted that the administration of THC completely abolished spontaneous seizures in an animal model of epilepsy. Dr. William B. O'Shaughnessy reported on the anticonvulsive properties of cannabis in 1842. And the Shafer Commission, appointed by President Nixon, cited a 1949 study on the effect of THC on epileptic children. All the children had severe symptomatic grand mal epilepsy with mental retardation. The results after treatment with THC homologues were reported as follows: "Three children responded at least as well as to previous therapy. Fourth child—almost completely seizure free. Fifth child—entirely seizure free." The authors of this study recommended that cannabinoids be explored further as a treatment for epilepsy. Dr. Van Sim, chief of clinical research at Edgewood Arsenal in the 1950s and early 1960s, also noted the anticonvulsant effects of small doses of cannabinoids. Virginia Commonwealth University scientists discerned a link between the dysregulation of the endocannabinoid system and the development of epilepsy (K. W. Falenski et al., "Temporal Characterization of Changes in Hippocampal Cannabinoid CB(1) Receptor Expression Following Pilocarpine-Induced Status Epilepticus," *Brain Research* 1262[2009]: 64–72). Researchers at the University of Rome in Italy observed low levels of the endocannabinoid anandamide in the cerebrospinal fluid in patients with untreated newly diagnosed temporal lobe epilepsy (A. Romigi et al., *Epilepsia*, October 8, 2009). According to studies at Radboud University in Nijmegen, Netherlands, the endocannabinoid system protects against seizures (C. M. van Rijn et al., "Endocannabinoid System Protects Against Cryptogenic Seizures," *Pharmacology Reports* 63[1][2011]: 165–68).

incorporated WAMM as a nonprofit and received state approval for their charitable endeavors. Founded with the explicit intention of catering to the needs of low-income and unemployed people, WAMM was a unique club, an agrarian health collective that specialized in cannabis therapeutics. One had to literally be dying to get into WAMM. Eighty-five percent of its members were terminally ill. The cemetery on the Corrals' 106-acre plot was the final resting place for the ashes of many WAMM members.

Described as "socialists in the woods," they were like an extended family—several hundred ailing Americans engaged in therapeutic horticulture, sharing the joys of tending an outdoor garden (if they were physically able). Every WAMM member contributed in some way to preparing their own medicine—watering plants, trimming leaves and stems, baking marijuana muffins, making hashish, ghee capsules, cannabis rubbing oil, and ointments. The buds were reserved for smoking; every other part of the plant was utilized in a variety of nonsmokable forms. "We come together around the marijuana, but it's not just the marijuana. It's the community," Valerie emphasized.

The Corrals felt that the psychoactive properties of cannabis were germane to the healing process. "Of all the things that marijuana does," said Valerie, "the most important is that it shifts your consciousness. It might relieve some pain, or awaken your appetite. It may slow down your neuropathy tingling sensations and let you walk more normally, instead of with drunken legs that won't behave. But the way that it works most remarkably is that it allows people to think differently about their illnesses and their symptoms. It really opens a possibility of looking at the illness in a different way. And, personally, I think that is one of the most profound and important effects that it has."

WAMM was a political nightmare for U.S. drug-war authorities. For several years, it functioned openly as a successful experiment in community health care despite federal marijuana prohibition. The Corrals were giving away cannabis to people who used it strictly for medical purposes. Unlike other cannabis clubs that were raided by the DEA, WAMM was not involved in commercial sales. But this fact was irrelevant to the narcs who invaded WAMM's collective farm on the morning of September 5, 2002. Suzanne Pfiel, a paraplegic WAMM board member and postpolio patient who needed an assisted breathing device, was sleeping at the Corrals' home when two dozen DEA agents barged in screaming and waving their semiautomatic weapons. Paralyzed from the waist down, Pfiel was awakened at gunpoint and handcuffed to her bed while men in paramilitary gear tore apart the living quarters. They chain-sawed 167 pot plants growing in the garden and arrested the Corrals.

But the narcs were in for a rude surprise when they tried to leave the premises. As word spread that a raid was in progress, more than a hundred outraged WAMM members and supporters, some in wheelchairs, gathered at the edge of the property and blocked the only road that led back to town. The DEA agents were trapped behind the makeshift barricade, while TV crews covered the confrontation. "Shame on you!" the protestors shouted at the ganja gestapo. Some held signs that said WARNING: FEDERAL CRIME IN PROGRESS and MARIJUANA IS MEDICINE. The standoff continued for three hours until the Corrals were released from police custody. They were never charged with a crime.

The widely publicized WAMM raid was a PR fiasco for the feds. On September 17, U.S. Constitution Day, Santa Cruz officials rallied behind the med-pot collective as the Corrals defiantly distributed marijuana to WAMM members on the steps of City Hall. "Everybody knows this group isn't about recreational drug use," said Mayor Emily Reilly, who attended the cannabis handout along with 1,300 demonstrators. Elvy Musikka, one of six surviving federal pot patients, addressed the crowd and expressed her solidarity with WAMM. It was an ironic moment, to be sure: Musikka held up a canister of marijuana cigarettes that she had recently received from the U.S. government as she spoke to a crowd of desperately ill patients whose marijuana had just been taken away by the U.S. government.

Attorney General Ashcroft and drug czar Walters understood that if American society embraced medical marijuana it could set the stage for a radically different kind of discussion regarding drug prohibition. Consequently, Dubya's drug warriors lashed out against America's most vulnerable citizens. The WAMM raid marked the twenty-second time since September 11, 2001, that federal officials had taken action against California patients, growers, and medicinal cannabis facilities, according to California NORML.

"The dinosaur is thrashing its tail. It's dying," said Valerie Corral. She and several WAMM members sued Ashcroft, Walters, and the acting head of the DEA for violating their constitutional rights. Unfazed by the federal government's heavy handed tactics, the Corrals replanted their pot garden the next spring and every spring thereafter. And they never stopped providing cannabis to the sick and needy.

Show Trials

On the evening of February 12, 2002, Asa Hutchinson, director of the DEA, stood behind the podium with his hands on his hips and gave a speech at the prestigious Commonwealth Club in San Francisco. The former congressman from Arkansas, who had played a leading role in the GOP's drive to impeach President Clinton, knew he was facing a hostile crowd.

"Maybe it is not such a bang-up idea to defend our nation's drug policy in the city of San Francisco, which has such an extraordinary tradition of toleration for drug use," Hutchinson ventured. "From the popularity of the opium dens of the late nineteenth century, to the drug culture thriving in the Haight-Ashbury district of the Sixties, to the Cannabis Buyers' Club of the New Century, San Francisco has been a hot spot for challenging current thinking on drug laws."

Cheers emanated from the audience.

"What science has told us thus far is that there is no medical benefit from smoking marijuana," said Hutchinson. "It is not recommended for the treatment of any disease."

"Liar!" someone shouted as boos ricocheted throughout the auditorium.

Undeterred, Hutchinson called for continued vigilance in the war on drugs. He claimed that more Americans entered substance-abuse treatment for cannabis than for any other drug. "Adolescent admissions to substance-abuse facilities for marijuana grew from 43 percent of all adolescent admissions in 1994 to 60 percent in 1999," said Hutchinson, who neglected to cite a pertinent fact. Few of those who enrolled in drug treatment for "marijuana abuse" were there of their own free will. In most cases, their "treatment" had been mandated by employers, schools, or judges.

While Hutchinson reiterated the prohibitionist party line, hundreds of medical-marijuana supporters outside the building banged drums and chanted, "DEA—Go away!" Among the demonstrators were several city council members and District Attorney Terence Hallinan, who exhorted the protestors through a bullhorn. "This city has been declared a sanctuary," Hallinan declared. "I call on the DEA to respect the wishes of the people of California and stay out of the marijuana clubs in San Francisco!"

On the same day, as if in honor of the DEA director's visit, federal narcotics agents dynamited the front door of the Sixth Street Harm Reduction Center in San Francisco's Mission District. The city-authorized Harm Reduction Center had been serving two hundred medical-marijuana patients daily without any complaints. That was irrelevant to the DEA agents who seized more than six hundred cannabis starter plants and arrested four people associated with the club. The feds simultaneously raided the private homes of several Bay Area medical-marijuana activists, including author-publisher Ed Rosenthal, known for his print and online gardening-advice column. "Ask Ed" Rosenthal grew clones and plants at a West Oakland warehouse, which was also raided during the early-morning dragnet on February 12.

"I was a trophy arrest. They were going to make an example out of me," Rosenthal asserted after the raid, adding: "The government antidrug policy is a big lie supported by a thousand other lies. My crime is that I'm willing to challenge those lies."

Rosenthal's arrest sent shock waves through California's medical-marijuana scene. The next day, the Cannabis Action Network called an emergency meeting to discuss the implications of the latest federal assault and what to do to help their friend Ed. "When those raids happened," recalled CAN member Don Duncan, "it was a wake-up call to how fragile our movement was."

Duncan and his comrades were upset by the paltry coverage the raids received in the local press. They decided to mount a media campaign on behalf of Rosenthal and others who had been busted by the feds. Americans for Safe Access (ASA), a group cofounded by Duncan and CAN activist Steph Sherer, would spearhead this effort. Sherer, aged twenty-six, became a convert to the med-pot cause after she was clubbed and badly injured by police while protesting against the World Trade Organization in Washington, D.C., in the spring of 2000. The meds her doctor prescribed for chronic pain were causing kidney failure, so Sherer tried marijuana. She found that the herb worked better as a painkiller than federally sanctioned pharmaceuticals—and cannabis didn't damage her internal organs. With Sherer and Duncan leading the charge, ASA would play a key role in the ensuing courtroom drama that pitted Ed Rosenthal against Uncle Sam.

Medical-marijuana patients and hemp activists crammed the visitors' gallery during the five-day trial. The stakes were high for Rosenthal—he faced a maximum of life in prison if convicted—and for the medical-marijuana movement as a whole. If the prosecution prevailed in this case, it would embolden federal authorities to intensify their attacks on cannabis dispensaries, growers, caregivers, and patients in California.

The trial of Ed Rosenthal was nothing short of Kafkaesque. Rosenthal had been deputized by the city of Oakland to grow medical marijuana for certified patients. Beholden to federal rules, Judge Charles Breyer (the brother of U.S. Supreme Court Justice Stephen Breyer) barred Rosenthal's attorneys from calling witnesses who could attest to his status as an officially authorized horticulturist who was carrying out city policy. Breyer deigned that only federal officials, not city officials, could grant immunity from federal law. And because pot cultivation was illegal under federal law, Rosenthal's motivation for growing cannabis was irrelevant in U.S. District Court. Thus the defendant wasn't allowed to utter a word about medical marijuana throughout the proceedings. Rosenthal, aged fifty-nine, found himself starring in a show trial, a kangaroo court where only one side's arguments would be heard. The prosecution pegged him as a felonious drug dealer, and the jury, not surprisingly, found him guilty as charged.

What happened next, however, surprised everyone. ASA buttonholed the jurors as they were leaving the courthouse. When they learned that Rosenthal was involved in a medical grow operation with city approval, five outraged jurors publicly renounced their own verdict and urged a retrial. “I’ve been devastated that I wasn’t given the whole truth,” said the jury foreman, Charles Sackett, who felt used and railroaded by the feds. “It’s totally appalling that they can bend and twist things. They expected me to play fair as a juror, but they weren’t playing fair with us.”

The unprecedented jurors’ revolt got extensive media play and sparked a national conversation about medical marijuana and federal policy. Rosenthal—the acerbic Yippie who once dressed as Uncle Sam and got arrested at a D.C. July 4 smoke-in—appeared on the pages of *The New York Times* wearing a white clinician’s coat, even though he wasn’t a doctor. No doubt he was stoned when the picture was taken. Since the federal government refused to distinguish between medical and recreational marijuana use, neither would Rosenthal. “All marijuana should be legal,” he insisted.

The courtroom was a mob scene on the day of Rosenthal’s sentencing. Spectators erupted in cheers when Judge Breyer imposed a punishment of one day in jail, time already served. The lenient sentence was, needless to say, a radical departure from federal guidelines. Med-pot advocates claimed victory. But the federal government—in cahoots with state and local law enforcement—would continue to target medical-marijuana proponents who lacked Rosenthal’s celebrity and resources. And a multitude of cannabis convicts would languish in prison for much longer than a single day.

Americans for Safe Access shifted into high gear after the Rosenthal trial. With backing from dispensary operators, ASA emerged as the preeminent watchdog and support group for the emerging medical-marijuana industry. ASA activists kept a close eye on law enforcement and maintained a database of legal cases involving medical-marijuana users. As the Bush administration turned up the heat, ASA rose to the occasion. “We have to protect patients and their access to medical marijuana, so we have to escalate our tactics,” Sherer vowed.

Unlike the Cannabis Action Network, ASA enrolled members. It quickly grew into a nationwide network of more than thirty thousand activists with chapters and affiliates in most states (as well as in Canada and other countries). In anticipation of future raids, ASA developed an emergency response strategy. The word went out to dispensaries: Back up your records off-site so you can reopen immediately if authorities seize your membership lists. ASA emphasized preparedness—chapters were trained to respond at a moment’s notice to DEA raids. ASA members kept placards, blow horns, water bottles, and energy bars in their cars; some carried digital cameras to record police conduct. As soon as a raid was reported, ASA activists appeared on the scene. They alerted reporters, and ASA-trained spokespeople addressed the media while protestors, many sick and lame, shouted their disapproval at the cops.

ASA held demonstrations at federal buildings and DEA offices across the country to decry the harassment of medical-marijuana patients and the U.S. government's obstinate refusal to recognize the therapeutic value of cannabis. "This is a proactive measure to put the federal government on notice," Sherer explained on a national day of protest during Bush's first term. "We have played by the rules, we got laws passed in various states, we worked with state governments, we worked with local law enforcement, we've done everything by the book, and still this campaign of terror against medical-marijuana patients and providers continues. The Bush administration is pushing us to the next level. Bush cannot attack the democratic process like this. We are taking a zero-tolerance stance on federal interference with medical marijuana in the states."

The ASA attorneys Joe Elford and Kris Hermes filed suit against several California cities and counties that banned medical-marijuana facilities. ASA also tutored five hundred public defenders on successful strategies for medical-marijuana cases, and it lobbied local officials to pass sensible laws that regulated dispensaries while protecting patient access. ASA sued the California Highway Patrol, the state's largest law-enforcement agency, forcing a policy change so that CHP officers would no longer confiscate the cannabis of patients in transit. Another precedent-setting ASA suit involved the return of marijuana to a patient after cops seized his medicine at a traffic stop.

Americans for Safe Access joined a coalition of organizations that filed a comprehensive federal rescheduling petition seeking the removal of cannabis from Schedule I classification to allow access for medical use. The 2002 petition was researched and written by scholar-activist Jon Gettman, a senior fellow at the George Mason School of Public Policy. Gettman's brief stint as executive director of NORML in the late 1980s coincided with DEA administrative law judge Francis Young's ringing endorsement of an earlier rescheduling petition—which was brusquely overruled by DEA higher-ups. Gettman maintained that drug scheduling is supposed to be based on scientific analysis of safety and efficacy, not DEA policy or preference. He noted in the new petition that there had been a number of key scientific advances since the last time rescheduling was rejected by the feds. The discovery of the endocannabinoid receptor system shed significant light on how marijuana worked as a medical therapy—a subject addressed in the 1999 Institute of Medicine report, which recognized cannabis as a herbal medicine of last resort and recommended the development of cannabis-based pharmaceuticals. Gettman also noted that hundreds of thousands of Americans were using cannabis as a medicine under state law, making its designation as a Schedule I substance a flagrant absurdity. And so it remained.

Gettman did extensive research into the economics of cannabis. Over twenty-five years beginning in 1981, domestic marijuana production increased tenfold. By 2002, as much as 10,000 metric tons of homegrown marijuana was cultivated annually, according to a U.S. State Department estimate. Gettman extrapolated and crunched the numbers. Despite ongoing government eradication campaigns, marijuana ranked as America's top cash crop throughout the Bush years. In 2006, homegrown cannabis was worth $35.8 billion, exceeding the combined market value of corn ($23.3 billion) and wheat ($7.45 billion), according to a widely quoted Gettman report. He found that five states produced more than $1 billion worth of marijuana apiece. The street value of California's twenty million pot plants topped $14 billion in 2006, accounting for more than a third of the entire U.S. yield.

Gettman also analyzed arrest statistics on a state-by-state basis. Annual marijuana arrests had nearly tripled nationwide since the early 1990s, surpassing three quarters of a million in 2005. An inordinate concentration of pot busts (38 percent of the national total) occurred in only ten counties, Gettman noted. Five of the top ten least-reefer-friendly counties in America were in Texas, while Pennsylvania had the nation's lowest percentage of pot arrests per capita, followed by North Dakota and Hawaii.

New York City was far and away the pot-arrest capital of America. From 1992 to 2002, the Big Apple experienced an 882 percent growth in marijuana arrests. A ganja smoker in Gotham was nine times more likely to be busted than a pot smoker in Nassau County, a suburb of NYC. Prior to the election of Mayor Rudolph Giuliani in 1994, the New York City Police Department pursued a low-key approach toward marijuana; petty pot busts weren't a priority and typically resulted in a ticket. Giuliani inaugurated an era of aggressive policing, characterized by warrantless stop-and-frisk searches of black and Latino youth, who, if they had any marijuana on them, would be arrested on a "public nuisance" charge.

Did busting pot smokers reduce violent crime in New York? No, according to University of Chicago Law School professors Bernard Harcourt and Jens Ludwig, who analyzed NYPD crime stats. "New York City's policing strategy is having exactly the wrong effect on serious crime—increasing it, rather than decreasing it," they concluded. Marijuana arrests went through the roof and clogged the courts while police units that could have been focusing on more important matters squandered time and public resources on pot prohibition.

The surge of pot arrests in New York City and the racist enforcement patterns that characterized the Giuliani years continued under Mayor Michael Bloomberg. Low-level pot possession became the number one cause of arrest in New York City. Yet Bloomberg acknowledged his own use of pot in the past, and when a reporter asked Bloomberg if he had liked it, the billionaire media-mogul-turned-pol responded, "You bet I did!"

Marijuana may have helped some Manhattan residents cope with the trauma of September 11. Data from the NYC Department of Health, which tracked the health effects of 9/11, indicated that as many as 70,000 New Yorkers may have developed PTSD as a result of the terrorist attacks. At least seven underground cannabis buyers' clubs were operating discreetly in the Big Apple when the Twin Towers toppled. One club, the Patients' Cooperative, run by Kenneth Toglia, had registered more than a thousand members and regularly provided pot to people with AIDS, glaucoma, MS, and, increasingly after 9/11, PTSD.

Pot arrests were sky-high in New York City, but California remained ground zero in the federal war on weed. The Bush administration pursued cannabis-related cases with a zealotry that mystified folks on both sides of the Atlantic. On February 24, 2003, the DEA launched Operation Pipe Dreams, a nationwide crackdown on pot paraphernalia—water pipes, bongs, vaporizers, and the like. Twelve hundred federal agents (from the DEA, Secret Service, U.S. Marshals Service, Customs, and the U.S. Postal Inspection) raided more than one hundred homes and businesses around the country that day. Fifty-five people were arrested during the sting operation. But only one person would go to jail for Pipe Dreams—Tommy Chong.

Erstwhile of Cheech and Chong, the Canadian-born comedian was woken up at 5:30 a.m. by the sound of helicopters hovering over his Los Angeles home. A SWAT team with automatic weapons kicked in the front door and arrested him at gunpoint. Chong was the owner of Nice Dreams, a family glass-blowing business that made bongs and advertised in *High Times*. Chong had no criminal record, but his reputation as a stoner comic and his success as a writer, director, and actor riled U.S. law enforcement. During the trial of Tommy Chong, federal prosecutor Mary McKeen Houghton actually cited his fictional character as proof of his frivolous attitude toward the law. "The defendant has become wealthy throughout his entertainment career by glamorizing the illegal distribution and use of marijuana," Houghton asserted. She admonished Chong for making light of "law-enforcement efforts to combat marijuana trafficking and use." Chong said that busting him was "like jailing all of the *Police Academy* people for making fun of cops."

Chong copped a plea when the feds threatened to press drug paraphernalia distribution charges against his wife and son. On September 11, 2003, the second anniversary of the Twin Towers terrorist attack, he was sentenced to nine months in federal prison. Chong had to forfeit $120,000 in business assets and pay a $20,000 fine and six-figure attorney fees. "I went to jail for my beliefs," an unchastened Chong declared after serving time. "I was a political prisoner, so I see it as a badge of honor."

Chong later reunited with Cheech for their first tour in twenty-five years. They called their act "Light Up America"—though "lighten up America" would have been an appropriate message for the drug-war die-hards that called the shots in D.C. Chong's bizarro encounter with federal law enforcement fired his enthusiasm as a cannabis activist. He became a sought-after speaker at drug-policy-reform gatherings and headlined a fund-raiser for Ed Rosenthal, who was facing another go-round in U.S. district court.

The Feds v. Rosenthal 2.0 brought to mind Karl Marx's famous adage about history repeating itself—"first as a tragedy, second as a farce." Both sides took issue with the initial verdict and got their wish for a new trial. After an appeals court overturned Rosenthal's pot-growing conviction on a technicality, he was reindicted by federal prosecutors. Only this time they tacked on nine additional criminal charges. Judge Charles Breyer threw out the new charges, issuing a rare finding that the U.S. attorney's office was engaged in a "vindictive prosecution."

The brightly bow-tied Breyer strongly urged the prosecutors to drop the entire case. The feds persisted anyway, knowing that they would not be able to seek additional punishment beyond the original one-day sentence. The retrial was utterly pointless, a farce that underscored the idiocy of the U.S. government's crusade against cannabis. Rosenthal showed up in court dressed in a blue wizard cape emblazoned with a large gold marijuana leaf. Judge Breyer once again wouldn't let the jury hear that Rosenthal was growing medicinal plants for the City of Oakland. And once again Rosenthal was convicted. The only drama during the proceedings came when Debby Goldsberry and several other cannabis activists defied a court order and refused to testify against Rosenthal. Judge Breyer, weary of the spectacle, opted not to issue contempt citations.

Physicians in the Crosshairs

Dr. Tod Mikuriya observed the coarse, puffy complexion and overweight bearing of the man who complained of a sore shoulder, stress, and poor sleep. During the twenty-minute examination in January 2003, Mikuriya deduced that his patient had a problem with alcohol and urged him to stop drinking and get more exercise. The Berkeley-based psychiatrist provided a letter recommending the use of cannabis to ease his ailments. At the time, Mikuriya was not aware that the person in his office was actually an undercover narcotics agent named Steve Gossett, who lied about his symptoms in order to bust California's foremost authority on medical marijuana.

Mikuriya had had a bull's-eye on him ever since he helped draft the Compassionate Use Act. It was Mikuriya who insisted on including the most critical phrase, which asserted that a doctor has a right to recommend cannabis for "any . . . illness for which marijuana provides relief." Dr. Tod was sixty-two when California voters legalized medical marijuana. He had already amassed considerable experience studying the effects of marijuana professionally—as a drug-abuse-treatment program director at Princeton, as a research psychiatrist for the NIMH, as a traveler to indigenous cannabis communities in Morocco and Nepal, and as a clinician who examined and counseled thousands of Bay Area cannabis club members.

Initially, Mikuriya was almost alone as a physician willing to recommend marijuana. Accompanied by his assistant John Trapp, Mikuriya traveled to various cities and towns to preside at ad hoc clinics for Californians who couldn't make the journey to the Bay Area. "Tod's patients were mostly poor uninsured folks who couldn't afford to pay spiraling health-care costs," according to Trapp.

Mikuriya churned out medical-marijuana recommendations—often more than twenty a day. He treated people with a wide range of ailments, including many for chronic pain. He was not averse to recommending cannabis for stress or depression. Nor did he try to hide the fact that he smoked pot, usually in the morning with his coffee. "Medical cannabis is legal here, for God's sake," Mikuriya said with a shrug. Given the latest science and his own experience as a clinician, Dr. Tod opposed the notion of restricting the use of cannabis to a short list of permissible conditions—the norm in other states with legal medical marijuana. Mikuriya rejected the short-list strategy as an unnecessary political compromise that excluded many people who could benefit from cannabis.

Mikuriya felt a sense of urgency in the aftermath of 215. "We expected that the feds and the state would marshal their forces and try to shut down the movement," said Trapp, his office manager. "We expected the DEA to smash through our doors any day." Mikuriya sought to authorize "as many patients as fast as possible so that more people would be invested in the new law and more people would be willing to fight to keep it when the anticipated crackdown came," Trapp explained.

To the cops, Mikuriya was a public nuisance, a quack who endorsed pot for nearly everything under the sun. To thousands of patients, he was an angel of mercy, a physician of last resort who risked a great deal for those in need. It was immensely satisfying to Mikuriya as a psychiatrist "to be able to remove the stigma of criminality from an individual," he explained after testifying in court for an alcoholic Vietnam vet who'd been busted for pot. "The litmus test for a real doctor," said Mikuriya, "is whether you're willing to go out on a limb for your patients. There's always a price to be paid when you follow science instead of fashion, especially when some results differ from the official line. But you can live with yourself and sleep well at night."

After 215 passed, the state attorney general's office ordered all California police departments and narcotics units to contact Sacramento whenever there was a bust involving a patient with a recommendation from Mikuriya and a handful of other physicians who had the *cojones* to recommend cannabis early and often drew intense scrutiny from the California Medical Board, a regulatory agency with an investigative branch made up entirely of career law-enforcement officers. The Medical Board had the power to revoke or suspend a doctor's license.

Of California's 300,000 doctors, only an estimated 1,500—mostly oncologists and AIDS specialists—authorized medical marijuana for at least one patient during the five and a half years that the ACLU's class action suit on behalf of all physicians (*Conant v. McCaffrey*) played out in federal court. The vast majority of recommendations during this period came from about fifteen MDs, who were dismissively dubbed "pot docs" in press accounts. Many "not-pot docs" decided it just wasn't worth the risk to certify patients for cannabis.

Mikuriya had foreseen that government pressure on the medical community would result in widespread reluctance on the part of physicians to recommend marijuana. He predicted, accurately, that this would give rise to a new professional niche—the cannabis consultant. Dr. Tod mentored a small circle of cannabis specialists who were willing to risk the wrath of officialdom. In 2000, they coalesced into the California Cannabis Research Medical Group (later called the Society of Cannabis Clinicians). They pooled research data, authored reports, and strategized about how to deal with the federal and state authorities that were breathing down their necks. Mikuriya and his acolytes were the lifeblood of California's fragile medical-marijuana scene. Had these conscientious physicians capitulated in the face of police pressure, the medical-marijuana movement might not have survived.

When Mikuriya attended medical school, his Temple University professors didn't teach him anything about undercover cops posing as patients and feigning illness in order to entrap physicians. Dr. Tod learned the hard way. "Never before had a fake witness infiltrated my practice and created a fraudulent medical record. It's most upsetting," Mikuriya asserted at a legal hearing instigated by the California Medical Board, which accused him of negligence, incompetence, and furnishing dangerous drugs without adequate prior examination in recommending marijuana to sixteen patients. The case contrived by undercover cop Steve Gossett brought the number of complaints against Mikuriya to seventeen. All the complaints against him were filed by disgruntled local DAs and narcs who lost cultivation cases involving medical-marijuana patients with a recommendation from Mikuriya. None of Dr. Tod's legitimate patients ever filed a complaint about him or said they suffered from his medical advice.

And so it began: another Kafkaesque episode in American jurisprudence. The first prosecution witness called during Dr. Mikuriya's six-day disciplinary hearing in September 2003 was none other than Deputy Sheriff Gossett, who headed the Sonoma County narcotics task force. Cross-deputized Detective Gossett also served as senior investigator for the federally funded CAMP eradication program. At the annual California Department of Justice CAMP conference in 2002, Gossett received an outstanding-service award for exceeding the scope of his duties. When duty called, this gung-ho narc was ready.

Gossett testified that he visited Mikuriya at a medical office in Oakland and obtained a letter of recommendation by making up a story. "I lied on a lot of issues," Gossett stated under oath, "and I told the truth on a lot of issues . . . It's hard to remember lies."

It was a textbook case of entrapment—a dubious tactic often used by the DEA and police departments in street drug busts. Prior to the Nixon presidency, it wasn't legal for an undercover cop to induce someone to commit a crime. But that changed thanks to a 1974 U.S. Supreme Court decision that condoned entrapment by law-enforcement personnel. What exactly did Gossett prove when he secured a medical-marijuana recommendation from Mikuriya under false pretenses? That a physician could be lied to. And that lying and entrapment were critical components of the government's increasingly desperate campaign against medical marijuana.

The only other witness for the prosecution was Laura Duskin, a San Francisco psychiatrist who had never issued a medical-marijuana recommendation. While marijuana might help ease a patient's symptoms, Duskin maintained, "it can actually be very dangerous to recommend a palliative treatment without treating the underlying problem." She obviously knew zilch about the endocannabinoid system. Given that the Medical Board hired her as an expert witness to study seventeen cases of suspect record-keeping and questionable medical exams, it was odd that Duskin chose not to speak with any of Mikuriya's patients. Yet Duskin told the court that she found "an extreme departure from the standard of care" whenever Mikuriya issued a medical-marijuana recommendation stating that a patient was under his "supervision and care."

That's not how Mikuriya's patients saw it. Nine patients, whose cases were under scrutiny, testified on Dr. Tod's behalf. They all agreed that he had carefully reviewed their medical histories and dispensed caring advice during his fifteen-to-twenty-minute examinations. All were self-medicating with cannabis when they saw Dr. Tod. Many were visibly ill and brought records from other doctors confirming their ailments. When cross-examined about Mikuriya's billing practices, one patient, a grizzled chap in his sixties, testified that he had paid $120 for an initial consultation and that three follow-up visits were free. "What are you doing to this guy, anyway?" the witness asked. "He helped me! And you're trying to screw him!!! Even my regular doctor at Kaiser told me to smoke as much pot as I wanted—off the record. He wouldn't give me a letter because he didn't have enough guts."

When he testified in his own defense, Mikuriya acknowledged that as a psychiatrist he frequently didn't take his patients' vital signs, but that he carefully observed their physical demeanor, asked them to fill out a detailed research questionnaire, and relied heavily on their self-reported symptoms. Dr. Tod considered himself a medical consultant; he never pretended to be a primary care physician. He kept records on every patient, but some of his paperwork may have been lax in part because he was so convinced of the benignity of cannabis. "My job is simply to ascertain whether, when presented with a set of symptoms, cannabis would or could help. Nothing more," Mikuriya asserted.

Although the California Medical Board failed to show that a single person was harmed in any way by Mikuriya's practice, Judge Jonathan Lew concluded that the defendant had committed "gross acts of negligence" for failing to properly examine his patients before recommending marijuana. Mikuriya and his supporters later learned that the judge served on the advisory board of Powerhouse Ministries, a right-wing Christian group that equated marijuana "addiction" with slavery. Lew sentenced Mikuriya to five years of medical practice probation and fined him $75,000 to cover the prosecution's legal costs—a hefty sum that underscored the major effort the Medical Board had devoted to dredging up charges against California's top pot doc.*

* The legal lynching of Mikuriya occurred at a time when CIA doctors and other American medical personnel were secretly using "enhanced interrogation techniques"—a euphemism for torture—on detainees in U.S.-occupied Iraq. The infamous "torture memos" by Bush administration lawyers sought to justify waterboarding and other acts of psychological and physical cruelty as a necessary part of the war on terror. Some U.S. military leaders begged

On October 14, 2003, the U.S. Supreme Court let stand a Ninth Circuit appeals court decision blocking federal efforts to yank the prescription-writing licenses of physicians who recommend cannabis to their patients. By not ruling on the case, the Supremes, in essence, reaffirmed that medical practice should be regulated by the states, not by D.C. politicians. The doctors had prevailed—with the caveat that they could not disclose to a patient how or where to obtain marijuana. The high court sent a strong signal that Uncle Sam had gone too far by threatening doctors and trying to intercede in the examination room. But many physicians, still fearful and poorly educated about marijuana, would continue to shun cannabis therapeutics. The toxic seed of self-censorship had taken root within the medical community.

With the feds handcuffed by the *Conant* decision, state law enforcement took the lead in going after several cannabis-recommending clinicians. Dr. Frank Lucido, a Berkeley-based family physician who devoted about a third of his practice to working with medical-marijuana patients, was investigated for a case involving a teenager with severe hyperactivity disorder. The troubled teen did not respond well to a raft of pharmaceuticals, including Ritalin and Prozac. The mere fact that Lucido had recommended marijuana for a minor raised hackles at the Medical Board. Board sleuths eventually dropped the matter when they learned that the youngster in question had benefited from cannabis edibles. His behavior at home and in school showed marked improvement along with his grades and his social relations.

As far as Lucido was concerned, the official probe of his practice was another example of the law-enforcement tail wagging the Medical Board dog. He launched MedBoardWatch.com and began to monitor cases of doctors who were under investigation for having recommended cannabis. Lucido showed up at Medical Board meetings and hearings, asked pointed questions, and called for an independent audit of the board's activities. He noted that physicians who prescribed sleeping pills for insomniacs were not at risk of being punished for failing to do a hands-on exam. Why the double standard? "Top priority should go to investigating complaints from patients with loved ones who allege harm induced by a practitioner," Lucido argued. "Lowest priority should go to complaints from third parties that don't allege harm to a patient."

---

to differ. Alberto J. Mora, U.S. Navy general counsel (2001–2006), told a congressional hearing that the "policy decision to use so-called harsh interrogation techniques . . . was a mistake of massive proportions." But no doctor would be held accountable by any medical board for "gross acts of negligence" while inflicting torture at the behest of the U.S. government.

David Bearman, a Santa Barbara–area physician, maintained that the Medical Board was on "a witch hunt" against doctors who okayed cannabis. The board subpoenaed the records of one of Bearman's patients—a twenty-one-year-old migraine sufferer—who got busted by a park ranger while camping in the woods. When Bearman refused to turn over the records, the board threatened him with a thousand-dollar-a-day fine. Bearman wouldn't budge even as the tally topped $100,000. He felt an ethical obligation to defend the confidentiality of doctor-patient discourse. The case dragged on for almost three years, until a state appeals court ruled that Bearman's records should never have been subpoenaed to begin with because the California Medical Board "failed to demonstrate sufficient facts to support a finding of good cause to invade the patient's right of privacy." The appellate judge noted in his decision that the Medical Board's case "included *no fact*s [italics in the original] even suggesting Dr. Bearman was negligent or that he indiscriminately recommended marijuana." Said Bearman: "This is a message to the Medical Board staff that they cannot go on fishing expeditions. It's more than a victory for Proposition 215, it's a victory for civil liberties."

Dr. Philip A. Denney had practiced family and occupational medicine for thirty years in California prior to Proposition 215. He never had a problem with law enforcement until he began specializing in medical-marijuana recommendations. An early member of the Society of Cannabis Clinicians, Denney saw patients at offices in Sacramento, Redding, and Orange County. He testified about cannabis therapeutics as a court-certified expert witness throughout the Golden State.

Half of Denney's recommendations were for chronic pain—accident victims, military veterans, seniors with degenerative bone loss and rheumatoid arthritis. "They are your friends and neighbors, they're fixing your tires, working in your banks. They're rich and poor, business owners and blue-collar workers, people of every ethnicity. I've seen a wide range of political viewpoints, liberals and conservatives. I've seen police officers . . . They teach me humility. Hearing their stories is one of the great privileges of being a doctor, and not a day goes by that I don't hear one that moves me deeply."

Dr. Denney was peeved when a whistle-blower sent him a Redding Police Department report indicating that in the fall of 2005 Steve Decker, an undercover Alcohol, Tobacco, and Firearms (ATF) special agent, had visited his office and lied to obtain a recommendation for cannabis. The document indicated that the DEA had also opened a case file on Denney. "I examine patients in good faith and it bothers me to be treated this way . . . It has a very chilling effect, to put it mildly," he confessed. "If I can't trust my patients, it makes it difficult for me to practice medicine ethically."

What was Denney supposed to do? Make his patients take a lie detector test? He dashed off an irate letter to Decker at the Redding ATF branch. Denney said he was "troubled by how much taxpayer money was spent on this operation and how you justify spending any taxpayer money investigating legal cannabis users when methamphetamine abuse is such a scourge in our community. I would hate to think of any law-enforcement officer as cowardly, but infiltrating a physician's office certainly seems less risky than pursuing violent criminals."

The narcs claimed that Denney was not the target of their investigation. Their sole motive, they said, was to use Denney's letter of recommendation to gain entrance to Dixon Herbs, a medical-marijuana dispensary in Redding that was under investigation. In others words, Denney would be an unwitting party to entrapment. The feisty physician unsuccessfully sued the ATF, the DEA, and the Redding Police Department. Denney wasn't after money. Rather, he proactively sought a court injunction to bar cops and spooks from pretending to be patients in a doctor's office. Denney decried the collusion between federal and state law-enforcement agencies that were trying to overturn the will of the voters: "I don't understand how state law enforcement can justify that. They work for the people of California."

And the people of California had spoken when they passed Proposition 215, which declared in no uncertain terms: "[N]otwithstanding any other provision of law, no physician in this state shall be punished, or denied any right or privilege, for having recommended marijuana to a patient for medical purposes."

The Supreme Court Punts

"The DEA has never targeted the sick and dying." That was the standard refrain from Drug Enforcement Administration officials, who insisted that the DEA targeted only "criminals engaged in drug cultivation and trafficking." Medical-marijuana patients supposedly were not on the federal government's law-enforcement radar. But the DEA's public-relations mantra didn't jive with what was happening on the ground in the Golden State.

Diane Monson, aged forty-five, was growing half a dozen marijuana plants outdoors on her rural property in Butte County in August 2002, when several DEA agents turned up at her home. Monson, a bookkeeper for a local landscaping company, explained that she had a doctor's recommendation to use cannabis for chronic pain due to a degenerative spinal disease. She asked the local sheriff's deputies who accompanied the DEA contingent to verify that she was in compliance with state law and Butte County's six-plant limit. They did. But that failed to sway the feds (even though the DEA usually didn't concern itself with small pot plots). As the narcs uprooted and confiscated her medicinal garden, Monson recited aloud the entire text of Proposition 215. "I thought they needed to hear it," she later recounted.

Few people would have heard about Monson's case had it not been for the resolve and determination of Angel McClary Raich, a desperately ill mother of two who suffered from a laundry list of maladies. This rail-thin woman from Oakland had an inoperable brain tumor, scoliosis, endometriosis, a seizure disorder, fibromyalgia, a degenerative joint condition, chronic nausea—"so many diseases I can't remember them all," as Raich put it. She and Monson would join forces and wage an uphill legal battle against the federal government in an effort to defend the use of their last-ditch drug of choice.

Partially paralyzed and confined to a wheelchair, Angel was in constant pain. She had no appetite. The doctors pumped her full of potent pharmaceuticals and heavy narcotics, but nothing helped. She was withering away. In 1997, she attempted suicide. Raich was offended when a nurse suggested she try medical marijuana. The erstwhile conservative Christian believed, as many people do, that marijuana is a bad drug. She had never smoked pot before and she wasn't keen on breaking the law. But she had little to lose at this

In June 2005, the Supreme Court ruled against Angel Raich and denied her the right to use marijuana as a medicine

(Courtesy of J. Scott Applewhite/Associated Press)

point, so she tried the herb and it did wonders for her. The pain ebbed. She could eat. She could move. She started smoking every couple of hours and eating cannabis-laced food, and in due course her strength returned. "There are no other treatments I can reasonably recommend for Angel," her physician, Dr. Frank Lucido, subsequently wrote in a legal deposition. "It could very well be fatal for Angel to forgo cannabis treatments."

Eighteen months after she started to medicate with cannabis, Raich was walking without assistance and advocating for patients' rights. "Cannabis gave me back my limbs," she declared. Embraced by the Bay Area medical-marijuana community, Angel took up the cause with a passion, speaking at press conferences and meetings, exhorting audiences, telling everyone within earshot about her phoenixlike transformation, and decrying federal policy that treated sick people like criminals.

Although she herself had never been charged with a crime, Raich opted to make her plight a test case to win protection for the nation's more than 100,000 medical-marijuana patients. She contacted Diane Monson after reading about her bust, and the two women proceeded to sue the U.S. government to prevent federal officials from interfering with their use of medicinal cannabis. They sought an injunction against the DEA. "We're sick," Raich stated emphatically, "and we shouldn't have to do this to stay alive." Filed in U.S. District Court in Oakland in October 2002, the lawsuit argued that U.S. Attorney General John Ashcroft and DEA director Asa Hutchinson were violating the Fifth, Ninth, and Tenth amendments as well as exceeding their authority under the Commerce Clause of the Constitution by cracking down on medical marijuana users.

Raich's attorneys framed the case in terms of states' rights and tailored their arguments to appeal to conservatives. Her legal team (which included her husband, Robert Raich) made a strategic decision to emphasize the Commerce Clause rather than other crucial issues such as medical necessity or the right to life. Federal drug laws are rooted in the Commerce Clause, which empowers Congress to regulate interstate commerce. This provision once served as an important tool for promoting progressive federal policies from the New Deal to Civil Rights, but over the years it became an all-purpose excuse for Congress to meddle in virtually every aspect of human behavior.

In December 2003, the Ninth Circuit Court of Appeals, in a split decision, ruled in Raich's favor. The three-judge panel determined that it was unconstitutional for the federal government to prosecute medical-marijuana growers and users under the 1970 Controlled Substances Act if the herb did not cross state lines and no money exchanged hands. Noncommercial medical use differed fundamentally from the kind of drug trafficking that the Nixon-era

Controlled Substances Act intended to prohibit and, therefore, according to the appellate court, the activities of Raich and Monson were outside of federal jurisdiction.

The Bush administration quickly announced that it would appeal the decision to the Supreme Court, thereby setting the stage for the most significant case involving medical freedom to face the high court since *Roe v. Wade*, which affirmed women's reproductive rights in 1973. During the eighteen-month interregnum before the Supremes ruled on *Raich*, the Ninth Circuit injunction applied in California and seven other Western states that had medical-marijuana laws. But this didn't help several medical-cannabis defendants in California's conservative Eastern District, where it was business as usual for antimarijuana law-enforcement officers. State and federal officials continued to play tag team in an effort to thwart the implementation of Proposition 215.

On the morning of January 13, 2004, Tehama County prosecutor Lynn Strom unexpectedly announced that the state of California was dropping charges against Cynthia Blake and David Davidson for possessing and growing cannabis with the intent to distribute. While the two medical-marijuana patients (both in their early fifties) waited in the courtroom, Strom and the defense attorneys disappeared inside the judge's chambers to discuss the motion to dismiss. Moments later, more than a dozen sheriff's deputies pounced on the hapless couple, handcuffed them, and shoved them into an unmarked police car waiting outside the Corning courthouse. They were already en route to jail in Sacramento when Strom informed their lawyers that the state was bowing out because the feds were taking over the case.

The well-coordinated hand-off was not the first time local officials in California had turned over a medical-marijuana case to federal authorities. But it was perhaps the most dramatic example of ongoing collusion between various levels of government to undermine California's medical-marijuana provision. Blake, a retired Federal Reserve employee, and her partner, Davidson, a retail shop owner, were booked on federal drug charges. If convicted, they each faced a mandatory minimum of ten years to life in prison for exercising a right they thought they had gained with the 1996 passage of the Compassionate Use Act. Their attorneys invoked the "Raich defense," insisting that no money had exchanged hands for herb. Blake and Davidson both had a physician's recommendation to ease their ailments with cannabis, and neither had a criminal history. They had been tending three dozen pot plants in a remote rural garden, which they shared with other patients. Their fate—and the fate of three dozen other medical-marijuana defendants—hung in the balance while the Supreme Court pondered the particulars of *Raich v. Ashcroft* (later renamed *Raich v. Gonzales*).

Much more was at stake than the status of a disputed herbal treatment. How the Supreme Court ruled in this instance could shift the legal boundaries between Washington and the states. The Raich case posed a difficult dilemma for the Robed Ones, who usually took a hard line on law-and-order issues but who also prided themselves as protecting states' rights from ever-encroaching federal power. Conservatives disagreed as to whether federal drug agents should have the authority to prosecute individuals who abide by their state's medical-marijuana law.

The importance of the case was reflected in the lineup of amicus briefs supporting Raich and Monson. Several conservative heavyweights and legal scholars, including former Justice Department officials under Reagan and Bush Sr., signed or authored briefs urging the court to recognize that federal power must not be allowed to reach this far. The attorneys general of Alabama, Mississippi, and Louisiana, even though they personally opposed legalizing medical marijuana, strongly endorsed the right of California and other states "in our federalist system to serve as 'laboratories for experimentation.'" Several Republican congressmen, meanwhile, filed a brief warning of terrible consequences if medical patients were exempted from federal marijuana laws. Any state that sanctioned medical marijuana, in their view, would become "a haven for drug traffickers" and America would return to "the 19th century age of quack medicine."

Dozens of people, some with blankets, were camped outside the Supreme Court on the morning of November 29, 2004, waiting to hear the justices debate the Raich case. Protestors from across the political spectrum had gathered on the steps of the building. One group called for liberalizing marijuana laws to protect medical users. Another sign-carrying crew demanded no letup in the war on drugs. Inside the hallowed halls, the Bush administration, represented by Acting Solicitor General Paul Clement, argued that states' rights are, indeed, a good thing—unless the state in question legalizes marijuana for therapeutic purposes. Clement asserted that marijuana has "no approved medical use" and a high potential for abuse. And if doctors were allowed to prescribe cannabis, it would set a bad example and undermine the war on drugs. Even a brain tumor patient like Angel Raich must not be permitted to use the herb, according to Clement, because "any little island of lawful possession of non-contraband marijuana . . . poses a real challenge to the statutory regime."

In his oral argument, Clement tried to have it both ways—insisting that cannabis has no medical value, while also stating that marijuana's curative effects could be obtained legally via Marinol. "To the extent there is anything beneficial, health-wise, in marijuana, it's THC, which has been isolated and provided in a pill form," Clement asserted. (Clement was wrong: Herbal cannabis contains many medicinal compounds, not just THC.) The pretzel logicians in the Justice Department maintained that the price of illicit marijuana in other states could be affected if Californians grew their own pot or gifted it to a medically needy neighbor. Clement averred that the legalization of medical marijuana would also impact interstate commerce by hurting sales of Marinol (a "more helpful substance") and undermining "the incentives for research and development into new legitimate drugs." He expressed concern that "excepting drug activity for personal use or free distribution from the sweep of the Controlled Substances Act could discourage the consumption of lawful controlled substances." In other words, wider cannabis use might cut into Big Pharma profits.

Raich's team countered by citing a precedential 1925 Supreme Court ruling (*Linder v. United States*), which held that the states, not the federal government, are responsible for regulating medical practice. Her attorneys pointed out that twice during the past ten years the high court had struck down laws that could not be justified as commerce-related. They contended that busting sick or dying patients who don't buy or sell marijuana—and justifying such behavior under the guise of regulating interstate commerce—was a blatant example of federal overreach. If the federal government prevailed on this issue, it could affect virtually everything, Raich's lawyers argued. Where do you draw the line? Will Congress ban breast-feeding because it has an economic impact on the interstate sale of milk?

Chief Justice William Rehnquist was too sick to attend the oral arguments. When Angel Raich learned that he was undergoing chemotherapy for thyroid cancer, she said she hoped it "would soften his heart about the issue . . . I think he would find that cannabis would help a lot." But Rehnquist was no softie when it came to the war on drugs. As assistant attorney general under President Nixon, he played a significant role in drafting the Controlled Substances Act, which codified marijuana as a Schedule I substance with no medical value. With Rehnquist at the helm, the Supreme Court functioned as a reliable law-and-order auxiliary in the drug war, issuing rulings (with few exceptions) that favored police power at the expense of constitutional rights. The Rehnquist court condoned random, warrantless searches for marijuana and other drugs and the eviction of public housing tenants for any illegal drug activity by any household member or guest.

The Raich case upset the Supreme Court's ideological applecart. On June 6, 2005, six judges ruled against Raich, while three others, including Rehnquist, swung the other way. Archconservative Anthony Scalia, usually a Rehnquist ally, joined liberal Ruth Bader Ginsburg for the majority, which found that Congress has the constitutional authority to ban the use of homegrown marijuana, even when a state approves it for medical purposes, because backyard bud could affect or contribute to the illicit interstate market for weed. Justice John Paul Stevens called the case "troubling." Writing for the majority, Stevens went out of his way to note that Raich and Monson had made "strong arguments that they will suffer irreparable harm, because, despite a congressional finding to the contrary, marijuana does have valid therapeutic purposes."

The antimarijuana lobby reacted with glee. The 6–3 decision marked "the end of medical marijuana as a political issue," drug czar John Walters gloated. But Walters overstated the practical impact of the Raich decision. The narrow ruling focused only on the applicability of the Commerce Clause, while steering clear of other dicey issues. Had the Supreme Court sided with the patients, the federal government's irrational, antidemocratic campaign against medical marijuana would have ground to a halt. Instead, little changed. California law remained intact. The Compassionate Use Act was not preempted by the Controlled Substances Act as a result of the *Raich* decision. "It is our conclusion that the use of medicinal marijuana under state law is unaffected by *Raich,*" Attorney General Bill Lockyer of California asserted. The Supreme Court ruling did not nullify legislation in any states with medical-marijuana statutes.

Justice Stevens in his written decision expressed hope that Raich and Monson and the voice of their supporters would "one day be heard in the halls of Congress." Stevens later indicated that he personally favored Proposition 215 and would have voted for it had he lived in California. But his suggestion that those who need medical marijuana should demand—or wait for—appropriate congressional approval was weak medicine at best, if not downright insulting to vulnerable patients who bore the brunt of callous federal policies.

Despite widespread popular support for medical marijuana and solid scientific evidence of its utility, Congress continued to block drug-policy reform. Pot prohibition skewed the moral compass of politicians who denounced medical marijuana as a sham while raking in campaign contributions from Big Pharma pill pushers. Bills introduced to stop federal interference in states trying to implement their own medical-marijuana laws continually came up short in Congress. Impervious to pleas from ailing Americans, Congress twice nixed the "Truth in Trials Act," championed by Democratic and Republican representatives from California, which would have allowed individuals accused of violating federal marijuana laws to introduce evidence in federal court that they were using cannabis for therapeutic purposes in accordance with state law. Congress also voted down the Hinchey-Rohrabacher amendment by a wide margin every year since 2003. This bipartisan bill would have prevented the U.S. Justice Department, which includes the DEA, from spending taxpayer money to raid, arrest, and prosecute patients in states where medical marijuana is legal.

In the aftermath of her David-versus-Goliath struggle, Angel Raich was in the same predicament as before. In order to stay alive, she had to violate federal law. She had no choice but to continue using marijuana as a medicine. "I consider cannabis my miracle," she stated. "I really owe my life to it, and I'm not going to let anyone, including the government, take it away from me."

The Long Arm of the DEA

The Canadian courts were kinder to medical-marijuana patients. On December 10, 1997, a provincial judge in Ontario found Terry Parker of Toronto not guilty of marijuana possession and cultivation by reason of medical necessity. Parker, an epileptic, had suffered frequent grand mal seizures since age four. Big Pharma pills prescribed by his doctors had nasty side effects and did little to improve his condition. Nor did surgery. As a young man, he discovered he could substantially reduce the incidence and severity of seizures by using cannabis. For twenty years he had smoked the herb while keeping a low profile until Toronto police raided his apartment and snagged seventy-one plants. His case would mark a turning point in Canadian drug policy.

Justice Patrick Shepherd dismissed the charges against Parker and ruled that Canada's marijuana laws were unconstitutional, a decision upheld by the Ontario Court of Appeals, which declared on July 31, 2000: "Forcing Parker to choose between his health and imprisonment violates his right to liberty and security of person." Furthermore, the court decreed that the Canadian Parliament had a year to craft new legislation to ensure that medical-marijuana patients could access their indispensable remedy. If the government neglected to implement a workable program to accommodate the needs of patients, marijuana prohibition would be deleted from the criminal code.

Exactly a year later, Canada became the first country in the world to legalize marijuana for medical purposes. Canada would also be the first country to offer tax relief for authorized patients who purchased the herb. But Ottawa's medical-marijuana regulations were so onerous and restrictive that only a small percentage of qualified individuals signed up for the program. A doctor had to fill out a complex 33-page application for each patient.

Health Canada, the government heath agency, offered three ways for sick people to obtain cannabis: They could get a permit to grow it themselves; have a designated grower cultivate it for them; or they could buy it from the Canadian government, which contracted with a single supplier, Prairie Plant

Systems, to manage a marijuana plantation in an abandoned mine shaft deep below Lake Manitoba. This heavily secured underground grow-op produced several hundred pounds of poor-quality pulverized pot for distribution to certified patients. "Leave it to the federal government to screw up something that even stoners can get right," remarked Russell Barth, a disgruntled Canadian medical-marijuana "exemptee."

Frequent complaints about red tape, delays, and lousy, irradiated reefer prompted Canada's high court to admonish Ottawa for its failure to comply with the appellate order mandating that Health Canada provide patients with adequate legal access to cannabis. The Canadian government had been a reluctant supplier of herb ever since a series of legal rulings forced it into the medical-marijuana business. In October 2003, the high court reminded the federal government that official foot-dragging on the medical front contravened the Canadian Charter of Rights and Freedoms. Without a viable medical-marijuana distribution system in place, the laws against cannabis were unconstitutional. Misbegotten from the get-go, Ottawa's medical-marijuana program was designed to prop up antiquated prohibitionist legislation that never should have been enacted in the first place.

The Canadian parliament had criminalized cannabis in 1923 following the publication of *The Black Candle,* a sensationalistic antimarijuana diatribe by Emily F. Murphy, who wrote under the pen name Janey Canuck. A juvenile court judge in Edmonton, Murphy spewed racist venom about "the dregs of humanity" that smoked the evil weed. All marijuana users are "non-white and non-Christian, wanting only to seduce white women," she proclaimed. Murphy warned of "an international conspiracy of yellow and black drug pushers" whose ultimate goal is "the domination of the bright proud races of the world." Her ravings could have easily been lifted from Hearst's yellow press: "Persons using marijuana smoke dried leaves of the plant, which has the effect of driving them completely insane. The addict loses all sense of moral responsibility. Addicts to this drug, while under its influence, are immune to pain, become raving maniacs, and are liable to kill or indulge in any form of violence to other persons." Although it trumpeted dangers to society that did not actually exist, *The Black Candle* became a bestseller north of the forty-ninth parallel and succeeded in influencing Canadian lawmakers who banned marijuana without any debate or scientific evidence to support the new prohibition. Lengthy jail sentences—up to seven years for possession and life in prison for trafficking—were meted out to cannabis convicts.

When U.S. draft resisters fled to British Columbia in the late 1960s and early 1970s to avoid fighting in Vietnam, they brought with them, literally and figuratively, the seeds of a nascent marijuana industry, which would blossom into "BC Bud," the generic name for high-quality cannabis that became one of Canada's leading industries and exports. Before long, British Columbia would be a net exporter of marijuana.

What goes around comes around: Three decades after U.S. conscientious objectors smuggled THC genetics to safe havens across the border, a Canadian cannabis advocate named Marc Scott Emery built a profitable business by mail-ordering millions of marijuana seeds mainly to ganja growers in the United States. Emery, the self-proclaimed "Prince of Pot," was something of a cult figure in North America's cannabis subculture. He vaulted into the headlines as a bookstore proprietor in London, Ontario, in the late 1980s when he challenged Canadian censorship laws that banned pro-cannabis literature. Brash, outspoken, and a glutton for controversy, he defiantly broke the law by selling copies of *High Times* and Jack Herer's *The Emperor Wears No Clothes*. He also broke the law by keeping his shop open on Sundays. Thanks to Emery's upstart antics, shopping on Sunday and the sale of marijuana-related literature were both legalized in Canada within a few years.

In 1994, Emery moved to Vancouver and founded Hemp BC, a store that retailed smoking paraphernalia, hemp clothing, and pot seeds over the counter. (Bongs and water pipes were then illegal in Canada.) After *The Wall Street Journal* published a front-page article about Emery's seed business, Hemp BC was raided by Vancouver cops. The alpha-male impresario reopened his store the next day. He later paid a fine for illicit sales.

By 1997, Emery had expanded his operations to include the Little Grow Shop, the Legal Assistance Center, and the Cannabis Café, a bring-your-own pot parlor. Emery's Cannabis Café was the first of several smoke-easies in Vancouver, where patrons could puff weed in public. Emery rarely passed up a chance to proselytize. Profiled by CNN, *USA Today*, the *Sunday Times* of London, and other major media, he promoted pot as a health aid and an economic stimulus. "Being an anti-prohibition advocate is about providing for a decent, safe, honest social system." He asserted. "It's not just about getting high."

More raids followed and more fines were levied, but Emery kept selling seeds. When city officials declined to renew his commercial license, he shifted gears and turned his seed company into an Internet-only operation. "Overgrow the government!" was his catchphrase as well as his strategy for spreading marijuana faster than drug agents could eradicate it. Emery continually flouted the law, mailing copies of his seed catalog to every member of the Canadian parliament. His online enterprise provided nearly four hundred different strains to customers around the world. With sales topping well over a million dollars a year, Marc Emery Direct Seeds was quite possibly the largest pot seed supplier on the planet.

Emery dutifully paid his taxes, listing "marijuana seed vendor" as his occupation on his returns and noting the sizable sums he accrued each year from hawking cannabis genetics. He used the profits to finance the pro-marijuana movement. But Emery was hardly a left-wing radical out to smash the state. He was, rather, a die-hard libertarian capitalist and an unabashed devotee of Ayn Rand's hyperindividualist, social Darwinist *shtick*. Blending business and activism, Emery channeled millions of loonies (Canadian dollars) into cannabis legalization and defense efforts across North America and beyond.

In 2000, Emery launched the British Columbia Marijuana Party (BCMP), which ran candidates for public office and lobbied for drug-policy reform. The BCMP's bustling headquarters on West Hastings Street in downtown Vancouver looked like a huge head shop with a cannabis-only smoking section upstairs and a small retail depot in the rear that featured an array of psychedelic botanicals. Down in the basement, Emery's stoned lieutenants staffed the offices of *Cannabis Culture,* a glossy bimonthly, and Pot TV, an online marijuana news channel.

Situated in a low-income neighborhood not far from where a city-sanctioned "safe injection" site for hard-drug addicts would be established in 2002, the BCMP headquarters spearheaded an economic revival in what became known as "the Pot Block" or "Vansterdam." This thriving, if shabby, entrepreneurial oasis of hemp stores, hydroponics outlets, head shops, and smoke-easies attracted tourists and local tokers. Soon travel agencies were hyping the trendy reefer hangouts that sprang up on West Hastings and in other parts of picturesque Vancouver, where a permissive attitude toward marijuana prevailed. In Canada, like in the Netherlands, laws were established nationally but implemented locally, and Vancouver officials for the most part winked at the flourishing pot scene. One would never know that cannabis was illegal while walking around much of the city.

On the south end of Commercial Drive, the British Columbia Compassion Club Society offered a variety of marijuana medicaments to three thousand patients with a doctor's note. For those unable to visit the office, the daily menu was accessible via recorded phone messages with a cheerful voice that occasionally broke into song: "*We have Queen Jane, an indica sativa, tasty, fragrant, and good for appetite . . . Purple Pine Berry, good for pain relief . . .*" The police turned a blind eye "because there's no dealing out the back door," said Hilary Black, the founder of Canada's first and largest nonprofit compassion club, which opened four years before the government legalized medical marijuana. Black, a former Hemp BC employee, was the prime mover of a pioneering women's collective that transformed the Vancouver pot club into an all-purpose wellness center, featuring massage, acupuncture, nutritional counseling, and other holistic healing alternatives in addition to cannabis. This therapeutic example would be emulated by several medical-marijuana dispensaries in Canada and the United States.

At the dawn of the new millennium, a majority of Vancouverites, including the city council, favored across-the-board marijuana legalization. Much of the country felt that way. A 2002 Canadian Senate committee report condemned marijuana prohibition as an abject failure. "The continued prohibition of cannabis jeopardizes the health and well-being of Canadians much more than does the substance itself," the report declared. This exhaustive study of Canadian drug policy reached the same conclusion as the Le Dain Commission thirty years earlier: Cannabis is not a gateway drug, and antimarijuana laws should be replaced by the same kind of regulations that apply to alcohol and tobacco.

In 2003, when the prohibition of cannabis seemed to be in limbo because of flaws in the government's medical-marijuana program, Emery staged a cross-country "summer of legalization" tour. He dared the authorities to arrest him—and they did on several occasions—as he smoked weed in front of police stations in eighteen cities, pontificating to the press at every opportunity.

The Canadian Justice Ministry, meanwhile, was mulling requests for political asylum from several California reefer refugees who claimed they faced persecution by the U.S. government because of their use and advocacy of medical marijuana. "The draconian policies of the Bush administration triggered an exodus of reefer refugees," said Renee Boje, who fled the United States after federal agents tried to get her to testify against several cohorts in connection with the notorious 1997 "marijuana mansion" bust in Beverly Hills. Arrested and charged with growing and conspiring to sell cannabis, she decamped to Vancouver, where a small community of American medical-marijuana exiles were able to blend in with the burgeoning ganja scene and experience life "on the freedom side of the cannabis curtain," as Steve Kubby, the adrenal cancer survivor from Squaw Valley, California, put it.

Kubby also sought political asylum in Canada after fleeing from California's inhospitable Eastern District with his wife and two young children. While in British Columbia, Kubby was granted permission by Health Canada to grow his own marijuana. Other U.S. drug-war refugees hitched a ride on BC's underground reefer railway, an elusive network of safehouses and sympathetic contacts that transported expats up the Canadian coast or into the mountainous interior where they could lie low and, if need be, disappear. Emery provided financial assistance for Boje, Kubby, and other reefer refugees who challenged authorities on both sides of the border by applying for asylum in Canada.

The expatriates faced an uphill battle. Canada had a long history of welcoming American refugees—from Sitting Bull's Lakota Indians and runaway slaves in the nineteenth century to the Vietnam-era draft resisters who came to Canada to avoid military service; the 2002 Iraq war would fuel another round of renegade border-crossers from the United States. But no one had ever been granted refugee status in Canada because of the war on drugs. If Canada gave political asylum to a medical-marijuana exile, it would have major legal and political ramifications. In addition to sending a pointed message that Canada believed U.S. drug policies were too harsh, it would constitute an unprecedented rebuke to America's self-image as a beacon of human rights.

But Ottawa was reluctant to offend "its steroidal southern neighbor," as Richard Cowan, a veteran pot activist from Texas, referred to Uncle Sam. Discouraged by America's war on drugs, Cowan moved to Vancouver, where he published a pithy Internet broadsheet and hosted a show on Emery's Pot TV. "Canada is a special problem for American prohibitionists because it is too white to invade, but too close to ignore," Cowan mused. In the end, the Canadian government refused to grant refugee protection to U.S. medical-marijuana patients.

The United States and Canada were on different trajectories when it came to the war on drugs. While Canadians were liberalizing their laws and attitudes and moving closer to a European harm-reduction model, the U.S. government was pushing hard in the opposite direction. Canada had broken with the United States when it legalized industrial hemp in 1998 and medical marijuana three years later. U.S. antidrug officials worked feverishly behind the scenes to impede plans by the ruling Liberal Party to decriminalize possession of small amounts of marijuana for adult use, a policy shift endorsed by prominent Canadian newsmedia and the Canadian Association of Chiefs of Police. Everyone from President George Bush and drug czar John Walters warned of serious political repercussions if Canada resisted American demands. Walters criticized Ottawa for being "soft on drugs" and raised the specter of tighter border restrictions and trade penalties. He urged Canadian officials to clamp down on the production of BC Bud, "the crack of marijuana," according to Walters, who downplayed the fact that the vast majority of cannabis consumed by U.S. citizens was either homegrown or imported from Mexico.

After September 11, the United States beefed up patrols along the increasingly militarized 3,987-mile border with Canada, deploying Blackhawk helicopters and unmanned aircraft ostensibly to catch terrorists, illegal immigrants, and pot smugglers. Customs officials claimed the right to ban foreigners from entering the United States if they admitted to having tried marijuana, even once, at some point in their lives. A Canadian mother searching for her missing daughter was denied entry because of a twenty-one-year-old drug conviction.

Long a thorn in the side of the U.S. drug-war establishment, Marc Emery seemed to operate with relative impunity in Canada. The Canadian government's tacit acceptance of Emery's activities was a sore point with Washington, which wanted his scalp for peddling pot seeds to Americans through the Internet.

On July 29, 2005, the Royal Canadian Mounted Police, acting on a request from the DEA, arrested Emery in Nova Scotia, where he was speaking at a hempfest. Police units simultaneously raided the offices of the British Columbia Marijuana Party, busted two of Emery's seed-selling associates, and shut down his seed company for good. Three dozen other Canadian pot seed firms remained in business. By this time, the commercial cultivation of cannabis, once largely confined to British Columbia, had spread to every Canadian province en route to becoming the nation's most lucrative agricultural crop—a development that Emery was instrumental in facilitating.

It was the twenty-second time that Emery had been arrested, but he had never faced U.S. charges before. He agreed to plead guilty to a single count of conspiracy to manufacture marijuana so as to ensure that his two employees would not have to serve jail time. DEA chief Karen Tandy (the Bush-appointed successor to Asa Hutchinson) called Emery's arrest "a significant blow to the marijuana legalization movement."

To shirts in the drug czar's office, Emery was one of the world's most notorious drug dealers, an arrogant, high-profile loudmouth who deserved to be muzzled and punished severely. To others, Emery was a symbol of the drug war run amok, a political victim of the U.S. government's hypocritical, over-the-top vendetta against marijuana.

The Canadian parliament was poised to legalize cannabis when the long arm of the DEA reached across the border and grabbed Emery. A few months later, the scandal-tainted Liberals lost the 2006 Canadian elections and a minority Conservative government, led by Stephen Harper, took over on a platform promising harsher drug laws and no marijuana decriminalization. Harper was hell-bent on following Washington's discredited, hard-line approach to narcotics enforcement. After a series of senior-level meetings between U.S. and Canadian officials, Walters praised the regime change in Ottawa.

A surge in Canadian pot arrests followed, along with more prison construction, more aerial patrols and eradication sweeps, more bogus search warrants and clogged courts, more reefer-related civil forfeitures—much like in the United States. While Canadians toked in record numbers (the United Nations ranked Canada first among industrialized nations in marijuana use),

Harper pushed mandatory-minimum jail terms for cannabis offenders. Ironically, the rollback in Canada occurred at a time when conservative U.S. politicians and cash-starved state governments were starting to rethink the social and economic costs of overstuffed prisons. "It boggles my mind that anyone can look to the United States as a model for anything except colossal failure," said Eugene Oscapella, a University of Ottawa criminology professor and director of the Canadian Foundation for Drug Policy.

Ninety-three percent of Canadians polled in 2006 favored legal access to therapeutic cannabis, but the bureaucratic mandarins at Health Canada continued to drag their feet when it came to implementing a viable medical-marijuana program. Ottawa imposed arbitrary rules that made cannabis more difficult to obtain than opium. Authorized patients were allowed to buy only one poorly grown strain at exorbitant prices. "We have no money as it is. Most of us are on full disability for life," explained Alison Myrden, a former corrections officer who used marijuana to treat multiple sclerosis and tic douloureux, a neurological condition that causes extreme facial pain. Myrden, a leading Canadian spokeswoman for LEAP, the drug-policy reform group, was forced to seek out illicit sources for her medicine: "I'm constantly on the street because I'm choosing a strain the government doesn't offer."

Mistreated by Health Canada, many medical-marijuana patients broke the law by patronizing compassion clubs that operated without official sanction in every province. Several med-pot clubs were raided, setting the stage for courtroom challenges that invariably found the Canadian government's medical-marijuana regulations to be unconstitutional. In June 2009, the court struck down Health Canada's monopoly on the distribution of herbal cannabis so that patients could legally obtain strains from other sources.

Later that year, Marc Emery was extradited to the United States, where he faced more prison time—five years—than some violent offenders who left their targets dead or in wheelchairs. "There isn't a single victim in my case, no one can stand up and say, 'I was hurt by Marc Emery.' No one . . . I feel proud about everything I've done," he told reporters as he turned himself in.

Unbowed, the Prince of Pot declared: "To win this battle, one has to be willing to go to jail."

Ten Years After

Three top executives of Purdue Pharma didn't go to jail. They each pled guilty to one misdemeanor count of misbranding a product—the painkiller Oxycontin (the trade name for oxycodone)—and paid $34.5 million in fines, but none spent a day in prison. The company itself copped to a single felony and paid a bigger fine for misleading the public when it underplayed the dangers of this highly addictive slow-release opioid. Known as "Oxy" or "hillbilly heroin" on the street, Purdue Pharma's multibillion-dollar blockbuster was linked to thousands of overdose deaths. Of the almost 500,000 hospital emergency-room visits in the United States in 2004, more than 36,000 involved oxycodone, according to federal government estimates.

Fixated on medical marijuana, the drug czar's office was caught off guard by the nationwide surge in prescription painkiller abuse. All of a sudden it seemed that a lot of Americans were living in a world of pain and popping pills to get by. During the two-term presidency of George W. Bush, prescription painkiller abuse became the fastest-growing drug problem in the United States. "Legal" painkillers were the number one drug of choice for teenagers as well as middle-aged women in Middle America. Peddled by Internet pharmacies and purloined from their parents' medicine cabinets, Oxy was a fave at "pharm" parties, an increasingly popular form of recreation among U.S. high school students who were oblivious to the dangers of dabbling with daddy's meds. In 2006, seven million Americans engaged in the nonmedical use of prescription pharmaceuticals and nearly two million were dependent on or addicted to pain pills.

Accidental overdoses involving high-profile media figures were symptomatic of the widespread misuse and abuse of lethal prescription drugs. Many celebrities, including Rush Limbaugh, the insufferable right-wing radio talk show host, publicly confessed to their struggles with Oxy and other government-approved painkillers. For years, Limbaugh had upbraided others about "personal responsibility" while sneering at the calamitous consequences of the war on drugs, especially for people of color. Evenhandedness, he brayed, did not require less incarceration of black and brown youth, but rather an increase in incarceration of irresponsible white people, those "maggot-infested dopers" who all too often got away with illegal drug use. Limbaugh regularly told his listeners that drug users should be jailed: "Convict them and send them up the river."

Limbaugh could dish it out, but he couldn't take it when he was under investigation for possible crimes related to his longtime addiction to prescription painkillers. He complained he was unfairly targeted by law enforcement because of his celebrity status. In Florida, where Limbaugh lived and doctor-shopped, buying large amounts of powerful narcotics without a proper prescription could get you five years in the joint. Over the previous decade, more people had been sentenced to Florida state prisons for drug offenses than for any other crime. Limbaugh, a wealthy, influential Republican, took out full-page newspaper ads to attack prosecutors who were probing his pain-med purchases. He eventually plea-bargained his way out of a possible jail term without admitting guilt.

Like millions of Americans, Limbaugh had an addiction problem. Unlike most Americans, he was rich enough to purchase a pass from the criminal-justice system. No such luck for poor whites in the American Midwest, where methamphetamine was king. Highly addictive crystal meth took hold in the heartland after the Reagan administration sided with the pharmaceutical industry against the regulation of ephedrine, the main ingredient of street speed. By the time George W. Bush ascended to the Oval Office, illegal meth labs by the hundreds had moved into "red state" America, the GOP stronghold, tearing apart rural communities, destroying families, rotting gums, and straining local law enforcement. Some farm-country sheriffs longed for the good old days when a roadside patch of feral hemp was considered a major drug threat.

For several years, the Bush administration made marijuana the centerpiece of its antidrug strategy. Meth was virtually off the drug czar's radar. (Of the sixty-seven print ads featured in the feds' 2005 antidrug campaign, most focused on pot; only one mentioned meth.) The failure of this ostrichlike policy was becoming ever more apparent to local officials and members of Congress from both parties. "What I've never understood is why they took marijuana so much more seriously than methamphetamine, when methamphetamine is a much more serious drug," said Senator Charles Grassley, the Iowa Republican.

Bob Doran, a spokesman for the Iowa Association of Chiefs of Police and Peace Officers, cut to the chase: "Marijuana is old news . . . The longtime argument has been that marijuana is the first step into drug use, but I think that argument has gone by the wayside. We're finding many kids skipping pot and going straight to meth." Surveyed by the National Association of Counties (NAC) in the summer of 2005, five hundred local law-enforcement officers from throughout the country identified meth as the number one scourge. The NAC chastised Team Bush for obsessing over weed while ignoring the savage, real-world consequences of methedrine addiction.

Bolstered by the June 2005 Supreme Court ruling against Angel Raich and Diane Monson, which put a federal exclamation point on marijuana's illegality, the Drug Enforcement Administration stepped up its attacks against the medical-cannabis infrastructure in the Golden State. Pot clubs were most at risk in the wake of the Raich decision. Patients could keep a low profile and growers could try to remain anonymous, but California's 150 aboveground reefer retail outlets were very vulnerable, even in presumed safe havens such as San Francisco, where some 40 pot clubs allowed on-site smoking and vaporizing for members.

The U.S. government bore down heavily on several medical-marijuana defendants whose litigation had been put on hold until *Raich* was settled. Case in point: Steve McWilliams, San Diego's foremost medical-marijuana advocate. A former cowboy, McWilliams served as codirector of a medical-marijuana dispensary with an affiliated coffeehouse, where patients could gather, share information, and use their medicine. In 2002, McWilliams staged a public handout of medical marijuana on the steps of San Diego City Hall to protest official obstruction of Proposition 215. ("It's like the law never passed," McWilliams lamented. "None of us ever imagined it would be this hard.") A few days later, he was busted by DEA agents and local narcs who had been cross-deputized by the feds.

Unable to present a medical argument in federal court, McWilliams was convicted of violating the Controlled Substances Act. He remained free on appeal while *Raich* was still in play, but a judge banned him from using medicinal cannabis and ordered regular drug tests to assure compliance, thereby forcing McWilliams to take Big Pharma narcotics with dopey side effects. When the Supreme Court gave Raich a thumbs-down, McWilliams sank into a deep depression. Wracked with pain from cancer and worried that he would be sent to federal prison, he took his own life on July 11, his fifty-first birthday, by overdosing on prescription meds. McWilliams left a suicide note saying that he had a "right to use a medicine that works for me" and denouncing the government for trying to control his life. He signed the letter, "No retreat. No surrender."

Shortly after the *Raich* decision, local fuzz joined federal agents in busting a dozen medical-marijuana storefronts in San Diego, California's second-largest city, where county authorities were particularly hostile toward therapeutic cannabis. The San Diego County district attorney's office rolled out the red carpet for the DEA. In no other area of California did local authorities so brazenly cooperate with the feds to shut down medical-marijuana facilities. Repeated law-enforcement sweeps effectively closed every dispensary in the region. The state of siege lasted for several years, while the San Diego County Board of Supervisors mounted a spurious legal challenge in federal court to overturn the Compassionate Use Act.

The board voted not to abide by state legislation that required all counties to issue identification cards to qualified medical-marijuana patients so that cops could easily verify which pot smokers were legit. The ID program was mandated by California Senate Bill 420. Championed by State Senator John Vasconcellos and enacted in 2004, the ironically named bill (4:20 being the pot smoker's happy hour) also sanctioned nonprofit medical-marijuana collectives and cooperatives. Many patients and activists interpreted this as a green light to open storefront dispensaries, although commercial cannabis transactions were not explicitly authorized by Proposition 215 or SB420. More than a hundred new medical-marijuana retail outlets cropped up in California within a year, some in previously unthinkable locations.

In 2006, San Diego County sued the state of California, contending that the Controlled Substances Act (CSA) nullified Proposition 215 because of the Supremacy Clause of the U.S. Constitution; that is, federal law trumps state law. But this argument failed to gain traction. "The purpose of the CSA is to combat recreational drug use, not to regulate states' medical practice," a federal appeals court ruled in rejecting San Diego's lawsuit. (An appellate panel concluded that the issuance of state ID cards for pot patients did not prevent the U.S. government from enforcing federal law.) The ruling, which the U.S. Supreme Court declined to review, showed that states need not march in perfect lockstep with federal drug policy.

Forced to take a stand on the issue, elected officials in more than one hundred California cities and counties opted to ban storefront dispensaries, while other jurisdictions scrambled to regulate the surge of med-pot facilities that ensued during Bush's second term. Numerous media reports warned that "young, able-bodied males" were buying weed from dispensaries for the sole purpose of getting high. These dispensaries, according to critics, were nothing more than unscrupulous moneymaking operations that sold marijuana to anyone with an easy-to-get doctor's note for almost any alleged ailment. The notion that cannabis could be an effective remedy for more than a hundred diseases seemed utterly preposterous to the antipot crowd.

Dustin Costa, a diabetic Marine Corps veteran in his late fifties, formed the Merced Patients Group, a nonprofit cultivation collective, and waged an effective publicity campaign on behalf of medical marijuana. A prominent cannabis activist in California's Central Valley (part of the Eastern District), Costa led a delegation of patient-protestors to the office of Congressman Dennis Cardoza, the sole California Democratic representative who refused to support an amendment that would have stopped the DEA from raiding growers and dispensaries in states with medical-marijuana laws. Costa and his colleagues rallied behind medical-marijuana defendants; they turned up in San Joaquin County Superior Court, for example, to show their support for Aaron Paradiso, a wheelchair-bound quadriplegic facing cannabis cultivation and, of all things, firearms charges, despite the fact that he couldn't move his finger to pull the trigger of a gun.

In running his patient collective and tending his pot garden, Costa followed California law to the letter. He paid his quarterly taxes on time and abided by all local ordinances. He earned the respect of his neighbors by sponsoring a graffiti-removal project that was well received in Merced County. City officials in Modesto led him to believe that his med-pot grow-op was okay; then they called in the DEA. An undercover agent with a false doctor's recommendation posed as a patient and obtained cannabis from Costa's club. Busted by Merced County sheriffs, Costa was dragged through eighteen months of state court proceedings. When it became apparent that the Compassionate Use Act made it impossible to convict him under California law, local officials went to the feds. After the *Raich* decision, Costa was rearrested and tried in federal court on the same charges he beat in Superior Court—marijuana cultivation and possession with intent to distribute. But this time he was convicted and sentenced to a mandatory minimum of ten years in federal prison.

Costa was one of tens of thousands of Californians whose love of cannabis had brought them persecution and imprisonment. Ten years after the passage of Proposition 215, medical-marijuana patients continued to inhabit a twilight zone where marijuana was no longer illegal but not quite legal. Local regulations pertaining to dispensaries and growers differed from one county to the next. Caught in a political maelstrom, patients were still waiting for police and prosecutors to declare a cease-fire in the war against therapeutic cannabis. Hardly a week would pass without a DEA raid somewhere in the Golden State. Southern California was hit particularly hard with repeated med-pot sweeps in Los Angeles, Bakersfield, Riverside, and Orange County, as the DEA continued to wage a low-intensity war of attrition, picking off cultivators, distributors, and persons of interest up and down the state.

Cops often insist that they don't make the law, they just enforce it. For years, however, police associations in California and other states had lobbied public officials to toughen antidrug statutes. In a letter dated October 2, 2006, California Police Chiefs Association president Steve Krull urged DEA administrator Karen Tandy to use her authority to close medical-marijuana distribution centers, seize their profits, and prosecute club operators in federal court. Krull beseeched the DEA to "send a message to local and county governments that medical marijuana is not allowed." California NORML's director, Dale Gieringer, who helped draft Proposition 215, described the letter as "a smoking gun" that proves top California law-enforcement officials "sought to undermine state law rather than enforce it. The police chiefs have blatantly betrayed their public duty under the state constitution."

California's elected officials were, with few exceptions, weak and passive in response to federal law-enforcement attacks on medical-marijuana patients and the facilities that served them. The lack of leadership from Governor Arnold Schwarzenegger was all the more glaring given his notorious history as a pot-smoking muscleman. After he won an international weight-lifting competition in 1975, Schwarzenegger celebrated by sparking a victory joint in a scene captured for posterity in the documentary *Pumping Iron*. Thirty years later, the governor told a journalist that marijuana "is not a drug, it's a leaf," a comment that triggered a quick damage-control two-step by his press handlers. Arnold was just kidding, we were told. But Schwarzenegger wasn't kidding when he appeared in an ad for a nicotine-laden energy drink and when he stumped for steroids in a bodybuilding magazine.

America was awash in pills, but the drug czar's office kept insisting that pot was the main problem—and the problem included medical marijuana as well as industrial hemp. Governor Schwarzenegger acted like a ninety-pound weakling when he kowtowed to the Bush administration and vetoed a bill on October 30, 2006, that would have allowed California farmers to cultivate nonpsychoactive industrial hemp. Hemp-industry sales in the United States exceeded $270 million that year. California legislators figured that a policy that allows Americans to buy products they can't make is absurd.

During his tenure as governor, Schwarzenegger oversaw the costliest and largest ever expansion of California's prison system at a time when the state faced a massive budget shortfall and big cuts in social programs. The prisons were bursting at the seams, thanks to mandatory drug-violation sentencing, lock-'em-up-for-life "three strikes" laws, the deinstitutionalization of the mentally ill, and parole strictures that all but guaranteed the highest recidivism rate in the country. Thirty thousand Californians incarcerated for nonviolent drug offenses were sardined among more than 170,000 inmates in prisons designed to hold half that number. In 2005, a federal judge ordered federal authorities to take control of the California prison system's health-care program, which the judge described as "barbaric." Instead of releasing pot prisoners to ease extreme overcrowding, the governor went on a deficit spending spree, allocating $7.4 billion for new prison construction.

The war on drugs had spawned a huge prison-industrial complex all across "the land of the free." Between 1995 and 2005, some thirteen million Americans had been arrested for cannabis (overwhelmingly for possession). In 2006, there were 829,625 marijuana arrests, an average of one every forty one seconds. By year's end, approximately one out of every hundred adults in the United States was behind bars. Counting those on parole or probation, some seven million U.S. citizens were caught in the criminal-justice system.

But all was not doom and gloom statistically speaking for marijuana proponents. A decade after California voters passed Proposition 215, a Gallup poll found that 78 percent of Americans felt a doctor should be allowed to prescribe cannabis. Most significant, support for medical marijuana had risen in each of the eleven states that legalized it. Dire predictions of an onslaught of marijuana abuse, particularly by kids, in med-pot states did not materialize.

The sky had not fallen. On the contrary, California, with its medical-marijuana market topping $2 billion per year, registered a modest decline in recreational pot consumption by youth after 215 was approved.

Medical marijuana had prevailed on the cultural battlefield. The hearts and minds of Middle America were strongly pro-choice with respect to cannabis therapeutics. On no other issue were the American people so united in their belief that the U.S. government was lying. California cannabis activists paved the way and there would be no going back.

9

MELLOW MAYHEM

Senior Stoners

The Baby Boomers were aging—and not very gracefully. Americans turning fifty-five during the first decade of the twenty-first century were fatter, weaker, more stressed and depressed, more susceptible to chronic ailments, and, in general, less healthy than the generation before them, despite significant advances in medical technology. More than half of America's seniors took three or more Big Pharma meds every day, but the results were dismal: epidemic levels of obesity, heart disease, diabetes, cancer, Alzheimer's, arthritis, hypertension, and sleep disorders. Even when properly prescribed by FDA standards, all too often these government-approved drugs proved to be dangerous, resulting in the deaths of more than 100,000 hospitalized patients and serious side effects for more than two million others each year.

The Baby Boom generation, those born between 1946 and 1964, was also the first demographic to smoke grass en masse. Back in the day, pot was for the most part a happy high, a "reality kick," as Ginsberg would say. Young tokers weren't thinking in medical terms; they just felt there was something good about cannabis. Many Sixties veterans continued to puff until they reached retirement age. Some found that marijuana helped assuage the aches and pains of growing old. And they weren't shy about letting other people know. The graying of the Baby Boom generation, which was favorably disposed toward marijuana because of direct experience, coincided with an explosion of interest in cannabis therapeutics in the United States.

It turns out that a fling with Mary Jane could do wonders for the aging brain. The medicinal benefits of cannabis were well suited for seniors who wished to avoid the toxic and debilitating effects of corporate pharmaceuticals.

Like most Americans, they wanted remedies that didn't ravage their bodies, medicine more in sync with natural processes. The Baby Boomers weren't afraid of marijuana, a plant whose safety had been verified by personal observation and generational consensus. At a time of spiraling health-care costs, the uninsured and elders on fixed income increasingly turned to cannabis for health reasons.

Cannabis was just what the doctor ordered, literally and figuratively, for Joe Schwartz, a ninety-year-old great-grandfather and World War II vet who had a few puffs of pot each night to calm his nerves before he went to bed in one of America's largest retirement communities, in Southern California. He was one of 150 senior citizens—ganja geezers—that joined an Orange County medical-marijuana collective.

The introduction of antibiotics during the last century catalyzed an "epidemiological transition," a worldwide change in disease patterns. As more people lived longer thanks to penicillin and public-health campaigns, the leading cause of death in the United States and elsewhere shifted from infectious illnesses, such as tuberculosis, to chronic, degenerative, inflammatory maladies—cardiovascular, autoimmune, and neurological disorders, the big C, and other age-related diseases.

A great deal of scientific data suggests that many problems associated with growing old stem from the inability of the aging organism to protect itself against free-radical-induced inflammation and oxidative stress. Free radicals are highly reactive chemicals composed of unstable atoms or molecules with jumpy, unpaired electrons that collide with other molecules in the body, causing cellular damage and a degenerative domino effect, an ionic chain reaction that exacerbates the aging process and leads to various chronic ailments. Produced when animals use oxygen to burn food for fuel, free radicals are implicated in the formation of protein amyloid plaques, which disrupt neural synapses and prevent normal brain function in Alzheimer's patients. Major sources of free-radical stress include food additives and preservatives, corn syrup and artificial sweeteners, hydrogenated fats, herbicides and pesticides, air and water pollutants, synthetic household chemicals, prescription pharmaceuticals, alcohol, radiation, and cigarette smoke.

Antioxidants are natural compounds that protect the body from the wear and tear of free radicals. Found in certain vitamins, minerals, and other botanical nutrients, antioxidants neutralize free radicals by donating an electron that binds to unstable molecules and captures them. U.S. government-funded research has determined that THC and other cannabinoid compounds are potent antioxidants that can slow disease progression. In 2003, as mentioned previously, the U.S. Department of Health and Human Services secured a patent titled "Cannabinoids as Antioxidants and Neuroprotectants," which asserts that "Cannabinoids have been found to have antioxidant properties [and] are found to have particular application as neuroprotectants, for example in limiting neurological damage following ischemic insults, such as stroke and trauma, or in the treatment of neurodegenerative diseases, such as Alzheimer's disease, Parkinson's disease and HIV dementia."

The antiaging properties of cannabis were recognized and revered in Eastern cultures. Hindu sages attributed longevity and good health to this plant. They worshipped ganja as "an extender of life." In traditional Chinese medicine, cannabis was also prized for its life-enhancing and life-extending qualities. Medicinal hemp was considered an unusual herb because it possessed both strong "yin" and "yang" energies (the passive feminine principle and the active masculine force). The ancient sages were on to something: Within the marijuana plant are various compounds that have opposite effects in the body.

The Food and Drug Administration dissed the entire history of cannabis therapeutics when it issued an advisory memo on April 20, 2006, reasserting that marijuana has no medical value. According to the FDA, "No sound scientific studies supported medical use of marijuana for treatment in the United States, and no animal or human data supported the safety or efficacy of marijuana for general medical use." It was an outright lie. The apparent intent of the FDA's latest antimarijuana missive, released on 4/20, the pot smokers' holiday, was to taunt proponents of medicinal cannabis and to counter state efforts to legalize the herb for therapeutic purposes.

The Economist, the blue-chip British magazine, editorialized that the FDA's stance lacked "common sense," adding: "If cannabis were unknown, and bioprospectors were suddenly to find it in some remote mountain crevice, its discovery would no doubt be hailed as a medical breakthrough. Scientists would praise its potential for treating everything from pain to cancer, and marvel at its rich pharmacopoeia—many of whose chemicals mimic vital molecules in the human body."

Several U.S. publications took the federal government to task for obstructing therapeutic-oriented research while claiming there are no scientific studies that prove marijuana's medical utility and safety. "More research is needed" is both an obvious truism (more science is always welcome) and a variation on the Big Lie that as yet not enough data existed to substantiate whether cannabis has healing properties. "It's a sad commentary on the state of modern medicine and U.S. drug policy that we still need 'proof' of something that medicine has known for 5,000 years," Dr. Lester Grinspoon observed in the *Boston Globe*.

Truth be told, there was a large body of scientific reports and journal articles from around the globe that underscored the plant's medicinal potential. Long hobbled by America's reefer madness, international scientific inquiry blossomed after the discovery of the brain's cannabinoid receptors in the late 1980s. During the next two decades, some seventeen thousand research papers probed the biochemistry and pharmacology of plant, animal, and synthetic cannabinoids. European scholars Arno Hazenkamp and Franjo Grotenhermen reviewed the medical literature and compiled an annotated bibliography of more than a hundred clinical studies, assessing more than six thousand patients, which showed that cannabis and single-molecule cannabinoids had a measurable therapeutic impact on a wide range of maladies.

Dr. Andrew Weil, head of the University of Arizona's integrative medicine clinic and a renowned expert in holistic healing, rejected the notion that more data was necessary to figure out what's up with cannabis. "We know more about marijuana than we do about penicillin," said Weil. "Marijuana has been researched to death. Marijuana is one of the safest drugs known to medicine. It has a startling lack of toxicity compared to other drugs."

A half dozen clinical trials involving herbal marijuana were conducted in the United States under the auspices of a University of California program established by the state legislature in 1999 in response to Proposition 215. "We focused on illnesses where current medical treatment does not provide adequate relief or coverage of symptoms," explained Dr. Igor Grant, the UC San Diego psychiatrist who directed the program. Published in various scientific journals, the results of four state-funded clinical trials showed that cannabis significantly relieved neuropathic pain and muscle spasms, while reducing the need for opiates.

Unlike the studies funded by California, most of the research supported by NIDA sought to establish that marijuana has adverse effects. But instead of documenting harm, NIDA-funded scientists explored the inner workings of the endocannabinoid system and the mystery of neurogenesis. Within the scientific community, the discovery of the endocannabinoid system was increasingly recognized as a seminal advancement in our understanding of human biology. "It's still not part of the medical-school curriculum," says journalist Fred Gardner. "But there is no scientific controversy regarding the existence of the endocannabinoid system. It's an established fact that cannabinoids regulate many systems within the body." In 2003, Gardner, a former editor at *Scientific American*, helped Dr. Tod Mikuriya launch a journal focused on what physicians and scientists were learning about marijuana and its components. They called it *O'Shaughnessy's* in honor of the Irish-born physician who introduced "gunjah" to Western medicine. Each issue described new advances in the emerging field of cannabinoid therapeutics.

What had California doctors learned about the safety and efficacy of cannabis? In 2006, *O'Shaughnessy's* aggregated the findings of eighteen cannabis clinicians who had issued a total of approximately 160,000 recommendations in the Golden State. Patient testimonials were diverse yet contained common elements. Many people reported that medical-marijuana helped ease psychological as well as physical pain. "The range of conditions that patients are treating successfully with cannabis is extremely wide," Dr. Jeffrey Hergenrather noted. "Patients get relief with the use of cannabis that they cannot achieve with any other pharmaceuticals . . . No other drug works like cannabis to reduce or eliminate pain without significant adverse effects."

A cofounder and future president of the Society of Cannabis Clinicians (SCC), Dr. Hergenrather maintained that marijuana "helps with muscle relaxation, and it has an anti-inflammatory action. Patients with rheumatoid arthritis stabilize with fewer and less destructive flare-ups with the regular use of cannabis . . . In my opinion, there is no better drug for the treatment of anxiety disorders, brain trauma and post-concussion syndrome, ADD and ADHD, obsessive compulsive disorder, and PTSD." According to Hergenrather, cannabis also normalizes circadian rhythms and gastrointestinal function. All the SCC docs found that in addition to easing symptomatic distress, marijuana can in some cases moderate disease progression.

Many of the health benefits claimed by medical-marijuana patients and doctors were substantiated by worldwide scientific inquiry, which showed that human beings have a biphasic cannabinoid infrastructure, a yin-yang grid of cell receptors (CB-1 and CB-2) that functions 24/7 throughout the body. Activated by our own natural cannabinoid compounds (anandamide and 2-AG) as well as by components of marijuana, these receptors play a crucial role in life's complex, biochemical balancing act, modulating our physiological tempo in both directions, faster and slower; hence the emerging concept of the endocannabinoid system as the "master regulator" of homeostasis, the Tao of health.*

* The emerging consensus within the scientific community was summarized by Dr. Maurizio Bifulco, from the University of Salerno in Italy, in the journal *Pharmacological Research*: "It is becoming clear that an underlying mechanism for most human diseases is shared by the endocannabinoid system . . . The auto-protective role of endocannabinoids has been widely documented." Systemic inflammation perturbs and depletes endocannabinoid tone, thereby setting the stage for all manner of chronic illness. "Alteration of the endocannabinoid system," Bifulco noted, is "implicated in the pathogenesis of several cardiovascular diseases, ranging from hypertension, atherosclerosis, myocardial infarction, to . . . heart failure and cardiovascular complications of liver cirrhosis" (Maurizio Bifulco, "The En-

Israeli and Spanish scientists were the first to link the onset of Alzheimer's to the brain's failure to produce enough of its own neuroprotective endocannabinoids. A devastating terminal illness characterized by memory loss, cognitive dysfunction, and a growing inability to carry out daily tasks, Alzheimer's afflicts some five million elderly Americans—and that number is expected to triple by 2050. Close to half of the U.S. population aged eighty-five or above is encumbered by dementia, which is *not* a natural, old-age phenomenon. There are no Big Pharma cures that can stop the progression of Alzheimer's. But hope is on the horizon.

In February 2005, less than a year after Ronald Reagan died of Alzheimer's, the *Journal of Neuroscience* reported that WIN 55,212–2 (a synthetic THC analog) reduced inflammation in human brain tissue and slowed the development of Alzheimer's in a rat model by downregulating overactive microglia immune cells that damage neurons in the brain. A subsequent study by investigators at the Scripps Research Institute in La Jolla, California, showed that THC inhibits the enzyme responsible for the accumulation of amyloid plaque that disrupts communication between cells, the hallmark of Alzheimer's-related dementia. Additional research indicated that depleted blood flow to the brain, resulting in insufficient glucose metabolism, acts as an Alzheimer's trigger. Cannabis, a vasodilator, facilitates oxygenation and glucose metabolism by relaxing blood vessels.

According to scientists at the University of Saskatchewan in Canada, cannabinoid remedies could also help adults with dementia by fostering neurogenesis in the hippocampus, the area of the brain associated with memory and learning. In November 2005, the *Journal of Clinical Investigation* disclosed that HU-210, a potent synthetic cannabinoid, stimulated the growth of new brain cells in the hippocampus of rats. The results suggested that cannabis or its derivatives somehow might activate the brain's intrinsic repair mechanism. Of all the so-called drugs of abuse, only marijuana contains compounds that promote neurogenesis.

Could smoking pot prevent Alzheimer's? "It might actually work," says Ohio State University professor Gary Wenk, whose research lab "demonstrated that stimulating the brain's marijuana receptors may offer protection by reducing inflammation and by restoring neurogenesis." A team of scientists at King's College in London showed that cannabinoid receptor signaling regulates stem

docannabinoid System: From Biology to Therapy," *Pharmacological Research* 60[2][2009]: 75–140; Epub May 15, 2009).

cell formation in two regions of the adult human brain, the subgranular zone of the hippocampus and the subventricular zone of the lateral ventricles.*

Cathy Jordan, a fifty-year-old Floridian with amyotrophic lateral sclerosis (ALS), didn't need any fancy experiments to convince her that cannabis prolonged and improved the quality of her life. There is no recognized cure for ALS, otherwise known as Lou Gehrig's disease, a neurological illness that is usually fatal within two to five years after symptoms first appear. Jordan learned she had ALS when she was thirty-six. Twenty-six years later, she was still using cannabis on a daily basis, even though she resided in a state where marijuana is not a legal medicine. Jordan credited cannabis with keeping her alive. "We don't know why it works, it just does," her husband, Bob, told the *Bradenton Herald.* He and Cathy became outspoken advocates for legalizing the herb for therapeutic purposes. "We are in this fight to the end," Bob insisted.

Scientists at the Pacific Medical Center in San Francisco reported that treatment with THC effectively staved off disease progression and prolonged survival in animals if administered *either before or after* the onset of symptoms of ALS. Researchers in North American, European, and Israeli laboratories found that pretreatment with cannabinoids limited stroke-induced brain damage in rodents, and cannabinoid exposure after a stroke reduced the size of the infarct and promoted the recovery of white and gray matter. Stroke survivors also found that marijuana can relieve the angst, stress, and pain one suffers following an abrupt traumatic brain injury (TBI). About one million people in the United States are treated in emergency rooms each year for TBI, resulting from traffic accidents, war wounds, strokes, and sports-related concussions.

The preponderance of data—preclinical, clinical, and anecdotal—attests to the overall protective nature of the endocannabinoid system, which plays a crucial role in the prevention and suppression of illness, including heart disease and cancer, the two leading killers in the United States. Marijuana, a herb uniquely capable of activating the endocannabinoid system, is the human body's natural ally. Peer-reviewed studies in several countries have shown that

* Stem cells are "pluripotent" master cells that can differentiate and produce many types of specialized cells within the body. Researchers have been able to induce brain plasticity—the process whereby learning and adaptation occur on a cellular level—with transplanted embryonic stem cells. Transplanted stem cells have shown promise in reversing brain damage caused by strokes and degenerative neurological diseases, such as Parkinson's, Huntington's, and Alzheimer's.

THC and other plant cannabinoids are effective not only for cancer symptom management (pain, nausea, loss of appetite, fatigue, and so on), but "they have a direct antitumoral effect as well," according to Dr. Donald Abrams, who coauthored the textbook *Integrative Oncology* with Dr. Andrew Weil. U.S. officials knew of THC's antitumoral properties since 1974, when NIH-sponsored researchers at the Medical College of Virginia, seeking to assess whether cannabis had a detrimental effect on the immune system, observed that THC injections inhibited the growth of three kinds of cancer in mice. But this tantalizing lead was buried and ignored for many years.

Animal experiments conducted by Manuel Guzmán at Madrid's Complutense University in the late 1990s revealed that a synthetic cannabinoid injected directly into a malignant brain tumor could eradicate it. Reported in *Nature Medicine,* this remarkable finding prompted additional studies in Spain and elsewhere that confirmed the anticancer properties of marijuana-derived compounds. Guzmán's team administered pure THC via a catheter into the tumors of nine hospitalized patients with glioblastoma (an aggressive form of brain cancer) who had failed to respond to standard therapies. This was the first clinical trial assessing the antitumoral action of cannabinoids on human beings, and the results, published in the *British Journal of Cancer,* were very promising. THC treatment was associated with significantly reduced tumor cell proliferation in all test subjects.

Guzmán and his colleagues found that THC and its synthetic emulators selectively killed tumor cells while leaving healthy cells unscathed. No Big Pharma chemotherapy drugs could induce apoptosis (cell death) in cancer cells without trashing the whole body. Up to 90 percent of advanced cancer patients suffer cognitive dysfunction from "chemo brain," a common side effect of corporate cancer meds that indiscriminately destroy brain matter, whereas cannabinoids are free-radical scavengers that protect brain tissue and stimulate brain cell growth.

There is mounting evidence that cannabinoids may "represent a new class of anticancer drugs that retard cancer growth, inhibit angiogenesis [the formation of new blood vessels] and the metastatic spreading of cancer cells," according to the scientific journal *Mini-Reviews in Medicinal Chemistry*. Studies from scientists around the world have documented the anticancer properties of cannabinoid compounds for various malignancies, including (but not limited to):

- *Prostate cancer.* Researchers at the University of Wisconsin found that the administration of the synthetic cannabinoid WIN-55,212–2, a CB-1 and CB-2 agonist, inhibited prostate cancer cell growth and also induced apoptosis.

- *Colon cancer.* British researchers demonstrated that THC triggers cell death in tumors of the colon, the second leading cause of cancer deaths in the United States.
- *Pancreatic cancer.* Spanish and French scientists determined that cannabinoids selectively increased apoptosis in pancreatic cell lines and reduced the growth of tumor cells in animals, while ignoring normal cells.
- *Breast cancer.* Scientists at the Pacific Medical Centers in San Francisco found that THC and other plant cannabinoids inhibited human breast cancer cell proliferation and metastasis and shrank breast cancer tumors. 1.3 million women worldwide are diagnosed yearly with breast cancer and a half million succumb to the disease.
- *Cervical cancer.* German researchers at the University of Rostock reported that THC and a synthetic cannabinoid suppressed the invasion of human cervical carcinoma into surrounding tissues by stimulating the body's production of TIMP-1, a substance that helps healthy cells resist cancer.
- *Leukemia.* Investigators at St. George's University and Bartholomew's Hospital in London found that THC acts synergistically with conventional antileukemia therapies to enhance the effectiveness of anti-cancer agents *in vitro* (in a test tube or petri dish). Scientists had previously shown that THC and cannabidiol were both potent inducers of apoptosis in leukemic cell lines.
- *Stomach cancer.* According to Korean researchers at the Catholic University in Seoul, WIN-55,212–2, the synthetic cannabinoid, reduced the proliferation of stomach cancer cells.
- *Skin carcinoma.* Spanish researchers noted that the administration of synthetic cannabinoids "induced a considerable growth inhibition of malignant tumors" on the skin of mice.
- *Cancer of the bile duct.* The administration of THC inhibits bile-duct cancer cell proliferation, migration, and invasion and induces biliary cancer cell apoptosis, according to experiments conducted at Rangsit University in Patum Thani, Thailand.
- *Lymphoma, Hodgkin's and Kaposi's sarcoma.* Researchers at the University of South Florida ascertained that THC thwarts the activation and replication of the gamma herpes virus. This virus increases a person's chances of developing cancers such as Hodgkin's, non-Hodgkin's lymphoma, and Kaposi's sarcoma.

- *Liver cancer.* Italian scientists at the University of Palermo found that a synthetic cannabinoid caused programmed cell death in liver cancer.
- *Lung cancer.* Harvard University scientists reported that THC cuts tumor growth in common lung cancer in half and "significantly reduces the ability of the cancer to spread." Lung cancer is the number one cancer killer in the world. More Americans die of lung cancer each year than any other type of cancer.

What about smoked cannabis? Pure THC is not the same as marijuana smoke. How credible are oft-repeated claims by U.S. officials that smoking pot harms the lungs? "Numerous studies have shown marijuana smoke to contain carcinogens and to be an irritant to the lungs. In fact, marijuana contains 50–70 percent more carcinogenic hydrocarbons than tobacco smoke," a fact sheet from the National Institute on Drug Abuse correctly asserts. But extensive epidemiological research sponsored by NIDA and other federal agencies failed to substantiate a real-world link between smoking marijuana and lung cancer.

UCLA pulmonologist Donald Tashkin, M.D., NIDA's go-to expert on cannabis and the lungs for thirty years, was the logical choice to conduct a comprehensive, government-funded, case-control study that would prove, once and for all, marijuana's detrimental effects on lung function. Tashkin's earlier work had shown that cannabis smoke includes cancer-causing chemicals as harmful as those in tobacco and, therefore, he assumed that marijuana smoke must cause cancer. "We hypothesized that there would be a positive association between marijuana use and lung cancer and that the association would be more positive with heavier use," he explained. "What we found instead was no association at all, and even a suggestion of some protective effect."

In June 2005, Tashkin presented his findings to the International Cannabinoid Research Society prior to publication. His team at UCLA compared the lung health of 2,252 participants—nonsmokers, pot smokers (including some who reported smoking more than 22,000 joints in their lifetime), cigarette smokers, and people who smoked both marijuana and tobacco. Not surprisingly, tobacco-only smokers showed high rates of cancer and emphysema compared with nonsmokers. Pot smokers, however, were found to have lower rates of cancer than nonsmoking subjects. Folks who smoked marijuana and tobacco fared slightly better than the tobacco-only group.

Tashkin's research corroborated a 1997 epidemiological analysis of more than 64,000 patients by researchers from the Kaiser Permanente HMO in Oakland and the California School of Public Health in Berkeley. They concluded that regular marijuana smoking did not lead to lung cancer or to premature mortality. A 2002 Johns Hopkins medical school study reached the same conclusion. Ten years later, research data published in the *Journal of the American Medical Association* indicated that long-term exposure to marijuana smoke is not associated with adverse effects on pulmonary function.

Why, if marijuana smoke contains known carcinogens, does it not cause cancer? The crucial difference between cannabis and tobacco cigarettes is that the former delivers nontoxic THC and other health-enhancing phytocannabinoids while the latter imparts nicotine and toxic chemical additives. THC, a bronchodilator, protects against cancer and many other diseases, including asthma. (Scientific studies lent credence to reports from asthmatics who said that marijuana relieves bronchial constriction and permits freer airflow to the lungs.) The only knock on smoked cannabis: Chronic consumption could irritate the esophagus and respiratory organs, a problem easily remedied by using a vaporizer or ingesting cannabinoids via tinctures or edibles.

Despite several U.S. government-sponsored studies showing that pot smoking does not cause lung cancer, the regime of confusion still held sway in state capitals and in Washington, D.C., where entrenched bureaucrats spun misleading factoids about the risks of cannabis. Sacramento's Office of Mental Health Hazard Assessment and the California Environmental Protection Agency went so far as to add marijuana smoke—but not the plant itself—to the Golden State's official list of carcinogens. It was more fodder for drug-war die-hards and ignorant law-enforcement martinets who maintained that no matter how much someone suffered, or how close they were to death, a person should not be allowed to use herbal cannabis.

An Industry Emerges

It was not what she wished for on her birthday. On January 17, 2007, the day JoAnna LaForce turned fifty-five, 120 heavily armed Drug Enforcement Administration agents wearing masks and bulletproof vests descended upon eleven Los Angeles–area medical-marijuana dispensaries. Assisted by the LAPD, the feds seized 5,000 pounds of pot and detained several dispensary proprietors in the largest single-day law-enforcement operation aimed at medical-marijuana clubs in California to date.

"They raided and pillaged," recalled LaForce, cofounder and director of the Farmacy, an innovative West Hollywood dispensary. "We were not able to get credit card service because of the nature of our business, so we had a lot of cash on hand. They took $250,000 worth of product and $60,000 in cash and wrote us a receipt for only $42,000."

The Farmacy, with it's "Very Open" neon window sign, was back in business two days later. "We practice civil disobedience every time we open our doors," said LaForce, a confident, even-tempered woman who prides herself on being the only registered pharmacist in America to manage a medical-marijuana dispensary. LaForce maintains that cannabis should be regulated as an herbal remedy, not as a pharmaceutical and certainly not as a controlled substance.

Before launching the Farmacy in November 2004, LaForce specialized in geriatric pharmacology and hospice care for dying patients. "I saw the value of alternative medicine, particularly cannabis, in helping with appetite, pain management, and anxiety," she told *The New Yorker*. "I found that I could use cannabis to decrease pain medication, which in turn made patients able to spend their last days talking to their friends, spouses, to share good times."

Upscale but modest, the Farmacy established branches in Venice and Westwood, in addition to West Hollywood. Each store offered a variety of Chinese medicaments, Ayurvedic remedies, and traditional North American healing herbs, as well as several dozen marijuana strains, imparting a mélange of therapeutic aromas ("a riot of perfumes," as Rimbaud once said). The Farmacy's family-friendly atmosphere appealed to young professionals, stay-at-home moms, stiletto stoners, and senior citizens who learned about the nuances of indicas and sativas from helpful attendants behind the counter. The Farmacy also produced its own array of cannabinated beverages, tinctures, sprays, and topicals. Some patients who never smoked pot came to get cannabis lotion for their arthritis—lotion that did not make them feel high.

The Farmacy was at the forefront of a belated surge of dispensaries in Los Angeles. The film industry took notice and Showtime developed a series using the emerging industry as a backdrop. Set in a fictional Los Angeles suburb, *Weeds* featured a sympathetic soccer mom who becomes a pot dealer out of necessity to support her family after her husband's death. Cannabis was depicted as a harmless, ordinary part of everyday life in America. The show's banality and success was one of many examples that underscored how far the serrated pot leaf had penetrated popular culture—in song lyrics, on T-shirts, at hempfests and hip-hop concerts, on medical-marijuana and hydroponics billboards. Acceptance of the weed seemed to be growing throughout the land. "In the court of public opinion, marijuana has been charged and been found relatively innocent," observed psychologist Dan Rose, director of a counseling center at Columbus State University in Georgia.

In 2005, when *Weeds* debuted on prime-time cable TV, there were 4 medical marijuana dispensaries operating openly in Los Angeles. By 2007, 187 reefer retail outlets were operating in LA County, which was home to one third of California's 300,000 authorized medical-marijuana patients, according to estimates by Americans for Safe Access. Thanks to a pent-up demand and entrepreneurial energy, the number of storefront dispensaries in LA would quadruple by the end of the decade. *Newsweek* called Los Angeles "the wild West of weed." No other city in California had seen such an explosion of medical-marijuana facilities. At least four local ad-filled glossy magazines served a burgeoning weed-smoking clientele. Hundreds of medical-cannabis dispensaries and delivery services advertised on websites such as WeedMaps and WeedTracker. In Hollywood (dubbed "Hollyweed" by stoners), there were more pot clubs than Starbucks.

On July 6, 2007, the DEA sent threatening letters to more than one hundred landlords in Los Angeles whose buildings were being leased to medical-marijuana dispensaries. A spokeswoman for the DEA told the *Los Angeles Times* that the letters were meant to "educate" landlords that they could face federal prosecution, the forfeiture of their property, and up to twenty years in prison if they rented space to anyone engaged in selling a controlled substance. The DEA also sent menacing missives to property owners in Santa Barbara, San Francisco, Marin, Alameda, and several other counties. Some landlords capitulated. Many dispensaries kept lawyers on retainer. When an attorney representing the Arts District Healing Center in LA argued that a landlord had no right to evict a medical-marijuana dispensary if the tenant had not broken the terms of the lease, the judge agreed.

Medical-cannabis providers in the Golden State, meanwhile, braced themselves in anticipation of more federal attacks. On July 25, 2007, DEA agents in combat gear, flanked by LAPD officers, raided ten more pot clubs in the Los Angeles area, including the California Patients Group (CPG), which served, among others, more than a thousand patients over the age of fifty. Directed by Don Duncan, cofounder of Americans for Safe Access, the CPG had become a focal point of local activism, hosting meetings for patients and dispensary operators. Duncan viewed the DEA's latest heavy-handed maneuvers as paramilitary theater designed to send an intimidating message rather than to enforce the law.* The timing of the raids coincided with a press conference by Los Angeles City Council members announcing a one-year moratorium to block new medical-marijuana storefronts from opening while officials fashioned a

---

* Armed with M-16s, DEA agents handcuffed California Patients Group employees, did a snatch and grab at the store, and froze the organization's bank accounts, but no one was arrested. The DEA also drained the bank account of the CPG's sister club in the Bay Area, the Berkeley Patients Group, a direct offshoot of the Cannabis Action Network.

comprehensive ordinance to regulate the fledgling industry. The measure was widely seen by local dispensary operators as sanctioning already existing pot clubs.

The DEA was also intent on sending a message when it targeted medical-marijuana users and providers outside California during the summer of 2007. In August, a multiagency drug task force composed of DEA and local law-enforcement officers raided the home of Leonard French, a forty-four-year-old paraplegic in Malaga, New Mexico, who had state approval to medicate with cannabis; the raid came shortly after New Mexico became the twelfth U.S. state to legalize medical marijuana. A few weeks later, the DEA raided a medical-marijuana dispensary in Portland, Oregon. But California continued to bear the brunt of Uncle Sam's anticannabis obsession.

"The medical-marijuana business is not an endeavor for the risk-averse," said Michael Backes, founder of the Cornerstone Collective, a state-of-the-art dispensary in Los Angeles. "When it got out that there was going to be a moratorium," Backes explained, "hundreds more clubs opened so they could register before the moratorium started. And then the landlord letters hit, which meant that some clubs might be forced to move. So they put in a hardship exemption drafted by the city attorney's office with very vague language that appeared to present a loophole." The hardship exemption was widely exploited and before long nearly one thousand (mostly small) pot clubs had taken root in Los Angeles County, while city officials bickered over how to handle the situation.

Councilman Dennis Zine, a former LAPD officer, called upon the federal government to cease its attacks on medical-marijuana facilities. Wearing pink armbands to show their support for therapeutic cannabis, Zine and several like-minded city council members asked the LAPD to review its policy of co-operating with the DEA. But prohibitionists on the city council and in the city attorney's office opposed any regulations that would legitimize the distribution of medical marijuana. They denounced cannabis clubs as "crime magnets" without offering any statistics to back up this claim. LAPD Chief Charlie Beck, hardly a medical-marijuana advocate, set the record straight when he asserted that armed robbers were far more likely to target a bank than a cannabis dispensary.

Mired in reefer madness and legislative paralysis, a split LA City Council did nothing for several years. As a result, unlicensed dispensaries continued to operate near playgrounds, schools, and senior centers. An increasingly competitive marketplace led to gaudy promotional gimmicks, such as scantily clad "nurses" on roller skates and carnival barkers handing out invitations to a hash bar on Venice Beach. A handful of pot clubs in LA stayed open all night, barely maintaining a medical pretense.

The Farmacy, Cornerstone, and fifty other high-caliber, community-oriented medical-cannabis providers formed the Greater Los Angeles Caregivers Alliance (GLACA). In the absence of sensible regulations from local officials, this trade association developed accreditation standards and other guidelines for organic-only med-pot stores. In 2010, when the city council finally got around to issuing a draconian ordinance that would have banned most medical-marijuana facilities, a Superior Court judge ruled it invalid.

Amid all the chaos in Los Angeles, support for medical marijuana grew. According to public opinion polls, three-quarters of LA residents favored regulating dispensaries rather than eliminating them. In November 2010, 60 percent of the voters went for Measure M, a citywide ballot provision that imposed new taxes on the sale of marijuana at brick-and-mortar dispensaries. The measure levied a 5 percent sales tax on medical-cannabis transactions in the city. To voters, it was easy money for a cash-strapped metropolis. While not in principle against a med-pot tariff, GLACA and Americans for Safe Access denounced Measure M on the grounds that it wasn't fair to patients for the tax on medicinal cannabis to be ten times higher than the next highest business license tax in the city.

LA County District Attorney Steve Cooley wasn't keen on the medical-marijuana tax, either. A drug-war die-hard, Cooley kept insisting that all pot sales were illegal under federal as well as state law, despite a 2005 California appellate court ruling (*People v. Urziceanu*), which reaffirmed that nonprofit consumer cooperatives could accept money in exchange for medicine.* In 2009, the California Board of Equalization announced for the first time that all medical-marijuana retailers must pay a state sales tax, a requirement opposed by some dispensary operators who worried that any information they reported to the Franchise Tax Board in Sacramento could be used against them by the federal government. And why should they fill the state's coffers with cash when California law-enforcement officers continued to assist the DEA's remorseless campaign against medicinal cannabis?

While Los Angeles caused chaos by failing to rein in its dispensaries, Oak-

---

* In *People.v. Urziceanu*, September 2005, the Third District Court of Appeals affirmed the legality of nonprofit medical-marijuana collectives and cooperatives involved in growing, storing, distributing, and selling cannabis (Pebbles Trippet, "*Urziceanu* Ruling Protects Sales, Distribution," *O'Shaughnessy's*, Spring 2006).

land authorities crafted regulations for medical-marijuana outlets with positive results. In 2004, Oakland became the first municipality in California to issue permits to cannabis clubs. The city council limited the number of dispensaries to four and banned on-site smoking.

The Harborside Health Center, situated on a scenic stretch of the Oakland waterfront, emerged as a model medical-marijuana facility, a media showcase that exudes professionalism and entrepreneurial panache. Friendly uniformed security guards monitor Harborside's hundred-car parking lot and check personal ID and doctor's notes before waving patient-members through the front door. A steady stream of customers are ushered into a spacious, tastefully designed room with hemp carpets, blond wood trim, natural light, and fresh flowers. A statue of a large laughing Buddha watches over eight glass display cases featuring the latest product line—flawlessly manicured green lumpy buds, tinctures, concentrates, and rubbing ointments, all labeled according to strain and THC content. A sophisticated point-of-sale system tracks inventory.

Within a year, Harborside had nearly fifty thousand members. Steve DeAngelo, Harborside's high-profile, pigtailed CEO, was featured in a 2009 *Fortune* magazine cover story entitled "How Pot Became Legal: Medical Marijuana Is Giving Activists a Chance to Show How a Legitimized Pot Industry Can Work. Is the End of Prohibition Upon Us?" As DeAngelo explained, "Whenever a patient comes into the clinic for the first time, they sign a collective cultivation agreement. They authorize all the other patients in the collective to grow medical cannabis on their behalf. That sets up a 100% closed loop distribution system that isolates my patients from any contact with the illicit market . . . For a variety of very valid reasons, most patients are unable to grow their own medicine. We act as a clearinghouse between patients who are able to grow and patients who aren't able to grow."

DeAngelo was a veteran cannabis activist who had accrued considerable business experience dealing weed and marketing hemp apparel prior to founding Harborside, his dream project, in October 2006. His roots in the marijuana movement stretched back three decades to his teenage years in the nation's capital, when he teamed up with a cadre of Yippie holdovers and organized a series of July 4 smoke-ins to protest marijuana prohibition. DeAngelo campaigned for Proposition 59, the D.C. medical-marijuana ballot measure that passed by a huge majority in 1998, only to have the vote discounted by Congress. Three years later he moved to the Bay Area, where he reunited with Rick Pfrommer, his trustworthy Nut House comrade. After DeAngelo was licensed by Oakland to open Harborside, Pfrommer came on board as the dispensary's chief purchasing agent.

During his day job, Pfrommer handled and sniffed more varieties of bud than anyone else on the planet. He urged growers to adopt techniques developed by the Clean Green certification program, a grassroots self-regulatory effort modeled after the U.S. Department of Agriculture's organic labeling process. Founded by Chris Van Hook in 2004, Clean Green visited cultivation sites, edibles manufacturers, and medical dispensaries to confirm that the herb was being grown, processed, and packaged in accordance with defined best practices. It was a nasty little secret within the marijuana world that many growers sprayed their plants with chemical contaminants, not unlike your typical American farmer.

Some of the cash generated by cannabis sales was plowed back into patient-oriented projects. Harborside provided free marijuana for low-income members and counseling for patients with substance abuse problems. DeAngelo's business partner, David Wedding Dress, was Harborside's director of holistic services, which included free acupuncture, chiropractic adjustments, naturopathy consultations, hypnotherapy, Reiki, and yoga sessions. A large, full-bearded heterosexual man, "Dress" wore a woman's gown every day to make a political statement against gender stereotyping. Dress oversaw Harborside's patient activist resource center, which included a computer station so members could sign online petitions, write letters to politicians and newspaper editors, or correspond with pot prisoners.

By 2009, Harborside employed seventy-four people and took in about $20 million in annual gross earnings. Workers got paid vacations and 401(k) plans. This dispensary contributed $2 million annually in state sales tax and another $360,000 to the city of Oakland. Before long, Harborside expanded into San Jose, California's third-largest city, where cannabis clubs went from zero to nearly sixty in 2010. DeAngelo eyed opportunities in other medical-marijuana states, as well. "It's a great growth industry," he declared on National Public Radio. "Anybody who's interested in a career, there's a great future in cannabis." But Stevie D also issued a warning: "Anybody who opens a dispensary has to be ready to go to federal prison."

Harborside tried to play the role of exemplary community citizen, but its bank accounts were closed several times and the Internal Revenue Service initiated an audit of its finances. The IRS also notified several other medical-marijuana dispensaries, including the Farmacy in Los Angeles, that they were under investigation for allegedly misreporting expenses and shirking their tax obligations. Specifically, the IRS cited a section of the federal tax code known as "280E." This section, aimed at drug lords, prohibited companies from deducting any expenses if they are "trafficking in controlled substances"—which meant that Harborside and other medical-marijuana providers could not subtract rent, payroll, and other standard business expenditures when calculating what they owed Uncle Sam.

Why would the federal government harass a thriving economic sector during an economic downturn? Why would banks shun a business that created dozens of new jobs at a time of high unemployment? "We do not deserve to have our accounts frozen or to be taxed out of existence," DeAngelo asserted. "280E was intended for cocaine kingpins, international smugglers and meth dealers. It was not intended for community organizations like ours and should not be applied to organizations like ours."

Wheelchair-bound ever since a freak accident left him paralyzed from the waist down as a young man, Richard Lee migrated from Texas to California after the passage of Proposition 215. In 1999, he launched the Bulldog, a medical marijuana dispensary in Oakland that was named after Amsterdam's infamous Bulldog Café, one of the first Dutch coffee shops. Lee quickly established himself as one of the most influential players in the California cannabusiness circuit. In 2004, he launched a local ballot initiative, Measure Z, which made adult use of reefer the lowest law-enforcement priority in the city. It passed with 65 percent of the vote. Several other municipalities—Berkeley, San Francisco, Santa Barbara, Santa Cruz, West Hollywood, and Santa Monica—did the same, but Oakland voters went a step further by declaring that "the city . . . shall establish a system to license, tax and regulate cannabis for adult use as soon as possible under California law."

Lee anticipated that waves of people would be interested in making a cannabis-related living. In 2008, he founded Oaksterdam University, a trade school in downtown Oakland that offered classes in horticulture, cannabis cuisine, bud-tending, business administration, marijuana law and history, economics, and political activism. Within three years of its launch, more than 13,000 students would graduate from this unique institution of higher learning, which moved to a four-story, 30,000-square-foot building to accommodate a waiting list of applicants. Oaksterdam University was so successful that it opened a Los Angeles branch and inspired imitators in California and other medical-marijuana states.

Though physically disabled, Lee considered himself first and foremost an adult cannabis consumer. Dubbed "the mayor of Oaksterdam," he saw vast commercial potential in his community's de facto legalization of marijuana. "I was trying to figure out the best way to promote the idea of a cannabis industry," Lee told the *Los Angeles Times,* "instead of all these nonprofit cooperatives, a bunch of hippies, peace and love, sharing their bud together, like a Coca-Cola commercial—you know, 'teach the world to sing.' No, this is like Budweiser and Jack Daniel's. It's a business."

Oaksterdam University, a trade school for the marijuana industry in downtown Oakland, was raided by federal agents in April 2012
(Courtesy of Michael Lam/Thomson Reuters)

Perhaps it was just a pipe dream, but Lee envisioned cannabis as a salve for California's financial woes. He would spearhead a statewide ballot initiative in 2010 to legalize marijuana for adult use. Although this effort came up short, businesses associated with medical marijuana would continue to flourish while much of the country struggled. The demand was real and kept growing, no matter how hard the DEA tried to suppress cannabis commerce. What started as a social-justice movement was evolving fitfully into a full-fledged, multifaceted industry with ample opportunities for young entrepreneurs and buttoned-down professionals who were smitten by "the great California weed rush," as *Rolling Stone* called it.

The market for medicinal cannabis was estimated to be $1.7 billion in 2011—and it was poised for dramatic expansion, as more states edged closer to legalizing cannabis for therapeutic purposes. Like health food and hip-hop, cannabis was going corporate. Various stakeholders sought to build brands and boost profit margins. The medical-marijuana scene fractured into competing camps. Some erstwhile political allies became bitter business rivals. Hard-core profiteers into get-rich-quick schemes vied with those who sincerely championed the cause of patients' rights. As a wave of newbies began to challenge the old guard, some movement veterans recalled the difficult days before Proposition 215 when there were no medical-marijuana storefronts selling sinsemilla to certified patients. "The younger generation doesn't understand how much sacrifice the preceding generations had to make to get to the point we're at now," said Rick Pfrommer, the cannabis sommelier, during a break between shifts at Harborside. "A lot of people want to cash in or get a nice safe job. But they really don't have an appreciation of what it took to get here. They don't know the history."

Healing Without the High

"If there is any future for marijuana as a medicine, it lies in its isolated components, the cannabinoids and their synthetic derivatives," the Institute of Medicine declared in 1999, keeping the door open for Big Pharma. By this time, scientists had an array of sophisticated tools at their disposal to study cannabinoid pharmacology and biology, including genetically altered "knockout" mice that lacked CB-1 receptors, CB-2 receptors, or both. Several start-ups and a dozen major drug companies launched their own cannabinoid research programs, and numerous patents were filed, mostly for cannabinoid-like designer drugs and nonsmoking delivery devices.

The FDA's fast-tracking of Marinol (the pure THC pill) and Eli Lilly's Naboline (a synthetic analog of THC) in the mid-1980s indicated that U.S. officials favored the development of single-molecule cannabinoids as a counterstrategy against medical marijuana. Initially, the focus was on creating THC substitutes and alternative modes of administration, such as transdermal patches and inhalers. University of Mississippi scientist Mahmoud ElSohly, director of the U.S. government's pot farm, developed a rectal suppository that could supply a steady dose of THC without causing psychoactive effects. It seems that Uncle Sam preferred anything to smoking a joint, even if it meant saying "up yours" to medical-marijuana patients.

After the brain's THC receptor was discovered, Big Pharma saw dollar signs and drug-company labs got the green light to explore ways to pharmaceuticalize the ancient herb. The plant itself would fade into the scientific background, or so it appeared, as academic researchers on corporate and U.S. government dole increasingly focused on crafting newfangled molecules that attached directly to cannabinoid receptors. Why mess with oily compounds from a crude, illegal botanical when single-molecule synthetics could reliably activate or blockade the same receptors? Synthetic cannabinoids, some hundreds of times stronger than THC, were utilized extensively in preclinical research. Their formulas were published in scientific journals and freelance chemists were able to reproduce and market some of these compounds as "herbal incense" products. One such concoction, a potent CB-1 receptor stimulant called JWH-108, escaped from the Clemson University lab where it originated and resurfaced years later on the black market as the street drug Spice.

The French pharmaceutical giant Sanofi-Aventis was the first to market a cannabinoid antagonist drug. SR141716, a Sanofi compound that blocked the CB-1 receptor, was utilized in the 1990s as a research tool. By antagonizing this receptor and seeing which functions were altered, scientists advanced their understanding of the endocannabinoid system. The "munchies," scientists confirmed, are linked to stimulation of CB-1 receptors in the part of the brain that regulates hunger and satiety. If activated, CB-1 receptors induce appetite; if blocked, they reduce it. Sanofi strategists believed they had the perfect diet pill: Turn off the CB-1 receptor and effortlessly shed a few pounds. They recast SR141716 as a therapeutic substance, called it Rimonabant (or Accomplia in some countries), and began marketing it as an appetite suppressant. Approved by European regulators in 2006, Rimonabant was hailed as "the first of the cannabinoid blockbusters" by a British pharmaceutical-business newsletter.

But Rimonabant didn't live up to the hype. People who used the diet pill for a year lost an average of 14 pounds, but they quickly gained it back when they stopped taking the drug, indicating that it would have to be prescribed indefinitely to work. Rimonabant's side effects, however, were dodgy if not downright scary for an alarming number of patients: increased blood pressure, nausea, vomiting, anxiety, mood swings, depression, headaches, seizures, sleep disorders, and heightened risk of suicide. One woman with no prior history of neurological illness manifested symptoms of multiple sclerosis. These symptoms abated after she discontinued the medication.

Cannabinoid antagonists proved to be blunt instruments. "One of the major functions of the endocannabinoid system is the protection of nerve cells from damage by overactivation of neurotransmitters," explains Dr. Franjo Grotenhermen, director of the International Association for Cannabis as Medicine in Germany. "The long-term use of [endocannabinoid] receptor antagonists may impair this neuroprotective effect with an accelerated loss of nerve cells and negative consequences on brain functions such as memory." A daily dose of Rimonabant triggered the same adverse conditions that CB-1 activity normally protects against—the same medical conditions for which cannabis provides relief. Sanofi sought U.S. approval for its CB-1 antagonist in 2007, shortly after the FDA had to recall Vioxx, an antiarthritis drug that caused thousands of fatal heart attacks and strokes. Still reeling from the Vioxx debacle, the FDA prudently gave Rimonabant the thumbs-down. European regulators took another look and winced, and Sanofi withdrew the drug from circulation.

Big Pharma's initial foray into designer cannabinoids failed miserably. If nothing else, the CB-1 antagonist debacle provided further evidence that a well-functioning endocannabinoid system is essential for good health. But U.S. government scientists saw other applications for Rimonabant. NIDA officials were keen on utilizing CB-1 blockers to treat various addictions, including "cannabis dependence." The administration of 40 milligrams of Rimonabant for eight consecutive days reduced subjective measures of intoxication after marijuana inhalation, according to NIDA-sponsored studies. Could a brave new cure for marijuana craving be a receptor tweak away? NIDA investigators, channeling Huxley, saw advantages in jamming the brain's receptor sites for THC—even if this interfered with everything crucial that CB-1 receptor signaling does.

The fact that Rimonabant blocked the euphoric effects of cannabis was a big plus, from NIDA's perspective. The psychiatric establishment defined "the high" as an adverse reaction. Harnessing the medicinal potential of cannabinoids without altering mood or thinking became an idée fixe among corporate pharmaceutical researchers. No one bothered to explain what's so objectionable about elevating the mood of a patient whose life is miserable. Dr. Donald Abrams, among others, questioned whether the herb's psychoactive properties are necessarily undesirable: "I am an oncologist as well as a specialist in AIDS, and I don't think a drug that creates euphoria in patients with terminal diseases is having an adverse effect."

Big Pharma was hot on the trail of a certain type of synthetic cannabinoid—a "selective CB-2 agonist"—that would bypass the brain while acting on the peripheral nervous system. The corporados were still pursuing a single-molecule approach to medical science, but the focus shifted from blocking CB-1 to activating CB-2, the cannabinoid receptor that regulates immune function and counters inflammation. Tinkering with molecules that stimulate CB-2 receptors—which are not concentrated in the brain and, therefore, are not associated with psychoactivity—raised the prospect of healing without the high.

Drug-company scientists envisioned a new series of highly selective cannabinoid-like compounds to treat a wide array of inflammatory ailments, including, at long last, a painkiller without abuse potential. That was the pharmaceutical Holy Grail, the druggist's dream—a nonaddictive analgesic bereft of adverse side effects. Michael Meyer, from Abbott Laboratories, cited studies involving CB-2 agonists and knockout mice that "demonstrated efficacy in preclinical models of inflammatory, moderate-to-severe post-operative, and neuropathic pain." Neuropathic pain, in particular, was difficult, if not impossible, to treat with conventional pharmaceuticals, according to University of Georgia neuroscientist Andrea Hohmann, who predicted that painkillers targeting CB-2 would not be psychoactive or addictive because CB-2 receptors "are localized predominantly outside the central nervous system."*

Medical researchers also explored ways to induce therapeutic outcomes by manipulating levels of the body's own cannabinoids. Various studies showed that it's possible to attenuate a wide range of pathological conditions by preventing or delaying the enzymatic breakdown of endogenous cannabinoids. Scientists developed synthetic compounds that raise endocannabinoid levels by suppressing fatty acid amide hydrolase (FAAH), the enzyme that deactivates anandamide. (Less FAAH means that more anandamide remains in the body for longer duration, and more anandamide means greater CB-1 receptor signaling.) Several new developments regarding FAAH inhibitors were discussed at the 2008 International Cannabinoid Research Society conference in Scotland. Virginia Commonwealth University scientist Joel Schlosburg reported that FAAH suppression reduced itching and scratching among rodents with experimentally induced pruritus. University of Calgary scientist Keith Sharkey disclosed that drugs targeting endocannabinoid degradation relieved experimentally induced colitis. And Sándor Bátkai at the U.S. National Institutes of Health found that a synthetic FAAH inhibitor lowered the blood pressure of hypertensive rats, suggesting that FAAH suppression may be a remedy for hypertension. Other studies indicated that FAAH inhibition ameliorated neuropathic pain and arthritis in animal models and blunted withdrawal symptoms in mice dependent on morphine.

Honest scientists who still paid attention to the plant's therapeutic qualities didn't have to look very far for a FAAH inhibitor. A team of Italian researchers led by Tiziana Bisogno was the first to point out that cannabidiol (CBD), a nonpsychoactive component of marijuana as well as fiber hemp, suppresses FAAH, the enzyme that metabolizes and destroys anandamide. By inhibiting this enzyme, CBD strengthens the body's autoprotective endocannabinoid signaling system. Cannabidiol enhances endocannabinoid tone and actually counters the psychoactive effects of THC.

Curiously, CBD has little binding affinity for either the CB-1 or CB-2 receptors. Instead it exerts its therapeutic impact on a molecular level through

* The first international science conference devoted wholly to the CB-2 cannabinoid receptor was convened in the Canadian Rockies, May 31–June 2, 2007. The CB2 Cannabinoid Receptors: New Vistas Conference was sponsored by Big Pharma heavyweights such as Abbott, AstraZeneca, Wyeth, and Amgen, as well as the National Institute on Drug Abuse. "I've never seen such a strong corporate presence at a cannabinoid conference, and I've been to several of these meetings," a veteran U.S. researcher commented. Marijuana, the venerable plant, was rarely mentioned at the CB-2 meeting.

various receptor-independent channels and by directly activating or antagonizing other (noncannabinoid) receptors. CBD activates a particular type of serotonin receptor, for example, thereby conferring an antidepressant effect.

Raphael Mechoulam, the Israeli scientist best known for isolating and synthesizing THC, elucidated the chemical structure of cannabidiol in 1963. But for a handful of early studies in Israel and Brazil, CBD's therapeutic potential was largely ignored while researchers focused on THC and public officials obsessed over the marijuana menace. (All cannabinoids in the plant were automatically placed in Schedule I because they fall under the definition of marijuana as stipulated in the Controlled Substances Act; although CBD doesn't make people feel euphoric and has no known adverse effects, U.S. authorities deemed it a dangerous drug with no medical utility and kept it in Schedule I along with heroin and LSD.) Cannabidiol remained a Schedule I substance even after scientists at the National Institute of Mental Health documented the extraordinary antioxidant and neuroprotective qualities of CBD in the late 1990s. Subsequent animal model experiments would show that CBD blocked the formation of Alzheimer's plaque. And a preclinical study published in the journal *Cell Communication and Signaling* reported that the administration of cannabidiol stimulated adult brain cell growth in laboratory mice.

José Crippa and his colleagues at the University of São Paulo conducted pioneering clinical research that showed that CBD significantly decreased social anxiety in psychiatric patients, an effect that scientists linked to changes in regional cerebral blood flow. Another Brazilian study showed that CBD mitigated THC-induced anxiety in human subjects. CBD also neutralized other unwanted reactions that THC occasionally may precipitate—rapid heartbeat, confusion, panic, and, in rare instances, transitory psychotic symptoms.

CBD interacts with THC in complex ways, diminishing certain effects (the munchies, sleepiness, the high) while augmenting others. Cannabidiol balances the buzz and softens the euphoria—or, in some cases, the dysphoria—induced by THC, which, in concentrated form, can make people feel very loopy and weird. CBD is the yin of THC's yang. They work together synergistically, complementing and magnifying each other's anti-inflammatory and painkilling impact.

Dr. Sean McAllister's research at the Pacific Medical Center in San Francisco yielded dramatic evidence attesting to the synergistic interplay between CBD and THC. McAllister discovered that cannabidiol reduces human breast cancer cell proliferation, invasion and metastasis. Best results were obtained when CBD was utilized in conjunction with THC. Pacific Medical Center scientists also showed that CBD strengthened the inhibitory effect of THC on human brain cancer cells. McAllister told the BBC that cannabidiol "offers hope of a non-toxic therapy" that could treat aggressive forms of cancer "without any of the painful side effects" of chemotherapy.

A gifted compound with a wide spectrum of action, cannabidiol shows great promise as a remedy for cardiovascular disease, diabetes, metabolic disorders and other chronic, diet-related conditions.* British researchers found that cannabidiol can suppress cardiac arrhythmias in lab animals after a stroke. (There are no safe and effective Big Pharma drugs for irregular heartbeat.) Other tests indicated that CBD lowers glucose levels, improves insulin sensitivity, and protects the health of diabetic patients' hearts. Cannabidiol, according to several scientific reports, can help prevent the onset of diabetes, which afflicted more than 285 million people worldwide in 2009. The U.S. Centers for Disease Control and Prevention predicts that one-third of all American adults will be diabetic by 2050. This debilitating illness and its complications already imposed a huge emotional and economic burden, accounting for one-fourth of America's $2.3 trillion national health-care bill—a staggering statistic that underscores the potential significance of CBD-rich medicine as a treatment for diabetes and related ailments.

CBD, the Cinderella molecule, the little substance that could—nontoxic, nonpsychoactive, and multicapable. Cannabinoid scientists, as a matter of professional decorum, were loath to speak in terms of a miracle drug, but cannabidiol came pretty close. In 2007, investigators at the National Center for Scientific Research in France reported that the administration of CBD stopped the progression of "Mad Cow" disease by inhibiting the development of deadly, infectious, misshaped protein particles known as prions. "Our results suggest that CBD may protect neurons against the multiple molecular and cellular factors involved in the different steps of the neurodegenerative process, which takes place during prion infection," the French research team concluded.

Infectious, antibiotic-resistant bacteria also got hammered by CBD in a petri dish. Cannabidiol, THC, and three other natural plant cannabinoids were shown to be effective against multiresistant bacterial strains, including Methicillin-resistant *Staphylococcus aureus* (MRSA), the deadly, infectious

---

* For example, a 2011 study by Japanese scientists demonstrated that CBD inhibits the activity of artery-clogging lipoxygenase, an enzyme involved in the development of atherosclerosis (S. Takeda et al., "Cannabidiol-2',6'-Dimethyl Ether as an Effective Protector of 15-Lipoxygenase-Mediated Low-Density Lipoprotein Oxidation in Vitro," *Biological & Pharmaceutical Bulletin* 34[8][2011]: 1252–56).

superbug that evolved from overuse of increasingly powerful antibiotics. The World Health Organization cited antibiotic resistance as one of the most serious public-health threats of the twenty-first century. Medical science had run amok and the allopaths found themselves outmatched by cunning, lethal bacteria that morphed into ever more virulent strains. A major global health crisis loomed. MRSA was already a serious problem in U.S. hospitals and prisons, killing 100,000 Americans a year, and the bug was spreading to the general population.

Canadian Marc Emery contracted MRSA while serving a five-year federal prison term in the United States for selling cannabis seeds over the Internet. But Emery had little opportunity to avail himself of marijuana's germ-fighting components. And if he managed to score some weed in the slammer, it wouldn't have had much CBD in it, according to a forensic study by Mahmoud ElSohly, supervisor of the federally sanctioned ganja grow-op at the University of Mississippi. The DEA commissioned ElSohly to analyze more than 46,000 samples of marijuana seized in raids from 1993 to 2008. Overall, THC content was found to have increased steadily from a mean of 3.4 percent in 1993 to 8.8 percent twenty-five years later, while CBD, with few exceptions, was barely detectable in the specimens tested.

The dearth of CBD-rich cannabis reflected a trend that began when domestic sinsemilla cultivation took root in the United States during the 1970s. Whereas traditionally plants grown abroad for hashish contained THC and CBD in roughly equal amounts, North American cannabis breeders selected plants for maximum psychoactivity to accommodate a growing consumer demand. Because CBD levels decrease as THC increases, they unwittingly bred cannabidiol out of the underground supply.

As of 2008, the only people in North America who could legally access CBD were Canadian multiple sclerosis patients with a doctor's prescription to use Sativex, the under-the-tongue cannabis spray developed by GW Pharmaceuticals. Sativex contained a 50/50 mix of THC and CBD, plus "minor cannabinoids" and a blend of aromatic terpenes and flavonoids. Rather than trying to isolate one compound and tailor it into a silver-bullet medication, GW bucked the Big Pharma trend and successfully introduced a whole plant extract with all of marijuana's active chemicals. The reduced psychoactivity of CBD-rich Sativex—which was clinically effective without causing the high that some patients find undesirable—made GW's flagship product more palatable to government officials. The fact that Sativex wasn't smoked and that each spray dispensed a precise, measured dose of medicine were also key selling points.

In the United States, however, cannabis users who might have benefited from cannabidiol were out of luck. Physicians in the Society of Cannabis Clinicians were intrigued by scientific studies indicating CBD's therapeutic potential, but the doctors were dismayed to hear experts conjecture that only trace amounts of CBD were present in marijuana strains accessible to patients. In 2005, *O'Shaughnessy's* predicted that the field of cannabis therapeutics would "really take off once California growers have access to an analytical test lab and can determine the cannabinoid content of their plants. Then patients can begin treating their given conditions with strains of known composition."

The breakthrough came in 2008 when Steve DeAngelo, CEO of the Harborside Health Center in Oakland, decided to back a start-up analytical lab that would test cannabis for THC and CBD levels. Harborside became the first medical-marijuana dispensary in the United States to offer certified CBD-rich cannabis to its members after several strains (out of many thousands tested) were identified as containing more than 4 percent CBD.

Before long, a dozen more labs were calibrating cannabinoid ratios and finding the occasional CBD-rich strain in California, Colorado, Montana, Michigan, and Washington. Analytical labs were one of many niche businesses that sprang up to serve the medical-marijuana community. Some breeders shifted gears and set their sights on conjuring CBD-rich hybrids, and several dispensary operators were eager to feature their products.

Testing marijuana strains and posting THC and CBD percentages in display cases were both effective marketing tools for medical-marijuana retail outlets and a genuine attempt to serve the needs of patients. Savvy pot-club proprietors recognized the importance of providing CBD-rich herb, edibles, tinctures, and topical ointments in addition to—not instead of—the typical high-THC fare. The decision to carry CBD-rich medicaments that don't make people high was a poke in the eye of drug-war apologists who slandered the medical-marijuana movement as a front for stoners. Offering CBD-rich meds was also shrewd business strategy that anticipated a vast new market for patients seeking the therapeutic benefits of the weed without any of the funny stuff.

"I am seeing many older patients who would like to try cannabis for pain, muscle spasms, insomnia, and management of various cancers," Dr. Jeffrey Hergenrather noted. "One thing that most of these cannabis-naïve patients are not interested in is 'getting high.' My hope is that CBD-rich strains will enable them to use cannabis and get its benefit without—or with less of—the usual 'high.' "

For decades, U.S. officials had been pushing the idea that THC was *the* active ingredient in marijuana. Marinol, "the pot pill," precluded the need for medical marijuana, they maintained. The Bush administration explicitly argued as much before the Supreme Court in the *Raich* case, asserting that synthetic THC, available as an approved pharmaceutical, was medically equivalent, if not superior, to herbal marijuana. Scientific research into cannabidiol and CBD's fortuitous reappearance in the grassroots medical supply exposed the falsity of this claim.

In addition to THC and CBD, the marijuana plant produces dozens of "minor cannabinoids," which are biologically active (meaning they interact with living cells). These compounds combine synergistically to produce an overall "entourage effect," as Mechoulam put it, so that the medicinal impact of the whole plant surpasses the sum of marijuana's individual components. Dr. John McPartland, a practicing osteopath and research scientist, compared the whole-plant "synergistic shotgun" versus Big Pharma's "single-ingredient silver bullet" approach. The latter, according to McPartland, is inherently self-limiting and much more likely to generate adverse side effects. Sure enough, no pattern of adverse effects had developed among medical-marijuana patients in California since the passage of Proposition 215, while pharmaceutical companies were forced to recall a battery of FDA-approved drugs that turned out to be dangerous and, in some cases, deadly.

Nature works in complex, synergistic ways. One compound is never the whole story, especially for cannabis, "a dialectical plant with opposite effects," as Fred Gardner put it. Twenty-three flavonoids, which are powerful antioxidants in their own right, have been found in marijuana, and two of these phytonutrients are unique to ganja. Scientists have also identified a total of 120 aromatic terpenoids that ooze from marijuana's resin glands and give each plant its distinct smell and flavor. Most of the qualities that distinguish specific marijuana strains are attributable to different terpenoid profiles. These fragrant essential oils contribute significantly to the entourage effect that "tames" THC's sassy psychoactivity and enhances its therapeutic impact.*

The science was amazing; the field of inquiry was exploding. Yet through it all, the U.S. government kept up the charade that miscategorized marijuana as a Schedule I drug with no medical utility. At the same time, the feds bent over backward to accommodate Big Pharma's single-molecule schemes, un-

* In 2008, the Swiss scientist Jürg Gertsch reported that beta-caryophyllene, a terpenoid compound present in marijuana and many edible plants, directly activates the CB-2 receptor. Gertsch described this common terpene as "a dietary cannabinoid." Certain terpenes dilate capillaries in the lungs, which allows THC and CBD to enter the bloodstream more easily.

derwriting research into the endocannabinoid system and fast-tracking potential reefer rivals or replacements. Drug-war strategists were playing a waiting game; they assumed that Big Pharma would eventually develop synthetic cannabinoid products with greater therapeutic efficacy than the herb. Modern medicine was all about controlled doses of single-molecule compounds. Federal regulators sought to discredit cannabis by harping on the difference between the "crude" botanical and the "pure" pharmaceutical. "You want to get as pure a medication as you can to minimize side effects," explained NIDA director Nora Volkow.

Of course, pure, single-molecule meds cause terrible side effects, but, unlike cannabis, they allegedly withstood "the rigorous scientific scrutiny of the FDA approval process," or so the authorities claimed.* Some drug-policy critics suspected the FDA frowned on marijuana because synthetic pharmaceutical makers stood to lose billions if they competed against cannabis on a level playing field. The reduced or discontinued use of pharmaceuticals, including prescription painkillers, was a recurring theme among medical-marijuana patients. In some cases, cannabis mitigated the toxic side effects of corporate pharmaceuticals. And best of all, many patients could grow their own medicine for next to nothing.

Despite the pipe dreams of the drug-war establishment, synthesized corporate concoctions will never make the whole plant obsolete. While cannabinoid designer drugs may indeed work wonders in the future—let's hope so—these synthetic products can never replace the widespread use of cost-effective, organically grown, backyard bud with its pungent, antioxidant-rich mixture of cannabinoids, terpenes, and flavonoids, which interact synergistically to produce a holistic, therapeutic effect that exceeds the capacity of single-molecule remedies. The plant's only drawback: It's against the law.

Booze or Bud?

A grapevine and a cannabis plant are depicted side by side on a bas-relief from a ruined Roman temple at Baalbek in Lebanon's fertile Bekaa Valley. One of the world's sweet spots for growing cannabis, this region is also known for its

* The FDA's hypercritical approach toward cannabis was in sharp contrast to the alacrity with which the FDA approved synthetic pharmaceuticals like Vioxx that turned out to have serious, even fatal, side effects.

fine wines. It is a place where wine and hashish mix geographically as well as culturally.

Poets and thinkers in the Muslim world have long debated the virtues and pitfalls of alcohol and marijuana. An epic poem written by Muhammad Ebn Soleiman Foruli, a sixteenth-century Turkish poet from Baghdad, portrays a dialectical battle between wine and hashish. The two inebriants engage in an allegorical fencing match as the poet describes the euphoric properties of both substances and their consequences, a subject much discussed among Muslim scholars. Foruli viewed wine as the drink of the rich, "while hashish," he said, "is a friend of the poor, the Dervishes and the men of knowledge."

One of the outstanding features of hashish was its inexpensiveness, which made the resinous herb accessible to nearly anyone desirous of the joy and repose that it may confer. Large numbers of Muslims used cannabis because, unlike alcohol, it was not expressly forbidden under Koranic law. Islam is the only major religion that banned booze, while cannabis remained a subject of theological dispute among Muslim intellectuals.

As the Islamic faith expanded, the use of cannabis spread across the Middle East. Symptomatic of its far-reaching cultural impact, hashish acquired numerous Arabic appellations—"rouser of thought," "bush of understanding," "branch of bliss," "shrub of emotion," "medicine of immortality," and so on. By the thirteenth century, cannabis consumption had become commonplace in Persia and the Arab lands, giving rise to many colorful legends. In *A Thousand and One Nights,* several characters take hashish and fantasize about a better life. One down-and-out fellow swallowed the potent resin and imagined that "a great Lord was shampooing him." In another story, two hashish eaters encounter the Sultan and mock him while dancing in the street.

An antiauthoritarian streak characterized the hashish-imbibing Sufis, the marginalized Muslim sect that embraced cannabis as a means of spiritual uplift. To the mystical Sufi, eating hashish was "an act of worship." Sufism always had a subversive edge because the claim of the direct experience of God threatened the prerogatives of the orthodox religious establishment. The brutal Ottoman emir Soudoun Scheikhouni, seeking to enforce religious and social conformity, issued the first edict against the use of hashish in the Muslim world in 1378. Several more such edicts would follow amid allegations that hashish caused immorality, sloth, poverty, mental derangement, and a disrespectful attitude toward the true faith. Growing cannabis for use as an intoxicant was forbidden, but growing the herb for medicinal purposes was allowed in keeping with the long tradition of cannabis therapeutics in the Middle East and North Africa. Muslim leaders recognized that hashish had important medicinal properties that were lacking in wine.*

The dialectical struggle between wine and weed continues to unfold in twenty-first-century America, where the alcohol industry funds organizations that seek to maintain marijuana prohibition. Such influence peddling by Booze Inc. is a preemptive strike against a mood-altering competitor. Drug-war posturing is also smooth public relations for liquor companies given the well-documented deleterious health and social costs of their products. Alcohol is a pivotal factor in some two-thirds of all cases of spousal abuse in the United States. Booze is implicated in more than 100,000 sexual assaults each year and 100,000 annual deaths in the United States due to drunk driving and alcohol-related violence. Worldwide, alcohol kills more than 2.5 million people annually. If drugs were classified on the basis of the harm they do, alcohol would be ranked right up there with heroin and crack cocaine, if not higher.

Although small amounts of wine can protect against certain illnesses such as heart disease (due in part to resveratrol, a flavonoid compound in grape skin), excessive alcohol intake poses serious health risks. Heavy drinking shrinks the brain, causes painful neuropathy, cirrhosis of the liver, and kidney damage, and increases the likelihood of breast cancer, colon cancer, and stomach ulcers. Yet booze is not only legal in our society, it is so pervasive and accepted that many people don't even think of alcohol as a drug. "In my era, everybody smoked [cigarettes], everybody drank, and there was no drug use," then DEA chief Thomas Constantine blithely asserted in 1998. That year, the World Health Organization published a toothless report that had originally described cannabis as less harmful than alcohol and tobacco—a conclusion deleted under pressure from U.S. officials.

In the United States, an estimated 60 percent of adults consume alcohol regularly. Fifteen million Americans—one-tenth of the adult U.S. population—are either addicted to or seriously debilitated by booze. Ten to 20 percent of all the alcohol guzzled in America is consumed by underage drinkers. The level of alcohol consumption among U.S. youth far exceeds the use of marijuana. Ditto for young people in Great Britain, where a fifth of ten- to fifteen-year-olds admit to getting drunk regularly.

While the harmful effects of alcoholism are well known, scientists have

* Within the Ottoman Empire, which encompassed parts of Spain and southern Europe during the Moorish conquest, hashish was employed as an anesthetic, a digestive aid, and a remedy for epilepsy, migraines, syphilis, flatulence, anxiety, and many other ailments.

only recently begun to investigate and understand the critical role that the endocannabinoid system plays in alcohol addiction and related mood disorders. According to several studies, ethanol exposure alters endocannabinoid levels in different regions of the mammalian brain. The amount of 2-AG, the most prevalent endocannabinoid in the brain, increases in direct proportion to the amount of ethanol consumed. When a person drinks booze and gets a little tipsy, his or her 2-AG levels increase slightly; when someone gets drunk, a lot of 2-AG sloshes around the brain; and as inebriation fades, 2-AG returns to its normal baseline level.

Why does the endocannabinoid system kick into high gear when a person hits the bottle? It is well known that ethanol is metabolized into acetaldehyde, a carcinogen and a mutagen that causes many harmful effects in vital organs. Simply put, alcohol is protoplasmic poison, and scientists have determined that a basic function of the endocannabinoid system is neuroprotective in nature: hence the spike in 2-AG in various parts of the brain during ethanol exposure.

The human brain is a delicate organ, stoutly defended by a thick skull and a blood-brain barrier primed to keep unwanted foreign substances from penetrating. The endocannabinoid system is a crucial component of the brain's protective apparatus. In 2009, the scientific journal *Neurotoxicology and Teratology* presented clinical data indicating that compounds in marijuana helped to "protect the human brain against alcohol-induced damage." This study, conducted at the University of California in San Diego, found that adolescents who smoke marijuana may be less susceptible to brain damage from binge drinking. Researchers at the National Institute of Mental Health have demonstrated that CBD reduces alcohol-induced cell death in the hippocampus, which plays an important role in memory and spatial navigation.

Whereas acute alcohol exposure temporarily increases endocannabinoid levels in the brain, chronic alcohol use results in a systemic decline in endocannabinoid signaling and deficient endocannabinoid baseline levels.* Long-

---

* Larry Parsons and his colleagues at the Scripps Research Institute report that prolonged ethanol exposure causes "reduced baseline extracellular 2-AG levels in the amygdala," less-efficient CB-1 receptor binding activity, and "diminished CB-1 receptor expression." Chronic alcohol consumption also desensitizes and weakens CB-1 receptor function in the brain region known as the ventral striatum. Dysfunction of CB-1 signaling in the ventral striatum correlates with increased vulnerability to alcohol addiction and suicidal tendencies. In 2009, writing in the *Journal of Psychiatric Research*, Yaragudri Vinod and his colleagues proposed that pharmacological agents which "modulate the endocannabinoid tone or CB-1 receptor function might have therapeutic potential in the treatment of alcohol addiction and prevention of suicidal behavior" (K. Yaragudri Vinod et al., "Selective Altera-

term alcohol abuse induces endocannabinoid deficits, and this, in turn, has an adverse impact on numerous physiological processes that are modulated by the endocannabinoid system. If alcoholism is an endocannabinoid deficit disorder, then it makes perfect sense that some people might successfully wean themselves from booze by smoking marijuana, which amplifies cannabinoid receptor signaling.

Recent advances in brain science have validated the practice of cannabis substitution as a harm-reduction strategy for treating alcoholism. There is compelling evidence that alcohol consumption diminishes among those who "self-medicate" with cannabis. A NIDA-funded investigation in Jamaica in the mid-1970s concluded that ganja smokers drank much less alcohol than non-smokers, lending credence to the idea that widespread marijuana use accounts for significantly lower levels of alcoholism in Jamaica than anywhere else in the Caribbean. But the notion of substituting marijuana for alcohol and other addictive substances would remain strictly taboo in NIDA-contracted scientific laboratories. The corporate medical establishment wasn't high on the idea of smoking pot to get off booze.

While working for the NIMH in the late 1960s, Dr. Tod Mikuriya discovered many references in the medical literature that supported the use of marijuana in the treatment of drug and alcohol addiction. Cannabis was found to be an effective medicine for withdrawal from a broad spectrum of addictive substances, including opiates and barbiturates. In 1891, Dr. J. B. Mattison, writing in the *St. Louis Medical and Surgical Journal*, described cannabis as a "remarkable" treatment for drug and alcohol dependence. Fifty years later, Dr. Roger Adams, writing about cannabis as a remedy for alcohol addiction, noted that THC "was useful in alleviation or elimination of withdrawal symptoms . . . The feeling of euphoria produced by tetrahydrocannabinol helped in rehabilitating the physical condition and in facilitating [the patients'] social reorientation."

But meaningful research into the possible benefits of using cannabis as an alternative to alcohol was all but impossible until the passage of Proposition 215. After Californians voted to legalize medical marijuana, Mikuriya and a small circle of like-minded physicians recommended the herb for many alcoholics—often with good results. In 2003, Mikuriya reported his findings in *O'Shaughnessy's*. Ninety-two patients were identified as successfully utilizing cannabis to treat alcohol abuse and related problems. "Although medicinal use of cannabis by alcoholics can be dismissed as 'just one drug replacing

tions of the CB1 Receptors and the Fatty Acid Hydrolase in the Ventral Striatum of Alcoholics and Suicides," *Journal of Psychiatric Research* 44[9][2010]: 59–97).

another,' lives mediated by cannabis and alcohol tend to run very different courses," Mikuriya observed. "Even if use is daily, cannabis replacing alcohol (or other addictive, toxic drugs) reduces harm because of its relatively benign side-effect profile . . . The chronic alcohol-inebriation-withdrawal cycle ceases with successful cannabis substitution. Sleep and appetite are restored, ability to focus and concentrate is enhanced, energy and activity levels are improved . . . Family and social relationships can be sustained as pursuit of long-term goals ends the cycle of crisis and apology."*

Getting stoned on weed is a very different experience from getting drunk on booze. The mild, swimmy-headedness that many cannabis smokers feel is not caused by a toxic insult to the central nervous system, as is the case with alcohol. Nor does marijuana damage the esophagus, the spleen, the digestive tract, or the liver like alcohol and so many Big Pharma meds. In a cruel twist of fate, an unknown number of patients would die after being denied liver transplants because they tested positive for cannabis. (Medical-marijuana users suffer many kinds of discrimination. Some have lost government-subsidized housing, custody of their children, the right to adopt, the right to raise foster children, as well as employment opportunities.) To disqualify someone who needs a liver transplant—usually the result of alcohol abuse—on the grounds that they smoke or eat marijuana is particularly perverse given that plant cannabinoids can "suppress the immunity reaction that causes rejection of organ transplants," as the *Washington Post* reported.

After a University of Colorado freshman died of alcohol poisoning during a fraternity pledge in 2004, a group of Rocky Mountain cannabis activists formed SAFER—Safer Alternative for Enjoyable Recreation—to highlight the contrasting risk profiles of cannabis and booze. Backed by the D.C.-based Marijuana Policy Project, SAFER argued that booze is much more dangerous than reefer, and to reduce alcohol problems on campus, the university should lessen penalties for pot possession and cut its cozy ties with Coors, the Colo-

---

* A study by sociologist Amanda Reiman (*Harm Reduction Journal* [December 3, 2009]) provided additional evidence that for those unable or disinclined to stop using psychoactive substances completely, marijuana offered a viable alternative to Alcoholics Anonymous, which emphasizes complete abstinence as a rehab requirement. Reiman surveyed 350 members of the Berkeley Patients Group, a city-licensed medical-marijuana dispensary. Forty percent of respondents said they used marijuana as an effective substitute for alcohol. Twenty-six percent of those surveyed said they used marijuana to replace more dangerous illegal drugs. Fifty-seven percent asserted that marijuana provided better relief for their symptoms than conventional medications, and 66 percent said they used cannabis as a replacement for prescription pills.

rado brewery that sponsored frat parties and other UC events. "Marijuana is a safer intoxicant for partying. It's that simple," said Mason Tvert, the twenty-two-year-old leader of SAFER, who denounced pot prohibition and the legal double standard that privileges booze over bud. Tvert's harm-reduction advocacy rang true to the student majority in Boulder that voted to equalize punishment for on-campus weed and alcohol infractions. The SAFER movement quickly spread to other colleges around the country.

"This isn't about being pro-drug. This is about being pro-safety, pro-health, and pro–good public policy," Tvert explained. "It's about allowing adults to make the rational, safer choice to use marijuana instead of alcohol, if that's what they prefer, so we're no longer driving people to drink."

SAFER took its campaign to Denver, which became the first major metropolis in the United States to wipe out all criminal and civil penalties for adults possessing a small amount of marijuana. In the run-up to the November 2005 vote, SAFER unveiled a billboard proclaiming, "Alcohol use makes domestic violence eight times more likely . . . Marijuana use does not." Emphasizing public safety and personal freedom, Tvert spearheaded the citywide ballot initiative—backed by 54 percent of the electorate—that legalized adult marijuana use in the Mile High City.

But Denver cops, citing state law, ignored the will of the people and cranked up the number of local pot citations. So SAFER sponsored another ballot measure—making marijuana arrests Denver's lowest law-enforcement priority—and this passed easily, as well. SAFER went on the offensive during the 2008 presidential campaign, organizing protests at the Democratic National Convention in Denver. (Coors and Anheuser-Busch were prominent corporate sponsors of the convention that nominated Barack Obama.) SAFER also took Cindy McCain, wife of Republican nominee John McCain, to task, calling her a "drug dealer" because of her ownership stake in a major beer company.

SAFER's message was catching on. A Zogby poll during Bush's second term indicated that a majority of U.S. citizens living on the east and west coasts thought marijuana should be regulated much like alcohol. Another survey found that Colorado residents were smoking more marijuana and drinking less booze than in previous years. Tvert considered this good news. If legalizing marijuana resulted in a decline in alcohol use, it would be a positive development from a public-health perspective, according to SAFER, and if legalization resulted in the wider use of marijuana, with its demonstrable neuroprotective properties, then so much the better.

The Green Rush

Medical marijuana in Colorado got off to a bumpy start. In November 1998, 57 percent of voters in the Rocky Mountain state approved Amendment 19, which would have legalized the use of cannabis for therapeutic purposes, but the results, like in Washington, D.C., that year, did not count. Shortly before the election, the Colorado secretary of state announced that the sponsors of the initiative had failed to obtain the required number of signatures to qualify for the ballot—even though the initiative was already on the ballot. Two years later, Coloradans went to the polls again and passed another medical-marijuana measure. For much of the next decade, however, foot-dragging by the state bureaucracy made it very difficult for qualified patients to do what the law allowed.

As Denver's district attorney, Democrat Bill Ritter adamantly opposed medical marijuana. But after he became governor in 2007, Ritter turned to cannabis to balance the budget. Medical-marijuana providers and other reefer-related businesses paid for state licenses, and taxes on officially sanctioned for-profit sales began pouring into the treasury. By the end of Ritter's four-year gubernatorial tenure, the number of authorized pot patients in Colorado climbed from fewer than two thousand to more than a quarter of a million, comprising 2 percent of the state's population.

Medical-marijuana facilities opened throughout Colorado, including at least 230 in Denver, giving rise to predictable jokes about "the Mile High City." Storefronts with giant pot leaves were prevalent all along a hemp-themed stretch known as "the Green Mile" or "Broadsterdam." As in California, some pot shops offered holistic healing services, including acupuncture and massage. *The Denver Post* regularly carried medical-marijuana ads, and the local weekly, *Westword*, hired a writer to cover the dispensary beat. A restaurant specializing in cannabis cuisine for patients got rave reviews.

Colorado was already the fastest-growing medicinal-cannabis market in the country when the Obama administration told federal prosecutors that they "should not focus resources . . . on individuals whose actions are in clear and unambiguous compliance with existing state laws providing for the medical use of marijuana." Dated October 19, 2009, the directive, written by Deputy Attorney General David Ogden, was riddled with vague, conditional language and major loopholes "that give prosecutors broad discretion to determine what they think is legal," warned Dale Gieringer of California NORML. Nevertheless, the Ogden memo triggered a surge of entrepreneurial activity in states where cannabis was allowed as a curative. From Montana to Michigan to Maine, medical-marijuana dispensaries were popping up like mushrooms after the prohibitionist reign.

Obama's ascension to the White House engendered high hopes for substantive change in federal policy regarding marijuana and many other areas of governance. He seemed less uptight about cannabis than his Oval Office predecessors. "I inhaled frequently. That was the point," candidate Obama remarked in response to a question about pot smoking. But he also said that marijuana would have to pass muster with the FDA in order to qualify as medicine. Obama promised that as president he would respect science and end federal law-enforcement raids against medical-marijuana targets in states where it was legal to take the herb: "The Justice Department going after sick individuals using this as a palliative instead of going after serious criminals makes no sense."

On November 4, 2008, the day Obama was elected president, voters approved nine out of ten marijuana law reform measures around the country. That year, 25.8 million U.S. citizens, or 10.3 percent of the population aged twelve or older, smoked the herb. More than 100 million Americans had tried marijuana, and ten states (led by Rhode Island, Vermont, Alaska, and Colorado) had a higher per capita cannabis usage than California. Roughly a quarter of all Americans resided in a state where medical marijuana was legal. What was once seen as a dangerous habit of a deviant counterculture had become deeply woven into the fabric of mainstream social life. Weed smoking was so widespread that even the FBI, eager for new recruits, changed its practice of not hiring people with a history of marijuana use.

Would the new president seize the moment and remove cannabis from Schedule I to allow research and medical access? Would Obama pull an FDR and put an end to an unpopular prohibition?

Alas, lip service and mixed signals, rather than fresh thinking and novel approaches, characterized Obama's stance on marijuana. To head the Justice Department, Obama tapped Eric Holder, who had been appointed to serve as a Superior Court judge in the District of Columbia by that fervent pot foe Ronald Reagan. As deputy attorney general under Clinton, Holder had proposed stiffening federal marijuana penalties after California legalized medicinal cannabis. As attorney general under Obama, Holder reappointed the Bush holdover Michele Leonhart to head the DEA.*

* Michele Leonhart's crowning moment as interim DEA chief under Bush was her refusal to issue a license to Professor Lyle Craker, a University of Massachusetts botanist, to cultivate

Instead of abolishing the budget sinkhole known as the Office of National Drug Control Policy, Obama named Seattle police chief Gil Kerlikowske as the new drug czar. In his first on-the-job interview, Kerlikowske said it was time to retire the phrase "war on drugs." "We're not at war with people in this country," he told *The Wall Street Journal*. But DEA squads kept right on raiding dispensaries in California with automatic weapons drawn. Who was calling the shots? Had the DEA gone rogue? In the topsy-turvy, quasi-legal world of medical marijuana, it appears that rogue was policy.

The massive economic stimulus bill enacted by Congress in 2009 included $3.8 billion for state and local law enforcement, much of it destined for multi-jurisdictional antimarijuana task forces—the same units involved in busting medical-marijuana providers. This cushy government jobs program guaranteed that law enforcement would continue arresting, prosecuting, and jailing pot smokers, usually for possessing small quantities of weed. In addition to receiving government subsidies earmarked for combatting cannabis, police agencies used cash seizures and forfeited property from marijuana suspects to pad their budgets. "Marijuana is where the money is," Sheriff Tom Bosenko of Shasta County acknowledged.

Many a cannabusiness entrepreneur surely would agree. Their revenues were based on production and distribution of a commodity for which there was real consumer demand. In a dismal economy, the marijuana sector was creating jobs for thousands of people, including young workers who were anything but amotivated. It provided employment for pot trimmers, couriers, edibles vendors, clone providers, bud tenders, medical consultants, staff at analytical labs and hydroponics shops, electricians, carpenters, Web designers, security guards, bakers, confectioners, tincture makers, lawyers, real estate and insurance agents, accountants, clerical workers, and more. Existing businesses were forced to compete with pot industry wages ($20 per hour off the books

---

marijuana for FDA-approved research. In so doing, Leonhart overruled a decision by the DEA administrative law judge Mary Ellen Bittner, who had concluded that it would be "in the public interest" to grant Craker's request. As a result, the University of Mississippi's pot farm would remain the only legal source of cannabis for scientists, and NIDA would continue to block access. Nearly any fourteen-year-old could get weed from street sources, but scientists and doctors in the United States still could not obtain the herb to investigate its therapeutic efficacy or lack thereof. In 2011, NIDA blocked proposed research on medical marijuana to treat PTSD. That same year, NIDA announced it was setting aside $10 million in grants for institutions to study the effects of the movement to legalize medical marijuana (Fred Tasker, "South Florida Man Smokes Marijuana at Taxpayers' Expense," *Miami Herald*, January 11, 2011).

for seasonal bud trimmers); consequently wages tended to rise in marijuana-growing regions. Word got out. Zonker, the *Doonesbury* cartoon character, told his comic-strip parents that he was moving to Humboldt County to grow pot just like thousands of other recession-driven green rushers who pulled up stakes and settled in Northern California.

There was a saying in the late 1960s: "Pot will get you through times of no money better than money will get you through times of no pot." Four decades later, the marijuana industry was thriving like never before, "raking in what is estimated to be tens of billions of dollars nationwide," according to CNBC. Colorado's for-profit medical-marijuana market was the envy of cannabusiness owners across the country. The political terrain in California was more problematic. In 2008, the attorney general, Jerry Brown, issued legal guidelines stipulating that medical-marijuana providers must operate as nonprofit collectives. But structuring a business as a nonprofit didn't mean that it couldn't generate lots of cash.

Rooted in an outlaw subculture, the medical-marijuana industry contributed more than $105 million in tax revenues to the state treasury in 2009, according to the California Board of Equalization. By the end of the decade there were an estimated one million doctor-recommended medical users in California—and certified patients accounted for less than 10 percent of the pot-smoking vox populi. The flourishing gray market for medical marijuana overlapped with a much larger black market for ganja. Californians consumed 500 tons of marijuana or one billion joints annually. The state's mostly untaxed pot crop in 2010 was said to be worth $13.8 billion. The vast majority of the harvest was destined for out-of-state consumers.

Since people were going to smoke pot no matter what, why not treat bud like booze, tax it, and harmonize the state's finances? The economic argument for legalization was compelling at a time when California was drowning in debt, jobs in general were hard to come by, and a quarter of the population lacked health insurance. The California Board of Equalization estimated the Golden State could earn nearly $1.4 billion per year in extra tax revenue from legalized cannabis commerce.

Harvard economist Jeffrey Miron did the math: In addition to gaining a huge tax windfall, California would save $981 million a year in police, court, and jail costs by no longer enforcing the ban on marijuana. "A policy that prohibits marijuana makes no more sense than a policy that prohibits alcohol, ice cream, or driving on the highway," said Miron, the author of a 2005 study on the budgetary implications of cannabis prohibition. Endorsed by five hundred economists (including several Nobel laureates), Miron's report projected that ending pot prohibition nationwide would save $7.7 billion in combined state and federal spending, while taxing the herb would bring in $6.2 billion annually—a potential net gain of close to $14 billion. Miron maintained that federal officials had "hyperbolized" marijuana use, which "just makes them look like idiots."

Miron was one of several notables who supported Proposition 19, the California ballot measure that would allow adults twenty-one and over to possess an ounce of marijuana and to grow a few plants on 25 square feet of land. Cities and counties would decide whether to permit and tax marijuana sales within their boundaries. That was the bait—a chance to tax and regulate reefer transactions. It appeared that California, one of the first states to ban cannabis nearly twenty-five years before the Marihuana Tax Act, was poised to become the first state to relegalize the weed. The tax issue was paramount in 1937 when a medically ignorant bureaucrat convinced the federal government to impose a de facto ban on cannabis by requiring physicians to purchase exorbitant tax stamps that were never available, a legislative sleight-of-hand that consigned the herb to decades of legal oblivion. And now, in a biphasic reversal of sorts, the possibility of lucrative tax revenue was aiding the legalization effort.

By coincidence, the 1972 California Marijuana Initiative—which gained a third of the vote in favor of legalizing "backyard marijuana" for personal use (no tax provisions included)—was also called Proposition 19. The new Prop. 19, the Regulate, Control and Tax Cannabis Act of 2010, attracted broad-based support that cut across class, gender, ideological, and racial lines. Several labor unions and civil rights groups endorsed the measure.

For Alice Hoffman, head of the California chapter of the NAACP, marijuana law reform was a racial-equality issue. She recognized that pot prohibition took a heavy toll on minority communities. "Proposition 19 is about eliminating enforcement practices that are targeting and creating a permanent underclass of citizens, of African Americans, caught in the criminal-justice system while other people, a more privileged class, go free," said Hoffman. An October 2010 report commissioned by the NAACP and the Drug Policy Alliance documented pervasive racist law-enforcement patterns in the Golden State: "In every one of the 25 largest counties in California, blacks are arrested for marijuana possession at higher rates than whites, typically double, triple or even quadruple the rate of whites." The National Black Police Association, citing similar concerns, also backed Proposition 19.

And guess who turned up during the heat of the campaign? None other than Captain Howard Wooldridge and his faithful horse, Misty, who traversed the length and breadth of California in the months leading up to the vote. The former Michigan police detective had already ridden across the United States twice to make a statement against the war on drugs. Now he was back in the

Retired police captain Howard Wooldridge and his horse, Misty, trekked across the United States to protest marijuana prohibition

(Courtesy of Steve Cookinham)

Golden State, wearing his cowboy hat and the T-shirt that said in large letters: COPS SAY LEGALIZE POT. ASK ME WHY. Wooldridge, a founding member of Law Enforcement Against Prohibition (LEAP), likened himself to a modern-day Paul Revere who took to the streets on horseback to sound the alarm and get out the vote for Proposition 19.

After witnessing firsthand the manifold lunacies of the war on drugs, Wooldridge concluded that his colleagues were chasing the tail of a very old dragon they could never slay. Prohibition hadn't worked since Adam and Eve bit the apple in the Garden of Eden, and it wouldn't keep people from smoking marijuana. The kind bud was either too much fun or too essential a balm for too many folks. If a "tough on drugs" approach worked, the goal of a drug-free America would have been achieved a long time ago. Instead, the drug warriors had little to show for their efforts "except prisons full of the wrong people," according to Wooldridge.

Ex–San Jose police chief Joseph McNamara, another member of LEAP, was featured in pro-19 television ads during the final week of the campaign. "Proposition 19 will tax and control marijuana just like alcohol," he claimed. "It will generate billions of dollars for local communities, allow police to focus on violent crimes."

No-on-19 forces countered with fearmongering and hair-on-fire hysterics.

"Prop. 19 would allow big-rig drivers and even school bus drivers to smoke marijuana right up until the moment they climb behind the wheel," GOP Assemblyman Jim Nielsen warned in a TV spot. The No-on-19 website posted images of smashed-up cars and wrecked school buses, implying that marijuana was to blame for fatal accidents. Insinuations that stoned drivers posed a threat to road safety were not supported by data. A study by the Institute for the Study of Labor found that in states with legal medical marijuana, traffic fatalities declined due to lower alcohol consumption.

"There's no earthly reason to make another mind-altering substance, particularly one that's carcinogenic, more available to people," argued No-on-19 spokesman John Lovell, the Sacramento lobbyist for the California Narcotics Officers' Association, the California Police Chiefs Association, and several other state law-enforcement organizations. Lovell was also formerly a troubleshooter for Gallo Winery. California law enforcement and alcohol producers were allied in their opposition to marijuana legalization. Concerned that people would drink less alcohol if pot were legal, the California Beer and Beverage Distributors contributed financially to the No-on-19 campaign. Police groups were also major donors.

A chorus of high-profile California politicians, both Democrats and Republicans, weighed in against Proposition 19, much as they had opposed Proposition 215 fourteen years earlier. Governor Arnold Schwarzenegger said the ballot measure, if passed, would "make California a laughingstock." A few weeks before the vote, he signed legislation that reduced the punishment for possession of less than an ounce of marijuana from a misdemeanor to an infraction equivalent to a parking ticket.

President Obama wasn't exactly a profile in courage on this issue, either. As drug czar Kerlikoswke proclaimed, "Legalization is not in the president's vocabulary, nor is it in mine." Attorney General Holder denounced Proposition 19 and vowed to aggressively enforce the Controlled Substances Act no matter what the outcome of the vote. In the months ahead, the DEA would reject a long-standing petition filed by several groups, which sought to remove cannabis from Schedule I so that medical patients could use the herb and scientists could analyze it. Marijuana "has a high potential for abuse . . . no accepted medical use . . . [and] lacks accepted safety for use under medical supervision," the DEA declared.* So much for Obama's promise to restore scientific integrity to government. The stubbornness of the DEA in insisting

---

* In July 2010, the DEA issued a fifty-four-page booklet, "DEA Position on Marijuana," which asserted that medical marijuana is a "fallacy," that "smoked marijuana is not medi-

that cannabis lacked medical value was reminiscent of the priests who refused to look through Galileo's telescope.*

On Election Day 2010, 4,643,592 Californians out of nearly 10 million voters, or 46.5 percent, cast their ballot in favor of Proposition 19—an impressive number but not enough to turn the tide. Only eleven out of fifty-eight counties supported the legalization initiative. Mendocino, Humboldt, and Trinity, the Emerald Triangle counties where marijuana was the economic lifeline, all rejected Proposition 19. The prospect of legalization upset everyone's applecart and gave pause to thousands of small- to mid-size cannabis cultivators that formed the backbone of the region's economy. Many mom-and-pop growers, who had paid their dues over the years, feared that Prop. 19 would open the door for Big Tobacco and corporate megafarms to get involved in cannabis production. (Philip Morris had already filed a trademark application for "Marley" brand cannabis cigarettes.) The Marlborization of marijuana loomed as potentially catastrophic for first- and second-generation ganja green thumbs in Northern California. How could they compete if massive farming operations caused a precipitous drop in pot prices? Anna Hamilton, an Emerald Triangle radio host, foresaw economic apocalypse: "We're going to be ruined." Bumper stickers began appearing: "Save Humboldt County—Keep Pot Illegal."

"I got into this to just legalize it. I didn't get into it to protect the small grower or the big grower," said Prop. 19's instigator and chief financial backer, Richard Lee. The proverbial Mayor of Oaksterdam was eminently pragmatic about marijuana: "For a lot of people it's just another brand of beer." His cavalier attitude did not endear him to Emerald Triangle veterans, who felt threatened by the city of Oakland's decision to license four large, industrial-scale indoor grow facilities that could potentially supply marijuana to much of the state. Eager to cash in on the pot trade, Oakland officials saw the move as a way to boost the city's economy in the event that Proposition 19 passed. Old-time ganja farmers were also wary of weGrow, California's first hydroponics superstore, which promoted itself as "the Walmart of Weed" when it opened in the

cine," and "there is no sound scientific evidence that smoked marijuana can be used safely and effectively as medicine."

* Shortly after the DEA formally rejected the rescheduling petition, the *British Journal of Pharmacology* published yet another study documenting the neuroprotective effects of THC and CBD, the dynamic plant cannabinoid duo; this particular report showed that these compounds were able to blunt the progression of Huntington's disease and Parkinson's disease, two neurodegenerative brain disorders that do not respond to conventional treatments (J. Fernández-Ruiz et al., "Prospects for Cannabinoid Therapies in Basal Ganglia Disorders," *British Journal of Pharmacology* 163[7][2011]: 1365–78).

East Bay in January 2010. Some joked about the rise of "Starbuds," a fictional dispensary chain with identical franchises, uniformed budtenders, standardized customer greetings, and the same strains of overfertilized, mass-produced, THC-heavy, indoor-grown herb.

The marijuana business was changing rapidly, eclipsing its founding political movement and forcing a shakeout within the industry as weaker players folded. Enterprising cannabusinessmen and women were building trade associations and hiring lobbyists. Instead of betting on dot-coms, venture capitalists eyed pot-coms as the next big thing, a huge, about-to-be-unfettered market ripe for speculation and IPOs. "We're past the days when people call here to ask if marijuana will give men breasts," Allen St. Pierre, executive director of NORML in Washington, D.C., told *The New York Times*. "Now, the calls are from angel investors . . . people who are looking for ways to invest or offer their services."

All of this was disconcerting to old-guard marijuana activists who had blazed a treacherous trail for therapeutic access. Valerie Corral from Santa Cruz, the conscience of the medical-marijuana movement, lamented "the corporatization of cannabis," a sentiment shared by hemp guru Jack Herer, who decried proposals to tax and regulate the herb. Dennis Peron, the guiding force behind Proposition 215, also took umbrage at the thought of medical marijuana becoming a business driven by the bottom line. "Taxes? We shouldn't pay taxes," he said. "The government should pay us reparations for all the lives they ruined."

Peron, who had stayed on the sidelines in recent years running a bed-and-breakfast at his house in the Castro and volunteering in a San Francisco soup kitchen, urged voters to reject Proposition 19. Especially irksome to pro-pot opponents of Prop. 19 was wording in the ballot measure that would make a felon of someone if they smoked a joint in the presence of anyone under age twenty-one. This meant that adults with children wouldn't be able to use marijuana in the privacy of their home without committing a crime punishable by a three-year mandatory-minimum prison sentence. It also meant that cops would continue to arrest huge numbers of black and brown youth.

Professional campaign consultants, who previously worked for Bill Clinton and other mainstream antimarijuana Democrats, had convinced Lee that the initiative had a better chance of succeeding if it appealed more to soccer moms and others who might be inclined to vote yes on 19 if tight restrictions were included. But pandering to fears about cannabis and kids may have backfired by reinforcing decades of government propaganda that portrayed pot as perilous for adolescents. Although the economic argument for legalization made sense, it did not address deeply ingrained misgivings and misperceptions about marijuana. Those who thought that marijuana was a dangerous drug before the campaign evidently still felt the same way afterward.

Suffer the Children

"Kids at play, keep the pot away!" they chanted as the procession marched along a busy boulevard in Anaheim, California. Upset over a new medical-marijuana dispensary in their neighborhood, about a hundred residents protested in front of the controversial storefront on a Friday night in February 2011. They were concerned that children would be exposed to marijuana if the dispensary stayed opened. One demonstrator held a sign that said, YES KIDS, NO POT.

Although medical-marijuana dispensaries were not associated with an uptick in crime and in many cases they helped to revitalize California neighborhoods, the presence of reefer retail outlets sometimes met with local resistance. Kids were a key concern. Federal and state authorities maintained that marijuana deserved special criminal sanctions because of its presumed danger to children. Antimarijuana laws entailed additional penalties for pot crimes within a thousand feet of places where kids regularly gather, such as schools and playgrounds. "Unfortunately," as Clare Wilson wrote in *New Scientist*, "the idea that banning drugs is the best way to protect vulnerable people—especially children—has acquired a strong emotional grip, one that prohibitionists are happy to exploit."

Drug warriors claimed that tough laws were needed to keep kids away from marijuana and other illicit substances. They often warned that legalizing marijuana for medical purposes or for general adult use would "send the wrong message" to young people by implying that pot is okay. But Proposition 215 proved them wrong: There was no explosion of cannabis consumption among youth after its passage.

That's because ubiquitous black-market marijuana was already easy for young people to get. Nearly half of America's teenagers tried marijuana before graduating from high school and by their senior year more than 20 percent were occasional users.

Medical-marijuana dispensaries were strictly off-limits to minors. Doctors would not write letters recommending marijuana for underage patients unless they had a very serious medical problem *and* the consent of a parent. Some California youth "got legal" as soon as they turned eighteen. It was an open secret that nearly anyone with the right ID could visit a scrip mill and obtain a doctor's note by complaining of poor sleep, anxiety, or headaches. For-profit clinics and physicians specializing in ersatz medical-marijuana recommendations cropped up in several states. Young adults came in droves and left with notes from doctors that served as get-out-of-jail-free cards, ostensibly exempting them from state marijuana laws—a form of harm reduction in its own right.

Ever since the 1960s, smoking pot was both a rite of passage for adolescents around the world and a way for teens to socialize. Most youth who puffed weed went through a period of limited experimentation without suffering acute harm or lasting untoward effects. The assumption that only messed-up kids used marijuana was not borne out by a 2007 Swiss study, which found that teen pot smokers were generally well adjusted and did not report more frequent psychosocial problems than abstainers. According to researchers at Cardiff University in Britain, above-average intelligence among youth is a "risk factor" for cannabis use later in life—that is, smart kids are more likely to become pot smokers.

Weed wasn't just for losers—that was obvious from the parade of prominent actors, musicians, athletes, politicians, business leaders, and other role models who were outed as marijuana smokers. Baseball fans were nonplussed when Cy Young Award winner Tim Lincecum of the San Francisco Giants was arrested in the fall of 2009 after police found a pot pipe in the long-haired pitcher's car. Earlier that year, a picture surfaced of fourteen-time Olympic gold medalist Michael Phelps taking a bong hit at a college dorm party in South Carolina. Apparently one could smoke marijuana on occasion and still be successful in sports and life.

Several guidebooks for parents—with tips on how to "drug proof" kids—explained what to look for if your child is using marijuana. Utah criminology professor Gerald Smith identified several warning signs such as "excessive preoccupation with social causes, race relations, environmental issues, etc." A 2005 study of parental attitudes toward teen drug use, conducted by the Partnership for a Drug-Free America, found that nearly half the grown-ups surveyed would not be upset if their children experimented with marijuana. Some parents smoked pot with their sons and daughters when they got to be of a certain age. Chronic-pain patients reported that their child-rearing capabilities improved considerably when they used cannabis to ease somatic distress.

In an interview with *GQ* magazine, film star Johnny Depp said that if his kids were going to smoke pot, he'd prefer that they got marijuana from him rather than from someone on the street. "I have nothing to hide," said Depp, the proud owner of Jack Kerouac's raincoat and other Beat memorabilia. "I'm not a great pothead or anything like that . . . but weed is much, much less dangerous than alcohol." Ironically, Depp got his start on the TV series *21 Jump Street* playing a police officer, Tom Hanson, who went undercover in high schools to bust nickel-bag pot dealers and other teenage miscreants.

It took some creative acting on the part of an attractive young cop in order to pretend to be a high school senior and convince several male students in Falmouth, Massachusetts, to sell her marijuana, resulting in nine real-life arrests. Similar snitch scenarios unfolded in other parts of the country. The courts found it acceptable for police informants to purchase and peddle illicit substances and to use deceptive tactics, including sexual overtures, to entrap young people. School districts in several states paid students (sometimes as much as $1,000) to finger classmates who used marijuana. Police raids, drug-sniffing dogs, student locker searches, pat-downs and strip searches, closed-circuit security cameras in bathrooms, and random urine tests became part of the American high school experience—all in the name of protecting children from drugs.

From the moment Harry Anslinger began spewing invective about the evil weed, the feds maintained that pot prohibition was necessary above all to protect American youth. High school and college students were among those most affected by the war on drugs. Young marijuana users, especially ethnic minorities, suffered the highest arrest rates for possession. According to a 2006 national assessment by the American College Health Association, almost 34 percent of U.S. college students (some six million young men and women) had tried marijuana. One in five students (more than two million) said they smoked pot every month.*

American officials warned that young people were putting themselves at serious risk by smoking marijuana. Cannabis, the naysayers insisted, is a harmful drug that saps resolve, destroys brain cells, causes infertility and sexual dysfunction, impairs the immune system, blurs thinking, diminishes IQ, and leads to schizophrenia and addiction. "Numerous deleterious consequences are associated with [marijuana's] short and long term use, including the possibility of becoming addicted," Nora Volkow of NIDA alleged. Young people were told repeatedly that today's marijuana is superstrong—"not like the pot your father smoked." Apparently the weed that Dad smoked wasn't

* Since Congress passed the 1998 Higher Education Act, which barred federal grants or loans to any student with a drug conviction, more than 200,000 American students had lost their financial aid because of a drug bust (Students for Sensible Drug Policy, "Harmful Drug Law Hits Home: How Many College Students in Each State Lost Financial Aid Due to Drug Convictions?" [2006]: www.ssdp.org/states/ssdp-state-report.pdf).

so devilish after all, so the panicmeisters had to conjure a new specter: high-potency marijuana.

The stronger stuff was good news for seasoned pot smokers, who took fewer puffs for relief and/or relaxation. But drug warriors in the United States and elsewhere depicted high-THC herb as more addictive, more brain damaging, more disorienting, more psychosis-producing, and more of a threat to youth than the relatively mellow reefer of yesteryear. Stronger pot meant more warped young minds, according to British psychiatrist Robin Murray, who ruminated on the supposed dangers of "skunk," as high-THC sinsemilla was called in the UK, where a million and a half blokes smoked it each year. "Most people who drink alcohol, and most people who smoke cannabis, don't come to any harm," Murray conceded. "However, just as drinking a bottle of whisky a day is more of a hazard to your health than drinking a pint of lager, so skunk is more hazardous than traditional cannabis . . . because it may contain three times as much of the active ingredient tetrahydrocannabinol (THC)."

The skunk and whiskey comparison betrays the willful scientific ignorance of someone who has made a career out of claiming that marijuana causes schizophrenia. Numerous medical studies have proven that THC is not toxic to the human body.* Unlike alcohol, it does not destroy brain cells; on the contrary, extensive research has shown that THC and other phytocannabinoids protect brain cells and promote neurogenesis, the creation of new brain cells.†

Marijuana does not make one into an addict any more than food makes a

* In 2006, scientists at the Nathan Kline Institute in New York reported that cannabis exposure is not toxic to the developing adolescent brain (Lynn E. DeLisi et al., "A Preliminary DTI Study Showing No Brain Structural Change Associated with Adolescent Cannabis Use," *Harm Reduction Journal* 3[2006]: 17). Several studies indicate that regular cannabis use has limited effects on long-term cognitive functioning. Experienced marijuana consumers exhibit virtually no change in cognitive functioning immediately after smoking pot, according to clinical trial data published in the journal *Pharmacology, Biochemistry, and Behavior* in 2010. Research published in the *American Journal of Epidemiology* in 2011 showed that cannabis users' memories were as good, if not better, than nonusers'.

† In an effort to marshal data to show that marijuana harms the brain, NIDA sponsored animal studies involving megadoses of THC and a potent synthetic CB-1 agonist developed by Pfizer. Neuroscientist David Robbe injected these drugs into restrained rats' brains and found that it caused aberrant brain wave activity (David Robbe et al., "Cannabinoids Reveal Importance of Spike Timing Coordination in Hippocampal Function," *Nature Neuroscience*, published online November 19, 2006). Although the study had nothing to do with the real-world use of marijuana by teenagers, it became grist for the mill of alarmist assertions about pot's adverse effects on the developing brain.

person become a compulsive eater. THC, a substance safe enough to be classified as Schedule III by the federal government, is not addictive, regardless of potency, and it is incapable of causing a fatal overdose. If given the opportunity to self-administer THC, lab rats quickly lose interest (whereas rats keep lever-pressing for more heroin, cocaine, nicotine, and alcohol). The U.S. National Academy of Sciences, the British Advisory Council on the Misuse of Drugs, the Canadian Special Committee on Illegal Drugs, and dozens of other inquiries reached the same conclusion: Withdrawal symptoms are typically mild and short-lived, even when habitual users cease taking marijuana. A person who quits smoking after a lengthy dalliance with cannabis might feel grumpy or have low energy or be somewhat depressed; he or she might not sleep well. In short, they'd feel much like they did before they started to relieve stress by puffing herb on a consistent basis. But they wouldn't go through anything like the agony of kicking opiates or booze.

Psychological dependency is a trickier issue. "Marijuana is indisputably reinforcing for many people," according to the Institute of Medicine, which found that fewer than 10 percent of those who try cannabis go on to use it regularly. Drug warriors who claim that pot is addictive point to the large number of kids in treatment for "cannabis-related disorders," a NIDA-concocted syndrome of dubious clinical relevance. Most people entering reefer rehab were arrested for possession and referred to treatment by the courts in lieu of prison. Of the estimated 288,000 people who enrolled in substance-abuse treatment programs for marijuana in 2007, 34 percent of these alleged pot addicts said they hadn't used cannabis during the month prior to their admission, and another 16 percent admitted using it three times or fewer in the month before they started court-ordered rehab.

It became a self-perpetuating myth: Kids busted for smoking pot are forced into useless, boring treatment programs, and these treatment admissions are touted as proof that marijuana addiction is rampant among American youth. When the main character in the 1998 stoner comedy *Half Baked* attends a substance-abuse meeting, he's mercilessly heckled because hard-drug users think that so-called marijuana addiction is a joke. "Half baked" would be an apt description of NIDA's decision to fund a "Center for Cannabis Addiction" at the grant-hungry Scripps Research Institute. American taxpayers shelled out millions of dollars "to support research studies that focus on the identification, and pre-clinical and clinical evaluation, of medications that can be safe and effective for the treatment of cannabis-use and -induced disorders." NIDA claimed that "therapeutic interventions" for marijuana dependence are important for adolescents and young adults "given the extent of the use of cannabis in the general population."

Troubled adolescents who start smoking marijuana at a young age are more likely than others to become "problem users"—the small percentage of youth who obsessively seek out and smoke the herb morning, noon, and night. Onset of heavy use typically correlates with a drop in school performance, strained family relationships, and various behavioral issues. These kids are in a rut. But is their compulsive cannabis consumption the cause of their problems or a symptom of them?

NIDA broad-brushed chronic marijuana smokers with the deceptive phrase *cannabis-related disorders*. Recent research suggests that *cannabinoid deficiency disorders* might be a more apt term. Some people may be predisposed toward substance abuse by virtue of a systemic enzyme imbalance that results in pathologically low levels of endogenous cannabinoids. Scientists have linked a mutated version of the gene that encodes FAAH, the enzyme that breaks down the brain's own marijuana, to higher levels of alcoholism and drug addiction. People with this condition may need extra cannabinoid stimulation just to feel "normal."

For many medical-marijuana patients, a daily doobie is more like insulin than heroin. Add less psychoactive, CBD-rich cannabis into the grassroots therapeutic mix and the insulin analogy seems all the more appropriate. From this perspective, chronic marijuana use is a symptom of—if not a remedy for—an underlying imbalance rather than the cause of a syndrome of disorders.

In 2010, Brazilian scientists reported that cannabidiol helped chronic marijuana users wean themselves from high-THC habituation. Holy smokes! A cure for "marijuana addiction" had been discovered and the cure turned out to be . . . CBD-rich marijuana! Laboratory and clinical trials in several countries also showed that CBD has antipsychotic properties and reduces schizophrenic symptoms.

The causes of schizophrenia, an illness that afflicts three million Americans and 1 percent of the world's population, are not fully understood. But researchers agree on this much: Schizophrenics are more likely to smoke pot than people who aren't schizophrenic. That's because many schizophrenics self-medicate with cannabis to cope with the stress of their illness. Some schizophrenics claim that marijuana decreases their anxiety, helps them focus, relaxes them, and increases their sense of self-worth—benefits similar to those reported by "normal" pot smokers. High-THC cannabis can exacerbate symptoms of an existing mental illness, just as it can amplify feelings of good mood.

Prohibitionists seized upon elevated rates of association between pot puffing and schizophrenia and twisted this into scare stories about cannabis making people go crazy. Young males were said to be especially vulnerable. The old trope that marijuana triggers mental illness returned with a vengeance, but the evidence did not support a causal link. Although cannabis use in the United States and elsewhere had increased by many orders of magnitude since the 1960s, there was no rise in the incidence of schizophrenia. The findings of Samuel Allentuck and Karl Bowman, the La Guardia Commission scientists, still rang true: "Marihuana will not produce psychosis de novo in a well-integrated, stable person."

But what about those who are not well integrated or stable? What impact will marijuana have upon an impressionable adolescent whose sense of self is still very much a work in progress? Never one to pull punches, Dr. Tod Mikuriya maintained that marijuana is a useful, safe, and appropriate treatment for various childhood mental disorders. Given the herb's benign-side-effect profile and its exceptional versatility, Mikuriya felt that cannabis should be considered a "first line medicine" for depression, anxiety, bipolar disorder, obsessive-compulsive behavior, PTSD, and other mental diseases.

Some families discovered that marijuana was nothing short of miraculous for children with severe autism. Long known as an effective anticonvulsant, cannabis was particularly helpful for autistic kids who also suffered from seizures. A spectrum of diseases that affects more than 1 percent of American children, autism is found among all social strata in every part of the world. Worried about the toxic side effects of Risperdal and other antipsychotic meds prescribed for kids with autism, a few desperate parents turned to cannabis.

Marijuana muffins proved to be a life-safer for Joey, a severely disabled African American boy in Los Angeles who had been diagnosed with autism when he was sixteen months old. At age ten Joey weighed forty-six pounds and could not speak or walk. He was on six powerful pharmaceuticals that destroyed his appetite, ruined his sleep, and wasted his body. The doctors told his mother, Meiko Hester-Perez, that longevity was not in the cards for Joey. Meiko, who had never smoked cannabis, would do anything to help her son, even if it meant breaking federal law. Meiko's uncle, a career LAPD officer, frowned upon marijuana, but he, too, was impressed by the dramatic changes that occurred after Joey started eating ganja edibles. The mute, autistic child became more responsive and more energetic, his body weight nearly doubled, and he took fewer Big Pharma meds. Cannabis "is an alternative for parents who have exhausted all other means," said Hester-Perez. She formed a group called the Unconventional Foundation for Autism, which emphasized marijuana therapy as a treatment option for autistic children.

The Internet was buzzing with testimonials from parents who touted the benefits of medical marijuana for adolescents with attention deficit hyperactivity disorder (ADHD), a diagnostic label applied increasingly to school kids who behaved in a manner that irritated and frustrated teachers and often alienated other students. Medicinal cannabis was showing up in classrooms, according to a 2010 *Christian Science Monitor* article, which reported that "high schoolers are bringing pot to school, and they're doing it legally. Not to get stoned, but as part of prescribed medical treatment."

But the thousand or so school kids who were eating cannabis edibles under a doctor's supervision paled in comparison with the almost four million American youth diagnosed with ADHD who were on addictive amphetamines such as Ritalin and Adderall, which cause neurological damage, heart attacks, and sudden death in children. Another 1.5 million American kids were taking risky pharmaceutical antidepressants and atypical antipsychotics that worked no better than a placebo—drugs that were far more mind-altering and dangerous than marijuana. Big Pharma antidepressants and ADHD pills—unlike cannabis—figured in scores of emergency room visits. The mass overmedication of American youth was the flip side of the war on drugs.

Amphetamines can often quell the fidgety, impulsive symptoms of ADHD, but speed doesn't address the underlying disorder, which has been linked to food additives and environmental pollutants. In addition to recommending dietary changes and less screen time, a handful of physicians risked the wrath of the California Medical Board when they began treating difficult ADHD kids with cannabis. For some children, the herb was much more effective than corporate pharmaceuticals—without any nasty collateral effects.

For kids with attention deficit disorder, pot doesn't impair—it helps them focus. "My son was diagnosed with ADHD when he was six," a woman from Grass Valley, California, acknowledged. "He was hyperactive and had trouble in school, but we didn't want to put him on Ritalin. Too many side effects. When he got to high school, I suddenly noticed that he'd calmed down and could concentrate. I couldn't figure it out. Then he told me that he started smoking pot."

The rise in marijuana's popularity among American youth since the late 1960s coincided with a surge in diagnosed cases of attention deficit disorder and its hyperactive variant, ADHD, a condition that Dr. Tom O'Connell likened to a "pediatric anxiety syndrome." A retired thoracic surgeon and former captain in the U.S. Army Medical Corps, O'Connell had treated hundreds of wounded American soldiers during the Vietnam War. He came out of retirement in 2000 and began seeing medical-cannabis applicants in Oakland. Over the years he would compile a database and analyze usage patterns of six thousand patients. His findings would challenge both prohibitionists and drug-policy reformers who concurred that reefer ought to be a no-no for under-twenty-one-year-olds. "Each side in the modern pot debate is wedded to its own fairytale," O'Connell blogged. He bemoaned that reform leaders "were nearly as clueless as the Feds—and equally susceptible to doctrinaire thinking when it comes to adolescent drug initiation and usage."

Why do some young people who experiment with cannabis become daily users? Are their claims of medical use credible? Dr. O'Connell found that the vast majority of medical-marijuana applicants were already chronic users before they walked through the door of the dispensary. (People who try marijuana and have an unpleasant experience generally don't go to physicians for letters of recommendation.) The everyday smokers he interviewed had remarkably similar medical and social histories. O'Connell determined that the main reason young people smoke pot on a regular basis is because it is a safe and effective way to relieve anxiety and other mood disorders associated with insecurity and low self-esteem.

Repetitive drug use usually entails a more serious purpose than mere recreation, according to O'Connell, who maintains that since the 1960s young Americans have embraced marijuana en masse to assuage the same emotional symptoms "that made anxiolytics, mood stabilizers and antidepressants Big Pharma's most lucrative products." "The need to self-medicate symptoms of adolescent angst is much more important than simple youthful hedonism," O'Connell concluded.

For America's youth, cannabis was like catnip for a cat, a poorly understood but nonetheless efficient herbal means of navigating the ambient anxiety and frenetic complexity of modern life. The emergence of marijuana as the anxiolytic drug of choice and its durable popularity among tense teens and anxious adults made sense in light of scientific research that has documented the stress-buffering function of the endocannabinoid system.

Whereas activation of the body's innate stress response ("fight or flight") is essential for responding and adapting to acute survival threats, too much stress can damage an organism in the long run by depleting endocannabinoid tone. A compromised endocannabinoid system sets the stage for a myriad of disease symptoms and ups the risk of premature death. Chronically elevated stress levels boost anxiety and significantly hasten the progression of Alzheimer's dementia. Emotional stress has been shown to accelerate the spread of cancer. Stress alters how we assimilate fats.

On a cellular level, stress is the body's response to any change that creates a physiological demand on it. When a person is stressed, the brain generates cortisol and other steroid hormones, which, in turn, trigger the release of naturally occurring marijuana-like compounds: anandamide and 2-AG. These endogenous cannabinoids bind to primordial cell receptors that restore homeostasis by down-regulating the production of stress hormones. Marijuana, an herbal adaptogen, essentially does the same thing.

Twenty-first-century children are under assault from an unprecedented array of debilitating stressors, including junk food, electromagnetic radiation, information overload, and a noxious swill of eighty thousand unregulated synthetic chemicals, all of which wreak havoc on metabolism and brain development. The cumulative effect can be seen in skyrocketing rates of childhood obesity, ADHD, autism, hypertension, depression, and strokes among adolescents. For all the talk about protecting the children, kids haven't been faring very well in America. Among twenty developed nations, the United States and Great Britain ranked as the two worst places to be a child, according to a 2007 UNICEF study that assessed six criteria: material well-being, health, education, relationships, behaviors and risks, and young people's own sense of happiness.

Economic inequality is socially divisive, emotionally stressful, and hugely damaging in terms of health outcomes, especially for the poor, who comprise 50 percent of the population in early twenty-first-century America. Massive inequalities disgrace and sicken the United States. Extensive research has shown that health and social problems by almost every measure—from mental and physical illness to violence and drug abuse—are more prevalent in countries with large income disparities.

With millions of stressed-out teens smoking pot, some parents are apt to attribute their children's problems to marijuana's malevolent influence. The adult temptation to blame the weed is reinforced by public officials who continually inflate the dangers and deny the benefits of cannabis. But U.S. authorities have long since forfeited any claim to credibility with respect to marijuana. The facts, meanwhile, speak for themselves: Carcinogens in our food, water, and air are legal; cannabis is not.

Marijuana prohibition is symptomatic of a deep cultural pathology. Its persistence as government policy is indicative of a body politic with a failing immune system, a society unable to heal itself. There is no moral justification for a policy that criminalizes people for trying to relieve their suffering. Reefer madness has nothing to do with smoking marijuana—for therapy or fun or any other reason—and everything to do with how the U.S. government has stigmatized, prosecuted, and jailed users of this much maligned and much venerated plant.

POSTSCRIPT

On the third weekend of August, several hundred thousand people converge at Myrtle Edwards Park, a mile-long strip of greenery and winding asphalt paths along the Seattle waterfront, to celebrate their favorite botanical. The Seattle Hempfest is by far the biggest pro-pot gathering in the world. Revelry and civic-mindedness mix as ganja lovers from all corners join a throng of locals in a crowd so large that people are shoulder to shoulder much of the time in many areas. They squeeze past hundreds of information exhibits, tents, and booths selling organic food, hemp clothing, books, vaporizers, rolling papers, and more. Speakers on five different stages discuss marijuana law reform, the many uses of industrial hemp, and the benefits of medicinal cannabis, which was legalized in the state of Washington in 1998. Young moms with baby strollers, aging hippies, working-class kids in T-shirts proclaiming WAKE AND BAKE, patients in wheelchairs, and wannabe scene-makers lounge on the grass, listening to live music.

Musicians and entertainers perform throughout the day and many folks smoke marijuana openly. But the cops on the scene are appropriately laid-back, not making arrests for pot possession in keeping with the Emerald City's reputation as a cannabis-friendly bastion. "Hempfest is one of the easier events that we do," said police spokesman Mark Jamieson. "There has always been great cooperation between the organizers and the Seattle Police Department." An ethic of "leave no trace" animates the all-volunteer crew that cleans up meticulously afterward.

The purpose of Hempfest is unequivocally political, according to Vivian McPeak, the dreadlocked cofounder and prime mover of the yearly convocation. At its core, it is about decriminalizing marijuana. "Hempfest is about promoting the freedom to choose and human rights," McPeak asserted, adding: "No political or human rights movement in America has made it this far without eventually winning. It's just a matter of time."

Cannabinoid compounds interact synergistically for maximum effect; so, too, with social-justice movements—they're far more potent in combination than as single-issue endeavors. The Seattle Hempfest grew out of a peace vigil opposing the 1991 Gulf War. Allen Ginsberg visited and sat with the vigil during the six months that it lasted. Shortly thereafter, McPeak and several cohorts organized the inaugural Washington Hemp Expo, which drew five hundred people. The keynote orator was Jack Herer, the bombastic hemp evangelist, who gave a barn-burner of a speech at this "humble gathering of stoners." Renamed the Seattle Hempfest the following year, it was destined to become a major Northwest summer attraction, a flagship event of today's sprawling, global cannabis culture. More than 20,000 people showed up in 1994, and the crowds kept increasing year after year, feted by the likes of Dennis Peron, Valerie Corral, Debby Goldsberry, and other stoner activists who starred in the hemp movement.

On the tenth anniversary of Hempfest in 2001, an estimated 150,000 attendees heard Woody Harrelson denounce America's "injustice system" and the "war on all natural, noncorporate drugs." In October of that year, the Drug Enforcement Administration tried to ban hemp food products, even though they packed about as much of a psychoactive punch as a potato. Emboldened by the authoritarian fervor that followed the 9/11 terrorist attacks, the narcs tried to pull a fast one. They thought they could get away with a sneak attack against a wide range of hemp food items, including nutrient-dense hempseed oil, one of the few complete, plant-based protein sources on the planet.

The DEA, citing THC concerns, pegged the hemp industry and medical marijuana as a smokescreen for folks who just want to smoke pot. But Uncle Sam's attempt to destroy hemp food commerce in America would falter largely due to the efforts of David Bronner, the young CEO of Dr. Bronner's Magic Soaps, who funded and coordinated the Hemp Industry Association's protracted litigation against the DEA. The industrial hempsters scored a major victory in February 2004 when the Ninth Circuit Court of Appeals rejected the DEA's hemp food ban on substantive grounds.

Hemp, the world's foremost agricultural crop in the eighteenth century, reemerged as the textile of choice among eco-conscious shoppers in twenty-first-century America. New processing techniques made hemp cloth silky soft, but federal law stopped American farmers from growing the plant. The DEA claimed that industrial hemp crops must not be permitted in the United States because hemp farmers might hide marijuana plants in their fields. Actually, marijuana growers wouldn't want their pot plants anywhere near fiber hemp, given that cross-pollination would ruin a cannabis harvest. For a while in 2010, it seemed like industrial hemp might become legal in California by piggybacking on Proposition 19. Had voters in the Golden State chosen to legalize marijuana, it would have unshackled industrial hemp, as well, boosting a domestic growth industry. And if hemp pollen blew their way, cannabis cultivators, ironically, would have been in a tough spot.

"Tall hemp plants that followed man . . . To bind his loads and ease his mind," poet Robert Creeley wrote in 1972. In olden times, people all over the world marked the planting and harvesting of hemp with communal festivities. So, too, in modern America, where intimations of something vaguely primal were felt in the resurgence of hemp celebrations across the country—Hempstalk in Portland, Oregon; the Great Midwest Harvest Festival in Madison; the Raleigh Marijuana Rally; the Boston Freedom Rally; Hempstock in Maine; and many more.

And beyond the United States, hempfests thrive, including the Festival du Chanvre in Paris, the London Hemp Fair, and Mardi Gras in Nimbin, New South Wales, Australia. There's also the annual springtime Global Marijuana March in more than two hundred cities from Helsinki to Johannesburg and Buenos Aires, 420 powwows at colleges and universities, and a plethora of cannabis cups, regional bud contests, and other neo-hippie conclaves where organically grown weed is a given.

Of all these law-breaking, pot-friendly jamborees, none could top the Seattle Hempfest, which enjoyed widespread support among local residents and city officials. In 2003, a solid majority of Seattle voters passed Initiative 75, making marijuana possession the city's lowest law-enforcement priority. Seven years later the state's medical-marijuana law was expanded so that a variety of health care professionals, including naturopaths and nurse practitioners, could recommend the herb. By this time, a vibrant medical-marijuana scene with at least seventy-five storefront dispensaries had blossomed in Seattle, brightening the overcast metropolis. Like Vancouver, its scenic counterpart across the border, Seattle was something of a pro-cannabis autonomous zone.

The situation was much different in Spokane, Washington's second-largest municipality, on the other side of the Cascade Mountains. In the summer of 2011, the biggest federal crackdown in the thirteen-year history of Washington's medical-marijuana law shuttered every dispensary in Spokane, driving providers underground and making life a lot more difficult for ailing Americans. At the time of the raid, there were thirty-four entries in the new "medical-marijuana" section of the Spokane Yellow Pages. "The display ads now read like a list of the indicted," the *Seattle Times* reported after the heavy-handed attacks. Most of the pot clubs in Spokane would remain closed; those that continued to operate did so discretely by word-of-mouth. It was, in essence, a tale of two cities. In Seattle, where the city council passed legislation to license and regulate medical-marijuana dispensaries like other businesses, large-scale ganja grow-ops serviced thousands of people without police interference. In the eastern part of the state, a rheumatoid arthritis patient could go to jail for cultivating a few plants.

During this period of retrenchment, the DEA mounted aggressive, SWAT-type raids against medical-marijuana storefronts, cannabis-testing labs, and grow-ops (many of which were run by patients) in a half dozen states that had legalized the herb for therapeutic use. It was a bit like watching the same sorry scene from a Samuel Beckett play over and over again. Obama-era federal raids on med-pot targets exceeded the frequency of attacks during the Bush years, prompting Americans for Safe Access to give the president a failing grade on his midterm medical-marijuana report card. Obama's massive drug-war budget reflected the same skewed priorities as his Oval Office predecessor, allocating lavishly for prosecutions and prisons while scrimping on education and harm reduction.

On June 29, 2011, the Obama Justice Department issued a memo to all U.S. attorneys, emphasizing its "core priority" commitment to enforcing the Controlled Substances Act in all states: "Congress has determined that marijuana is a dangerous drug and that the illegal distribution and sale of marijuana is a serious crime that provides a significant source of revenue to large scale criminal enterprises, gangs, and cartels." Written by Deputy Attorney General James M. Cole, this masterpiece of sophistry reiterated that "it is likely not an efficient use of federal resources to focus enforcement efforts on individuals with cancer or other serious illnesses who use marijuana as part of a recommended treatment regimen consistent with applicable state law . . ." But "commercial operations cultivating, selling or distributing marijuana" are another matter entirely, according to Cole, whose carefully worded policy clarification signaled that a major crackdown on the medical-marijuana industry was imminent. While going after individual patients might not be "an efficient use of federal resources," dispensaries that serviced the patient community were fair game for law enforcement.

With the green light strobing from D.C., federal prosecutors sent another round of menacing letters to landlords in several medical-marijuana states, indicating that their property could be seized and forfeited if they continued to rent to cannabusinesses. The feds also threatened various supporting industries, including newspapers that ran ads for medical-marijuana storefronts and banks that held ganja *gelt*. U.S. attorneys even threatened to arrest state workers who followed state law by helping to regulate distribution of the herb. It appeared that these stern missives were deliberately timed to intimidate elected officials as they mulled whether and how to regulate medical-marijuana dispensaries.

Several state governments capitulated. After she got a threatening letter from the feds, Governor Chris Gregoire of Washington vetoed a bill that she herself had supported previously, which would have created a statewide regulated dispensary system. Governor Lincoln Chafee of Rhode Island suspended a plan to license three dispensaries. Arizonans, who passed yet another medical-marijuana ballot initiative in 2010, were supposed to have access to 125 dispensaries, but the program stalled as Governor Jan Brewer deferred to the feds. Governor Chris Christie of New Jersey, an outspoken opponent of cannabis, did everything possible to ensure that the medical-marijuana program mandated by the state legislature in 2010 would fail. Five hundred and thirty-three days after the law was enacted, New Jersey issued retro rules that absurdly capped THC levels at 10 percent for medicinal strains and barred certified patients from growing their own cannabis.

The burgeoning medical-marijuana industry in Michigan was undermined in August 2011, when a state appellate court ruled that the Michigan Medical Marihuana Act of 2008, which carried every county and won with 63 percent statewide, did not permit the sale of cannabis. Medical marijuana was still legal in Michigan—but it was illegal to buy it. Despite the precarious legal situation, the medical-marijuana trade continued to flourish in some pockets of the state, thanks to defiant dispensary operators and law-enforcement officials into a hands-off approach. Regulations pertaining to medical marijuana varied significantly among the sixteen states and the District of Columbia where the herb was allowed for therapeutic purposes, but in most places patients confronted the same dilemma: There was nowhere to go to obtain cannabis legally.

Robin Prosser, a fifty-year-old Missoula, Montana, resident who used marijuana to manage the painful symptoms of systemic lupus, committed suicide in 2007 after the DEA intercepted her personal supply of herb, which had been sent by an authorized provider. Five years earlier, Prosser, a former concert pianist, went on a sixty-day hunger strike to call attention to the need for legal medicinal cannabis. She became the poster child for Initiative 148, which passed with 62 percent of the vote in red-state Montana in 2004, but medical-marijuana retail outlets didn't emerge from the shadows until the end of the decade. Soon nearly 3 percent of Montanans had medical-marijuana recommendations.

In December 2010, prospective jurors in Missoula staged a marijuana mutiny and just said no to rendering judgment in a criminal case that involved a small amount of pot. This had never happened before anywhere in the country. The would-be jury nullifiers thought it was a waste of time and money to prosecute a minor marijuana infraction as a felony. "Sanity broke out in Missoula, Montana, today," the *Huffington Post* declared.

Three months later, the DEA raided two dozen medical-marijuana dispensaries and grow-ops in Big Sky country. Several medical-marijuana providers were arrested and some would serve time in federal prison. Among the targets were marijuana breeders and facilities that specialized in rare CBD-rich cannabis strains with reduced psychoactivity and unique therapeutic potential. Precious plant genetics were squandered as a result of these federal incursions, which came on the eve of the Montana state legislature's debate on whether to pull the plug on a thriving network of medical-marijuana storefronts.

Hundreds of jobs disappeared and a fledgling industry was nipped in the bud when elected officials in Montana, citing the need to protect children from the marijuana "scourge," banned the sale (but not the possession) of medicinal cannabis. Reefer madness was entrenched among state legislators who warned of an uncontrolled epidemic of marijuana abuse. Although surveys showed a decrease in cannabis use among Montana high school students during the previous two years, House Majority Leader Tom McGillvray (R-Billings) sounded the alarm: "Do we want our schools infiltrated with this powerful, addictive drug? I think not. Our culture is being corrupted. Our children are being exploited."

Cherrie Brady, the leader of a vocal antipot parents' group, Safe Community, Safe Kids, was quoted in the press saying that she had heard from unnamed school officials that Montana was flooded with marijuana, children were selling it on school grounds, and kids were prostituting themselves to get it. "It's crossing boundaries," Brady fretted. "It's not just the bad kids. They have star athletes [using marijuana, too]." Her rant about marijuana destroying America's next generation would have made Harry Anslinger proud.

Mike Hyde, a parent in Missoula, had a different perspective on cannabis. When it comes to young people using marijuana, he said, "I'd be more concerned about kids eating McDonald's or playing with plastic toys with lead-based paint from China. Cannabis is the last thing they need to really worry about." Hyde's two-year-old son, Cash, was the youngest certified medical-marijuana patient in Montana, if not the country. Diagnosed with a malignant brain tumor and late-stage cancer, Cash was on life support for fifty-one days. He suffered septic shock, stroke, and pulmonary hemorrhaging while undergoing intense rounds of radiation and chemotherapy. As a last resort, Mike Hyde slipped a potent cannabis oil extraction into his son's feeding tube without telling the doctors. He gave him the oil twice a day for two weeks, and the boy with the cannabinated brain started eating again and playing with toys. Soon he was off all pharmaceuticals. His doctors, who expected that Cash would die, were astonished by the transformation. Mike credited his son's survival to the healing powers of the cannabis extract.

Unconfirmed accounts of miraculous outcomes following the administration of cannabis oil concentrates have become the stuff of Internet legends as well as fodder for sweeping claims by true believers that marijuana cures cancer. Had they forgotten that Bob Marley died of cancer? That said, those who would dismiss marijuana's curative qualities as hokum should consider the rigorous science that has documented the antitumoral and anticancer properties of cannabinoid compounds.

Homemade CBD-rich oil extracts were already circulating underground, albeit sporadically, in Northern California in October 2011, when the feds announced stepped-up enforcement efforts against medical-marijuana dispensaries and the growers that supplied them. Proposition 215 "has been hijacked by profiteers," U.S. Attorney Melinda Haag asserted. Instead of going after crooked bankers and mortgage brokers who defrauded the American economy of trillions of dollars, the U.S. Justice Department fumed about earnings from taxed and regulated med-pot transactions. "Federal antidrug bureaucrats are afraid because the dispensaries are proving that it's possible for marijuana to become a safe, legal, taxpaying industry and so expose their own last-century policies as bankrupt and obsolete," said Dale Gieringer of NORML.

After all these years, patient advocates were still waiting for police and prosecutors to declare a cease-fire in their fight against therapeutic cannabis. Many local and state officials were eager accomplices in the latest smackdown on the California medical-marijuana industry. They weren't just going after the bad apples—they were going after every apple in the barrel. Unincorporated Sacramento County proceeded to shut all sixty-three of its dispensaries, while med-pot storefronts inside Sacramento city limits continued to operate under duress. Americans for Safe Access kept a running tally: 168 California cities and 17 counties had banned dispensaries and another 80 cities enacted moratoria on medical-marijuana storefronts; only about 40 cities and 10 counties passed ordinances that allowed cannabis clubs. How many jobs were lost? How many patients were denied access to cannabis or forced to drive long distances to obtain their medicine?

"Pot smokers are a small minority. They are containable," the *Christian Science Monitor* stated smugly in an editorial that decried marijuana's "well documented adverse side effects, notably upon teens" and applauded the federal government's hard-line prohibitionist stance. Because of stiff opposition at all levels of government, access to legal medicinal cannabis was limited geographically in California and elsewhere. In effect, the antipot forces succeeded in restricting availability to certain reefer-friendly enclaves while effectively thwarting access in most areas where medical marijuana was supposedly the law of the land.

Proposition 215 called upon elected officials to come up with a viable statewide distribution system so that California's patients could obtain their herbal medicine without hassle. It never happened. Instead, local jurisdictions were allowed to make their own rules. County cops claimed that medical-marijuana law was ambiguous and confusing, but this excuse was convenient camouflage to conceal their personal disapproval of pot smoking. To a significant degree, the conflict between federal and state law was a media-inflated alibi, a pretext for local authorities who had been consistently hostile to medicinal cannabis in California since 215 was enacted in 1996 and who continued to block its implementation.

Did law enforcement succeed in containing the medical-marijuana groundswell? Yes and no. Yes—if one considers that a million people constitutes a relatively small percentage of Californians who could benefit from the herb's wide-ranging medicinal applications. No—to the extent that law enforcement was unable to stop the medical-marijuana industry from spreading and taking firm root in a patchwork of communities across North America, from Seattle to Denver to Ann Arbor to Portland, Maine.

Yes and no. Contained, yet not contained. In a story replete with doubles, here's another: In trying to limit the medical-marijuana movement, the authorities played upon the apparent dichotomy between recreational and therapeutic use. The young, able-bodied twentysomethings striding into dispensaries didn't look sick to Peeping Tom police on surveillance duty. (Didn't the cops have anything better to do?) Recreational use was driving cannabis commerce under the guise of medical need, according to the narcs. And recreational users were red meat for law enforcement. But how could a peace officer tell who was a legitimate patient and who was a pothead putting on airs when many men and women were obtaining medical-marijuana recommendations for anxiety, stress, insomnia, and psychological reasons? Properly titrated, cannabis confers preventive as well as palliative benefits in a way that muddles the distinction between therapeutic and recreational use.

Dr. Lester Grinspoon, the Harvard psychiatrist and professor emeritus, predicts that "medical uses are going to be the undoing of prohibition." He believes that marijuana will eventually be recognized as a wonder drug. "[T]he full potential of this remarkable substance, including its full medical potential, will be realized only when we end the regime of prohibition," says Grinspoon. The fate of medical marijuana and the broader legalization movement would remain entwined if only because the fallacious arguments used to justify the banning of recreational reefer have had an adverse impact on the medical sphere, impeding research and clinical access.

The edifice of cannabis prohibition seemed increasingly shaky in 2012 as voters in several states prepared to weigh in on ballot measures to relegalize marijuana for adult consumption. In Colorado, Mason Tvert, director of the Campaign to Regulate Marijuana Like Alcohol, was spearheading a ballot measure that would legalize possession of up to one ounce of cannabis and six plants per person. Tvert and his colleagues felt that marijuana legalization should be debated on its own merits, not just as a quick fix for the economy. In their view, pot prohibition had such terrible consequences that it needed to be ended regardless of how much money the government could make by taxing it.

Even soccer moms were stumping for legalization in the Rocky Mountain state. "Our stance isn't just about endorsing the behavior of 95 million Americans who have used pot, and it's not even about endorsing the medical use of marijuana by the hundreds of thousands of medical-marijuana patients across the nation," said Jessica Corry, a pro-life Republican mother and a high-profile cannabis activist from Denver. "This is about something so much greater. We are coming together to reclaim our country. For our children. For our pocketbooks. And for the long-forgotten American ideal that in the absence of harm to others, government should not interfere in our personal lives."

By this time, several prominent "family values" conservatives had called for a truce in the cannabis culture war—a sign that the Great Pot Moment may indeed have arrived. Christian broadcaster Pat Robertson lamented the failure of tough drug laws (which he had long supported) on his *700 Club* TV show: "It's costing us a fortune and it's ruining young people." Erstwhile Alaska governor and GOP vice presidential candidate Sarah Palin conceded that marijuana smoking was "a minimal problem" that should not be a priority for police, a sentiment shared by a growing number of law-enforcement veterans.

Former U.S. attorney John McKay had the temerity to admit that the policy he implemented as a federal prosecutor in Seattle was wrong. It was McKay who put Marc Emery, the Canadian "Prince of Pot," behind bars in the United States for selling cannabis seeds via the Internet. McKay generated headlines in the Pacific Northwest when he announced his decision to back a statewide marijuana legalization initiative sponsored by New Approach Washington. If passed, Initiative 502 would allow adults to purchase up to an ounce of marijuana at state-regulated cannabis dispensaries. The eminently mainstream *Seattle Times* endorsed the measure, hoping it would have a domino effect:

"To end marijuana prohibition at the federal level, several states need to defy federal authority. That's how politics works. The legislature will not do it, nor [the governor]. But the people of Washington can, through a ballot initiative."

A huge issue for McKay was the deteriorating situation in Mexico, where half the population lived in poverty and black-market commerce in cannabis and other illicit substances fueled a stunningly brutal drug war that had claimed more than 40,000 lives and 10,000 "disappeared" during a five-year conflict with no end in sight. McKay recognized that the enormous popularity of marijuana among Yankee consumers was a driving force behind the horrific violence in Mexico. He argued that legalizing marijuana would greatly benefit Mexico and the United States by depriving ruthless criminals of a major source of funds.

Nearly a quarter of a million Mexicans had been forced to flee their homes since President Felipe Calderón decided to militarize operations against the so-called drug cartels, whose tactics included beheading their opponents and posting the evidence on YouTube. Human rights groups also documented numerous cases of torture and extrajudicial killings by Mexican soldiers. The CIA and DEA made matters worse by dispatching advisers to Mexico to train security personnel and formulate antidrug strategies. Calderón's predecessor, Vicente Fox, had sought to decriminalize (not legalize) possession of small amounts of marijuana in his country, but Uncle Sam pressured Fox to abandon this plan and he did.*

Although men and women in many cultures have used cannabis for thousands of years, U.S. legislators and their international counterparts did not impose a global prohibitionist regime until well into the twentieth century. The first antimarijuana laws in the United States were primarily a racist reaction against Mexican migrants. Two decades after the federal government banned marijuana, the Beat writers introduced the jazz cat's herb to Middle America, where cannabis tinctures and rubbing ointments were once widely available for multiple clinical indications. Adopted as a safe, effective, and medically unsupervised anxiolytic by millions of Baby Boomers during the 1960s, marijuana became the central focus of a deceitful and disastrous war on drugs

---

* Against a backdrop of surreal, drug-war-related bloodletting in Mexico, the Obama administration ignored the findings of a 2009 Latin American commission, headed by former Presidents Ernesto Zedillo of Mexico, Fernando Henrique Cardoso of Brazil, and César Gaviria of Colombia, which condemned harsh, one-note U.S. prohibition policies that are based, in Gaviria's words, "on prejudices and fears and not on results" (Neal Peirce, "Obama's Take on the Drug War," *Denver Post*, July 9, 2009).

launched by a Machiavellian president. The drug war that Nixon set in motion would escalate and metastasize under Reagan and his Oval Office successors.

Marijuana legalization has long been a "big tent" issue that galvanized activist energy on the left and the right, from antiglobalization protestors to free-market capitalists. Like the plant itself, the social movement that coalesced around cannabis contained components with opposite characteristics. The turf was fertile for strange bedfellows—pro-pot liberals embracing states' rights, conservative libertarians begging for government regulation, ganja growers consorting with ex-cops, all united by their opposition to the federal government's hyperbolic crusade against marijuana, the cheap hippie high that spurred America's leading growth industry.

Recent demographic trends would appear to favor marijuana legalization, perhaps in the not-too-distant future. A nationwide Angus Reid poll in August 2011 found that two-thirds of Americans thought the war on drugs has been a failure and 55 percent of adult respondents supported the legalization of marijuana. Younger voters were more in favor of ending pot prohibition than other age groups. The notion that weed should be regulated like wine was obvious to a growing number of folks who recognized that when it came to marijuana the public had been bamboozled on a grand scale. They understood that it's irrational and hypocritical for the federal government to subsidize alcohol, tobacco, and dangerous pharmaceuticals, while prohibiting cannabis, "one of the safest therapeutically active substances known to man," in the memorable words of DEA administrative law judge Francis Young.

How long could a society endure such a venal and dishonest policy? For more than thirty years, the federal government has been dispensing government-grown reefer to a handful of medical-necessity patients, while the DEA, FDA, and NIDA pretend that marijuana lacks therapeutic value. Riddled with contradictions, federal policy ranks Schedule I cannabis as more dangerous than Schedule II crack cocaine. It makes no sense. Why is it legal for a corporation to sell THC, but it's not legal to get the very same compound by growing a plant in your own garden? What's up with that? To ponder the history of marijuana in America is to embark upon a political landscape so illogical as to be perverse, a world where facts and votes don't count and common sense is ignored, a world so full of paradox and doublespeak that you might need to smoke some of the *good shuzzit* just to wrap your mind around it all.

ACKNOWLEDGMENTS

There are times while writing a book when a particular event or encounter changes the trajectory of the narrative. That happened when I met Fred Gardner, editor of *O'Shaughnessy's*, the journal of cannabis in clinical practice. Fred introduced me to the remarkable world of cannabinoid science, a subject little known outside of academic research circles. I was fortunate to have Fred as a friend and sounding board, and his suggestions for improving the manuscript were invaluable.

Very special appreciation to Carolyn Garcia for her hospitality and her recollections; Patrick McCartney for his probe of official efforts to crush the medical marijuana movement in California; Immy Humes for sharing her father's unpublished writings on cannabis; the great investigative poet Ed Sanders for opening his archive and refusing to be burnt out; and hemp historian Michael Aldrich for his generous scholarship.

Special thanks also to Michael Horowitz, cofounder of the Fitz Hugh Ludlow Memorial Library; Judy Goldhaft of the Planet Drum Foundation; Jason Schechter of Cortical Systematics; Scott Thompson of the Walter Benjamin Research Syndicate; and Sarah Russo, my colleague at Project CBD.

Thanks to those who were interviewed for this book or who helped in various ways, including Dennis Peron, Dale Gieringer, Debby Goldsberry, Rick Pfrommer, Steve DeAngelo, Jonathan Trapp, DJ Short, JoAnna LaForce, Mason Tvert, Valerie Corral, Michael Backes, Jim Ketchum, Irv Rosenfeld, Elvy Musikka, Dr. Jeffrey Hergenrather, Al Byrne and Mary Lynn Mathre, Jeff and Dale Sky Jones, Michelle Aldrich, Cindy Palmer, Sreedhar Thakkun, Michael Krawitz, Chris Conrad and Mikki Norris, Dr. Tom O'Connell, Bill Panzer, Doug McVay, Miles, Freek Pollak, Chris Bennett, Ralph Metzner, Vivian McPeak, Mike Hyde, Steve Kubby, Ethan Nadlemann, Marc Emery, Renee Boje, Oliver Trager, Richard Cowan, Robert Melamede, Don Wirtshafter, Eddie Lepp, Chris Miller, Wayne Justmann, David Watson, Meiko Hester-Perez, Phillipe Lucas, David Malmo-Levine, Ed Rosenthal, Aron Kay,

Dana Beal, Jonathan Bevier, Larry Brooke, Eva Jenkins, Sam Sabzehzar, Todd McCormick, Geoff Olsen, Rik Musty, Dr. Geoffrey Guy, Chris Blum, Diamond Dave Whitaker, and Bruce Shlain.

And thanks to these valuable sources that keep the information flowing: Paul Armentano, editor of NORML's weekly e-newsletter; Franjo Grotenhermen of the International Association for Cannabis as Medicine and his cannabinoid science e-newsletter; and the Media Awareness Project of www.DrugSense.org.

A tip of the hat to Brant Rumble at Scribner for guiding this project to fruition; Anna deVries for her excellent line editing; and Colin Robinson, formerly of Scribner, for acquiring this book.

And to those who passed away while this book was being written: David Solomon, Simon Vinkenoog, Steve Ben Israel, Tod Mikuriya, and my close friend Peter Berg. It‘s a great privilege to have known them all.

My heartfelt thanks to those who were there when it mattered most: Norman Solomon, Lloyd Williams, Pia Gallegos, Helen and Craig Thomas, Neal Gates, John Downing, Len Ochs, Alana Lee, and Michael Lardner. And to Bob Katz and Jeff Cohen, who can't be thanked enough.

My deepest gratitude to my wife, Tiffany Devitt; my son Kai Devitt-Lee, guitarist extraordinaire, for playing the music that kept me alive; and my youngest son, Adrian, whose brilliance is beyond description.

NOTES

PROLOGUE

2 **"the most dysfunctional, immoral domestic policy":** Howard Wooldridge, letter to the editor, *Dowagiac Daily News*, January 13, 2009. All Wooldridge quotations in the prologue are from letters he has written to various newspapers.

3 **Fifteen million U.S. citizens use marijuana:** Paul Armentano, "Over 100 Million Americans Have Smoked Marijuana—And It's Still Illegal?" AlterNet, September 10, 2009.

3 **"felt that the road to Hades . . .":** Lester Grinspoon, M.D., *Marihuana Reconsidered*, p. 1.

4 **Recent archaeological findings:** Ethan B. Russo et al., "Phytochemical and Genetic Analyses of Ancient Cannabis from Central Asia," *Journal of Experimental Botany* 59(15) (2008): 417–82.

5 **"If one takes it over a long period . . .":** Shen Nung, *Pen Ts'ao Ching*, cited in Hakim Bey and Abel Zug, eds., *Orgies of the Hemp Eaters*, p. 281.

5 **an ingredient of holy anointing oil:** Chris Bennett, "Early/Ancient History," in Julie Holland, ed., *The Pot Book*, pp. 17–26. "There can be little doubt about a role for cannabis in Judaic religion," says Carl Ruck, professor of classical mythology at Boston University. Sula Benet, a Polish etymologist from the Institute of Anthropological Sciences in Warsaw, discerned references to hemp *(kanna-bosm)* in the Old Testament, "both as incense, which was an integral part of religious celebration, and as an intoxicant." The Talmud, written in the early Middle Ages (AD 500–600), mentions the euphoric qualities of cannabis. Canadian scholar-activist Chris Bennett maintains that Jesus and his disciples used anointing oil that contained cannabis. (Messiah means "anointed one.") Applied as a topical, the cannabinated oil had legendary healing properties. "In the Christian Scriptures," Bennett notes, "Jesus does not baptize any of his own disciples, but rather, in the oldest of the synoptic Gospels, Jesus sends out his followers to heal with the anointing oil."

5 **Galen, the influential Greek:** William A. Embolden, "Ritual Use of Cannabis Sativa L.: A Historical-Ethnographic Survey," in Peter T. Furst, ed., *Flesh of the Gods*, p. 220.

5 **The first botanical illustration:** Michael Aldrich, "History of Therapeutic Cannabis," in Mary Lynn Mathre, ed., *Cannabis in Medical Practice*, p. 40.

5 **covering inflamed body parts:** Raphael Mechoulam and Lumír Hanuš, "Anandamide and More," in Holland, ed., *The Pot Book*, p. 67.

6 ***Marijuana* is a Spanish-language colloquialism:** Alan Piper, "The Mysterious Origins of the Word 'Marihuana,'" *Sino-Platonic Papers* 153 (July 2005).

6 **2009 United Nations survey:** United Nations Office on Drugs and Crime, *World Drug Report 2009.*

6 **"wrapped in wild observation . . .":** In Ann Charters, ed., *Jack Kerouac: Selected Letters, 1940–1956,* p. 231

6 **"italicization of experience":** Michael Pollan, *The Botany of Desire,* p. 166.

CHAPTER 1: HERBLORE

10 **I had myself a ball:** Laurence Bergreen, *Louis Armstrong,* pp. 282–83; and Louis Armstrong, *In His Own Words,* p. 114.

10 **We all used to smoke marijuana:** Bergreen, *Louis Armstrong,* p. 284.

10 **That's one reason we appreciated pot:** Max Jones and John Chilton, *Louis,* p. 134.

11 **If ya ain't got it in ya:** David Huddle, "Search This World Over," *Harvard Review* 34 (Spring 2008), p. 89.

11 **"In this bag, we would keep . . .":** 1993 documentary film *The Unknown Marx Brothers* cited in http://www.veryimportantpotheads.com/site/groucho.htm. The publicity shot for the 1946 film *A Night in Casablanca* showed the Marx Brothers happily smoking a large hookah.

11 **"Vic and I were blasting . . .":** Mike Pinfold, *Louis Armstrong,* p. 65.

11 **Dr. Jerry Zucker:** James Lincoln Collier, *Louis Armstrong: An American Genius,* p. 324.

11 **"It puzzles me to see Marijuana . . .":** Armstrong, *In His Own Words,* p. 112.

12 **"We always looked at pot as a sort of medicine . . .":** Jones and Chilton, *Louis,* p. 133.

12 **"go out by the railroad tracks . . .":** Ibid., pp. 134–35.

12 **"It makes you feel good, man":** Bergreen, *Louis Armstrong,* p. 327.

12 **"Danger was dancing all around you":** Pinfold, *Louis Armstrong,* p. 47.

12 **Armstrong "refused to let anything . . .":** Dizzy Gillespie, *To Be, or Not . . . to Bop,* p. 295.

13 **brought tears to the eyes of Kwame Nkrumah:** Penny von Eschen, *Satchmo Blows Up the World,* p. 63.

13 **"I know it now. I came from here . . .":** Ibid., p. 61.

14 **Pollen samples indicate the presence:** Ethan B. Russo, "History of Cannabis and Its Preparations in Saga, Science, and Sobriquet," *Chemistry & Biodiversity* 4 (2007).

14 **Portuguese seamen traveling from India:** The Portuguese explorer and botanist Garcia da Orta visited India in the mid-sixteenth century and wrote about Indian hemp in *Colloquies on the Simples and Drugs of India* (1563). In 1578, the Portuguese doctor and natural historian Cristóbal Acosta published a book, *On the Drugs and Medicines from the East Indies,* which also discussed cannabis.

14 **"Dagga deepens and makes men wiser":** Brian M. du Toit, "Dagga: The History and Ethnographic Setting of *Cannabis sativa* in Southern Africa," in Vera Rubin, ed., *Cannabis and Culture,* pp. 81–115.

14 **Earth-smoking . . . keeled over:** Christian Rätsch, *Marijuana Medicine,* pp. 127–31; Ernest L. Abel, *Marihuana: The First Twelve Thousand Years,* pp. 136–47; Embolden in Furst, ed., *Flesh of the Gods,* p. 226; and Tod H. Mikuriya, M.D., ed., *Marijuana: Medical Papers,* p. 215.

14 **a treatment for asthma:** Mikuriya, *Marijuana,* p. 219. Science would confirm that cannabis is a bronchial dilator.

14 **The roots of jazz and blues:** Thomas Brothers, *Louis Armstrong's New Orleans,* p. 62.

14 **"my ancestors came from here . . .":** Von Eschen, *Satchmo Blows Up the World,* p. 61.

15 **how cannabis took root in Brazil:** Alvaro Rubim de Pinho, "Social and Medical Aspects of the Use of Cannabis in Brazil," in Vera Rubin, *Cannabis and Culture,* pp. 293–94.

15 **Linguistic evidence in this case:** Harry William Hutchinson, "Patterns of Marihuana Use in Brazil," in Vera Rubin, *Cannabis and Culture,* pp. 173–83; Chris Conrad, *Hemp: Lifeline to the Future,* p. 191; and Albert Goldman, *Grass Roots,* p. 91.

15 ***marijuana* may have come from *mariguango*:** Alvaro Rubim de Pinho, "Social and Medical Aspects of the Use of Cannabis in Brazil," in Vera Rubin, *Cannabis and Culture,* p. 294.

15 **The aboriginal peoples of the New World:** See, in general, Johannes Wilbert, *Tobacco and Shamanism in South America.* Of the approximately 120 psychotropic plants known to exist, 90 percent are found in the Western hemisphere or, to a lesser extent, in Siberia.

15 **medicinal applications in Latin America and the Caribbean:** Hutchinson in Vera Rubin, *Cannabis and Culture,* p. 180.

16 **hemp grew twice as high:** Conrad, *Hemp,* p. 24; and Abel, *Marihuana,* pp. 78–80.

16 **Hemp farming and processing:** John Roulac, *Hemp Horizons,* pp. 32–33.

16 **served as a substitute for legal tender:** Abel, *Marihuana,* p. 90.

16 **Robert "King" Carter, an ancestor of President Jimmy Carter:** Ronald Siegel, *Intoxication,* p. 256.

16 **"substance of a hundred operations":** Abel, *Marihuana,* p. 65.

16 **an English-language guidebook:** Edmund Quincy, "A Treatise of Hemp-Husbandry," reprinted in Jack Frazier, *The Marijuana Farmers: Hemp Cults and Cultures,* pp. 93–126. Thanks to Michael Aldrich for bringing this to my attention.

17 **Washington wrote in his diary:** George Andrews and Simon Vinkenoog, eds., *The Book of Grass,* p. 34.

17 **"Make the most of Indian hempseed":** Washington's diaries, U.S. Library of Congress, 1794, vol. 33, p. 270.

17 **"Washington not only didn't smoke pot . . .":** Author's interview with Michael Aldrich.

18 **Franklin owned a mill:** Abel, *Marihuana,* p. 80; and Mitch Earleywine, *Understanding Marijuana,* pp. 5–6.

18 **Thomas Paine hyped hemp:** Thomas Paine, *Common Sense and Related Writings,* p. 104.

18 **"The greatest service which can be rendered . . .":** Saul Rubin, *Offbeat Marijuana,* p. 143; Conrad, *Hemp,* p. 27; and Rowan Robinson, *Hemp Manifesto,* p. 40.

18 **War of 1812:** Conrad, *Hemp,* p. 28.

19 **farmers established vast hemp-growing operations:** Abel, *Marihuana,* p. 96; Martin Booth, *Cannabis,* p. 36; and Grinspoon, *Marijuana Reconsidered,* p. 12.

19 **"Hemp is abundantly productive . . .":** E. M. Betts, ed., *Thomas Jefferson's Farm Book,* p. 252.

19 **on land where hemp grew:** Joshua Paddison, *A World Transformed: Firsthand Accounts of California Before the Gold Rush,* p. 273.

20 **"To have hemp in your pocket":** *Brewer's Dictionary of Phrase and Fable* (1895), reissued in 1993 by Wordsworth Editions.

20 **Young women in the Ukraine and England:** Sula Benet, "Early Diffusion and Folk Uses of Hemp," in Vera Rubin, *Cannabis and Culture,* pp. 39–49; and Abel, *Marihuana,* pp. 106–8.

21 **A familiar ingredient in European folk remedies:** Rätsch, *Marijuana Medicine,* pp. 9–30; Abel, *Marihuana,* p. 109; and Ralph Metzner, *The Well of Remembrance,* p. 289.

21 **Linked to witches' unguents and potions:** Jonathon Green, *Cannabis,* pp. 78–79.

21 **the Church's war on pre-Christian traditions:** "Among the ranks of the pre-modern peasantry, Christian faith remained relatively shallow, and was variously interwoven with many still-lively vestiges of paganism," writes John Demos in *The Enemy Within: 2,000 Years of Witch-Hunting in the Western World,* p. 15.

21 **Shakespeare . . . often wrote in coded language:** See, in general, Clare Asquith, *Shadowplay: The Hidden Beliefs and Coded Politics of William Shakespeare.*

21 **the Bard may have been alluding to hemp:** J. Francis Thackeray, "Trance, Art and Literature," *Antiquity* 79(303)(2005); and William Shakespeare, Sonnet 118.

21 **It sounds like someone had the munchies:** Shakespeare, Sonnet 118.

22 **fragments tested positive for hemp:** Shaun Smillie, "Did Shakespeare Puff on 'Noted Weed'?" *National Geographic News,* March 1, 2001; Alan Dunn, "Riddle of the Bard," *Independent* (UK), March 1, 2001; and Thackeray, "Trance, Art and Literature."

22 **imposed draconian punishments on smokers:** Steven B. Duke and Albert C. Gross, *America's Longest War,* p. 23.

22 **traces of hemp, as well as coca leaf:** The seafarer Sir Frances Drake, a major figure in the tobacco trade and a contemporary of Shakespeare's, brought coca leaf to England after seizing large quantities of it from Spanish galleons that were returning from Peru.

22 **they may not have known exactly what was in those mixtures:** Author's interview with Michael Aldrich. Traces of myristic acid (from nutmeg), which has hallucinogenic properties, were also found on the four-hundred-year-old English pipe fragments.

22 **Culpeper remarked in his compendium:** Harry Shapiro, *Waiting for the Man,* p. 9.

23 **Captain Bowrey recorded in his journal:** Maev Kennedy, "17th-Century Cannabis Pioneer's Journal Found," *The Guardian* (UK), February 25, 2006; and Abel, *Marihuana,* pp. 116–17.

23 **In the month of April:** *A Dissertation on the Sexes of Plants.* Translated from the Latin of Linnaeus by James Edward Smith, F.R.S., into English and published in 1786, pp. 32–35. I thank Michael Horowitz for bringing this rare document to my attention.

23 **A man of many talents:** Michael R. Aldrich, "The Remarkable W. B. O'Shaughnessy," *O'Shaughnessy's,* Spring 2006.

24 **"Almost invariably . . . the inebriation is . . .":** W. B. O'Shaughnessy, "On the Preparations of the Indian Hemp or Gunja," in Mikuriya, ed., *Marijuana,* p. 7.

24 **"In the popular medicine of these nations . . .":** Mikuriya, *Marijuana,* p. 3.

24 **After testing ganja tincture:** A tincture is a liquid extract containing high concentrations of the active ingredients of medicinal herbs.

24 **O'Shaughnessy noted the general effects:** O'Shaughnessy in Mikuriya, ed., *Marijuana,* pp. 22–23.

24 **"My experience would lead me to prefer *small* doses . . .":** Ibid., pp. 29–30.

25 **Drawing upon his analysis:** Ibid., p. 14; Abel, *Marihuana,* pp. 182–83; and Green, *Cannabis,* p. 108.

25 **more than a hundred articles had appeared:** Mikuriya, *Marijuana,* p. 216. In 1851, *The Dispensatory of the United States* reported: "Extract of hemp is a powerful narcotic [meaning sleep-inducing drug], causing exhilaration, intoxication,

delirious hallucinations, and, in its subsequent action, drowsiness and stupor, with little effect upon the circulation. It is asserted also to act as a decided aphrodisiac, to increase appetite . . . to allay spasm, to compose nervous disquietude, and to relieve pain. In these respects it resembles opium; but it differs from that narcotic in not diminishing the appetite, checking the secretions or constipating the bowels. It is much less certain in its effects, but may sometimes be preferably employed, when opium is contraindicated . . . The complaints in which it has been specially recommended are neuralgia, gout, rheumatism, tetanus, hydrophobia, epidemic cholera, convulsions, chorea, hysteria, mental depression, delirium tremens, insanity, and uterine hemorrhage" (Edward Brecher and the Editors of *Consumers Union Reports, Licit & Illicit Drugs*, p. 405).

26 **a key ingredient in dozens:** Conrad, *Hemp*, p. 14; and Green, *Cannabis*, pp. 186–88.

26 **In 1860, the Ohio State Medical Society:** R. R. McMeens, "Report of the Ohio State Medical Committee on Cannabis Indica," in Mikuriya, ed., *Marijuana*, pp. 117–40.

26 **Sir William Osler, often called the founder:** Robert Clarke, *Hashish!*, p. 294

26 **"When pure and administered carefully . . .":** J. Russell Reynolds, "Therapeutic and Toxic Effects of Cannabis Indica," in Mikuriya, ed., *Marijuana*, pp. 145–49, reprinted from *Lancet*, (1) (March 22, 1890).

26 **"[W]ine and liquors are a thousand times more dangerous":** J.-J. Moreau in Mike Jay, *Emperors of Dreams*, p. 101.

27 **"To understand the ravings of a madman . . .":** Moreau, *Hashish and Mental Illness*, p. 17.

28 **They gathered beneath vaulted ceilings:** Gautier in Kimmens, ed., *Tales of Hashish*, pp. 86–104.

28 **Gautier wrote of his initiation:** Moreau, *Hashish and Mental Illness*, pp. 11–14.

29 **Alexandre Dumas, a notorious hashish eater:** Dumas, *The Count of Monte Cristo*, in Abel, *Marihuana*, pp. 162–63.

29 **"It is as though one lives several lifetimes . . .":** Charles Baudelaire, *The Poem of Hashish*, p. 87.

30 **"You have scattered your personality . . .":** Ibid., p. 95.

30 **"reveals nothing to the individual but himself":** Ibid., pp. 116–17.

30 **"a magnifying mirror":** Ibid., p. 71.

30 **"nothing miraculous, absolutely nothing . . .":** Abel, *Marihuana*, pp. 157–59.

30 **"I would have thought it better if you hadn't blamed hashish . . .":** Jay, *Emperors of Dreams*, p. 112.

30 **"If by means of a teaspoonful of sweetmeat . . .":** Baudelaire, *The Poem of Hashish*, p. 113.

30 **Dr. François Lallemand viewed the healing potential of hashish:** Kimmens, ed., *Tales of Hashish*, pp. 113–24.

31 **"I had to travel, divert the spells . . .":** Arthur Rimbaud, *A Season in Hell*, p. 65.

31 **"systematic derangement of all his senses:** Rimbaud, *Illuminations*, p. xxx.

31 **"Hell hath no power over pagans":** Rimbaud, *A Season in Hell*, p. 29.

31 **Finally I came to regard as sacred:** Ibid., p. 55.

31 **"all things curative and preventive":** Fitz Hugh Ludlow, *The Hasheesh Eater*, p. 15.

31 **"an aromatic invitation to scientific musing":** Ibid.

32 **"hysteria, chorea, gout, neuralgia . . .":** Larry Sloman, *Reefer Madness*, p. 210.

32 **"I was encompassed by a sea of light . . .":** Bayard Taylor, "A Slight Experience of Hashish," in Kimmens, ed., *Tales of Hashish*, pp. 143–55.

32 **"smitten by the hashish thrill . . .":** Ludlow, *The Hasheesh Eater,* p. 50.

32 **"A vision of celestial glory . . .":** Ibid., pp. 34, 51.

32 **"uncontrollable terror":** Ibid., p. 20.

33 **"the agonies of a martyr":** Ibid., p. 66.

33 **"to experiment with the drug of sorcery no more":** Ibid., p 85.

33 **Brown University student John Hay:** Donald P. Dulchinos, *Pioneer of Inner Space,* p. 87.

33 **Lincoln's widow was prescribed:** Conrad, *Hemp,* p. 195.

33 **"If someone does not propose a new and interesting amusement . . .":** Louisa May Alcott, "Perilous Play," in Cynthia Palmer and Michael Horowitz, eds., *Sisters of the Extreme,* pp. 45–52.

34 **"It will burst upon you . . .":** John Patrick Deveney, *Paschal Beverly Randolph,* p. 70. Thanks to Chris Bennett for bringing Randolph to my attention.

34 **"the largest importer of hashish into the United States":** Ibid., p. 69.

34 **Randolph developed a formula:** Ibid., pp. 71, 418.

34 **"Hashish multiplies one's life a thousand-fold . . .":** H. P. Blavatsky in Bey and Zug, *Orgies of the Hemp Eaters,* p. 440. Blavatsky tried hashish for the first time in Egypt in the early 1850s in the company of her lifelong friend A. L. Rawson, who was "an occultist, a 33rd degree Freemason, a founder of the Mystic Order of the Shrine (the 'Shriners'), and a claimant of middle-eastern initiations" (Bey and Zug, *Orgies,* p. 351).

35 **Dr. Louis-Alphonse Cahagnet . . . had been experimenting:** Siegel, *Intoxication,* pp. 166–67. The French hashish eater Victor-Émile Michelet, a symbolist poet and occultist in the theosophical mode, asserted that "Hashish always encourages, and sometimes provokes spontaneously, the projection of the astral body" (James Webb, *The Occult Underground,* pp. 174–75).

35 **Yeats much preferred hashish:** Jay, *Emperors of Dreams,* p. 215.

35 **Fitz Hugh Ludlow's evocative comment:** Aleister Crowley, *The Psychology of Hashish,* p. 6; on Crowley's and Lovecraft's admiration of Ludlow, see Dulchinos, *Pioneer of Inner Space,* p. 11, and Marcus Boon, *Road of Excess,* p. 146. On Crowley in general, see Martin Booth, *A Magick Life.*

36 **"a terrible joy":** William Butler Yeats, *The Plays,* p. 655.

36 **"the voluptuous enjoyment of eternal emptiness":** Friedrich Nietzsche, *The Will to Power,* p. 20.

36 **"two great European narcotics":** Nietzsche, *Twilight of the Idols,* in Walter Kaufmann, ed., *Portable Nietzsche,* p. 507.

36 **"To escape from unbearable pressure . . .":** Nietzsche, *Ecce Homo,* p. 6.

36 **Gunjah Wallah Hasheesh Candy:** Brecher and the Editors of *Consumers Union Reports, Licit & Illicit Drugs,* p. 409.

36 **"[L]ast night was like a thousand years . . .":** Jack London, *John Barleycorn* (1913) in Dale Gieringer, "Jack London, California Cannabis Pioneer," 2005. www.canorml.org/history/London-CannabisPioneer.pdf.

36 ***Scientific American* reported:** *Consumers Union Reports, Licit & Illicit Drugs,* p. 407.

37 **"All visitors, both male and female . . .":** "A Hashish-house in New York: The Curious Adventures of an Individual Who Indulged in a Few Pipefuls of the Narcotic Hemp," *Harper's Magazine* 67 (1883) in John Strausbaugh and Donald Blaise, eds., *The Drug User,* pp. 164–72.

CHAPTER 2: PROHIBITION

38 **widely employed as a folk remedy:** Roberto Williams-Garcia, "The Ritual Use of Cannabis in Mexico," in Vera Rubin, *Cannabis and Culture,* pp. 133–45; Emboden in Furst, ed., *Flesh of the Gods,* p. 229; and Siegel, *Intoxication,* p. 157.

39 **hemp plants escaped from cultivation:** Isaac Campos-Costero, "Marijuana, Madness and Modernity in Mexico, 1521–1920" (PhD diss., Harvard University, 2006).

39 ***"Esta ya le dio las tres":*** Richard J. Bonnie and Charles H. Whitebread, *The Marijuana Conviction,* p. 33.

40 ***Narcocorridos,* a subgenre of folk songs:** Curtis Marez, *Drug Wars,* p. 143; and Juan Gonzalez, *Harvest of Empire,* p. 220.

40 **"After the guard went down to Mexico . . .":** Bonnie and Whitebread, *The Marijuana Conviction,* p. 35. Marijuana was prohibited at the Fort Sam Houston military base in Texas in 1921 by order of the commanding general.

41 **Smoking grass became commonplace:** Marez, *Drug Wars,* pp. 110–11; and Sloman, *Reefer Madness,* p. 29.

41 **"a web of social controls":** Marez, *Drug Wars,* p. 152.

41 **Under the auspices of the Pure Food and Drug Act:** Dale H. Gieringer, "The Origins of Cannabis Prohibition in California," originally published as "The Forgotten Origins of Cannabis Prohibition in California," *Contemporary Drug Problems* 26(2) (1999); and Bonnie and Whitebread, *The Marijuana Conviction,* p. 37.

41 **a bare-knuckle drive to prevent physicians:** "Report on Drug Addiction—II," *Bulletin of the New York Academy of Medicine* 39 (1963): 466; Wayne Morgan, *Drugs in America,* p. 125; and Erich Goode, *Drugs in American Society,* p. 232. At the turn of the century, there were roughly 250,000 opiate addicts in the United States (out of a 75 million population), and two-thirds of these were genteel middle-aged women.

42 **drug statutes have been aimed:** See, in general, David F. Musto, *The American Disease.*

42 **"arrests and convictions of 'Mexican' workers . . .":** Marez, *Drug Wars,* pp. 136–37.

42 **Law-enforcement operations against alleged "reds":** Gonzalez, *Harvest of Empire,* p. 101; and Marez, *Drug Wars,* pp. 111–12, 128–29. According to Marez, there were "hundreds of incidents between 1915 and 1916 in the lower Río Grande Valley of South Texas," involving "los sediciosos" (Mexican anarchists and revolutionaries), who "tore up railroad tracks, burned bridges, sabotaged irrigation pumps, raided ranches, and skirmished with U.S. Army units and Texas Ranger patrols. . . . Mexican revolutionary, anti-imperial attacks were met by a ruthless counterinsurgency that combined white nativist vigilantes, the Texas Rangers, and various state militias."

43 **first official U.S. inquiry into cannabis:** Abel, *Marihuana,* pp. 206–7; and Bonnie and Whitebread, *The Marijuana Conviction,* pp. 132–36.

43 **the Narcotic Farms Act:** Bonnie and Whitebread, *The Marijuana Conviction,* p. 137; and David Musto, "The 1937 Marihuana Tax Act," in Mikuriya, ed., *Marijuana,* pp. 424–25.

44 **"The prestige of the government . . .":** David E. Rowe and Robert J. Schulmann, *Einstein on Politics,* p. 245.

44 **The cocktail was invented:** Edward Behr, *Prohibition,* p. 89. Deborah Blum reported in *Slate* (February 19, 2010) that government officials, frustrated by wide-

spread booze consumption during Prohibition, purposely poisoned industrial alcohol manufactured in the United States, a product that was regularly stolen by bootleggers and resold as drinkable spirits (Blum, "The Chemist's War: The Little-Told Story of How the U.S. Government Poisoned Alcohol During Prohibition with Deadly Consequences").

44 **"see things in a wonderful, soothing . . .":** Mezz Mezzrow, *Really the Blues,* p. 73.

45 **They called him "the Reefer King":** Ibid., p. 210.

45 **a byword in black hip-speak:** *Cab Calloway's Hepster's Dictionary* (1944) defined Mezz as "anything supreme, genuine." http://www.mcsweeneys.net/articles/actual-entries-from-cab-calloways-hepsters-dictionary-revised-1939-edition.

45 **more "Lo Zee Rose" and "Orchestrations":** Armstrong's letter to Milton Mezzrow, reproduced in Jack Herer, *The Emperor Has No Clothes,* p. 96.

45 **"hobo jungles" that sprang up near rail terminals:** Nels Anderson, *On Hobos and Homelessness,* p. 44.

45 **"Marijuana is popular because . . .":** Box-Car Bertha Thompson in Palmer and Horowitz, *Sisters of the Extreme,* pp. 103–5.

46 **"Poppa, you never smacked your chops . . .":** Mezzrow, *Really the Blues,* p. 215.

46 **"We were on another plane in another sphere . . .":** Ibid., p. 94.

46 **"acres of marijuana" being smoked:** Ibid., p. 236.

46 **"anybody from all walks of life . . .":** Jones and Chilton, *Louis,* p. 132.

47 **He lived in Paris for the rest of his days:** Mezzrow died in Paris in 1972 at the age of seventy-two. He is buried in the Père Lachaise cemetery, where his grave shares the same hallowed ground as the Hashish Eaters' Club members Honoré de Balzac and Gérard de Nerval.

47 **French surrealist writers:** Michel Boujut, *Louis Armstrong,* p. 11.

47 **Baroness Elsa von Freytag-Loringhoven graced the dance floors:** Palmer and Horowitz, *Sisters of the Extreme,* pp. 94–95.

47 **Walter Benjamin was one of several:** See, in general, the Walter Benjamin Research Syndicate, http://www.wbenjamin.org/walterbenjamin.html.

47 **"Under the influence of hashish we are . . .":** Benjamin, *On Hashish,* p. 53.

47 **a hashish-inspired "profane illumination":** Ibid., p. 132.

47 **"to win the energies of intoxication . . .":** Ibid., p. 133.

47 **"commingle with the cosmic powers":** Ibid., p. 130.

48 **"After smoking this you will see . . .":** Errol Flynn in Andrews and Vinkenoog, eds., *The Book of Grass,* pp. 82–85.

48 **imposing harsh penalties was the only way:** For first-time infractions, Anslinger urged a minimum of six months in jail and a fine of not less than $1,000; for second violations, two to five years' imprisonment and a fine of $5,000 to $50,000.

48 **"The greatest dangers to liberty lurk . . .":** Brandeis in Duke and Gross, *America's Longest War,* p. 122.

48 **marked by dancing in the streets:** A national cheer could be heard at 3:52 p.m. Mountain Time on Tuesday, December 5, 1933, when Utah joined thirty-six other states and ratified the Twenty-first Amendment, which lifted federal alcohol prohibition.

49 **The stuff grows "like dandelions":** Musto, *The American Disease,* pp. 221–22.

49 **"If the hideous monster Frankenstein . . .":** *Washington Herald,* April 12, 1937, cited in Bonnie and Whitebread, *The Marijuana Conviction,* p. 117.

49 **"the most violence-causing drug . . .":** Anslinger in Rudolph Joseph Gerber, *Legalizing Marijuana,* p. 7.

49 **a plant that provided the paper:** More than 75 percent of the world's paper manufactured before 1883 was made from hemp fiber, including the Gutenberg Bible.

50 **suffering from a form of nervous strain . . .":** Jill Jonnes, *Hep-Cats, Narcs, and Pipe Dreams,* p. 104.

50 **a strong ally in the press baron William Randolph Hearst:** Ibid., p 158.

50 **"Murder Weed Found Up and Down Coast":** *Los Angeles Examiner,* November 5, 1933.

51 **a policy of ethnic cleansing:** Gonzalez, *Harvest of Empire,* p. 103. Vicente Serrano's documentary, *A Forgotten Injustice,* examines the mass deportation of Mexican immigrants in the 1930s.

51 **Hearst also cheered the rise of fascist forces:** George Seldes, *Witness to a Century,* p. 102.

51 **"Mussolini Leads Way in Crushing Dope Evil":** Winifred Black, "Mussolini Leads Way in Crushing Dope Evil: Italy Jails Smugglers & Peddlers for Life with No Hope of Pardon; US Acting at Last," in Hearst papers, March 9, 1928, cited in Harry Shapiro, *Shooting Stars,* p. 18; and Conrad, *Hemp,* p. 201. The American Federation of Teachers went so far as to call Hearst the "chief exponent of Fascism in the United States" (Gary Brechin, *Imperial San Francisco,* p. 234).

51 **Hearst Sunday papers published columns by German Nazi leaders:** Brechin, *Imperial San Francisco,* p. 235.

51 **the "combating of drugs" to promote racial hygiene:** Scott J. Thompson, "Thoughts on Hitler's War on Drugs" in Werner Pieper, ed., *Nazis on Speed: Drogen im 3. Reich,* Bd. I (Vol. I), pp. 155–59.

51 **"Mexicans, Greeks, Turks, Filipinos, Spaniards, Latin Americans . . .":** *Union Signal* in Bonnie and Whitebread, *The Marijuana Conviction,* p. 106.

52 **"Marijuana causes white women to seek sexual relations . . .":** Margaret J. Goldstein, *Legalizing Drugs,* p. 29.

52 **"voodoo-satanic music":** Hearst papers cited in Ed Sanders, *America: A History in Verse,* vol. 1, p. 361.

52 **The sprawled body of a young girl:** Harry Anslinger, "Assassin of Youth," *American Magazine,* July 1937.

52 **financed by major distilling companies:** Booth, *Cannabis,* p. 151. Marijuana was depicted as having a sedating effect in *Night of Terror* (1933), starring Bela Lugosi, who asks a policeman guarding him if he could smoke. The cop agrees, takes a cigarette for himself, lights up, and inhales. "Hey, what kind of cigarette is that?" he asks. "It is an oriental cigarette," says Lugosi in a thick Transylvanian accent, as the detective falls asleep.

53 **"voodoo pharmacology":** Jacob Sullum, *Saying Yes,* p. 10.

53 **an exorbitant tax:** Treasury Department General Counsel Herman Oliphant is credited with the idea of a marijuana transfer tax as a solution to the problem that the federal government lacked the constitutional authority to outlaw a drug—which is why alcohol prohibition required a constitutional amendment (Kathleen Grammatico Ferraiolo, "Popular 'Medicine': Policymaking by Direct Democracy and the Medical Marijuana Movement of the 1990s" [PhD diss., University of Virginia, 2004], 26).

53 **When he testified before the House:** U.S. Congress, House Committee on Ways and Means, 75th Cong., 1st Sess., H Rept. No. 792, Hearings on H.R. 6385. An-

slinger played up stories of young men murdering people while high on marijuana. Victor Licata, a once "sane, rather quiet young man" from Tampa, Florida, according to Anslinger, killed his family with an axe in 1933 after becoming "pitifully crazed" from smoking "muggles." Actually, the Tampa police tried to have Licata committed to a mental hospital before he started to smoke marijuana. Many of Anslinger's tall tales about cannabis-induced crimes were debunked by John Kaplan in *The New Prohibition,* pp. 91–104.

53 **Woodward, the legislative counsel for the [AMA]:** "It may serve to deprive the public of benefits of a drug that on further research may prove to be of substantial value." Dr. William Woodward in Richard Glen Boire and Kevin Feeney, *Medical Marijuana Law,* p. 19.

55 **"Marijuana destroys life":** Sloman, *Reefer Madness,* p. 104.

55 **"Marijuana has become our greatest problem . . .":** Ibid.

55 **a confidential memo to all his district supervisors:** Ibid.

55 **"It can be grown easily almost anywhere . . .":** "The Weed," *Time,* June 19, 1943.

55 **a young hustler known as Crazy Red:** *Autobiography of Malcolm X,* p. 110.

55 **an estimated 50,000 Americans:** Saul Rubin, *Offbeat Marijuana,* p. 202.

55 **that number had doubled:** "Reefers on KPFA" *Newsweek,* May 10, 1954.

56 **Anslinger habitually exaggerated:** Bonnie and Whitebread, *The Marijuana Conviction,* p. 181.

56 **removed from the *United States Pharmacopeia*:** *Dispensatory of the United States of America,* 21st ed. (1926).

56 **memo dated September 7, 1943:** Anslinger to all district supervisors, September 7, 1943, in Bonnie and Whitebread, *The Marijuana Conviction,* p. 183.

57 **a special FBN file, "Marijuana and Musicians":** Ibid., p. 184.

57 **"I smoked some grass":** Anita O'Day, *High Times Hard Times,* pp. 28, 116.

57 **FBN agents weren't able to infiltrate:** Bonnie and Whitebread, *The Marijuana Conviction,* p. 185.

58 **generous government subsidies for farmers:** Roulac, *Hemp Horizons,* p. 45. Registered hemp farmers and their sons were exempted from military service during World War II.

58 **to eradicate barely psychoactive "ditch weed":** Homegrown slang developed for wild marijuana: Kentucky Bluegrass, Missouri Mud, Kansas Krap, Nebraska Nonsense, Tahoe Trouble, New Jersey Swamp (William Novak, *High Culture,* p. 192).

59 **"It accentuates the senses":** OSS Memorandum for the File, Subject: Truth Drug (T.D.), April 5, 1946, in Martin A. Lee and Bruce Shlain, *Acid Dreams,* p. 4.

59 **he visited Manhattan Project security officer John Lansdale:** Douglas Valentine, *The Strength of the Wolf,* pp. 46–47.

59 **an overdose of T.D.:** Undated OSS document, "Memorandum Relative to the Use of TD in Interrogation," in Lee and Shlain, *Acid Dreams,* pp. 4–5.

59 **"The drug defies all but the most . . .":** OSS Memorandum for the File, Subject: Truth Drug (T.D.), April 5, 1946, in Lee and Shlain, *Acid Dreams,* p. 5. When T.D. didn't pan out as hoped, an OSS consultant suggested further study of "synhexyl," another cannabis derivative. But this, too, fell by the wayside.

60 **a "regime of truth":** Clare O'Farrell, *Michel Foucault,* p. 153; see also, John F. Galliher, David P. Keys, and Michael Elsner, "Lindesmith v. Anslinger: An Early Government Victory in the Failed War on Drugs," *Journal of Criminal Law & Criminology* (Winter 1998).

61 **"cannabis is a mild euphoriant":** Editor's note in 1973 republication of the Mayor's Committee, *The Marihuana Problem in the City of New York* (La Guardia Report), p. iii.

61 **"Prolonged use of the drug . . .":** S. Allentuck and K. M. Bowman, "The Psychiatric Aspects of Marihuana Intoxication," *American Journal of Psychiatry* 99(51) (1942): 248.

61 **marijuana is not addictive:** Mayor's Committee, *The Marihuana Problem in the City of New York,* p. 25.

61 **"The lessening of inhibitions and repressions . . .":** Ibid., p. 218.

61 **"a government-printed invitation to youth . . .":** Harry J. Anslinger, *The Murderers,* p. 40.

61 **no link between juvenile delinquency and marijuana smoking:** Mayor's Committee, *The Marihuana Problem in the City of New York,* p. 25.

62 **"A constant observation was the extreme willingness . . .":** Ibid., p. 10.

62 **the AMA continued to raise the possibility:** *JAMA* editorial, December 1942, in Grinspoon, *Marihuana Reconsidered,* p. 27.

62 ***Journal of the American Medical Association* excoriated:** Bonnie and Whitebread, *The Marijuana Conviction,* p. 201.

62 **"has already done great damage . . .":** Anslinger in John Kaplan, *Marijuana,* p. 151.

62 **Anslinger also received the support of drug companies:** Sloman, *Reefer Madness,* pp. 46–47.

62 **buried a summary of the La Guardia Report:** *New York Times,* January 12, 1945, cited in Jerome L. Himmelstein, *The Strange Career of Marihuana,* p. 43. A 1934 *New York Times* article described marijuana as a "poisonous weed which maddens the senses and emaciates the body of the user." From the same publication, same year: "Users of marijuana become stimulated as they inhale the drug and are likely to do anything." In 1937, the *Times* erroneously reported that smoking marijuana "may produce criminal insanity and causes juvenile delinquency."

62 **all use was abuse:** Wayne Morgan, *Drugs in America,* p. 147. "Whereas the opiates can be a blessing when properly used, marijuana has no therapeutic value and its use therefore is always an abuse and vice," Anslinger insisted in a 1953 book on the drug problem.

62 **cannabis was now part of a Commie plot:** John C. McWilliams, *The Protectors,* pp. 149–52; and Bonnie and Whitebread, *The Marijuana Conviction,* p. 209.

63 **led the user to hard drugs:** Marijuana is more dangerous than alcohol, *Newsweek* reported in 1954, because "it makes the switch to heroin easy" ("Reefers on KPFA," *Newsweek,* May 10, 1954, cited in Himmelstein, *The Strange Career of Marihuana,* p. 85).

63 **"They took to the needle . . .":** Anslinger testimony before U.S. Congress, House of Representatives, Committee on Ways and Means Hearings on H.R. No. 3490, 82nd Congress, 1st Session, 1951, p. 206, in Abel, *Marihuana,* p. 253.

63 **a Communist conspiracy to weaken the United States:** "Dope's Flow Said to Have Red Backing," Bonnie and Whitebread, *The Marijuana Conviction,* p. 209.

63 **Anslinger accused the Japanese of pushing narcotics:** Eric Schlosser, *Reefer Madness,* p. 21.

63 **The FBN chief ominously warned:** Anslinger in Jonnes, *Hep-Cats, Narcs, and Pipe Dreams,* pp. 176–77. A few critics were openly skeptical of the new laws. Speaking at a conference of federal judges, James V. Bennett, director of the U.S. Bureau of

Prisons, called the Boggs bill a hysterical overreaction. Bennett was subsequently tailed by FBN agents, who reported on his movements and his speaking engagements (Bonnie and Whitebread, *The Marijuana Conviction*, p. 211; Schlosser, *Reefer Madness*, p. 43).

64 **arranged a regular supply of morphine:** Anslinger, *The Murderers*, p. 181.

64 **none other than Senator Joseph McCarthy:** McWilliams, *The Protectors*, pp. 98–99.

64 **The FBN chief faithfully subordinated:** Valentine, *The Strength of the Wolf*, pp. 68–69, 230–32, 392.

64 **Anslinger concealed evidence:** Ibid., p. 18.

64 **the CIA-backed Chinese Nationalist Kuomintang Army:** See, in general, Alfred McCoy, *The Politics of Heroin*.

64 **the FBN turned a blind eye to dope smuggling:** See, in general, Valentine, *The Strength of the Wolf*.

64 **Eisenhower called for "a new war on narcotics . . .":** Jonnes, *Hep-Cats, Narcs, and Pipe Dreams*, p. 262.

64 **"Mary Warner, honey, you sure was good . . .":** Jones and Chilton, *Louis*, p. 138.

65 **Young gave Jack Kerouac, the fledgling writer:** Lewis McAdams, *Birth of the Cool*, p. 47; and John Leland, *Why Kerouac Matters*, p. 48.

65 **"a tenor man drawing a breath . . .":** Leland, *Why Kerouac Matters*, p. 122.

66 **"All that we knew was that we . . .":** Allen Ginsberg, *Composed on the Tongue*, p. 72.

67 **"I smoke marijuana every chance I get":** Ginsberg, "America," in *Howl and other Poems*, pp. 31–32.

67 **"I guess you might say that we're a beat generation":** Kerouac in John Leland, *Hip: The History*, p. 147.

67 **"to be in a state of beatitude . . .":** Ann Charters, *Kerouac*, p. 298.

67 **"a community of the excluded":** Ted Morgan, *Literary Outlaw*, p. 289.

67 **"out of his mind with real belief":** Jack Kerouac, *On the Road*, p. 39. "Translated into 40 languages, millions of copies of the Beat Generation classic have sold worldwide since the novel was published in 1957, placing it among the 20th century's most influential books," writes Scott James, *Bay Citizen*, April 16, 2011.

67 **"Gone on the road":** Leland, *Why Kerouac Matters*, p. 4.

68 **he journeyed to the Amazon jungle:** William S. Burroughs and Allen Ginsberg, *The Yage Letters*.

68 **Burroughs had been "searching . . .":** Eric Mottram, *William Burroughs: The Algebra of Need*, p. 94.

68 **"to make people aware of the true criminality . . .":** Burroughs in Dennis McNally, *Desolate Angel*, p. 336.

69 **a landmark obscenity case:** On July 7, 1966, the Massachusetts Supreme Court determined that *Naked Lunch* was not "utterly without socially redeeming value" and therefore was not obscene. This ruling effectively marked the end of government-imposed literary censorship in the United States.

69 **men who "screamed with joy":** Ginsberg, *Howl*, p. 12.

69 **"narcotic tobacco haze of capitalism":** Ibid.

69 **"Holy the groaning saxophone!":** Ibid., p. 21. Ginsberg said that in publishing "Howl" he sought "to leave behind after my generation an emotional time bomb that would continue exploding in U.S. consciousness in case our military-industrial-nationalist complex solidified into a repressive police bureaucracy" (Jason Shinder, ed., *The Poem That Changed America: "Howl" Fifty Years Later*, p. 146).

70 **Caen mockingly referred:** Herb Caen in Barry Miles, *Ginsberg,* p. 244; and Martin Torgoff, *Can't Find My Way Home,* p. 66.
70 **Ginsberg visited him in prison:** Bill Morgan, *I Celebrate Myself,* p. 294.
70 **"It was becoming clear to me . . .":** Ginsberg in Torgoff, *Can't Find My Way Home,* p. 67.
70 **Marijuana was never mentioned in Hollywood films:** Booth, *Cannabis,* p. 175.
70 **"the latrine laureate of Hobohemia":** *Time* magazine in Deborah Baker, *A Blue Hand,* p. 122.
71 **what the Sixties would bring:** Bill Morgan, *I Celebrate Myself,* p. 307.

CHAPTER 3: REEFER REBELLION

72 **"The three biggest threats to America . . .":** Hoover in *Daily News* cited in Sloman, *Reefer Madness,* p. 181.
72 **"Woe unto those who spit . . .":** Kevin J. Hayes, ed., *Conversations with Jack Kerouac,* p. 11.
73 **a marijuana user "becomes a fiend . . .":** Grinspoon, *Marijuana Revisited,* p. 17.
73 **Hoover pegged Ginsberg:** Ed Sanders, *The Poetry and Life of Allen Ginsberg,* p. 59. See also Herbert Mitgang, *Dangerous Dossiers.*
73 **"lucid advertisement for pot":** Ginsberg in Bill Morgan, *I Celebrate Myself,* p. 325.
73 **"a lot of alarmist nonsense . . .":** Sloman, *Reefer Madness,* p. 219. A Treasury Department representative, handpicked by Anslinger, claimed that marijuana was so damaging to dogs that cannabinated canines had to be destroyed!
73 **rabid fictions still held sway.** The 1963 edition of Roget's Thesaurus listed "marijuana" under the heading "poison." David Hajdu, *Positively 4th Street,* p. 135.
74 **Ginsberg tried to persuade commercial publishers:** Extensive selections from the La Guardia Report were included in *The Marijuana Papers* (1969), edited by David Solomon.
74 **"It was the first time I ever had solid evidence . . .":** Ginsberg in Sloman, *Reefer Madness,* p. 180.
74 **"Marijuana consciousness is one that . . .":** Allen Ginsberg, "First Manifesto to End the Bringdown," in Solomon, *Marijuana Papers,* p. 239.
74 ***muerta blanca,* or "white death":** William Carter, ed., *Cannabis in Costa Rica,* pp. 125, 129.
75 **"Instinctively, Leary stayed away from marijuana . . .":** Author's interview with Ralph Metzner.
75 **stoked the interest of American spies and military strategists:** See, in general, Lee and Shlain, *Acid Dreams.*
75 **one of the hottest topics:** By the mid-1960s, more than two thousand published, peer-reviewed research papers discussed LSD experimentation involving more than forty thousand patients.
77 **Corruption was rampant among FBN agents:** Jonnes, *Hep-Cats, Narcs, and Pipe Dreams,* pp. 192, 268.
77 **a scandal waiting to blow:** Ibid., pp. 264–65.
77 **White House Conference on Narcotics and Drug Abuse:** Himmelstein, *The Strange Career of Marihuana,* pp. 90–91; and Dr. William H. McGlothlin, "Cannabis Intoxication and Its Similarity to That of Peyote and LSD," in Andrews and Vinkenoog, *Book of Grass,* p. 174.
77 **"We've got it locked up so tightly now . . .":** Anslinger in Kaplan, *Marijuana,* p. 369.

77 **whispers alleging that Kennedy:** Michael O'Brien, *John F. Kennedy: A Biography,* p. 696; and Ed Dwyer, "I Was JFK's Dealer," *Best of High Times,* pp. 6–13.

78 **the recent Cuban revolution:** Peter Guralnick in *Dream Boogie* described Cuban premier Fidel Castro's impromptu visit to Harlem's Apollo Theater, across the street from a funky hotel where Castro stayed during a 1960 United Nations visit. The Cuban leader mixed easily at the Apollo with R&B stars, with whom he shared an interest in "chorus girls, cigars and marijuana."

78 **Zimmerman first came into contact with marijuana:** Author's interview with Diamond Dave Whitaker, who turned Dylan on to pot.

78 **"It was Ginsberg and Kerouac who inspired . . .":** Dylan quoted in McNally, *Desolate Angel,* p. 307. "Howl" "said more to me than any of the stuff I'd been raised on," Dylan remarked (Colleen J. Sheehy and Thomas Swiss, eds., *Highway 61 Revisited: Bob Dylan's Road from Minnesota to the World,* p. 252). "I came out of the wilderness and just naturally fell in with the beat scene, the Bohemian, Bebop crowd, it was all pretty much connected," Dylan wrote of his time in Minneapolis (quoted in Shinder, *The Poem That Changed America,* p. 234).

79 **Richard and Bob shared a "fondness for marijuana":** Hajdu, *Positively 4th Street,* p. 135.

79 **"to begin the world over again":** Thomas Paine, *Collected Writings,* p. 52.

80 **"We were kind of proud . . .":** Barry Miles, *McCartney,* p. 189.

80 **whenever John Lennon felt like getting stoned:** Al Aronowitz, *Bob Dylan and the Beatles,* pp. 24, 228; and Carol Sherman and Andrew Smith, *Highlights,* p. 91. The Delmonico Hotel has a plaque mounted on its lobby wall highlighting the meeting between Dylan and the Beatles.

81 **Mechoulam . . . announced his discovery:** Raphael Mechoulam, "A Total Synthesis of DL-Delta-1-Tetrahydrocannabinol, the Active Constituent of Hashish," *Journal of the American Chemical Society* 87 (1965): 3273–75.

81 **"a medicinal treasure trove":** "Conversation with Raphael Mechoulam," *Addiction* 102 (2007): 887–93; see also "The New Science of Cannabinoid-Based Medicine: An Interview with Dr. Raphael Mechoulam," in David Jay Brown, ed., *Mavericks of Medicine.*

81 **Everyone "had a different reaction":** Patrick Matthews, *Cannabis Culture,* p. 101.

81 **"We weren't looking for medical benefits":** Unless otherwise indicated, all quotes from Col. Jim Ketchum are from the author's interviews with James Ketchum. See also Martin A. Lee, "The Counterculture Colonel," *North Bay Bohemian,* July 2–8, 2008.

82 **"war without death":** "The Hallucination Battlefield" in Lee and Shlain, *Acid Dreams,* pp. 35–43.

84 **synthetic variant of THC that could clobber people:** Author's interview with James Ketchum; see also James S. Ketchum's self-published memoir, *Chemical Warfare: Secrets Almost Forgotten.*

84 **"There was no doubt in my mind . . .":** Ibid.

84 **"Everything seems comical . . .":** Ibid., pp. 38–41.

85 **a mixture of eight stereoisomers of THC:** Two Edgewood Arsenal research scientists, Herbert S. Aaron and C. Parker Ferguson, reported their findings in "Synthesis of the Eight Stereoisomers of a Tetrahydrocannabinol Congener," *Journal of Organic Chemistry* 33(2) (1968): 684–89.

85 **"This hypotensive [blood pressure reducing] property . . .":** Author's interview with James Ketchum.

86 **a delirium-inducing ass-kicker:** The glycolate compound BZ is a belladonna-like substance similar to atropine. *Acid Dreams,* pp. 41–43.

86 **"a large black steel barrel . . .":** Author's interview with James Ketchum; and Ketchum, *Chemical Warfare.*

88 **"stop the coming end of the world":** Dennis McNally, *A Long Strange Trip,* pp. 162–63.

88 **"With Cassady at the throttle . . .":** Robert Stone, *Prime Green,* p. 120.

88 **"He never ate, never slept . . .":** Ibid., p. 159.

89 **"an entire nation's burning material madness":** Lee and Shlain, *Acid Dreams,* p. 123.

89 **"great rucksack revolution":** Jack Kerouac, *Dharma Bums,* pp. 77–78. "Kerouac opened a million coffee bars and sold a million Levi's to both sexes. Woodstock rises from his pages," said William Burroughs (*High Times Reader,* p. 117).

89 **"the world capital of madness . . .":** Hunter S. Thompson, *Songs of the Doomed,* p. 118.

90 **Dr. Isbell concluded that a very high dose:** H. Isbell and D. R. Jasinksi, "A Comparison of LSD-25 with Delta-9-Trans-THC and Attempted Cross-Tolerance Between LSD and THC," *Psychopharmacologia* 14(2) (1969): 115–23. While under CIA contract, Isbell gave LSD and psilocybin, the magic mushroom extract, to prisoners for seventy-seven consecutive days at the Lexington Narcotics Hospital in Kentucky in the late 1950s.

90 **LSD madness:** Lee and Shlain, *Acid Dreams,* pp. 150–51.

90 **He maintained that cannabis was essentially a Christian herb:** Author's interview with Carolyn Garcia.

90 **"[T]o be peaceful without being stupid . . .":** Kesey in Nick Jones, *Spliffs,* p. 65.

90 **"We smoked a lot of pot":** Author's interview with Carolyn Garcia.

91 **"out the door and into the street . . .":** Stone, *Prime Green,* p. 161.

91 **"salted with revelation":** Author's interview with Ken Kesey, August 1978.

91 **all types of personal and social experimentation:** Peter Braunstein, "Forever Young," in Peter Braunstein and Michael William Doyle, *Imagine Nation,* p. 257.

92 **"out of step together":** McNally, *A Long Strange Trip,* p. 240.

92 **"Why San Francisco?":** Herb Caen, *One Man's San Francisco,* pp. 125–26.

92 **this riveting episode of "guerrilla theater":** Author's interview with Peter Berg and Judy Goldhaft.

93 **"The arrests were made under a law . . .":** Joel Selvin, *The Summer of Love,* p. 132.

94 **marijuana made a quantum leap:** William McGlothlin, "Sociocultural Factors in Marihuana Use in the United States," in Vera Rubin, *Cannabis and Culture,* p. 531.

94 **"Dope Invades the Suburbs":** Robert Goldman, "Dope Invades the Suburbs," *Saturday Evening Post,* April 4, 1964; and Jeremy Larner, "The College Drug Scene," *Atlantic Monthly,* November 1965. Both articles cited in Himmelstein, *The Strange Career of Marihuana,* p. 3.

94 **As the times changed, so did the arguments:** *Time* magazine reported in 1965 that marijuana "affects the user's judgment and if used daily will dull a student's initiative" (Himmelstein, *The Strange Career of Marihuana,* p. 122).

95 **these drugs were often misused:** Some three thousand Americans died from prescription drug overdoses in 1965.

95 **"the rarest or most abnormal form of behavior . . .":** Duke and Gross, *America's Longest War,* p. 12.

95 **"When a young person took his first puff . . .":** Lee and Shlain, *Acid Dreams,* p. 129.

95 **There's an old joke among stoners:** David Lenson, *On Drugs,* p. 110.

96 **"You couldn't separate laws against drugs . . .":** Krassner in Larry Sloman, *Steal This Dream,* p. 55; and Paul Krassner, "LSD as Gateway Drug," *San Francisco Bay Guardian* Online, August 19, 2009.

96 **the "heads" and the "fists":** Laurence Leamer, *The Paper Revolutionaries.*

96 **an axis of division among rebellious youth:** Certain left-wing sectarian groups tried to enforce a cultural conservatism among their ranks, sometimes expelling members who used marijuana. "Nobody will need to take drugs when the revolution comes," a Young Socialist pamphlet declared.

97 **the bridge . . . the culture carrier . . .":** Ted Morgan, *Literary Outlaw,* p. 376.

97 **broadened the very definition of politics:** The 1962 Port Huron Statement, a founding document of Students for a Democratic Society (SDS), the leading New Left youth organization, included "private problems" and "personal alienation" as examples for the kinds of issues a viable New Left must address. "Men have unrealized potential for self-cultivation . . . ," declared the Port Huron Statement, which fashioned a political analysis of alienation and loneliness in advanced industrial America.

97 **"to the right of Goldwater":** Author's interview with Michael Aldrich.

98 **"to get people who use marijuana":** Ed Sanders, *Fug You,* p. 143.

98 **"My life changed overnight":** Sanders in Ronald Sukenick, *Down and In,* p. 95.

99 **churned out pro-cannabis leaflets:** Sanders called for the legalization of marijuana in 1963 in an editorial in *Fuck You/A Magazine of the Arts* (Sanders, *Fug You,* p. 79).

99 **"liberate pot from the grouches":** Ibid., pp. 121, 389.

100 **I am part of a movement:** Ed Sanders, "Ode to d.a. levy," in Larry Smith and Ingrid Swanberg, eds, *d.a. levy & the mimeograph revolution,* pp. 129–49; and Sanders, *Fug You,* pp. 190–91.

101 **a satiric pamphlet about pot smoking:** Albert Goldman, *Ladies and Gentlemen—LENNY BRUCE!!,* p. 272.

101 **visiting Professor Alfred Lindesmith:** Alfred Lindesmith was one of the few academic experts who challenged Anslinger's notion that drug addicts were criminals; Lindesmith suggested that addicts suffered from a disease and should be treated like they were ill, not illegal. Anslinger went ballistic and tried, unsuccessfully, to get Lindesmith fired from his job at Indiana University.

101 **Ginsberg penned a prose essay:** Published initially in the *Atlantic Monthly,* "First Manifesto to End the Bringdown" was the centerpiece of *The Marijuana Papers,* a 1967 anthology compiled by David Solomon, former editor of the jazz magazine *Metronome.* Solomon's mass-market anthology included a reprint of much of the La Guardia Report, per Ginsberg's recommendation.

101 **the government's list of suspicious persons:** Bill Morgan, *I Celebrate Myself,* p. 464.

101 **"reported engagement in drug smuggling":** Shinder, *The Poem That Changed America,* p. 276.

102 **a photograph of the famous poet:** Lee and Shlain, *Acid Dreams,* p. 226.

102 **"I feel like the noose of the police state . . .":** Miles, *Ginsberg,* p. 390.

102 **"It wasn't being done openly . . .":** Sanders in Torgoff, *Can't Find My Way Home,* p. 107.

102 **Composed while he chain-smoked reefers:** Hajdu, *Positively 4th Street,* p. 234.

102 **couldn't fall asleep at night:** Albert Lloyd on Dylan in Clinton Heylin, *Behind the Shades,* p. 677.

103 **"open his head":** Scaduto cited in Shapiro, *Waiting for the Man,* p. 144. "I wouldn't advise anybody to use drugs—certainly not the hard drugs," Dylan told *Playboy* (November 1966). As for natural substances like marijuana and hashish, he declaimed: "Now these things aren't drugs; they just bend your mind a little. I think everybody's mind should be bent once in a while."

103 **"The political and societal juggernaut . . .":** Tom Robbins in *High Times,* November 2005.

103 **"entirely about pot":** Miles, *McCartney,* p. 290.

103 **"We were smoking marijuana for breakfast":** Barry Miles, *Hippie,* p. 76.

104 **two overarching concerns of Sixties rebels:** *The Fifth Estate,* an underground newspaper in Detroit, filled its front page in January 1968 with a list of New Year's resolutions, beginning with "Legalize marijuana" and "Overthrow the government."

104 **"Changing the lifestyle and appearance . . .":** Miles, *McCartney,* p. 293.

105 **Mick Jagger of the Rolling Stones:** Busted again in 1969, Jagger claimed that marijuana had been planted by a corrupt cop who then demanded money to ensure the charges were dropped.

106 **also arrested by Pilcher:** Sergeant Pilcher of London's Drug Squad was immortalized as "Semolina Pilchard" in John Lennon's "I Am the Walrus" on the *Magical Mystery Tour* album.

106 **"If I smoke, will I get caught?":** Richard Neville in *Power Play,* cited in Shapiro, *Waiting for the Man,* p. 150.

106 **"You are a pest to society":** Barry Miles, *In the Sixties,* pp. 190–92.

106 **"Hoppy's friends held an emergency summit":** Ibid., p. 192.

106 **SOMA (an affiliate of LEMAR):** SOMA, the acronym for Abrams's "Society of Mental Awareness," was also the name of the ancient mystical drug mentioned in the Vedas and the rapturous narcotic featured in Aldous Huxley's *Brave New World.*

107 **"Do you know what caused *Pepper*?":** Miles, *McCartney,* p. 347.

107 **The Wootton Report drew a clear distinction:** Wootton Commission Report, November 1, 1968, http://www.druglibrary.org/schaffer/library/studies/wootton/wootton_toc.htm. See also Steve Abrams, "Hashish Fudge: The Times Advertisement and the Wootton Report," May 10, 1993. http://www.druglibrary.org/schaffer/library/studies/wootton/soma1.htm.

108 **"looked like the legions of Sgt. Pepper's band":** Mailer in Maurice Isserman and Michael Kazin, *America Divided,* p. 184.

109 **"A new man was born while besieging the Pentagon . . .":** Torgoff, *Can't Find My Way Home,* p. 230.

109 **Every time I smoke pot is a revolutionary act:** Hoffman in Janet Farrell Brodie and Marc Redfield, eds., *High Anxieties,* p. 144.

109 **One clandestine Yippie caper:** Sanders, *Fug You,* p. 333.

110 **some of whom went so far as:** Bonnie and Whitebread, *The Marijuana Conviction,* p. 227.

110 **"a lot of marijuana money was re-channeled . . .":** Rubin in Torgoff, *Can't Find My Way Home,* p. 238.

110 **a large victory flag:** Miles, *Hippie,* p. 289; Miles, *In the Sixties,* p. 240.

110 **"With pupils dilated from the drug":** *Krokodil,* December 1970, in *Marijuana Review* 1(6) (January–June 1971).

110 **protestors adopted the song "San Francisco":** *Marijuana Review* 1(4) (October–December 1969).

111 **"We will burn Chicago to the ground":** Lee and Shlain, *Acid Dreams,* p. 219.

111 **"We are dirty, smelly, grimy . . .":** Ibid.

111 **conspiracy theories:** An article in the August 1968 issue of the *Mensa Journal* suggested that police pass out free pot at political demonstrations to keep things cool.

111 **cannabinoid compounds have significant neuroprotective properties:** See, for example, Raphael Mechoulam et al., "Cannabinoids and Brain Injury: Therapeutic Implications," *TRENDS in Molecular Medicine* 8(2) (2002): 58–61; and Anat Biegon, "Cannabinoids as Neuroprotective Agents in Traumatic Brain Injury," *Current Pharmaceutical Design* 10(18) (2004): 2177–83.

112 **one out of six protestors in Chicago:** *CBS News* report based on declassified U.S. Army intelligence documents cited in Lee and Shlain, *Acid Dreams,* p. 224.

112 **quarter of a million Americans were under "active surveillance":** Robert Justin Goldstein, *Political Repression in Modern America,* p. 463.

112 **"We were definitely a happy group . . .":** Cril Payne, *Deep Cover,* pp. 124–37.

113 **"And since there was a certain aura of mystery . . .":** Ibid., p. 162.

113 **"My undercover experiences brought me . . .":** Ibid., p. 124.

113 **"Since the use of marijuana and other narcotics . . .":** FBI Memorandum from Director, FBI, to SAC, Albany, "Counter-Intelligence Program—Internal Security, Disruption of the New Left," July 5, 1968, cited in Lee and Shlain, *Acid Dreams,* p. 225.

114 **While in jail, Sinclair wrote:** John Sinclair, "The Marijuana Revolution," in *Marijuana Review* 1(6) (January–June 1971).

114 **there was not a single fight:** Kaplan, *Marijuana,* p. 131.

114 **"It was a chance to show the world . . .":** Wavy Gravy, *Something Good for a Change,* p. 19.

114 **estimates of the number of pot smokers:** Bonnie and Whitebread, *The Marijuana Conviction,* p. 238, citing U.S. Congress, Senate Committee on the Judiciary, Subcommittee to Investigate Juvenile Delinquency, 91st Congress, 1st Sess., 1969.

115 **Vietcong, "love," and "legalized marijuana":** Miles, *Hippie,* p. 312.

115 **"just another effort to break down . . .":** Kaplan, *Marijuana,* p. 9.

115 **Condemning cannabis was a way:** Himmelstein, *The Strange Career of Marihuana,* pp. 130–36.

115 **"an immeasurably costly game of cops and robbers":** Stone, *Prime Green,* p. 228.

CHAPTER 4: THE BIG CHILL

116 **This unilateral interdiction effort:** For a discussion of Operation Intercept, see Brecher and the Editors of *Consumer Union Reports, Licit & Illicit Drugs,* pp. 434–50.

116 **The amount of reefer seized:** Ibid., p. 440.

117 **"For diplomatic reasons the true purpose . . .":** G. Gordon Liddy, *Will,* p. 135.

117 **"Since marijuana is not addictive . . .":** *San Francisco Chronicle,* September 14, 1969, cited in Kaplan, *Marijuana,* p. 169.

117 **Brotherhood of Eternal Love, an elusive underground network:** See, in general, Stewart Tendler and David May, *The Brotherhood of Eternal Love.*

119 **"The unfortunate scheduling which groups together . . .":** Hollister in Leslie L.

Iversen, *The Science of Marijuana,* pp. 266–67. Hollister was associated with the Veterans Administration hospital in Palo Alto, California.

119 **"They're all on drugs":** Thanks to Doug McVay and Common Sense for Drug Policy, a Washington-based nongovernmental organization, for reporting on the contents of the infamous Nixon tapes.

119 **"You know it's a funny thing . . .":** Kevin Zeese, "Once-Secret 'Nixon Tapes' Show Why the U.S. Outlawed Pot," AlterNet, March 21, 2002, www.alternet.org/story/12666.

119 **"you have to face the fact that the whole problem . . .":** Haldeman in Dan Baum, *Smoke and Mirrors,* p. 13.

120 **"America's public enemy number one . . .":** Nixon in Michael Massing, *The Fix,* p. 112.

120 **"A memo by Egil "Bud" Krogh":** Peter Guralnick, *Careless Love,* p. 420.

120 **Elvis died of a polydrug overdose:** According to investigators, Presley had taken more than 19,000 doses of medications during the last two and a half years of his life. An autopsy revealed that his body contained dozens of different pharmaceuticals—valmid, Quaalude, codeine, Demerol, thallium, morphine, Placidyl, pentobarbital, butabarbital, phenobarbital, and several barbiturates, narcotics, stimulants, sedatives, and antidepressants.

121 **"Then, at night," a commission member:** Patrick Anderson, *High in America,* p. 93.

121 **"had very strong feelings" about marijuana:** Zeese, "Once-Secret 'Nixon Tapes.'"

121 **"motivated primarily by curiosity . . .":** National Commission on Marihuana and Drug Abuse, *Marihuana: A Signal of Misunderstanding,* p. 95.

121 **"Why has the use of marijuana . . .":** Ibid., p. 6.

122 **"Many see the drug as fostering . . .":** Ibid., p. 8.

122 **"a symbol of the rejection of cherished values":** Ibid., p. 9.

122 **"Seldom in the nation's history . . .":** Raymond Shafer in foreword to 1972 paperback edition of National Commission on Marihuana and Drug Abuse, *Marihuana.*

122 **"The time for politicizing . . .":** Shafer in Thomas Szasz, *Ceremonial Chemistry,* p. 133.

122 **No evidence that marijuana causes:** National Commission on Marihuana and Drug Abuse, *Marihuana,* p. 78.

122 **"the nation's philosophical preference . . . We believe that government must show . . .":** Ibid., pp. 140, 142.

122 **"possession of marijuana for personal use":** Ibid., p. 152.

123 **"My sister and I were shot at . . .":** Mikuriya quoted in David Duncan, "In Memoriam: Tod Mikuriya," National Association of Public Health, May 21, 2007, http://www.naphp.org. See special issue of *O'Shaughnessy's* honoring Tod Mikuriya, M.D., Winter/Spring 2008; and the film *Dr. Tod,* www.drtod.com/.

123 **"just to see that it wasn't poison":** Author's interview with Tod Mikuriya.

124 **Mikuriya traveled to North Africa:** Tod H. Mikuriya, "Kif Cultivation in the Rif Mountains," *Economic Botany* 21(3) (1967): 231–34.

124 **Princeton-based researcher Carl C. Pfeiffer:** Author's interview with Tod Mikuriya; Lee and Shlain, *Acid Dreams,* p. 25; Tod H. Mikuriya, "Authoritarianism: Social Disease," http://www.mikuriya.com/sp_authority.html; and Carl Pfeiffer, Henry Murphee, and Tod Mikuriya, "Biomonitored Effects of Charas, Extract" http://www.mikuriyamedical.com/about/cw_charas.html.

124 **helped smooth the way for his next job:** "I was vetted [by CIA-contracted scientists] at Princeton," Mikuriya stated in a 2005 interview with this author.

124 **He was rather idealistic at the time:** Author's interview with John Trapp.

124 **He combed through 3,281 pages:** Mikuriya compiled a digest of the findings of the Indian Hemp Commission; this digest was published in the Spring 1968 issue of the *International Journal of the Addictions.*

125 **"The government wanted bad things found out . . .":** Author's interview with Tod Mikuriya; and Tom Gorman, "Dr. Mikuriya's Medicine," AlterNet, November 3, 2004.

125 **"One also had to worry about antediluvian congressional types . . .":** Bonnie and Whitebread, *The Marijuana Conviction,* p. 231.

125 **Mikuriya crafted a detailed position paper:** *O'Shaughnessy's,* Winter/Spring 2008.

125 **"I was assigned by the NIMH to spy . . .":** Author's interview with Tod Mikuriya.

126 **In March 1968, he participated in a panel discussion:** Tod H. Mikuriya, M.D., "Marijuana in Medicine: Past Present and Future," guest speaker's address before the Second General Meeting of the 97th Annual Meeting of the California Medical Association, San Francisco, March 23 to 27, 1968; printed in *California Medicine,* January 1969.

126 **"In light of such assets as minimal toxicity . . .":** Mikuriya, *Marijuana,* pp. xii–xiv.

127 **he networked with cannabis agitators:** Author's interview with Michael Aldrich.

128 ***"What we want is free, legal . . .":*** Author's interview with Michael Aldrich. Amorphia quickly embraced the findings of the Shafer Report, even though Aldrich and his comrades felt that the Commission should have come out for legalization rather than decriminalization.

128 **"the existing anti-marijuana laws . . .":** *Marijuana Review* 1(9): 12. Buckley confessed he once tried pot on a sailboat in ocean waters beyond the three-mile territorial limit, where U.S. law did not apply, but it didn't do anything for him and apparently he never smoked another joint.

128 **"The hysterical myths about marijuana . . .":** Richard Cowan, "Why Conservatives Should Support the Legalization of Marijuana," *National Review,* December 6, 1972.

129 **"The lack of government credibility on marijuana . . .":** Brownell, May 1, 1972, press conference, in *Marijuana Review* 1(9).

129 **"In Tod, I found another libertarian Republican . . .":** Brownell in *O'Shaughnessy's,* Winter/Spring 2008.

130 **a prudent fiscal move:** Michael R. Aldrich and Tod H. Mikuriya, M.D., "Savings in California Marijuana Law Enforcement Costs Attributable to the Moscone Act of 1976—A Summary," *Journal of Psychoactive Drugs* (January–March 1988).

131 **"The one thing that can be said about marijuana . . .":** "Ex-Federal Justice Led Drug-Use Probe," *Vancouver Sun,* December 20, 2007.

131 **an official government inquiry gave cannabis:** *Le Dain Commission of Inquiry into the Non-Medical Use of Drugs*; see also Brecher and the Editors of *Consumers Union Reports, Licit & Illicit Drugs,* which summarizes the Le Dain report, pp. 451–72.

131 **"So flower power didn't work":** Lennon in Lester Bangs, *Psychotic Reactions and Carburetor Dung,* p. 99.

132 **"If Lennon's visa was terminated . . .":** Rick Perlstein, *Nixonland,* p. 713.

132 **A July 1972 FBI memo:** Jon Wiener, *Gimme Some Truth,* p. 27.

133 **The original plan to bypass:** See, in general, Edward Jay Epstein, *Agency of Fear.*

133 **Deputy Attorney General Kleindienst envisioned:** Perlstein, *Nixonland,* p. 381.

133 **"Peace Pot Promiscuity . . .":** Ibid., p. 713.

133 **"A person doesn't drink to get drunk . . .":** Tom McNichol, "Tricky Dick's Guide to Drinking and Toking," *Salon,* April 15, 2002.

134 **"a walking box of short-circuits":** *Newsweek*'s John Lindsay in Anthony Summers, *The Arrogance of Power,* p. 95.

134 **"If the president had his way . . .":** George Carver, the CIA's top Vietnam expert, reported that in 1969 Nixon ordered a tactical nuclear strike against North Korea. "The Joint Chiefs were alerted and asked to recommend targets, but Kissinger got on the phone to them. They agreed not to do anything until Nixon sobered up in the morning" (Summers, *The Arrogance of Power,* p. 372).

134 **When Lieutenant Colonel Oliver North needed bagmen:** Martin A. Lee, "How the Drug Czar Got Away," *The Nation,* September 5, 1987.

134 **the DEA dutifully looked the other way:** See, in general, McCoy, *The Politics of Heroin.*

134 **in a macabre, metaphoric twist:** Hank Messick, *Of Grass and Snow,* p. 19.

135 **the use of heroin by U.S. servicemen:** Wayne Morgan, *Drugs in America,* p. 154. See, in general, McCoy, *The Politics of Heroin.*

135 **"It was a privilege just . . .":** Herr, *Dispatches,* p. 66.

135 **As many as three out of four American servicemen:** Saul Rubin, *Offbeat Marijuana,* p. 75; and Grinspoon, *Marihuana Reconsidered,* p. 267.

135 **"Even in combat situations . . .":** Novak, *High Culture,* p. 168.

135 **Congressional Medal of Honor winner:** Brecher and the Editors of *Consumers Union Reports, Licit & Illicit Drugs,* p. 426.

136 **"Vietnamese pot became our path to sanity . . .":** Dr. Dalat, "Heart of Dankness," *High Times,* August 2005.

136 **"the American system of government":** Isserman and Kazin, *America Divided,* p. 35.

136 **"subversive groups played a significant role . . .":** Subcommittee Hearings to Investigate the Administration of the Internal Security Act and Other Internal Security Laws, *Marihuana-Hashish Epidemic and Its Impact on United States Security* in Patrick Anderson, *High in America,* p. 129.

136 **"If the epidemic is not rolled back . . .":** Eastland in Alan Bock, *Waiting to Inhale,* p. 151.

136 **"We make no apology . . .":** Eastland in Patrick Anderson, *High in America,* p. 130.

136 **Nahas claimed to have uncovered:** G. G. Nahas et al., "Inhibition of Cellular Mediated Immunity in Marihuana Smokers," *Science* 183 (1974): 419–20; see also Iversen, *The Science of Marijuana,* p. 67.

137 **Nahas wrote two alarmist books:** Arnold Trebach, *The Great Drug War,* pp. 126–33; Iversen, *The Science of Marijuana,* p. 67; and Renée Downing, "Marijuana World," *Tucson Weekly,* November 17, 2005. A January 25, 1974, press release announced the results of Nahas's research that purported to show "the first direct evidence of cellular damage from marijuana in man." The press release stated that the marijuana smokers he examined had claimed "that they did not use any other mind-altering drugs." Yet in the next sentence, Nahas noted, "They drank alcoholic beverages and smoked cigarettes, as did members of the control group." As Arnold Trebach wrote in *The Great Drug War*: "No marginally literate student would dare refer to alcohol as anything but a mind-altering drug, and many experienced researchers view tobacco in the same light. Also there is scientific evidence that both of these latter drugs could account for some depression in the activity of the im-

mune system"—a finding that Nahas attributed solely to cannabis, even though his cell assays had been exposed to nicotine and alcohol. Unable to repeat his earlier findings, Nahas eventually renounced his petri dish extrapolations.

137 **zealots invoked the amotivational syndrome:** Lynn Zimmer and John P. Morgan, *Marijuana Myths, Marijuana Facts,* p. 63.

137 **"amotivation [is] a cause of heavy marijuana smoking . . .":** Andrew Weil, *The Natural Mind,* p. 51

138 **"a kind of latter-day *Malleus Maleficarum*":** Grinspoon, *Marijuana Reconsidered,* p. 323.

138 **"No one is more controllable . . .":** Anne Wilson Schaef, *When Society Becomes an Addict,* p. 65.

139 **the steady drumbeat of deceptions:** The deliberate creation of scientific uncertainty regarding marijuana would serve as a prototype for subsequent corporate-driven efforts to foster doubt and confusion about the impact of human activity on global climate change and the greenhouse effect.

139 **"slowed the growth of lung cancers . . .":** "Cancer Curb Is Studied," *Washington Post,* August 18, 1974, cited in Raymond Cushing, "Pot Shrinks Tumors; Government Knew in '74, AlterNet, May 31, 2000. The original report by A. E. Munson et al., "Anticancer Activity of Cannabinoids," was published in the *Journal of the National Cancer Institute* 55 (September 1975): 597.

139 **rediscovered the cancer-fighting qualities of THC:** Ismael Galve-Roperh et al., "Anti-Tumoral Action of Cannabinoids," *Nature Medicine* (March 2000); and Raymond Cushing, "Pot Shrinks Tumors," AlterNet, May 31, 2000.

139 **THC successfully minimized chemotherapy-induced nausea:** S. E. Sallan, N. E. Zinberg, and E. Frei, "Antiemetic Effect of Delta-9-Tetrahydrocannabinol in Patients Receiving Cancer Chemotherapy," *New England Journal of Medicine* 293(16) (1975): 795–97.

139 **Dr. Raj K. Razdan, a senior scientist at Arthur D. Little:** Organix Inc., http://www.organixinc.com/founders.html.

140 **Mechoulam predicted a bright future:** Bock, *Waiting to Inhale,* p. 149.

140 **"You smoke pot, your eye strain goes away . . .":** Lester Grinspoon and James B. Bakalar, *Marihuana: The Forbidden Medicine,* p. 47.

140 **"more than a recreational drug":** Robert C. Randall and Alice M. O'Leary, *Marijuana Rx,* p. 11.

141 **a copy of a recent NIDA report:** *Marijuana and Health Report for 1974,* published by the Department of Health, Education and Welfare; and Randall and O'Leary, *Marijuana Rx,* pp. 19–20.

141 **he reported his findings in the *American Journal of Ophthamology*:** R. S. Hepler and R. Petrus, "Experiences with Administration of Marijuana to Glaucoma Patients," in S. Cohen and R. C. Stillman, eds., *The Therapeutic Potential of Marihuana,* pp. 63–76.

142 **"Medical evidence suggests that the prohibition . . .":** Fred Gardner, "The Judge Who Ruled Marijuana Is Medicine," *CounterPunch,* March 2, 2009.

142 **"Having won, why go mum?":** Randall in Irvin Rosenfeld, *Pot Luck,* p. 61.

143 **residents claim that ganja "brainifies" them:** Vera Rubin and Lambros Comitas, *Ganja in Jamaica,* p. 128. "If you have something to consider, you smoke ganja to help you," a Jamaican worker explained. Several other Jamaican marijuana smokers voiced similar sentiments to a U.S. research team.

143 **an Old Testament–oriented Christian mystical sect:** Rastafarians comprise a small minority of Jamaica's 2.6 million residents, but ganja use is "culturally entrenched," according to the anthropologist Barry Chevannes in Steven Wishnia, *The Cannabis Companion,* p. 28.

143 **They cited biblical passages:** "Thou shalt eat the herb of the field" (Genesis 3:18) and "eat every herb of the land" (Exodus 10:12).

145 **"Herb is the healin' of the nation":** Sherman and Smith, *Highlights,* p. 103; and Bob Marley on Very Important Potheads, website maintained by Ellen Komp, www.veryimportantpotheads.com/marley.htm. "The leaves of the tree are for the healing of the nation" (Revelation 22:2).

145 **"You mean they can tell God that it's not legal?":** Komp, ibid.

145 **the lengthy NIDA report:** Rubin and Comitas, *Ganja in Jamaica,* pp. 161–62; and Michael H. Beaubrun, "Cannabis or Alcohol: The Jamaican Experience," in Vera Rubin, *Cannabis and Culture,* p. 493.

145 **lower levels of alcoholism in Jamaica:** Rubin and Comitas, *Ganja in Jamaica,* pp. 149, 155.

145 **NIDA's Jamaica study also called into question:** Ibid., p. 154.

146 **two other major long-term-use studies:** Carter, ed., *Cannabis in Costa Rica:* "One of our principal objectives was to identify gross or subtle changes in major body and central nervous system functions which could be attributable to marijuana. We failed to do so" (p. 205); and Costas Stefanis, Rhea Dornbush, and Max Fink, eds., *Hashish: Studies of Long-Term Use.* Hashish use in Greece is closely associated with "rebetika," a style of folk music with pro-cannabis lyrics, which developed in the early twentieth century.

146 **"smoking and drinking ganja was good for the mother . . .":** Wei-Ni Lin Curry, "Hyperemesis Gravidarum and Clinical Cannabis: To Eat or Not to Eat?" in Ethan Russo, Melanie Dreher, and Mary Lynn Mathre, eds., *Women and Cannabis,* p. 75.

146 **Older women recommended that newborns:** Rubin and Comitas, *Ganja in Jamaica,* p. 53.

146 **"make them smarter and stronger":** Ibid., p. 50; and M. C. Dreher, "Cannabis and Pregnancy," in Mathre et al., eds., *Cannabis in Medical Practice.*

146 **In her NIDA study, Dreher matched thirty:** Melanie C. Dreher, Kevin Nugent, and Rebekah Hudgins, "Prenatal Marijuana Exposure and Neonatal Outcomes in Jamaica: An Ethnographic Study," *Pediatrics* 93(2) (1994): 25–60.

147 **"alertness was higher . . .":** Ibid.

147 **subsequent epidemiological investigation:** R. E. Westfall et al., "Survey of Medicinal Cannabis Use Among Childbearing Women: Patterns of Its Use in Pregnancy and Retroactive Self-Assessment of Its Efficacy Against 'Morning Sickness,'" *Complementary Therapies in Clinical Practice* 12 (2006): 27–33. Several studies found no association between prenatal exposure to marijuana and low birth weight, neurobehavioral deficits, or childhood leukemia.

148 **NIDA gave her the cold shoulder:** "Dreher Recounts Jamaican Study on Cannabis Use in Pregnancy," *O'Shaughnessy's,* Spring 2006. In 2005, Dreher returned to Jamaica on her own dime and located forty of her original subjects, who by then were adults and many were parents. They all appeared to be "doing quite well," Dreher observed.

148 **To the midwives on the Farm, cannabis seemed:** Author's interview with Dr. Jeffrey Hergenrather; and Hergenrather, "Prescribing Cannabis in California," in Holland, ed., *The Pot Book,* pp. 416–17.

148 **Humes, a literary wunderkind:** In addition to writing two highly acclaimed novels (*The Underground City* and *Men Die*), Humes was a cofounder of *The Paris Review,* a prestigious literary journal.

148 **"among the most forgiving medicines we know":** All quotes from Humes are from Doc Humes, "Marijuana in Medicine: Past, Present and Future," unpublished manuscript provided by his daughter Immy Humes, who made *Doc,* a PBS documentary about her father.

150 **anti-Castro Cubans with CIA and Mob connections:** Messick, *Of Grass and Snow.*

150 **editorial that listed the names of local narcotics agents:** Abe Peck, *Uncovering the Sixties,* p. 190; Bill Weinberg, "Tom Forçade: Unsung Hero of the Counter-Culture," *World War 4 Report,* http://ww4report.com/node/3495.

151 **"The movement was over . . .":** Torgoff, *Can't Find My Way Home,* p. 265.

151 **"under any circumstances, period":** David Armstrong, *A Trumpet to Arms,* p. 260.

151 **"a vast underground society . . .":** Goldman in Torgoff, *Can't Find My Way Home,* p. 267.

151 **visually compelling photobotanical genre:** See, for example, Jason King's Cannabible series and Ed Rosenthal's *Big Book of Buds.*

152 **"drugs paradoxically sparked a spiritual renaissance . . .":** Armstrong, *A Trumpet to Arms,* p. 261.

153 **a hypercapable high school dropout:** Author's interview with Steve DeAngelo.

153 **Penalties against drug use should not:** President Jimmy Carter, message to Congress, August 2, 1977.

154 **The U.S. Justice Department disclosed:** Philip Jenkins, *Decade of Nightmares,* p. 125.

154 **"We should concentrate on prosecuting . . .":** Quayle in Dan Baum, *Smoke and Mirrors,* p. 92.

154 **"a haze of marijuana smoke hung heavy . . .":** *Ladies' Home Journal* (December 1978) cited in Marcelo Ballve, "Legal Pot: Are Hard Times Leading to Higher Times?" AlterNet, March 13, 2009.

154 **458,000 people were arrested:** Patrick Anderson, *High in America,* p. 225.

154 **nationwide household survey:** Jonnes, *Hep-Cats, Narcs, and Pipe Dreams,* p. 313; and Goldman, *Grass Roots,* p. 11.

154 **a cream pie landed on Nellis's face:** Author's interview with Aron Kay.

155 **Paraquat, the herbicide used in Mexico:** In 2007, the European Union revoked its approval for Paraquat, citing scientific evidence that farmworkers exposed to the herbicide had more than double the risk of contracting Parkinson's. Paraquat is used to create animal models of Parkinson's for medical science research.

155 **"It was probably the stupidest thing . . .":** Stroup in Peter Carlson, "Exhale, Stage Left: Keith Stroup Retiring from NORML," *Washington Post,* January 4, 2005.

155 **Forçade had been donating $50,000:** Torgoff, *Can't Find My Way Home,* p. 268.

156 **so many people were smoking pot in America:** In 1979, 68.2 percent of eighteen-to-twenty-five-year-olds admitted to government surveyors that they had used marijuana or hashish at least once. Among high school seniors, the perception that regular marijuana smoking is harmful hit a low of 35 percent in 1978.

CHAPTER 5: JUST SAY NEVER

157 **So she smoked some grass to calm her nerves:** Patti Davis, *The Way I See It,* pp. 248–49.

157 **"the most dangerous drug in America":** Schlosser, *Reefer Madness,* p. 24. "Exagger-

ations are a severe addiction of the anti-marijuana cultists," wrote William F. Buckley, "On the Right: The DEA Strikes Back!," Universal Press Syndicate, August 3, 1993.

158 **We're making no excuses for drugs:** Reagan in Torgoff, *Can't Find My Way Home*, p. 288.

159 **1982 study, comprising six years of research:** National Research Council of the National Academy of Sciences, "An Analysis of Marijuana Policy," 1982, in Baum, *Smoke and Mirrors*, p. 162, and Green, *Cannabis*, p. 156.

159 **Law-enforcement jobs at every government level:** Baum, *Smoke and Mirrors*, p. 306.

160 **distinction between military ops and civilian policing:** In December 1981, President Reagan issued an executive order that directed the CIA and the entire U.S. intelligence community to provide guidance to civilian drug law enforcement.

160 **"Where the military sees 'enemies' . . .":** Col. Charles J. Dunlop, "The Thick Green Line," in Peter B. Kraska, ed., *Militarizing the American Criminal Justice System*, p. 35. Lawrence Korb, former assistant secretary of defense under Reagan, put it this way: "The military [is] trained to vaporize, not Mirandize." The militarization of the police encouraged the maximal use of force in situations when no force at all was necessary. Law-abiding American citizens who had nothing to do with the drug trade would be killed by trigger-happy soldiers and gung-go narcs (Kraska, p. 78).

160 **"indoctrinated to hate drug users . . . The drug war is a holy war . . .":** McNamara quoted in Ann Harrison, "Counting the Costs of the Drug War," AlterNet, May 7, 2004; and Lanny Swerdlow, "It's NORML to Smoke Pot," AlterNet, June 20, 2002.

161 **Gross receipts of seizures nationwide:** Christian Parenti, *Lockdown America*, p. 51.

161 **80 percent of all forfeited property:** Congressman Henry Hyde in Saul Rubin, *Offbeat Marijuana*, p. 57.

161 **"Forfeiture, contrary to its purported goals . . .":** Parenti, *Lockdown America*, p. 53. Under the 1984 federal crime bill, state and local law-enforcement agencies that collaborate with the federal government get to keep up to 80 percent of the proceeds from seizures.

161 **"the drug exception to the Bill of Rights . . .":** Duke and Gross, *America's Longest War*, p. 133.

161 **"the veritable national crises in law enforcement . . .":** Baum, *Smoke and Mirrors*, pp. 206–7; and Duke and Gross, *America's Longest War*, p. 124.

161 **Rehnquist was often pixilated on Placidyl:** David Garrow, "Mental Decrepitude on the U.S. Supreme Court: The Historical Case for a 28th Amendment," *University of Chicago Law Review*, Fall 2000.

161 **An FBI probe noted that in 1981:** "FBI Releases Rehnquist Drug Problem Records," Associated Press, January 4, 2007.

162 **according to Rehnquist the real issue:** Patrick Anderson, *High in America*, p. 305. "The war on drugs is a war on poor people using street drugs waged by rich people on prescription drugs," said Roseanne Barr during her HBO special *Blonde and Bitchin'*.

162 **"There is no moral middle ground":** Mikki Norris et al., *Shattered Lives*, p. 5; and Parenti, *Lockdown America*, p. 56.

162 **"If you're a casual user . . .":** Duke and Gross, *America's Longest War*, p. 106; and Baum, *Smoke and Mirrors*, p. 253.

162 **"To my knowledge she never addressed . . .":** Patti Davis, *The Way I See It*, pp. 228, 298–99.

162 **"We're in danger of losing our whole next generation":** Trebach, *The Great Drug War*, p. 135.

162 **NIDA director William Polin ordered his staff:** Baum, *Smoke and Mirrors,* p. 164; and Musto, *The American Disease,* p. 272. Blacklists were back in vogue during the Reagan years. FCC obscenity regulations prohibited "Howl," Allen Ginsberg's marijuana-inspired masterpiece, from being broadcast on radio except after midnight. Ginsberg was among several prominent Americans who were blacklisted by the U.S. Information Agency in the 1980s and banned from government-sponsored overseas speaking engagements. The USIA blacklist included James Baldwin, Ralph Nader, Coretta Scott King, and other Reagan policy critics.

163 **pot makes men grow large breasts!:** *Grass* (1999), the documentary by Ron Mann.

163 **an alarming three-part series:** *Reader's Digest,* December 1981. Three articles by antipot polemicist Peggy Mann in *Reader's Digest* between 1979 and 1981 warned parents about the dangers of marijuana. Mann expanded those articles into a book, *Marijuana Alert* (1985), which was praised in the foreword by First Lady Nancy Reagan as "a true story about a drug that is taking America captive."

163 **the tax-deductible coffers of the Partnership for a Drug-Free America:** Cynthia Cotts, "Hard Sell in the Drug War," *The Nation,* March 9, 1992; and Mike Males, "Pot Boiler: Why Are Media Enlisting in the Government's Crusade Against Marijuana?" *Extra!,* July/August 1997.

163 **School kids were instructed to rat:** D.A.R.E. recruited schoolchildren to act as police informants. D.A.R.E.-encouraged tattling to cops resulted in several arrests of parents and promoted a culture of snitching that had more in common with a dictatorship than a democracy. Some kid snitches ended up in foster homes thanks to D.A.R.E.

163 **casual drug users were guilty of "treason":** Duke and Gross, *America's Longest War,* p. 223.

163 **Subsequent studies called into question:** See, for example, the U.S. General Accounting Office report, *Youth Illicit Drug Use Prevention: DARE Long-Term Evaluations and Federal Efforts to Identify Effective Programs,* January 15, 2003, which found that D.A.R.E. had "no statistically significant long-term effect on preventing youth illicit drug use."

164 **"The kids try marijuana and say . . .":** Mikuriya in *Marijuana Review* 1(9): 59.

164 **Anderson . . . criticized the federally approved D.A.R.E.:** Kristen Stewart, "Anderson Calls D.A.R.E. a Fraud," *Salt Lake Tribune,* June 22, 2000.

164 **"harmed scores of American kids . . .":** Trebach, *The Great Drug War,* p. xvi.

164 **"Because we so irrationally fear drugs . . .":** Ibid., p. xxi.

164 **"the fallacy of misplaced concreteness":** Alfred North Whitehead, *Science and the Modern World,* p. 64.

164 **pro-pot enthusiasts made a similar mistake:** The Yale law professor Charles Reich, author of *The Greening of America,* described marijuana as "a maker of revolution, a truth serum."

164 **"There are no good or bad drugs . . .":** Andrew Weil and Winifred Rosen, *From Chocolate to Morphine,* p. 29.

164 **"an insoluble marijuana problem . . .":** Weil, *Natural Mind,* p. 31.

164 **intoxication persists as a fundamental drive:** See, in general, Siegel, *Intoxication.*

164 **"The ubiquity of drug use is so striking . . .":** Weil in Stuart Walton, *Out of It,* p. 23.

165 **"was sentenced to a year in federal prison . . .":** Baum, *Smoke and Mirrors,* p. 243. Burton's eyesight worsened while in prison without cannabis. Bereft of land and lodging when released from jail, he and his wife moved to the Netherlands, where Burton had access to government-sanctioned marijuana.

166 **"They could obey the law . . .":** Zeese in George McMahon and Christopher Largen, *Prescription Pot,* p. 138.

166 **"Grandma Marijuana":** Randall and O'Leary, *Marijuana Rx,* p. 227.

167 **In a March 1982 letter:** *JAMA* cited in Bock, *Waiting to Inhale,* p. 156.

167 **"The medical case for the use of marijuana . . .":** Gingrich in Randall and O'Leary, *Marijuana Rx,* p. 275.

167 **Irvin Rosenfeld became the second person:** Irv tells his story in Rosenfeld, *Pot Luck.*

168 **"It's a lethal irony, that's for sure . . .":** McMahon and Largen, *Prescription Pot,*, p. 135.

168 **"Compared to all the patients . . .":** Ibid.

169 **"I'm living proof that cannabis works . . .":** Rosenfeld in Bruce Mirken, "Psst . . . Government-Supplied Marijuana Program Turns 30," AlterNet, May 7, 2008.

169 **"Results demonstrate clinical effectiveness . . .":** Ethan Russo et al., "Chronic Cannabis Use in the Compassionate Investigational New Drug Program: An Examination of Benefits and Adverse Effects of Legal Clinical Cannabis," *Journal of Cannabis Therapeutics* 2(1), 2002. The Missoula study was sponsored by Patients Out of Time, a medical marijuana advocacy group, and MAPS (Multidisciplinary Association for Psychedelic Studies).

169 **federal money for research into risks:** Zimmer and Morgan, *Marijuana Myths, Marijuana Facts,* p. 13.

169 **"For many years, we tried to determine . . .":** Schuster in Michael Massing, *The Fix,* p. 186.

170 **"the patient is better able to control the dose . . .":** Affidavit of Tod H. Mikuriya in the Matter of Marijuana Rescheduling Petition to U.S. Justice Department, DEA, September 1, 1987.

171 **"We have no reason to believe . . .":** Weil in Chapkis and Webb, *Dying to Get High,* p. 74.

172 **clinically depressed patients:** Clinical depression, a life-wrecking illness characterized by chronic feelings of sadness and poor self-esteem, is linked to high blood pressure, heart disease, elevated stress hormones, brain shrinkage, cognitive decline, and poor health in general (Thomas H. Maugh, "A Varied Assault on Depression Yields Gains," *Los Angeles Times,* March 23, 2006). Twice as many people taking SSRIs committed suicide than did depressed people who took placebos (John Abramson, *Overdosed America,* p. 116).

172 **The FDA approved these drugs:** Marcia Angell, "The Epidemic of Mental Illness: Why?" *New York Review of Books,* June 23, 2011, and "The Illusions of Psychiatry," *New York Review of Books,* July 14, 2011.

172 **nasty side effects:** Carey Goldberg, "New Life Inside the Depressed Brain," *Boston Globe,* November 19, 2007; Shweta Govindajaran, "Ban Antidepressant, Watchdog Group Says," *Los Angeles Times,* October 30, 2003; Will Boggs, "Painkillers, Antidepressants a Risky Combination," Reuters, October 30, 2007; Elizabeth Shogren, "FDA Sat on Report Linking Suicide, Drugs," *Los Angeles Times,* April 6, 2004; and Francis Elliot and Sophie Goodchild, "Drug Crisis: Prozac Nation," *Independent* (UK), April 16, 2006.

172 **fetal exposure to Prozac:** Michael Day, "Prozac During Pregnancy 'Can Damage Unborn Child,'" *Daily Telegraph,* February 22, 2004. Antidepressants have been linked to an increased risk of miscarriage. Women who took SSRIs while pregnant were twice as likely to give birth prematurely than those who did not take these drugs, according to a 2010 study published in the *Archives of Pediatrics & Adolescent Medicine.*

172 **antidepressant properties of cannabis:** Iversen, *The Science of Marijuana,* pp. 172–73; and Ed Rosenthal et al., *Marijuana Medical Handbook,* pp. 57–58.

173 **A peer-reviewed study** Thomas F. Denson and Mitchell Earleywine, "Decreased Depression in Marijuana Users," *Addictive Behaviors,* June 2005. An extensive survey by researchers at the University of Southern California disclosed that people who smoked marijuana daily or weekly were more likely to report positive moods and fewer somatic complaints, such as sleeplessness. In a separate survey of Oregon medical-marijuana patients, 64 percent reported significant psychiatric benefit from cannabis and 56 percent reported reduced use of prescription meds (*O'Shaughnessy's,* Spring 2006).

173 **brain receptors that modulate the ebb and flow:** Ethan B. Russo et al., "Agonistic Properties of Cannabidiol at 5-HT1a Receptors," *Neurochemical Research* 30(8) (2005): 1037–43; and Martin A. Lee, "Enzymes and the Endocannabinoid System," *O'Shaughnessy's,* Summer 2009.

173 **marijuana produces an antidepressant effect:** Fabricio A. Moreira, "Serotonin, the Prefontal Cortex, and the Antidepressant-Like Effect of Cannabinoids," *Journal of Neuroscience* 27(49) (2007):13369–370; Gino Serra and Walter Fratta, "A Possible Role for the Endocannabinoid System in the Neurobiology of Depression," *Clinical Practice and Epidemiology in Mental Health,* published online November 19, 2007; and Kurt Blass, "Treating Depression with Cannabinoids," *Cannabinoids* 3 (2) (2008): 8–10. There is evidence that marijuana in low doses increases serotonin, conferring an antidepressant effect, according to preclinical trial data published in December 2005 in the journal *Proceedings of the National Academy of Sciences.*

173 **"We should be thinking of cannabis . . .":** Mikuriya in Bock, *Waiting to Inhale,* p. 246.

173 **laughter is therapeutic:** Norman Cousins, *Anatomy of an Illness.*

174 **homegrown cannabis seized that year:** Steve Chapple, *Outlaws in Babylon,* pp. 66–67.

174 **15 percent of the total amount of marijuana:** Ralph Weisheit, *Domestic Marijuana,* pp. 32–33.

175 **"Two hits of this stuff . . .":** Author's interview with Carolyn Garcia.

175 **"I had a whole circle of friends . . .":** Torgoff, *Can't Find My Way Home,* p. 254.

175 **"Thai farmers pray and meditate . . .":** Mountain Girl, *Primo Plant,* p. 91.

175 **He studied Rudolph Steiner's writings:** Author's interview with Carolyn Garcia.

176 **surpassed sugar to become the biggest cash crop:** Messick, *Of Grass and Snow,* pp. 123–24.

177 **"The range of flavors expressed . . .":** Author's interview with DJ Short; and DJ Short, "Mapping the Pot Palate," in Ed Rosenthal, *The Big Book of Buds,* p. 53.

177 **"There is always a hint of danger . . .":** Kevin Stewart, *Tales of the Emerald Triangle,* p. 145.

178 **Weed was the new wampum:** Dr. Loon, "Tusk Shell Gold Dollar Pulp Note & Weed: Four Principles of Economy in the Six Rivers/Humboldt Bay Region," in Peter Berg, ed., *Reinhabiting a Separate Country,* pp. 157–83.

178 **some 30,000 pot growers took part:** Chapple, *Outlaws in Babylon,* p. 49.

178 **Farmers in the early 1980s:** Roger Warner, *The Invisible Hand,* p. 196.

178 **"As far as I'm concerned . . .":** Ibid., p. 230.

178 **"fit in with the tradition of rural anarchy . . .":** Ray Raphael, *Cash Crop,* p. 177.

178 **"the first truly populist form of agriculture . . .":** Ibid., pp. 170–72.

179 **"rejoined, operationally speaking . . .":** Thomas Pynchon, *Vineland,* p. 49.

179 **"There [was] a visceral hostility . . .":** Rick Del Vecchio, "Dispute on Humboldt County Pot Raid Boiling Over," *San Francisco Chronicle,* August 6, 1990. "Marijuana sits on the San Andreas fault of contemporary American culture," said Eric Sterling, president of the Criminal Justice Policy Foundation, an anti-drug-war think tank (Paul Van Slambrouck, "Marijuana Still Divides California," *Christian Science Monitor,* May 4, 1998).

179 ***"War on drugs! War on drugs!"*:** Torgoff, *Can't Find My Way Home,* p. 289.

179 **Local residents banded together:** Ibid., p. 284.

179 **The judge also ordered federal and local police:** Trebach, *The Great Drug War,* pp. 206–8. It was perhaps the first time in the history of the United States, as Arnold Trebach noted, "that police forces have been forced to operate under direct judicial supervision."

179 **"That's my price support system":** Confidential source.

179 **an economic lifeline for an estimated:** Weisheit, *Domestic Marijuana,* p. 39. In 1986, the federal government estimated there were between 90,000 and 150,000 commercial pot growers in the United States and more than one million people who grew for their personal use.

180 **American farmers struggling to keep afloat:** Schlosser, *Reefer Madness,* p. 37; Daniel Levitas, *The Terrorist Next Door,* p. 173.

180 **the largest coordinated antimarijuana crackdown:** Trebach, *The Great Drug War,* p. 149.

180 **"The plant adapted more brilliantly . . .":** Pollan, *The Botany of Desire,* p. 134.

181 **"that the creation of a powerful new taboo . . .":** Ibid., p. 128.

181 **Dutch radicals unrolled reams of newsprint:** Lee and Shlain, *Acid Dreams,* p. 213.

181 **When denied a permit for a demonstration:** Teun Voeten, "Dutch Provos," *High Times Reader,* p. 379.

182 **two erstwhile Provo ringleaders:** Lee Foster, "Lowlands Seed Company," *High Times,* Spring 1975; Voeten, "Dutch Provos," pp. 372–73.

182 **"A few tokes of good cannabis . . .":** Nol van Schaik, *The Dutch Experience,* p. 50.

182 **a handful of imitators:** Ibid., pp. 69–84.

183 **"it's more sensible for a society . . .":** Grinspoon, *Marijuana Reconsidered,* p. 366.

184 **The expression 'going Dutch':** Van Schaik, *The Dutch Experience,* p. 43.

185 **"Marijuana is our medicine . . .":** Pete Brady, "Double Dutch cannaversary," *Cannabis Culture,* http://www.cannabisculture.com/v2/articles/2936.html.

186 **"the pothead's answer to Ann Landers . . .":** Dean E. Murphy, "Clash on Medical Marijuana Puts a Grower in U.S. Court," *New York Times,* January 21, 2003.

186 **"I just give advice on how . . .":** Jim Herron Zamora, "Pot-growing Icon Takes Raid in Stride," *San Francisco Chronicle,* February 25, 2002.

187 **Seal had made more than $50 million:** Jonathan Kwitny, "Dope Story: Doubts Rise on Report Reagan Cited in Tying Sandinistas to Cocaine," *Wall Street Journal,* April 22, 1987; and Lee, "How the Drug Czar Got Away."

188 **Seal's aviation talents:** Joel Millman, "Who Killed Barry Seal?" *Village Voice,* July 1, 1986; Kwitny, "Dope Story"; and Lee, "How the Drug Czar Got Away." In late December 1984, Seal got caught flying a cargo of marijuana into Louisiana. He continued to smuggle drugs while serving as a DEA informant and a CIA contract employee. Michael Tolliver, a pilot recruited by Seal to fly arms to the contras, was arrested on drug charges in 1987. Tolliver said he landed twelve tons of marijuana at Homestead Air Force Base near Miami on one return leg from Central America.

188 **"The whole thing is too sleazy . . .":** Alexander Cockburn and Jeffrey St. Clair, *Whiteout,* pp. 284–85.

188 **Frank Castro, a longtime CIA asset:** Robert Parry, *Lost History,* pp. 202, 233–35; and Peter Dale Scott and Jonathan Marshall, *Cocaine Politics,* p. 25.

188 **"Drugs and covert operations go together . . .":** Lee and Shlain, *Acid Dreams,* p. 296.

189 **more than fifty contras and contra-related entities:** Report by CIA Inspector General Frederick Hitz in Parry, *Lost History,* pp. 204–5, 224–43.

189 **"a bad breath drug":** Torgoff, *Can't Find My Way Home,* p. 327.

189 **"the 'fast food' of the cocaine world":** Marcus Reeves, *Somebody Scream!,* p. 55.

189 **the use of marijuana declined:** Trebach, *The Great Drug War* pp. 12–13; and Booth, *Cannabis,* p. 256.

189 **Cannabis is not a gateway drug:** National Academy of Sciences, *An Analysis of Marijuana Policy,* 1982. "Medical researchers in Jamaica reported that ganja was used to minimize the negative effects of smoking crack, including paranoia and weight loss. Rather than functioning as a gateway, ganja provided a way out for 33 former crack addicts in one study. For these Jamaicans, cannabis cigarettes were the cheapest, most effective and most easily available therapy for discontinuing cocaine consumption" (Melanie Dreher, "Crack Heads and Roots Daughters: The Therapeutic Use of Cannabis in Jamaica," in Russo et al., *Women and Cannabis,* pp. 121–33).

189 **"the legislative equivalent of a cattle stampede":** Joel Miller, *Bad Trip,* p. 165.

190 **"drugs are a threat worse than nuclear warfare . . .":** Cockburn and St. Clair, *Whiteout,* p. 75.

190 **A 1986 *New York Times*/CBS poll:** Jonnes, *Hep-Cats, Narcs, and Pipe Dreams,* p. 398.

190 **the Anti–Drug Abuse Act:** Douglas Husak, *Legalize This!,* pp. 45–46; and Baum, *Smoke and Mirrors,* p. 245.

190 **"cottage industry of cooperators":** Ethan Brown, *Snitch,* p. 206.

190 **Incarceration rates exploded:** Parenti, *Lockdown America,* p. 58; and Duke and Gross, *America's Longest War,* p. 179. "The United States, with about 5 percent of the world's population, accounts for nearly 25 percent of its prisoners—largely as a consequence of draconian drug laws," wrote *Atlanta Journal-Constitution* columnist Cynthia Tucker (October 31, 2010). As of 2010, the rate of incarceration in the United States was five times that of Great Britain, nine times that of Germany, and twelve times more than Japan. China, with four times more people than the United States, had far fewer people in prison.

190 **"so ubiquitous that they might be said . . .":** Douglas Husak, "Do Marijuana Offenders Deserve Punishment?" in Mitchell Earleywine, ed., *Pot Politics,* p. 194.

190 **Even though whites and blacks:** See, in general, Michelle Alexander, *The New Jim Crow;* and Mark Mauer, *Race to Incarcerate.*

190 **particularly young African Americans:** Baum, *Smoke and Mirrors,* p. 249. Baum reports that 99 percent of drug-trafficking defendants nationwide between 1985 and 1987 were African Americans.

190 **black prisoners outnumbered white inmates:** Mike Gray, *Drug Crazy,* p. 110.

191 **longer sentences for possessing crack:** The 1986 Anti–Drug Abuse Act set a 100-to-1 sentencing ratio between possession of crack and powder cocaine, which meant that possession of 5 grams of crack carried a minimum five-year federal prison sentence, while it took 500 grams of powder cocaine to trigger the same mandatory minimum.

191 **"barred from voting because . . .":** Ira Glasser, "How the Drug War Targets Black

Americans," *Times-Picayune,* December 6, 2007. See also Michelle Alexander, *The New Jim Crow.*

191 **widened the gap between rich and poor:** See, in general, Kevin Phillips's critique of the Reagan '80s, *The Politics of Rich and Poor.*

191 **The war on drugs served as a pretext:** Parenti, *Lockdown America,* pp. 43–45; see also Clarence Lusane, *Pipe Dream Blues.* "I think people believe that the only strategy we have is to put a lot of police officers on the street and harass people and make arrests for inconsequential kinds of things," said Chief Daryl Gates of the LAPD. "Well, that's part of the strategy, no question about it" (Mike Davis, *City of Quartz,* p. 284).

191 **required to take random urine tests:** Musto, *The American Disease,* p. 276; and Mauer, *Race to Incarcerate* p. 183.

191 **a majority of Fortune 500 companies:** Goode, *Drugs in American Society,* p. 284.

192 **Urine tests don't measure:** "Detection of THC in Blood Not Necessarily Indicative of Recent Pot Use, Study Says," NORML e-Zine, October 8, 2009.

192 **ignored by the American press:** *New York Times* reporter Keith Schneider commented on the reluctance of corporate media to pursue the contra drug connection. The implications of such a story, Schneider told *In These Times* magazine, were "so damaging" and "so extraordinary" that it could "shatter the Republic" (Cockburn and St. Clair, *Whiteout,* p. 46).

192 **There was substantial evidence of drug smuggling . . . :** The Kerry Report, *Drugs, Law Enforcement and Foreign Policy,* a Report of the Senate Committee on Foreign Relations, Subcommittee on Terrorism, Narcotics and International Operations, 1989, pp. 2, 36, 41.

192 **This region became the largest source:** Cockburn and St. Clair, *Whiteout,* pp. 264–65. See also McCoy, *The Politics of Heroin.*

193 **The 1988 Anti-Drug Abuse Act:** Husak, *Legalize This!,* p. 46; and Parenti, *Lockdown America,* p. 61.

193 ***"What do we want legalized?":*** Marla Donato, "Pot Rally Brings Whiff of the '60s," *Chicago Tribune,* April 26, 1989.

195 **"I was a normal American nerd":** Jack Herer, *High Times* interview, April 1990.

195 **"She tried three times . . .":** Ibid.; and Matthews, *Cannabis Culture,* p. 109.

195 **"You mean there's something else . . .":** Author's interview with Michael Aldrich.

195 **The USDA extolled hemp:** Matthews, *Cannabis Culture* pp. 115–16.

196 **the article predicted a bonanza:** "New Billion-Dollar Crop," *Popular Mechanics,* February 1938.

196 **"the most profitable and desirable crop . . .":** George A. Lower, "Flax and Hemp: From the Seed to the Loom," *Mechanical Engineering,* February 1938.

196 **despite assurances from top narc Harry Anslinger:** Hemp is "the finest fiber known to mankind," Harry Anslinger told Congress. "My God! If you ever have a shirt made out of it, your grandchildren would never wear it out."

196 **"If hemp had not been made illegal . . .":** Herer, *The Emperor Wears No Clothes,* p. 26.

197 **would have been in Hearst's interest:** Steven Wishnia, "Debunking the Hemp Conspiracy Theory," AlterNet, February 21, 2008.

197 **"We have found a way . . .":** Gary Libman, "Businessman Calls Marijuana a Cure for the Environment," *Los Angeles Times,* June 11, 1990.

198 **Herer got ahold of the fourteen-minute:** Herer got a copy of *Hemp for Victory* from Oregon cannabis activist Bill Conde.

198 **"Jack had an almost messianic ability . . .":** Author's interview with Rick Pfrommer.
198 **"We had this little fire going . . .":** Author's interview with Steve DeAngelo.
199 **"The plant financed her own liberation":** Ibid.

CHAPTER 6: FROM BLUNTS TO BALLOTS

201 **"Marijuana in its natural form . . .":** Francis L. Young, *In The Matter of MARIJUANA RESCHEDULING PETITION,* September 6, 1988, Docket No. 86-22. http://www.druglibrary.org/olsen/MEDICAL/YOUNG/young1.html.
202 **"When the child ate these cookies . . .":** Ibid.
202 **"When your kid is riding a tricycle . . .":** Ibid.
203 **"While this mode of treatment is illegal . . .":** Ibid.
203 **"marijuana is far safer than many foods . . .":** Ibid.
203 **Cannabis would remain a Schedule I substance:** DEA administrator John Lawn formally rejected Judge Francis Young's recommendation that cannabis be rescheduled on December 29, 1989. Six years later, the U.S. Court of Appeals for the D.C. circuit ruled that the DEA had the right to ignore its own administrative law judge.
203 **"The chief opposition to the drug . . .":** *Merck Manual of Diagnosis and Therapy* in William F. Buckley, "On the Right: The DEA Strikes Back!," Universal Press Syndicate, August 3, 1993.
204 **"impart the message that you can use drugs . . .":** Bennett in Duke and Gross, *America's Longest War,* p. 227.
204 **"Somewhere along the way . . .":** Bennett in Massing, *The Fix,* p. 198.
204 **Urban African Americans and Latinos bore the brunt:** Baum in *Smoke and Mirrors* (p. 323) cites a *USA Today* story, "Drug War Focused on Blacks," which led: "Urban blacks are being detained in numbers far exceeding their involvement" in the drug trade.
204 **By 1990, there were 610,000 black males:** Reeves, *Somebody Scream!,* p. 106.
204 **Bennett complained that drug suspects:** Baum, *Smoke and Mirrors,* pp. 276, 298.
204 **Sixty-two percent of Americans said:** Ibid., p. 263.
204 **rollback of marijuana decriminalization:** A 1975 Alaska Supreme Court decision, *Ravin v. Alaska,* made marijuana legal for personal use. A 1990 voter referendum recriminalized marijuana possession in Alaska by a narrow margin—only to be reversed by the Alaska Court of Appeals in 2003.
205 **More than 90 percent of the cannabis plants:** Michael Poole, *Romancing Mary Jane,* p. 70.
205 **"They offered us women, guns, and money . . .":** Ray Boyd, "Operation Green Merchant," *Cannabis Culture,* October 15, 2005.
205 **Green Merchant had snagged $17.5 million:** Jon Gettman, "Federalization of Marijuana Cultivation Offenses," DrugScience.org, 2006.
205 **"They used the law . . .":** Peter Gorman, "Operation Green Merchant," *High Times,* January 1990.
206 **after Congress revised civil forfeiture laws:** Joel Miller, *Bad Trip,* p. 133. At the outset of the Bush presidency, the Justice Department directed all U.S. attorneys to "convert personnel from other activities" if need be to meet their commitment "to increase forfeiture production."
206 **Police had an incentive:** Ibid., p. 130.

206 **"created a great temptation . . .":** Henry J. Hyde, *Forfeiting Our Property Rights,* p. 9.
206 **Jim Montgomery, a paraplegic:** Schlosser, *Reefer Madness,* p. 28.
206 **Okie justice saddled William Foster:** Norris et al., *Shattered Lives,* pp. 23, 84.
206 **More than twenty million Americans:** NIDA's 1990 National Household Survey in Lusane, *Pipe Dream Blues,* p. 81.
207 **"We need at least to consider . . .":** Shultz in Associated Press, November 6, 1989.
207 **"If doctors can prescribe morphine . . .":** Nofziger in Baum, *Smoke and Mirrors,* p. 74.
207 **"Your mistake is failing to recognize . . .":** Milton Friedman to William Bennett in *Wall Street Journal,* September 7, 1989.
207 **Drug-policy critics in the late 1980s:** Duke and Gross, *America's Longest War,* p. 199.
207 **"when the largest military-industrial complex . . .":** Kraska, *Militarizing the American Criminal Justice System,* pp. 20–21. President Bush put the Defense Department in charge of detecting and monitoring drug runs into the United States, while Lockheed and other military contractors, which made radar devices for tracking smugglers, lobbied hard for a bigger piece of the drug-busting pie.
208 **"We wouldn't have been able . . .":** Raphael Mechoulam in PBS special, *The Botany of Desire,* based on Michael Pollan's book.
209 **American researchers at Johns Hopkins University:** Candace B. Pert, *Molecules of Emotion.*
209 **a government-funded study at the St. Louis University School of Medicine:** W. A. Devane, F. A. Dysarz, M. R. Johnson, L. S. Melvin, and A. Howlett, "Determination and Characterization of a Cannabinoid Receptor in Rat Brain," *Molecular Pharmacology* 34(13) (1988): 605–13.
209 **mapping the locations of cannabinoid receptors:** Miles Herkenham et al., "Characterization and Localization of Cannabinoid Receptors in Rat Brian: A Quantitative in vitro Autoradiographic Study," *Journal of Neuroscience* 11(2) (February 1991): 563–83.
210 **genetically engineered "knockout" mice:** A team of NIH scientists created CB-1 and CB-2 knockout mice in 1997.
210 **Researchers soon identified a second:** S. Munro, K. L. Thomas, and M. Abu-Shaar, "Molecular Characterization of a Peripheral Receptor for Cannabinoids," *Nature* 365(6441) (1993): 61–65.
210 **found a novel neurotransmitter:** W. A. Devane et al., "Isolation and Structure of a Brain Constituent That Binds to the Cannabinoid Receptor," *Science* 258(5090) (1992): 1946–49.
210 **his group discovered a second major:** R. Mechoulam et al., "Identification of an Endogenous 2-Monoglyceride, Present in Canine Gut, That Binds to Cannabinoid Receptors," *Biochemical Pharmacology* 50(1) (1995): 83–90. See also "Conversation with Raphael Mechoulam," *Addiction* 102 (2007): 887–93; and "The New Science of Cannabinoid-Based Medicine: An Interview with Dr. Raphael Mechoulam" in David Jay Brown, ed., *Mavericks of Medicine.*
211 **this ancient internal signal system:** J. M. McPartland and G. Guy, "The Evolution of Cannabis and Coevolution with the Cannabinoid Receptor—A Hypothesis," in Guy et al., eds., *The Medicinal Uses of Cannabinoids*; and J. M. McPartland et al., "Evolutionary Origins of the Endocannabinoid System," *Gene* 370 (2006): 64–74. See also "The Brain's Own Marijuana," *Scientific American,* November 22, 2004.

211 **annual conclaves hosted by:** The International Cannabinoid Research Society was formed in 1992. The first ICRS conference was held as a satellite meeting of the College on Problems of Drug Dependence, a NIDA-supported effort.

212 **"guardian angel" or "gatekeeper":** Mauro Maccarrone, "Role of the CB2 Receptor in Reproduction," presentation at CB-2 Cannabinoid Receptors: New Vistas Conference in Banff, Canada, June 30–July 2, 2007; Mauro Maccarrone, "The Endocannabinoid 2-Arachidonoylglycerol Promotes Sperm Development Through Activiation of Cannabinoid-2 Receptors," *Cannabinoids* 4(4) (2009): 4–6; and Haibin Wang, Sudhansu K. Dey, and Mauro Maccarrone, "Jekyll and Hyde: Two Faces of Cannabinoid Signaling in Male and Female Fertility," *Endocrine Reviews* 27(5) (2006): 427–48.

212 **misfiring of the endocannabinoid system:** M. Maccarrone et al., "Low Fatty Acid Amide Hydrolase and High Anandamide Levels Are Associated with Failure to Achieve an Ongoing Pregnancy after IVF and Embryo Transfer," *Molecular Human Reproduction* 8(2) (2002): 188–95.

212 **endocannabinoids in maternal milk:** Uberto Pagotto et al., "The Emerging Role of the Endocannabinoid System in Endocrine Regulation and Energy Balance," *Endocrine Reviews* 27(1) (2006): 73–100.

212 **"failure to thrive" syndrome:** E. Fride et al., "Critical Role of the Endogenous Cannabinoid System in Mouse Pup Suckling and Growth," *European Journal of Pharmacology* 419(2–3) (2001): 207–14.

212 **a dysfunctional endocannabinoid system:** Ethan B. Russo, "Clinical Endocannabinoid Deficiency," *Neuroendocrinology Letters* 25 (1–2) (2004).

212 **An "animal model" of osteoporosis:** O. Ofek et al., "Peripheral Cannabinoid Receptor, CB2, Regulates Bone Mass," *Proceedings of the National Academy of Sciences USA* 103(3) (2006): 696–701.

214 **only during the embryonic development:** Roger A. Nicoll and Bradley E. Alger, "The Brain's Own Marijuana," *Scientific American,* November 22, 2004.

214 **"a broad array of developmental processes . . .":** John M. McPartland, "The Endocannabinoid System: An Osteopathic Perspective," *Journal of the American Osteopathic Association* 108(10) (2008): 586–600.

214 **regulates adult neurogenesis:** M. B. Goncalves et al., "A Diacylglycerol Lipase-CB2 Cannabinoid Pathway Regulates Adult Subventricular Zone Neurogenesis in an Age-dependent Manner," *Molecular Cell Neuroscience* 38(4) (2008): 526–36; and M. J. Oudin et al., "DAGL-Dependent Endocannabinoid Signaling: Roles in Axonal Pathfinding, Synaptic Plasticity and Adult Neurogenesis," *European Journal of Neuroscience* 34(10) (November 21, 2011): 1634–46.

214 **attesting to the neuroprotective function:** R. Mechoulam et al., "Cannabinoids and Brain Injury: Therapeutic Implications," *TRENDS in Molecular Medicine* 8(2) (2002): 58–61; Anat Biegon, "Cannabinoids as Neuroprotective Agents in Traumatic Brain Injury," *Current Pharmaceutical Design* 10(18) (2004): 2177–83; and J. Fernández-Ruiz et al., "Role of CB2 Receptors in Neuroprotective Effects of Cannabinoids," *Molecular Cell Endocrinology* 286(1–2 Suppl. 1) (2008): 591–96.

214 **the body's "general protective network . . .":** C. Pope, R. Mechoulam, L. Parsons, "Endocannabinoid Signaling in Neurotoxicity and Neuroprotection," *Neurotoxicology* 31(5) (2010): 562–71.

215 **"We were motivated . . .":** Author's interview with Debby Goldsberry.

215 **"Everywhere we went . . .":** Ibid.

216 **"a sexy urgency":** Rob Buchanan, "The New Pot Party," *Mademoiselle,* November 1993.
216 **"We never wanted to be . . .":** Author's interview with Debby Goldsberry.
217 **"If you smoke or eat marijuana . . .":** Author's interview with Elvy Musikka; and Norris et al., *Shattered Lives,* p. 90.
217 **"Those kids were wonderful . . .":** Author's interview with Elvy Musikka.
217 **"The medicinal aspect was crucial . . .":** Author's interview with Debby Goldsberry.
218 **"It's a holy weed . . . I enjoy the high":** Margery Eagan, "Back to Woodstock in the Hub," *Boston Herald,* September 15, 1991; and Tom Puleo, "Legalization of Marijuana Pressed by Supporters," *Hartford Courant,* September 29, 1991.
218 **"If looks could kill . . .":** Author's interview with Elvy Musikka.
218 **once known for its abundant hemp fields:** Kentucky produced 24 million pounds of hemp a year in the mid-1800s. There were more than 150 hemp factories in Kentucky, employing more than 16,000 people.
218 **"Why does your husband . . .":** Weisheit, *Domestic Marijuana,* p. 151.
218 **Gary Earl Shepherd, a crippled forty-five-year-old:** Norris et al., *Shattered Lives,* p. 67.
219 **"Industrial hemp can help . . .":** Sherman and Smith, *Highlights,* p. 133.
219 **"one of the most promising crops . . .":** John Mintz, "Splendor in the Grass?" *Washington Post,* January 5, 1997.
219 **"Hemp is petroleum . . .":** Willie Nelson, *High Times* interview, January 1991.
220 **"The highest killer on the planet . . .":** Willie Nelson on Very Important Potheads, http://www.veryimportantpotheads.com/site/nelson.htm.
220 **"There's value in actually looking . . .":** Author's interview with Debby Goldsberry.
220 **an increase in marijuana use among Americans:** Andrew Golub, ed., *The Cultural/Subcultural Contexts of Marijuana Use at the Turn of the Twenty-First Century,* p. 8.
221 **"Legalizing marijuana could bring . . .":** Saul Rubin, *Offbeat Marijuana,* p. 177.
221 **the kind of tidal wave . . .":** Jeff Chang, *Can't Stop Won't Stop,* p. 41.
222 **The hip-hop community's high-profile involvement:** Hip-Hop Summit Action Network, "Hip-Hop Rallies Against Drug Laws," AlterNet, May 15, 2003.
222 **A 2001 study of twenty-three U.S. cities:** Greg Krikorian, "Pot's Rise Reported in Young Arrestees," *Los Angeles Times,* June 30, 2001.
222 **"a prism through which . . .":** Kevin Starr, *California: A History,* p. 132.
223 **"the spiritual Bethlehem . . .":** Brownell in *Marijuana Review* 1(9), p. 23.
223 **"Saigon was filled with . . .":** *Brownie Mary's Marijuana Cookbook and Dennis Peron's Recipe for Social Change,* p. 26.
223 **"parental stress syndrome . . .":** Author's interview with Dennis Peron.
224 **"And the right to smoke it . . .":** Peron in Fred Gardner, "Dennis Peron and the Passage of Proposition 215," *O'Shaughnessy's,* Winter/Spring 2007.
224 **"It was the only restaurant in the world . . .":** *Brownie Mary's Marijuana Cookbook,* pp. 28–29.
224 **"It was kind of one-stop . . .":** Torgoff, *Can't Find My Way Home,* pp. 296–97.
224 **"It became a home . . .":** *Brownie Mary's Marijuana Cookbook,* pp. 228–29.
224 **"It was a little oasis . . .":** Michael Simmons, "The Madness Continues," in Sloman, *Reefer Madness,* pp. 399–400.
225 **Milk used the Island restaurant:** Author's interview with Dennis Peron; see, in general, Randy Shilts, *The Mayor of Castro Street.*
225 **Considerable animosity toward homosexuals:** Ibid., p. 62.
226 **more likely than others to use:** A survey by Massey University researchers in New

Zealand indicated that "Gay, lesbian and bisexuals drink more, do more drugs," stuff.co.nz, July 4, 2007.

226 **Mackavekias shot an unarmed Peron:** Author's interview with Dennis Peron; and "The Miracle Ounce," *Blacklisted News,* pp. 274–75.

226 **"He's the opposite of a profiteer . . .":** "The Miracle Ounce," *Blacklisted News.*

226 **"Hey, sweetheart . . .":** Author's interview with Dennis Peron.

226 **"Watch the light from San Francisco . . .":** "Peron's Prison Message," *High Times,* February 1979.

227 **"Harvey was not just for gay rights . . .":** *Brownie Mary's Marijuana Cookbook,* p. 32. See also Robert McRuer, "Gay Gatherings," in Braunstein and Doyle, *Imagine Nation,* pp. 229–30. In 2009, Harvey Milk was posthumously awarded the Presidential Medal of Freedom by President Obama for civil rights work and Governor Arnold Schwarzenegger signed legislation that designated May 22 as Harvey Milk Day in the Golden State.

228 **her "magically delicious" brownies:** Alice B. Toklas, Gertrude Stein's companion, included a recipe for hash brownies in her celebrated 1954 cookbook.

228 **"I'm going to be vindicated . . .":** Torgoff, *Can't Find My Way Home,* pp. 442–43; and Jane Meredith Adams, "Brownie Mary's Recipe for Controversy," *Dallas Morning News,* October 3, 1992.

229 **"Florence Nightingale of the medical . . .":** Marianne Costantinou, "Friends Pay Tribute to Brownie Mary's Life," *San Francisco Chronicle,* April 18, 1999.

229 **At the peak of her baking operation:** Richard C. Paddock, "Is Smoking Pot Good Medicine?" *Los Angeles Times,* February 26, 1995.

230 **"Every place I turn . . .":** Ibid.

230 **"Donald, we are the National Institute . . .":** Leschner in Clint Werner, *Marijuana Gateway to Health,* p. 119.

230 **Cannabis helped AIDS patients:** Donald Abrams et al., "Short-Term Effects of Cannabinoid in Patients with HIV-1 Infection: A Randomized, Placebo-Controlled Clinical Trial," *Annals of Internal Medicine* 139(4) (2003): 258–66.

230 **A subsequent study:** Donald Abrams et al., "Cannabis in Painful HIV-Associated Sensory Neuropathy: A Randomized Placebo-Controlled Trial," *Neurology* 68(7) (2007): 515–21.

230 **"I think marijuana is a very good medicine":** UPI.com, "Medical Marijuana Debate Increases," November 8, 2001.

231 **"Do you know what AIDS means?"** Author's interview with Dennis Peron.

231 **it came to him in a dream:** *Brownie Mary's Marijuana Cookbook,* p. 75.

231 **"He lived to testify . . .":** Fred Gardner, "Dennis Peron and the Passage of Proposition 215," *O'Shaughnessy's,* Winter/Spring 2007.

232 **"I can't explain to anyone . . .":** Sylvia Rubin, "They Smoke Pot, But Not to Get High," *San Francisco Chronicle,* March 13, 1992.

232 **"It's not just about marijuana":** Author's interview with Dennis Peron.

232 **"I am sensitive and compassionate . . .":** Paddock, "Is Smoking Pot Good Medicine?"

233 **"might be less likely to practice . . .":** Mason in Randall and O'Leary, *Marijuana Rx,* p. 390.

234 **"If it is perceived . . .":** Mason in Grinspoon and Bakalar, *Marihuana,* p. 22.

234 **A 1991 Harvard University survey:** R. E. Doblin and M. A. Kleiman, "Marijuana as Antiemetic Medicine: A Survey," *Journal of Clinical Oncology* 9(7) (1991): 1314–19.

235 **"scientifically, legally and morally wrong":** Dr. Lester Grinspoon, "Marihuana as Medicine: A Plea for Reconsideration," *Journal of the American Medical Association,* 273(23) (1995): 1875–76.

236 **"People in the autumn or sunset . . .":** "AIDS Patients Offered Pot," Associated Press, March 21, 1995.

237 **"People are smoking pot openly here!":** CBS *48 Hours,* April 10, 1996. *The New York Times* ran a sympathetic portrait of "an arthritic, HIV-positive cabaret performer" (Carey Goldberg, "Marijuana Club Helps Those in Pain," *New York Times,* February 25, 1996).

237 **"Mix, in a big country . . .":** *Brownie Mary's Marijuana Cookbook,* p. 25.

237 **"Marijuana is part of it . . .":** *O'Shaughnessy's,* Spring 2005.

237 **"Sick people tend to withdraw . . .":** Ibid.

237 **the "San Francisco model":** Harvey W. Feldman and R. Jerry Mandel, "Providing Medical Marijuana: The Importance of Cannabis Clubs," *Journal of Psychoactive Drugs* 30(2) (April–June 1998): 179–86; and Amanda E. Reiman, "Self-Efficacy, Social Support and Service Integration and Medical Cannabis Facilities in the San Francisco Bay Area of California," *Health and Social Care in the Community* 16(1) (2008): 31–41.

238 **played a crucial, salutary role:** Lester Grinspoon, "Cannabis Clubs: Public Nuisance or Therapy?" *Playboy,* November 1998.

238 **"unique research opportunity":** Mikuriya in Fred Gardner, "Take Two Tokes and Call Me in the Morning," *Village Voice,* November 12, 1996.

238 **"Further clinical study . . .":** Tod H. Mikuriya, "Cannabis Medicinal Uses at a Buyers' Club," http://druglibrary.net/schaffer/hemp/sfbc1.htm.

238 **"Tod Mikuriya convinced us . . .":** Author's interview with Debby Goldsberry.

238 **"Nobody was thinking . . .":** Ibid.

239 **another pro-cannabis stronghold:** Seventy-seven percent of Santa Cruz County voters backed a 1992 medical-marijuana advisory measure.

240 **"We have a lot of sick and dying people . . .":** Carey Goldberg, "Marijuana Club Helps Those in Pain," *New York Times,* February 25, 1996.

241 **"When the going gets weird . . ."** Hunter S. Thompson, ed., *Ancient Gonzo Wisdom,* p. 172.

241 **"A drug-free America is simply not possible . . .":** George Soros, *Washington Post,* 1997, in Michael Kaufman, *Soros,* p. 294.

241 **Soros became interested in drug policy:** Kaufman, *Soros,* p. 180.

242 **merged with another organization:** Arnold Trebach's Drug Policy Foundation.

242 **a citizen action achievement award:** *Brownie Mary's Marijuana Cookbook,* pp. 74–75; and author's interview with Ethan Nadelmann.

243 **pro-215 TV ads:** Kathleen Grammatico Ferraiolo, "Popular 'Medicine': Policymaking by Direct Democracy and the Medical Marijuana Movement of the 1990s" (doctoral dissertation, 2004), pp. 158–59.

243 **The opposition:** Attorney General Dan Lungren and Orange County Sheriff Brad Gates cochaired the campaign against Proposition 215.

244 **"more than 10,000 studies":** U.S. Department of Justice, "Say It Straight: The Medical Myths of Marijuana," http://library.findlaw.com/1999/Mar/3/129051.html.

244 **"The key is medical access . . .":** Cowan in Bock, *Waiting to Inhale,* p. 22.

244 **"This bill was written by . . .":** Fred Gardner, "Dennis Peron and the Passage of Proposition 215," *O'Shaughnessy's,* Winter/Spring 2007.

245 **"This is nothing more than . . .":** Simmons in Sloman, *Reefer Madness,* p. 410.
245 **"a cheap political trick":** Martin Espinoza, "Canna-bust," *San Francisco Bay Guardian,* August 7, 1996.
245 **"I can't get hold of any pot . . .":** *Doonesbury* cartoon reprinted in Ed Rosenthal et al., *Medical Marijuana Handbook,* p. 128.
246 **"There is not a shred of scientific evidence . . .":** Nick Brownlee, *This Is Cannabis,* p. 61.
246 **"increased drug abuse . . .":** Faye Fiore, "U.S. Drug Czar Calls State Marijuana Measure 'Tragedy,'" *Los Angeles Times,* November 16, 1996.
246 **"What in the world . . .":** Dennis Peron quoted in Bob Condor, "Marijuana's Therapeutic Value Impresses the Ill," *Chicago Tribune,* January 5, 1997.
247 **"all marijuana use is medical":** Christopher S. Wren, "Votes on Medical Marijuana Are Stirring Debate," *New York Times,* November 17, 1996; and author's interview with Dennis Peron.

CHAPTER 7: FIRE IN THE BELLY

248 **"This thing is a disaster . . .":** Michael Simmons in Sloman, *Reefer Madness,* p. 415; and Pat McCartney, "California and U.S. Officials Conspired to Block Prop 215," *O'Shaughnessy's,* Autumn 2004.
249 **"the challenge that the new law . . .":** *Metropolitan News-Enterprise,* November 7, 1996.
249 **"to determine how they will enforce . . .":** McCartney, "California and U.S. Officials Conspired to Block Prop 215."
249 **"The decision to bring appropriate criminal . . .":** Office of National Drug Control Policy, press release, November 9, 1996.
249 **California law-enforcement heavies huddled privately:** McCartney, "California and U.S. Officials Conspired to Block Prop 215." Among the attendees were the leaders of several powerful California law-enforcement organizations, including the District Attorneys Association, the Chiefs of Police Association, the Sheriffs' Association, and the California Narcotics Officers' Association; aides of four U.S. senators; and officials from the Justice Department, the DEA, Health and Human Services, Education, Transportation, and the Office of National Drug Control Policy.
250 **"the interagency working group":** Pat McCartney and Martin A. Lee, "The Dis-Implementation of Prop 215," *O'Shaughnessy's,* Winter/Spring 2007.
250 **asked the DEA to deputize California cops:** McCartney, "California and U.S. Officials Conspired to Block Prop 215."
250 **"The other side would be salivating . . .":** McCartney and Lee, "The Dis-Implementation of Prop 215."
250 **"We hope to establish the right . . .":** "Lungren Warns Prosecutors of 'Challenge' Presented by Medical Marijuana," *Metropolitan News-Enterprise,* November 7, 1996.
251 **McCaffrey promised to come up with big bucks:** Daniel Forbes, "Fighting 'Cheech and Chong' Medicine," *Salon,* July 27, 2000.
251 **"Emergency All Zones Meeting":** Among the 300 attendees were 27 state district attorneys, 22 sheriffs, 15 police chiefs, and dozens of peace officers and prosecutors representing 60 cities and 55 of California's 58 counties.
251 **"not incumbent on a police officer . . .":** Bock, *Waiting to Inhale,* p. 61.
251 **"What Proposition 215 does is create . . .":** McCartney, "California and U.S. Officials Conspired to Block Prop 215."

252 **"State and local law enforcement officials will . . .":** Ibid.; and "Preliminary Injunction Protects Physicians from Federal Prosecution and License Revocation," *215 Reporter,* March–April 1998.

252 **"Federal law-enforcement provisions remain . . .":** Bock, *Waiting to Inhale,* p. 57.

253 **"is effective and has a reasonable place . . .":** Marcus Conant, "This Is Smart Medicine," *Newsweek,* February 3, 1997; Conant also quoted in Carey Goldberg, "Marijuana Club Helps Those in Pain," *New York Times,* February 25, 1996.

253 **The suit, called *Conant v. McCaffrey*:** Coplaintiffs of the class action suit included Keith Vines, a former prosecutor in the San Francisco DA's office who had AIDS and who used cannabis to counter the wasting syndrome; former S.F. police commissioner Jo Daly, who smoked pot when she underwent chemotherapy for cancer; Santa Cruz activist Valerie Corral and several other medical-marijuana patients; two nonprofit associations; and nine physicians who treated people with AIDS and cancer.

253 **"I believe that a federal policy . . .":** *New England Journal of Medicine,* January 30, 1997. The rights of "those at death's door" are subservient to "the absolute power of bureaucrats whose decisions are based more on reflexive ideology and political correctness than on compassion."

253 **"When politicians say . . .":** Rosenfeld, *Pot Luck,* p. 187.

253 **"physicians have been censoring . . .":** "Doctors Free to Recommend Medical Use of Marijuana, Federal Judge Rules," *NORML News,* April 11, 1997.

254 **a memo to all California law-enforcement:** McCartney, "California and U.S. Officials Conspired to Block Prop 215."

255 **"There's no sense in having a law . . .":** Peron in *San Francisco Examiner,* November 11, 1996.

255 **"People who are sick are not . . .":** Peron in *215 Reporter,* March/April 1997.

255 **"nation at peace with itself":** *Brownie Mary's Marijuana Cookbook,* p. 89.

256 **Lungren gave local fuzz carte blanche:** McCartney and Lee, "The Dis-Implementation of Prop 215."

256 **"You would not ask the doctor . . .":** *Brownie Mary's Marijuana Cookbook,* p. 89.

257 **"police harassment, raids on gardens . . .":** Bock, *Waiting to Inhale,* p. 71.

257 **argued at a pretrial hearing:** "Hearing Sought in Medical Pot Case," *Press Democrat* (Santa Rosa), April 15, 1997.

257 **"He was pretty stressed out":** "Marijuana Activist Dies in Crash," *San Francisco Chronicle,* July 10, 1997.

257 **"the first death directly caused . . .":** *The Chronology of Implementation,* a detailed, post-215 time line compiled by Fred Gardner and Pebbles Trippet.

257 **"The state's position . . .":** Tom Philp, "Ailing Woman, 72, Travels Great Lengths for 'Legal' Pot," *Daily News of Los Angeles,* February 9, 1997.

258 **Hallinan told the feds:** "Hallinan Knocks Feds over Pot Raid," *San Francisco Examiner,* April 22, 1997.

259 **"My Dad Is Not a Criminal":** Americans for Safe Access, "Medical Marijuana Patient's Federal Appeal Today," press release, June 16, 2004.

259 **San Jose club was raided:** "San Jose Cannabis Center Raided on Day After Chief Resigns," *215 Reporter,* May/June 1998.

260 **"It sounded like you . . .":** Sabin Russell, "S.F. Club's Style Rankles Medical Pot Advocates," *San Francisco Chronicle,* January 3, 1998; and Bill Ainsworth, Copley News Service, January 12. 1998.

261 **"the haunting fear that someone . . .":** Vincent Fitzpatrick, *H. L. Mencken,* p. 37.

261 **Latter-day zealots for zero tolerance:** A 1999 survey found that 55 percent of the total sample population agreed that "using marijuana is morally wrong." Belden, Russonello, and Stewart, *National Survey on Marijuana,* ACLU, 1999, in Earleywine, ed., *Pot Politics,* p. 236.

261 **"It was a direct action campaign":** Author's interview with Debby Goldsberry.

262 **"We don't want to be . . .":** John Hendren, "California's Marijuana Clubs Remain Outlaws Despite 'Legalization,'" Associated Press, June 6, 1997.

262 **The OCBC was one of:** The six Northern California clubs named in the federal civil suit were the Oakland Cannabis Buyers' Cooperative, Dennis Peron's Cannabis Cultivators' Club, Flower Therapy in San Francisco, the Marin Alliance for Medical Marijuana, the Ukiah Cannabis Buyers' Club, and the Wo/Men's Alliance for Medical Marijuana in Santa Cruz.

263 **the narrow ruling:** The Supreme Court declared that "medical necessity is not a defense to manufacturing or distributing marijuana," but it was a narrow ruling; the court did not hold that federal law trumps state law.

264 **"Yes, I did sell marijuana . . .":** Maria Alicia Gaura, "S.F. Pot Club Owner Starts Campaign," *San Francisco Chronicle,* January 15, 1998.

264 **"the Jim Crow laws . . .":** Sands in Tammy Stables Battaglia, Freep.com, January 23, 1998.

264 **"Except in a few areas . . .":** Alan Bock, *Orange County Register,* May 3, 1998. Bock is the author of *Waiting to Inhale,* an early account of the enactment of Proposition 215 and its immediate aftermath.

265 **strains rich in cannabidiol (CBD):** Author's communication with Todd McCormick.

265 **"I thought I could share . . .":** *215 Reporter,* March/April 1998.

266 **"Not only is cannabis a vasodilator . . .":** Peter Gorman, "Sister Somayah Kambui: Burning the Bush for Sickle Cell," hightimes.com, December 17, 2002.

267 **"Sister Somayah has been a pioneer . . .":** Eidelman on http://dreidelman.org/Eidelman_polyMVA_jawsDEATH.html.

267 **"You've got kids so sick . . .":** Gorman, "Sister Somayah Kambui."

267 **Questioned by Chavez's attorney:** Bock, *Waiting to Inhale,* pp. 93–97.

267 **Chavez's lawyer also asked:** Dana Parsons, "A Charter Member of O.C.'s Cannabis Club," *Los Angeles Times,* July 19, 2007.

268 **Judge Borris later wrecked his car:** Bock, *Waiting to Inhale,* pp. 106–7.

269 **The inside joke:** Selena Roberts, "Marijuana Use Goes Unchecked, Many in NBA Say," *New York Times,* October 26, 1997.

269 **"From my own personal experience . . .":** Mark Donald, "Cannabis: The Elixir of Champions!" *Dallas Observer,* October 31, 2002.

269 **"marijuana culture is widely accepted . . .":** Kevin Parnell, "Infamous Olympic Medalist Wants Another Shot in 2010," *Kelowna Capital News* (British Columbia), March 11, 2007. Rebagliati was barred by U.S. immigration officials from entering the United States in 2002 because he had tested positive for marijuana four years earlier.

270 **During Clinton's second term:** "Clinton Kicks Off $2 Billion Anti-Drug Media Blitz," Reuters, July 9, 1998.

270 **"If Corporate America uses . . .":** Christopher Wren, "Teen-agers and Marijuana; Scaring Them Straight Has Lost Its Edge," *New York Times,* September 14, 1997; and "Anti-Drug Ads to Bombard Airwaves," *Seattle Times,* July 9, 1998.

270 **"there is a carefully camouflaged . . .":** Brownlee, *This Is Cannabis,* p. 61.

270 **The general's military experience:** As commander of the 24th Infantry Division during the 1991 Gulf War, McCaffrey had ordered a relentless attack on retreating Iraqi troops—the infamous "left hook" maneuver—that was wholly disproportionate to any real threat. He later served as head of the U.S. Southern Command in Panama.

271 **McCaffrey said it was:** Frank Davies, "Extra Drug-War Funds Urged for Latin America," *Miami Herald,* July 17, 1999; and Larry Rohter with Christopher S. Wren, "U.S. Anti-Drug Chief Proposes $1 Billion for Colombian War," *New York Times,* July 17, 1999.

271 **militarization of U.S. narcotics policy:** Timothy J. Dunn, "Waging a War on Immigrants at the U.S.-Mexico Border," in Kraska, ed., *Militarizing the American Criminal Justice System,* pp. 65–81.

271 **the crux of McCaffrey's antidrug strategy:** Massing, *The Fix,* p. 223.

271 **"a guy of absolute, unquestioned integrity":** Shapiro, *Shooting Stars,* p. 240.

271 **He rejected recommendations:** In April 1998, the U.S. Senate passed a "sense of the Senate" resolution ordering the drug czar not to fund any future medical-marijuana research or any scientific research that might suggest that the U.S. government should redirect funding from antitrafficking busts into medical treatment of addicts.

272 **superfungus to attack:** Jed Gottlieb, "The Temptation of Dr. Weed," *Missoula Independent,* March 6, 2003.

272 **"an unmitigated disaster":** CNN, July 9, 1998, in Mike Gray, ed., *Busted,* p. 127.

272 **"The murder rate in Holland . . .":** Reuters, July 17, 1998.

272 **Point of fact:** *Los Angeles Times,* July 21, 1998. The murder rate in the United States was 8.2 per hundred thousand; the murder rate in the Netherlands was 1.7 per hundred thousand.

272 **The Dutch Foreign Office:** Mike Gray, ed., *Busted,* p. xi.

272 **"Human Rights and the Drug War":** Organized by American activists Virginia Resner, Mikki Norris, and Chris Conrad, the "Human Rights and the Drug War" exhibit was displayed in various venues in North America and elsewhere during the mid- and late 1990s.

272 **Borst told McCaffrey:** "U.S. Drug Czar at Odds with Dutch," BBC, July 17, 1998.

272 **"As for a possible switch . . .":** "Cannabis Policy, an Update" by the Netherlands Institute of Mental Health and Addiction, cited in "Government Report from the Netherlands Criticizes Marijuana's Label as a 'Gateway' Drug," *NORML News,* May 1, 1997.

273 **This pattern would continue:** Americans consume marijuana at rates more than double those of their Dutch counterparts, according to a study published by the Centre for Drug Research of the University of Amsterdam in 1999. The study found that 15.6 percent of Dutch persons aged twelve and over had tried marijuana; of these, 4.5 percent reported using marijuana in the past year. By contrast, 32.9 percent of Americans above eleven years of age tried marijuana, and 9 percent indicated that they had used the herb during the past year. A 2002 report from the European Monitoring Centre for Drugs and Drug Addiction said that "problem drug use" in the Netherlands is the lowest among countries in the European Union and dramatically less than in United States.

273 **"The coffee shops are living proof . . .":** Author's interview with Frederick Polak.

273 **a continent-wide shift:** In France, the Henrion Commission, the official state commission on drug policy, called for a two-year trial in the regulated sale of cannabis; the French government rejected this advice, prompting more than a hundred intellectuals and artists to risk prosecution by signing a petition that acknowledged their use of marijuana.

273 **"Most of Europe prefers . . .":** Rick Steves, speech to NORML conference, in *O'Shaughnessy's*, Autumn 2005.

273 **The British legal system:** *Cannabis: The Scientific and Medical Evidence* (November 11, 1998), HM Government: House of Lords Science and Technology Select Committee on Science and Technology Ninth Report (Session 1997–98), HL 151. A 2002 British survey found that 43 percent of MS patients used marijuana therapeutically.

273 **"What's extraordinary is to have . . .":** Ibid.

274 **"They were almost relieved . . .":** Author's interview with Geoffrey Guy.

274 **Spooked by the prospect:** A 2002 survey of British multiple sclerosis patients found that 43 percent of respondents used marijuana therapeutically to alleviate spasms and relieve pain.

274 **Clinical trials in several European countries:** According to a 2009 clinical study conducted at the University of Rome, Sativex did not cause psychopathological states or cognitive deficits in patients with multiple sclerosis.

274 **studies by American scientists:** For example, Denis Petro, "Marihuana as a Therapeutic Agent for Muscle Spasm or Spasticity," *Psychosomatics* 21(1) (1980): 81–85; J. T. Ungerleider et al., "Delta-9-THC in the Treatment of Spasticity Associated with Multiple Sclerosis," *Advances in Alcohol and Substance Abuse* 7(1) (1987): 39–50; and Paul Consroe et al., "The Perceived Effects of Smoked Cannabis on Patients with Multiple Sclerosis," *European Neurology* 38(1) (1997): 44–48.

275 **"I'm breaking the law . . .":** Associated Press, "Montel Williams Backs Legalized Marijuana," *Los Angeles Times,* May 6, 2004. The U.S. National Multiple Sclerosis Society's 2008 Expert Opinion Paper concluded from its research that marijuana is effective in controlling the symptoms of MS, and it can stop the progression of the disease.

275 **"I agree that marijuana laws . . .":** Dear Abby column, March 1, 1999. A 1999 Gallup poll found 73 percent of Americans in favor of "making marijuana legally available for doctors to prescribe in order to reduce pain and suffering."

275 **"This is democracy held hostage":** Associated Press, December 18, 1998.

276 **Clinton Justice Department announced:** Ryan Grim, "Congressional Malpractice," AlterNet, November 9, 2005; Colbert I. King, "Glossing over Mistreatment in the Magbie Case," *Washington Post,* April 8, 2006; and *NORML News*, December 10, 1998.

276 **He died four days later:** Assisted by the ACLU National Prison Project, Magbie's mother sued the D.C. government and was awarded a "substantial" undisclosed settlement. Judge Judith Retchin was never sanctioned for judicial homicide.

277 **"overly zealous in opposing . . .":** "New California A.G. Says Legalizing Medical Marijuana Will Be a Priority," *NORML News*, December 31, 1998.

278 **"If local law enforcement is supportive . . .":** Edward Epstein, "Lockyer Gives Quiet OK to SF Pot Clubs," *San Francisco Chronicle,* March 20, 1999.

278 **"You know, if you take away . . .":** Personal communication with the author.

278 **ill from childhood diabetes:** In May 2010, experiments conducted by Portuguese

scientists showed that THC improves the insulin sensitivity of cells (D. Teixeira et al., "Modulation of Adipocyte Biology by δ(9)Tetrahydrocannabinol," *Obesity* 18[11][May 2010]: 2077–85). Also in May 2010, Italian researchers reported that endocannabinoid levels were significantly elevated in diabetics and obese individuals as part of an adaptive response to dietary and lifestyle stress (G. Annuzzi et al., *Lipids Health Disease* 9[1][2010]: 43).

278 **"My health was all . . .":** "Man Pleads for Marijuana," *Modesto Bee*, March 19, 1998.

279 **a 1991 DEA analysis:** Chris Conrad, *Cannabis Yields and Dosage*.

279 **his conviction was subsequently overturned:** "Medicinal Marijuana Advocate Dies," *Union Democrat* (Sonora, CA), October 17, 2006; and Americans for Safe Access, *Patients in the Crossfire*, pp. 38–39.

280 **"I don't have a medicine . . .":** All quotes from Steve Kubby are from author's interview with Kubby.

281 **"Only Kubby had survived":** Martin A. Lee, "Reefer Refugees," *Razor*, April 5, 2005.

281 **The Mayo Clinic:** Steve Kubby, *The Politics of Consciousness*, p. 120.

282 **"I asked him not to handcuff . . .":** Michael Pulley, "Search Unwarranted," *Sacramento News & Review*, January 20, 2000; see also Patrick McCartney, "Last Ones Standing," *Sacramento News & Review*, February 28, 2002.

283 **"fresh, green and still moist":** Ibid.

283 **They all shopped at:** Ibid.

283 **"Just the fact that people shop . . .":** Ibid.

284 **an eighteen-month jail sentence:** McCartney, "Last Ones Standing," See also Robert and Shawna Whiteaker, "Sacramentro Area Injustice," May 5, 2002, http://forum.grasscity.com/real-life-stories/4991-sacramento-area-injustice.html.

284 **"On the basis of the facts conceded . . .":** Penne Usher, "Deputies Could Face Trial over Pot Raid," *Auburn Journal*, May 6, 2005; *Michael W. Baldwin v. Placer County*, No. 04–15848, U.S. Appeals Court, Ninth Circuit, April 19, 2005; Eron Ben-Yehuda, "Court Rejects Qualified-Immunity Defense for Deputies," *Daily Journal Extra*, May 9, 2005; and Claire Cooper, "Placer Deputies Face Trial Linked to Pot Raids in '90s," *Sacramento Bee*, April 20, 2005.

285 **"The passage of Proposition 215 has made . . .":** *O'Shaughnessy's*, Summer 2010.

285 **The IOM delegation:** Author's interviews with Jeff Jones and Michael Aldrich.

285 **a lengthy technical exegesis:** Janet E. Joy et al., eds., *Marijuana and Medicine* pp. 33–81.

286 **"[F]ew users develop dependence":** Ibid., pp. 6, 177.

286 **"In fact, most drug users . . .":** Ibid., p. 99.

286 **"Smoked marijuana is a crude . . .":** Ibid., p. 4.

286 **cannabinoid effects cannot be separated:** Ibid., p. 5.

286 **"rapid-onset, reliable, and safe . . .":** Ibid., p. 10.

286 **"there is little future . . .":** Ibid., p. 178.

286 **"Prohibition is right up there . . .":** Barbara Ehrenreich, "Kicking the Big One," *Time*, February 28, 1994.

287 **the problems of military vets:** Jeremy Manier and Judith Graham, "Mental Health Problems Plague Vets," *Press Democrat* (Santa Rosa, CA), March 13, 2007; and Deborah Sontag and Lizette Alvarez, "Across America, Deadly Echoes of Foreign Battles," *New York Times*, January 13, 2008.

287 **"PTSD is not a disorder . . .":** Al Byrne, "The Recurring Terror of Combat," *O'Shaughnessy's,* Spring 2006.

287 **"Eighty to ninety percent of the vets . . .":** Author's interview with Al Byrne and Mary Lynn Mathre.

287 **"Guys would come up to me and say . . .":** Ibid. Grinspoon and Bakalar write: "The odor of marijuana is said to be omnipresent on some V.A. hospital paraplegia and quadriplegia wards" (*Forbidden Medicine,* p. 84).

288 **In 1995, Mathre and Byrne formed:** Patients Out of Time was the direct successor to Robert Randall's Alliance for Cannabis Therapeutics. Randall got the ball rolling two decades earlier when he successfully sued the federal government for access to cannabis. He handed the baton to Mathre and Byrne as he withdrew from full-time activism to attend to his health needs.

288 **"regarding current, evidence-based . . .":** American Nurses Association resolution June 2003: http://www.medicalcannabis.com/Healthcare-Professionals/nurses.

288 **"Cannabis use enhances the quality . . .":** Tod Mikuriya, "Cannabis Eases Post-Traumatic Stress," *O'Shaughnessy's,* Spring 2006.

289 **"I told them, 'I've done nothing . . .":** Bock, *Waiting to Inhale,* p. 98.

289 **"the largest, most sophisticated . . .":** http://stopthedrugwar.org/chronicle/353/tworaids.shtml.

290 **A kamikaze pilot for cannabis:** Fred Gardner, "Eddy Lepp Busted by DEA," *Anderson Valley Advertiser,* August 25, 2004.

290 **The analgesic effects of THC:** R. Noyes Jr. et al., "Analgesic Effect of Delta-9-Tetrahydrocannabinol," *Journal of Clinical Pharmacology* 15(2) (1975): 139–43; and M. Staquet et al., "Effect of a Nitrogen Analog of THC on Cancer Pain," *Journal of Clinical Pharmacology and Therapeutics* 23 (1978): 397–401.

290 **Subsequent scientific studies:** Ethan Russo and Geoffrey W. Guy, "A Tale of Two Cannabinoids: The Therapeutic Rationale for Combining Tetrahydrocannabinol and Cannabidiol," *Medical Hypotheses* 66 (2005): 234–46. Long before the days of Hippocrates, Ayurvedic healers in India utilized ganja to soothe pain, while Chinese physicians employed medicinal hemp as an anesthetic for surgery. Pliny the Elder, the Roman naturalist born in AD 23, cited the painkilling properties of cannabis in his encyclopedia. In nineteenth-century America, patent medicines containing cannabis tinctures were widely used to treat migraines and other kinds of pain.

291 **"substances similar to or drawn from . . .":** Ulysses Torassa, "UCSF Study Backs Claim Pot Kills Pain," *San Francisco Examiner,* September 23, 1998.

291 **California cannabis clinicians:** "Medical Marijuana in California, 1996–2006," *O'Shaughnessy's,* Winter/Spring 2007.

291 **Some opiate addicts used cannabis to blunt:** Ethan B. Russo, M.D., "Cannabis: From Pariah to Prescription," *Journal of Cannabis Therapeutics* 3(3) (2003): 1–29. See also, Ethan Russo, "The Role of Cannabis and Cannabinoids in Pain Management," in Richard S. Weiner, ed., *Pain Management,* CRC Press, American Academy of Pain Management.

292 **The IOM cited cases:** Joy et al, eds., *Marijuana and Medicine,* pp. 139–44. In 2006, researchers in Basel, Switzerland, found that THC reduces spasticity in patients with spinal cord injuries (*European Journal of Neuroscience* 27[7] [2008]: 1722–30); and animal studies reported in the journal *Anesthesiology* 108(4) (2008): 722–34, showed that activation of the CB-2 receptor in the spinal cord reduces pain after

nerve injury. See also, J. Guindon and A. G. Hohmann, "Cannabinoid CB2 Receptors: A Therapeutic Target for the Treatment of Inflammatory and Neuropathic Pain," *British Journal of Pharmacology* 15(2) (January 2008): 319–34.

292 **Traumatic brain injuries cause:** "Glutamate is to the brain like coffee is to our bodies," reports a Georgetown University Medical Center press release, "Understanding the Brain's Natural Foil for Over-Excited Neurons," October 19, 2009; and "Enzyme Is the Culprit in Neuronal Death after Stroke and Brain Trauma," June 8, 2009. http://insciences.org/article.php?article_id=5518.

292 **greater antioxidant potency:** A. J. Hampson, M. Grimaldi, J. Axelrod, and D. Wink, "Cannabidiol and Delta-9-Tetrahydrocannabinol Are Neuroprotective Antioxidants," *Proceedings of the National Academy of Sciences USA* 95(14) (1998): 8268–73.

292 **"Cannabinoids as antioxidants and neuroprotectants":** A. J. Hampson, J. Axelrod, and M. Grimaldi, "Cannabinoids as Antioxidants and Neuroprotectants," United States Patent, US 6,630,507, awarded in October 2003, was held by the United States of America as represented by the Department of Health and Human Services.

292 **Thousands of U.S. soldiers:** A low-ball, 2007 Pentagon estimate put the number of soldiers returning from Iraq and Afghanistan with PTSD at 360,000, or 20 percent. According to another Pentagon study, equal number of returning soldiers have suffered traumatic brain injuries. Nearly one-third of Afghanistan and Iraq vets have sought mental health services. By 2010, veteran suicides outnumbered U.S. military deaths in Iraq and Afghanistan (David Goldstein, "Study: A Fifth of War Veterans Have Mental Health Issues," *Truthout,* October 5, 2011; Asha Bandele and Tony Newman, "Traumatized Veterans Turning to Alcohol, Drugs," *Santa Cruz Sentinel,* March 25, 2007; Penny Coleman, "10 Reasons Why the US Military Should [Officially] Use Pot," AlterNet, December 29, 2009; and Nadias Prupis, "Veteran Suicides Outnumber US Military Deaths in Iraq and Afghanistan," *Truthout,* October 22, 2010).

293 **"Frankly, I felt like I deserved . . .":** Author's interview with Michael Krawitz.

CHAPTER 8: GROUND ZERO

294 **"A new drama of invention . . .":** "New Debates for a New Year," *New York Times* editorial, January 1, 2001.

294 **"Bush's shallow intellect . . .":** Juliet Roper, Christina Holtz-Bacha, Gianpietro Mazzoleni, *The Politics of Representation: Election Campaigning and Proportional Representation,* p. 158.

295 **"You know why? Because . . .":** Jefferson Morley, "Secret Tapes Indicate Bush Used Drugs as Youth," *Washington Post,* February 24, 2005.

295 **the Bush twins smoked pot:** Stephen M. Silverman, "Kutcher Sips and Tells on Bush Twins," *People,* May 8, 2003.

295 **"I want to escalate the war . . .":** Ashcroft on *Larry King Live,* CNN, February 7, 2001.

295 **"Walters' record reveals . . .":** Mike Males, "Moral Poverty and Body Counts," AlterNet, May 1, 2001.

296 **"the great urban myths of our time":** *Weekly Standard,* March 6, 2001, cited in Kevin Nelson, "2001: A Year in the Life of Marijuana Prohibition," AlterNet, January 27, 2002.

296 **"the Doctor Strangelove of our . . .":** *Austin Chronicle,* November 30, 2001.

296 **He sent a letter to:** Dominic Holden, "Czar Struck," *DrugSense Weekly,* February 13, 2009.

296 **"For Walters, its all marijuana . . .":** Robert Dreyfuss, "Bush's War on Pot," *Rolling Stone,* July 28, 2005.

296 **referred to cannabis as "poison":** Bruce Mirkin, "Marijuana and the Media" in Earleywine, *Pot Politics,* p. 145.

296 **"Marijuana use, especially during . . .":** White House press release, "White House Drug Czar, Research and Mental Health Communities Warn Parents That Marijuana Use Can Lead to Depression, Suicidal Thoughts and Schizophrenia," cited in "Teen 'Self Medication' for Depression Leads to More Serious Mental Illness, New Report Reveals," *ScienceDaily,* May 9, 2008.

297 **"Faith plays a powerful role . . .":** Walters in Paul Armentano, "Bush's Born-Again Drug War," AlterNet, August 12, 2004.

297 **the teachings of the United Methodist Church:** While favoring decriminalization, the United Methodist Church cautioned against recreational drug use: "The medical use of any drug should not be seen as encouraging recreational use of the drug. We urge all persons to abstain from marijuana. Unless it has been legally prescribed in a form appropriate for treating a particular medical condition" (Charles Thomas, "Detailed Analyses of Religious Groups' Divergent Positions on Marijuana," in Earleywine, *Pot Politics,* p. 252).

297 **"a conservative cultural revolution":** Baum, *Smoke and Mirrors,* p. 104.

297 **covert operations against U.S. peace groups:** James Ridgeway, "Cops and Former Secret Service Agents Ran Black Ops on Green Groups," *Mother Jones,* April 11, 2008.

297 **Bush defended the Patriot Act:** John Tierney, "A Taste of His Own Medicine," *New York Times,* May 6, 2006.

297 **tracking terrorists got short shrift:** Arianna Huffington, "Did the Drug War Claim Another 3,056 Casualties on 9/11?" AlterNet, June 6, 2002; Dreyfus, "Bush's War on Pot"; and *NORML News,* August 1, 2002.

298 **"If you use drugs, you are standing . . .":** Ellis Henican, "Drug-Fighters High on Their Own Nonsense," *Newsday,* September 15, 2004.

298 **The drug war was all the more necessary:** *The 9/11 Commission Report* subsequently found "no reliable evidence that bin Laden was involved in or made his money through drug trafficking" (p. 171).

298 **"make marijuana seem more dangerous . . .":** Robinson, coauthor of *Lies, Damn Lies, and Drug War Statistics,* cited in Russell Goldman, "Is the Nation's Marijuana Policy Misguided?" ABC *World News Tonight,* August 2, 2007.

299 **"When science is falsified . . .":** Adrianne Appel, "Top Scientists Want Research Free from Politics," Inter Press Service, February 14, 2008; and "Hundreds of EPA Scientists Report Political Interferences over Last Five Years," press release, Union of Concerned Scientists, April 23, 2008.

299 **national polls that showed:** A *Time* magazine/CNN poll conducted in 2002 found that 80 percent of respondents supported allowing adults to "legally use marijuana for medical purposes."

299 **"They threw me down on the ground . . .":** Chuck Seidel, "Reefer Madness," *Sacramento News & Review,* November 29, 2001.

299 **"The whole idea was to get . . .":** Ibid.

300 **"There are not enough jails . . .":** Vanessa Nelson, *Cool Madness.*

300 **On the same day the feds busted:** Michael Simmons, "The Other War," *LA Weekly,* October 31, 2001; and Eric Bailey, "DEA Targets Landlords of Pot Outlets," *Los Angeles Times,* July 17, 2007.

300 **"running wild in the laboratories . . .":** Jacob Sullum, column, August 1, 2007.

301 **incorporated WAMM as a nonprofit:** In 1998, the federal Internal Revenue Service nixed WAMM's nonprofit status that had been granted by the state of California. Suddenly WAMM found itself responsible not only for taxes on future income but also for two years of penalties and interest from the period when they had been operating as an approved nonprofit. The financial blow was substantial for an organization that never had an annual budget exceeding $145,000 (Chapkis and Webb, *Dying to Get High,* p. 47).

301 **"We come together around . . .":** Chapkis and Webb, *Dying to Get High,* p. 107.

301 **"Of all the things that marijuana does . . .":** Valerie Corral interview by David Brown, http://mavericksofthemind.com/valerie-corral and http://mavericksofthemind.com/valerie-corral-2.

303 **The standoff continued for three hours:** Chapkis and Webb, *Dying to Get High,* pp. 176–77.

303 **"Everybody knows this group isn't . . .":** Eric Bailey, "Santa Cruz Clinic Leads Medical Marijuana Charge," *Los Angeles Times,* August 11, 2003.

303 **The WAMM raid marked the twenty-second time:** *NORML News,* September 6, 2002.

303 **"The dinosaur is thrashing . . .":** *California NORML Newsletter,* October 2002. In 2005, WAMM, the City of Santa Cruz, and the County of Santa Cruz agreed not pursue the lawsuit if the federal government agreed not to act against WAMM—with the caveat that WAMM reserves the right to resume the lawsuit if the U.S. government breaks the terms of the settlement.

304 **"Maybe it is not such a bang-up . . .":** "Let's Not Punt on Third Down," Asa Hutchinson's speech to Commonwealth Club, San Francisco, February 12, 2002, http://www.justice.gov/dea/speeches/s021202.html.

304 **Few of those who enrolled in drug treatment:** According to statistics released by the Department of Health and Human Services, 57 percent of the 255,000 people admitted for marijuana treatment in 2001 were referred by the criminal-justice system; many were first-time offenders. In 2007, the criminal-justice system was the single largest source of referrals to the substance-abuse treatment system, states a report ("Substance Abuse Treatment Admissions Referred by the Criminal Justice System") by the U.S. Substance Abuse and Mental Health Services Administration. See also the SAMHSA report "Substance Abuse Treatment Admissions Referred by the Criminal Justice System," August 13, 2009, cited in *NORML News,* "Pot Arrests Responsible for Majority of Marijuana Treatment Referrals," October 22, 2009; and SAMHSA, Office of Applied Studies. *Treatment Episode Data Set (TEDS) Highlights—2007 National Admissions to Substance Abuse Treatment Services,* OAS Series #S-45, DHHS Publication No. (SMA) 09–4360.

304 **"I call on the DEA . . .":** Dan Evans and Nina Wu, "Feds vs. S.F. on Pot," *San Francisco Examiner,* February 13, 2002.

304 **federal narcotics agents dynamited:** Ann Harrison, "Potshot," *San Francisco Bay Guardian,* January 22, 2003.

304 **"I was a trophy arrest . . .":** Andrew Gumbel, "Ganja Guru," *Independent,* May 1, 2003; and Schlosser, *Reefer Madness,* p. 68.

305 **"When those raids happened . . .":** John Geluardi, *Cannabiz,* p. 59.

306 **"I've been devastated . . .":** Dick Polman, "US Drug Net Snares State-Backed Grower," *Philadelphia Inquirer,* March 10, 2003.

306 **"We have to protect patients . . .":** Sherer in David Borden, "Medical Marijuana Wars Heat Up," DRCNet, May 22, 2002.

307 **"This is a proactive measure . . .":** Ibid.

307 **written by scholar-activist Jon Gettman:** The Cannabis Rescheduling Petition, http://www.drugscience.org/petition_intro.html.

308 **as America's top cash crop throughout the Bush years:** Eric Bailey, "Pot Is Called Biggest Cash Crop," *Los Angeles Times,* December 18, 2006.

308 **The street value of California's:** The other states boasting billion-dollar cannabis harvests in 2006 were Tennessee, Kentucky, Hawaii, and Washington. Of the estimated cannabis crop grown in America, 17 percent was thought to be cultivated indoors under controlled conditions.

308 **arrest statistics on a state-by-state basis:** See Gettman's state-by-state analysis at www.norml.org/facts/arrestreport.

308 **An inordinate concentration of pot busts:** Don Hazen, "Pot Busts Much More Likely in Some States, Counties," AlterNet, July 25, 2000.

308 **"New York City's policing strategy . . .":** Bernard E. Harcourt and Jens Ludwig, "Broken Windows: New Evidence from New York City and a Five-City Social Experiment," *University of Chicago Law Review* 73 (2006).

308 **Marijuana arrests went through the roof:** Harry G. Levine, "Arrest Statistics and Racism," in Holland, ed., *The Pot Book,* p. 202. In 2008, blacks were about 26 percent of New York City's population, but more than 54 percent of the people arrested for possession. Latinos were about 27 percent of New Yorkers, but 33 percent of the pot arrestees. Whites were more than 35 percent of the city's population, but fewer than 10 percent of people arrested for possessing marijuana.

309 **"You bet I did!":** Jennifer Steinhauer, "Bloomberg Says He Regrets Marijuana Remarks," *New York Times,* April 10, 2002.

309 **Data from the NYC Department of Health:** Verena Dobnik, "Study: 70,000 May Suffer Post-9/11 Stress Disorder," Associated Press, September 11, 2008.

309 **Patients' Cooperative, run by Kenneth Toglia:** Sharon Lerner, "Up In Smoke," *Village Voice,* May 15, 2001.

309 **"The defendant has become wealthy . . .":** Torsten Ove, "Tommy Chong's Hopes May Be Up in Smoke," *Pittsburgh Post-Gazette,* September 10, 2003.

309 **"like jailing all of the . . .":** Paul Krassner, "Pipe Dreams vs. Nice Dreams," *High Times,* January 2007.

310 **"I went to jail for my beliefs":** Chris Cobb, "On Golden Bong," *Ottawa Citizen,* September 1, 2008.

311 **"Tod's patients were mostly poor . . .":** Author's interview with John Trapp.

311 **"Medical cannabis is legal here . . .":** Peter Gorman, "Dr. Mikuriya's Medicine," AlterNet, November 3, 2004.

311 **"We expected the DEA . . .":** Author's interview with John Trapp.

311 **"as many patients as fast as . . .":** Ibid.

312 **"The litmus test for a real doctor . . .":** Bock, *Waiting to Inhale,* p. 243.

313 **"I lied on a lot of issues . . .":** "The Prosecution of Tod Mikuriya," *O'Shaughnessy's,* Winter/Spring 2008, p. 11.

313 **"it can actually be very dangerous . . .":** Henry K. Lee, "Medical Pot Doctor Faces His Accusers," *San Francisco Chronicle,* September 4, 2003.

313 **"an extreme departure from the standard of care":** Robert Gammon, "Witch-Hunt Victim or Shoddy Docs?" *East Bay Express,* October 20, 2004.

314 **"What are you doing to this guy . . .":** Fred Gardner, "Medical Board Says It Won't Investigate Doctors Just for Approving Cannabis Use; So Why Is Tod Mikuriya, MD, Being Punished?" *O'Shaughnessy's,* Autumn 2004.

315 **investigated for a case involving a teenager:** *O'Shaughnessy's,* Spring 2004.

315 **"Top priority should go to investigating . . .":** *O'Shaughnessy's,* Spring 2003.

316 **"failed to demonstrate sufficient facts . . .":** David Bearman, "My Civil Rights Suit Vs. the Medical Board," *O'Shaughnessy's,* Winter/Spring 2007.

316 **"They are your friends . . .":** Dr. Philip A. Denney, "A Day in the Life of the Cannabis Consultant," *O'Shaughnessy's,* Spring 2006; and Peter Larsen, "Doctor Believes Medical Marijuana Holds Promise," Knight Ridder newspapers, November 2, 2005, record online.

317 **"troubled by how much taxpayer money . . .":** Fred Gardner, "The Investigation of Dr. Denney," *Anderson Valley Advertiser,* February 22, 2006.

317 **"I don't understand how state law . . .":** Tim Hearden, "Redding Doctor Sues DEA," *Record Searchlight* (Redding, CA), December 1, 2006.

318 **"I thought they needed to hear . . .":** Fred Gardner, "Ashcroft v. Raich," *O'Shaughnessy's,* Spring 2005.

319 **"There are no other treatments . . .":** Lucido's declaration to the U.S. District Court filed on behalf of Angel Raich on October 30, 2002, http://www.justice.gov/osg/briefs/2004/3mer/2mer/2003-1454.mer.ja.html.

319 **"Cannabis gave me back my limbs":** Steven Wishnia, "The Supremes Debate Medical Pot," AlterNet, November 30, 2004.

320 **charges against Cynthia Blake and David Davidson:** McCartney and Lee, "The Dis-Implementation of Prop 215," *O'Shaughnessy's,* Winter/Spring 2007.

320 **Their fate—and the fate of three dozen other:** Facing the prospects of a decade in federal prison, David Davidson left Cynthia Blake and became a fugitive. Blake pled guilty to a single felony and was sentenced to eighteen months in federal custody.

321 **amicus briefs supporting Raich and Monson:** Jeff Taylor, "Nullification Makes a Comeback—and Not Just on the Right," *The American Conservative,* July 1, 2010.

321 **a brief warning of terrible consequences:** Bob Egelko, "Medical Marijuana Before Supreme Court," *San Francisco Chronicle,* November 28, 2004.

321 **"any little island of lawful possession . . .":** Wishnia, "The Supremes Debate Medical Pot."

321 **"To the extent there is anything beneficial . . .":** Fred Gardner, "Ashcroft v. Raich."

322 **"the incentives for research and development . . .":** Fred Gardner, "Ashcroft v. Raich," *CounterPunch,* November 27–29, 2004.

322 **"would soften his heart . . .":** Gina Holland, "Court Questions Possible Abuse of Pot Laws," Associated Press, November 29, 2004.

323 **"strong arguments that they will suffer . . .":** *Oakland Tribune,* June 8, 2005.

323 **"It is our conclusion . . .":** Bill Lockyer, "Bulletin to all California Law Enforcement Agencies," June 22, 2005.

324 **"I consider cannabis my miracle":** Evelyn Nieves, "'I Really Consider Cannabis My Miracle,'" *Washington Post,* January 12, 2005.

324 **"Forcing Parker to choose . . .":** Drew Edwards, *West Coast Smoke,* p. 198.

324 **Exactly a year later, Canada:** Several other countries would also allow the use of marijuana for medical purposes, including the Netherlands (which began supplying cannabis through pharmacies to patients with a doctor's prescription in 2003), Israel, and Finland.

325 **"Leave it to the federal government . . .":** Russell Barth, letter to *North Island Gazette,* October 28, 2008.

325 **Murphy spewed racist venom:** Canuck in Booth, *Cannabis,* pp. 136–37.

326 **"Being an anti-prohibition advocate . . .":** Ian Kaufman, "American Hands in the Canadian Pot," *The Argus* (Seattle), September 26, 2009.

327 **"because there's no dealing . . .":** MarijuanaNews.com, March 28, 1999.

328 **"The continued prohibition of cannabis . . .":** Canadian Senate Special Committee on Illegal Drugs, *Cannabis: Our Position for a Canadian Public Policy,* Vols. 1 & II, September 2002.

328 **"on the freedom side of the cannabis curtain":** Martin A. Lee, "Reefer Refugees," *Razor,* April 5, 2005.

329 **Internet broadsheet:** MarijuanaNews.com.

329 **"Canada is a special problem . . .":** Author's interview with Richard Cowan.

329 **Canadian Association of Chiefs of Police:** Booth, *Cannabis,* p. 325.

329 **Walters criticized Ottawa:** "Marijuana and the Media," in Earleywine, *Pot Politics,* p. 145.

329 **Canadian mother searching:** Phillip Smith, "Canadian Mom Searching for Missing Daughter Denied Entry to US Over 21-Year-Old Drug Conviction," stopthedrugwar.org, June 7, 2007. A fifty-four-year-old British Columbia woman who suffered from multiple sclerosis was turned away at the border because she used medical marijuana.

330 **the nation's most lucrative agricultural crop:** "Cannabis Now Top Canadian Cash Crop," *NORML News,* October 6, 2005.

330 **"a significant blow . . .":** Jacob Sullum, "DOJ Denies Marc Emery's Transfer Request," Reason blog, April 27, 2011.

330 **Walters praised the regime change:** "US Drug Czar Praises Canada," *Packet & Times* (Ontario), February 23, 2007; and "US Shows Us What Not To Do," Victoria *Times Colonist* (British Columbia), December 13, 2006.

330 **Canadians toked in record numbers:** 16.8 percent of Canadians smoke marijuana, according to the 2007 World Drug Report by the United Nations Office on Drugs and Crime.

331 **"It boggles my mind . . .":** Patrick Lejtenyi, "Prohibition, Pot and Politics," *Mirror* (Montreal), April 24, 2008.

331 **"We have no money . . .":** "Medical Pot Users Want Health Canada to Butt Out," *Hamilton Spectator* (Ontario), June 18, 2007.

331 **patronizing compassion clubs:** As of mid-2011, about forty compassion clubs provided medical marijuana illegally to patients across Canada.

331 **"There isn't a single victim . . .":** Ian Mulgrew, "Prince of Pot's Sentence Reeks of Injustice and Mocks Our Sovereignty," *Vancouver Sun,* September 28, 2009.

331 **"To win this battle . . .":** Author's interview with Marc Emery.
332 **thousands of overdose deaths:** Martin Zimmerman, "Painkiller Maker to Pay Millions," *Los Angeles Times,* May 11, 2007.
332 **addicted to pain pills:** Tim Reiterman, "Prescription Overdose," *Los Angeles Times,* May 18, 2008.
332 **"Convict them and send them . . .":** Rush Limbaugh radio show, October 5, 1995.
333 **Highly addictive crystal meth:** Ellen Komp, "Hillary's Uninspiring Drug Reform Plan," AlterNet, April 14, 2008.
333 **"What I've never understood . . .":** Ben Wallace-Wells, "How America Lost the War on Drugs," *Rolling Stone,* December 13, 2007.
333 **"Marijuana is old news . . .":** Russell Goldman, "Is the Nation's Marijuana Policy Misguided?" ABC *World News Tonight,* August 2, 2007.
333 **the National Association of Counties:** Kate Zernike, "White House Searches for Balance in Drug Fight," *New York Times,* August 19, 2005.
333 **chastised Team Bush:** Kate Zernike, "Officials Across U.S. Describe Drug Woes," *New York Times,* July 6, 2005.
334 **"No retreat. No surrender":** San Diego Cannabis Support Group, "Steve McWilliams Remembered," July 11, 2008.
335 **"The purpose of the CSA . . .":** Jeff McDonald, "Medical Pot Dispensaries Promoted," *San Diego Union Tribune,* September 8, 2006.
336 **"a smoking gun":** California NORML Press Release, December 12, 2008.
337 **"is not a drug, it's a leaf":** Associated Press, "Governor Says Marijuana Is Not a Drug, 'It's a Leaf,'" *Los Angeles Times,* October 29, 2007.
337 **California prison system's health-care:** Daniel Abrahamson, "The Failed War on Drugs Is What's Packing California's Prisons," *San Jose Mercury News,* June 16, 2011. "In 2009, suicide rates in California's prisons were 80 percent higher than the national average, while roughly one inmate a week died because of constitutionally deficient medical care."
337 **a Gallup poll found:** Debra J. Saunders, "Hazy Thinking on Medical Marijuana," *San Francisco Chronicle,* May 13, 2008.
338 **The sky had not fallen:** Mitch Earleywine and Karen O'Keefe, "Marijuana Use by Young People: The Impact of State Medical Marijuana Laws," a report for the Marijuana Policy Project, September 2005; and S. Harper et al., "Do Medical Marijuana Laws Increase Marijuana Use? Replication Study and Extension," *Annals of Epidemiology* 22(3) (2012): 207–12.

CHAPTER 9: MELLOW MAYHEM

339 **Americans turning fifty-five:** Teresa E. Seeman et al., "Disability Trends Among Older Americans," *American Journal of Public Health* 100(1) (2010): 100–107.
339 **these government-approved drugs:** Julie Steenhuysen, "Dangerous Drug Combos Pose Risk for Elderly," Reuters, December 23, 2008.
339 **an explosion of interest in cannabis therapeutics:** In February 2006, the American Association of Retired Persons (AARP) announced the results of a national survey that it had commissioned about medical marijuana. Posted on AARP's website, the poll numbers indicated that seniors overwhelmingly supported an individual's right to use cannabis for therapeutic purposes with a doctor's approval. Seventy-two percent of Americans age forty-five and older were bullish on medical marijuana as a treatment option; one-third admitted that they had smoked it; and

55 percent said they would seek to obtain the herb for themselves or a loved one if they needed it. By the end of the decade, according to U.S. government statistics, nearly 10 percent of American men age fifty to fifty-four were using cannabis. In 2010, *Time* magazine, which had deemed medical marijuana as "legitimate" a few years earlier, reported that 5.1 percent of Americans age fifty-five to fifty-nine smoked pot regularly (*NORML News,* February 4, 2010; and *Time* cited in Gerald Ensley, "Legalizing Marijuana Is Just a Matter of Time," *Tallahassee Democrat,* March 24, 2010).

340 **a ninety-year-old great-grandfather:** Gillian Flaccus, "Medical Pot Collective Splits Retirement Community," Associated Press, June 9, 2011.

340 **"change in disease patterns":** Kate Pickett and Richard Wilkinson, *The Spirit Level,* p. 73.

340 **U.S. government-funded research has determined:** A. J. Hampson, M. Grimaldi, J. Axelrod, and D. Wink, "Cannabidiol and Delta-9-Tetrahydrocannabinol Are Neuroprotective Antioxidants," *Proceedings of the National Academy of Sciences USA* 95 (14) (1998): 8268–73.

340 **secured a patent titled:** "Cannabinoids as Antioxidants and Neuroprotectants," US Patent 6,630,507, awarded in October 2003.

341 **traditional Chinese medicine:** The world's oldest pharmacopoeia from China, the *Shen Nung Pen Ts'ao Ching,* listed more than a hundred ailments helped by "ma," medicinal hemp. Taoist adepts embraced "ma" as a means to achieve immortality.

341 **"If cannabis were unknown . . .":** "Reefer Madness," *The Economist,* April 27, 2006.

341 **"It's a sad commentary . . .":** Lester Grinspoon, "Marijuana as Wonder Drug," *Boston Globe,* March 1, 2007.

342 **an annotated bibliography:** Arno Hazenkamp and Franjo Grotenhermen, "Clinical Studies with Cannabis and Cannabinoids, 2005–2009," *O'Shaughnessy's,* Summer 2010.

342 **"We know more about marijuana . . .":** C. T. Revere, "Voters, Medical-Pot Okay May Yet Go Up in Smoke," *Tucson Citizen,* November 16, 1998.

342 **"We focused on illnesses . . .":** Victoria Colliver and Wyatt Buchanan, "Clinical Trials Show Medical Benefits of Pot," *San Francisco Chronicle,* February 18, 2010.

342 **results of four state-funded clinical trials:** Center for Medicinal Cannabis Research (CMRC), "Report to the Legislature and Governor of the State of California Presenting Findings Pursuant to California Senate Bill 847 Which Created the CMCR and Provided State Funding," February 11, 2010. Another CMCR study showed that vaporization, a cleaner way of inhaling phytocannabinoids, delivered the same levels of THC as smoking a joint. Because the federal government had no role in funding these studies, it was not incumbent upon NIDA to deny access to government-grown cannabis for research purposes.

342 **"It's still not part of the medical-school curriculum":** Fred Gardner, personal communication with author.

343 **What had California doctors:** "Medical Marijuana in California, 1996–2006," *O'Shaughnessy's,* Winter/Spring 2007.

343 **"The range of conditions . . .":** Ibid.

344 **slowed the development of Alzheimer's:** Belén G. Ramirez et al., "Prevention of Alzheimer's Disease Pathology by Cannabinoids: Neuroprotection Mediated by Blockade of Microglial Activation," *Journal of Neuroscience* 25(8) (2005): 1904–13.

344 **THC inhibits the enzyme:** L. M. Eubanks et al., "A Molecular Link Between the Active Component of Marijuana and Alzheimer's Disease Pathology," *Molecular Pharmacology* 3(6) (2006): 73–77.

344 **stimulated the growth of new brain cells:** Wen Jiang, Yun Zhang, Lan Xiao et al., "Cannabinoids Promote Embryonic and Adult Hippocampus Neurogenesis and Produce Anxiolytic- and Anti-Depressant-like Effects," *Journal of Clinical Investigation* 115(11) (2005): 3104–16.

344 **the brain's intrinsic repair mechanism:** "Contrary to dogma, the human brain does produce new nerve cells in adulthood," two neurobiologists reported in *Scientific American* in May 1999.

344 **Of all the so-called drugs of abuse:** Michael Smith, "Marijuana May Grow Neurons in the Brain," *MedPage Today*, October 14, 2005; and Susanne A. Wolf et al., "Cannabinoid Receptor CB1 Mediates Baseline and Activity-Induced Survival of New Neurons in Adult Hippocampal Neurogenesis," *Cell Communication and Signaling* 8 (2010): 12.

344 **"It might actually work":** Canwest News Service, "Marijuana May Stimulate Ageing Brains," December 1, 2008; and Gary Wenk, "Maintaining Memories with Marijuana," *Psychology Today* blog, July 14, 2010, in Werner, *Marijuana Gateway to Health*, p. 34. See also Y. Marchalant et al., "Cannabinoids Attenuate the Effects of Aging upon Neuroinflammation and Neurogenesis," *Neurobiology of Disease* 34(2) (2009): 300–307.

344 **A team of scientists at King's College:** M. B. Goncalves et al., "A Diacylglycerol Lipase-CB2 Cannabinoid Pathway Regulates Adult Subventricular Zone Neurogenesis in an Age-Dependent Manner," *Molecular and Cellular Neuroscience* 38(4) (2008): 526–36; M. J. Oudin et al., "Endocannabinoids Regulate the Migration of Subventricular Zone-Derived Neuroblasts in the Postnatal Brain," *Journal of Neuroscience* 31(11) (2011): 4000–4011. And M. J. Oudin et al., "DAGL-Dependent Endocannabinoid Signalling: Roles in Axonal Pathfinding, Synaptic Plasticity and Adult Neurogenesis," *European Journal of Neuroscience* 34(10) (2011): 1634–46.

345 **"We don't know why it works . . .":** Beth Burger, "Local Group Pushes for Medical Marijuana," Bradenton.com, February 21, 2008.

345 **Scientists at the Pacific Medical Center:** Raman et al., "Amyotrophic Lateral Sclerosis: Delayed Disease Progression in Mice by Treatment with a Cannabinoid," *Amyotrophic Lateral Sclerosis & Other Motor Neuron Disorders* 5(1) (2004): 33–39; see also Gregory T. Carter et al., "Cannabis and Amyotrophic Lateral Sclerosis: Hypothetical and Practical Applications, and a Call for Clinical Trials," *American Journal of Hospice & Palliative Medicine,* published online May 3, 2010.

345 **pretreatment with cannabinoids:** Tetsuya Nagayama et al., "Cannabinoids and Neuroprotection in Global and Focal Cerebral Ischemia and in Neuronal Cultures," *Journal of Neuroscience* 19(8) (1999): 2987–95; P. Pacher and G. Haskó, "Endocannabinoids and Cannabinoid Receptors in Ischaemia-Reperfusion Injury and Preconditioning," *British Journal of Pharmacology* 153(2) (2008): 252–62; and K. Hayakawa et al., "Cannabidiol Prevents a Post-Ischemic Injury Progressively Induced by Cerebral Ischemia Via a High-Mobility Group Box1-Inhibiting Mechanism," *Neuropharmacology* 55(8) (2008): 1280–86.

345 **"they have a direct antitumoral effect . . .":** In March 2011, the National Cancer Institute acknowledged on its website that cannabis is used "not only for symptom management but also for its possible antitumor effect." But a few days after

this statement was posted, the website was changed to read: "physicians caring for cancer patients who prescribed medicinal Cannabis predominantly do so for symptom management" while omitting any reference to marijuana's antitumoral effects.

346 **THC injections inhibited the growth:** A. E. Munson et al., "Anticancer Activity of Cannabinoids," *Journal of the National Cancer Institute* 55(3) (1975): 597–602; and Raymond Cushing, "Pot Shrinks Tumors; Government Knew in '74," AlterNet, May 31, 2000.

346 **Animal experiments conducted by:** Ismael Galve-Roperh et al., "Anti-Tumoral Action of Cannabinoids," *Nature Medicine* 6(3) (March 2000): 313–19.

346 **the first clinical trial:** M. Guzmán et al., "A Pilot Clinical Study of Delta(9)-Tetrahydrocannabinol in Patients with Recurrent Glioblastoma Multiforme," *British Journal of Cancer* (June 27, 2006) (electronic publication ahead of print).

346 **There is mounting evidence:** *Mini-Reviews in Medicinal Chemistry,* October 2005. See also Donald Abrams and Manuel Guzmán, "Cannabis and Cancer" in Donald Abrams and Andrew Weil, eds., *Integrative Oncology*; this chapter was also published in *O'Shaughnessy's,* Summer 2009.

346 **Prostate cancer:** *Cancer Research,* March 1, 2005.

347 **Colon cancer:** A. Greenhough et al., *International Journal of Cancer,* June 21, 2007.

347 **Pancreatic cancer:** *Journal of the American Association of Cancer Research*, July 2006, in NORML News Release, July 6, 2006.

347 **Breast cancer:** S. D. McAllister et al., "Pathways Mediating the Effects of Cannabidiol on the Reduction of Breast Cancer Cell Proliferation, Invasion, and Metastasis," *Breast Cancer Research and Treatment,* September 22, 2010 (Epub ahead of print).

347 **Cervical cancer:** Robert Ramer and Burkhard Hinz, "Inhibition of Cancer Cell Invasion by Cannabinoids Via Increased Expression of Tissue Inhibitor of Matrix Metalloproteinases-1," *Journal of the National Cancer Institute* 100(1) (2008): 59–69.

347 **Leukemia:** W. M. Liu et al., *Leukemia and Lymphoma* 30 (2008): 1–10.

347 **Stomach cancer:** J. M. Park et al., *Journal of Cellular Biochemistry,* February 10, 2011 (in press).

347 **Skin carcinoma:** M. Casanova et al., "Inhibition of Skin Tumor Growth and Angiogenesis *in vivo* by Activation of Cannabinoid Receptors," *Journal of Clinical Investigation* 111(1) (2003): 43–50.

347 **Cancer of the bile duct:** S. Leelawat et al., *Cancer Investigations* 28(4) (2010): 357–63.

347 **Lymphoma, Hodgkin's, and Kaposi's sarcoma:** M. Medveczky et al., "Delta-9 Tetrahydrocannabinol (THC) Inhibits Lytic Replication of Gamma Oncogenic Herpesviruses *in vitro,*" *BMC Medicine* 2 (2004): 34.

348 **Liver cancer:** M. Giuliano et al., *Biochimie,* November 27, 2008 (electronic publication ahead of print).

348 **Lung cancer:** Angela Zimm, "Marijuana Stops Growth of Lung Cancer Tumors in Mice," Bloomberg News, April 17, 2007.

348 **"Numerous studies have shown . . .":** NIDA InfoFacts: Marijuana," www.nida.nih.gov/infofacts/marijuana.html.

348 **"We hypothesized that there would be . . .":** Marc Kaufman, "Study Finds No Cancer-Marijuana Connection," *Washington Post,* May 26, 2006.

348 **Tashkin presented his findings:** "Study Finds No Link Between Marijuana Use and Lung Cancer," *ScienceDaily,* May 26, 2006.

348 **UCLA compared the lung health:** M. Hashibe et al., "Marijuana Use and the Risk of Lung and Upper Aerodigestive Tract Cancers: Results of a Population-Based Case-Control Study," *Cancer Epidemiology, Biomarkers and Prevention* 15 (2006): 1829–34.

348 **researchers from the Kaiser Permanente HMO:** S. Sidney et al., "Marijuana Use and Cancer Incidence," *Cancer Causes and Control* 8 (1997): 722–28. See also M. Hashibe et al., "Epidemiologic Review of Marijuana Use and Cancer Risk," *Alcohol* 35(3) (2005): 265–75; and Amanda Chen et al., "Hypothesizing That Marijuana Smokers Are at a Significantly Lower Risk of Carcinogenicity Relative to Tobacco-Non-Marijuana Smokers: Evidence Based on Statistical Reevaluation of Current Literature," *Journal of Psychoactive Drugs* (September 2008).

349 **A 2002 Johns Hopkins medical school study:** M. Hashibe et al., "Marijuana Smoking and Head and Neck Cancer," *Journal of Clinical Pharmacology* 42 (2002): 103S–107S.

349 **Ten years later, research data:** Mark J. Pletcher, M.D. et al., "Association Between Marijuana Exposure and Pulmonary Function Over 20 Years," *Journal of the American Medical Association* 307(2) (2012): 173–81.

349 **Despite several U.S. government-sponsored studies:** In January 2008, a Reuters headline screamed: "Cannabis Bigger Cancer Risk Than Tobacco." *Fox News* blustered: "Smoking one joint is equivalent to 20 cigarettes, study says." An Australian broadcast network warned of a pending worldwide "cannabis cancer 'epidemic.'" These sensational stories were based on a small, methodologically flawed study by New Zealand researchers who never bothered to answer or even ask the obvious question—If marijuana causes cancer, where are all the bodies? (Fred Gardner, "The Greatest Story Never Told," *O'Shaughnessy's,* Summer 2009; Paul Armentano, "Outrageous Anti-Pot Lies," AlterNet, March 10, 2008; S. Aldington et al., "Cannabis Use and Risk of Lung Cancer," *European Respiratory Journal* 31[1] [2008]: 280–86; and R. A. Sewell et al., "Doubts about the Role of Cannabis in Causing Lung Cancer," *European Respiratory Journal* 32[3] [2008]: 815–16).

349 **"They raided and pillaged":** Author's interview with JoAnna LaForce.

350 **"We practice civil disobedience . . .":** Ibid.

350 **"I saw the value . . .":** David Samuels, "Dr. Kush," *New Yorker,* July 28, 2008.

350 **"In the court of public opinion . . .":** Sonya Sorich, "Pop Culture Can Make Marijuana's Dangers Harder for Students to Learn," *Ledger-Enquirer* (Columbus, GA), October 21, 2008.

351 ***Newsweek* called Los Angeles:** Matthew Philips, "The Wild West of Weed," *Newsweek,* October 14, 2009. http://www.thedailybeast.com/newsweek/2009/10/14/the-wild-west-of-weed.html.

351 **Hundreds of medical-cannabis dispensaries:** Brian Doherty, "How Los Angeles Became the 'Wild West' of Medical Marijuana," *Reason,* AlterNet, April 14, 2010.

351 **the Arts District Healing Center in LA:** "DEA Launches Statewide Offensive Against Medical Cannabis Dispensaries," Cal *NORML Newsletter,* December 2007.

352 **New Mexico became the twelfth U.S. state:** In 2009, New Mexico added PTSD to the list of medical conditions covered by its State Medical Cannabis Program.

352 **"The medical-marijuana business is not . . .":** Author's interview with Michael Backes.

352 **Chief Charlie Beck:** Doherty, "How Los Angeles Became the 'Wild West' of Medical Marijuana."

353 **three-quarters of LA residents:** Steve Elliott, "Chronic City: L.A. Panels Reject Ban on Medical Marijuana Sales," *SF Weekly* Blog, November 17, 2009.

354 **"Whenever a patient comes . . .":** Roger Parloff, "How Pot Became Legal," *Fortune,* September 28, 2009.

355 **It was a nasty little secret:** Josh Harkinson, "Which Dangerous Toxins Are in Your Marijuana?" AlterNet, posted February 4, 2011.

355 **By 2009, Harborside employed:** Solomon Moore, "Los Angeles Prepares for Clash Over Marijuana," *New York Times,* October 17, 2009.

355 **"It's a great growth industry":** *NPR Marketplace,* June 22, 2009.

355 **"Anybody who opens a dispensary . . .":** Ryan Grim, *This Is Your Country on Drugs,* p. 216.

356 **they owed Uncle Sam:** In 2011, the IRS informed Harborside that it owed $3 million in back taxes.

356 **"We do not deserve to have . . .":** *Macon Telegraph,* March 31, 2011.

356 **"I was trying to figure out . . .":** John Hoeffel, "Proposition 19 Backer Is Committed to His Cause," *Los Angeles Times,* October 4, 2010.

357 **"the great California weed rush":** Vanessa Grigoriadis, "The Great California Weed Rush," *Rolling Stone,* February 22, 2007.

357 **The market for medicinal cannabis:** Dana Mattioli, "High Hopes at Miracle-Gro in Medical Marijuana Field," *Wall Street Journal,* June 14, 2011.

357 **"The younger generation doesn't understand . . .":** Author's interview with Rick Pfrommer.

358 **"If there is any future . . .":** Joy et al., eds., *Marijuana and Medicine: Assessing the Science Base,* p. 178.

358 **developed a rectal suppository:** L. John Cummins, "Research Center Looks for Profit Amid Pharmaceutical Advances," Associated Press, March 29, 1999; and Mark Robichaux, "Researchers Aim to Develop Marijuana Without the High," *Wall Street Journal,* February 28, 2001.

359 **the street drug Spice:** John Huffman's presentation at the International Cannabinoid Research Society conference, Lund, Sweden, July 2010.

359 **Approved by European regulators:** Fred Gardner, "Adieu, Rimonabant," *O'Shaughnessy's,* Summer 2009.

359 **Rimonabant's side effects:** R. Christensen et al., "Efficacy and Safety of the Weight-Loss Drug Rimonabant: A Meta-Analysis of Randomised Trials," *Lancet* 370(9600) (2007): 1706–13. *Lancet* linked Rimonabant to "severe adverse psychiatric effects," including two suicides. See also Fabricio A. Moreira and José Crippa, "The Psychiatric Side-Effects of Rimonabant," *Revista Brasileira de Psiquiatria* 31(2) (2009): 145–53.

359 **"One of the major functions . . .":** Paul Armentano "So Much for Big Pharma's 'Anti-pot' Pill," AlterNet, June 15, 2007.

360 **NIDA officials were keen on:** Fred Gardner, "California MJ Research Program Stretches Mandate to Hold 'Cannabinoid Therapeutics' Event in Italy," *O'Shaughnessy's,* Autumn 2004.

360 **The administration of 40 milligrams of Rimonabant:** "Oral Pill Arrests Marijuana 'High,' Study Says," NORML Press Release, July 19, 2007.

360 **a big plus, from NIDA's perspective:** Fred Gardner, "The Year of the Antagonist," *CounterPunch*, July 24–25, 2004.

360 **"I am an oncologist . . .":** *O'Shaughnessy's*, Autumn 2005.

360 **molecules that stimulate CB-2 receptors:** See special issue on the CB-2 receptor in the *British Journal of Pharmacology*, January 8, 2008.

360 **"demonstrated efficacy in preclinical models":** Michael Meyer at CB-2 Cannabinoid Receptors: New Vistas Conference in Banff, Canada, May 31–June 2, 2007.

361 **"are localized predominantly . . .":** Martin A. Lee, "CB2-Receptor Research May Lead to Drugs That Heal Without the High," *O'Shaughnessy's*, Winter/Spring 2008.

361 **new developments regarding FAAH inhibitors:** Martin A. Lee, "Enzymes and the Endocannabinoid System," *O'Shaughnessy's*, Summer 2009; and Jean Marx, "Drugs Inspired by a Drug," *Science* 311(5759) (2006): 322–25.

361 **Other studies indicated:** Stefania Petrosino and Vincenzo Di Marzo, "FAAH and MAGL Inhibitors: Therapeutic Opportunities from Regulating Endocannabinoid Levels," *Current Opinion in Investigational Drugs* 11(1) (2010): 51–62; S. Shahidi et al., "Behavioral Effects of Fatty Acid Amide Hydrolase Inhibition on Morphine Withdrawal Symptoms," *Brain Research Bulletin* 86(1–2) (2001): 118–22. D. Ramesh et al., "Blockade of Endocannabinoid Hydrolytic Enzymes Attenuates Precipitated Opioid Withdrawal Symptoms in Mice," *Journal of Pharmacology and Experimental Therapeutics* 339(1) (2011): 173–85; and Jean Marx, "Drugs Inspired by a Drug," *Science* 311(5759) (2006): 322–25.

361 **A team of Italian researchers:** T. Bisogno et al., "Molecular Targets for Cannabidiol and Its Synthetic Analogues: Effect on Vanilloid VR1 Receptors and on the Cellular Uptake and Enzymatic Hydrolysis of Anandamide," *British Journal of Pharmacology* 134(4) (2001): 845–52.

361 **CBD has little binding affinity:** Martin A. Lee, "CBD: How It Works," *O'Shaughnessy's*, Summer 2011; http://www.projectcbd.org/CBDiary.html#Apr20.11.

362 **CBD activates a particular type:** Ethan B. Russo et al., "Agonistic Properties of Cannabidiol at 5-HT1a Receptors," *Neurochemical Research* 30(8) (2005): 1037–43.

362 **Mechoulam . . . elucidated the chemical structure:** R. Mechoulam and Y. Shvo "Hashish-I. The Structure of Cannabidiol," *Tetrahedron* 19 (1963): 2073–78. Roger Adams had published a provisional structure of cannabidiol in 1942 (R. Adams, "Marijuana," *Bulletin of the New York Academy of Medicine* 18 (1942): 705–30, reprinted in Mikuriya, ed., *Marijuana: Medical Papers*, pp. 345–74).

362 **the extraordinary antioxidant and neuroprotective qualities:** A. J. Hampson et al., "Cannabidiol and Delta-9-Tetrahydrocannabinol Are Neuroprotective Antioxidants," *Proceedings of the National Academy of Sciences USA* 95(14) (1998): 8268–73.

362 **CBD blocked the formation:** For example, T. Iuvone et al., "Neuroprotective Effect of Cannabidiol, a Non-Psychoactive Component from *Cannabis sativa*, on Beta-Amyloid-Induced Toxicity in PC12 Cells," *Journal of Neurochemistry* 89(1) (2004): 134–41.

362 **stimulated adult brain cell growth:** S. A. Wolf et al., "Cannabinoid Receptor CB1 Mediates Baseline and Activity-Induced Survival of New Neurons in Adult Hippocampal Neurogenesis," *Cell Communication and Signaling* 8 (2010): 12.

362 **CBD mitigated THC-induced anxiety:** P. Fusar-Poli et al., "Distinct Effects of Delta 9-Tetrahydrocannabinol and Cannabidiol on Neural Activation During

Emotional Processing," *Archives of General Psychiatry* 66(1) (2009): 95–105; J. A. Crippa et al., "Neural Basis of Anxiolytic Effects of Cannabidiol (CBD) in Generalized Social Anxiety Disorder: A Preliminary Report," *Journal of Psychopharmacology* 25(1) (2011): 12–30; and A. W. Zuardi et al., "Action of Cannabidiol on the Anxiety and Other Effects Produced by Delta 9-THC in Normal Subjects," *Psychopharmacology* 76(3) (1982): 245–50.

362 **They work together synergistically:** Ethan Russo and Geoffrey W. Guy, "A Tale of Two Cannabinoids: The Therapeutic Rationale for Combining Tetrahydrocannabinol and Cannabidiol," *Medical Hypotheses* 66 (2006): 234–46. A randomized clinical trial of 177 subjects in Great Britain indicated that GW Pharmaceuticals' Sativex spray, a whole-plant formula with a one-to-one mix of CBD and THC, provided greater relief from cancer pain than THC alone.

362 **cannabidiol reduces human breast cancer:** S. D. McAllister et al., "Pathways Mediating the Effects of Cannabidiol on the Reduction of Breast Cancer Cell Proliferation, Invasion, and Metastasis," *Breast Cancer Research and Treatment* (September 22, 2010) (Epub ahead of print).

362 **CBD strengthened the inhibitory effect of THC:** J. P. Marcu et al., "Cannabidiol Enhances the Inhibitory Effects of Delta 9-Tetrahydrocannabinol on Human Glioblastoma Cell Proliferation and Survival," *Molecular Cancer Therapeutics* 9(1) (2010): 180–89; Epub January 6, 2010.

363 **"offers hope of a non-toxic therapy":** "Cannabis Compound 'Halts Cancer,'" BBC News, November 19, 2007.

363 **suppress cardiac arrhythmias:** S. K. Walsh et al., "Acute Administration of Cannabidiol *in vivo* Suppresses Ischaemia-Induced Cardiac Arrhythmias and Reduces Infarct Size When Given at Reperfusion," *British Journal of Pharmacology* 160(5) (2010): 1234–42.

363 **prevent the onset of diabetes:** In an experiment conducted at Hadassah University Hospital in Jerusalem, CBD dramatically reduced the incidence of diabetes in mice. L. Weiss et al., "Cannabidiol Lowers Incidence of Diabetes in Non-Obese Diabetic Mice," *Autoimmunity* 39(2) (2006): 143–51.

363 **"Our results suggest that CBD . . .":** S. Dirikoc et al., "Nonpsychoactive Cannabidiol Prevents Prion Accumulation and Protects Neurons Against Prion Toxicity," *Journal of Neuroscience* 27(36) (2007): 9537–44. "When combined with its ability to target the brain and its basic lack of toxic side effects, CBD may represent a promising new anti-prion drug," the researchers concluded.

363 **Infectious, antibiotic-resistant bacteria:** Giovanni Appendino of the University of the Eastern Piedmont and his team studied the five most common cannabinoids—THC, CBD, CBG (cannabigerol), CBC (cannabichromene), and CBN (cannabinol). All were found to halt the spread of antibiotic-resistant bacterial strains. See G. Appendino et al., "Antibacterial Cannabinoids from *Cannabis sativa*: A Structure-Activity Study," *Journal of Natural Products* 71(8) (2008): 1427–30.

364 **THC content was found to have increased:** Z. Mehmedic et al., "Potency Trends of Delta 9-THC and Other Cannabinoids in Confiscated Cannabis Preparations from 1993 to 2008," *Journal of Forensic Sciences* 55(5) (2010): 1209–17.

364 **The dearth of CBD-rich cannabis:** J. R. Burgdorf et al., "Heterogeneity in the Composition of Marijuana Seized in California," *Drug and Alcohol Dependence* 117(1) (2011): 59–61.

365 **"really take off once California growers . . .":** "Continuing Mutual Education," *O'Shaughnessy's,* Autumn 2005.

365 **"I am seeing many older patients . . .":** Fred Gardner, "Doctors to Study Effectiveness of CBD," *O'Shaughnessy's,* Summer 2010.

366 **In addition to THC and CBD:** Among the dozens of so-called minor cannabinoids are cannabigerol (CBG), cannabichromene (CBC), tetrahydrocannabivarin (THCV), cannabidivarin (CBDV), tetrahydrocannabinolic acid (THCA), and cannabidiolic acid (CBDA).

366 **an overall "entourage effect":** The phrase "entourage effect" was introduced in a 1998 paper by the Israeli scientists S. Ben-Shabat et al., "An Entourage Effect: Inactive Endogenous Fatty Acid Glycerol Esters Enhance 2-Arachidonoyl-Glycerol Cannabinoid Activity," *European Journal of Pharmacology* 353(1) (1998): 23–31.

366 **the whole-plant "synergistic shotgun":** John McPartland, "A Molecular View of the Synergistic Shotgun," presentation at Patients Out of Time conference, April 16, 2010, in Providence, Rhode Island.

366 **"a dialectical plant with opposite effects":** Fred Gardner, personal communication with the author.

366 **These fragrant essential oils:** For a review of the medicinal properties of terpenes, see Ethan Russo, "Taming THC: Potential Cannabis Synergy and Phytocannabinoid-Terpenoid Entourage Effects," *British Journal of Pharmacology* 163(7) (2011): 1344–64.

367 **"You want to get as pure a medication . . .":** Chapkis and Webb, *Dying to Get High,* p. 71.

367 **Roman temple at Baalbek:** Matthews, *Cannabis Culture,* pp. 4–5.

368 **Foruli viewed wine as the drink of the rich:** C. Stefanis et al., "Sociocultural and Epidemiological Aspects of Hashish Use in Greece," in Vera Rubin, *Cannabis and Culture,* p. 309.

368 **Growing cannabis for use:** Franz Rosenthal, *The Herb,* p. 132.

369 **Muslim leaders recognized:** Ibid., p. 105.

369 **the alcohol industry funds organizations:** Ryan Grim, "California Pot Initiative Opposed by Beer Industry," *Huffington Post,* September 21, 2010.

369 **Alcohol is a pivotal factor:** Steve Fox et al., *Marijuana Is Safer,* pp. 27–29.

369 **"In my era, everybody smoked . . .":** David Guard, "This Week in History," July 1, 1998, http://stopthedrugwar.org/taxonomy/term/100?page=17.

369 **the World Health Organization published:** *New Scientist,* November 21, 1998.

369 **In the United States, an estimated:** Maia Szalavitz, "The Binge and the Bias," AlterNet, April 19, 2005; and Ian Ross, "Fifth of 10- to 15-Year-Olds 'Get Drunk Regularly,'" *Independent* (UK), November 16, 2007.

370 **the critical role that the endocannabinoid system:** Martin A. Lee, "Alcoholism and the Endocannabinoid System," *O'Shaughnessy's,* Summer 2010.

370 **a basic function of the endocannabinoid system:** C. Pope, R. Mechoulam, and L. Parsons, "Endocannabinoid Signaling in Neurotoxicity and Neuroprotection," *Neurotoxicology* 31(5) (2010): 562–71.

370 **"protect the human brain against . . .":** J. Jacobus et al., "White Matter Integrity in Adolescents with Histories of Marijuana Use and Binge Drinking," *Neurotoxicology and Teratology* 31(6) (2009): 349–55; Epub July 23, 2009.

371 **lower levels of alcoholism in Jamaica:** Rubin and Comitas, *Ganja in Jamaica,*

pp. 149, 155; and Michael H. Beaubrun, "Cannabis or Alcohol: The Jamaican Experience," in Vera Rubin, *Cannabis and Culture,* p. 490.

371 **treatment of drug and alcohol addiction:** J. B. Mattison, M.D., "Cannabis Indica as an Anodyne and Hypnotic," *St. Louis Medical and Surgical Journal* 61(5) (November 1891), reprinted in Mikuriya, ed., *Marijuana,* pp. 265–71.

371 **"was useful in alleviation or elimination . . .":** Roger Adams, M.D., "Marijuana," in Mikuriya, ed., *Marijuana,* pp. 345–74.

371 **"Although medicinal use of cannabis by alcoholics . . .":** Tod Mikuriya, M.D., "Cannabis as a Substitute for Alcohol," *O'Shaughnessy's,* Summer 2003.

372 **In a cruel twist of fate:** Gene Johnson, "Medical Marijuana Patients Face Transplant Hurdles," Associated Press, April 26, 2008; Carol M. Ostrom, "Is Medical-Marijuana Use Reason to Deny Someone an Organ Transplant?" *Seattle Times,* May 3, 2008; and Anna Gorman, "Medical Marijuana Jeopardizes Liver Transplant," *Los Angeles Times,* December 3, 2011.

372 **"suppress the immunity reaction . . .":** "Cancer Curb Is Studied," *Washington Post,* August 18, 1974, cited in Raymond Cushing, "Pot Shrinks Tumors; Government Knew in '74," AlterNet, May 31, 2000. The original report by A. E. Munson et al., "Anticancer Activity of Cannabinids," was published in the *Journal of the National Cancer Institute* 55 (September 1975): 597.

373 **"Marijuana is a safer intoxicant for partying . . .":** Author's interview with Mason Tvert.

374 **what the law allowed:** The Colorado law allows marijuana use by patients with at least one of eight debilitating conditions, including AIDS, cancer, and chronic pain.

374 **the fastest-growing medicinal cannabis market:** By the end of 2011, there were 667 cannabis dispensaries, 926 grow-ops, and 246 infused-product manufacturers operating under Colorado law, according to figures from the state revenue department. The United Food and Commercial Workers Union recruited hundreds of new members from the medical-marijuana industry in Colorado and California.

374 **"should not focus resources . . .":** David W. Ogden, "Memorandum for Selected United State Attorneys on Investigations and Prosecutions in States Authorizing the Medical Use of Marijuana," October 19, 2009, http://blogs.usdoj.gov/blog/archives/192.

374 **"that give prosecutors broad discretion . . .":** Bob Egelko, "Medical-Pot Backers React to New Obama Policy," *San Francisco Chronicle,* October 20, 2009.

375 **"The Justice Department going after sick . . .":** Peter Schrag, "Obama Sends Mixed Messages on Marijuana," *Sacramento Bee,* December 9, 2008.

375 **As deputy attorney general under Clinton:** Malcolm Maclachian, "CA Medical Marijuana Advocates Concerned About Obama Appointments," *Capitol Weekly* (Sacramento), November 20, 2008.

376 **"We're not at war with people . . .":** Gary Fields, "White House Czar Calls for End to 'War on Drugs,'" *Wall Street Journal,* May 14, 2009.

376 **"Marijuana is where the money is":** Justin Scheck, "Strapped Police Run on Fumes, and Federal Pot-Fighting Cash," *Wall Street Journal,* July 3, 2010.

377 **"raking in what is estimated . . .":** CNBC, "Marijuana Inc: Inside America's Pot Industry," January 22, 2009.

377 **more than $105 million in tax revenues:** Marc Lifsher, "State to Collect Sales Tax on Medical Marijuana," *Los Angeles Times,* February 24, 2011.

377 **one million doctor-recommended medical users:** Ray Stern, "In a Strange About-

face, the President Tries to Hack Medical Marijuana Off at the Knees," *Phoenix New Times,* October 20, 2011.

377 **Californians consumed 500 tons:** Guy Kovner, "2 Sides of Pot Debate," *Press Democrat* (Santa Rosa), October 17, 2010.

377 **"A policy that prohibits marijuana . . .":** Jeffrey Miron, "A Cost-Benefit Analysis of Legalizing Marijuana," in Holland, ed., *The Pot Book,* p. 453; and Jeffrey Miron, "The Budgetary Implications of Marijuana Prohibition," published by the Marijuana Policy Project.

377 **Endorsed by five hundred economists:** Jeffrey Miron, "A Cost-Benefit Analysis," in Holland, ed., *The Pot Book,* p. 453.

378 **Miron maintained that federal officials:** Sarah Husk, "Economist Speaks Against 'Just Say No,'" *Brown Daily Herald,* September 25, 2008.

378 **"Proposition 19 is about eliminating . . .":** Patrick McGreevy, "NAACP Leader's Ouster Is Sought," *Los Angeles Times,* July 8, 2010.

378 **"In every one of the 25 largest counties . . .":** Harry G. Levine et al., "Targeting Blacks for Marijuana: Possession Arrests of African Americans in California, 2004–8," published by the Drug Policy Alliance.

379 **"except prisons full of the wrong people":** Wooldridge, letter to *Wall Street Journal,* March 7, 2006.

379 **"Proposition 19 will tax and control marijuana . . .":** http://www.youtube.com/watch?v=L_oIpIyZRu0.

379 **"Prop. 19 would allow big-rig drivers . . .":** John Hoeffel, "Prop. 19 Battle Shifts to TV, Radio," *Los Angeles Times,* October 26, 2010.

380 **Insinuations that stoned drivers:** Earleywine, *Understanding Marijuana,* p. 211.

380 **study by the Institute for the Study of Labor:** Stephen C. Webster, "Study: Legalizing Medical Marijuana Reduces Traffic Fatalities," AlterNet, November 29, 2011.

380 **"There's no earthly reason . . .":** Duane W. Gang and Jim Miller, "Efforts to Legalize Pot Meet Stiff Resistance," *Press-Enterprise* (Riverside, CA), September 12, 2009.

380 **law enforcement and alcohol producers were allied:** Ryan Grim, "California Pot Initiative Opposed by Beer Industry," *Huffington Post,* September 21, 2010.

380 **"make California a laughingstock":** Arnold Schwarzenegger, "SEIU Is Off-Base on Legalizing Pot," *Los Angeles Times,* September 24, 2010.

380 **"Legalization is not in the president's vocabulary . . .":** Marcus Wohlsen, "Pot Legalization Gains Momentum in California," Yahoo! News, Associated Press, October 7, 2009.

380 **Holder denounced Proposition 19:** Evan Perez, "U.S. Casts Vote Against Pot," *Wall Street Journal,* October 16, 2010.

380 **"has a high potential for abuse . . .":** DEA, "Denial of Petition to Initiate Proceedings to Reschedule Marijuana," *Federal Register* 76(131) (Friday, July 8, 2011): 40552–89.

381 **"We're going to be ruined":** Geluardi, *Cannabiz,* p. 167.

381 **"Save Humboldt County . . .":** Ibid., p. 154.

381 **"I got into this to just legalize it . . .":** John Gravois, "The Closing of the Marijuana Frontier," *Washington Monthly,* November–December 2010.

381 **"For a lot of people . . .":** Jesse McKinley, "Push to Legalize Marijuana Gains Ground in California," *New York Times,* October 27, 2010.

382 **"We're past the days":** David Segal, "When Capitalism Meets Cannabis," *New York Times,* June 28, 2010.

382 **"the corporatization of cannabis":** Author's interview with Valerie Corral.

382 **"Taxes? We shouldn't pay taxes":** Geluardi, *Cannabiz,* p. 139.

383 ***"Kids at play, keep the pot away!":*** Eric Carpenter, "Neighbors Protest Marijuana Dispensary," *Orange County Register,* February 12, 2011.

383 **medical-marijuana dispensaries were not associated:** Americans for Safe Access, "Impact of Dispensaries and Regulations on Communities," updated June 2011, http://www.safeaccessnow.org/article.php?id=4339.

383 **"the idea that banning drugs . . .":** Clare Wilson, "Better World: Legalise Drugs," *NewScientist,* September 10, 2009.

383 **no explosion of cannabis consumption:** Mitch Earleywine and Karen O'Keefe, "Marijuana Use by Young People: The Impact of State Medical Marijuana Laws," a report for the Marijuana Policy Project, September 2005.

383 **ubiquitous black-market marijuana:** "We couldn't make this drug any more available if we tried," said retired Orange County Superior Court judge James Gray, an adamant drug-war critic, in Alison Stateman, "Can Marijuana Help Rescue California's Economy?" *Time,* March 13, 2009.

383 **Nearly half of America's teenagers:** *Science Daily* cited in Linda Stahl, "Teenagers and Marijuana," *Courier-Journal* (Louisville, KY), July 10, 2008. NIDA's 2011 Monitoring the Future Survey indicated that pot smoking was more common among tenth graders than cigarette smoking.

384 **a 2007 Swiss study:** J. C. Suris et al., "Some Go Without a Cigarette: Characteristics of Cannabis Users Who Have Never Smoked Tobacco," *Archives of Pediatrics & Adolescent Medicine* 161(11) (2007): 1042–47.

384 **above-average intelligence among youth:** J. White and G. David Batty, "Intelligence Across Childhood in Relation to Illegal Drug Use in Adulthood: 1970 British Cohort Study," *Journal of Epidemiology and Community Health* (November 14, 2011); and "Brightest Kids 'More Likely to Take Drugs,'" *New Zealand Herald,* November 17, 2011.

384 **"excessive preoccupation with social causes . . .":** Julian Borger, "Is Your Teenager Concerned about Inequality and Pollution? Call a Drug Counsellor," *The Guardian* (UK), October 8, 1998.

384 **2005 study of parental attitudes:** Larry McShane, "Parental Attitudes Toward Drugs Increasingly Mellow," Associated Press, February 22, 2005.

384 **Chronic-pain patients reported:** Jeffrey Hergenrather, "Prescribing Cannabis in California," in Holland, ed., *The Pot Book,* p. 419.

384 **film star Johnny Depp:** *GQ,* October 2003.

384 **"I have nothing to hide":** *Film Review,* June 2001.

385 **"It took some creative acting:** Otis L. Sanford, "Cops Posing as Kids Just Does Not Seem Right," *Commercial Appeal* (Memphis, TN), December 21, 2008.

385 **School districts in several states paid:** "Oregon Schools Offer Students $1000 Incentive to Snitch on Classmates," NORML News Release, February 4, 1999.

385 **According to a 2006 national assessment:** John W. Cox, "Pot Is Part of Life," *Miami Herald,* June 4, 2007.

385 **"Numerous deleterious consequences . . .":** Volkow in Sanjay Gupta, "Why I Would Vote No on Pot," *Time,* November 6, 2006.

386 **"Most people who drink alcohol . . .":** "What Is the Long-Term Effect of Cannabis?" *The Observer* (UK), August 26, 2007.

387 **If given the opportunity to self-administer THC:** Robert J. MacCoun and Peter Reuter, *Drug War Heresies*, p. 349.

387 **"Marijuana is indisputably reinforcing . . .":** Joy et al., eds., *Marijuana and Medicine*, p. 87. By contrast, the Institute of Medicine reported that 32 percent of tobacco users, 23 percent of heroin users, 17 percent of cocaine users, and 15 percent of alcohol users meet the criteria for "drug dependence."

387 **Most people entering reefer rehab:** The Substance Abuse and Mental Health Services Administration (SAMHSA), "Substance Abuse Treatment Admissions Referred by the Criminal Justice System," August 13, 2009, cited in "Pot Arrests Responsible for Majority of Marijuana Treatment Referrals," NORML News Release, October 22, 2009.

387 **Of the estimated 288,000 people:** Substance Abuse and Mental Health Services Administration (SAMHSA), Office of Applied Studies. *Treatment Episode Data Set (TEDS) Highlights—2007 National Admissions to Substance Abuse Treatment Services*, OAS Series #S-45, HHS Publication No. (SMA) 09–4360, cited in NORML News Release, March 26, 2009.

387 **"to support research studies that focus . . .":** Paul Armentano, "The Feds Are Addicted to Pot—Even If You Aren't," AlterNet, November 30, 2009.

388 **Scientists have linked a mutated version:** Jack C. Sipe et al., "A Missense Mutation in Human Fatty Acid Amide Hydrolase Associated with Problem Drug Use," *Proceedings of the National Academy of Sciences USA* 99(12) (2002): 8394–99; and D. Proudnikov et al., "Association of Polymorphisms of the Cannabinoid Receptor (*CNR1*) and Fatty Acid Amide Hydrolase (*FAAH*) Genes with Heroin Addiction: Impact of Long Repeats of *CNR1*," *Pharmacogenomics Journal* 10(3) (2010): 232–42. This same FAAH gene polymorphism, according to German researchers, is often present in patients with obesity and irritable bowel disease; see Timo D. Müller et al., "Mutation Screen and Association Studies for the Fatty Acid Amide (FAAH) Gene and Early Onset and Adult Obesity," *BMC Medical Genetics* (January 1, 2010). See also Martin A. Lee, "Alcoholism and the Endocannabinoid System," *O'Shaughnessy's*, Summer 2010.

388 **Brazilian scientists reported:** José Crippa, M.D., "Cannabidiol for the Treatment of Neuropsychiatric Disorders: Past, Present and Future," presentation at the Patients Out of Time conference, April 17, 2010, Providence, Rhode Island.

388 **CBD has antipsychotic properties and reduces:** See, for example, Celia J. A. Morgan and H. Valerie Curran, "Effects of Cannabidiol on Schizophrenia-like Symptoms in People Who Use Cannabis," *British Journal of Psychiatry* 192(4) (2008): 306–7; and A. Zuardi et al., "Cannabidiol for the Treatment of Psychosis in Parkinson's Disease," *Journal of Psychopharmacology* 23(8) (2009): 979–83 (Epub November 21, 2008).

388 **Schizophrenics are more likely to smoke pot:** N. Francoeur and C. Baker, "Attraction to Cannabis Among Men with Schizophrenia: A Phenomenological Study," *Canadian Journal of Nursing Research* 42(1) (2010): 132–49. See also G. Schwarcz et al., "Synthetic Delta-9-Tetrahydrocannabinol (Dronabinol) Can Improve the Symptoms of Schizophrenia," *Journal of Clinical Psychopharmacology* 29(3) (2009): 255–58; and Franjo Grotenhermen, "THC Can Improve Symptoms of Schizophrenia," *Cannabinoids* 4(4) (2009): 1–3. Doctors at a hospital in Izmir, Turkey, reported on a case study in which cannabis effectively relieved the tardive dyskine-

sia (involuntary movements) of schizophrenics, a side effect of standard antipsychotics (Y. Beckmann et al., "Tardive Dystonia and the Use of Cannabis," *Türkiye Psikiyatri Derneği* 21[1] [2010]: 90–91).

389 **evidence did not support a causal link:** See, for example, M. Frisher et al., "Assessing the Impact of Cannabis Use on Trends in Diagnosed Schizophrenia in the United Kingdom from 1996 to 2005," *Schizophrenia Research* 113(2–3) (2009): 123–28 (Epub June 26, 2009).

389 **"Marihuana will not produce psychosis de novo . . .":** S. Allentuck and K. M. Bowman, "The Psychiatric Aspects of Marihuana Intoxication," *American Journal of Psychiatry* 99 (1942): 248.

389 **Mikuriya felt that cannabis should be considered:** Tod Mikuriya, M.D., "Cannabis as a First-Line Treatment for Childhood Mental Disorders," *O'Shaughnessy's*, Winter/Spring 2008.

389 **"is an alternative for parents who have exhausted . . .":** Author's interview with Meiko Hester-Perez; and Scott Martindale, "Marijuana Advocates Flock to Anaheim Expo," *Orange County Register,* August 29, 2010.

390 **"high schoolers are bringing pot to school . . .":** Brad Knickerbocker, "Marijuana in the Classroom? Sometimes It's Legal," *Christian Science Monitor,* January 23, 2010.

390 **addictive amphetamines such as Ritalin and Adderall:** Madelyn S. Gould et al., "Sudden Death and Use of Stimulant Medications in Youths," *American Journal of Psychiatry* 166 (2009): 992–1001.

390 **antipsychotics that worked no better than a placebo:** Marcia Angell, "The Epidemic of Mental Illness: Why?" *New York Review of Books,* June 23, 2011, and "The Illusions of Psychiatry," *New York Review of Books,* July 14, 2011.

390 **scores of emergency room visits:** Linda A. Johnson, "ADHD Drugs Likely Send Thousands to ER," *Seattle Post-Intelligencer,* May 25, 2006.

390 **linked to food additives and environmental pollutants:** Kristin Wartman, "ADHD: It's the Food, Stupid," *Civil Eats,* CommonDreams.org, March 25, 2011.

390 **"My son was diagnosed with ADHD . . .":** Catey Hill, "Doctors Recommend Medical Marijuana for Minors with ADHD in California," *New York Daily News,* November 25, 2009.

390 **"Each side in the modern pot debate . . .":** Dr. Tom O'Connell blog, May 20, 2006.

391 **"were nearly as clueless as the Feds":** Ibid., August 27, 2006.

391 **similar medical and social histories:** Author's interview with Tom O'Connell; and O'Connell blog, September 11, 2006.

391 **effective way to relieve anxiety:** In 2009, Canadian researchers reported that many teenagers who smoke marijuana are trying to find a way to cope with mental and physical problems (Joan L. Bottorff et al., "Relief-Oriented Use of Marijuana by Teens," *Substance Abuse, Treatment, Prevention, and Policy* [April 23, 2009]). A subsequent study published in the *American Journal of Sports Medicine* (November 2011) noted: "In adolescents and young adults, cannabis also helps in coping with negative moods and emotional distress."

391 **"that made anxiolytics, mood stabilizers and antidepressants . . .":** O'Connell blog, June 29, 2008.

391 **"The need to self-medicate symptoms . . .":** Ibid., March 16, 2008.

391 **the stress-buffering function of the endocannabinoid system:** See, for example, Matthew N. Hill et al., "Endogenous Cannabinoid Signaling Is Essential for Stress

Adaptation," *Proceedings of the National Academy of Sciences USA* 107(20) (2010): 9406–11; and Matthew N. Hill et al., "Functional Interactions Between Stress and the Endocannabinoid System: From Synaptic Signaling to Behavioral Output," *Journal of Neuroscience* 30(45) (2010): 14980–986.

391 **On a cellular level, stress:** See, in general, Hans Selye, M.D., *The Stress of Life.*

391 **When a person is stressed, the brain generates:** B. B. Gorzalka et al., "Regulation of Endocannabinoid Signaling by Stress: Implications for Stress-Related Affective Disorders," *Neuroscience and Behavioral Reviews* 32(6) (2008): 1152–60; and M. N. Hill et al., "Recruitment of Prefrontal Cortical Endocannabinoid Signaling by Glucocorticoids Contributes to Termination of the Stress Response," *Journal of Neuroscience* 31(29) (2011): 10506–515.

392 **Among twenty developed nations:** Maggie Farley, "UNICEF Ranks the Well-Being of Youngsters in Developed Countries," *Los Angeles Times,* February 15, 2007.

392 **50 percent of the population:** Hope Yen, "Census Shows 1 in 2 People Are Poor or Low-Income," Associated Press, December 15, 2011.

392 **Massive inequalities disgrace and sicken:** See, in general, Pickett and Wilkinson, *The Spirit Level,* a must read.

POSTSCRIPT

393 **"There has always been great cooperation . . .":** "World's Largest Pro-Pot Rally Rolls into Town, Police Not Worried," *Seattle Post-Intelligencer* Blog, August 15, 2008.

393 **"Hempfest is about promoting the freedom . . .":** Casey McNerthney, "Where There's Smoke, There's Hempfest," *Seattle Post-Intelligencer,* August 17, 2007.

394 **Seattle Hempfest grew out of a peace vigil:** Author's interview with Vivian McPeak, January 2, 2012.

394 **On the tenth anniversary of Hempfest:** Vivian McPeak, *Protestival,* p. 67.

394 **the young CEO of Dr. Bronner's Magic Soaps:** David Bronner was arrested in October 2009 for planting hemp seeds on a lawn at DEA headquarters in Washington, D.C.

395 **Robert Creeley:** Handwritten poem published in *Marijuana Review* 9(1): 45.

395 **"The display ads now read . . .":** Jonathan Martin, "Medical Pot OK in Seattle, in Trouble in Spokane," *Seattle Times,* September 18, 2011.

396 **Obama-era federal raids on med-pot targets:** "Medical Marijuana Report Card Gives Obama Failing Grade for Broken Promises & Half-Measures," Americans for Safe Access press release, April 21, 2011.

396 **"Congress has determined that marijuana . . .":** James M. Cole, Deputy Attorney General, "MEMORANDUM FOR UNITED STATES ATTORNEYS," June 29, 2011, cited in "The Medical Marijuana Mess," *Los Angeles Times* editorial, October 14, 2011.

397 **Brewer deferred to the feds:** In January 2012, an Arizona state judge ordered Governor Jan Brewer to fully implement the 2010 voter-approved Medical Marijuana Act, saying she acted illegally by holding it up.

397 **Governor Chris Christie of New Jersey:** Michael Alan Goldberg, "Medical Marijuana in New Jersey: 'This Law Was Designed to Fail,'" *Philadelphia Weekly,* December 12, 2011. While Governor Christie dawdled, multiple sclerosis patient John Ray Wilson faced a five-year prison term for growing twenty-seven pot plants. "Criminal convictions do not get more absurd than this one," the *Atlantic City Press*

asserted in an editorial urging Governor Christie to commute Wilson's sentence (January 30, 2012).

397 **jurors in Missoula staged a marijuana mutiny:** Jesse McKinley, "Montana Jurors Raise Hopes of Marijuana Advocates," *New York Times,* December 23, 2010.

398 **"Sanity broke out in Missoula":** "Montana Jury Stages 'Mutiny' in Marijuana Case," *Huffington Post,* December 22, 2010; and Gwen Florio, "Missoula Jury Pool Creates Uproar Across Nation After Marijuana 'Mutiny'," *Billings Gazette,* January 3, 2011.

398 **Precious plant genetics were squandered:** Sarah Russo, "Sabotage of Research in Montana," CBDiary, June 22, 2011, www.projectcbd.org.

398 **"Do we want our schools infiltrated . . .":** Charles S. Johnson, "Foes Call Medical Marijuana a 'Scourge'," *Helena Independent Record,* February 11, 2011.

398 **"It's crossing boundaries . . .":** Charles S. Johnson, "Group to Run Ads on Repealing Medical Marijuana Law," *Helena Independent Record,* February 17, 2011.

398 **"I'd be more concerned about kids . . .":** Gwen Florio, "Kids' Use of Medical Marijuana Stirs Debate over Future in Montana," *Missoulian,* March 27, 2011.

398 **Hyde slipped a potent cannabis oil extraction:** "Dad: Pot Saved Cancer-Ridden Son's Life," UPI.com, May 5, 2011: http://www.upi.com/Science_News/2011/05/05/Dad-Pot-saved-cancer-ridden-sons-life/UPI-55851304608184/print/#ixzz1gu8zFFDs.

399 **Mike credited his son's survival:** Author's interview with Mike Hyde.

399 **U.S. Attorney Melinda Haag:** Thomas D. Elias, "Medipot Hijack Is Behind Federal Prosecutions," *Ukiah Daily Journal,* November 5, 2011.

399 **"Federal antidrug bureaucrats are afraid . . .":** "Californians Protest Federal Crackdown on Medical Marijuana Dispensaries," California NORML Press Release, October 7, 2011.

399 **Americans for Safe Access kept a running tally:** "Cities Can Ban Marijuana Dispensaries, CA Court Rules," Philip Smith, stopthedrugwar.org, November 13, 2011.

399 **How many jobs were lost?** Chris Roberts, "Jobs, Revenue Lost in Pot Dispensary Crackdown," *San Francisco Chronicle,* November 25, 2011. An estimated 2,500 people statewide lost their jobs between September and November 2011 during the federal crackdown on medical-marijuana facilities.

399 **"Pot smokers are a small minority . . .":** *Christian Science Monitor* editorial, October 12, 2011.

400 **who was a legitimate patient:** A 2011 survey by researchers at the University of California in Santa Cruz found that 73 percent of certified medical-marijuana patients were male and heaviest use was in the twenty-five-to-forty-four age group. The most common reasons patients cited for using medical marijuana were pain relief, spasms, headache, and anxiety, as well as to improve sleep and relax. Half of those surveyed indicated that they used cannabis as a substitute for prescription medication, suggesting that medical marijuana may offer significant health-cost savings.

400 **"the undoing of prohibition":** Gary Greenberg, "An Interview with Lester Grinspoon, M.D.," *Mother Jones,* October 17, 2005.

400 **"[T]he full potential of this remarkable substance . . .":** Grinspoon and Bakalar, *Marihuana,* p. 175.

401 **marijuana legalization should be debated:** Author's interview with Mason Tvert.

401 **Jessica Corry, a pro-life Republican mother:** Daniela Perdomo, "The Secret to

Legal Marijuana? Women," AlterNet, December 5, 2010; and Jessica Corry, "A Mother's Day Pro-Marijuana Tea Party," *Huffington Post,* May 5, 2010.

401 **"It's costing us a fortune . . .":** Pat Robertson cited in Conrad Black and Evan Wood, "Wrong on Crime," *National Post,* May 14, 2011.

401 **Sarah Palin conceded . . . :** Kyle Smith, "End of the Culture Wars," *New York Post,* June 27, 2010.

401 **McKay generated headlines:** Nina Shapiro, "The Evolution of John McKay," *Seattle Weekly,* September 28, 2011.

402 **"To end marijuana prohibition at the federal level . . .":** "Legalize Marijuana in Washington State," *Seattle Times* editorial, June 22, 2011.

402 **Human rights groups also documented numerous cases:** "Torture Will Not Win the Mexican Drug War," Toronto *Globe and Mail* editorial, November 14, 2011; Human Rights Watch, "Neither Rights Nor Security: Killings, Torture, and Disappearances in Mexico's 'War on Drugs,'" November 10, 2011.

402 **Calderón's predecessor, Vicente Fox:** Connie Littlefield, "In the Heart of a Drug War," *Ottawa Citizen,* March 2, 2001.

403 **Angus Reid poll:** Kristen Gwynne, "New Poll: Most Americans Consider War on Drugs a Failure and Support Legalization of Marijuana," AlterNet, August 10, 2011.

BIBLIOGRAPHY

Abel, Ernest L. *Marihuana: The First Twelve Thousand Years.* New York: Plenum, 1980.

———. *A Marihuana Dictionary.* Westport, CT: Greenwood, 1982.

Abrams, Donald, and Andrew Weil. *Integrative Oncology.* New York: Oxford University, 2009.

Abramson, John. *Overdosed America: The Broken Promise of American Medicine.* New York: Harper Perennial, 2005.

Alexander, Michelle. *The New Jim Crow: Mass Incarceration in the Age of Colorblindness.* New York: New Press, 2012.

Alexander, Tom. *Sinsemilla Tips.* Corvaliss, OR: New Moon, 1988.

Americans for Safe Access. *Patients in the Crossfire.* 2004.

Anderson, Nels. *On Hobos and Homelessness.* Chicago: University of Chicago, 1999.

Anderson, Patrick. *High in America.* New York: Viking, 1981.

Andrews, George, and Simon Vinkenoog, eds. *The Book of Grass: An Anthology of Indian Hemp.* New York: Grove Press, 1968.

Angell, Marcia. *The Truth about Drug Companies.* New York: Random House, 2005.

Anslinger, Harry J. *The Murderers.* New York: Farrar, Straus and Cudahy, 1961.

Armstrong, Louis. *Louis Armstrong: In His Own Words.* New York: Oxford, 1999.

Aronowitz, Al. *Bob Dylan and the Beatles.* Bloomington IN: 1st Books Library, 2003.

Asquith, Clare. *Shadowplay: The Hidden Beliefs and Coded Politics of William Shakespeare.* New York: PublicAffairs, 2005.

Baker, Deborah. *A Blue Hand: The Beats in India.* New York: Penguin, 2008.

Balko, Randy. *Overkill: The Rise of Paramilitary Police Raids in America.* Washington, DC: Cato Institute, 2006.

Ball, Gordon, ed. *Allen Verbatim: Lectures on Poetry, Politics, Consciousness by Allen Ginsberg.* New York: McGraw-Hill, 1975.

Bangs, Lester. *Psychotic Reactions and Carburetor Dung.* New York: Anchor, 1988.

Barich, Bill. *Big Dreams: Into the Heart of California.* New York: Vintage, 1995.

Barlett, Donald L., and James B. Steele. *Critical Condition: How Health Care in America Became Big Business—and Bad Medicine.* New York: Broadway, 2006.

Barton, Lee V., ed. *Illegal Drugs and Governmental Policies.* New York: Nova Science, 2007.

Baudelaire, Charles. *Artificial Paradises.* New York: Citadel, 1998.

———. *The Poem of Hashish.* New York: Perennial, 1971.

———. *On Wine and Hashish.* London: Hesperus Press, 2010.

Baum, Dan. *Smoke and Mirrors: The War on Drugs and the Politics of Failure.* New York: Back Bay, 1996.

Behr, Edward. *Prohibition: Thirteen Years That Changed America.* New York: Arcade, 1996.
Bello, Joan. *The Benefits of Marijuana: Physical, Psychological and Spiritual.* Boca Raton, FL: Lifeservices, 2000.
Benjamin, Walter. *Illuminations.* New York: Schocken, 1969.
———. *On Hashish.* Cambridge, MA: Harvard University, 2009.
Bennett, Chris, and Neil McQueen. *Sex, Drugs, Violence and the Bible.* Gibsons, BC: Forbidden Fruit, 2001.
Benson, Doug, Arj Barker, and Tony Camin. *The Marijuana-Logues.* New York: Three Rivers, 2005.
Berg, Peter, ed. *Reinhabiting a Separate Country: A Bioregional Anthology of Northern California.* San Francisco: Planet Drum, 1978.
Bergreen, Laurence. *Louis Armstrong: An Extravagant Life.* New York: Broadway, 1997.
Betts, E. M., ed. *Thomas Jefferson's Farm Book.* Princeton, NJ: Princeton University, 1953.
Bey, Hakim. *T.A.Z.* New York: Autonomedia, 1985.
Bey, Hakim, and Abel Zug, eds. *Orgies of the Hemp Eaters: Cuisine, Slang, Literature and Ritual of Cannabis Culture.* New York: Autonomedia, 2004.
Blacklisted News: Secret Histories, from Chicago '68 to 1984. New York: Bleecker Publishing, 1983.
Bock, Alan. *Waiting to Inhale: The Politics of Medical Marijuana.* Santa Ana, CA: Seven Locks, 2000.
Boire, Richard Glen and Kevin Feeney. *Medical Marijuana Law.* Oakland, CA: Ronin, 2006.
Bonnie, Richard J., and Charles H. Whitebread. *The Marijuana Conviction: A History of Marijuana Prohibition in the United States.* New York: Lindesmith, 1999.
Boon, Marcus. *The Road of Excess: A History of Writers on Drugs.* Cambridge, MA: Harvard University, 2002.
Booth, Martin. *A Magick Life: A Biography of Aleister Crowley.* London: Coronet, 2000.
———. *Cannabis: A History.* New York: St. Martin's, 2003.
Boujut, Michel. *Louis Armstrong.* New York: Rizzoli International, 1998.
Braunstein, Peter, and Michael William Doyle. *Imagine Nation: The American Counterculture of the 1960s and '70s.* New York: Routledge, 2002.
Brecher, Edward M., and the Editors of *Consumers Union Reports. Licit & Illicit Drugs.* Mount Vernon, NY: Consumers Union, 1972.
Brechin, Gary. *Imperial San Francisco: Urban Power, Earthly Ruin.* Berkeley: University of California, 1999.
Breton, André. *Manifestoes of Surrealism.* Ann Arbor: University of Michigan, 1972.
Brewer's Dictionary of Phrase and Fable (1895). London: Wordsworth Editions, 1993.
Brightman, Carol. *Sweet Chaos: The Grateful Dead's American Adventure.* New York: Pocket, 1998.
Brodie, Janet Farrell, and Marc Redfield, eds. *High Anxieties: Cultural Studies in Addiction.* Berkeley: University of California, 2002.
Brothers, Thomas. *Louis Armstrong's New Orleans.* New York: W. W. Norton, 2006.
Brown, David J., ed. *Mavericks of Medicine.* Petaluma, CA: Smart, 2006.
Brown, Ethan. *Snitch: Informants, Cooperators & the Corruption of Justice.* New York: PublicAffairs, 2007.
Brownie Mary's Marijuana Cookbook & Dennis Peron's Recipe for Social Change. San Francisco: Trail of Smoke Publishing, 1996.
Brownlee, Nick. *This Is Cannabis.* London: Sanctuary, 2002.
Burroughs, William S. *Naked Lunch.* New York: Grove Press, 1959.

Burroughs, William S., and Allen Ginsberg, *The Yage Letters.* San Francisco: City Lights, 1990.

Buzzell, Linda, and Craig Chalquist, eds. *Ecotherapy.* San Francisco: Sierra Club, 2009.

Cab Calloway's Hepster's Dictionary (1944).

Caen, Herb. *One Man's San Francisco.* Sausalito, CA: Comstock, 1979.

Callenbach, Ernest. *Ecotopia.* New York: Bantam, 1975.

Campos-Costero, Isaac. "Marijuana, Madness and Modernity in Mexico, 1521–1920." PhD diss., Harvard University, 2006.

Canadian Government Commission of Inquiry into the Non-Medical Use of Drugs, *Le Dain Commission of Inquiry into the Non-Medical Use of Drugs.* Ottawa, 1972.

Canadian Senate Special Committee on Illegal Drugs, *Cannabis: Our Position for a Canadian Public Policy,* vols. I & II, September 2002.

Carter, William E., ed. *Cannabis in Costa Rica: A Study of Chronic Marijuana Use.* Philadelphia: Institute for the Study of Human Issues, 1980.

Case, John, and Rosemary C. R. Taylor. *Co-ops, Communes & Collectives: Experiments in Social Change in the 1960s and 1970s.* New York: Pantheon, 1979.

Center for Public Integrity. *Harmful Error: Investigating America's Local Prosecutors.* Washington, DC: Center for Public Integrity, 2003.

Chang, Jeff. *Can't Stop Won't Stop: A History of the Hip-Hop Generation.* New York: St. Martin's, 2005.

Chapkis, Wendy, and Richard J. Webb. *Dying to Get High: Marijuana as Medicine.* New York: New York University, 2008.

Chapple, Steve. *Outlaws in Babylon.* New York: Long Shadow, 1984.

Charters, Ann, ed. *Jack Kerouac: Selected Letters, 1940–1956.* New York: Penguin, 1996.

Charters, Ann. *Kerouac: A Biography.* San Francisco: Straight Arrow, 1973.

Chong, Tommy. *The I Chong.* New York: Simon Spotlight, 2006.

Clarke, Robert Connell. *Hashish!* Los Angeles: Red Eye, 1998.

———. *Marijuana Botany.* Berkeley, CA: Ronin, 1981.

Clecak, Peter. *America's Quest for the Ideal Self.* New York: Oxford University, 1983.

Clements, Marcelle. *The Dog Is Us.* New York: Penguin, 1987.

Cockburn, Alexander, and Jeffrey St. Clair. *Whiteout: The CIA, Drugs and the Press.* New York: Verso, 1999.

Cohen, Peter. *Drugs as a Social Construct.* Utrecht: Universiteit van Amsterdam, 1990.

Coleman, Peter. *The Liberal Conspiracy.* New York: Free Press, 1989.

Collier, James Lincoln. *Louis Armstrong: An American Genius.* New York: Oxford University, 1983.

Conrad, Chris. *Cannabis Yields and Dosage: A Guide to the Production and Use of Medical Marijuana.* El Cerrito, CA: Creative Xpressions, 2005.

———. *Hemp for Health: The Medicinal and Nutritional Uses of Cannabis Sativa.* Rochester, VT: Healing Arts, 1997.

———. *Hemp: Lifeline to the Future.* Los Angeles: Creative Xpressions, 1994.

Cooke, Mordecai. *The Seven Sisters of Sleep.* Rochester, VT: Park Street, 1997.

Courtright, David T. *Dark Paradise.* Cambridge, MA: Harvard University, 2001.

———. *Forces of Habit: Drugs and the Making of the Modern World.* Cambridge, MA: Harvard University, 2001.

Cousins, Norman. *Anatomy of an Illness.* New York: Bantam, 1979.

Critser, George. *Generation Rx.* New York: Mariner, 2005.

Crowley, Aleister. *The Diary of a Drug Fiend.* York Beach, ME: Samuel Weiser, 1991.

———. *The Psychology of Hashish.* Edmonds, WA: Holmes, 2001.
Davis, Mike. *City of Quartz.* New York: Vintage, 1992.
———. *Ecology of Fear.* New York: Vintage, 1998.
Davis, Patti. *The Way I See It.* New York: Putnam, 1992.
Dean, Alan. *Chaos and Intoxication.* New York: Routledge, 1997.
Delsohn, Gary. *The Prosecutors: A Year in the Life of a District Attorney's Office.* New York: Dutton, 2003.
Demos, John. *The Enemy Within: 2,000 Years of Witch-Hunting in the Western World.* New York: Viking, 2008.
Deveney, John Patrick. *Paschal Beverly Randolph.* Albany: State University of New York, 1997.
Devereux, Paul. *The Long Trip: A Prehistory of Psychedelia.* New York: Penguin, 1997.
Didion, Joan. *Where I Was From.* New York: Knopf, 2003.
Dispensatory of the United States of America, 21st ed. Philadelphia: J. B. Lippincott, 1926.
Doidge, Norman. *The Brain That Changes Itself.* New York: Penguin, 2007.
Drake, William Daniel. *The Connoisseur's Handbook of Marijuana.* San Francisco: Straight Arrow, 1971.
Duerr, Hans Peter. *Dreamtime: Concerning the Boundary between Wilderness and Civilization.* Oxford: Basil Blackwell, 1985.
Duke, Steven B., and Albert C. Gross. *America's Longest War: Rethinking Our Tragic Crusade Against Drugs.* New York: Tarcher, 1993.
Dulchinos, Donald P. *Pioneer of Inner Space: The Life of Fitz Hugh Ludlow, Hasheesh Eater.* New York: Autonomedia, 1998.
Earleywine, Mitch, ed. *Pot Politics: Marijuana and the Costs of Prohibition.* New York: Oxford University, 2007.
Earleywine, Mitch. *Understanding Marijuana: A New Look at the Scientific Evidence.* New York: Oxford University, 2002.
Eddy, Paul, and Sara Walden. *Hunting Marco Polo.* New York: Little, Brown, 1991.
Edwards, Drew. *West Coast Smoke.* Toronto: Warwick, 2000.
Ehrenreich, Barbara. *Dancing in the Streets.* New York: Holt, 2007.
Ellison, Ralph. *Invisible Man.* New York: Vintage, 1989.
Epstein, Edward Jay. *Agency of Fear.* New York: Putnam, 1977.
Farber, David. *The Age of Great Dreams: America in the 1960s.* New York: Hill and Wang, 1994.
———. *Chicago '68.* Chicago: University of Chicago, 1994.
Farber, David, and Jeff Roche, eds. *The Conservative Sixties.* New York: Peter Lang, 2003.
Ferraiolo, Kathleen Grammatico. "Popular 'Medicine': Policymaking by Direct Democracy and the Medical Marijuana Movement of the 1990s." PhD diss., University of Virginia. 2004.
Fichtner, Christopher Glenn. *Cannabinomics.* Northbrook, IL: Well Mind, 2010.
Fitzpatrick, Vincent. *H. L. Mencken.* Macon, GA: Mercer University, 2004.
Foucault, Michel. *Power/Knowledge: Selected Interviews & Other Writings, 1972–1977.* New York: Pantheon, 1980.
Fox, Steve, Paul Armentano, and Mason Tvert. *Marijuana Is Safer.* White River Junction, VT: Chelsea Green, 2009.
Fried, Stephen. *Bitter Pills.* New York: Bantam, 1999.
Friedman, Lawrence M. *Crime and Punishment in American History.* New York: Basic, 1993.
Furst, Peter T., ed. *Flesh of the Gods: The Ritual Use of Hallucinogens.* Prospect Heights, IL: Waveland, 1990.

Garcia, Jerry, Charles Reich, and Jann Wenner: *Garcia: A Signpost to New Space.* New York: Da Capo, 1972.
Gaskin, Ina May. *Spiritual Midwifery.* Summertown, TN: Book Publishing, 1978.
Geluardi, John. *Cannabiz.* Sausalito, CA: PoliPoint, 2010.
George, Nelson. *Hip Hop America.* New York: Penguin, 1998.
Gerber, Rudolph Joseph. *Legalizing Marijuana: Drug Policy Reform and Prohibition Politics.* Westport, CT: Praeger, 2004.
Gertz, Stephen J. *Dope Menace: The Sensational World of Drug Paperbacks, 1900–1975.* Los Angeles: Feral House, 2008.
Giddins, Gary. *Satchmo: The Genius of Louis Armstrong.* New York: Da Capo, 2001.
Gillespie, Dizzy. *To Be, or Not . . . to Bop.* New York: Da Capo, 1979.
Gilmore. Mikal. *Stories Done: Writings on the 1960s and Its Discontents.* New York: Free Press, 2008.
Ginsberg, Allen. *Composed on the Tongue.* Bolinas, CA: Grey Fox, 1980.
———. *Howl and Other Poems.* San Francisco: City Lights, 1956.
Goffman, Ken, and Dan Joy. *Counterculture Through the Ages: From Abraham to Acid House.* New York: Villard, 2004.
Goldman, Albert. *Grass Roots: Marijuana in America Today.* New York: Warner, 1979.
———. *Ladies and Gentlemen—LENNY BRUCE!!* New York: Random House, 1971.
Goldstein, Margaret J. *Legalizing Drugs,* Minneapolis, MN: Twenty-First Century Books, 2010.
Goldstein, Robert Justin. *Political Repression in Modern America.* Cambridge, MA: Schenkman, 1978.
Golub, Andrew, ed. *The Cultural/Subcultural Contexts of Marijuana Use at the Turn of the Twenty-First Century.* New York: Haworth, 2005.
Gonzalez, Juan. *Harvest of Empire: A History of Latinos in America.* New York: Penguin, 2001.
Goode, Erich. *Drugs in American Society.* New York: Knopf, 1989.
Gould, Jonathan. *Can't Buy Me Love.* New York: Harmony, 2007.
Gravy, Wavy. *Something Good for a Change.* New York: St. Martin's, 1993.
Gray, James P. *Why Our Drug Laws Have Failed and What We Can Do About It.* Philadelphia: Temple University, 2001.
Gray, Mike, ed. *Busted.* New York: Thunder's Mouth, 2002.
Gray, Mike. *Drug Crazy: How We Got into This Mess and How We Can Get Out.* New York: Routledge, 2000.
Green, Jonathon. *Cannabis.* New York: Thunder's Mouth, 2002.
Greider, Katharine. *The Big Fix: How the Pharmaceutical Industry Rips Off American Consumers.* New York: PublicAffairs, 2003.
Grim, Ryan. *This Is Your Country on Drugs.* New York: Wiley, 2009.
Grinspoon, Lester. *Marihuana Reconsidered.* Cambridge, MA: Harvard University, 1971.
Grinspoon, Lester, and James B. Bakalar. *Marihuana: The Forbidden Medicine.* New Haven, CT: Yale University, 1993.
Guralnick, Peter. *Careless Love.* New York: Back Bay, 1999.
———. *Last Train to Memphis.* New York: Back Bay, 1994.
Guy, Geoffrey et al., eds. *The Medicinal Uses of Cannabis and Cannabinoids.* London: Pharmaceutical Press, 2004.
Hajdu, David. *Positively 4th Street.* New York: North Point, 2002.
Halberstam, David. *The Fifties.* New York: Villard, 1993.

Halperin, Steve, and Steve Bloom. *Pot Culture.* New York: Abrams, 2007.
Hamowy, Ronald, ed. *Dealing with Drugs.* Lexington, MA: Lexington, 1987.
Hayes, Kevin J., ed. *Conversations with Jack Kerouac.* Oxford, MS: University Press of Mississippi, 2005.
Henman, Anthony et al. *Big Deal: The Politics of the Illicit Drugs Business.* London: Pluto, 1985.
Herer, Jack. *The Emperor Wears No Clothes.* 11th ed. Van Nuys, CA: AH HA Publishing, 2000.
Herr, Michael. *Dispatches.* New York: Vintage, 1991.
Heylin, Clinton. *Bob Dylan: Behind the Shades.* New York: HarperCollins, 2003.
High Times editors. *High Times Greatest Hits.* New York: St. Martin's, 1994.
Himmelstein, Jerome L. *The Strange Career of Marihuana: Politics and Ideology of Drug Control in America.* Westport, CT: Greenwood, 1983.
Holland, Julie, ed. *The Pot Book.* Rochester, VT: Park Street, 2010.
Hornblum, Allen M. *Acres of Skin.* New York, Routledge: 1998.
Hoskyns, Barney. *Beneath the Diamond Sky: Haight-Ashbury 1965–1970.* New York: Simon and Schuster, 1997.
House of Lords Science and Technology Select Committee on Science and Technology Ninth Report (Session 1997–98). *Cannabis: The Scientific and Medical Evidence.* London, November 11, 1998.
Humes, H. L. *Men Die.* New York: Random House, 2007.
———. *Underground City.* New York: Random House, 2007.
Husak, Douglas. *Legalize This! The Case for Decriminalizing Drugs.* London: Verso, 2002.
Hyde, Henry J. *Forfeiting Our Property Rights: Is Your Property Safe from Seizure?* Washington, DC: Cato Institute, 1999.
Hyde, Lewis. *The Gift.* New York: Vintage, 1983.
———. *Trickster Makes This World.* New York: North Point, 1999.
Isserman, Maurice, and Michael Kazin. *America Divided: The Civil War of the 1960s.* New York: Oxford University, 2000.
Iversen, Leslie L. *The Science of Marijuana.* New York: Oxford University, 2000.
Jay, Mike. *Emperors of Dreams: Drugs in the Nineteenth Century.* London: Dedalus, 2000.
Jeffries, Debbie, and LaRayne Jeffries. *Jeffrey's Journey.* Oakland, CA: Quick American, 2005.
Jenkins, Philip. *Decade of Nightmares: The End of the Sixties and the Making of the Eighties America.* New York: Oxford University, 2006.
Johnson, Joyce. *Minor Characters.* New York: Anchor, 1994.
Jones, LeRoi. *Blues People.* New York: Perennial, 2002.
Jones, Max, and John Chilton. *Louis: The Louis Armstrong Story, 1900–1971.* New York: Da Capo, 1988.
Jones, Nick. *Spliffs: A Celebration of Cannabis Culture.* New York: Black Dog & Leventhal, 2003.
Jonnes, Jill. *Hep-Cats, Narcs, and Pipe Dreams: A History of America's Romance with Illegal Drugs.* New York: Scribner, 1996.
Joy, Janet E., Stanley J. Watson, and John A. Benson Jr., eds. *Marijuana and Medicine: Assessing the Science Base.* Washington, DC: National Academy Press, 1999.
Kaplan, John. *Marijuana: The New Prohibition.* New York: Pocket Books, 1971.
Kamstra, Jerry. *Weed: Adventures of a Dope Smuggler.* New York: Bantam, 1974.
Kaufman, Michael T. *Soros: The Life and Times of a Messianic Billionaire.* New York: Vintage, 2003.
Kaufmann, Walter, ed. *The Portable Nietzsche.* New York: Penguin, 1982.

Kempton, Richard. *Provo: Amsterdam's Anarchist Revolt.* New York: Autonomedia, 2007.
Kerouac, Jack. *Desolation Angels.* New York: Riverside, 1995.
———. *Dharma Bums.* New York: Penguin, 1991.
———. *On the Road.* New York: Signet, 1958.
———. *Visions of Cody.* New York: Penguin, 1993.
Ketchum, James S. *Chemical Warfare: Secrets Almost Forgotten.* ChemBook, 2006.
Kimmens, Andrew C., ed. *Tales of Hashish: A Literary Look at the Hashish Experience.* New York: William Morrow, 1977.
King, Jason. *The Cannabible Collection.* 3 vols. Berkeley, CA: Ten Speed, 2007.
Kohn, Marek. *Dope Girls: The Birth of the British Drug Underground.* London: Granta, 1992.
Kraska, Peter B., ed. *Militarizing the American Criminal Justice System: The Changing Roles of the Armed Forces and the Police.* Boston: Northeastern University, 2001.
Krassner, Paul. *Pot Stories for the Soul.* New York: Trans-High, 1999.
Kubby, Steve. *The Politics of Consciousness.* Port Townsend, WA: Loompanics, 1995.
Kuipers, Dean. *Burning Rainbow Farm.* New York: Bloomsbury, 2006.
Lash, John. *Twins and the Double.* New York: Thames and Hudson, 1993.
Leamer, Laurence. *The Paper Revolutionaries: The Rise of the Underground Press.* New York: Simon and Schuster, 1972.
Lee, Martin A., and Bruce Shlain. *Acid Dreams: The Complete Social History of LSD—The CIA, the Sixties, and Beyond.* New York: Grove Press, 1986.
Lee, Martin A., and Norman Solomon. *Unreliable Sources.* New York: Lyle Stuart, 1990.
Leland, John. *Hip: The History.* New York: Ecco, 2004.
———. *Why Kerouac Matters: The Lessons of "On the Road."* New York: Viking, 2007.
Lenson, David. *On Drugs.* Minneapolis: University of Minnesota, 1995.
Levine, Michael. *Deep Cover: The Inside Story of How DEA Infighting, Incompetence and Subterfuge Lost Us the Biggest Battle of the Drug War.* New York: Delacorte, 1990.
Levitas, Daniel. *The Terrorist Next Door: The Militia Movement and the Radical Right.* New York: St. Martin's, 2004.
Lewin, Louis. *Phantastica.* Rochester, VT: Park Street, 1998.
Liddy, G. Gordon. *Will.* New York: St. Martin's, 1996.
Ludlow, Fitz Hugh. *The Hasheesh Eater.* San Francisco: City Lights, 1979.
Lusane, Clarence. *Pipe Dream Blues: Racism and the War on Drugs.* Boston: South End, 1991.
Lytle, Mark Hamilton. *America's Uncivil Wars: The Sixties from Elvis to the Fall of Richard Nixon.* New York: Oxford University, 2006.
MacAdams, Lewis. *Birth of the Cool: Beat, Bebop, and the American Avant-Garde.* New York: Free Press, 2001.
MacCoun, Robert, and Peter Reuter. *Drug War Heresies.* London: Cambridge University, 2001.
Malcolm X, as told to Alex Haley. *The Autobiography of Malcolm X.* New York: Grove Press, 1965.
Mann, Peggy. *Marijuana Alert.* New York: McGraw-Hill, 1985.
Maran, Meredith. *Dirty: A Search for Answers Inside America's Teenage Drug Epidemic.* New York: HarperCollins, 2004.
Marez, Curtis. *Drug Wars: The Political Economy of Narcotics.* Minneapolis: University of Minnesota, 2004.
Margolis, Jack, and Richard Clorfene. *A Child's Garden of Grass.* New York: Pocket Books, 1970.
Marijuana: Report of the India Hemp Commission, 1893–1894. Silver Spring, MD: Thomas Jefferson Co., 1969.

Markoff, John. *What the Dormouse Said: How the Sixties Counterculture Shaped the Personal Computer Industry.* New York: Viking, 2005.

Marks, Howard. *Mr. Nice: An Autobiography.* London: Vintage, 1998.

Marshall, Jonathan. *Drug Wars.* Forestville, CA: Cohan and Cohan, 1991.

Martien, Jerry. *Shell Game.* San Francisco: Mercury House, 1996.

Massing, Michael. *The Fix.* Berkeley: University of California, 2000.

Masters, Bill. *Drug War Addiction: Notes from the Front Lines of America's #1 Policy Disaster.* St. Louis: Accurate Press, 2001.

Mate, Gabor. *In the Realm of Hungry Ghosts.* Berkeley, CA: North Atlantic, 2010.

Mathre, Mary Lynn et al., eds. *Cannabis in Medical Practice: A Legal, Historical and Pharmacological Overview of the Therapeutic Use of Marijuana.* Jefferson, NC: MacFarland, 1997.

Matthews, Patrick. *Cannabis Culture.* London: Bloomsbury, 1999.

Mauer, Marc. *Race to Incarcerate.* New York: New Press, 1999.

Mayor's Committee on Marihuana. *The Marihuana Problem in the City of New York* (La Guardia Report). New York: Jacques Cattell, 1944.

McCoy, Alfred W. *The Politics of Heroin: CIA Complicity in the Global Drug Trade.* Chicago: Lawrence Hill, 1991.

McKenna, Terence. *Food of the Gods.* New York: Bantam, 1992.

McMahon, George, and Christopher Largen. *Prescription Pot: A Leading Advocate's Heroic Battle to Legalize Medical Marijuana.* Far Hills, NJ: New Horizon, 2003.

McNally, Dennis. *Desolate Angel: Jack Kerouac, the Beat Generation, and America.* New York: Delta, 1990.

———. *A Long Strange Trip: The Inside History of the Grateful Dead and the Making of Modern America.* London: Corgi, 2003.

McPeak, Vivian. *Protestival.* Austin, TX: AH HA Publishing, 2001.

McVay, Douglas, ed. *Drug War Facts.* 5th ed. Common Sense for Drug Policy, 2006.

McWilliams, Carey. *California: The Great Exception.* Berkeley: University of California, 1999.

McWilliams, John C. *The Protectors: Harry J. Anslinger and the Federal Bureau of Narcotics, 1930–1962.* Newark: University of Delaware, 1990.

Mechoulam, Raphael, ed. *Cannabinoids as Therapeutics.* Basel: Birkhäuser Verlag, 2005.

Meggyesy, Dave. *Out of Their League.* New York: Warner, 1971.

Meier, Barry. *Pain Killer.* New York: Rodale, 2003.

Mendel-Reyes, Meta. *Reclaiming Democracy: The Sixties in Politics and Memory.* New York: Routledge, 1995.

Merlin, Mark David. *Man and Marijuana: Some Aspects of Their Ancient Relationship.* South Brunswick, NJ: Perpetua, 1973.

Messick, Hank. *Of Grass and Snow.* Englewood Cliffs, NJ: Prentice-Hall, 1977.

———. *John Edgar Hoover.* New York: McKay, 1972.

Metzner, Ralph. *The Well of Remembrance.* Boston: Shambala, 1994.

Mezzrow, Mezz, and Bernard Wolfe. *Really the Blues.* New York: Citadel, 1990.

Mikuriya, Tod H., ed. *Marijuana: Medical Papers, 1839–1972.* Oakland, CA: Medi-Comp, 1973.

Miles, Barry. *Ginsberg: A Biography.* New York: Simon and Schuster, 1989.

———. *Hippie.* New York: Sterling, 2005.

———. *In the Sixties.* London: Pimlico, 2003.

———. *Paul McCartney: Many Years from Now.* New York: Henry Holt, 1997.

Miller, Henry. *The Time of the Assassins.* New York: New Directions, 1962.

Miller, Joel. *Bad Trip: How the War Against Drugs Is Destroying America.* Nashville, TN: WND Books, 2004.

Miller, Richard Lawrence. *Drug Warriors and Their Prey.* Westport, CT: Praeger, 1996.

Miller, Timothy. *The 60s Communes: Hippies and Beyond.* Syracuse, NY: Syracuse University, 1999.

Mooney, Chris. *The Republican War on Science.* New York: Basic, 2003.

Moreau, J.-J. *Hashish and Mental Illness.* New York: Raven, 1973.

Morgan, Bill. *I Celebrate Myself: The Somewhat Private Life of Allen Ginsberg.* New York: Viking, 2006.

Morgan, Ted. *Literary Outlaw: The Life and Times of William S. Burroughs.* New York: Henry Holt, 1988.

Morgan, Wayne H. *Drugs in America: A Social History, 1800–1980.* Syracuse, NY: Syracuse University, 1981.

Mottram, Eric. *William Burroughs: The Algebra of Need.* Buffalo, NY: Intrepid Press, 1971.

Mountain Girl. *Primo Plant: Growing Marijuana Outdoors.* Oakland, CA: Quick American Archives, 1998.

Mulgrew, Ian. *Bud Inc.: Inside Canada's Marijuana Industry.* Toronto: Random House, 2005.

Musto, David F. *The American Disease: Origins of Narcotics Control.* New York: Oxford University, 1983.

Nadelmann, Ethan A. *Cops Across Borders.* University Park, PA: Penn State, 1993.

National Academy of Sciences. *An Analysis of Marijuana Policy.* Washington, DC: National Academies Press, 1982.

National Commission on Marihuana and Drug Abuse. *Marihuana: A Signal of Misunderstanding.* The First Report of the National Commission on Marihuana and Drug Abuse, and Technical Papers to the First Report. 2 vols. Washington, DC: Government Printing Office, 1972.

National Commission on Terrorist Attacks Upon the United States. *The 9/11 Commission Report.* New York: Cosimo, 2010.

Nelson, Vanessa. *Cool Madness: The Trial of Dr. Mollie Fry and Dale Schafer.* Sacramento: Medical Marijuana of America, 2008.

———. *U.S. vs. Ed Rosenthal 2.0.* Sacramento: Medical Marijuana of America, 2007.

New York Times Information Bank. *The Middle East: Issues and Events of 1978.* New York: Arno, 1980.

Nietzsche, Friedrich. *Ecce Homo.* New York: Oxford, 2007.

———. *The Will to Power.* New York: Vintage, 1968.

Nocenti, Annie, and Ruth Baldwin, eds. *The High Times Reader.* New York: Nation, 2004.

Norris, Mikki, Chris Conrad, and Virginia Resner. *Shattered Lives: Portraits from America's Drug War.* El Cerrito, CA: Creative Xpressions, 1998.

Novak, William. *High Culture: Marijuana in the Lives of Americans.* Cambridge, MA: Cannabis Institute of America, 1980.

Oakes, Kaya. *Slanted and Enchanted: The Evolution of Indie Culture.* New York: Holt, 2009.

O'Brien, Michael. *John F. Kennedy: A Biography.* New York: St. Martin's, 2005.

O'Day, Anita, with George Eells. *High Times Hard Times.* New York: Limelight, 1997.

O'Farrell, Clare. *Michel Foucault.* London: Sage, 2005.

Okrent, Daniel. *Last Call: The Rise and Fall of Prohibition.* New York: Scribner, 2010.

Osburn. Judy. *Spectre of Forfeiture.* Frazier Park, CA: Access Unlimited, 1991.

Paddison, Joshua. *A World Transformed: Firsthand Accounts of California Before the Gold Rush.* Berkeley, CA: Heyday, 1999.

Paine, Thomas. *Collected Writings.* Washington, DC: Library of America, 1995.
———. *Common Sense and Related Writings.* New York: St. Martin's, 2000.
Palmer, Cynthia, and Michael Horowitz, eds. *Sisters of the Extreme: Women Writing on the Drug Experience.* Rochester, VT: Park Street, 2000.
Parenti, Christian. *Lockdown America: Police and Prisons in the Age of Crisis.* London: Verso, 1999.
Parry, Robert. *Lost History: Contras, Cocaine, the Press & "Project Truth."* Arlington, VA: Media Consortium, 1999.
Parsons, Edward E. *Humboldt Homegrown: The Golden Age.* Eureka, CA: Egret, 1985.
Payne, Cril. *Deep Cover: An FBI Agent Infiltrates the Radical Underground.* New York: Newsweek, 1979.
Peck, Abe. *Uncovering the Sixties: The Life and Times of the Underground Press.* New York: Citadel, 1991.
Pendell, Dale. *Pharmako/Dynamis: Stimulating Plants, Potions & Herbcraft.* San Francisco: Mercury House, 2005.
———. *Pharmako/Gnosis: Plant Teachers and the Poison Path.* San Francisco: Mercury House, 2005.
———. *Pharmako/Poeia: Plant Powers, Poisons, and Herbcraft.* San Francisco: Mercury House, 1995.
Perlstein, Rick. *Nixonland.* New York: Scribner, 2008.
Pert, Candace B. *Molecules of Emotion: The Science Behind Mind-Body Medicine.* New York: Touchstone, 1997.
Phillips, Kevin. *The Politics of Rich and Poor.* New York: HarperCollins, 1991.
Pickett, Kate, and Richard Wilkinson. *The Spirit Level: Why Greater Equality Makes Societies Stronger.* New York: Bloomsbury, 2011.
Pieper, Werner, ed. *Nazis on Speed: Drogen im 3. Reich,* Bd. I (Vol. I). Badan: Löhrbach, 2002.
Pinchbeck, Daniel. *Breaking Open the Head.* New York: Broadway, 2003.
Pinfold, Mike. *Louis Armstrong.* New York: Universe, 1987.
Plana, Manuel. *Pancho Villa and the Mexican Revolution.* New York: Interlink, 2002.
Plant, Sadie. *Writing on Drugs.* New York: Farrar, Straus and Giroux, 1999.
Pollan, Michael. *The Botany of Desire: A Plant's-Eye View of the World.* New York: Random House, 2001.
Poole, Michael. *Romancing Mary Jane: A Year in the Life of a Failed Marijuana Grower.* Vancouver: Greystone, 2003.
Potter, Beverly, and Dan Joy. *The Healing Magic of Cannabis.* Berkeley, CA: Ronin, 1998.
Powers, Ann. *Weird Like Us.* New York: Da Capo, 2001.
Preston, Brian. *Pot Planet: Adventures in Global Marijuana Culture.* New York: Grove, 2002.
Pynchon, Thomas. *Vineland.* New York: Little, Brown, 1990.
Quirk, Robert. E. *The Mexican Revolution, 1914–15.* New York: Norton, 1970.
Randall, Robert C., and Alice M. O'Leary. *Marijuana Rx: The Patients' Fight for Medicinal Pot.* New York: Thunder's Mouth, 1998.
Raphael, Ray. *Cash Crop: An American Dream.* Mendocino, CA: Ridge Times, 1985.
Raskin, Jonah. *American Scream.* Berkeley: University of California, 2004.
Rätsch, Christian. *Marijuana Medicine.* Rochester, VT: Healing Arts, 2001.
Reed, Ray. *Mendocino Sinsemilla.* Mendocino, CA: Old Growth, 1989.
Reeves, Marcus. *Somebody Scream!* New York: Faber and Faber, 2008.

Rimbaud, Arthur. *Illuminations.* New York: New Directions, 1957.

———. *A Season in Hell.* New York: New Directions, 1961.

Robinson, Matthew B., and Renee G. Scherlen, eds. *Lies, Damned Lies, and Drug War Statistics.* Albany: State University of New York, 2007.

Robinson, Rowan. *The Hemp Manifesto.* Rochester, VT: Park Street, 1997.

Rock and Roll Hall of Fame and Museum. *I Want to Take You Higher.* San Francisco: Chronicle, 1997.

Roffman, Roger A. *Marijuana as Medicine.* Seattle: Madronna, 1982.

Rogin, Michael. *Ronald Reagan, The Movie and Other Episodes on Political Demonology.* Berkeley: University of California, 1987.

Romain, Joseph. *Marijuana for Dopes.* Toronto: Warwick, 2001.

Roper, Juliet, Christina Holtz-Bacha, and Gianpietro Mazzoleni. *The Politics of Representation: Election Campaigning and Proportional Representation.* Bel Air, MD: Peter Lang, 2004.

Roselle, Mike. *Tree Spiker.* New York: St. Martin's, 2009.

Rosenbaum, Thane. *The Myth of Moral Justice: Why Our Legal System Fails to Do What's Right.* New York: HarperCollins, 2004.

Rosenfeld, Irvin. *Pot Luck.* Santa Barbara, CA: Open Archive, 2010.

Rosenthal, Ed. *The Big Book of Buds: Marijuana Varieties from the World's Great Seed Breeders.* Vol. 1. Oakland, CA: Quick American Archives, 2001.

———. *The Big Book of Buds: Marijuana Varieties from the World's Great Seed Breeders.* Vol. 2. Oakland, CA: Quick American Archives, 2004.

———. *The Big Book of Buds: Marijuana Varieties from the World's Great Seed Breeders.* Vol. 3. Oakland, CA: Quick American Archives, 2007.

———. *Ed Rosenthal's Marijuana Grower's Handbook.* Oakland, CA: Quick American Archives, 2010.

Rosenthal, Ed, Dale Gieringer, and Tod Mikuriya. *Marijuana Medical Handbook.* Oakland, CA: Quick American Archives, 1997.

Rosenthal, Ed, and Steve Kubby. *Why Marijuana Should Be Legal.* New York: Thunder's Mouth, 1996.

Rosenthal, Franz. *The Herb: Hashish Versus Medieval Muslim Society.* Leiden: Brill, 1971.

Ross, John. *The Annexation of Mexico: From the Aztecs to the IMF.* Monroe, ME: Common Courage, 1998.

Rotolo, Suze. *A Freewheelin' Time.* New York: Broadway, 2008.

Roulac, John W. *Hemp Horizons: The Comeback of the World's Most Promising Plant.* White River Junction, VT: Chelsea Green, 1997.

Rowe, David E., and Robert J. Schulmann. *Einstein on Politics.* Princeton, NJ: Princeton University, 2007.

Rubin, Jerry. *Do It!* New York: Simon and Schuster, 1970.

Rubin, Saul. *Offbeat Marijuana: The Life & Times of the World's Grooviest Plant.* Santa Monica, CA: Santa Monica, 1999.

Rubin, Vera, ed. *Cannabis and Culture.* The Hague: Mouton, 1975.

Rubin, Vera, and Lambros Comitas. *Ganja in Jamaica: The Effects of Marijuana Use.* New York: Anchor, 1976.

Rublowsky, John. *The Stoned Age.* New York: Putnam's, 1974.

Ruck, Carl A. P. et al. *The Hidden World: Survival of Pagan Shamanic Themes in European Fairytales.* Durham, NC: Carolina Academic, 2007.

Rudgley, Richard. *Essential Substances.* New York: Kodansha International, 1993.

Rudgley, Richard, ed. *Wildest Dreams.* London: Abacus, 1999.

Russo, Ethan, Melanie Dreher, and Mary Lynn Mathre, eds. *Women and Cannabis: Medicine, Science, and Sociology.* New York: Haworth, 2002.

Sabbag, Robert. *Loaded: A Misadventure on the Marijuana Trail.* New York: Little, Brown, 2002.

Sagan, Carl. *The Dragons of Eden.* New York: Ballantine, 1977.

Sanders, Edward. *1968: A History in Verse.* Santa Rosa, CA: Black Sparrow, 1997.

———. *America: A History in Verse, Volume 1: 1900–1939.* Santa Rosa, CA: Black Sparrow, 2000.

———. *America: A History in Verse, Volume 2: 1940–1961.* Santa Rosa, CA: Black Sparrow, 2000.

———. *America: A History in Verse, Volume 3: 1962–1970.* Boston: Black Sparrow, 2004.

———. *Fug You.* New York: Da Capo, 2011.

———. *The Poetry and Life of Allen Ginsberg.* Woodstock, NY: Overlook, 2000.

Saul, Scott. *Freedom Is, Freedom Ain't: Jazz and the Making of the Sixties.* Cambridge, MA: Harvard University, 2003.

Saunders, Frances Stonor. *The Cultural Cold War: The CIA and the World of Arts and Letters.* New York: New Press, 1999.

Sayres, Sohnya et al., eds. *The 60s Without Apology.* Minneapolis: University of Minnesota, 1984.

Schaef, Anne Wilson. *When Society Becomes an Addict.* San Francisco: Harper and Row, 1987.

Schaef, Anne Wilson, and Diane Fassel. *The Addictive Organization.* New York: Harper and Row, 1990.

Schlosser, Eric. *Reefer Madness: Sex, Drugs, and Cheap Labor in the American Black Market.* New York: Mariner, 2003.

Schultes, Richard Evans, Albert Hofmann, Christian Rätsch. *Plants of the Gods: Their Sacred, Healing, and Hallucinogenic Powers.* Rochester, VT: Healing Arts, 1998.

Scott, Peter Dale, and Jonathan Marshall. *Cocaine Politics: Drugs, Armies, and the CIA in Central America.* Berkeley: University of California Press, 1991.

Seldes, George. *Witness to a Century.* New York: Ballantine, 1987.

Selvin, Joel. *The Summer of Love.* New York: Cooper Square, 1994.

Selye, Hans. *The Stress of Life.* New York: McGraw-Hill, 1978.

Senate Committee on Foreign Relations, Subcommittee on Terrorism, Narcotics, and International Operations. *Drugs, Law Enforcement and Foreign Policy* (The Kerry Report). 1989.

Shakespeare, William. *The Sonnets.* New York: Signet, 1965.

Shannonhouse, Rebecca, ed. *Under the Influence: The Literature of Addiction.* New York: Modern Library, 2003.

Shapiro, Harry. *Shooting Stars: Drugs, Hollywood and the Movies.* London: Serpent's Tail, 2003.

———. *Waiting for the Man.* New York: William Morrow, 1988.

Sheehy, Colleen J., and Thomas Swiss, eds. *Highway 61 Revisited: Bob Dylan's Road from Minnesota to the World.* Minneapolis: University of Minnesota Press, 2009.

Sherman, Carol, and Andrew Smith with Erik Tanner. *Highlights: An Illustrated History of Cannabis.* Berkeley, CA: Ten Speed, 1999.

Shilts, Randy. *And the Band Played On.* New York: Penguin, 1988.

———. *The Mayor of Castro Street: The Life and Times of Harvey Milk.* New York: St. Martin's Press, 1982.

Shinder, Jason, ed. *The Poem That Changed America: "Howl" Fifty Years Later.* New York: Farrar, Straus and Giroux, 2006.

Short, DJ. *Cultivating Exceptional Cannabis.* Oakland, CA: Quick American Archives, 2003.

Siegel, Ronald. *Intoxication: Life in Pursuit of Artificial Paradise.* New York: Pocket, 1989.

Sloman, Larry. *Reefer Madness: The History of Marijuana.* New York: St. Martin's Griffin, 1998.

———. *Steal This Dream.* New York: Doubleday, 1998.

Smith, James Edward. *A Dissertation on the Sexes of Plants translated from the Latin of Linnaeus.* London: George Nicol, 1786.

Smith, Larry, and Ingrid Swanberg, eds. *d.a. levy & the mimeograph revolution.* Huron, OH: Bottom Hog Press, 2007.

Snyder, Solomon H. *Uses of Marijuana.* New York: Oxford University, 1971.

Solomon, David, ed. *The Marijuana Papers.* New York: Mentor, 1968.

Sontag, Susan. *Illness as Metaphor and AIDS and Its Metaphors.* New York: Picador, 1990.

Southern, Terry. *Red-Dirt Marijuana and Other Tastes.* New York: Signet, 1968.

Stamper, Norm. *Breaking Rank.* New York: Avalon, 2004.

Stansill, Peter, and David Zane Mairowitz. *BAMN: Outlaw Manifestos and Other Ephemera, 1965–1970.* Middlesex, U.K.: Penguin, 1971.

Starr, Kevin. *California: A History.* New York: Modern Library, 2007.

Stefanis, Costas, Rhea Dornbush, and Max Fink, eds. *Hashish: Studies of Long-Term Use.* New York: Raven Press, 1977.

Stewart, Kevin. *Tales of the Emerald Triangle.* Moreno Valley, CA: 1st Books, 2002.

Stone, Robert. *Prime Green: Remembering the Sixties.* New York: Ecco, 2007.

Strausbaugh, John, and Blaise, Donald, eds. *The Drug User: Documents 1940–1960.* New York: Blast, 1991.

Strick, Anne. *Injustice for All: How Our Legal System Betrays Us.* New York: Barricade, 1996.

Subcommittee Hearings to Investigate the Administration of the Internal Security Act and Other Internal Security Laws. *Marihuana-Hashish Epidemic and Its Impact on United States Security.* Washington, DC: U.S. Government Printing Office, 1974.

Sukenick, Ronald. *Down and In: Life in the Underground.* New York: Collier, 1987.

Sullum, Jacob. *Saying Yes: In Defense of Drug Use.* New York: Tarcher, 1973.

Summers, Anthony. *The Arrogance of Power: The Secret World of Richard Nixon.* New York: Viking, 2000.

———. *Official and Confidential: The Secret Life of J. Edgar Hoover.* New York: G. P. Putnam's, 1993.

Susann, Jacqueline. *Valley of the Dolls.* New York: Bantam, 1966.

Swanberg, W. A. *Citizen Hearst.* New York: Collier, 1986.

Szalavitz, Maia. *Help at Any Cost: How the Troubled-Teen Industry Cons Parents and Hurts Kids.* New York: Riverhead, 2006.

Szasz, Thomas. *Ceremonial Chemistry: The Ritual Persecution of Drugs, Addicts, and Pushers.* Holmes Beach, FL: Learning Publications, 1985.

Tart, Charles T. *On Being Stoned.* Lincoln, NE: iUniverse, 2000.

Teachout, Terry. *Pops.* Boston: Mariner, 2010.

Tendler, Stewart, and David May. *The Brotherhood of Eternal Love.* London: Panther, 1984.

Thompson, Hunter S. *Songs of the Doomed.* New York: Simon and Schuster, 2011.

Thompson, Hunter S., and Anita Thompson. *Ancient Gonzo Wisdom: Interviews with Hunter S. Thompson.* New York: Da Capo, 2009.

Torgoff, Martin. *Can't Find My Way Home: America in the Great Stoned Age, 1945–2000.* New York: Simon and Schuster, 2004.

Trager, Oliver. *Dig Infinity!: The Life and Art of Lord Buckley.* New York: Welcome Rain, 2001.
Trebach, Arnold S. *The Great Drug War: And Radical Proposals That Could Turn the Tide.* Bloomington, IN: Unlimited, 2005.
Twohig, Dorothy, ed. *George Washington's Diaries: An Abridgment.* Charlottesville: University of Virginia Press, 1999.
United Nations Office on Drugs and Crime, *World Drug Report 2007.*
———. *World Drug Report 2009.*
Valentine, Douglas. *The Strength of the Wolf: The Secret History of America's War on Drugs.* London: Verso, 2004.
Van Schaik, Nol. *The Dutch Experience.* The Netherlands: Real Deal Publishing, 2002.
Von Eschen, Penny M. *Satchmo Blows Up the World: Jazz Ambassadors Play the Cold War.* Cambridge, MA: Harvard University, 2004.
Wald, Elijah. *Narcocorrido.* New York: Rayo, 2001.
Walton, Stuart. *Out of It: A Cultural History of Intoxication.* New York: Harmony, 2001.
Warde, Ibrahim. *The Price of Fear: The Truth Behind the Financial War on Terror.* Berkeley: University of California Press, 2007.
Warner, Roger. *The Invisible Hand: The Marijuana Business.* New York: Beech Tree, 1986.
Webb, James. *The Occult Establishment.* LaSalle, IL: Open Court, 1976.
———. *The Occult Underground.* LaSalle, IL: Open Court, 1974.
Weil, Andrew. *The Natural Mind.* New York: Houghton Mifflin, 2004.
Weil, Andrew, and Winifred Rosen. *From Chocolate to Morphine.* New York: Houghton Mifflin, 2004.
Weiner, Richard S., ed. *Pain Management.* Boca Raton, FL: CRC, 2006.
Weisheit, Ralph A. *Domestic Marijuana: A Neglected Industry.* New York: Greenwood, 1992.
Weiss, Lawrence D. *Private Medicine and Public Health.* Boulder, CO: Westview, 1997.
Werner, Clint. *Marijuana Gateway to Health.* San Francisco: Dachstar, 2011.
White, Edmund. *Rimbaud: The Double Life of a Rebel.* New York: W. W. Norton, 2008.
White, Timothy. *Catch a Fire: The Life of Bob Marley.* New York: Henry Holt, 1989.
Whitehead, Alfred North. *Science and the Modern World.* Cambridge: Cambridge University, 2011.
Wiener, Jon. *Gimme Some Truth: The John Lennon FBI Files.* Berkeley: University of California, 1999.
Wilbert, Johannes. *Tobacco and Shamanism in South America.* New Haven, CT: Yale University, 1993.
Williams, Daniel E. *The Naked Truth About Drugs.* Bonita Springs, FL: Cronin House, 2004.
Williams, Montel. *Climbing Higher.* New York: New American Library. 2005.
Wishnia, Steven. *The Cannabis Companion.* Philadelphia: Running Press, 2004.
Wootton Commission Report (1968). http://www.druglibrary.org/schaffer/library/studies/wootton/wootton_toc.htm.
Yeats, William Butler. *The Collected Works of W. B. Yeats, Vol. II: The Plays.* New York: Simon and Schuster, 2001.
———. *Explorations: Essays and Plays.* New York: Collier, 1973.
Young, James. *The Toadstool Millionaires: A Social History of Patent Medicines in America Before Federal Regulation.* Princeton, NJ: Princeton University, 1961.
Zimmer, Lynn, and John P. Morgan. *Marijuana Myths, Marijuana Facts.* New York: Lindesmith Center, 1997.

APPENDIX 1

Text of Proposition 215—the Compassionate Use Act—passed by California voters on November 5, 1996.

The full text of the Compassionate Use Act, which proposed to add a section to the California Health and Safety Code, read as follows:

SECTION 1. Section 11362.5 is added to the Health and Safety Code, to read:

11362.5. (a) This section shall be known and may be cited as the Compassionate Use Act of 1996.

(b) (1) The people of the State of California hereby find and declare that the purposes of the Compassionate Use Act of 1996 are as follows:

(A) To ensure that seriously ill Californians have the right to obtain and use marijuana for medical purposes where that medical use is deemed appropriate and has been recommended by a physician who has determined that the person's health would benefit from the use of marijuana in the treatment of cancer, anorexia, AIDS, chronic pain, spasticity, glaucoma, arthritis, migraine, or any other illness for which marijuana provides relief.

(B) To ensure that patients and their primary caregivers who obtain and use marijuana for medical purposes upon the recommendation of a physician are not subject to criminal prosecution or sanction.

(C) To encourage the federal and state governments to implement a plan to provide for the safe and affordable distribution of marijuana to all patients in medical need of marijuana.

(2) Nothing in this section shall be construed to supersede legislation prohibiting persons from engaging in conduct that endangers others, nor to condone the diversion of marijuana for nonmedical purposes.

(c) Notwithstanding any other provision of law, no physician in this state shall be punished, or denied any right or privilege, for having recommended marijuana to a patient for medical purposes.

(d) Section 11357, relating to the possession of marijuana, and Section 11358, relating to the cultivation of marijuana, shall not apply to a patient, or to a patient's primary caregiver, who possesses or cultivates marijuana for the personal medical purposes of the patient upon the written or oral recommendation or approval of a physician.

(e) For the purposes of this section, "primary caregiver" means the individual designated by the person exempted under this section who has consistently assumed responsibility for the housing, health, or safety of that person.

SEC. 2. If any provision of this measure or the application thereof to any person or circumstance is held invalid, that invalidity shall not affect other provisions or applications of the measure that can be given effect without the invalid provision or application, and to this end the provisions of this measure are severable.

APPENDIX 2

Chronic Conditions Treated with Cannabis

Reported to California doctors between 1990 and 2005*

By Tod Mikuriya, M.D.

Medical conditions that Californians have been treating successfully with cannabis are listed here according to ICD-9 number. The International Classification of Disease system was developed by the World Health Organization to promote comparability in the collection, processing, classification, and presentation of mortality statistics. It is universally required by insurance companies to process claims.

Some 38,000 cases are coded by ICD-9 number in the Oakland Cannabis Buyers' Cooperative database, and 8,500 in my practice. The number would be larger if the Act-Up San Francisco contingent had not objected—because of privacy concerns—when the city's Department of Public Health set up their card system.

Genital Herpes 054.10
Herpetic infection of penis 054.13
AIDS-Related Illness 042
Post W.E. Encephalitis 062.1
Chemotherapy Convales 066.2
Shingles (Herpes Zoster) 053.9
Radiation Therapy E929.9
Viral B Hepatitis, chronic 070.52
Viral C Hepatitis, chronic 070.54
Other arthropod-borne diseases 088.
Lyme Disease 088.81
Reiter's Syndrome 099.3
Behcet's Syndrome++ 136.1
Post-Polio Syndrome 138.0
Osteoblastoma Ischium 170.6
Malignant Melanoma 172.x
Other Skin Cancer 173
Breast Cancer 174.x
Prostate Cancer 185
Prostate Cancer 186

* Published in *O'Shaughnessy's*, Autumn 2005.

Testicular Cancer 186.9
Adrenal Cortical Cancer 194.0
Brain malignant tumor 191
Glioblastoma Multiforme 191.9
Sarcoma: Head-neck 195.0
Cancer, site unspecified 199
Lympho & reticular cancer 200
Hodgkins disease 201.9
Myeloid leukemia 205
Uterine cancer 236.0
Lymphoma 238.7
Graves' Disease** 242.0
Acquired hypothyroidsm 244
Thyroiditis 245
Diabetes Adult Onset 250.0
Diabetes Type I, Unco ++ 250.01
Diabetes Type I Ctrld ++ 250.03
Diabetes Insulin Depend. 250.1
Diabetes Adult Ons Unctrl 250.2
Diabetic Renal Disease 250.4
Diabetic Ophthalmic Disease 250.5
Diabetic Neuropathy 250.6
Diabetic Peripheral Vasc 250.7
Hypoglycemia(s) 251
Lipomatosis 272.8
Arthropathy, gout 274.0
Mucopolysaccharoidosis 277
Porphyria 277.1
Amyloidosis 277.3
Obesity, exogenous 278.00
Obesity, morbid 278.01
Autoimmune disease 279.4
Thalasemia 282.4
Hemophilia A 286.0
Henoch-Schönlein Purpura 287.0
Senile Dementia+ 290.0
Delirium Tremens+ 291.0
Schizophrenia(s) 295.x
Schizoaffective Disorder 295.7
Mania 296.0
Major Depression, Sgl Epi 296.2
Major Depression, Recurr 296.3
Bipolar Disorder 296.6
Autism/Asperger's 299.0
Anxiety Disorder+ 300.00
Panic Disorder+ 300.01
Agoraphobia 300.22
Obsessive Compulsive Disorder 300.3
Dysthymic Disorder 300.4
Neurasthenia 300.5
Writers' Cramp**** 300.89
Impotence, Psychogenic 302.72
Alcoholism+ 303.0
Opiate Dependence+ 304.0
Sedative Dependence+ 304.1
Cocaine Dependence+ 304.2
Amphetamine Dependence 304.4
Alcohol Abuse+ 305.0
Tobacco Dependence 305.1
Psychogenic Hyperhidrosis 306.3
Psychogenic Pylorospasm** 306.4
Psychogenic Dysuria 306.53
Bruxism 306.8
Stuttering* 307.0
Anorexia Nervosa 307.1
Tic disorder unspec 307.20
Tourette's Syndrome 307.23
Persistent Insomnia 307.42
Nightmares 307.47
Bulemia 307.51
Tension Headache 307.81
Psychogenic Pain 307.89
Post Traumatic Stress Dis. 309.81
Org. Mental Dis. hd inj 310.1
Post-Concussion Syndrome 310.2
Nonpsychotic Org Bra Dis. 310.8
Brain Trauma 310.9
Intermittent Explosive Dis 312.34
Trichotillomania 312.39
ADD w/o hyperactivity 314.00
ADD w hyperactivity 314.01
ADD other 314.8
Psychogenic PAT 316.0
Parkinson's Disease 332.0
Huntington's Disease+ 333.4
Restless legs syndrome 333.99
Friedreich's Ataxia 334.0
Cerebellar Ataxia 334.4
Spinal mm atrophy II 335.11
Amytrophic Lateral Sclerosis 335.2
Other spinal cord disease 336
Syringomyelia 336.0
Reflex Sympath Dystroph 337.2
Multiple Sclerosis 340.0
Other CNS demyelinating 341.
Hemiparesis/plegia 342

Cerebral Palsy+ 343.9
Quadriplegia(s) 344.0x
Paraplegia(s) 344.1x
Paralysis, unspecified 344.9
Epilepsy(ies)+ 345.x
Grand Mal Seizures** 345.1
Limbic Rage Syndrome** 345.4
Jacksonian Epilepsy** 345.5
Migraine(s)+ 346.x
Migraine, Classical+ 346.0
Cluster Headaches 346.2
Compression of Brain 348.4
Tic Douloureux+ 350.1
Bell's palsy 351.0
Thoracic Outlet Synd 353.0
Phantom Limb Synd++ 353.6
Carpal Tunnel Syndrome 354.0
Mononeuritis lower limb 355
Charcot-Marie-Tooth 356.1
Neuropathy+ 357
Muscular dystrophies 359
Coats' Syndrome++ 362.12
Macular Degeneration** 362.5
Glaucoma 365.23
Dyslexic Amblyopia** 368.0
Color Blindness* 368.55
Conjunctivitis 372.9
Drusen of Optic Nerve 377.21
Optic neuritis 377.30
Strabismus & other binoc 378
Nystagmus, Congenital 379.5
Ménière's Disease 386.00
Tinnitus 388.30
Hypertension+ 401.1
Ischemic Heart Disease 411.X
Angina pectoris 413
Arteriosclerotic Heart Disease 414.X
Cardiac conduction disorder 426.X
Paroxysmal Atrial Tachycardia** 427.0
Congestive Heart Failure 428.0
Post Cardiotomy Syndrome 429.4
Raynaud's Disease 443.0
Thromboangitis Obliterans 443.1
Polyarteritis Nodosa 446.0
Acute Sinusitis 461.9
Chronic Sinusitis 473.9
Chronic Obst Pulmo Dis 491.90
Emphysema 492.8
Asthma, unspecified 493.9
Pneumothorax, Spontaneous 512.8
Pulmonary Fibrosis 516.3
Cystic Fibrosis 518.89
Dentofacial anomaly pain 524.
T.M.J Syndrome 524.60
GastroEsophgeal Rflx Dis 530.81
Acute Gastritis 535.0
Gastritis+ 535.5
Peptic Ulcer/Dyspepsia 536.8
Colitis, Ulcerative 536.9
Pylorospasm Reflux 537.81
Regional Enteritis & Crohn's 555.9
Colitis+ 558.9
Colon diverticulitis 562.1
Constipation 564.0
Irritable Bowel Synd. 564.1
Dumping Sydro Post Surgery 564.2
Peritoneal pain 568
Hepatitis-non-viral 571.4
Pancreatitis 577.1
Celiac disease 579.0
Nephritis/nephropathy 583.81
Ureteral spasm calculus 592
Urethritis/Cystitis 595.3
Prostatitis 600.0
Epididymitis** 604.xx
Pelvic pain 607.9
Testicular torsion 608.2
Pelvic Inflammatory Dis 614
Endometriosis** 617.9
Premenstrual Syndrome+ 625.3
Pain, Vaginal/Pelvic 625.9
Menopausal syndrome 627.2
Sturge-Weber Disease 759.6
Eczema 692.9
Pemphigus 694.4
Epidermolysis Bullosa 694.9
Erythema Multiforme 695.1
Rosacea 695.3
Psoriatic Arthritis 696.0
Psoriasis 696.1
Pruritus, pruritic+ 698.9
Neurodermatitis 698.3
Atrophie Blanche 701.3
Alopecia 709.x
Lupus 710.0
Scleroderma 710.1

Sjögren's Disease ++ 710.2
Dermatomyositis 710.3
Eosinophilia-Myalgia Syn. 710.5
Arthritis, Rheumatoid+ 714.0
Felty's Syndrome 714.1
Arthritis, Degenerative 715.0
Arthritis, post traumatic+ 716.1
Arthropathy, Degenerative+ 716.9
Patellar chondromalacia 717.7
Ankylosis 718.5
Multiple joints pain 719.49
Intervertebral Disk Disease 722.x
L-S disk dis sciatic N irrit 722.1
IVDD Cerv w Myelopathy 722.71
Cervical Disk Disease 722.91
Cervicobrachial Syndrome 723.3
Lumbosacral Back Disease 724.x
Spinal Stenosis 724.02
Lower Back Pain 724.5
Peripheral enthesopathies 726
Tenosynovitis 727.x
Dupuytren's Contracture 728.6
Muscle Spasm 728.85
Fibromyalgia/Fibrositis 729.1
Weber-Christian Dis++ 729.30
Legg Calvé Perthes Dis++ 732.1
Osgood-Schlatter 732.4
Osteoporosis 733.0
Tietze's Syndrome 733.6
Melorheostosis 733.99
Spondylolisthesis** 738.4
Cerebral Aneurysm 747.81
Polycystic Kidney 753.1x
Scoliosis 754.2
Club foot 754.70
Spina Bifida Occulta 756.17
Osteogenesis imperfecta 756.51
Ehlers Danlos Syndrome 756.83
Nail patella syndrome 756.89
Peutz-Jehgers Syndrome** 756.9
Mastocytosis 757.33
Darier's Disease 757.39
Marfan syndrome 759.82
Sturge-Weber Eye Syn** 759.6
Vater Syndrome++ 759.89
Insomnia+ 780.52
Sleep Apnea Unspecified 780.57
Chronic Fatigue Synd 780.7
Tremor/Invol Movements 781.0
Myofacial Pain Syndrome** 782.0
Anorexia+ 783.0
Bulemia 783.6
Hyperventilation 786.01
Cough+ 786.2
Hiccough+ 786.8
Vomiting 787.01
Nausea+ 787.02
Diarrhea 787.91
Pain, Ureter 788.0
Cachexia 799.4
Vertebral disloc unspec 839.4
Whiplash 847.0
Back Sprain 847.9
Shoulder Injury Unspec 959.2
Fore Arm/Elbow/Wrist 959.3
Hand except finger 959.4
Finger 959.5
Hip 959.6
Knee, ankle & foot injury 959.7
Motion Sickness 994.6
Anaphylactic or Anaphylactoid Reaction 995.0
Renal Transplant ++ 996.81
"Trachoria Growths"***

+ Represents citations from pre-1937 medical literature
++ Jeffrey Hergenrather, M.D.
* Eugene Schoenfeld, M.D.
** Dale Gieringer, PhD, CA NORML Hotline
*** Robert Wilson, Hayward Hempery. Uncodeable and thought to be a specious disease submitted by an undercover agent who presented a false physician's note.
**** Barry R. McCaffrey, 12-30-96 Press Conference

INDEX

Page numbers in *italics* refer to illustrations.